ARDOYNE:
THE UNTOLD TRUTH

Ardoyne Commemoration Project

First published 2002
by
Beyond the Pale
BTP Publications Ltd
Unit 2.1.2 Conway Mill
5-7 Conway Street
Belfast BT13 2DE

Tel: +44 (0)28 90 438630
Fax: +44 (0)28 90 439707
E-mail: office@btpale.ie
Website: http://www.btpale.ie

British Library Cataloguing-in-Publication Data.
A catalogue record for this book is available from the British Library.

Paperback ISBN 1-900960-17-6
Hardback ISBN 1-900960-18-4

Printed in Dublin by Colour Books Ltd.

Cover Photos: Pacemaker (front), Andersonstown News (back).

CONTENTS

Dedication

To all those who contributed to the book and who have since died:

Jimmy Barrett
Rose Craig
Tom Largey
Mickey Lagan
Patrick McBride
Agnes Mulvenna
Bobby Reid
Rose-Ann Stitt

Acknowledgements

Ardoyne Commemoration Project Committee

Tom Holland (Chairperson, co-editor and interviewer)
Patricia Lundy (co-editor, co-author and interviewer)
Mark McGovern (co-editor, co-author and interviewer)
Phil McTaggart (interviewer and treasurer)
Kelley McTaggart (transcribing)
Helen McLarnon (transcribing)

Additional help and support was provided by:

Mary Brady, Mickey Liggett, Ann Stewart, Geraldine Brown, Barry McCafferty, Mark Thompson, Jim Gibney, Sean Mag Uidhir, Maria Williams, Margaret McClenaghan, Kate Lagan, Claire Hackett, Mairead Gilmartin, Jacqueline Monahan, Dolores Hughes, Marie Murphy, Sam McLarnon, Uschi Grandel, Mike Tomlinson, Agnieszka Martynowicz and Bill Rolston.

The ACP would also like to thank the following groups and organisations:

The Joseph Rowntree Charitable Trust, Belfast Regeneration Office (North Team), Northern Ireland Voluntary Trust, Community Relations Council, The Lottery Charities Board, The Hans Bloeckler Foundation (Germany), Ardoyne Fleadh Cheoil, Amach agus Isteach, North Belfast News, Survivors of Trauma, Edge Hill College, Ormskirk.

List of those killed

1969

Sammy McLarnon – Killed by the RUC, Herbert Street, 15 August 1969
Michael Lynch – Killed by the RUC, Butler Street, 15 August 1969

1971

Barney Watt – Killed by the British army, Chatham Street, 5 February 1971
Sarah Worthington – Killed by the British army, Velsheda Park, 9 August 1971
Paddy McAdorey – Killed on active serviceby the British army, Jamaica Street,
    9 August 1971
John Laverty – Killed by the British army, Ballymurphy, 11 August 1971
Michael McLarnon – Killed by the British army, Etna Drive, 28 October 1971
Johnny Copeland – Killed by the British army, Strathroy Park, 30 October 1971
Joseph Parker – Killed by the British army, Toby's Hall, 12 December 1971
Margaret McCorry – Killed by the IRA, Crumlin Road, 20 December 1971
Gerard McDade – Killed on active service by the British army, Brompton Park entry,
    21 December 1971

1972

Charles McCann – Killed on active service, Lough Neagh, 5 February 1972
Bernard Rice – Killed by loyalists, Crumlin Road, 8 February 1972
David McAuley – Died as a result of 'accidental discharge' from an IRA weapon,
    Fairfield Street, 19 February 1972
James O'Hanlon – Killed by the IRA, Gracehill Street, 16 March 1972
Sean McConville – Killed by the UDA/UFF, Crumlin Road, 15 April 1972
Joseph Campbell – Killed by the British army, Eskdale Gardens, 11 June 1972
Terry Toolan – Killed on active service by the British army, Eskdale Gardens,
    14 July 1972
James Reid – Killed on active service by (persons unknown), Eskdale Gardens,
    14 July 1972
Joseph (Giuseppe Antonio) Rosato – Killed by (unknown), Deerpark Road, 21 July 1972
Patrick O'Neill – Killed by loyalists, Forthriver Drive, 22 July 1972
Charles McNeill – Killed by (unknown), Brompton Park, 14 August 1972

Joseph McComiskey – Killed on active service by the British army, Flax Street, 20 September 1972

Gerry Gearon – Killed by the UFF, Crumlin Road, 30 November 1972

Bernard Fox – Killed on active service by the British army, Brompton Park, 4 December 1972

Hugh Martin – Killed by the UVF, outside the Tip-Top bakery, East Belfast, 30 December 1972

1973

Elizabeth McGregor – Killed by the British army, Highbury Gardens, 12 January 1973

Pat Crossan – Killed by the UVF Woodvale Road, 2 March 1973

David Glennon – Killed by loyalists, Summer Street, 7 March 1973

Eddie Sharpe – Killed by the British army in Cranbrook Gardens, 12 March 1973

Pat McCabe – Killed on active service by the British army, Holmdene Gardens, 27 March 1973

Anthony McDowell – Killed by the British army, Etna Drive, 19 April 1973

Sean McKee – Killed on active service by the British army, Fairfield Street, 18 May 1973

1974

Terry McCafferty – Killed by loyalists, Rush Park estate, 31 January 1974

Martha Lavery – Killed by the British army, Jamaica Street, 5 August 1974

Thomas Braniff – Killed by loyalists, Sunflower Bar, Corporation Street, 16 July 1974

Albert Lutton – Killed by loyalists in the Ballyduff estate, 10 October 1974

Ciaran Murphy – Killed by loyalists, Hightown Road, 13 October 1974

James McDade – Killed on active service, Salt Lane, Greyfriars, Coventry, 14 November 1974

1975

Thomas Robinson – Killed by loyalists, Etna Drive, 5 April 1975

Francis Bradley – Killed by loyalists, Corporation Street, 19 June 1975

John Finlay – Killed by loyalists, Brougham Street, 21 August 1975

William Daniels – Killed by the UVF, Glenbank Place, 22 August 1975

Thomas Murphy – Killed by loyalists, Antrim Road, 2 October 1975

Seamus McCusker – Killed by 'Official' IRA, New Lodge Road, 31 October 1975

Francis Crossan – Killed by loyalists, Shankill Road, 25 November 1975

Christine Hughes – Killed by the IRA in Mountainview Parade, 21 December 1975

1976

Ted McQuaid – Killed by loyalists, Cliftonville Road, 10 January 1976

Paul McNally – Killed by loyalists, Brompton Park, 7 June 1976

Patrick Meehan – Killed by loyalists, Crumlin Road, 17 June 1976

Gerard Stitt – Killed by loyalists, Crumlin Road, 17 June 1976

Paul Marlow – Killed on active service, Ormeau Road Gasworks, 16 October 1976

Charles Corbett – Killed by loyalists, Leggan Street, 30 October 1976
John Maguire – Killed by the UVF in Glenbank Place, 30 October 1976
Geraldine McKeown – Killed by loyalists in Mountainview Gardens, 8 December 1976
John Savage – Killed by the British army, Springfield Road, 18 December 1976

1977

John Lee – Killed by IRA, Balholm Drive, 27 February 1977
Danny Carville – Killed by the UDA, Cambrai Street, 17 March 1977
Trevor McKibbin – Killed on active service by the British army, Flax Street, 17 April 1977
Sean Campbell – Killed by the UVF, Etna Drive, 20 April 1977
Sean McBride – Killed by the UVF, Etna Drive, 21 April 1977
Trevor McNulty – Killed by the IRA, Alexander Flats, 27 July 1977

1978

Dennis (Dinny) Brown – Killed on active service by the British army, Ballysillan Road, 21 June 1978
Jim Mulvenna – Killed on active service by the British army, Ballysillan Road, 21 June 1978
Jackie Mailey – Killed on active service by the British army, Ballysillan Road, 21 June 1978

1979

Frankie Donnelly – Killed on active service, Northwick Drive, 5 January 1979
Lawrence Montgomery – Killed on active service, Northwick Drive, 5 January 1979

1980

Alex Reid – Killed by loyalists, Shankill Road, 3 January 1980
Colette Meek – Killed by the IRA, Alliance Avenue, 17 August 1980

1981

Maurice Gilvary – Killed by the IRA, near Jonesboro, S. Armagh, 19 January 1981
Paul Blake – Killed by the UFF, Berwick Road, 27 March 1981
Patsy Martin – Killed by loyalists, Abbeydale Parade, 16 May 1981
Danny Barrett – Killed by the British army, Havana Court, 9 July 1981
Anthony Braniff – Killed by the IRA, Odessa Street, 27 September 1981
Larry Kennedy – Killed by the UDA/UFF, Shamrock Club, Flax Street, 8 October 1981
Bobby Ewing – Killed by the UFF, Deerpark Road, 12 October 1981

1983

Trevor Close – Killed by loyalists, Cliftonville Road, 26 May 1983

1984

Harry Muldoon – Killed by the UVF, Mountainview Drive, 31 October 1984

1986

Colm McCallan – Killed by loyalists, Millview Court, 14 July 1986
Raymond Mooney – Killed by loyalists, Holy Cross chapel, 16 September 1986

1987

Larry Marley – Killed by the UVF Havana Gardens, 2 April 1987
Eddie Campbell – Killed by loyalists, Horseshoe Bend, 3 July 1987
Thomas McAuley – Killed by loyalists, Crumlin Road, 16 November 1987

1988

Paul McBride – Killed by the UVF, Avenue Bar, Union Street, 15 May 1988
Seamus Morris – Killed by loyalists, Etna Drive, 8 August 1988

1989

Davy Braniff – Killed by loyalists, Alliance Avenue, 19 March 1989
Paddy McKenna – Killed by loyalists Crumlin Road, 2 September 1989

1991

Gerard Burns – Killed by the INLA, New Barnsley Park, West Belfast, 29 June 1991
Hugh Magee – Killed by loyalists, Rosapenna Street, 10 October 1991

1992

Liam McCartan – Killed by the UFF, Alliance Avenue, 12 March 1992
Isabel Leyland – Killed by the IRA, Flax Street, 21 August 1992
Martin Lavery – Killed by loyalists, Crumlin Road, 20 December 1992

1993

Alan Lundy – Killed by loyalists, Andersonstown, 1 May 1993
Sean Hughes – Killed by the UFF, Falls Road, 7 September 1993
Thomas Begley – Killed on active service, Shankill Road, 23 October 1993

1994

Martin Bradley – Killed by loyalists, Crumlin Road, 12 May 1994

1996

John Fennell – Killed by the INLA, Bundoran, 6 March 1996
Fra Shannon – Killed by the INLA, Turf Lodge, 9 June 1996

1998

Brian Service – Killed by loyalists, Alliance Avenue, 31 October 1998

Preface

Seamus Deane

The Ardoyne area in Belfast has endured for over 30 years the combined and co-ordinated assaults of the RUC, the B-Specials, the British army and the various loyalist groups with which these security forces have regularly colluded in their campaign to quench resistance to the injustices of the rump of the British state that is Northern Ireland. Most of the civilians whose stories are given here were murdered. Most were unarmed, most were Catholic – the two ingredients that best stimulate the appetite of these organizations for murder and torture. It may be said that the fact that some of these organizations no longer exist is an indication of the sea-change that has overtaken the military-political squalor of the state; the RUC is now the PSNI, the B-Specials have been transmogrified successively into the UDR and now the RIR. The theory seems to be that the scandal attached to these names disappears with the alphabetic rearrangement. But it does not. The additional scandal is that the crimes of these organizations have never been nor can ever be investigated, most especially by the ravenous media which feeds so greedily on their horror and on the press releases issued by those responsible. The first moments of the so-called 'troubles' in 1969 contained the history of all that has happened since. Any demand for justice or equality on the part of the minority in Northern Ireland was met and continuously has been met by state violence, unionist outrage, and a barrage of lies and propaganda. Northern Ireland is a criminal state now and was so then; it is less criminal now than it was then, but the modification will never really be enough to alter that fundamental status. Like the police and their paramilitary allies, it could be renamed and re-christened a dozen times over and it would remain the same. Only justice and equality can change Northern Ireland. If either one or both of these is ever achieved, Northern Ireland – even if the name is retained – will no longer exist.

One step towards justice would be the prosecution of all those who killed so many innocent people, including children, in Ardoyne between 1969 and the present. This will not happen. Many of the killers were British soldiers. They acted in line with government policy and were therefore obedient to their masters. Even in the case of Bloody Sunday in Derry, when the Paras characteristically slaughtered unarmed people, as they also did in Ardoyne, no soldier will be charged with murder, no politician will be identified as a criminal. When the chain of command is pulled, all one hears is the sound of evidence and responsibility being flushed away. But there are RUC men who cannot lurk any longer behind the army shield; there are loyalists who have never been questioned about collusion. It should be possible to find out who was responsible for many of the 'unsolved' deaths of the total of 99. The determination of the government and the media to find out who was responsible for the Omagh massacre should be matched by an equal determination to find out who was responsible for the Dublin and Monaghan bombings, for the bombing of McGurk's Bar, for the killing of Sammy McLarnon by the RUC, for the exposure of the murderous collusion between the official forces of the crown and their loyalist counterparts. Such determination does not exist. Rather the reverse. With the help of the media journalists, the British government in particular hopes to portray the conflict as the war of a legal state on terror. For it would not do to have it revealed that the system of legality in the northern statelet is and always has been itself founded upon terror.

The people who inevitably have faced the consequences of this terrible situation are those who are most exposed, physically and economically. Of all the exposed minority areas in the province, Ardoyne is perhaps the most vulnerable, although it has also been the most resistant. To be a Catholic in Northern Ireland has never been an enviable position; worse, to be a Catholic and a nationalist; worse again to be a Catholic and a nationalist and member of the working class; worse again to be a Catholic and a member of the working class and a republican. 'Fenian' is the catch-all loyalist term for all those who occupy these positions; anyone not a Catholic who otherwise supports them is a 'fenian-lover'. In order to sanction injustice, all political positions must be rewritten as sectarian, most especially those which do not accept the legitimacy of the state itself.

It is perfectly legitimate to say the state is illegitimate. But the point of this volume is that many people who would not have been particularly bothered about the question of legitimacy in itself have been compelled to address it, largely on the grounds of their own safety and survival. States traditionally protect their citizens. The Northern Irish state has traditionally attacked large sections of its citizens – in the 1920s and 1930s and since the late 60s in particular – and thereby made its own survival, which it was proposing thereby to defend, indefensible. The citizens so attacked are inhabitants of the Catholic ghettoes of Belfast and Derry and more recently of Portadown, the new capital of unionism. Among these, Ardoyne has had the fiercest history, has faced the most unrelenting assault, even to the present day.

Was Northern Ireland, in David Trimble's weasel euphemism, merely a 'cold house' for Catholics since 1922? The phrase has now migrated, in the mouths of Protestant clergy, famously silent on state injustices since 1922, to apply to the present state of Protestants. There is no equivalence between the two conditions. The present state of Protestants is rooted simply in the fact that there no longer is a Protestant state. That is the sum of their fears and anxieties. The present state of Catholics is that they have some hope of achieving justice in present conditions. It is badly needed.

There may be some therapeutic value in being able to speak and write of what happened to members of one's own family. There may be some relief in being able to say publicly that someone was a victim of a murder which has scarcely been noticed in a place so given to cataloguing its own grisly record, especially of victims of the IRA and other republican organizations, and including victims of their internecine quarrels. But there never has been a question of condemnation of the IRA or of any republican organization. That is routine.

The harder question is the condemnation of the forces of the state and of its collusion with loyalist paramilitaries. Every attempted inquiry has been aborted. What this book does is to increase the pressure for further inquiry, to ask the state, before the world to justify its behaviour in Ardoyne. Or even simply to tell the truth.

This book is an instance of what the truth sounds like. It is difficult to listen to; for many it will be impossible to hear it. But this is a necessary as well as a courageous book and for all the pain it exposes it offers, proportionately, the prospect of a future peace and justice so long desired and so cruelly denied. Ardoyne, precisely because of what it has undergone, may be the first to arrive at a world elsewhere. This book is not only a tribute to the dead; it is also a tribute to the living and the power of commemoration.

Seamus Deane, May 2002

Ardoyne, 1953.
The mural celebrates the 150th anniversary
of the rebellion of Roger Emmet
(courtesy Daniel Wasson)

Aerial photograph of Ardoyne and surrounding areas, late 1980s

Introduction

'To give testimony is to bear witness; it is to tell the unofficial story, to construct a history of people, of individual lives, a history not of those in power, but by those confronted by power, and becoming empowered.' (Perks and Thomson, 1998)

This book tells the story of 99 ordinary people, living ordinary lives, who became victims of political violence in a small close-knit, working class, nationalist community in North Belfast. The deaths occurred between 1969 and 1998 and the victims were from Ardoyne. Because of the ongoing nature of the conflict, victims' names and the traumatic circumstances of their death were often forgotten or overshadowed by further tragedy and loss. Most of the people who have given testimony in this book are the relatives, neighbours and friends of the 99 victims. Almost all have never spoken publicly about the death of their loved one and the personal costs to their family, friends and community. Their very moving accounts of loss and pain have up until now been private, unspoken and 'silenced'. To recall such traumatic memories was an emotional and sometimes difficult process for individuals and families to undertake. Until now no one has taken the time to listen to these voices and record their memories of the past. There is evidence from countries emerging from conflict around the world that public recognition of such loss and human rights abuse can provide a cathartic experience for many victims' families. It is clear from our own discussions with victims' relatives that it was important for them to be given the opportunity to 'tell their story', in their own words without constraints or censorship. What is more, to document such experiences prevents history from being lost, rewritten or misrepresented. It opens the possibility for a society to learn from its past.

What is also apparent from the testimonies is the number of relatives who have never been told 'the truth' about the death of their loved one. Many of these testimonies speak of the brutality of a system that treated ordinary people with utter contempt and colluded to ensure lack of disclosure, accountability and justice. Others recall, and have since learnt, personal details that were lost in the pandemonium and confusion that followed such traumatic events. These very vivid and personal accounts tell the 'hidden' story of powerlessness, marginalisation and resistance. To compound personal and collective grief, sections of the media have intruded, misrepresented events and given less than equal recognition to all victims. Over the years they have demonised and labelled Ardoyne a 'terrorist community',

1

thus implying, in some distorted way, that the community got what it deserved. To add insult to injury, a growing number of books on 'the Troubles' have published details about victims', often incorrectly and without consent, causing further distress to relatives. What distinguishes this book from others is the painstaking effort by the Ardoyne Commemoration Project (ACP) to ensure all participants were given space and time to speak about their experiences, in order to capture the essence of their loved one. Another important feature was that participants were given complete editorial authority over the final draft. This was a huge and time-consuming process given that over 300 people were eventually interviewed. It also explains why the process took almost four years to complete.

In short, this book has sought to give control and ownership over what is written about victims to their relatives and friends. It is primarily a community project and one defined by the importance of writing 'history from below'. The book offers a platform for the community to 'write back' and set the record straight. It puts a human face on statistics, contextualises the deaths in terms of historical events and gives social recognition to the victims of the conflict. It is a collective memory of the community, researched and written by members of that community. The testimonies describe unspeakable loss and pain. It means that this book makes neither easy nor comfortable reading, but given its subject matter, this cannot and should not be. We are, though, deeply conscious that many readers may find these pages difficult and harrowing. The story can feel unrelenting. For some people, too, it may stir up traumatic memories of their own. Such experiences will reflect something of the impact that the project has had on all those involved. Yet, the testimonies also describe resistance and survival in the face of adversity. This has also shaped the experience of being part of the ACP. It is one reason that the members of the project feel a deep sense of gratitude to every person that agreed to be interviewed. The willingness of interviewees to talk about deeply personal and often disturbing memories can only be admired, and only their courage in speaking made this book possible. The project's aim is to ensure that these unheard voices of ordinary people will enter the public discourse. In doing so they will reclaim an important part of their history for future generations. Who better to tell that story than those who have experienced political violence first hand? If the history of the conflict is to be written well, we believe these very powerful and poignant testimonies can, and must, be allowed to speak for themselves.

The following sections explain the concept, practical stages and processes, methodology and structure of the book. It is hoped that other communities intending to embark on a similar project will find the following practical information useful and the lessons we have learnt helpful.

Why a book?

The concept for the book came about as a result of informal discussions between victims' relatives, concerned individuals and members of community groups. The political conditions produced by the cease-fires and the Good Friday Agreement created the space for people to begin to reflect upon and discuss the past thirty years of political conflict. As part of that process there has been a period of reflection and reassessment at the individual and community level, in both the private and public sphere. The sense of loss produced by so many deaths, injuries and the various other costs of the conflict created a growing focus on how to deal with the legacy of the past. In Ardoyne people were beginning to reflect upon and discuss these highly contentious issues in what were essentially uncharted waters.

At the same time, in the political aftermath of the Good Friday Agreement, the 'victims agenda' came to the fore. As part of the Agreement an early release scheme for political prisoners was announced. Unionist anti-agreement groups and parties seized upon this aspect of the Agreement and linked the 'victims agenda' and prisoner releases for political purposes to oppose the Good Friday Agreement. The unionist anti-agreement lobby argued that political prisoners should not be given early release. At the same time they sought to differentiate between victims and to imply that such a 'hierarchy of victimhood' should guide public debate and policy on the issue. The British Secretary of State had already established a Victims Commission in October 1997, with Sir Kenneth Bloomfield at its head. Following the publication of the Bloomfield Report (*We Will Remember Them*) in late 1998, a Victims Liaison Unit was set up and Adam Ingram was appointed as the Minister for Victims. It is through this framework that the government has pursued its response to the victims issue. In themselves, many nationalists regarded the appointments of both Sir Kenneth Bloomfield and Adam Ingram to their respective positions as particularly insensitive. The former had been a long-serving senior civil servant in the Northern Ireland Office, whilst the latter was also in post as the Minister for Armed Forces. With such backgrounds both were seen as lacking impartiality and were viewed as unlikely to be neutral custodians of the needs of all victims of the conflict. The Bloomfield Report was also criticised for having established an exclusive and hierarchical approach to the victims' agenda, with an implicit suggestion that there were more deserving, and less (if not un-) deserving victims. The 'undeserving' victims were inevitably nationalists and republicans killed by British security forces and their agents. Whilst Bloomfield suggested that there should be no such thing as 'guilt by association' many of those involved with the relatives of nationalist/republican victims have argued that is precisely the perception which was fostered. The sense has been that, although the Good Friday Agreement was supposed to herald a new era of equality, the Bloomfield Report sowed anew the old seeds of ostracism.

The 'hierarchy of victims' and the distinction made increasingly by anti-agreement unionists and others between 'innocent' and 'non-innocent' victims angered many in the Ardoyne community. To them it seemed as though the anti-agreement unionists had become self-appointed advocates for all victims of the conflict – the supposed 'legitimate' voice for victims. Many victims' families felt that they were at the bottom of this hierarchy, or that they and their lost loved ones were not regarded as victims at all. Their sense of injustice was heightened by the fact that those in the British security forces responsible for many deaths in Ardoyne had never been arrested, interrogated or served time in prison.

It was against this backdrop that in July 1996 a number of victims' relatives, concerned individuals and representatives from community groups called a meeting to discuss the 'victims agenda' and to explore ways in which the community could commemorate their own victims of the conflict, in their own way. No concrete decision was reached at the initial meeting. The general consensus was that something should be done to record the experiences of ordinary people in Ardoyne during the past thirty years of conflict and to mark the sense of loss produced by so many deaths. It was clear from the meeting that people felt angry. They wanted an opportunity to 'set the record straight', to 'tell their story' from the community's perspective. After several further meetings, much discussion and debate, the idea of a commemoration book emerged. The Ardoyne Commemoration Project was born and a committee was elected.

The general view was that a book offered the best way to challenge the 'hierarchy of victims' agenda and provided the means for the community to tell its own story. It was important to the integrity of the project that the community, as opposed to someone 'outside' of the community, should undertake the work. Community participation has therefore been a defining feature of the project, guiding and shaping the project's development over the past four years. During all stages of the project the ACP made every effort to seek the views and opinions of the participants and the wider community. This process has meant that right from the start the community in effect took 'ownership' and control of the design, research process, editing, return phase and production of the book. This makes the project, and the book, unique. This work is the outcome of ordinary people taking charge of their history, rather than being objects in someone else's study. The people who have given their testimonies, along with those who have listened, recorded, and edited them, are from within or have strong links with the Ardoyne community. In retrospect the complexity of researching and writing a book was totally underestimated and with the best will in the world naïvely misjudged. At this stage none of us appreciated the extent of the task, the toll it would take on individuals both giving and receiving testimonies and the number of years it would take to complete. As well as the practical problems to be dealt with, those involved in the project had to grapple with a wide range of difficult issues that often took much soul-searching in what was unforeseen terrain for us all.

Defining Victims

One of the first issues that arose at the start of the project was establishing what victims were to be included in the book. This initially seemed straightforward but in reality a number of unforeseen, complex and far from uncontentious issues soon emerged. Even though Ardoyne is an overwhelmingly nationalist/republican community, there exists within it a diversity of groups, opinions and politics. The aim of the ACP was to be inclusive and not to alienate any particular individual, family or group. At the outset the ACP discussed and debated the issue of who should be included in the study and consulted widely with relatives and interested groups who had, up until that point, not participated directly in the ACP. After this process of broad consultation, and much reflection (which was a learning process for all of us), it was agreed that the research project should focus on all those victims who, at some point in their lives, had been Ardoyne residents, irrespective of who killed them. There were a number of reasons as to why this specific focus was arrived at, although it was never intended to imply that the suffering of other victims' relatives and communities is any less worthy of note. The view of the ACP is that everyone's grief should be respected, that all victims are equal and that no one has a monopoly on grief and loss. What is more, the ACP was highly sensitive to the potential problem of creating an alternative 'hierarchy of victims', between and within particular communities.

A major reason for restricting the research to Ardoyne residents was essentially bound up with the manageability of the project. The ACP was a small group of volunteers with limited resources at its disposal. By way of contrast to many other works dealing with the stories of victims and their families a decision was taken early on that substantial time and space needed to be given to each individual story. This was so that their lives, as well as their deaths, could be described. By seeing those who had been killed through the eyes of those who knew them best, the aim was to reveal the human face so often lost amid the welter of statistics, supposedly 'objective' historical accounts and media misrepresentations. Such a task presented huge logistical problems that demanded defining a very specific constituency, given the dimensions of the conflict. Of the roughly 3,630 conflict fatalities that have resulted from the war in Ireland during the last three decades almost half occurred in Belfast. Just under 550 deaths occurred in the north of the city alone. Most of these (some 396) were civilians, and the majority of civilian casualties in North Belfast were from the nationalist community.[1] The decision to focus on the residents of Ardoyne was, in part, the result of these realities.

Yet even if only those killed in and around Ardoyne were to be considered, issues not only of scale but also of contact and access soon became all too apparent. Of its nature the project was dealing with deeply traumatic and often highly sensitive matters. As a result it was imperative to provide those giving testimonies with a sufficient sense of comfort and ease to speak openly and freely about their experiences. However, the conflict has left a legacy of doubt, fear and suspicion of strangers in places like North Belfast, not least because of the 'dirty war' carried out there by the state's intelligence agencies. One of the key strengths of the ACP was that those who conducted the interviews were from the district itself, people who were trusted because of their community, family and friendship ties. That the project was very much rooted in Ardoyne was not only useful, it was essential. Quite simply, these stories could not have been told unless those being interviewed were talking to someone they could place. Only this could offset the old (and often all too necessary adage): 'whatever you say, say nothing'. However, given the divided geography of North Belfast and the inevitable limits of inter-communal contact engendered by years of conflict, that very 'rootedness' precluded easy access to other areas, other (mainly non-nationalist) communities and, as a consequence, other people's stories. The 'rootedness' of the ACP was, in other words, both a prerequisite for the project and an important factor in defining its inevitable limits.

Given this context, the decision taken early on by the ACP, that they would deal with the cases of all those Ardoyne residents who had been killed, was of the utmost importance. In spite of the difficulties of access it ensured that, within the limits set, no victim would be excluded because of their religious or political beliefs, the circumstances of their death, or the agency responsible for it. This reflected the ethos that defined the raison d'être of the ACP; the equality of all victims. Ardoyne is a community that has known its history to be hidden and humanity denied. That is why there has been such a need for its story to be told. But in telling its own story there has been no desire to imply that others should be left untold, or that any death is unimportant. Given its constituency the Ardoyne story is inevitably dominated by victims from particular backgrounds. However, amongst the names of the 99 victims there can be found those of Catholics and Protestants, nationalists and non-nationalists, civilians and combatants, those killed by the RUC, the British army, loyalist paramilitaries and Irish republicans. This remit raised all manner of difficulties, but it was a decision driven by the desire to challenge the 'hierarchy of victimhood'.

Whilst lying outside the focus of the book it is also important to recognise and acknowledge the wider context of human costs and sense of loss that were the outcome of three decades of war. As well as the 99 Ardoyne residents killed during the conflict there were other civilians (both nationalist and unionist), members of the state security forces (the

British army, RUC, UDR) and combatants who died within or on the fringes of the district. It is difficult to establish definitive figures for all such victims and what is outlined below is merely by way of illustration. Certainly there were several nationalist civilians and IRA members from other parts of the North killed within the district. There were also at least a dozen civilians from unionist areas who were killed in the streets that lie within or are immediately adjacent to Ardoyne. Many of these, and the far larger number of victims who died in other parts of North Belfast, were killed (in a very wide range of circumstances) by Irish nationalists and republicans, some of whom came from Ardoyne. An unknown number of loyalist paramilitaries were also killed by people from Ardoyne. Unsurprisingly most of these took place outside the district's boundaries. Most such deaths occurred after the onslaught of loyalist sectarian killings launched in the early to mid-1970s against Ardoyne and other isolated nationalist areas, exemplified in the activities of the Shankill Butchers. There were also at least eight members of the RUC/UDR and 22 members of the British army killed within the district. Most of the state security forces that died in Ardoyne were killed by the local IRA. Virtually all of these deaths took place in the early years of the conflict. For example, at least 19 British soldiers had been killed in Ardoyne by the end of 1973. It is worth noting, perhaps, that before the introduction of internment (in August 1971) there had been just three such casualties; in the next 14 months a further 15 were to follow. The last member of the regular British army killed in Ardoyne was shot dead in 1977, almost a quarter of a century ago. As has already been stated, whatever its focus, it is not the intention of this book to try to in any way diminish or marginalise the sense of loss that such deaths brought in their wake for the friends and relatives of such victims of the conflict. The intention is, however, to tell the stories of the loved ones of the dead of Ardoyne, who have for many years suffered from having their stories, their lives and their suffering diminished, marginalised and wilfully misrepresented.

Having established that the book would be concerned only with those people who had at some point been residents of Ardoyne, the next practical task for the group was to draw up a list of victims' names and contact addresses. No definitive list existed. We compiled our own list from a number of different sources, including the republican plaque in Ardoyne, books, pamphlets and word of mouth. This was a difficult process because a number of residents had changed address or moved out of the district. Tracking them down wasn't easy. The database was continually updated and as the research uncovered more and more victims' names, the number initially thought to be 75 increased to 99 victims. Indeed, this may not be a definitive total but is as close to one that the ACP have been able to establish. The names and addresses of all relatives, eyewitnesses and friends were also included on the database. This was a huge, difficult and time-consuming task to undertake given the number of people who were eventually interviewed. However, the database was essential in order for interviewers to make initial contact with relatives and friends, to set up interviews and eventually return edited testimonies for comment and approval.

Unlike many other parts of the North, the people of Ardoyne suffered attacks and fatalities throughout every phase of the conflict. While bare statistics cannot tell the true story of loss it might be useful to outline a general profile of the Ardoyne dead. Of the 99 men, women and children from the Ardoyne community who were killed, the first (Sammy McLarnon and Michael Lynch) were shot dead by the RUC on the night of the 14/15

August 1969, in the earliest days of the 'Troubles'. The latest (Brian Service) was killed by loyalists on Halloween 1998. However, reflecting wider patterns, there were a greater number of victims in the earliest years. By the end of 1973 Ardoyne had already suffered 33 deaths, roughly a third of all those who were to die throughout the conflict. Of these, a large majority (19) had been killed by members of the RUC or the British army. The state was ultimately to be directly responsible for 26 deaths of people from the district, 28 per cent of the total. Loyalists killed a further 50. Of the various republican groups the IRA was responsible for nine deaths (roughly nine per cent), the 'Official' IRA for one and the INLA for three. Six more people were inadvertently killed whilst on active service with the IRA. One other died accidentally and in three cases it has not proven possible to clearly ascribe responsibility. Of the 99 killed eight were women. The youngest victim was Anthony McDowell, aged 12, shot dead by the British army on April 19, 1973, and the oldest was Elizabeth McGregor, aged 76, shot dead by the British army on January 12, 1973.

Community and Clarifying Geographical Boundaries

Given that the criterion used to draw up the list of victims was one-time residence within Ardoyne, a key issue was clarifying the actual geographical boundaries of the district. This also raised some important questions about the nature of community and the role of collective memory within it. Ardoyne is a readily identifiable place, both historically and today. However, the boundaries of communities do not exist merely, or even primarily, due to lines on maps. They exist in the way, and with whom, people live their lives, share their experiences and identify themselves. Ardoyne is a particular place because the people who make up this tight-knit community live it as such. Indeed, that very collective solidarity proved to be one of the community's most vital resources during the most difficult days of the conflict. To be from Ardoyne usually means to have been born and grown up in certain streets. It is, in other words, to share a certain sense of place and belonging and to live that out in the contacts, actions and institutions that make up everyday life. This is hardly unusual. Most people and places exist in just this way. It is, more particularly, what the 'working class city' invariably looks like. When people in Ardoyne therefore sought to remember their dead and commemorate their lives it was, in many ways, simply a reflection of this seemingly obvious, almost unconscious sense of identity and belonging.

The stories of the people who died from Ardoyne are, in the first place (and most importantly), the personal memories of those who knew and loved them. In another way they are also, however, a key component of a collective memory through which a shared identity takes shape. They are part of the fabric of what makes this community see itself as a community. Indeed, the strong bonds of interdependence that helped hold the area together also ensured that the (unquestionably more distressing and traumatic) individual loss experienced by those closest to the victims had a powerful impact on the rest of the community. This was perhaps particularly so for those who lived through the worst days of the conflict. It was this sense of place also, therefore, which informed the way that the geographical boundaries of the project were clarified, and moulded the focus of the study.

In practical terms this approach still required that very specific lines defining the geographical limits of the area be drawn up. For those who come from Ardoyne, and those (both nationalist and unionist) who live around it, where Ardoyne starts and ends is, generally speaking, very clearly understood. Who is and is not from Ardoyne is generally seen as a matter of common sense. Of course, the boundaries of Ardoyne are to some degree defined by the political divisions, sectarian geography and history of conflict that has shaped North Belfast. Ardoyne is an overwhelmingly nationalist/republican area of around 11,000 people, surrounded on three sides by unionist/loyalist areas. Certain parts of Ardoyne were at one time more 'mixed'. However, during the 1969-1971 period there was a substantial movement of people into and out of the district. This not only ensured that the population of the area became more homogenous but that its boundaries were also increasingly clear and socially and politically significant. Ardoyne became a nationalist island in a loyalist sea, shaping a growing sense of siege and isolation.

However, for those unfamiliar with North Belfast it is perhaps important to stress that by no means all such boundaries are 'sectarian'. Indeed, even within Ardoyne there was a traditional (if generally good natured) 'divide' between the older, narrow streets of 'Old Ardoyne' and the somewhat more substantial houses of Glenard that had more to do with relative affluence than anything else. There are local boundaries that demarcate the district from other neighbouring and mostly nationalist communities like the Bone, Ligoniel, Cliftonville and Mountainview. These boundaries also shape local identity. For example, the Bone is a small nationalist/republican area (originally of no more than three or four streets, though much expanded today) that lies directly adjacent to Ardoyne. Yet the Bone has its own distinctive sense of history and place in the mosaic of territories that make up this part of the city. It is a place unto itself with its own sense of identity. All that said, some geographical boundaries have altered and become slightly more blurred over the years, largely as a result of demographic shifts and urban redevelopment. Streets that were once regarded as the Bone are now part of Ardoyne and vice versa.

Therefore, having decided on the limits of the project, it was necessary to clearly define and agree upon which particular streets were to be included and, more importantly, which were not. The ACP was very aware of the sensitivities of neighbouring communities who have suffered equally as a result of the conflict. There was a particular concern that other areas should not feel excluded by the work of the project. As a result, a number of approaches were made to community groups (for example, in the Bone and Ligoniel) to explain the reasons for restricting the research project to Ardoyne and to encourage them to undertake similar projects. Again, this reflected a key approach by the ACP that only communities themselves can tell their own stories. It is because of this that, for example, a number of civilians killed in Ardoyne (both nationalist and non-nationalist) who were not, and had never been, residents of the district, were not also included in the book. However, there were a small number of victims, from areas adjacent to Ardoyne, (for example, Geraldine McKeown from Mountainview and Joseph Rosato from the Deerpark Road) that were included because they did not readily fit in with any particular community and had well-established links or roots in Ardoyne. In addition, several victims from the Bone (Jim Mulvenna and Sean Campbell) have been included because they died alongside victims from Ardoyne in the same incident. Such decisions were the subject of a great deal of thought and it was a process that finally produced the list of 99 that make up the lives told in this work.

Methodology and Processes

This book is based on interviews with over 300 people. Interviews were carried out with victims' relatives, friends, eyewitnesses and key individuals within the Ardoyne community. Each victim's story is made up of a case study that usually contains at least two or three (sometimes more) interviews. In the main the interviews also provided the basis for the biographical detail contained in the boxes that proceed each case. Photographs of the victims were also, wherever possible, obtained directly from the closest relatives. Driven again by the desire to avoid any 'hierarchy of victimhood', cases were kept to an equal length as far as possible. However, some cases are longer or shorter than others. This was usually due to the varying levels of detail and insight given by different interviewees. It was notable, for example, that there was often less material available for many of the younger victims. This did not reflect any lack of concern or desire to tell such stories in full. Rather, it says much about the lost opportunities that such young lives being cut so short entails. The testimonies were also edited, with the consent of the interviewees. This was a task that took a great deal of time and work.

In a small number of cases there were less than the average of two or three interviews, in a few, no interviews at all. This was usually because, in spite of strenuous and exhaustive efforts, no relevant interviewee could be found to provide their testimony. In such instances, and in others where it was felt that the interviews needed to be supplemented, the ACP has tried to compile information from alternative sources. These included newspaper articles, coroner's reports and other relevant official and media material. Given that such sources have not always been seen to provide reliable objective information, where possible reliance upon them was kept to a minimum or cross-referenced with other available evidence. Throughout the project sought to prioritise the voices contained in the testimonies and the wishes and views of the relatives. This was reflected in the way that the list of possible interviewees was drawn up. Initial contact was made with the closest next of kin (i.e. mother, father, husband, wife) whose permission was sought for an interview to be carried out. If it was granted, the victims' families were then asked to suggest a close friend, eyewitness or other significant person to be interviewed. Over time other possible avenues were pursued to try to build up a rounded portrait of the life and death of each victim. This process took a great deal of time and effort but helped to ensure that relatives were always kept central to the research process.

Individuals interviewed for the history chapters were 'selected' after consultation with a variety of sources within the community. The ACP objective was to interview a sample of people that would reflect a broad spectrum of views in the district. These interviews were carried out by those charged with the responsibility of producing the historical context sections of the book. The interviews therefore informed and shaped the content of the history chapters that in turn reflect the themes, issues and concerns raised by the community members consulted. The ACP felt that it was important to put victims' deaths into historical context and illustrate that they did not take place in a political vacuum. As discussed in the historical chapters, there are clear discernible patterns, linked in particular to British state strategies, that contextualise the deaths. Although direct interviews are the basis of the information used in the history chapters, other primary and secondary sources were utilised to back up the analysis and highlight contradictions in official accounts and discourse (see select bibliography). That said, it is important to stress that the book does not claim to be a definitive oral history of Ardoyne or even an exhaustive political analysis of the conflict played out in Ardoyne. It is one community's attempt to try and make sense of events that contributes to a much wider jigsaw of lived experience throughout the Six Counties. The book deals primarily with a specific period in recent history and a particular overarching theme – political violence and its impact on the members of this working class nationalist community. Having said that, the testimonies do provide fascinating insights into the broader social, political and economic conditions of the time. A number of those interviewed for the historical sections have since died, including Jimmy Barrett, Rose Craig, Mickey Lagan, Tom Largey, Patrick McBride, Agnes Mulvenna, Bobby Reid, and Rose-Ann Stitt.

Carrying out the testimony interviews involved a fairly steep learning curve. In retrospect a number of 'mistakes' were made in the early stages, largely probably due to lack of experience. For example, the designing of the interview question schedule, method of recording the testimony and means of collecting the interviews all evolved over time. Similarly, some of the recording equipment initially used was found to be unsuitable. The individuals who carried out the interviews were Ardoyne residents or people who have very close links with the community. As has already been noted, this was essential in order to gain the trust and confidence of those being interviewed. All interviews were recorded and transcribed, after which they were carefully edited. Volunteers who had a deep personal and political commitment to the project undertook all these tasks. It was felt that, wherever possible, interviews should be carried out in the participant's home or a venue of their choosing. This is what usually occurred. Given the very sensitive nature of the interviews it was hoped this approach would help put those interviewed at their ease and give them a sense of control over the proceedings. Nonetheless the interviews were an emotional and sometimes difficult experience for individuals and families. Conducting this large number of often lengthy and difficult interviews was also a time-consuming process that undoubtedly took its toll, not only on relatives, but also the volunteers, who recorded the testimonies and transcribed and edited their words. That said, the feedback received from relatives does suggest that the process was important and in general had a very positive and cathartic effect on family and friends.

An absolutely critical aspect of the project was the 'return' phase. Every effort was made to ensure that all individuals interviewed received a copy of the victim's edited case study (i.e. two/three/four interviews). The testimonies were hand-delivered to participants' homes with a letter explaining that they were free to make changes or include additional information to their own testimony. They were also invited to make comment on the overall case study but changes to other testimonies, could only be authorised by the person interviewed. Several weeks later testimonies were collected. Volunteers spent considerable time in people's homes talking through, clarifying and meticulously documenting any changes individuals had requested. Participants were asked to sign the returned testimony indicating consent for publication. The final case presented in the book had to be approved by the family or closest relative.

The process of returning testimonies was fundamental to the project. However, the extent of the task was completely underestimated. Moreover it presented the ACP with a whole series of sensitive issues we had certainly never anticipated. The sheer length of time the process demanded and the patience and commitment it required is simply impossible to convey and quantify. Yet for all of us involved in the research the community's control and ownership was the essence of the project. It is what distinguishes this book from other similar pieces of work. We regarded this aspect of the work, despite the complications, as an essential process to undertake.

There were, at least, three reasons for the decision to return complete edited case studies to participants. Firstly, the ACP felt that it was important that those interviewed had control and ownership over what was written. It was felt essential that they had an opportunity and space to comment on their edited testimony and to give their consent for publication. Secondly, it was important that relatives were given an opportunity to read what other participants had said about their loved one during interviews. While the ACP made it clear that they could not change the words of other peoples' interviews we actively helped to resolve any misunderstandings or issues that arose. The ACP was called upon to undertake this mediating role on a number of occasions. Thirdly, returning the testimonies was a way of disclosing 'the truth' or details about the circumstances of death that had been 'hidden' or lost in the chaos of the time.

These issues will be discussed more fully in the conclusion of the book. However, at this point it is important to say that one of the striking things for those of us involved in the project was the realisation of how little relatives actually knew about the circumstances of the death. A surprising number of relatives had never spoken to eyewitnesses or individuals who had been with their loved ones when they died. This is completely understandable given the trauma, confusion and bewilderment in the circumstances of that time. Moreover, countless families up until now have never spoken about the death of their loved one, and as a result, such information was never shared or disclosed at a community level. The project has provided a mechanism for such stories to be told.

A further recurring theme in testimonies that will be examined later in the book was the complete sense of alienation people felt from the institutions of the British state and the whole process of investigation, inquest and disclosure. The hostility and obstruction ordinary people experienced when attempting to establish 'the truth' from a system that had long practised a culture of denial and secrecy was in the end too much for many people to cope with. This is evident in the testimonies of this book in particular where agents of the state were involved in the killing. This has meant that over the years some victims' relatives reluctantly resigned themselves to the fact that they were powerless in view of the odds stacked against them. In later years this created, for some relatives, a misplaced feeling of guilt. Yet in the face of adversity many individuals found ways to challenge the system, struggled and refused to accept. How the British state managed 'the truth', and the ways in which local people responded, are explored in some detail in the history sections and conclusion of the book.

The Value of Memory

The testimonies in this book are important for a number of reasons, not least because they allow ordinary people to tell their story. In doing so they challenge perceptions of the past. The last few years has seen a ground swell of community-based groups and projects that are raising the question of 'state-sanctioned forgetting' through oral history and commemoration projects. They share the demand for society not to forget and aim to preserve communal collective memories of the conflict, struggle and resistance as a counterweight to 'official histories' in the future. The collective memory recovery work being undertaken by groups like the Ardoyne Commemoration Project bear a strong resemblance to that of organisations such as the Recovery of Historical Memory project (REMHI) in Guatemala and other 'Never Again' projects initiated by civil society in Latin America.

However, what is apparent is that there are many families who have a deep and fundamental need to know the truth surrounding the death of their loved one. Uncovering the truth and public acknowledgement of wrongdoing by the British state are seen as an essential part of the healing process for many victims' families. But the fundamental problem remains: where there has been no radical change in government how can the state be persuaded to tell the truth?

It is within this context that groups and organisations like the ACP, operating within civil society, have taken up the challenge of 'truth-telling' by trying to establish unofficial mechanisms through which to confront the past. Such voices are becoming steadily louder and better heard; their discourse on truth and justice has come to occupy a more significant position in the public space than before. It is also apparent that these processes are creating awareness and politicising individuals and groups within nationalist communities. In essence a social movement for truth and justice is evolving in the North of Ireland. Until now many individuals and families have struggled privately and in silence with the unresolved issues surrounding the death of a loved one. These ordinary people have had first hand experience of a long-standing practice by the British state of marginalising their experiences, their status as victims and their memories. The growth of the sort of social action described in this book, and indeed the book itself, is a response to the 'state-sanctioned discourse of forgetting' explicit in the Bloomfield Report and which underpins the state's 'victims agenda'. Like many other societies experiencing conflict transition, there is need to establish truths, in part to preserve an accurate historical account of the conflict, and in so doing ensuring that such human rights abuses never happen again.

The process of 'post-conflict transition' presents difficulties in getting at 'the truth' in other ways. There have been 'silences' within a community like Ardoyne as well as surrounding it. For many years there has been a reticence to discuss fully and publicly events and issues that have touched on many aspects of the conflict. In large part this is a product of a 'secrecy is survival' mentality. That was the consequence of subjecting communities like Ardoyne to extreme levels of state surveillance and psychologically destructive counter-insurgency strategies. In addition, it could be argued, the Catholic working class culture that predominates in Ardoyne is not one that lends itself easily to public discussion or display of loss. Such things have also moulded the way that collective memories have been conditioned and shaped. The aftermath of conflict can open spaces for 'history from below' perspectives to challenge 'official' discourses and public memories. If they are to do so, however, there is also a need to overcome the (understandable) reluctance to place the 'hidden transcripts' of the community past on record. It may well be speech, rather than secrecy, that ensures the survival of such memories into the future.

Structure of the Book

The overall structure of the book is built around a series of chronologically organised chapters that are designed to highlight distinct phases of the conflict. In turn, those phases were largely defined by the changing counter-insurgency strategies and policies of the

British state that had such a devastating impact on Ardoyne. The consequences of these strategies are reflected in the changing circumstances of many of the victims' deaths and the testimonies. Each chapter therefore begins with an historical context section that describes how events developed within Ardoyne and elsewhere during a specific time frame. This is then followed by the individual cases of all of the Ardoyne victims who died during that period. Each case includes a photograph of the victim where one was available, key biographical details and the testimonies of the relatives, friends and eyewitnesses interviewed.

Six phases of the conflict were identified. The first was from 1969 to 1970. This was marked by the invasion of the district by the RUC and loyalist mobs on the night of 14/15 August 1969. Hundreds of houses in several streets were set alight and the district suffered its first two fatal casualties. These events are treated in some depth because they were seared into the collective consciousness of the community and did much to define what was to happen thereafter. The next chapter, and one of the most extensive, deals with the period from 1971 through to 1973. Throughout the North 1972 witnessed more deaths than any other year and Ardoyne was to similarly suffer more losses at this time than in any other phase of the war. The introduction of internment in August 1971 and killing of 14 unarmed civilians on 'Bloody Sunday' in Derry in January 1972 instigated open war. Such events also exemplified a particular phase of British counter-insurgency strategy that was characterised by militarisation and the mass use of the army in open confrontations and search operations in nationalist areas. This is one reason why British army casualties in Ardoyne were so high during this time. Over 90 per cent of all the British soldiers killed in the district throughout the 30 years of the conflict died in these years.

In part as a response to the extent of casualties being inflicted on the British army the state's strategy was already becoming more streamlined, concerted and guided by key counter-insurgency strategists by 1974. Ardoyne deaths from British army actions decreased from the 1971-73 highpoints, but still remained very high. Of growing significance, however, was the role of loyalist paramilitaries and the issue of collusion. The UVF and UDA embarked upon a nakedly sectarian murder campaign that grew in intensity and ferocity between 1974 and 1976. North Belfast became synonymous with such killings due, in particular, to the actions of the Shankill Butchers, who made the area their sectarian hunting ground. Marking this wave of terror the Cliftonville Road, which borders onto Ardoyne, was re-christened the 'murder mile'. In these two years 22 people from Ardoyne were killed, 16 in sectarian attacks at the hands of loyalists.

By 1976 the British strategy of Containment was being implemented through the three allied policies of Criminalisation, Ulsterisation and Normalisation. The notional return to 'police primacy', the revising of emergency legislation, the creation of special courts and 'interrogation centres' foreshadowed the attempt to criminalise resistance to the state. The newly built cells of the H-Blocks were soon filled with the young of (mainly nationalist) working class areas, including large numbers from Ardoyne. Such strategies culminated in the republican hunger strikes of 1980 and 1981, events that re-defined politics for decades to come. In the years immediately following the hunger strikes British state attempts to curtail opposition saw it adopt the 'supergrass' strategy. This again had a direct and potent impact upon the people of Ardoyne during the Christopher Black case. Throughout this period sectarian assassination continued to be the dominant cause of deaths in Ardoyne.

The next identified phase begins with the signing of the Anglo-Irish Agreement in 1985 and ends with the declaration of the IRA cease-fire in August 1994. Politically this period was defined by the long, slow and often unclear germination of the subsequent peace process. On the ground real change seemed a very distant prospect. Certainly the rate of fatalities suffered generally in the North had by this time achieved an unwelcome equilibrium, although from the late 1980s onward an increase in loyalist paramilitary activity once again drew attention to the spectre of collusion. Allegations of collusion between loyalist groups and various British intelligence agencies (MI5, Military Intelligence, including Force Research Unit and RUC Special Branch) came more and more to the fore, particularly after the 'shoot-to-kill' debate was made public during the Stalker affair in the mid-1980s. Certainly in Ardoyne the primary responsibility for deaths continued to be loyalist paramilitaries and although the numbers killed were far less than in the early to mid 1970s, there were nevertheless losses in most years. In a number of such cases evidence has pointed to the possibility of collusion playing a part.

The final chapter covers the period of the Irish Peace Process. While it was hoped that the Peace Process would ensure that tension was lessened and deaths from political violence would become a thing of the past this has not, unfortunately, proved to be the case. Certainly many things have changed and the signing of the Good Friday Agreement in April 1998 signalled a truly historic opportunity for real social and political progress. The Peace Process also engendered reflections on the history of the conflict as the chance emerged, for the first time in two generations, to consign deaths from political violence to the past. Yet these were years too when inter-communal tensions were enflamed, particularly during the months of the Orange 'Marching Season'. Whatever the possibilities of finding a better future, the legacy of issues from the past had clearly not yet been put to rest.

It was also in these years and within this environment that the ACP was established. The aim of the project has been to bring into the public arena the story of those people from Ardoyne who lost their lives during the many years of war. As has been stated, the desire is not to write a definitive history of the district or of the conflict, but to show, through the words of those most directly affected, how the conflict impacted upon the district. At the start of the project, in 1998, we had hoped that the last of the political killings had already occurred. Three months later Brian Service was killed by loyalists. Another family experienced grief and loss at first hand. Another name was added to the list of Ardoyne victims. It was a salutary reminder of why this book needed to be written. The hope is that by giving the families and friends of the dead to tell their truth, and contributing in the search for justice, it may be possible to help ensure that the latest victim becomes the last.

1. These figures are taken from a number of sources including; Fay, Marie-Therese et al. (1999) *Northern Ireland's Troubles: The Human Costs*, Pluto Press, London; McKitterick, D. et al. (1999) *Lost Lives: The Stories of the Men, Women and Children who Died as a Result of the Northern Ireland Troubles*, and Sutton, M. (1994) *Bear in Mind These Dead: An Index of the Deaths from the Conflict in Ireland 1969-1993*, Beyond the Pale Publications, Belfast

Top: Young lads posing at the junction of Butler Street and Crumlin Road, 1966. Left and below, the same view showing the British army rounding up young men, August 1971 (left) and barricading nationalists with armoured trucks while loyalists wait around the corner on Crumlin Road, 1970 (below).

Ardoyne as viewed from the Bone area, late 1960s. The waste ground to the fore was where Josie McComiskey was killed by the British army in September 1972.

1

1969-70
'Ardoyne Will Not Burn...'

The Song of 'Old Ardoyne'

In the middle of August in the year '69,
Chi-Chi called the Specials on Stormont's hotline.
'I want you to go to a place called Ardoyne,
to shoot all the Fenians for the sake of the Boyne.
On the 14th and 15th the B-men went mad,
with machine guns and whippets they tore up the 'Pad',
intending to shoot every Catholic in sight,
but the boys of Ardoyne did not easily take fright.
With sticks and with stones and with petrol bombs too,
the so-called long-haired ones stood steady and true.
'We need more help now', the B-men they roared,
so Chi-Chi obliged with the UVF hoard.
With hate in their hearts now these monsters came on,
they swore they'd destroy Old Ardoyne before dawn,
they burnt and they murdered and looted as well
but as hard as they tried Old Ardoyne never fell.
We'll never forget them as the years pass away,
we'll always remember they came here to slay,
those butchers of Chi-Chi some day we will meet
and for Ardoyne's long-haired ones revenge will be sweet.

(Local song composed by Bobby Rodgersand sung after the events of 1969)

After decades of unionist rule, the north of Ireland in the early 1960s appeared to be a place of relative calm. True, the IRA had launched a border campaign from 1956-62 (that saw a number of Ardoyne republicans interned) but it had all but run out of steam within a year or two. Its most lasting impact was to be the re-orientation of the republican movement in the coming decade. In 1966 the celebrations to mark the 50th anniversary of the Easter Rising led to street clashes. These were largely fomented by a young fundamentalist Protestant preacher called Ian Paisley. His anti-Catholic message also helped inspire some of those in the Protestant working class heartland of the Shankill Road (that bordered onto Ardoyne) to form themselves into a new paramilitary group, adopting the name Ulster Volunteer Force (UVF). They soon embarked upon a nakedly sectarian murder campaign that led to the death of three young Catholic men. But it was the civil rights agitation that gathered pace from the mid-1960s onward which brought to the fore nationalist grievances that, if often unspoken, had long bubbled just below the surface. The new mood of political mobilisation and the spiralling tumult of events that shaped the late 1960s would affect Ardoyne as elsewhere, if at first only at a distance.

If calm had reigned, it was not that of a society at ease with itself so much as the stagnation of a sectarian and conservative backwater. Years of unionist rule may have led many in the Catholic community to adopt a strategy of 'keeping their heads down' but they could still see the inequality that determined their limited life chances, and those of their children. In Catholic working class areas like Ardoyne unemployment, underemployment and deprivation were rife. The path of emigration to find work in England was a well-trodden one, breaking up families in the process and heaping the pain of separation from a tight-knit community on to that of endemic poverty. Housing conditions in (particularly 'Old') Ardoyne were deplorable, with vastly overcrowded abodes often lacking the most basic amenities. Many lived without access basic amenities such as indoor sanitation. People's health suffered as a consequence, most clearly indicated by the very high level of child mortality. The dire social and economic conditions in Ardoyne were to be a breeding ground for future dissent.

Nor did the image of inter-communal harmony promoted by the 'modernising' unionist Prime Minister Terence O'Neill fit with reality on the ground. In Ardoyne and the surrounding areas Protestant and Catholic neighbours lived more or less peacefully most of the time, although the Orange marching season helped to ensure that the fires of sectarianism were stoked on an annual basis. The communal divide was always there. It could not disappear in a society where being a Protestant or a Catholic mattered in economic and political terms. In Ardoyne that division affected almost every aspect of the social world in which people lived. Because of the sectarian nature of unionist rule it also determined what opportunities people in Ardoyne might have, or be denied.

By late 1968 and early 1969 people in nationalist areas watched what took place in Derry, Burntollet and other places with a growing sense of anger and unease. At the same time the early months of 1969 saw an increasing number of clashes between people from Ardoyne and the RUC. Although not always exactly 'political' in nature, such confrontations evidenced the slow gathering pace of heightened local tensions. Indeed, a visit of Terence O'Neill to Ardoyne in January 1969 helped spark the civil rights movement in the district into life. Joe Graham (an early civil rights activist and founding member of the Ardoyne Citizen Action Committee) describes what happened:

> There were only about 20 ardent civil rights activists in Ardoyne at first – people like Liam Mulholland, Patsy Quinn, Rebecca and Frank McGlade, the whole Corrigan family, myself and Martin Meehan. But what brought things into focus in the area was

when Terence O'Neill came into the district in January 1969. It was part of his attempt to enlist Catholic support. One local resident invited him in to her house and there were pictures in the papers of him having tea with her. That infuriated people because we were conscious of the problems that there were. Within minutes a crowd gathered and O'Neill was whisked away. After that an Ad Hoc Committee was formed from a public meeting one Sunday afternoon. By early May of 1969 we felt there was a need for a more formal grouping. We held a meeting one Sunday afternoon in Toby's Hall and the Ardoyne Citizen Action Committee [ACAC] was formed. Myself, Tony Cosgrove, Martin Meehan, Fr. Marcellus and Francie McGuigan were elected to it by a show of hands. By then there were more and more clashes with the local RUC building up. They were trying to criminalise the civil rights movement by arresting youths for alleged 'riotous behaviour' that the local RUC knew had a record for minor offences. That was a tactic they used. They also tried to divide us amongst ourselves. In late May we [the Committee members] went to the RUC headquarters in Castlereagh for a meeting with the head of the RUC. They took Fr. Marcellus aside and tried to say we were all IRA men and that he should not be involved with us. It caused division and left a stigma. But they were trying to undermine us because of the big reaction we were getting. The RUC were showing more and more signs of bitterness toward the area and the ACAC had shown them they were not representative of Ardoyne or welcome in it. One Sunday night in late May we had called a public meeting at the top of the Pad and the corner of Herbert Street. Literally thousands of people were at it. They voted to police themselves. After that we called for volunteers to act as what were called 'vigilantes' but we saw as local policing. We decided to go for middle-aged and moderate men. It took us about two hours to get all the names down. There was a queue three deep from the corner of Herbert Street down to the old Star Club at the bottom of the Pad. That was when the RUC knew they had to meet with us. But a monster was being unleashed that was going to hit us in August. It was a monster that would rage through burning row after row of houses. There would be no law, no order and no justice. (Joe Graham, Community activist)

Things began to come to a head during the Orange marching season in July. A Twelfth parade returning down the Crumlin Road was met with a tricolour flown from the window of Kilpatrick's pub. The RUC smashed down the door of the bar, beat out the occupants and arrested 'Topper' Deeds, Sammy Graham and Hughie Corrigan for the alleged 'offence'. It was noticeable thereafter that the RUC began to have a markedly more high-profile presence, something which tended to greatly accentuate rather than lessen people's anxiety. Anger and frustration in the area had also become more and more focussed on the giant union jack flown provocatively by local moneylender 'Skinny Lizzie' Gilmour from the wall of her house-cum-shop on the corner of Hooker Street and Chatham Street. Longstanding irritation over this insistent practice was becoming allied with a far more concrete sense of injustice. That growing frustration was somehow symbolised by this flag which was eventually guarded by two armed RUC men. On one occasion the RUC came into Hooker Street armed with pick shaft handles. Across the street from Skinny Lizzie's lived a young woman, Alice Sharpe. When she came to her door to see what the commotion was, she was hit on the head by one of the RUC men. Alice was expecting a child at the time. She lost her child as a result of this beating. For some people in the area that lost child was the first victim of the conflict. Alice Sharpe's husband Eddie would later be shot dead by the British army [Eddie Sharpe, killed by the British army, Cranbrook Gardens, 12 March 1973]. In the tinder-dry atmosphere of the summer of 1969 and in such a 'frontline' area these actions seemed to personify the second-class condition that was the tacitly accepted, if long resented lot of the Ardoyne Catholic population. It also led to more and more confrontations with the RUC.

Early reminders of Ardoyne's vulnerable position as an enclave community fuelled a growing sense of fear. From May onward Catholic families had been forced to flee their homes on the 'other' side of the Crumlin Road as loyalist intimidation began to make its presence felt. From mid-July, Protestant crowds were gathering virtually every night, often organised by John McKeague (soon to be prominent in loyalist paramilitary circles) and John McQuaid, later an MP in West Belfast. Catholics began to be burnt out of their homes, despite the close presence of the RUC. By early August dozens of Catholic families had been forced out of Chief Street, Cambrai Street and Leopold Street. The build up of tension, the frightening nature of these events and their long-term impact is reflected in the testimony of Charlie Toner who was just 17 years old in 1969. Charlie's family was burnt out of their home in Cambrai Street on the weekend of 2-5 August.

My family lived above our off-licence business in Cambrai Street after we moved to Belfast in 1955, until 1969. We had a small bar and at the back of that there was a pigeon club. Pigeon fanciers from all over north Belfast would gather there, Protestant and Catholic. We had tremendous neighbours and my mother in particular was very popular in the street. It was mainly a Protestant street, with just one or two Catholic families, but virtually all the licensed premise on either side of the Crumlin Road were Catholic-owned at that time. We got on with everyone all year round except during the marching season in July. At that time of year there was always a bit of hostility. You were made to feel as if you were not wanted and didn't really belong. Tensions started to build up from 1966 onward. One of our windows was broken that year after Gerry Fitt was elected. On the night of 11 July 1967 all our windows were put in. There were always some problems around July but in 1969 things got a lot worse. For months there was an undercurrent of unease. People passing the door of the bar would shout in that we would not be there in a few months time. Then my mother and father were warned that the house might be attacked. The RUC put a guard in the road and for two weeks my parents didn't get a single night's sleep. They had buckets of water ready in every room in case we were petrol bombed. It was an awful existence.

Then on Saturday 2 August there were clashes following an Orange parade near the Unity Flats and a confrontation on the Crumlin Road after the Wheatfield bar was attacked. Just after that a window in our house was broken. The whole family was in the house at the time. We went into the street where there were loads of people. The atmosphere was really electric. My father was boarding up the window when my oldest sister shouted that a big crowd of people was coming down the street. There were a couple of hundred of them marching down the middle of the road. They stopped just outside our house and started chanting. Then a petrol bomb was thrown through one of the downstairs windows. My mother and father put it out with water from the buckets. Another petrol bomb was thrown into the off-licence. All the windows of the off-licence were broken and some of the crowd started grabbing bottles of spirits. Some of our neighbours were trying to stop the crowd but they were threatened and had to just leave the scene. We thought the mob were coming into the house and I remember my mother praying on the stairs because she thought we were all going to be killed. We pushed all the wardrobes upstairs and stood them against the windows. A shower of bricks was being thrown and they were ripping into the wardrobes. You could smell petrol. The whole incident was absolutely terrifying.

It was over half an hour before the RUC arrived, even though their barracks was in Tennent Street, the road right next to ours. Until they turned up we were completely at the mercy of the crowd. After the RUC left again we just sat up all night. Every now and again a few bricks were thrown. Next morning, at about nine o'clock, the crowd gathered again and started chanting 'Taigs out, Taigs out!' The RUC came and even though my parents wanted to stay to protect the business they had built up, the RUC said they could not guarantee their safety. Some friends came over in three or four cars from Ardoyne to take us away and we went to stay with family. As we left the crowd was all around us chanting. It was really frightening. We were told that the house and the off-licence were completely looted that night. People were just sitting around outside drinking and all the furniture was taken out of the house. That nearly broke my mother's heart because she had built up a lovely home. The next day, my father went back and tried to secure the premises but a crowd soon gathered and he had to leave. The whole house was burnt out that night, Monday 4 August. There were three or four other Catholic families burnt out that night in Leopold Street as well. We lost things that could never be replaced, like family photographs and the wee things that make a house a home. We found out on the news the next morning that the house had been burnt out. My father was just broken by that. It was the first time I ever saw him cry. My mother took it very badly too and we had to get a doctor for her. I don't think she ever really got over it. Everything they had built up was wiped out in a couple of days of madness. My mother and father were very good people who had never done any harm to anyone and I could never understand why anyone wanted to do that to them. (Charlie Toner, Ardoyne resident and local shop owner)

At the same time a number of Protestants had to leave the area surrounding Hooker Street. Skinny Lizzie's house was attacked and burnt out. The ACAC tried to persuade Protestants not to leave. When this failed they liased with some families and groups in Protestant areas to arrange for people to swap their homes. Lines were becoming more clearly drawn, both politically and physically. Temporary barricades began to appear each evening on the roads facing onto the Disraeli Street area. The atmosphere grew more heated following attacks on Catholics in the isolated Unity Flats on the weekend of 2-5 August. A barricade built at the top of Hooker Street met with a massive RUC response. The RUC mounted a series of landrover-led charges into a Catholic crowd who replied with a hail of stones and petrol bombs. Two locals were badly injured and received the last rites. One was soon-to-be well-known republican Martin Meehan. The other was 16-year-old Neil Somers who lost his leg after being hit by a speeding RUC landrover and dragged by the vehicle for a considerable distance. A pattern to the confrontations was becoming established. So too was the need for a co-ordinated response. The ACAC set up in May to liase with the state authorities had been short-lived. However, it was a forerunner of the ad-hoc vigilante groups and defence bodies that began to emerge from this time on, evidence again of the growing sense of trepidation that was taking hold within the area. In early August a revamped ACAC was established made up of Joe Hughes, Joe Graham and Tony Cosgrove. Mary McGuigan was the chairperson. A number of local priests were also closely connected to this new committee, including Fr. Myles and the white-haired Fr. Marcellus. The latter would become a familiar figure on the streets in the coming dark nights. Some precautions were laid to try and fend off future attacks on the area. However, nothing had prepared anyone in Ardoyne for what was to happen on the night of 14 and 15 August.

The pent-up powder keg of politics in the Six Counties exploded on the streets of Derry on the 12th August 1969 when the annual Apprentice Boys parade led to the 'Battle of the Bogside'. The call went out from Derry to other Catholic working class areas that (in order to stretch the RUC and so relieve the pressure on the Bogsiders) a 'second front' needed to be opened up. Bernadette Devlin spoke at a hastily called street meeting in Ardoyne on the evening of 13 August. Such was the dynamic of tensions in the area, however, that confrontation was virtually a foregone conclusion anyway. That night a large crowd fought with the RUC in Hooker Street and Brompton Park whilst behind the RUC lines loyalist rioters set fire to Catholic homes, shops, businesses and bars.

By now dozens of families had been made homeless and many were being given refuge in the dinner hall of the Holy Cross Boys school in Butler Street. The makings of what would later become the Ardoyne Relief Committee was beginning to take shape as people fell back on their own resources to find practical answers to the precarious position they found themselves in. Learning how to find food, shelter and providing for the welfare of the 'refugees' was a lesson learnt through the trial and error of those days. As the momentum of events built up through July and early August, space for literally hundreds of families had to be found. Families were squatted into any empty, half-built or new houses that could be found. The Travellers who had a camp up on the old Brickyard provided their lorries in order that people could be moved out of increasingly dangerous areas. On the morning of 14 August as the bishop (somewhat ominously) walked around blessing the area, a number of buses were commandeered to transport women and children across the city to the relative safety of West Belfast. They would spend the next few days sleeping on hastily erected campbeds in school halls as the fear of what had happened the night before mounted further. Later many from the district would also flee over the border to 'refugee' camps set up by the 26-County government, such as that in Gormanstown, Co. Meath.

If things had been bad on 13 August, far worse was to follow the night after. The Stormont regime signalled its intentions when the then Deputy Minister for Home Affairs

John Taylor announced the mobilisation of the 11,000 Protestant members of the 'B' Specials. As the British army was being moved into Derry and fighting again broke out throughout the Six Counties, RUC men, 'B' Specials and a mob of several hundred loyalist rioters surged across the Crumlin Road down Hooker Street and set fire to houses there and in the adjoining Chatham Street and Brookfield Street. The throng of RUC, 'B' men and loyalist civilians were as one, wreaking destruction on people and property as they poured through Herbert Street and Butler Street. The Scarman Tribunal, set up later by the British government (supposedly to 'investigate' the upheavals of 1969) would politely chastise the RUC for permitting themselves to work in tandem with this loyalist mob. However, it stopped far short of actually denouncing these actions. Indeed, Scarman placed responsibility for the wholesale destruction and violence that occurred that night upon the people of Ardoyne themselves. The Scarman Report even suggested at one point that it may have been petrol bombs thrown by Catholics that burnt their own homes! Insult was added to grievous injury and further confirmed a lack of faith in the RUC that smouldering burnt-out houses left in their wake.

It is almost impossible, with the hindsight of the last thirty years, to comprehend the disbelief and cold fear that gripped everyone in the area that night. Their state of vulnerability in the face of this onslaught was made crystal clear in the most frightening of ways. The RUC came in armed and supported by armoured cars mounted with heavy machine guns. At around midnight they opened fire in Butler Street and Herbert Street. At first many were filled with bewilderment believing (wrongly) that they were shooting blanks. A sense of real dread and panic gripped all as the flames from burning houses leapt into the night sky and the air became filled with the shouts and screams of pitched street battles. People truly feared that a massacre was about to take place and that the aim of those invading Catholic Ardoyne was to end its existence. Something of the fear and dread people felt can be seen in the account of the night given by Kathleen O'Kane, whose brother Dandy would later be killed by loyalists [Trevor 'Dandy' Close, killed by UVF on the Cliftonville Road, 26 May 1983].

I remember the night of the 14/15 August very well. The Paisleyites came in, smashed all the windows and threw in petrol bombs. I was stuck in the house with two kids. My son Owen had just been born on 7 June that year. I was literally petrified. At one point I was sitting behind the door trying to keep the mob out. Then I remember running down the street with my two kids in my arms, screaming. I ended up in a neighbour's house, Jean Cooney's, and she put mattresses down on the floor for us. I was just sitting there with my two kids and I didn't even have a bottle for the child. The Paisleyites were looking to burn us all out. I couldn't believe it. I was so angry and at the same time I literally couldn't speak with fright. We were not brought up to be bigots and I was not into politics or anything. But after that, everyone in the whole street would have come out if something was happening, to help one another, because we were not going to let anyone else be burnt out. I called the Paisleyites every name under the sun for burning us out but my brother Dandy just said that they were ordinary people and they were scared and frightened too. (Kathleen O'Kane, Ardoyne resident and sister of Ardoyne victim Trevor Close)

Similarly the testimony of Alice Campbell gives a sense of the impact these events were to have on those burnt out on the night of 14/15 August.

In 1969 we lived in Brookfield Street. My husband was working as a joiner and I looked after our young children. I was very house-proud and I really loved that house. On the night of the 14/15 August I remember the Paisleyites coming down the street. They had guns and were shooting around them. Then they started burning the whole street, from top to bottom. My house was burnt out with all the rest. We lost everything we had, I wasn't able to get a single thing out of that house. We got some compensation but nothing compared to what we lost, and of course there were lots of sentimental things that you could never get again. We stayed in my mother-in-law's house afterward before we got a new one, in Farringdon Gardens. We started to build our home once more but I knew that someday the same thing would happen again, that the same men would come back and burn us out. I will never get the sight of them out of my mind.
(Alice Campbell, Ardoyne resident and mother of Ardoyne victim Eddie Campbell)

After suffering more sectarian harassment Alice and her family would be burnt out for a second time on the morning of the introduction of internment, 9 August 1971. Worse still, her son Eddie would be shot dead in a blatantly sectarian attack by the UFF in July 1987, his body being left in the laneway of a disused quarry [Eddie Campbell, killed by the UFF near Horseshoe Bend, 3 July 1987].

Certainly the thought burnt into the mind of many on the night of 14/15 August was that they should never again find themselves unable to fend off such an attack with no more than stones, sticks and petrol bombs. Because, despite RUC views to the contrary, there were virtually no weapons in Ardoyne at that time. A couple of shotguns and a broken rifle were the grand sum of the district's arsenal. As a result, people fought back with an adrenaline-driven resolution born out of necessity and made do with whatever came to hand. They broke up paving stones, rolled out oil drums as makeshift barricades, threw milk bottles and rapidly learnt how to make petrol bombs. Robert McCargo's evidence to the Scarman Tribunal takes up the story.

I had been looking down towards Hooker Street and I saw a crowd of people apparently being baton-charged towards the Butler Street area by the police. That was practically a common sight in Ardoyne for some time in the Hooker Street area. As I was standing in Herbert Street two police jeeps preceded a crowd of policemen, 'Specials' and civilians into Herbert Street and started to throw petrol bombs at the houses. On each side of the street petrol bombs were thrown; they set the houses afire on the right. They were all allied to one another. I happened to be enveloped in flames with a petrol bomb thrown by a policeman. I was shocked; I could not believe civilised people could come in and start firing petrol bombs. There was little I could do, but people who were further up Chatham Street, people who were at their doors, came running down with empty milk bottles and naturally enough I did my best to repel the people who were setting their property afire. I and the people I was standing with organised a chain of buckets of water. I am nearly certain he [Sammy McLarnon] was there giving me a hand in chaining buckets of water up the street. I was in a state of exhaustion. I had been running to and fro for the best part of an hour. There was an armoured car [that] came down Herbert Street going very slow. It seemed to rev up and increase its speed and reversed towards the Crumlin Road but as it got beyond Chatham Street, there was a burst of gunfire [from this vehicle]. It was replaced by men in uniform who knelt down at the top of the street and started to fire down the street. People who were close by McLarnon's house started to shout up the street that they required an ambulance, that they had a man dead in the house, and the police at the top of the street were shouting, 'And there'll be more of you dead before the weekend'. I went up into Butler Street and found there were 12 or 13 young fellas shot who actually thought the men at Butler Street corner were firing blanks. When the shooting commenced in Ardoyne the place was in utter chaos and for the police to say that there was automatic fire from the Ardoyne area is absolute nonsense. (There had been) mass migration of people in that area so there was practically nobody left in it. (Excerpts from the evidence of Ardoyne resident Robert McCargo to the Scarman Tribunal of the events of 14/15 August 1969)

By the next morning the RUC had shot dead two men, Sammy McLarnon killed in his home in Herbert Street and Michael Lynch, fatally wounded whilst standing on the corner of Butler Street. Sammy and Michael were the first people from the area killed by state violence during the recent conflict. Several others were also badly injured by the heavy RUC gunfire. In all at least twelve people were shot in the area that night. All were from Ardoyne. All were Catholic. The RUC received no gunshot casualties. Something of the attitude of the RUC can be garnered directly from the Scarman Report. Scarman argued that, in the hours after the invasion of Ardoyne and the killing of Sammy McLarnon and Michael Lynch, the RUC 'were thinking of the situation in terms of rebellion: and the rebels, in their view, were to be found in the Ardoyne'. For both the RUC and the British army who entered the area on the evening of 15 August, Protestant streets were regarded as 'friendly'. For the people of Ardoyne, as the testimony of Sean Colligan (a republican activist of the time) illustrates, things appeared very differently.

Everything was evolving and nobody could really see where things were going to go. I was up in Derry the day the soldiers went into there and then decided to make my way home to Ardoyne as best as I could. That was a bad night in the district but at first I couldn't get a lift home from Derry, so I didn't get to Ardoyne until four o'clock on the Friday [15 August 1969]. When I got there it was clear the area was all but defenceless. There were only two shotguns to be had, that was it. So Fr. Marcellus got my brother and I to go from street to street with the shotguns so the loyalists would think we had a whole lot of weapons. I was running about from just after four o'clock on the Friday afternoon till about eleven or twelve that night. The loyalists on the other side of the road had loads of guns and they were shooting into the area the whole time. They kept running up and firing bursts off into the streets of the district. At some point in the evening it was decided that in order to provide some kind of defence we should get the buses from the depot nearby in Glenard and block off the streets with them.

Everyone that could drive was sent up to the bus depot. That took a couple of hours but to be honest it felt like an eternity. I felt like I was in a time capsule, that time was standing still. Everyone was terrified about what might happen. We thought we were going to be torched, that the whole area was going to be burnt out by the loyalists. There was real panic and pandemonium at that point but the buses acted as a real deterrent. Oddly enough when they were taken away again in a couple of days that acted as a deterrent as well. It looked as if people in Ardoyne must have got hold of a stack of guns to defend itself, which was certainly not the case at that stage.

By then though there was a lot of enthusiasm to defend the area. People were not really 'political'; it was much more that they saw the need to defend themselves and the district. It was all a very spontaneous reaction. They could see the Brits coming in and treating us as if we were the ones causing the trouble. They set up their posts and had all their guns pointing down toward us. That certainly had a big effect on me. '69 is going to mean a lot of different things for different people but I know that as far as I was concerned it was all about defence and that meant there was a critical need to get hold of guns. I was far from alone in that; everybody wanted to get hold of guns to defend themselves. When the split in the republican movement came in early 1970 who was going to be able to provide the means to defend the district was my first and only priority when I had to decide who to support. Defending your neighbours was what it was all about in Ardoyne. This is an area with a militia mentality because of its geography. Our location dictated everything. We were surrounded and we had to stand up for ourselves because there was no one else to do it for us. That's Ardoyne. (Sean Colligan, Ardoyne resident and republican activist)

A surreal calm enveloped the district in the cold light of day as people tried to come to terms with the events of the previous night and the new reality they now faced. In the early evening the RUC withdrew and there were several hours of sustained fighting between loyalist crowds and men from the district, which included exchanges of gunfire. A double-decker bus was taken from the Crumlin Road and used to form a barricade at the top of Hooker Street. Afterwards, a large number of the Ardoyne men went down to the nearby bus depot and took over a dozen buses back into the area. Put in place, the buses formed a wall of defence across all the key roads into the district, at the same time creating one of the starkest images and abiding memories of the period. That evening also saw units of the British army move into positions on the Crumlin Road, as they were in other parts of Belfast and elsewhere. Also as elsewhere they were initially welcomed, and in the immediate months that followed, a relatively frictionless relationship developed. However, the sense that the district's protection might be dependent on action from within was already something that had taken, at least partial, hold. The argument over how best to defend the area and different reactions to the first British presence in the district are reflected in the words of Martin Meehan.

Just a few days before the big Troubles, about 10 or 11 August 1969, the leadership of the IRA disarmed us. We didn't have a terrible lot of weapons anyway but they came in and took away what gear we had. They said that they didn't want the conflict growing into a full-blown sectarian war and they saw Ardoyne as a potential catalyst for sectarianism. So they thought that if they disarmed us there was no need for them to worry about us. They left us with nothing; they left the whole district totally defenceless. All that we had was the buses out of the depot; without those buses we would have been overrun. The people of the district were terrified. At night time it was completely different but during the day there was a quietness, an eerie quietness. Then on the 15th the Brits came in and they were standing there with bayonets pointing towards us. Some of the women were carrying trays of tea and sandwiches and I started shouting that they were here to protect the mills, not us, that they had their bayonets pointing towards us, and it was this area that was being attacked. (Martin Meehan, Ardoyne resident and republican activist)

The decision of the British cabinet on 19 August not to follow the mobilisation of British troops on the streets of the North with the introduction of Direct Rule meant that their involvement was identified with propping up the Stormont regime. This set in motion a train of events that would insure a clash of interest and confrontation between the British state and the minority community. That said, the findings of the Cameron Commission (published in late 1969) that widespread discrimination had been practised against Catholics did hold out some promise of positive reform. Similarly, the recommendation of the Hunt Report (published in October) that the 'B' Specials should be disbanded was widely welcomed. However, the root of these problems was also seen to reside in the nature of the state itself. That Stormont was to be preserved was already unacceptable for many in the Catholic working class ghettos who had suffered the brunt not only of such discrimination but also of the summer's violence. Tom Fleming was the first chairperson of the Ardoyne Relief Committee and a stalwart of community activism and welfare efforts in the dark years ahead. He remembers how his attitude developed through this period and the impact that the events the district went through shaped his response.

I was an ex-serviceman myself. I had been in the navy from 1942 to 1946. In fact I had a brother in the navy and another who was in the British army for 22 years. But I was always aware of discrimination because it was always harder to get a job if you were a Catholic and, if you had a job, then it was difficult to get promotion. When the 'troubles' started you became aware of the civil rights movement and it filled you with pride to see people standing up and showing courage the way they did. When Ardoyne was attacked in August 1969, you also realised that you had to do something. It was an instinct to defend the area. At that time the rioting was mainly restricted to 'Old Ardoyne'. I lived in Northwick Drive in Glenard. It was mostly Protestants that lived at the top of the street and between us we organised a 'peace group' to try to stop trouble starting – although I remember one meeting with them where one fella asked me if I was willing to give my allegiance to the Queen. That left a bad taste in my mouth because, apart from the fact that I was an ex-serviceman, that sort of question was more about bigotry than anything else.

Soon afterwards a CDC (Civil Defence Committee) was set up in Ardoyne and I was asked to go on it. There were about seven of us in total and we held several public meetings to try to organise defence and get people to stay calm. Most of the measures taken to defend the area at that stage were very much makeshift. The CDC organised 'vigilantes', which was basically people from the area patrolling it and keeping watch for attacks. It also organised the first Relief Committee to deal with people coming into the area who had been put out of their homes. I was elected chairman of the Ardoyne Relief Committee around the start of 1970. In the end I could not identify myself with the CDC anymore. The CDC was based over in West Belfast and at one point they put a full page article in the *Irish News* saying 'stop the violence'. I found that attitude difficult because people were having to use force to protect themselves, their families and their areas. It didn't recognise that discrimination was a form of violence too. To me calling on people to 'stop the violence' was like asking them not to protect themselves. (Tom Fleming, Ardoyne resident and chairperson of the Ardoyne Relief Committee in the 1970s)

The failure of the IRA to carry through their 'traditional' role of defenders of the Catholics of the Six Counties during August was leading to growing antagonism and frustration with the republican leadership. Many of those involved in defending Ardoyne without guns that summer would be amongst the first to join the 'Provisionals' when they were formed following the split in the republican movement in late 1969 and early 1970. It was precisely because the Provos stepped forward with the promise of weapons that they appealed to so many in Ardoyne. The harvest of August 1969 was bearing its clearest fruit in the form of an over-riding desire to get guns for the defence of the district. That is not to say that everyone in the area supported such moves, or indeed that all were antagonistic toward the presence of the British army. Far from it. But the 'honeymoon' was always only partial and temporary, and perhaps nowhere more so than in Ardoyne given the context of what had taken place in the preceding months. Through early 1970 the consequence of the British state's decision to preserve the status quo and re-impose 'order' invariably brought them into an increasingly fractious relationship with Catholic working class communities.

This was to culminate in the confrontations of late June 1970. It was then that the 'Provisional' IRA in Ardoyne showed itself (essentially for the first time) capable of protecting the area through the inevitably tense months of the Orange marching season. On 26 June Bernadette Devlin was arrested and imprisoned for her part in the Battle of the Bogside. This was followed by rioting, first in Derry and then in Belfast. On Saturday 27 June, the 'Little Twelfth' marked the first occasion of the summer when the new Defence Committees in many areas were put to the test. An Orange parade on the Crumlin Road was the spark for furious rioting and the first sustained gun-battle undertaken by the IRA from Ardoyne. Three Orangemen were shot dead. Events in Ardoyne were echoed in enclave areas elsewhere. The Short Strand in the east of the city was besieged and here again it was members of 'Provisional' IRA who formed the only line of defence for a terrified community. A sense of changed times was clearly in the air, married to what, in hindsight, may appear to have been an almost naïve optimism as to what was achievable. Everyone was entering uncharted waters, as the testimony of Martin Meehan again shows:

When there was a split in the offing, there was a lot of manoeuvring and some underhand stuff done. It was touch and go who would win but eventually we [the 'Provisionals'] won the day. You see, people had been let down. Defending the area was paramount in people's minds and we had to retrieve that situation. Then we exposed the British army for what it was. We started to scratch their 'achilles heel' and they responded forthwith. Confrontations started on a weekly and nightly basis coming into 1970. There was a growing series of confrontations and then came 27 June, 1970. People say that '69 was the birth of the 'Provisionals' but I think it was 27 June that year. There was an Orange parade and the Orangemen tried to get into Hooker Street. That led to hand to hand fighting. Then the Orangemen began firing and our lads responded. In the end three Orangemen were shot dead and fifteen were wounded.

After that night every door in the district was opened up to the IRA. The 'Provisionals' were born because they proved they could do what they said they would do and they carried it out to the letter. They defended the area. For the community and the volunteers 27 June was a catalyst for believing in ourselves. In '69 we were still victims but after 27 June we believed in ourselves and the community began to come together. We opened up our first republican club. The first fleadh was held in August. You had a situation in 1970 where people said, 'We're going to do something different. We're not going to let this situation get on top of us and we're going to show that we can enjoy ourselves and get on with our lives'.

Everyone wanted to join the IRA. People in the area had been giving the 'Brits' their dinner, women were going to their dances and people were standing on street corners having a sing-song with them. We went from that to armed rebellion in the space of a year. That was unbelievable. In my eyes 1970 is a very significant year in the whole history of republicanism. I remember there was a feeling of invincibility amongst the volunteers. There was no fear and no hang-ups. We knew we were on the right course and no matter what was thrown against us we felt we could face it down. In reality, when you look back, it was very scary. Young men and women who believed they could defeat the British army militarily. If we had stood back for ten seconds we would have seen that it was naïvety in the extreme. But what happened was because the men and women on the ground propelled the situation. I don't think you will ever see the like of it again. (Martin Meehan, Ardoyne resident and republican activist)

To understand anything about Ardoyne it is necessary to see the indelible mark that the memory of August 1969 had left upon virtually everyone in the district. For both individuals and the community as a whole August '69 was to become a touchstone of all future experiences, a yardstick for the rightness or wrongness of all future decisions. Such was the very real sense that the area might literally have been burnt out of existence, that anything deemed likely to leave the district so vulnerable again would be treated with, at best, disbelief and more likely contempt. The lesson was simple. This was never to be allowed to happen again. The RUC may have for long been regarded with suspicion as an 'alien' force. That they were seen to have so clearly sided with loyalist crowds coming from the south side of the Crumlin Road in the August invasion of Ardoyne was to leave, as never before, a long-term and abiding sense of distrust in anything to do with them. The experience of the actions (and inactions) of the RUC in Ardoyne in 1969 forced this generation of the district's residents to conclude that they would never be acceptable. This lack of faith was further reinforced when the RUC's deeds were exonerated by the whitewash of the Scarman Report. No action was taken against anyone for the killing of Sammy McLarnon and Michael Lynch after wholly inadequate investigations. Another pattern to future proceedings had been established. Three decades later the families of Sammy McLarnon and Michael Lynch still await some sort of justice. Only three years ago Sammy McLarnon's son Sam (who was just two when his father was murdered) launched a campaign calling for a new inquiry.

The events of the 14/15 August also realised the darkest fears long-held by people within the area. Stories of pogrom and death from the '20s and '30s were not that often told but were still lodged in the collective mind. They seemed now, more than ever before, to make sense of a world that everyone was having to come to terms with. Those stories were also to tell people how and through whom they were to answer back. Ardoyne went into 1969 as a frightened, Catholic and 'nationalist' community. What emerged out of it was a politicised people, and the beginnings of 'republican' Ardoyne. Similarly, while 1969 brought people out onto the street to defend the area, at that stage Stormont rule was still regarded as the source of the problem. By 1970 people were identifying the British state as being at the root of things. The sense of vulnerability of 1969 would slowly give way to a stubborn resolve that, no matter what was to happen in the future, Ardoyne would continue to be. It was a message declared to the people of the district in the slogan that soon adorned the wall of Tom's shop on the corner of Herbert Street in the heart of 'Old Ardoyne': 'Ardoyne will not burn, under no circumstances'.

Apart from denying me my father they would deny me the memory of my father as well.

Sammy McLarnon
Killed by the RUC,
Herbert Street,
15 August 1969

Both the parents of Sammy McLarnon came to Ardoyne in the 1930s and were amongst the first families moved into Glenard. They had six boys, of whom Sammy was the second youngest, born in 1942. Sammy did well at the Holy Cross school and when he left at 16, he got a job as an invoice clerk for a firm in St George's fruit market. He worked 'with bananas and stuff like that'. This earned him the nickname 'Slippery Sam'. But, as his brother Patsy would say, Sammy 'didn't mind what you called him as long as you didn't call him too early!' The family was living in Herbert Street when Sammy met his future wife Ann, from nearby Kingston Street. In 1966 the two married and moved into their home in Herbert Street not long after. Ann worked in the mills whilst Sammy moved on to become a bus conductor. It was a job more suited to his sociable nature. Sammy was always a 'jokey, happy-go-lucky bloke'. Working the buses afforded him ample opportunity to chat and 'sleg' with all the people from 'old Ardoyne' that he knew as his own. That was in 1968. By 1969 Sammy and Ann had two children, young Sam and Ann-Marie, with a third (Samantha) on the way. It was a young family looking toward the future at the outbreak of the conflict. On the night of 14/15 August Sammy McLarnon was shot dead in his own living room by the RUC. He was 27 years old and the first person from Ardoyne killed in the conflict.

Ann McLarnon (wife)

Sammy had been up the street helping to put out a fire at a house just before he was shot. The Protestants had come across the Crumlin Road and attacked three Catholic houses. John's shop was also ablaze. As the Catholics were defending the houses they came under attack. There was a number of shots fired from the Protestant side of the Crumlin Road. So everybody went back into their own homes and Sammy came into our house. At about 11 pm I heard shooting but I thought it was blanks. Sammy said to me, 'We'll take the kids over to my mammy's'. I said, 'But it could start in your mammy's street tonight'. Sammy's mammy lived in the top half of Herbert Street. Things started to get bad and we brought the kids (Ann-Marie and young Sammy) downstairs. But I thought it was getting too bad to take them out so I put them back up in their cots again. Then Sammy and me were standing at the right hand side of the window. I remember that there was an awful bright light. There must have been a light on down the street because we didn't have a light on in the house. The TV was not on either. There was just this bright light coming from outside the house. We saw these two fellas kneeling down in the street. Then the RUC went over and talked to them. I thought at the time that it was our ones and the RUC was going to arrest them. But it wasn't. The RUC said something to them and then the two fellas and the RUC went away. The 'B' specials, loyalists and the RUC were together at the Crumlin Road that night. Then I walked away to go into the working kitchen. I came back into the living room again and then the shots came through the window. There were three bullets, very close together. The RUC tried to say at the inquest that they were ricochets but they were head height. They were obviously intended to kill. He was shot through the window. He was pulling down the blind because he must have seen something. The glass actually hit me in the face. Then I ran back into the working kitchen again. When I came out Sammy was on the ground of the living room. I thought he had dived to the ground. But then I realised he had been shot and I just screamed, 'My husband's shot, my husband's shot'. After that, all I can remember is someone saying turn on the light. Then a load of fellas came into the house. Up until the point that Sammy was killed the only shots that had been fired had come from the Protestant end of the road. There was only about five minutes between the time Sammy had been helping to put the fire out at the top of the street and his murder. Afterwards the RUC never came near the house. They were up the street in their armoured cars. At no stage did the RUC ever come to talk to me. They never asked me for a statement or anything. At no stage did the RUC admit what they had done. There was no apology or anything else. The only help I was given at the time was from the people of the district. Nobody from the state gave me any assistance or advice. I was four months pregnant at the time with Samantha. She was due in January. After Sammy's death I ended up leaving the district and stayed with my sister before going to Gormanstown for a week.

Sam McLarnon (son)

I was the eldest child in our family. At the time of my father's death Ann-Marie was a year and a half and Samantha was in my mother's womb. I was just two and a half years of age. So I have no memory as such of what my father was like. But you tend to build up a picture of what he looked like and the sort of man he was from photographs and what people tell you. You try to fill that void yourself. Because of the picture you built up in your mind it is as if he was a person you had actually encountered. But the one thing I can see of him in my memory is one time when he carried me across the brickyard. But I am not sure that even that actually happened.

When I grew up I always felt guilty when I visited my father's grave. That was because I felt that I did not know an awful lot about the circumstances of his death and had not done anything to help his memory. I felt that I had not done anything to try and get justice for my father. So I just blotted it out and tried to forget about it. But it just constantly came back to the fore. In the end there was a chain of accidental circumstances that made me think that I could do something to get some justice. I got involved with an organisation called the North Belfast Survivors of Trauma. Through that I began to talk to kids who had lost their parents through the conflict. We got on well because I had lost my father in similar circumstances. We seemed to know what we were going through together. They said that I was easy to talk to because they had suffered what I had suffered. We had the same thoughts, angers and fears. I found I was really good doing that. So things just got better and better in the place. We had an exhibition and a book which travelled the country. It was all about young people's experiences of growing up in the conflict. The organisers asked me if I would like to contribute something and I did. But when it went to Cultra [Folk and Transport Museum] the RUC removed my piece in the exhibition. So

I had written a piece that started off, 'My father was shot dead in the house by the police when I was two and half years of age'. The RUC had it removed from the exhibition saying that no one had ever been murdered in the house by the police. My name was not even on the quote, so the RUC was denying that they ever murdered anyone in a house. The museum withdrew the piece at the request of the RUC. But when the museum checked the authenticity of the piece with the organisers they replaced it. It was at that point that I said to myself, apart from denying me my father, they would deny me the memory of my father as well. That is when I decided to go and ask people questions and find out more. I had always wanted to ask my family about my father and the circumstances and details of what happened. Then I plucked up the courage and went and did it. It was hard to talk about something that had never been discussed before.

Up until this point I knew that my father had been murdered by the RUC; I knew he had been murdered in his own home and that they had got away with it. I knew they lied in court. One of the RUC men took deliberate aim and shot him dead. That is in the Scarman Tribunal. But they put it down to a ricochet. The Scarman Tribunal established that my father was killed by a 15mm bullet fired out of a Sterling sub-machine gun. They also said that the RUC did kill my father. But they still recorded an open verdict. That was even though one of the RUC men told them that one of the RUC officers did take careful aim. So it was a calculated action. There was no gun battle that night in Ardoyne. There were only a couple of rusty guns and seven bullets in the district at the time. There were 12 men shot by the RUC that night and two were shot dead. All the men shot were Catholics from Ardoyne. There were no RUC injuries, no bullet marks or holes in their vehicles. There were no bullet holes at the positions where they were standing. This was all checked out by the Scarman Tribunal. These facts speak for themselves. The RUC have never admitted shooting my father. The head of the RUC in the district at the time was District Inspector Montgomery. He said the RUC never did anything like that. He said that my father was probably shot by the IRA. That was even though the bullets used were standard RUC bullets from standard RUC weapons at that time and that they were the only ones firing that night facing our house. A large number of people living in Herbert Street that night saw the RUC firing. All that and they still deny it. But although I was aware of all this I wasn't angry when I used to see the RUC patrolling the streets of Ardoyne. I used to be afraid. They had put fear into me. Instead of feeling like throwing a petrol bomb at them I used to just get out of the road. I would never ever have stood at a window when there was trouble going on.

My quest now is to establish the truth behind what happened that particular night. The question that burns in my head now is what was different on the 14/15 August 1969 that the RUC went out and shot six Catholics dead? Before they had been content with beating people, harassing them, kicking their doors in and running them over in land rovers. Why all of a sudden did they start shooting? What order came from the barracks on 14 August? Were they told to keep down a republican uprising? Did some sort of directive go out? Were they told to quell this 'civil rights shit' once and for all? Were they told to use whatever force was necessary and not to worry about being made accountable for their actions? I just want it to be publicly known that the British government have sanctioned massive human rights abuses in this country. I want them to admit it. I don't want to hear it from Ronnie Flanagan. If he said anything it would just be part of a PR exercise. I want to hear it from the British government in the British parliament or in Europe. I want to hear them admit that they have committed serious human rights violations in the past and that they apologise for them. As for people who actively took part in any way in the murder of my father and the other actions against the people in Ardoyne that night, they should play no part in any new policing service. Neither my son nor my grandchildren will ever be putting on any police uniform until the hurt and the damage that they have caused to our community has been acknowledged. When I started to ask questions about my father's death my mother didn't really want me to dig things up again. She said, 'Sammy, just leave it'. It probably would be easier to leave it. But it wasn't easy for me to leave it. I have waited 30 years for this moment and I am not going to wait another 30 years. What is the alternative? Do we just let things go so that any new police service can do exactly the same as the last one? Sometimes you just have to stand up and say that these things must not be allowed to happen again.

A large part of my mother died the day my father was killed. As we were children growing up she didn't like us to be out playing any time there was trouble or shooting. That was a regular occurrence in Ardoyne. Even when we were well away from any type of trouble she would still come out and drag us off the streets. She would always imagine the worst possible scenario. That took a toll on her nerves. She had to have a lot of treatment to shut out the memory of what happened that night. In a way I am hoping that maybe what we have been doing might bring a bit of closure. I don't mean that she will forget about my father. My mother will never forget my father, but that she will be able to forget about the circumstances of his death. Sometimes I imagine what it was like when my father was killed but my mother was there. She saw him lying on the floor. She heard the shooting and saw the bullet holes in the windows. She saw us crying, ran into the street and screamed for help. People shouldn't see those things. No one should see that.

Michael Lynch
Killed by the RUC,
Butler Street,
15 August 1969

> *Mummy said all that she knows is that Michael ran to get home to her. That was when the bullet hit him.*

Like Sammy McLarnon, Michael Lynch's parents had moved into Ardoyne in the 1930s where they lived in Strathroy Park. Michael was born in 1940, the eldest of 12 (six boys and six girls) who crammed into the small two-bedroom house that was their home. From an early age Michael was an important breadwinner for the family. He left school at 14 and became 'Steak' Lynch when he got a job in a butcher's in Alliance Avenue. Michael was a quiet sort, the quietest of the 'quiet Lynchs'. He was also very close to and protective of his mother, to whom he always gave over most of his wages. Even when he briefly moved to London in the late 1960s in search (like so many others) of decent work, he never failed to send home a few pounds a week. Michael only had two real interests in life: a regular Saturday flutter on the horses and going to the pictures, which he did four or five times a week, often on his own. In the summer of 1969 Michael had returned home to Ardoyne and had just started a new job at the waterworks. On the evening of the 14/15 August he was on his way home from a picture house on the Crumlin Road. He stopped to see what all the commotion was in Butler Street. The RUC were coming down the street followed by a loyalist crowd. Michael was trying to make a run for home when he was shot dead by the RUC.

Joe McDade (friend)

I knocked about with Mickey's brother Danny in 1969. He was the same age as myself. Mickey was a bit younger. The actual night it happened was 14/15 August. Sammy McLarnon was shot first but I didn't even see Sammy. Sammy was in the house in Herbert Street and I was up towards Elmfield Street. Me, Seanie Rafferty out of the Bone and big Stanley Corbett were over in this pub in the Bone called Campbell's. When the pub closed at 10 pm or so, we got a carry-out over to the Bone Hills. We went up to the Bone Hills and saw Ardoyne burning. So we decided to go over. My ma and da were living in Elmfield Street at the time so I wanted to see that they were alright. All we saw was fire. The end house of the street was on fire. When we got over to Ardoyne somebody said, 'Sam McLarnon's after being shot'. Then I was up standing at Reid's shop. There was about ten of us standing there. That is where Mickey was, standing with us at Reid's corner. Then I could see that there was shooting. But somebody said, 'They are only bangs'. We thought they were shooting blanks. But the 'orangies' and 'B' specials were shooting into the area. The cops were all gathered around Paddy Cassidy's shop on the front of the road. The 'B' Specials and the other crowd were in the Grove grounds. They were shooting from there. The bullets were hitting Doherty's gable wall and they were sparking off it. But we didn't realise what was happening because somebody said they were blanks and I didn't know what a real shot sounded like. The next thing was we saw Mickey falling. All I saw was Michael falling and two people carried him up to Basil McAfee's house. When Michael Lynch was shot the only shooting that was happening was coming into Ardoyne, from the Grove. Michael Lynch was just standing about. He was no gunman. Then I went on up to Chatham Street and started throwing a few stones. The next thing I felt was my leg going numb. I didn't realise at first that I had been shot. I felt the blood running down my leg. So they brought me into John Doherty's in Elmfield Street. They took me to the Royal Hospital. I was in the Royal when Seamie McAuley and Seamie Donnelly came in and said that Mickey Lynch was up in a ward. The bullet went right through my leg and they said, 'If you get a chance, go up and see him'. But somebody told me that he died in the middle of the night. So I never got up to see him. The cops never interviewed me or came near me about it afterwards.

Mrs McAfee (eyewitness)

Thursday 14 August 1969 was a fine clear day. There had been rumours that trouble had started on the Falls Road at about teatime and people in Ardoyne were expecting a repetition of what had occurred over the previous few nights. Crowds would gather on the Crumlin Road and try to get into the district. We lived at the top of Elmfield Street which ran parallel to the Crumlin Road, from Kerrera Street to Butler Street and then down to Herbert Street. The mood of the people was quite light-hearted. No one was expecting anything serious to happen. Any trouble that had occurred on earlier nights had taken place at the lower end of the district and we had only heard the noise. We knew that the 'B' Specials had been driving up and down the Crumlin Road in 'whippets'. When it began to get dark we heard a lot of noise and bangs. Someone said that they [RUC] had driven into Herbert Street followed by a mob from across the road. We were told that Sammy McLarnon had been shot through the window of his house. The mob had got through Herbert Street to the junction with Butler Street and was being chased up towards the Crumlin Road. When I saw them, they had reached the old dinner hall that was about halfway. The 'B' Specials were mingling with the mob and there were a couple of 'whippets' there too. They were like miniature tanks with a turret for a man to stand upright. Men from the district were fighting with the crowd and throwing bricks at them. They managed to chase them out to the Crumlin Road opposite the chapel and then down to Chief Street.

There was a lull for a short time and then they started trying to get back in again through Butler Street and Kerrera Street. The men all ran towards the Crumlin Road and there was a lot of noise. There was a lot of shouting and banging. I did not realise that some of the bangs were gunshots. My children were in bed but all the doors of the houses were open and people were coming and going. Hannah McCallum and Geraldine Smart were in my house when a man I did not recognise stumbled into the living room. He collapsed on the floor. We put a pillow under his head and a blanket round him. His skin was cold and clammy and he was only semi-conscious. There was very little blood. There was just a small hole in the front of his shirt. We tried to keep him awake but he only said that his name was Michael Lynch. We knew he was badly hurt. Bridie McAllister lived across the street and she had seen him staggering into the house. She came over to see if she could help but there was nothing any of us could do. A few minutes later John Rice came in and he had been shot in the arm. But John was not too bad.

We were unable to get either of these men to hospital because there was still fighting on the Crumlin Road and we were hemmed in. We could not even get across to the chapel to get a priest. Eventually when it eased a bit, someone got a car and tied a white sheet to the bonnet and took them to hospital. By that time it was the early hours of the morning of 15 August. I was never asked to give a statement to the police or at an inquest. I did give evidence to the Scarman Tribunal at the request of lawyers for the district.

Rosaleen Matthews (sister)

We all went to England when we were younger. We would have been about 17 or 18. Everybody seemed to come to us. We were all living under the one roof. There were beds everywhere you looked. Then Michael came over. He was the quiet one. Michael never really bothered with anyone till he came to London and then he mixed with all us. Michael was one of those people who liked his own company. He never had a girlfriend in Belfast but he did in London. It widened his horizons a bit when we brought him over to London. But Michael always worked and he liked a bet on a Saturday. Michael was very good to my mummy and daddy. He was the breadwinner of the whole family. Whatever wages he got he gave to my mummy. Then mummy would just give him a half crown to go to the pictures. Michael loved the pictures. He didn't really have a great life because he was so quiet. But he probably enjoyed it his way. We all came back from London but Michael went back again, thinking he would see the same thing he did with all of us. But because we weren't there it wasn't the same. He came home the next day. If he just hadn't come back ... Mummy had packed his bags full of tinned custard and rice because Michael loved them. That was my mummy. I came round to go to work one morning and there was Michael hiding in the coal hole with his hand out for money. But I had no money. I'll never forget that because he died that week. He started work in the Waterworks the same week. Michael didn't even get to lift his first pay.

When Michael was shot, we didn't find out till 10 am later that morning. Mummy thought Michael had stopped with me because of all the trouble. You couldn't get out to see what had happened at the time. I went into Lilly Davison's shop the next morning and she said to me, 'That was terrible what happened to your Michael'. I said, 'What happened to him?' That is how I found out he had been shot. Daddy went to the Royal Victoria but Michael was already dead. He had been in intensive care and he never came through it. Nobody was ever charged with Michael's murder. We never heard from the Scarman Tribunal and nobody got in touch with the family about it. Mummy said all she knows is that Michael ran to get home to her. That is when the bullet hit him. He ran into a house. The women in the house said all he could say was, 'I'm dying. I want my mummy'. All he wanted was mummy. They said prayers in his ear.

It was a shame about poor Michael; he didn't deserve it. He didn't have a life and he was just coming out of himself. Mummy took it awful bad; she still does. Daddy has nightmares about it still. Mummy never got over it. She had all Michael's tools until a few years ago. It is still on her mind. It broke their hearts. They had to get away from Ardoyne after it. There were too many memories for them there. So the whole family moved away. Now we are spread all over. We are in Yorkshire, Cornwall, everywhere. We sort of broke away from each other. We still ring each other but it is not the same. We were a very close family and very quiet. We were always in mummy's. In our street we used to know everybody from the top of the street to the bottom. I used to love it. You could walk to the bottom of the path with the baby if it wouldn't get to sleep for mummy and you could stand there talking till 2 am in the morning. Then we came to England after Michael was shot. Everybody split up and it just hasn't been the same since. When you talk about Ardoyne, you need to talk about the ones that left too. It didn't stop just because you left home.

Funeral of the first political victim of conflict from Ardoyne. Sammy McLarnon's remains as they enter Milltown Cemetry, August 1969

Corner of Hooker Street and Crumlin Road, August 1969. Scene of burnt out homes and riots, prior to arrival of British troops

Remains of Catholic homes in Brookfield Street, burnt out by loyalists, August 1969 (above) and refugee Catholic families in Holy Cross Boys School, Butler Street, having been forced by loyalists to flee their homes with few or no belongings (left)

The remains
of the
Wheatfield Bar,
Crumlin Road,
after a loyalist
attack, 1969

Scene of rioting in Herbert Street, 27 June 1970 (above). Loyalists had earlier marched down past Ardoyne chapel and then attacked Hooker Street. The smoke (below) is from CS gas canisters fired by the British army in Chatham Street, between Herbert and Butler Street, the same day.

2

1971-73
'Hot and Heavy' – The War Begins

There was no single event through the latter half of 1970 and early 1971 that marked the total collapse of 'good' relations between the British army and the people of Ardoyne. Initially at least, fear and antagonism remained very much focused on the surrounding loyalist areas. Nor did the district witness a parallel to the Falls Curfew of July 1970, when much of nationalist West Belfast found itself under virtual martial law and saturation army occupation for over thirty-six hours. It was an event that had a devastating effect on nationalist attitudes toward the British military everywhere. However, what happened on a more gradual basis in Ardoyne echoed the military logic and tactics that lay behind the Falls Curfew. The British state was faced with a deteriorating political situation. It was also driven by a desire to impose order and suppress the challenge of nationalist working class resistance. A policy of evermore draconian military operations was the result. The primary aim of such actions was to stem the rising tide of support for the emerging republican movement. Initially, the principal means by which the British military sought to achieve this goal was through the discovery and capture of weapons. These had begun to find their way into the North in ever greater numbers after the events of August 1969. In other words, the very guns that had become for many Catholics (particularly in an enclave area like Ardoyne) an insurance of their own survival were the object of increasingly regular and sweeping searches by the British army. If the aim was the demise of support for militant republicanism the effect was undoubtedly the reverse.

That aim was the product of the thinking of certain British military strategists. In April 1970 Brigadier General Frank Kitson arrived at British army HQ in Lisburn to take command of the 39th Infantry Brigade. Around the same time General Anthony Farrar-Hockley was appointed the British Commander of Land Forces, Northern Ireland. Just under a year later, in March 1971, Lieutenant-General Tuzo was made General Officer Commanding British Forces in the North. These three shared much in common, not least a history of involvement in many of Britain's then recent colonial campaigns in places like Malaya, Kenya and Cyprus. Along with other leading figures of the British military and political establishment who were now directly involved in the emerging Northern conflict, Kitson, Farrar-Hockley and Tuzo personified the state's response to the ever-worsening political crisis in the North. The 'restoration of order' (or the imposition of British State rule) was to be the primary objective. It was to be achieved by methods previously employed in Britain's more far-flung colonial possessions.

In early 1971 Kitson published a British army training manual, *Low Intensity Operations*. This book outlined the way in which political opposition and guerrilla resistance to the state should be dealt with. It recommended, amongst other things, the granting of minimal political concessions in order to divide the popular movement and thus make it easier to undermine. It also suggested that 'intelligence gathering' was a key means of defeating opposition. This could be achieved by, for example, building up a portrait of what Douglas Hurd would later brand 'terrorist communities'. Regular spot checks, searches and the development of surveillance techniques were the tactics to be employed. It would also involve the infiltration of various groups and the use of informants. In addition, Kitson outlined the importance of 'psychological operations' and in particular, the dissemination of (dis)information to cause confusion, uncertainty and isolation. Such 'psy-ops' would work in tandem with the use of 'special forces', military intelligence units capable of conducting a 'dirty war' against insurgent organisations and communities. This would also involve the use of 'pseudo-gangs' for 'identifying and eliminating the enemy'.

Overall Kitson argued that military, political, legal and even media institutions should be directed in such a way as to form a co-ordinated onslaught on those challenging the status quo. *Low Intensity Operations* was, in many ways, a blueprint for the strategy subsequently (if gradually) adopted by the British throughout the 1970s. It was an approach that would have a shattering impact on the lives of the people of Ardoyne. Not until 1973 were many of the most chilling measures that Kitson recommended put fully into place. They were the result of the failure of the tactics the state employed until then. British strategy between 1971 and 1973 was designed to thwart armed opposition. The result was, if anything, the exact opposite – a process exemplified by what happened in Ardoyne.

The strategies introduced by the British state from 1970 onward ensured that, on a day-to-day basis, the face-to-face contact between British soldiers and virtually all members of the Ardoyne community became increasingly difficult, fractious and violent. People began to notice that the attitude of British soldiers during searches and spot-checks was changing. They were becoming more confrontational and aggressive as what certainly appeared a matter of policy rather than personality. Large sections of the district were increasingly swamped by ever-greater numbers of British soldiers. Whole streets would be cut off and any movement in or out of the area was prevented whilst destructive searches and more and more arrests were made. These became the sights and sounds ingrained on people's memories: armed British soldiers, often in full riot gear, spread in lines from path to path down the narrow streets of Ardoyne, moving slowly and ominously forward, the roar of armoured vehicles and the shouts of barked orders in the middle of the night as another raid began – households woken by the smashing down of doors and the heavy tread of boots on stairs.

Reaction was often swift, direct and, increasingly, too co-ordinated. Such responses took a variety of forms. Through 1970 and into 1971 the local IRA had significantly developed its organisation, building up their stock of weapons and recruiting more members. By early 1971 there were as many as thirty or so IRA volunteers in Ardoyne, supported by a wider circle of Auxiliaries and members of the Fianna, Cumann na mBan and Cumann na gCailíní. Anything up to a hundred republican activists were now in place in the district. At least for the time being, however, no direct attacks were being made upon British soldiers. Attention was being directed instead toward the threat coming from loyalist areas across the road. This was, however, soon to change. The build-up of tension would also ensure that for many, and for young people in particular, the IRA would increasingly be seen as the only group offering a solution. The impact of events on the life of local journalist Seán Mag Uidhír helps to illustrate how this happened.

My family lived in a mixed area at the start of the conflict and we were put out of our house just after 'Bloody Sunday'. They [loyalists] had started putting Catholics out up at the top end of our estate around June 1971. There was one old Catholic guy, Hughie Lynch, an ex-serviceman who had served in the British army for years. The loyalists came down and put a union jack up outside his home. Hughie objected, saying that he had served under that flag for years and that they weren't sticking it down his throat now. So they threw all the Catholics out of Hughie's street in the next couple of days. A couple more families went during internment. It was our turn by early 1972. They would come down as a mob and gather outside the house, put the windows in, that sort of thing. But my ma was a bit of a wild woman and she wouldn't move. She just said that no one was putting her out.

Then the IRA blew up a couple of supermarkets nearby; everyone's windows were blown in. We didn't care, we were putting up with so much all the time and so much was happening in nationalist areas. People were being gunned down. But it brought the war to the doorstep of those around us and they didn't like it. The thing that eventually moved us was when my aunt's house three doors down from us was attacked. My ma had started sending my sisters down there instead of all the way over to Mountainview. She expected our house to be the one that would get hit if anything was going to happen because she was the outspoken one. Then one night my aunt's house was blast-bombed. They [loyalists] threw bombs into the back of the house. My ma just thought, 'its alright me refusing to go but if it means my kids getting hurt or killed or something happens to them then it isn't worth it'. So we pulled out. My aunt pulled out too and so did one or two other families. There were a couple that hung around for another few months then eventually they got put out of their homes as well. I moved back to Ardoyne in April 1972. I was on the Crumlin Road when Sean McConville was shot by loyalists. Then Terry Toolan got shot, I knew him from the GAA. Then Josh Campbell was killed by the Brits. I knew Josh well and that had a big impact on me. People were getting shot all the time, that was just the general situation. From there, for me, it was just a case of joining the na Fianna Éireann and as time went on I progressed into the 'RA. (Seán Mag Uidhír, journalist and local resident)

But political activism was not restricted to the ranks of the IRA. The British army's actions in Ardoyne and the sense of threat from surrounding loyalist areas mobilised a far wider circle of people within the community. Very much to the fore in this were the women of the district. In late 1970 Ardoyne women organised one of the first nationalist demonstrations to take place in the middle of Belfast. This followed the arrest of several local men in connection with the shootings of 27 June. They were attacked by the RUC for their trouble. Shortly after, a local Women's Committee was established. It was designed to organise the various sit-ins, demonstrations, marches and other actions that women from the area increasingly undertook. This was not the only locally organised group set up during this period to meet the needs and wants of a community that found itself increasingly cut off from the channels of social and welfare provision. The Ardoyne Relief Committee continued to provide transport, shelter, food and advice for the continuing flow of those left homeless as the result of intimidation. Tom Fleming was by then chairman of the Relief Committee.

In 1969 Butler Street School was used to organise relief efforts for 'refugees'. That was during the school holidays so the building was available. We used to have families and their furniture in the classrooms for several weeks until they could be re-housed. After the school year started again we moved to Toby's Hall and that was where the Ardoyne Relief Committee was based for several years. The Relief Committee used to organise transport for moving people from their homes when they were intimidated or burnt out. Jimmy Lynch, an ex-serviceman, was in charge of the transport. Moving people out of their homes could be very scary because you didn't know what reception you would get. There were a number of people attacked so they used to keep the engine running on the lorry all the time in case they had to get out quick. At first we were just amateurs but we gradually got to know how things were done. We used to deal with the welfare office and the housing office for people. We provided camp beds, blankets and meals for displaced families, both those that were in the Hall and many who were living with relatives. There was a fella in Alliance Avenue who used to cook the meals and at any one time we would have been feeding about 60 people. Most families stayed about a fortnight then we would move them into houses that, as often as not, had become vacant because Protestant families were moving out. Now I don't remember any Protestants being forced out, that is not the way it happened, but I suppose, given the situation, they just felt safer if they moved.

I remember when the Knights of Malta was formed. They started first-aid lessons in the old school. With so many people being shot it was clear that there was going to be a need for it. Then about half a dozen of us went out and bought an old ambulance for the district. We found this ambulance in a scrapyard in Downpatrick and towed it back up to Ardoyne. On the way it broke down, in the middle of the Shankill Road of all places. But we got it into the district in the end. We didn't have any money to fix it so we just had a load of different people volunteering their time and effort. That was how the Ardoyne ambulance started. (Tom Fleming, Ardoyne resident and chairperson of the Ardoyne Relief Committee)

Vigilante groups and defence committees abounded, usually organised on a street by street basis, seeking to co-ordinate the defence of the area. A Catholic Ex-Servicemen's Association was set up to employ the skills learnt by those who had served in the British army for the protection of the community. The first-aid organisation, the Knights of Malta, established classes to train local people to deal with the various medical emergencies that both conflict and isolation brought with them. One of those who joined was a then young and initially apolitical Rose Craig, who passed away shortly after giving an interview for this book. For Rose community activism offered a way to contribute to the life of the area.

I was in the Knights of Malta and I was also on the Relief Committee. In 1970 the Knights of Malta started courses for first-aid. The best thing about it was that before that, if I had cut my hand, I would have panicked. When the first-aid started we had to do everything. You see at that time Ardoyne was sealed off. Once you got past the Oldpark Road you were running a gauntlet past all the Protestants. It was just too dangerous. Our ambulance had more bullet holes in it than enough, and in the end it was no use because of them. The first-aid workers were based in the school and in the dinner hall in Butler Street. But we would have been stationed in different houses throughout the district. People would see us going into a house and would know that we were there for the night. There was a need for it with everything that was going on and because we were cut off. But we weren't just there in case of trouble; we were there for anything that happened to anybody.

I was working in the Relief Centre too, with Tom Fleming. I was responsible for phoning up the welfare, to get the refugees clothes, food, that sort of thing. There were a couple of hundred families at least that went through the Relief Centre. It was in the school at that time [1971], and we would have had two families to a classroom, living there and sleeping on camp beds. We would also arrange lorries to go and collect the belongings of those people that were forced out of Protestant areas, what belongings they had left. The fellas that did that all the time, that drove those lorries, they were the unsung heroes. They deserve a lot of praise. (Rose Craig, Ardoyne resident and community activist)

There was even a relatively short-lived experiment in community-based democracy in the form of the 'People's Assembly'. This gathering set up in the latter part of 1971 adopted its own parliamentary procedures and included members elected to represent every street in the area. One of its first acts was to co-ordinate a peaceful protest against the lack of any street lighting in the area that cast Ardoyne into the depths of darkness every night. At a pre-set time on the night of 2 December 1971 everyone in the district placed a light outside their homes. By coincidence, a matter of minutes earlier, a number of IRA men (including leading local republicans Martin Meehan and Tony 'Dutch' Doherty) had broken out of Crumlin Road gaol. The light display thus appeared to an (undoubtedly astonished) military as an almost instantaneous demonstration of communal solidarity and celebration!

However, the co-ordination of community efforts tended in the main to flow from the less formal ties of family, friendship and neighbourhood that bound the people of Ardoyne together. In an isolated, tight-knit, working class community like Ardoyne contact and connections were everywhere. They were the unseen lifeblood of the place, creating a real sense of collective experience and mutual dependence. Virtually everyone in the district would know within minutes of any incident (of which there were increasingly daily examples), what had happened and who had been involved. The injury and insult inflicted by the British army were not therefore lived individually but passed rapidly into a common pool of feelings and memories. Even more importantly, it was such connections of community that then provided the main means of organising collective resistance and through which the women of Ardoyne, in particular, acted.

In every street in the district were women who slept little (if at all) throughout the night, waiting to run out into the road with whistles and bin lids to rouse the area if a British army patrol appeared. Similarly, if house raids were under way in one part of the district then this informal, but highly effective early warning system, would alert people elsewhere to come out and create some sort of diversion or distraction so as to stretch the Crown's forces to the full. The bin lid-toting 'harridans in hairnets' (as a British politician once described them) proved to be an astonishingly powerful weapon against British incursions and arms searches in the area. It often left the military frustrated, bemused and empty-handed in the face of such an unexpected response. Rose McAdorey, whose husband Paddy was to be shot dead on the morning internment was introduced [Paddy McAdorey, killed by the British army in Jamaica Street, 9 August 1971] was one of those women and describes what they did and the effect such activism had.

I would say that 1970 was the start of women coming out. There were things that happened then that I am really proud of. Six men were lifted on the Crumlin Road and everybody knew those six men were innocent. So we went down to Castle Street, about two or three hundred of us, and we blocked it off. There was women from Ardoyne, from the Bone, women from Ligoniel, all North Belfast women. It was the first time in the history of the north of Ireland that something like that had happened. Mind you we got a real beating for it. But this was all new ground that was being broken by women; we had an awful lot of strength and we hadn't used it before. Early in 1971, us women were protesting against the fact that a law had been rushed through in 24 hours that classed hurley bats as offensive weapons. These things needed to be brought forward so the public, especially the British public, knew exactly what this oppressive regime was like. So there was 38 women and we went down and protested. All of them bar, myself and Mary McGuigan, were released. As members of Sinn Féin we didn't recognise the court, so we were brought into Armagh gaol. Inside we just found our own way of fighting back. It was the same as when you were on the outside, you had to show some sort of resistance.

We used to patrol the streets with our whistles and bin lids. Sometimes I would have sat on the corner and watched to see if anyone was coming. There wasn't a single street where the women didn't come out to protect their street. It wasn't just a few women; you had enough women to do it in shifts. That made things easier because of the help they gave to each other. The women had to do a lot of the vigilante work around that time. The men couldn't do it. At that time if a man walked up the street he was lifted. And you were sometimes in a situation when you opened your door and some fella wanted through, to get out the back way because the peelers and the Brits were all about and he had to get to safety. Even though you might have had children playing you opened your door. Those Brits could have come in and stamped all over those children, so you were scared of that, but that was a way of fighting back. (Rose McAdorey, Ardoyne resident and political activist)

It was such women who also provided the network of safe houses (for arms and activists) that allowed the IRA to operate with such apparent impunity in the area during this period. This created what one local has called a 'free zone' in the heart of the city. It is often forgotten that many women were also active militarily in Cumann na mBan. One member of Cumann na mBan of those times recalls the role they played.

Women played a major role in a whole range of ways. It was mostly women who were organising relief when people were intimidated out of their houses, women like Vera McKenna, Lily McClenaghan, Sadie Grieve, Lily Largey and Mrs Rice. Women were always better at organising things than the men! Although Tom Fleming was at the centre of the Ardoyne Relief Committee, women always played a pivotal role within the community. In groups like the Green Cross or the Relatives Action Committee women were key. People would go to women like Rose Craig, myself, Mary McGuigan,

Maureen Hardy or Mrs McAdorey if their sons or husbands were arrested. That was because these were the women you knew had contacts so they knew who to phone and what to do. Women would also have been out with whistles and bin lids when the army were coming into the area. Maggie-Ann Magee was very, very vocal. She would come out roaring and shouting. Maggie-Ann was a great alarm system. If a house was being raided or a young fella was being stopped the women would go over and start having a shouting match. You would make a racket and just get as close to the house as possible.

It would have been mostly women involved in the local McCaughey/Saunders Sinn Féin Cumann as well. Some women played a leading role. Nan Saunders [mother of James Saunders, killed by the British army, in the Oldpark, 6 February 1971] from the Bone was one. Nan was in Cumann na mBan and Nan's front and back doors were always open. The woman me and a lot of others looked up to most was Mary McGuigan. Mary was OC of Cumann na mBan at that time. It is because of Mary that Cumann na mBan was so strong in Ardoyne. Women didn't join the army [IRA], they joined Cumann na mBan because Mary always saw the two as entirely equal. Mary was traditional in that respect and had no patience for any woman who would have suggested otherwise. I think at one stage there were as many as 14 Ardoyne women in Cumann na mBan. None were ever killed in Ardoyne though a lot ended up in prison. At one stage there were nine Ardoyne Cumann na mBan volunteers in gaol. Mary McGuigan liked it so much she was imprisoned six times! The average volunteer would have been involved in a range of things. You would have called round to various houses in the area getting updates on what was going on and was planned. We would bring back reports. There was a lot of intelligence work. In military terms women were involved in collecting weapons, bringing them to a particular point and removing them again after an operation. Women would also have been on bombing missions with IRA volunteers. There was no great difference between the volunteers in Cumann na mBan and the IRA, though I remember one time an IRA volunteer went to Mary McGuigan and said that he needed a 'bird' for an operation. Mary asked him if he was after a turkey for Christmas because otherwise he should be requesting the assistance of a Cumann na mBan volunteer properly. I would say that fella never referred to a Cumann na mBan volunteer as a 'bird' again as long as he lived! (Former Cumann na mBan volunteer, Ardoyne)

There were always divisions within Ardoyne about the use of violence and later events would make many people far more reluctant to be involved in this way. However, during this time republicans 'on the run' could find many homes throughout the district at their disposal and there was probably no period when IRA volunteers enjoyed so much popular support and access to houses. Whether or not 'every door was open' to 'the boys' is debatable but certainly a huge number were. Routes and pathways through the confusing complex of streets were forged that were known to those from the district but not to pursuing British soldiers. This was the 'water' in which the 'fish' flowed. It made Ardoyne, if briefly, uncontrollable and uncontainable.

More obviously, rioting in the area became more intense, regular and sometimes at least more purposeful. During early 1971 rioting was at first weekly, then nightly and, as the new year wore on, increasingly during the daytime as well. The numbers involved could differ greatly, depending on everything from the political climate of the day to the weather! So too could the level of violence employed by all concerned. However, there was a steady, seemingly unstoppable slide into open hostility and conflict. Certainly the new tactics of aggressive house searches and a heavy-handed military presence began to draw a direct response. In early February the worst rioting seen since 1969 followed a series of raids throughout the district. Involving mostly women, a number of whom were subsequently arrested and imprisoned, feelings ran particularly high in the immediate aftermath of these confrontations. Jackie Donnelly, who would later be interned, describes how the momentum of the riots built up.

> Rioting became extremely frequent. In the end there were even riots in daylight because people were so frustrated with the search policy of the Brits. At the beginning they used to come in and be almost apologetic. Then they started to get rougher. They were coming in with snatch squads and not only were they arresting people but they were beating them badly as well. In addition people were getting hit with the rubber bullets that the Brits were using all the time. They were also firing CS gas and smothering the district with it. That's when the situation started to get very, very serious and it was basically because of a noticeable shift in British strategy. They got very aggressive; it was like someone flicked a switch on. They were saturating and swamping the area when they were conducting searches because they wanted to try and get complete control of movement. They would put saracens and 'three tonners' at the end of every street. It was within that context that it went from people being out to riot as a pastime to rioting to stop them raiding houses and then rioting to get targets. (Jackie Donnelly, Ardoyne resident and republican activist)

Then on 6 February, the first casualties the area had suffered since '69 were inflicted. Barney Watt was shot dead during a riot in Butler Street and Jim Saunders (an IRA volunteer from the Bone) was killed during a gun battle shortly afterwards. As opposed to the events of two years earlier, however, both men had not been killed by loyalists or the RUC. Rather, they had been shot by the supposed 'saviours' of '69, the British army. A matter of hours later the first British soldier shot during the recent conflict, Gunner Robert Curtis, was killed by an IRA sniper on the New Lodge Road. The war was beginning in earnest.

The IRA in Ardoyne increasingly adopted a strategy of reacting swiftly and with force to events on the ground. This meant that they were amongst the most active units in this early period. In the main this was born out of that sense of isolation and potential vulnerability that conditioned the experience of the Ardoyne community, although it was driven by other factors too. Certainly the idea that any act taken against the district had to be met with a show of defiance, in whatever form that might have taken, was a key dimension. In many ways Ardoyne politics was primarily a politics of defiance. The approach of the IRA in North Belfast became crystallised in the months to come. In late February a crowd of, again mostly female, demonstrators, who were protesting against the recently introduced proscription against hurleys as offensive weapons, was set upon with batons by the RUC outside the Flax Street army barracks. Cecil Patterson was a locally based senior member of the Special Branch, well-known for his treatment of IRA suspects in the '50s. Within hours of the baton charge in Flax Street Patterson was shot dead with another RUC man, Constable Robert Buckley, in Alliance Avenue. The RUC (who had briefly been disarmed following the Hunt Report) was immediately re-armed following this event. At Patterson's funeral, perhaps not insignificantly, the British army was represented by Frank Kitson. By early March the level of British military violence in Ardoyne and other nationalist areas was significantly increasing, an indication that the drive to sap the will of the Catholic working class to resist was being intensified. Then, on 9 March three off-duty Scottish soldiers were found shot dead in Ligoniel on the outskirts of North Belfast. This marked a further turning point in the nature of the conflict. From April the IRA embarked upon a campaign of bombing economic targets in a concerted drive to bring down the Stormont government. That month there were 37 serious explosions, in May 47 and in June a further 50.

In mid-March Chichester-Clark had been forced to resign as leader of the Stormont regime by the right wing of his party, impatient as they were for more and more repressive measures. Brian Faulkner was his successor. Faulkner had been responsible for the introduction of internment during the IRA campaign of the late 1950s. He had also resigned from office in 1969 when the Cameron Commission (that accused unionists of systematic discrimination against Catholics) was set up. Faulkner made some attempt to win over middle ground Catholic support by proposing to set up three 'policy review' committees at Stormont. These were to include a proportion of Catholic representation. But spurred on by the ever louder and shrill voices of loyalists and Paisleyites for action, Faulkner also pressed for a tougher 'law and order' approach. On 25 May he declared that soldiers could shoot at people 'acting suspiciously'. In addition he looked to the British to support the introduction of internment again. There were plenty within the British establishment who echoed such sentiments. Both British army chiefs and the Conservative government under Edward Heath (that had come to power the previous June) were clearly contemplating a more hard-line strategy. A willingness to condone the killing of civilians as a means to 'deter' rioters was signalled in early July when Desmond Beattie and Seamus Cusack were shot dead by the British army in Derry. As a direct consequence, all nationalist representatives quit Stormont. Minister for Home Affairs John Taylor argued a few days later that 'it may be necessary to shoot even more in the forthcoming months'.

By now clashes and rioting were virtually daily events in Ardoyne. There were regular gun battles between local republicans and either the British military or loyalist gunmen, often against both at the same time. Streets and corners in the district most exposed to lines of fire from loyalist areas were now unsafe zones that people avoided whenever possible. More and more of the young people of the district were being lifted. The tension that such traumatic circumstances created was already beginning to take its toll on many people of the area. Given the apparent trajectory of British government policy everyone feared the worst and awaited what seemed the inevitable next step, the re-introduction of internment. It was not long in coming.

At 4.00 am on the morning of 9 August 1971, as in nationalist areas throughout the Six Counties, Ardoyne awoke to the sounds of armoured vehicles being driven down their streets and houses throughout the district being raided. Men, old and young, were dragged from their beds, pushed or beaten into the street and thrust into the back of waiting saracens, often being piled one on top of the other. Dozens were lifted in the area. Many had little or no involvement in the republican movement. They were the victims of poor intelligence on the part of British army or guilty of being the father, son or brother of an IRA suspect. Most were taken first to Girdwood army barracks. Then they were held along with 'suspects' from all over Belfast either in Crumlin Road gaol or on the Maidstone, a prison ship floating in Belfast Lough. In all 342 men were taken in this first wave of Operation Demetrius. 116 were released within 48 hours, some being deliberately dumped out onto the unsafe ground of loyalist areas. Mr Largey (who was even then an elderly man and who has only recently died) describes his experiences of being arrested on internment morning.

> I was lying in bed with my wife when the Brits came in. It was about 4.00 am and they just came smashing through the front door. My wife got up, still in her nightdress, and was the first one down the stairs. The Brits just pushed past her. I was still getting dressed when they came into the bedroom and forced me down the stairs. I remember my wife calling out that I had not even had anything to eat but they just pushed me through the door. I didn't even have on a pair of shoes. There was pandemonium in the street. There were people being lifted from other houses and it was crazy. The Brits threw me into the back of a 'pig' on top of a load of other fellas. Then they took us up to Girdwood barracks. We were put into a yard with a whole crowd of people who had been lifted from all over the place. It was very cold and they kept us there without any food or water for hours. Eventually they realised that they had picked up a lot of older men and the fathers of the younger ones. They must have been working off files going back to the forties. I was released later that morning but they didn't take us back to the district. They dropped me and another fella out of a jeep on the Cliftonville Road which was a dangerous place to be. A fella came out of a hotel on the corner and took us inside until someone came down from Adoyne to pick us up. The whole thing was a very terryifying experience. (Mr Largey, Ardoyne resident arrested on the morning of the introduction of internment)

By the end of the year 650 men had been interned. None of these were loyalists despite an upsurge in loyalist violence that had taken place in the preceding months. Those taken all had stories to tell of brutal beatings, degrading treatment. In the cases of the 'hooded men' (or 'guinea pigs' as they became known) there were also stories of new methods of physical and psychological torture being tried out by British military intelligence. One of these 'guinea pigs' was Ardoyne man Francis McGuigan, from Jamaica Street. Francis described his gruelling ordeal in a statement he gave shortly after his arrest and detention.

> It was 4.30 am, 9 August 1971. A soldier hit me with the butt of his rifle to awaken me. As soon as I had my trousers on I was forced at gunpoint down the stairs on to the street and forced to run about 400 yards barefoot. Me and about ten others were piled into the back of an army lorry, one on top of the other. I was on the bottom. When the military got into the back of the lorry they stood and sat on top of us. We were taken to Girdwood barracks, getting hit all the way. When we got there we were searched and photographed, marched to a gymnasium and left sitting with about 100 others. Then we were taken out one by one and routinely interrogated. This continued over the next forty eight hours. All that time we had one cup of tea. There were 300 men by then and we had six cups to use between us. We were told to go to sleep, then woken up in a couple of hours and interrogated.
>
> At roughly 3.00 am on the 11th the RUC Special Branch and military police came and started to take men out. When everyone had gone, there were just two of us left in the

hall. Then the officer commanding the military police came forward and told me they had something special in mind for me. I was then brought to one of the interrogation rooms and left under guard till daybreak. I saw others having a hood placed over their heads, then a hood was put over me. It blacked out all light and upon it being put on I felt very faint. I collapsed but was hit a severe punch in the stomach, which in its way revived me. With others I was then led out to a helicopter and placed inside. I then believed we were going to be thrown from the helicopter, as had been happening to other ones earlier, but it landed. I was taken into another room. Then I was medically examined, still with the hood on, and given a boiler suit overall, about ten times too big for me. They forced me to stand against the wall in the search position on my fingertips. I refused but they kept kicking and beating me. I decided to stand against the wall to get a break. There was continual noise going through the whole room and through my whole head. There were times when I would move my hands down to get a better position, then my two arms would be lifted up into the stretch position. Occasionally I would be punched, kicked and beaten. I could hear voices screaming all around me. I pulled the hood off, but I was instantly grabbed and thrown to the floor. Three boys put the hood back on, kicking away, pulling my hair, kicking my privates. Then I was placed against the wall.

This was just continuing. I tried to work out what was going on: nothing happening, but I was very tired and exhausted. I think I was three days against the wall without food or drink. I collapsed three or four times, completely exhausted, kicked and beaten then put back against the wall. After the last time I woke up in a lorry, handcuffed so they cut into my flesh and someone began to swing down on the cuffs. I was taken into a room and recognised that I was in Crumlin Road prison. Then I was given an awful severe kicking in the courtyard of the jail by the RUC. The battering continued when I was thrown into the back of a land rover. I came to handcuffed to a pipe. I had asked to use the toilet numerous times but I just had to urinate where I stood. Then I was taken and questioned, then hooded again and taken back to the room where the noise was, placed against the wall again and left there for a couple of hours. I was brought back to the same interrogator and he said that I was an officer in the IRA and he would give me time to think about it and get things off my chest. I was taken into the 'thinking room', told not to take the hood off or fall asleep. I came to with three guards kicking me, telling me not to sleep. Then I was taken back to the 'music box' [noise room].

I was interrogated about a dozen times, then sometimes taken to the thinking room, sometimes the noise room. When I was in the noise room there was a drop of inches; when you collapsed you were dragged by feet and hair and shoulders up and down it. I would hallucinate too, so that sometimes I couldn't feel the beating. I only got a few drops of water and a bit of bread to eat through the whole time. I was in such a state that my mind couldn't function properly. They kept pressing me very hard. They said I was responsible for explosions and deaths, they threatened my family and me with assassination. But one of the worst things was not knowing what was going to happen and the guards not speaking to you. (Francis McGuigan, Ardoyne resident and one of the 'Hooded Men', excerpts taken from his testimony published in Fr. Denis Faul and Fr. Raymond Murray (1974) *The Hooded Men*, pp. 36-42)

In reaction to internment people poured out on to the streets and pandemonium reigned. To the now familiar chorus of bin lids and whistles rioting broke out and gun battles ensued throughout Ardoyne. A group of boys were shot by the British army in Estoril Park. Two were injured and a third, 16-year old Leo McGuigan from the Bone, was killed outright. In the midst of this the well-known and much liked local IRA Volunteer Paddy McAdorey was shot dead by the British army during a gunbattle with the IRA. The next day his body was laid out 'in state' in the Holy Cross Boys School, flanked by a Fianna guard of honour. Driven by a 'backs against the wall' attitude and an ability to turn apparent adversity and setback into advantage this became a symbolic moment of resistance. It etched itself onto the memory of the many hundreds (if not thousands) who filed past his body paying their last respects. Again, it was the women of Ardoyne in particular who exemplified the response of the community, as Paddy McAdorey's widow Rose describes.

After interment and when my husband [Paddy McAdorey] was shot dead the women of Ardoyne couldn't do enough for me. They were absolutely fantastic. Without their help and support I don't know what I would have done. You see, women here stuck together. People don't realise what we were up against: soldiers with guns, the 'B' Specials and the RUC. We were women with babies, living at home, looking after our families. We had never, ever seen violence like that before, but we were living through it. You would see women looking bedraggled with their kids crying, going up to the Kesh. They had no money and they would bring whatever food they could up to their husbands. Then they would come back with their children wanting to be fed and there wouldn't be enough food in the house. But you had to do all those things. You had to fight back. A place like Ardoyne is small and enclosed so we all depended on each other. That is why the Brits tried to break our community spirit. That was the worst thing. It was their way to try to keep us down. (Rose McAdorey, Ardoyne resident and political activist)

As day dawned the mayhem continued. Angry clashes erupted throughout the area as the full implications of what had happened the night before became clear. The intermittent sound of gunfire was everywhere. Until this point several streets in Glenard (in the north west of the district) had still been occupied mainly by Protestants. Almost all of these now left. However, they first opened the gas valves and set fire to 194 houses in Farringdon Gardens, Velsheda Park and Cranbrook Gardens. This was in order that these homes could not then be used by the overcrowded crammed into Catholic Ardoyne. It was the second time in less that two years that a number of streets in the district had gone up in flames. It was the second time, too, that Alice Campbell had watched as her home was burnt to the ground.

After we had been burnt out in 1969 I moved into a house in Farringdon Gardens with my son Eddie and his wife. When Eddie was working on night shift loyalists used to come down and daub 'UVF' on my windows. That's how vicious it was. I was always afraid that we would be burnt out again, that the same men would come back. That's exactly what eventually happened. On the morning when internment was brought in my home was burnt out for the second time. I don't know why they wanted to do that to my house; I have never done any harm to anyone in my life. I forgive those that did it. I have learnt to forgive the men that burnt me out and I even pray for the ones who killed my son. I forgive, but it is hard to forget. You can't forget those memories. (Alice Campbell, Ardoyne resident, mother of Ardoyne victim Eddie Campbell)

As the three streets were engulfed in fire an indelible mark was left on people in the area. It was another image that became fixed in memories. As hundreds of houses burned Sarah Worthington, a 50-year old Protestant widow woman, was being helped by some of her nine children to move her belongings out of her home in Velsheda Park. As she waited in her living room a British soldier came into the house and shot her dead. At the same time May McGrandles was sitting in the house she had only just been allocated and moved into that morning in the neighbouring Farringdon Gardens. She remembers the excitement she had felt as a wife and mother expecting to bring her family into their new home. She also remembers the terrible events that were to mark the day.

My husband and I are a mixed marriage and we lived in Ligoniel, which was mostly Protestants then, right up until 1969. So I know that housing conditions were bad in those areas too. We were in a house with no gas, no electricity, no bath, no hot water. We had just one tap and an outside toilet. When you went to the toilet you had to stamp your feet to let the rats know you were coming. I had four kids sleeping in one room and when it rained the water ran down the inside walls. We had been trying for ages to get a house and we actually moved down to Cranbrook Gardens on the morning of internment. I was sitting there by myself when the loyalists came down to burn all the houses in these streets. I knew most of the people from here but I didn't recognise most of this crowd. I watched as the British army let the loyalists come in behind them. They just started wrecking and burning the houses, though a lot of them made sure to empty the meters first. They just smashed everything in sight. Everyone just ran away and in the end there was only myself and my son Billy in this street. But I saw what happened and I can tell you that it was not nationalists from this area that burnt those houses. I saw it with my own eyes. Some of those people burnt their own houses as they left so that Catholics would not move into them afterward. It was a terribly sad thing to watch houses being destroyed like that. It was particularly hurtful for me because I had lived here when I was a child and I actually knew a lot of those people. (May McGrandles, Ardoyne resident)

Throughout the North the 9 August saw two British soldiers, one IRA volunteer (Paddy McAdorey) and eleven civilians killed (nine of whom were Catholic). Two of the civilians (Leo McGuigan and Sarah Worthington) died in Ardoyne. Within four days a total of nineteen civilians were dead. One of these was John Laverty. John was born in Brookfield Street but moved to Ballymurphy when still a boy. Between 9 and 11 August the paras killed fourteen people in and around the Springhill and Ballymurphy areas of West Belfast. One night six had been shot dead in a single incident, including a Catholic priest. John had left his house in the early moring of 11 August when he heard the sound of bin lids. He was stopped and shot dead by a British army patrol. The paras who killed John later tried to claim that he had died during a gun battle. No prosecutions followed. This was testament to the ongoing legacy that the introduction of internment left behind. Before 9 August 34 people had been killed during 1971. In the remaining four and half months of the year 140 more people lost their lives. By the middle of August 7,000 people (most of them Catholic) had been made homeless. In the immediate wake of internment women and children had again been evacuated from Ardoyne, mainly to the old Irish army camp in Gormanstown, Co. Meath. Afterwards, another flood of intimidated refugees found themselves seeking refuge in Ardoyne. After 9 August barricades went up around Catholic areas throughout the North. Soon 26,000 families were on a rent and rates strike. Internment managed, as nothing else had done before, to solidify the anger and resolve of the nationalist community. It also left the ranks of the republican movement virtually intact. In every way imaginable internment manifestly failed to meet the goals its instigators sought to achieve. Something of its effect within Ardoyne is again captured in the words of Jackie Donnelly.

> For about three or four weeks before internment riots and raids were happening on a daily and nightly basis. But internment was a watershed. The Brits made a mistake by doing it through mass arrests and taking so many of the wrong men. People who half supported the IRA came out fully for them afterwards. The rent and rates strike proved that. It was a way of people saying, 'You've gone too far this time'. It all just added to the IRA's recruitment. Everybody wanted to join the IRA. I think it was the single biggest mistake the Brits ever made. The IRA had so many volunteers at that time it didn't know what to do with them. With this being a small area you would think that if the Brits saturated it they could close it down. But the IRA could operate because of the community. Without the community they couldn't have done it. They needed the conditions to use weapons and the community created those conditions. The Brits simply couldn't contain it. It was really unbelievable because out of it came a sense of camaraderie and not only amongst those from the district involved militarily. People joined all sorts of things to play a part because they knew that it wasn't going to stop. Given that situation, the IRA in this area became very, very strong. (Jackie Donnelly, Ardoyne resident and republican activist)

In Ardoyne the impact of the war was felt as acutely as anywhere else and the number of casualties from the area began to mount steadily. On 28 October Michael McLarnon was shot dead by British soldiers near his home in Etna Drive. On the same evening Johnny Copeland was also shot by British soldiers near his home in Strathroy Park, dying on 31 October. Then on 10 December British soldiers entered Toby's Hall while a disco was going on. They opened fire, shooting Joseph Parker and several other people. Joseph died two days later. On 20 December Margaret McCorry was killed as she was standing at a bus stop. An IRA unit opened fire on a British army patrol on the Crumlin Road and Margaret was shot. The next day IRA volunteer Gerard McDade was shot dead by British soldiers in Oakfield Street. He had been stopped, 'P'-checked by a foot patrol and cleared to proceed. Moments later the same patrol shouted to him to stop a second time. Fearing that he was about to be arrested and possibly interned, Gerard began to run down Oakfield Street toward Brompton Park entry. He was shot in the back by a British soldier.

Ominously too as the year wore on loyalism was very much on the march. In September the Ulster Defence Association was founded. It was set up to act as an umbrella organisation for the various locally based Protestant paramilitary groups that had emerged since 1969. On 30 October Ian Paisley formed the Democratic Unionist Party. The DUP founded its appeal on a mix of working class populism, rabid anti-republicanism and right-wing calls for oppressive measures to quell all opposition. From public platforms Paisley also increasingly called for the formation of what he termed a 'Third Force'. On 4 December the UVF planted a no-warning bomb in McGurk's bar, North Queen Street, in the New Lodge area of North Belfast. It killed 15 Catholics, including Thomas McLaughlin from the Bone. As part of the ongoing propaganda war British Intelligence initially fed a story to the press that this bombing was an IRA 'own goal'. This 'theory' was taken up and propagated by the then Stormont Security Minister John Taylor. Indeed, the death of an IRA volunteer in the Markets a few days later gave rise to a further lie that he had been 'disciplined' for having caused the McGurk bar bombing. It was not until some seven years later when members of the UVF were charged with this mass killlling that the truth came out. Attacks such as this were to become an increasingly regular feature of the conflict. So too were drive-by shootings and the more macabre and brutal killings carried out by certain gangs of loyalists. Enclave areas such as the New Lodge and Ardoyne would prove to be particularly susceptible to being targeted in this way.

On 8 February 1972, Bernard Rice was walking towards Ardoyne when he was shot dead on the Crumlin Road. Members of the recently formed Red Hand Commandos carried out the killing from a passing car before speeding away. Bernard was a founder member of the Catholic Ex-Servicemen's Association and had served for fifteen years in the British army. In many ways the killing of Bernard Rice marked a new turn in the loyalist campaign. It established a pattern of assassination that was to become all too depressingly and frighteningly familiar to people from the district in the years to come. Another worrying pattern to emerge was the disinformation deliberately spread by the RUC as to the supposed identity and motives of Bernard's killers. Newspapers reported that Bernard was shot by the IRA because he had been wearing a Glasgow Rangers scarf. Bernard was that very rare thing, a Catholic Rangers supporter. The aim of such 'black propaganda' was to turn the community against the republican movement. Certainly such nakedly sectarian killings as that of Bernard Rice cast a shadow on the lives of the people of Ardoyne throughout 1972. For example, on 15 April 17-year old Sean McConville was killed by loyalists. Like Bernard Rice he was shot at from a passing car as he walked along the Crumlin Road. Both murders were claimed, many years later, by Frankie Curry. Curry was a founder of the Red Hand Commandos, nephew of the leading UVF figure Gusty Spence and one of the most active loyalist killers in the early 1970s.

Bernard and Sean's deaths had also come in the wake of an event that was another critical watershed in the conflict, Bloody Sunday. On 30 January 1972, 14 unarmed civilians were shot dead by members of the British Parachute Regiment (paras) in broad daylight in Derry following a peaceful anti-internment march. The repercussions of Bloody Sunday were felt everywhere. Thousands of workers throughout Ireland went on strike. Thousands more marched in nationwide demonstrations. In Dublin the British embassy was burnt to the ground. In the wake of Bloody Sunday the 'Official' IRA also went on the offensive. As republicans stepped up their campaigns this invariably also brought with it the likelihood of greater loss of life within their own ranks too. Less than a week after Bloody Sunday, on 6 February, Charles McCann (an IRA volunteer who was born and bred in Ardoyne but who was then living in Toomebridge) died along with another IRA activist Phelim Grant. They were killed when a bomb they were moving in an arms dump on a barge on Lough Neagh exploded prematurely.

Bloody Sunday ensured that many, if not the majority, of people in Catholic working class areas of the North no longer believed that the British state would act impartially or (at least) uphold their own laws. This was particularly so after the whitewash of the report of the Widgery Tribunal, made public on 18 April, exonerated the paras of any wrongdoing. Widgery compounded the alienation produced by the Scarman Report (published less than two weeks earlier on 6 April) that cleared the RUC of any blame for the death and violence that had occurred in 1969. For the people of Ardoyne who had lived through those August nights, as for the people of the Bogside who had witnessed Bloody Sunday, it was as if their reality and experiences counted for nothing. It felt as if their voices were to be unheard and unheeded. What trust lingered thereby evaporated.

The day after Bernard Rice's death a movement called Vanguard was founded by the leading Ulster Unionist William Craig. Vanguard was a right wing quasi-fascist loyalist grouping that counted many unionist politicians (including a young David Trimble) as well as leading loyalist paramilitary figures in its ranks. At a public meeting held in the Ormeau Park in early March Craig argued that 'when the politicians fail us it may be our job to liquidate the enemy'. In the coming months Vanguard would grow in strength, giving political lead and credibility to the mass street mobilisation and ongoing campaign of loyalist violence that became such a feature of the period. The Stormont regime had essentially lost control of a society spinning into chaos. To all intents and purposes a state of virtual civil war now existed. Faulkner refused, however, to give up control of security decisions. As a result, on 30 March Stormont was suspended and Direct Rule from Westminster was introduced.

If the British had thought that this would lead to a lessening of the violence they were soon proved wrong. It was a forlorn hope anyway given the anger that both the Scarman and Widgery reports generated. Shootings and explosions were by now literally daily occurrences. On 13 and 14 April, for example, the IRA planted as many as 40 bombs throughout the Six Counties. In the aftermath of Bloody Sunday both the 'Provisional' and 'Official' IRA had declared that all members of the British army were 'legitimate targets'. On 21 May Private William Best, a soldier from Derry home on leave, was captured and killed by the 'Officials'. Such was the reaction to this event that the 'Officials' called a ceasefire a few days later. The 'Provisionals' also called a ceasefire in early July to allow negotiations to take place with the British government. On 7 July an IRA delegation (including both Gerry Adams and Martin McGuinness) met with senior British officials in London. However, the negotiations soon collapsed and the 'Provisionals' called off their ceasefire on 13 July. Just over a week later, on 21 July the IRA (as the 'Provisionals' will be referred to throughout, from this point onward) sent out a ferocious signal of their intent to return to the war when they exploded 26 devices in Belfast alone. Eleven people were killed on a day that would be remembered as 'Bloody Friday'. The atmosphere created by 'Bloody Friday' allowed the British the opportunity to give the counter-insurgency hawks their head. On 30 July 12,000 British troops, supported in places by heavy tanks, were employed in the biggest British military operation since Suez. Operation Motorman, led by General Tuzo, saw nationalist 'no-go areas' in Derry and Belfast invaded, swamped and occupied. Large British army forts were soon under construction. The British were bedding in for a long war.

However, the victims of IRA bombs had not been the only casualties of 'Bloody Friday'. On the same evening, 21 July 1972, Joseph Rosato was shot dead at his home on the

Deerpark Road in disputed circumstances. Joseph was a terrazzo worker and a member of one of North Belfast's Italian families. Even now the family are unsure which party to the conflict was responsible for his death. What is certain is that the list of Ardoyne dead from loyalists attacks kept getting longer. The day after Joseph Rosato was killed Patrick O'Neill from Jamaica Street was abducted along with Rose McCartney, a young folk singer from West Belfast. Patrick was severely beaten and then they were both shot dead by members of the UFF. Their bodies were found the next day dumped in a car in the Glencairn estate. On 11 November Gerard Gearon from Strathroy Park was making his way home in a taxi from his job as a barman at McGlade's pub in Donegall Street. Two fellow occupants got out at the Mater hospital and shot Gerard dead. They were also members of the UFF. Two years later Mary Sheppard (who worked in the taxi rank where all three had got into the cab) was shot dead by the UFF after she gave evidence at Gerard's inquest. As 1972 ended, on 30 December, 55-year-old Hugh Martin from Eskdale Gardens was killed by the UVF. Hugh had just finished his shift at the bakery in East Belfast, where he had worked in for twenty years, when he was shot dead. None of these victims had any political or military connection to any republican organisation. If the threat of loyalist death squads was to become a more fearsome reality in the mid-1970s, it had already impacted greatly on Ardoyne. This was part of a wide pattern. During the four months of 1972 a total of 40 civilians were killed thoughout the North. Of these 30 were Catholics killed in such circumstances.

In Ardoyne the conflict was also impacting heavily on the ranks of the republican movement. This was particularly so for members of na Fianna Éireann (the youth wing of the IRA). In many places Fianna members often fulfilled a largely supporting role to the volunteers of the IRA. However, the conflict in the relatively small area of Ardoyne was intense. As a result Fianna members were more likely to participate actively and directly in the district than elsewhere. Greater casualties were the result. On 19 February 15-year-old Davey McAuley from Fairfield Street was accidentally killed when a weapon he was nearby went off. At his funeral over two dozen members of the local Fianna in full dress uniform provided a guard of honour. On 19 March James O'Hanlon from Eskdale Gardens was accidentially killed during an IRA internal investigation. As his funeral entered Brompton Park the coffin was draped with a tricolour and accompanied by a guard of honour. On 11 June 17-year-old Josh Campbell from Havana Street was shot dead by British soldiers during a gun battle in Eskdale Gardens. On 20 September Fianna member Joseph McComiskey was shot dead by British soldiers on waste ground near Flax Street. Then on 4 December Bernard Fox from Etna Drive (still only 16-years-old) was shot and killed while on active service by a British army patrol on the Crumlin Road. Less than a year earlier Bernard Fox had been one of those providing the guard of honour for Davey McAuley. All in all the Fianna in Ardoyne lost four members during 1972. It was far and away more than the organisation lost in any other area at this or any other time.

Nor did the death toll for the area in this most bloody of all the years of the conflict for the North as a whole end there. IRA volunteer Jim Reid from Brompton Park was killed during a gun battle with British soldiers on the night of 13/14 July, just after the IRA ceasefire was called off. That same night Terry Toolan from Ladbrooke Drive was shot and killed by the British army in Eskdale Gardens. On 14 August Charles McNeill (a partially deaf pensioner of 68) was shot in disputed circumstances as he stood at the door of his home in Brompton Park. This was after a gun battle had broken out between an IRA unit and a British army patrol. The next day the IRA released a statement denying responsibility for Charles' death. No further investigation or prosecutions ensued. All in all the year had undoutedly had a devastating impact on Ardoyne. Prior to 1972 a total of ten people from the district had been killed as a result of the conflict since 1969. A further 15 had been added to that number by the end of the year.

However, terrible as it is, this catalogue of death suffered by Ardoyne in these years only tells part of the story. More difficult to quantify, but similarly destructive and alienating in its effect, was the brutality regularly employed by British soldiers on the ground to 'enforce the law'. The strategy of total military occupation ushered in by Operation Motorman ensured that systematic harassment became part and parcel of daily life. It created an extraordinarily oppressive atmosphere in the district. All the time more and more of the young of the area were being picked up, beaten, arrested and imprisoned. More and more people knew a friend, relative or neighbour inside. More and more mothers, sisters and wives began to make the long trek to Long Kesh for a brief visit with a son, brother or spouse. Then they would return to face the oppressive, mundane drudgery of keeping house and home intact. A number of young women of the district found themselves incarcerated in Armagh. There were also ongoing attempts to combat such treatment through community action. Tom Fleming again describes how this took shape.

> Even before internment there were a lot of people being 'lifted'. There was a Prisoners Defence Fund set up and then in 1973 the Green Cross Committee was established. Again, I was chairman of that in Ardoyne. But there were about six or seven people who were the main ones involved. The basic aim of the Green Cross was to raise funds to help the families of prisoners and internees. We were in Toby's Hall at first, then we moved down to where the Crumlin Star Social Club is now. We had a warehouse of food there that we used to distribute to the families. Aid came from all over, especially from America. People would send all sorts of things. For example, I remember one time someone donated six slaughtered pigs and we had to get a butcher in to carve them up for us. We acted as a point of contact and information for people after their friends or relatives were arrested. Brits like the paras used to come in with ten-ton trucks and just lift all the men in the clubs. It fell to us to phone up the barracks, see who was there and go down to try and make sure that they were being treated alright. We also got hold of a couple of old minibuses to transport the relatives of the prisoners to and from the jails for visits. A lot of these things were organised along with groups outside Ardoyne. But, to be honest, we generally did things in the district for ourselves. For instance, we had our own buses. If it is not quite right to say that Ardoyne was isolated, it was definitely a community on its own that took care of its own. (Tom Fleming, Ardoyne resident and Chairperson of the Green Cross Committee)

Many people remember with gratitude the tireless efforts of Tom Fleming and others to provide advice, help and support for them and their familes throughout this difficult period. For the (often very young) members of the community who were arrested his appearance on the scene to try to insure better treatment was a welcome sight and lasting memory. As well as a stalwart of the Relief Committee, Tom was also deeply involved with prisoner support organisations and later, the Anti-H-Block campaign and Sinn Féin. Tom worked tirelessly and selflessly for years providing help and support to 'refugees' and the families of the, literally hundreds, of prisoners and internees. Such work made him much-loved and respected throughout the district.

The extent of the conflict was, by now, virtually all-consuming in the district. For those still at school there was the knowledge that some of their classmates had been killed or injured. In addition the end of the schoolday brought regular clashes on the Crumlin Road with those from nearby Protestant estates. The 'lollipop' British army patrols that were established to police these clashes were the result. Attacks by the IRA on those patrols was the almost inevitable consequence. Jackie Donnelly illustrates the impact this situation had upon the relationship between the IRA and the community in this period.

> Such were the amount of operations being undertaken by the IRA in the areas where they were strong that the Brits were very reluctant to come in. They either came en masse or under the cover of darkness. Even then it wasn't safe for them. People think of 'no-go' areas like those in Derry where there were barricades up. But a 'no-go' area in Belfast was one where a Brit couldn't walk down the street because they would have been shot at. But when [Operation] Motorman came in it happened here too. They moved in from the Bone Hills and just swept down, coming in from all angles and creating a ring of steel. It was very frightening for the people here because there were vast amounts of Brits and major machinery.
>
> After that they were on the streets more and in greater numbers. There would be patrols coming from every direction, sequenced, targeting with each other. It made it much harder for the IRA to operate. But it by no means finished them off. They just had to be more careful about the type of operations they carried out. But the Brits surveillance equipment was getting more sophisticated. In a lot of ways the north of Ireland was like a training ground for their technology. There were also a lot more of what were called the 'five pound touts' [informers]. The Brits would arrest someone for nothing. Then they would take them up to Girdwood barracks and say to them, 'We know you're not in anything but you will have to tell us something, or keep an eye on such and such a person'. There was loads and loads of them. That was typical of British Intelligence. (Jackie Donnelly, Ardoyne resident and republican activist)

Patrols, raids, gun attacks, explosions, arrests, beatings: these became the ever-present possibilities defining the daily pattern of life in the district. Yet, at the same time, people adapted and created normality out of these extraordinary circumstances. Those fortunate enough to have work still had to go to it. Shopping still had to be done, children still had to be fed. The various clubs that sprang up in the area after the pubs of the Crumlin Road had been burnt out joined those long-established to provide new sites for the fleeting escape from the trials and tribulations of the day. The exhilaration experienced at such moments was, if anything, heightened by the tensions that were the peculiar norm of what the district was living through. Dancing went on at the discos held in Toby's Hall or the 'Shamrock'. Nights were spent drinking in the 'League', the 'Star' or the 'Saunders'. All the age-old rites and rituals of conviviality and courtship went on in an area increasingly cut off from a threatening outside world. Ardoyne turned toward itself to find the means to keep going. The Shamrock Social Club was one of those founded at this time. That was largely due to the efforts of Larry Kennedy, who was later killed by the UFF [Larry Kennedy, killed in Shamrock Social Club by the UFF, 8 October 1981]. Larry's friend Sean Murphy remembers how the Shamrock came into being.

> At the start of the 'troubles' a lot of the bars were burnt out. Then when the barricades were put up and the buses were used a number of us took the seats out and kept them. At one point the off licence at the bottom of Brompton Park was nearly burnt out but a crowd of us protected the shop and saved it. When the owner came back on the Sunday after the British soldiers came in he gave us a load of drink for saving his bar. Tommy Maguire suggested we went up to his attic to drink it and we swept it out and put the bus seats into it. That was the start of the Shamrock. After that we got a big wooden hut and just kept adding things on to it. The main man behind developing it was Larry Kennedy. Without Larry Kennedy there wouldn't be a Shamrock Club. He was 'Mr Shamrock'. (Sean Murphy, Ardoyne resident and friend of Ardoyne victim Larry Kennedy)

What also went on were the deaths. As 1973 began so too did a new year of killings of Ardoyne people by the now ever-present British army. On 12 January Elizabeth McGregor was killed. A British soldier shot Elizabeth dead when he fired at her from an observation post as she returned from mid-morning mass to her home in Highbury Gardens. Then a detachment of the 3rd battalion of the Parachute Regiment arrived in the area in March 1973. A spate of killings followed that showed their wilful disregard for life and a willingness to adopt a virtual shoot-to-kill policy. On 12 March Eddie Sharpe was shot dead by a para. Eddie was standing on his own doorstep taking the air and looking up at the evening sky when he was killed. As in the case of Elizabeth McGregor the British soldier fired from a nearby observation post. The British army at first tried to claim Eddie was a gunman. He was not. No prosecutions subsequently occurred. On 27 March a member of the local IRA was killed; 17-year-old Patrick McCabe was armed and making his way down Etna Drive. At the junction with Holmdene Gardens he was shot by a member of a para unit from a British army observation post on top of Flax Street Mill.

On 17 April IRA volunteer Brian Smyth from the Bone was shot dead. Brian was killed by a para lying in wait with his unit for some time in an empty house in Etna Drive. Brian Smyth was unarmed, as were three other men with him. Two of those were also injured. One suffered permanent brain damage. The manner in which the paras operated in the district is captured in the eyewitness accounts of the shooting of Brian Smyth and the others given by Betty and Margaret Doherty.

> *Betty:* A few of us had organised a food sale for the Green Cross. Some of the local lads were helping us gather and store the food. On the day Brian Smyth and the others were shot, they were helping us. One of them had gone to get a car and the rest were just standing on the corner of Brompton Park and Highbury at Etna Drive waiting for the car to return. Brian was actually using a walking stick at the time because he had hurt his ankle. He was in my house just before he went round to join the others. The next thing Margaret and I heard shooting. We ran round to the bottom of the entry between Highbury Gardens and Brompton Park with a number of other women. I

could see Pat Fennell lying on the ground and there was a British soldier standing over him. There was real hatred in this para's face. I will never forget how he looked till the day I die. He was really mad and started shouting and lunging at us. I knelt down beside Pat and the para was screaming at me to get away and pointing his gun. But I knew that if I had left Pat this guy was going to shoot him dead.

Margaret: The British soldiers were all lined along Etna Drive. When I went up the entry there was one soldier in particular who was waving his rifle around and going berserk. There was one wee girl called O'Connor from Etna Drive who knew first-aid and was trying to come up the entry to help. She had long hair and this soldier just grabbed her by it and threw her up the entry. His face absolutely terrified me. He just ran amok. The whole time we were in the entry there were only women there and the paras had them all up against a wall, torturing them. I was a nun at the time and the press made a big deal about how I was supposed to have been kicked in the face. It didn't happen the way they said and what always annoyed me was that by concentrating on that they took the focus away from what happened to those lads who were shot. The emphasis was taken away from where it should have been.

Betty: Apparently what happened was that the British army had an undercover unit in a disused house in Etna Drive for a couple of days. The lads were just standing waiting for the food for the Green Cross to arrive and the British soldiers opened fire. Pat Fennel tried to run up between Highbury and the entry at Brompton Park. He was shot in the body and the head. Jackie Meehan and Patsy McKinney were shot too. Brian Smyth had tried to run up Brompton Park but because of his bad ankle he couldn't get away. He was shot dead. Afterward the paras swamped the area. I fell to pieces straight afterward. I was covered in Pat's blood and a neighbour took me through to my house. The next thing some young lads came running in through my door begging me to hide them because the paras were after them. They were all about 15 and 16 years old and there was absolute terror on their faces. Saracens were coming down from both ends of the street and the paras were raiding every house. I just started praying to St Jude. In the state the paras were in I was sure there was going to be another killing. Just then the TV crews arrived and I thanked God because that is the only thing that stopped the paras.

Eddie McClafferty had been with the lads and he was sentenced to eight years. The British army said that their soldiers had been fired on first. They stood up in court and lied and even though I gave evidence I could see the judge just did not believe me. He didn't want to think that British soldiers would just start shooting like that. The truth only came out when one of the paras actually admitted it afterwards. He told the truth, that it had been an ambush and it was only then that Eddie got out on appeal. Those lads who got shot had just been doing me a good turn and the money we were raising was going to go to the families of people who had been interned. (Betty and Margaret Doherty, Ardoyne residents)

Unusually one of the paras later told the *Daily Mirror* that he had been directed to lie about the fact that none of the group were armed. In 1976 there was an appeal held in the case of an Ardoyne man charged for possession of a gun during this incident. During this appeal the same British soldier further argued that at the time of Brian Smyth's shooting his captain had declared that the three were IRA men. He then ordered his troops to fire because it was 'too good a chance to miss'. This was an early example of a 'shoot-to-kill' policy being adopted by the British army.

On 19 April 12-year-old Anthony McDowell was shot dead by the British army during a gun battle with a local IRA unit. At the time Anthony was just travelling in a car in Etna Drive, close to his home in Duneden Park. Once again a member of the paras was involved. On 18 May 17-year-old IRA volunteer Sean 'Sid' McKee was shot dead by a para as he came out of a house in Fairfield Street. The paras had set up covert surveillance from an empty house in Butler Street. Although they tried to claim that Sid had aimed a shot, eyewitnesses disputed this. The same eyewitnesses also suggested that Sid was still alive when he was dragged and beaten into an awaiting saracen. Sid McKee was therefore the fifth person to be shot and killed by the paras in the area in hotly disputed circumstances in a matter of weeks. Tom Fleming remembers the community reaction to the actions of the paras.

> When the paras came into Ardoyne there were five deaths. After that the Relief Committee was asked to organise a protest. The turnout was massive; there were thousands out that day. We had a lorry leading a parade that went all through the district. This was just an instantaneous reaction to what the paras were doing. We went up to Flax Street barracks to voice our anger at what had been happening. The next day I was sent for by the British army and told never to do anything like that again, but I never took any notice of things like that. The other thing that people did was to ignore the paras. You would pass them by and not allow them to get into confrontations with you. That was another form of resistance. (Tom Fleming, Ardoyne resident and Chairperson of the Green Cross Committee)

The systematic harrassment of the community was most evident when the routine of rotating troops every three months or so saw new British army units come in looking to 'leave their mark'. Certain regiments proved themselves more ready than others to employ all manner of violence on a massive scale; in this regard the paras were without peers. Even in the immediate wake of Operation Motorman Ardoyne had to all intents and purposes continued to be a 'no-go' area. The violence of the paras was specifically designed to end that situation. Periods when the paras came into Ardoyne to 'teach the district a lesson' are still vividly remembered by many for the fear and hatred generated by the constant and brutal use of force and torture during spot checks, searches and arrests. At such times people avoided any but absolutely necessary journeys on foot through the area, knowing that, at best, it might take an age to travel a few hundred yards because of being stopped and questioned repeatedly. At worst, and particularly at night, the consequences could be far more frightening and painful. Frank Burton was an English sociologist who lived in Ardoyne through much of this period. His classic study of Ardoyne, *The Politics of Legitimacy*, gives a flavour of what day-to-day contact between the residents of the district and British soldiers was like.

> British justice is recognised within Anro [Ardoyne] not only for the stamp of repressive law but by brutal enforcement. Soldiers not only apprehend and detain suspects, they beat them. They interrogate with illegal methods ranging from ill-treatment to torture. This 'enforcement' can be terrifying, as when the Paratroop Regiment entered Ardoyne. Reports

came in hourly about the latest beating, intimidation or act of destruction. A discotheque was interrupted by a foot-patrol who attacked the teenage dancers, putting one boy back into the hospital from which he had just been released. He had the stitches from a routine operation on his stomach reopened by the troops. A baker's hand was broken by the soldiers as he went about his delivery round. A store of furniture belonging to homeless, intimidated families was wrecked during a search. Local mill workers were kicked in the genitals as they were searched, twice daily, as they went to and from their workplace. I was hit in the ribs with a rifle as two paratroopers asked me if I was in the IRA. I said I was not and they said, 'Well, fucking well join so we can shoot you'. In addition to these and hosts of other examples, four people were shot dead by the regiment in heatedly disputed circumstances. (Frank Burton, sociologist resident in Ardoyne in 1972-73 and author of *The Politics of Legitimacy: Struggles in a Belfast Community*, Routledge, London, 1978)

There was also another Ardoyne victim of loyalist paramilitary violence in the early part of the 1973. February had seen severe rioting and attacks by loyalists (particularly in East Belfast) following the arrest of the first two non-republican internees. The recently founded Loyalist Association of Workers (LAW) also organised a brief strike of Protestant workers. It was a 'dry run' for what the following year would plunge the North into a greater political crisis. Not long after, on 2 March, Paddy Crossan from Ladbrooke Drive was killed by the UVF. Paddy was shot when he stopped the bus he was driving to pick up passengers on the Woodvale Road. Those close to him believe that he was chosen as a target because he would joke about Orange marches with work colleagues in the bus depot. Paddy was the third Catholic killed in a 24-hour period. Two years later Paddy's brother Frankie was also killed by loyalists. Frankie was a victim of the Shankill Butchers, the UVF gang that would terrorise Catholics (not least those of Ardoyne) for years. Less than a week after Paddy Crossan's death, on 8 March 1973, David Glennon was abducted by members of the UDA and shot dead. David was originally from Eskdale Gardens but was then living in Ballymurphy. His body was found hooded and bound in the boot of a car.

The deaths of Paddy Crossan and David Glennon came in the same week as a state-sponsored plebiscite on the future of the North took place. Its result was meaningless given the almost complete nationalist boycott of the poll. It did, though, indicate the direction in which British government policy was going. On the one hand (as events in Ardoyne could more than amply illustrate) there was the use of coercion. This was designed to undermine resistance and defeat (what was seen as) 'unacceptable' opposition. On the other hand there were minimal political reforms aimed at creating a new political consensus with 'sufficient' 'middle ground', cross-community support. This would then allow Britain to extract itself from direct rule whilst 'maintaining the union' and overall control. In terms of the latter strand of thinking the plebiscite had clearly failed. However, a more concerted and concrete attempt to carve out such a new 'consensus' for the basis of future political arrangements began to take shape in the latter half of the year. In June elections led to the setting up of a Northern Ireland Assembly. Then on 5 October the SDLP and Ulster Unionists began a series of talks with the British at Stormont. These talks were looking at the possibility of establishing a power-sharing executive. A further conference (also involving the Dublin Government) was held at Sunningdale in early December. On 9 December plans for a power-sharing government and an all-Ireland council were announced. Loyalists (who by this stage were co-operating closely with many leading unionist politicians) immediately created what they called the Ulster Army Council and vowed to bring down any new regime.

These political developments seemed a long way away from the reality of their lives for the people of Ardoyne. Of far more immediate impact was the other strand of British government policy. With the failure of internment to bring about a quick end to armed resistance the British began to put into place the cornerstones of a longer-term counter-insurgency strategy. Adapting the legal system to more readily serve the ends of the military was signalled by the introduction of the Emergency Provisions Act (EPA) in late 1973. The EPA gave a legal veneer to military occupation by granting the army and RUC sweeping powers of stop, search, arrest and detention. It gave soldiers a virtual free hand in the treatment of those whose paths they crossed. This helped create a culture of non-accountability that extended to state killings, as the circumstances of those shot dead in Ardoyne would clearly show. In addition the court system began to be changed. In December 1973 Lord Diplock recommended the ending of jury trials for 'scheduled offences' and substantially changed the rules governing the admissibility of evidence. This too would have important consequences for Ardoyne. Over one in three of the adult male population of the district would eventually find themselves in prison as a result of the conflict.

Surveillance was a mainstay of the military's approach. Numerous observation posts, the constant deployment of British army helicopters above the district and the use of both informers and spot checks by foot patrols to garner various grades of information subjected the whole community to blanket surveillance. Certainly this enabled the British army to build up a vast pool of information about the people of Ardoyne. This was then used by intelligence officers like the well-remembered 'Captain Burke' and his sidekick the 'Ball-licker'.

The oppressiveness of such constant prying and intrusion had another potential and much desired effect as far as the British army were concerned: demoralisation. 'Psy-ops' were intended by counter-insurgency thinkers to break people's spirit. The sense of being constantly watched, listened to and having every aspect of their lives observed and recorded cast a shadow on the community. The consequences of this (not least in terms of early death and ill-health) echo down to the present. For men and women, old and young alike, the British military presence seeped into virtually every aspect of their lives. The most apparently unimportant piece of information could be turned around to create insecurity and division in the community as a whole and even within people's own minds. Only through holding on to the bonds of community was this almost unseen onslaught offset. Those bonds were the last ultimate weapon at the people's disposal. They were to be severely put to the test in the years to come.

> ***When the British army came in, what they said went.***
> ***Whatever they did was the law and they got away with it.***

Barney Watt
Killed by the British army,
Chatham Street,
5 February 1971

B arney Watt was the child of a mixed marriage. His Protestant father Davy came from Crimea Street, just off the Shankill. His Catholic mother Peggy Donnelly had moved to Ardoyne with her family in 1919, having been burnt out of another area. They settled in Butler Street and had six children (three boys and three girls, one of whom died when still an infant). Barney was the eldest, born in 1943. Barney was christened Bernard, but nobody ever called him anything other than Barney. In October 1964 Barney met his wife-to-be, Theresa Parker. Theresa always said that it must have been love at first sight because they were married just three months later. The newly-weds moved into their home in 25 Hooker Street shortly after. Barney loved dog racing, horse racing and following football. Before 1969 he also did a brief spell in jail for fighting with the RUC for whom (like many others in the district) he had little affection. After 1969 Barney was involved in the street disturbances that engulfed the area. It was not untypical either that Barney found work in Ardoyne hard to come by. He worked for a while in McHugh's carrying timber. But the only really good job he had was when he got a start laying pipes in Wales in late 1970. Like many others Barney crossed back over the water for Christmas, arriving on the evening of 24 December. He stayed on for a while after. Barney was a 'League' man and had been there on the night of 5 February 1971. Later the same night he was shot dead by the paras in Chatham Street. Barney Watt's first child, Bernadene, was born just three months after his death.

Michael Mailey (friend)

Barney was a guy who made you laugh. He was a brilliant character, good craic and a great guy to be with in company. In those days Barney, his brother Robert, Mickey Murphy, Stanley Corbett and me all knocked about together. We were all from the district. There was never a dull moment with Barney, though he had a serious side too. If anybody said something, Barney would stick his point of view straight in. He would not have held back and he always stuck to his guns. Barney was in England until Christmas 1970. Then he decided to stay [home in Ardoyne] when he saw the state of what was going on here. Anybody right in the head would not have felt good leaving again. Barney would have been directed by the political circumstances of what was happening in Ardoyne at the time. Even when he was away he knew what was going on because he obviously kept in touch with home. I never asked him why he came home, but I would say that the political situation was one of the factors and once he knew what was going on, he decided to come back. Barney was very republican-minded anyway. So once he got the taste of rioting and once he saw the Brits, Barney felt that he was there to do something. Everybody was up for a riot then and Barney was one of the leaders.

The night he was shot, Barney and me were in Mickey Kane's wee room in the League [social club]. We left and went up to the pigeon club in Kerrera Street at the top corner of Chatham Street. You could get a wee late drink in there and a game of darts. It was a sort of shebeen and it was all shebeens, more or less, in those days. After a while somebody said, 'I hear rioting down at the corner'. So we decided to go down. Barney said, 'I'm away on down; my fans are waiting on me'. I told him to wait because I had to go to the toilet but he said that he would see me down at the corner. Like everyone, you went down to the corner when things were going on and then you were into it right away. So Barney went on by himself and I came down the stairs a couple of minutes after him. When I was standing there I heard a couple of cracks. Somebody said, 'That sounds like shooting'. So we went out and down Elmfield Street. As we were going down Elmfield Street there was a saracen burning at the corner of Chatham Street and Butler Street. Somebody came up and said, 'Barney Watt has been shot dead'. So we ran to the corner. The saracen was burning and there were crowds of people there. Everybody was squealing and shouting. We were looking around but could not see anything. Then I saw a stretcher with a white sheet being carried into Chatham Street. I ran over to it, pulled the sheet back and then just threw it back down again. It was Barney. It was just unbelievable. I was just totally shocked that it had happened. One minute I was with Barney and the next thing those fuckers banged him. There had only been a few minutes since I had told him to wait a wee minute for me. He had only got down there and the next minute, bang. There was no shooting before. It was just the Brits who were shooting. Apparently a petrol bomb had gone into the saracen and that was that.

Old Barney was always at the front line. Barney was full of bravado and always shouting. Maybe the guy that shot him just said, 'There's one; I'll take him'. That is probably what happened, just took him out for nothing. I was not there when he was hit but I was told that Barney was shot round by the saracen. Barney had nothing on him; he was not armed. He was shot in the chest so I think he just walked straight into it. The Brits were still there when I got down. They were towards the Crumlin Road end of the street. The rioting continued for a while afterwards. It was just the usual. Then everyone was just standing around talking about what had happened.

Nobody ever approached me in relation to an inquest. There was nothing like that. Inquests were just a case of, 'Let's get it out of the way' as far as the state was concerned. But that was Barney Watt. Barney was in the thick of things. He was a brave guy, as game as a badger. Barney was one of the characters and is sadly missed. The Brits just shot him because he was an Irishman. It is just plain and simple. That is all we were to them, just fucking Irish.

Theresa Watt (wife)

Barney was killed on Friday 5 February 1971. I was working in Edenderry [mill] that day and there had been rioting on the road. We had to be escorted out of Edenderry and came in to the district up Flax Street. I got to the house and when Barney came in, he said that he had been trying to get down to see me and make sure I got home. That was about 3 pm or 4 pm. Then Barney went down to the chippie and I went to the shops. When we got back to the house everything was laid out for him to go out that night. So he had his good suit on him that night that he was shot dead. Joe McDade and big Stanley Corbett came for him and they went out at about 8 pm. I didn't see him after that until he was brought home in a coffin.

That night Barney was up in the League. He was making his way down to his ma's house with one of the McDades, his cousins. Then there was a bomb attack on the paras and one of the saracens went up in the air. Barney was supposed to have cheered and they opened up on him from the saracen. At the inquest it said that he was shot twice. Apparently he got up and ran after being hit by the first one. His shoe came off and then he was shot again. At the time I was watching a John Wayne film in our house in Hooker Street. There was machine gun fire in the film and then there was gunfire outside the door just facing me as well. I was just sitting listening to both. Then my daddy came flying in and asked me where Barney was. I said that he was out. Then my daddy told me Barney had been shot. I thought he was probably exaggerating, and that Barney had been shot in the leg or something. But as I was going up Hooker Street I heard different people saying that he was dead. When I arrived he wasn't there. Some fellas had carried him into his aunt Sarah's in Chatham Street after he was shot. I didn't know until afterwards that they couldn't get him out. The paras had surrounded the place and nobody could get out. They would not let anything move. I was waiting in the Barrett's house and my ma couldn't even get round to me. Barney was in an ambulance in Brompton Park the whole time because the paras would not let the ambulance out. Barney was dead on arrival at the hospital.

I didn't see him then until he was brought back in the coffin. That night at the wake they [the IRA] opened up on the army post at the bottom of Hooker Street. They fired across the front and side of my house in Hooker Street. We all ended up having to go underneath the coffin. Some people coming down to the house had to hide under cars. Then Barney had a tricolour over his coffin at the funeral. The British army tried to say that was evidence that he was an IRA volunteer and that he was given an IRA funeral. But the tricolour was not there because he was connected but to show that he was republican-minded. As the men walked down Twaddell at Barney's funeral a lorry came down with a crowd of loyalists and they took the tricolour off his coffin. There was trouble in the wake of the funeral too. Barney had worked for a firm called McHugh and Dick's. The orangies burnt it down because Barney had worked there and put that in writing on the wall. His brother David had to go and get the police to take it off after Barney was shot dead. Then our Winnie and me were put out of Edenderry because they knew then that I was Barney's wife.

I was pregnant at the time of Barney's death without realising it. Barney was murdered on 5 February and our daughter Bernadene was born on 14 May 1971. It was a godsend because I think otherwise I might have done something stupid. But there were things that you were left to face that you couldn't talk to your ma or your da about. I only had one brother and ten months after Barney went, he was killed too [Joe Parker, killed by the British army in Toby's Hall, 12 December 1971]. The British army only came near me after Barney was dead and buried. The only ones that harassed me were the paras. They came into my mother's house when my Bernadene was only a couple of months old. I can still see this ginger bastard who asked me my name and details then turned round and said, 'Oh aye, that's the bastard we got that night; it was us that did it'. They were paras. I couldn't say anything because my brother was lying on the settee at the time. If anything had started he would have got it, which he did in the long run anyway. There was never any come-back for the family. No official bodies ever offered me help. You just had to help yourself and rely on your neighbours. Barney's death nearly killed his mother Peggy. She was about 50 or 60 then. It hit his family hard. At the inquest the British army said that Barney was a gunman. They didn't say who killed him. There were just statements from a soldier 'A' and a soldier 'B' saying that Barney was a gunman. They said that he was pointing a weapon; they fired and killed him. But he just put his hands up and cheered. Then they opened up. There was no gun. There was absolutely nothing. The inquest said that he was using a gun but he was that drunk coming out of the League that he couldn't even have thrown a stone. The British army told lies and we never got any justice. The result of the inquest was an open verdict and nobody charged with his murder. The media just went with the army version and made Barney out to be a volunteer. There is no hope in hell of bringing those responsible for his death to justice. It's the same with my brother. When the British army came in, what they said went. What they did was the law and they got away with it. There's no way that the like of me could have done anything about it. You just had to take what was going and that was it. I was happy enough that the community knew that Barney was not a gunman and that he was murdered in cold blood. When it boils down to it, it was a drunk man coming out of a club who cheered at them. It could have been anybody that night and it was just unlucky that he was there at the wrong time.

Robbie Watt (brother)

Barney thought he was a hard man but he couldn't beat his way out of paper bag. He loved the dogs. He kept a big greyhound for a pet though it was supposed to be a big racing dog. We used to call it a homing pigeon because he used to try to sell it but it was always brought back! I definitely had some laughs with Barney. He came home for Christmas 1970 and was supposed to go back again. He stayed to be with Theresa. On 5 February 1971 I had a phone call and a knock on my door in the middle of the night. I was working in England at the time. It was the English cops to tell me to make an emergency phone call home. That's when I found out what had happened. They just said they had bad news and I phoned my brother. If he had come back after Christmas things might have been different, but his heart was in Ardoyne and not in England. He hated England. I was in Belfast at the time of the inquest but the only one that went to it was Theresa. She was a bit sketchy about what happened. She was crying her eyes out and couldn't talk. Nobody can seem to tell me exactly what happened. I don't know, maybe they didn't want to offend me. Anything I heard was from people that were supposed to be there but when I approached them they said they weren't. The worst thing is that nobody will actually talk to you about it. Too many tell you different things. Barney's death nearly killed my mother. My ma was an alcoholic but she went into Graham's home and got electric shock treatment. Then she was off it for about seven years. After Barney went, she went back to the drink again. It really did nearly kill her. She loved Barney. I'd love to find out the exact circumstances. When I heard what young McLarnon was doing [campaigning for a new inquiry into the death of Sammy McLarnon, killed by the RUC in Herbert Street, 14/15 August 1969] it broke my heart. I thought that was great and good luck to the child. I loved hearing that and I would love to do it. I would love to find out how they killed Barney. Barney was a beautiful person. We loved each other and that was it. He would have done anything for you. He had a heart of gold. If it hadn't been for the Brits he would still be here. We lost him because of the Brits.

> *I saw a figure and I thought it was a gunman, and I fired my SLR from the hip and the figure fell. I went over to the body and it was only then I discovered it was a woman.*

Sarah Worthington
Killed by British army,
Velsheda Park
9 August 1971

Sarah Worthington was a 50-year-old Protestant woman who lived in Velsheda Park, Ardoyne. She was a widow with nine grown-up children. On 9 August Ardoyne was in chaos; Operation Demetrius signalled the introduction of internment without trial. There were heavy gun-battles between the IRA, British army and loyalists. Prior to 1971 Velsheda Park, Farringdon Gardens and Cranbrook Gardens were predominantly Protestant streets. On 9 August most Protestant families began systematically moving out of their homes. Mrs Worthington was one of those families. Men in lorries, vans and cars, some displaying loyalist flags, moved Protestant families from their homes before setting them alight; 194 houses were gutted. Loyalists later claimed that Protestant families had been 'burnt out' of their homes by nationalists.

That morning the British army entered Mrs Worthington's home in Velsheda Park apparently believing it to be empty. When they came upon her, they opened fire and fatally wounded Mrs Worthington. The British army admitted that Mrs Worthington's death had been a mistake. Neither internal disciplinary proceedings nor criminal sanction were sought against the British soldier responsible for her death.

Basil (Ardoyne resident)

It was 9 August 1971. The British army, Green Howards, were positioned across Cranbrook Gardens, Farringdon Gardens and Velsheda Park. They were preventing the people from Ardoyne getting up to stop the Protestants burning their houses. A lot of houses were on fire; there was chaos. It was the morning of internment and the Protestant people in those streets started moving out of their houses. But before they went, they set them on fire. The night before, from our front window in Northwick Drive, we watched British troops arriving; we counted at least 150 of them. They stood across the streets while the Protestants burnt their own homes rather than leave them to their Catholic neighbours. There were gun battles throughout the district. There was an engagement between the IRA and loyalists who were firing from a house in Cranbrook Gardens. The IRA returned fire and the British army fired relentlessly. A number of people were killed that day in Ardoyne: a British soldier, Paddy McAdorey, an IRA volunteer, young Leo McGuigan and Mrs Worthington.

The British army stood half way up Velsheda Park. Mrs Worthington lived at number 49; that was beyond the British army lines. There were quite a few people on the streets at the time. I remember seeing Mrs Martin from Eskdale Gardens whose husband was shot dead by loyalists and other people from Eskdale Gardens and Northwick Drive were there. The people from the top of Northwick and Eskdale Gardens would be the people who could verify the situation at the time.

In the next few days it was acknowledged that Sarah Worthington had been shot dead. I can remember the newspapers stating that a woman had been killed in crossfire. I can remember some reference to a British soldier saying he saw movement in a house and he fired shots. It was definitely the British army that shot Sarah Worthington because there is no way that the IRA could have fired in through her front door – not at that angle of the street. Just prior to 9 August there were four houses in Velsheda Park that displayed UVF slogans. Velsheda Park was predominately Protestant at that time. But the UVF slogans were definitely a source of provocation to the Catholic neighbours.

The Ardoyne Commemoration Project was unable to interview anyone else regarding Mrs Worthington's case. Below are inquest statements from the Public Record Office. They include statements from the British army and Mrs Worthington's family.

British Soldier 'A'

My platoon was held in reserve in Hesketh Road until 20.00 hours. During the waiting period I could hear the sound of gunfire in our immediate area although no shots were directed at my Platoon. I could see large clouds of smoke drifting up in the air from the Velsheda Park area and Farringdon Gardens. I could not see any flames. About 20.00 hours that night my platoon was ordered to move forward and take up position at Velsheda Park. I drove along Velsheda Park in an armoured vehicle and saw a large number of houses had been set on fire. I estimated that a third of the street was burning. My task allocated to me by 'Y' was to prevent looting and the burning of the remaining houses. At that time there was a heavy pall of smoke in the area, with large numbers of people running up and down.

We then deployed from the vehicles and as a sniper was firing somewhere in the area, my platoon were deployed in doorways of houses that had not been set on fire. This was also to prevent looting and the deliberate setting fire to property and also to prevent gunmen from using them as cover. I then approached an apparently empty house at number 49 Velsheda Park which had not been set on fire. The house was in darkness with the front door lying open. I shouted into the house enquiring if there was anyone inside. No reply came and I assumed that the house was empty of legal occupants, although the possibility was in my mind that gunmen could well be sheltering inside.

I entered the house through the open door to find a small hall immediately behind the door with stairs leading up to the bedroom. I again shouted if there was anyone in the house but all was quiet. My immediate impression was that no state of disorder existed in the house and that the occupants had left for safety as the nearby houses were on fire.

I looked up the stairs – no one was there – and then stepped through a half open door into a living room on my left. This room was clear and I could see the rear kitchen through a half-open door leading of from the living room. I then moved towards the door holding my rifle in the alert position with the muzzle pointing down to the ground, with a round in the breech and the safety catch off.

As I was half-way across the living room moving towards the door I saw a figure move across my front from left to right in the kitchen. I immediately thought that it was a gunman who had been hiding at the back of the house so I fired one shot from the waist position with my SLR. The figure dropped to the floor on its back with its arms outstretched. I moved forward nearer the door and it was only then that I saw the figure on the floor was that of a woman dressed in either a dress or a skirt. I immediately left the house via the front door and shouted for 'Y' to attend.

I remained just outside the front door while 'Y' entered the house where he remained for a few minutes and then came back out again and got medical assistance. I was then ordered away from the house to report to my Commanding Officer.

I would like to emphasise that when I first entered the house I was not aware of any person being present inside, more so as I had shouted on two occasions to anyone inside. I therefore assumed that when I first saw the figure move across my front it was one of the gunmen operating in that area.

Norman Worthington (son)

On Monday 9 August 1971 I received a telephone call at approx. 6.45 pm from my brother David and as a result I drove immediately to Ardoyne, Belfast. I stopped my car outside my mother's door at 49 Velsheda Park. I found my brother David, sister Sadie and my mother at home. They had been clearing furniture from the house. There was an alarming situation in the area. Most people were evacuating their homes. A number of lorries and cars in the street were being used by residents to take their belongings away. I loaded my car and then asked my mother and sister to go with me to my brother's home but my mother and Sadie refused. I then left with David and drove to his house and unloaded the car. We got a van from his employer and David and I got into the van with the driver and went to Ardoyne again but were stopped by two military at the top of Alliance Avenue.

The situation in Ardoyne was deteriorating. Gunshots were heard. Some houses at the top of Velsheda Park were on fire. There was an urgency on the residents to get out of the area. David and I got out of the van and were separated for a time at the rear of the bus depot. I eventually got into the back of a lorry that was reversing into Velsheda Park. I then got off this lorry and ran into the gardens of the houses. I then moved down the street by jumping over the fences between the houses. I eventually got to a house almost opposite my mother's and from here ran across to her home. As I walked along the passage towards the front door of my mother's house I saw an armed soldier standing in the hallway of her house. He called, 'Get back' and pointed his rifle at me. As I walked towards him I explained that I wanted to see my mother but he still insisted, 'Get back'. I moved across to the garden of the next house and spoke to Tommy Lannie. I asked him where my mother was. He didn't reply. I asked again and he said that he thought my mother had got hurt. I went back to the soldier but he still would not let me in. I then saw my mother inside the house when I looked through the ground floor bay window. She was lying in the rear scullery on her back with her head at the back door and her feet towards the front of the house. As I saw this, my brother David and sister Sadie arrived. On seeing my mother, David became very upset but the Sergeant Major who was standing in the door would not let us in. At this stage I saw a man aged about 23 years, dark hair, swarthy skinned, wearing a shirt and trousers. He spoke with an unusual accent that was definitely not Irish. I don't know where this man came from but he said something about a cartridge. An officer then arrived on the scene and permitted us to enter the house. I went in with David and Sadie and found my mother as already stated. She appeared to be dead. I found a wound under her right arm. She was dressed in a frock, apron and coat. My mother was then removed to an army ambulance. David and Sadie accompanied her to the Royal Victoria Hospital.

Sarah Baillie (daughter)

I reside at 11 Glenbank Place, Belfast. At approximately 6.40 pm on 9 August 1971, I left home to go to my mother's at 49 Velsheda Park, as I heard there was trouble in Ardoyne. I arrived at Velsheda Park at 7 pm. My brother David was assisting my mother to put her furniture and other articles out of the house and into the front garden. People in the area were in an alarmed state. Most of the residents were attempting to load their furniture into vehicles that were in the street. The soldiers were firing shots from behind their armoured vehicles towards the Berwick Road. My other brother Norman arrived from Kells. We loaded some of my mother's articles into Norman's car. Norman and David then took this load to Wallasey Park. As we cleared my mother's house I went across the road to Ellen Ditty, 54 Velsheda Park, to give her assistance to move her stuff. I left my mother alone in the front living room of her home. I spent approximately 10 minutes in Mrs Ditty's house and I remember during this period, I looked across to my mother's home and saw her standing at the bay window. I did not notice any other person in the vicinity of the house. After I had assisted Mrs Ditty I went across to my mother's house. When I arrived at the house my brother Norman was talking to a soldier who was standing in the hallway. Norman left the soldier and jumped across the railing into the next house. I went into the garden of this house. Norman asked me where my mother was. I said I didn't know. I was then told by Mrs Lannie's daughter, who was in the garden of number 51, that someone was lying in the kitchen of the house. I then knew something was wrong. At that stage a man spoke to me. No one seemed to know this lad who was in his early twenties, swarthy skinned, with shoulder-length black hair. He was not wearing a coat. This lad said something about a cartridge but due to his peculiar accent I couldn't make out what he was saying. An officer arrived on the scene and told the soldier to let us into the house. David went into the house followed by Norman and I. I immediately saw my mother lying on her back in the kitchen. Her head was at the back door while her feet were at the living room door. An army medical officer examined my mother and he could find no pulses. I saw blood on my mother's right side. I accompanied her to the Royal Victoria Hospital with my brother David in an army ambulance. I remember that when I first went into my mother's home I smelt a strong smell of fireworks or something similar.

He was very protective towards most people and especially towards his community.
He loved Ardoyne and he loved the people in it.

Paddy McAdorey
Killed on active service
by the British army,
Jamaica Street
9 August 1971

Paddy McAdorey was the son of Josie Kane from Butler Street and Daniel McAdorey, a joiner who hailed originally from the Falls Road. Shortly after their wedding in 1938 Daniel and Josie moved into Brompton Park. They had a family of three sons and four daughters, although the eldest daughter Ann died shortly after birth. Paddy was the fifth child, born in 1947. At 15 he left St Gabriel's school and went to work in a shirt factory in Ligoniel. Then he joined the merchant navy. 'Paddy Mac' was very outgoing and always up for the 'craic'. He is remembered for both his generosity and boundless good humour. Paddy loved music, going dancing, playing football and had a large group of friends in the district. Early on in the conflict he missed his boat and never went back to the merchant navy, although he always worked, latterly as a scaffolder. By then Paddy was already a member of the local Sinn Féin Cumann, through which he met his future wife, Rose Smith. They were married on 15 January 1971. They had little time left to enjoy married life. Paddy had also become a leading, highly active and renowned member of the local IRA. He held the position of quartermaster. As a result, he was spending most of his time on the run, billeted in the many safe houses to be found in the district. This also meant that Paddy was being specifically sought and targeted by both loyalists and the British army. In the early hours of 9 August 1971, the introduction of internment saw Paddy's family home being raided, along with so many others in Ardoyne. When Paddy was not found at his home, his aged and severely ill father was taken away in his place. He was later to be dumped out of a jeep by a roadside. Paddy McAdorey was engaged in a gun battle against both British soldiers and loyalists in Jamaica Street a few hours later when he was shot dead. He was 24 years old.

Frankie Kane (cousin)

> I knew Paddy when he was growing up; he was my cousin and he used to stay in our house on occasions. He was very adventurous, good craic and very kind-hearted. If you were skint, our Paddy would have taken you out. He was a private sort of person in some ways but he could also mix with anyone. He had a lot of friends but when he died, the movement would have been his closest friend. Paddy was a volunteer in the IRA. He joined in 1969, about the same time as myself. It was a reaction to the trouble and attacks in the area. We didn't know a great deal about republicanism at that stage. It was basically a defensive thing, a reaction to being attacked and seeing that the RUC and the government were the people to blame. Paddy remained a volunteer right up to his death. He also progressed in the movement. He was a very disciplined person and took his republican beliefs very seriously. Paddy was also very politically aware. He took an

interest in the whole history of the conflict. So he was astute, knew where he was coming from and where he intended to get to one day. But unfortunately that was not to be.

I can remember distinctly the morning Paddy was shot. It was on internment morning, 9 August 1971, around 9 am or 10 am. The Sunday night before that there had been a gun battle in Ardoyne. Paddy held an important position in the movement and he was involved in distributing weapons. Guns had to be given out, put away and maintained well. Paddy was very, very good at all of that. Paddy was the quartermaster. He used to make sure that weapons were checked, double-checked, cleaned and then checked by himself. That was because other people depended on them. He was also engaged in the gun battle himself that Sunday night. There were a number of us together all night. We knew that internment was on its way and so we decided to stay out of our houses. That morning we left the house we were in and I went to a different part of the area with 'Dutch' Doherty. I can remember my last conversation with Paddy, coming out of Butler Street just as the gun battles were starting. Dutch was slagging Paddy and giving him some stick. It was nothing serious. Then somebody said that the loyalists were shooting down Jamaica Street. Paddy went down to investigate and obviously took a weapon with him. A short while later news filtered through that somebody had been shot. It was Paddy. He was hit only about 20 minutes after I left him. Peter McGuigan came and told me and Dutch that there was a bit of a conflict going on. I ran down Northwick entry and ran across the back of Jamaica Street. Paddy was at Braniff's house in Jamaica Street. He had just been hit in the head. It was then you realised that this was no game. But Paddy was always a volunteer. He was killed during an operation against the British army. The British army were firing down Jamaica Street. There was also shooting from loyalists coming in from Alliance Avenue. Paddy returned fire and they [British soldiers] pinpointed him. Paddy must have been at that point for a while because he obviously fired quite a number of shots with a .303. He obviously stayed too long. He was shot once, clean through the head with an SLR. If he had moved he might have been alright. But he was a game sort of fella. He died instantly. The British army never claimed him. There was confusion surrounding who shot him because at the time there was a loyalist, an ex-Brit, who lived up there and he was firing too. He also got shot. I believe that it was the Brits who shot Paddy. When we went round, there were no Brits visible but they could have been in concealed positions.

Straight after his death everybody was in shock. There was so much going on. Young Leo McGuigan was shot the same morning [Leo McGuigan, killed by the British army in Estoril Park, 9 August 1971]. Things were snowballing. Reports were coming in that people had been shot over in Ballymurphy. The natural reaction was retaliation and so there were gun battles going on all that day. Then Paddy's body had to be removed in a baker's van and for security reasons he was buried from the Falls. There was a military funeral up the Falls and then he was buried in the republican plot. Before that, his body was in the assembly hall in the Holy Cross school so people could go in and offer their condolences. There was a guard of honour in full regalia. Paddy was a militant person. He was well thought of by the other volunteers because he was disciplined, stern and solid in his political beliefs. He guided others the right way and dedicated his life to the movement. I am sure that had he lived Paddy would have ended up at the political end of things. He was very well respected. It was just unfortunate that he ended up in a position when there was shooting coming from two attackers, the loyalists and the Brits. We know now about collusion but we didn't really realise it until years later.

Lena Murphy (sister)

Paddy was the life and soul of our family. He was just always cracking jokes and carrying on. I never knew him to be serious in my whole life. Anybody that knew Paddy before he got involved would tell you the same thing. He was never a serious person. He was just full of life and he loved his clothes. He used to play football and used to play for Kills Cubs in Flax Street. He liked to play a bit of 'catch kiss' as well. Paddy loved Irish dancing and jiving up in Ardoyne Hall and the Plaza. He used to go ceile dancing in St Gabriel's and over on the Falls. He loved music. He was just a very happy-go-lucky fella and he loved life. Nothing was a problem to him. He went out of his way to do things for people, even during the troubles. He always got the girls too. He just had that sort of personality. He wasn't what you would call a drinker but he would go out, down to Kilpatricks and the Saunders after it was built. I remember him always carrying on in the house. He would dress up and have concerts in the house in the winter nights. He loved playing with my children. I know there was a serious part to Paddy but he was never serious in the house. We were a very close family but there are only two of us left now. Everything that developed in the mid to late 1960s had a big impact on Paddy – things like Paisley, the Divis riots and the civil rights movement. We were not aware at that time that Paddy was involved in the republican movement. He kept it to himself until such time as he couldn't any longer. When the troubles started really bad, we used to live in Chatham Street. We knew Paddy was involved then because he used to come round to take my kids to my mummy's in a car. The parents in the street used to say, 'We better get the kids; there's the Murphys away'. At my mummy's Paddy would dismantle a bed, put the mattress on the floor and make a tent over the top of the kids, as if they were camping out for the night. That's the way he was with the children. Then he would go out and do whatever he had to do.

At the time internment came in I was in my own house in Chatham Street. I was sent for to come round to my mummy's house. On the way I was told that Paddy had been shot dead. When I got into the house I found out my daddy had been lifted the night before. They trailed him out of his sick bed in his bare feet. My uncle Frankie was held too. There was a whole crowd lifted. It was all the fathers of the sons that they were looking for. The Brits told my mummy that when they got Paddy my daddy would be let out. They knew my daddy wasn't well. My mummy had to just sit and wait. They held my daddy in Castlereagh and then the Brits threw him and a wee elderly man called Mr Quigley out of a jeep in Glengormley. That was once the Brits knew that Paddy was dead. Some fella (I don't know who he is to this day) picked the two of them up and brought them home. My daddy didn't know that Paddy was dead until he reached Brompton Park. After Paddy was killed, the boys were fixing him up in the Holy Cross school. Then when they were ready,

Martin Meehan came up for my mummy. As we were walking through the back gates we could see into the assembly hall. The curtains were wide open and through the windows we could see Paddy lying there. There were a lot of people standing around. So they put everybody out of the hall to let my mummy be alone for a wee while. The only ones there were the guard of honour. They were just four wee lads, God love them. Paddy was just lying there. It was nice of them to do it and they did the right thing by Paddy. They gave him his place. But the hall was so big and it was very cold. We also knew that the British army would come for Paddy and that there would be trouble. When the British army did come, they wanted the body. My mummy was worried most about the wee lads doing the guard of honour. But, God love them, they stood their ground until the lads took him away in an ambulance. Those wee boys wouldn't let them in. Paddy and Patsy McArdle got the ambulance and they brought him home to the house the following day. He was in my mummy's house until he was buried. There was heavy shooting coming in from the Bone Heights the whole time, so no one could get in or out. On the morning of Paddy's funeral he was taken out in the ambulance to the back of Chatham Street. Then he was put into a bread van, belonging to Gerry Morgan, the local bread man, and taken over to St Paul's. He had to be sneaked out because the British army still wanted him. Paddy's death was devastating for the whole family.

Rose (wife)

The first time I ever saw Paddy was when I joined the local Sinn Féin Cumman. Paddy was already in it. He was also in the IRA at that time. Mary McGuigan was the chairperson of the Cumann, and Amy Mulholland was in it. Those were people that I already knew. But I joined the Sinn Féin Cumman because I was always very political. My mummy told me about the troubles years ago. The 'B' Specials took my uncle Phil and my father and frog-marched them down to Tennent Street station. My uncle Phil did two years on the prison ship and was also interned for two years in Crumlin Road gaol. So I was brought up with politics, but never the Catholic or Protestant thing. We were never bigoted because we couldn't afford to be bigots. We had cousins that lived on the Shankill Road. My uncle Phil's first wife was a Protestant and a nicer woman you couldn't meet. So I had three cousins on the Shankill Road and I use to go over there and play when I was a child.

What I liked about Paddy was that he had a great sense of humour and he made me laugh. He was also a very strong person, both in terms of his character and his beliefs. He would never ask anybody to do something that he would not have done himself. He was also very protective. He was very protective towards me and towards most people, especially towards his community. He loved Ardoyne and he loved the people in it. The first night we went out, we went up to a bar in Ligoniel. He wasn't on the run then but it was a 'shoot to kill' thing with Paddy. They were really after him and we didn't want to go anywhere where it would be too easy for him to be caught. I remember he was driving a wreck of a car. Afterwards his mummy told me that he had everybody in the family out scrubbing it and cleaning the inside because he was taking me out in it. When we were driving up, the door of the car opened on the passenger side where I was sitting and I was hanging onto the door so that I wouldn't fall onto the road. He was hanging onto me so that I wouldn't fall out and he was trying to drive the car at the same time. We had a nice night. It was very friendly, talking and things like that. We got to know each other and started going out. Then we got to know each other very well. We got married on 15 January 1971 in a registry office. We had a reception at the Hunting Lodge and Frankie Kane was our best man. Afterwards as we drove at the back of the city hall, this cop drove along beside us. My heart went into my mouth because we were just married. Of course Paddy had armed bodyguards there and I just saw everybody's hands going into their pockets. I thought, 'Jesus, Mary and Joseph'. Luckily they drove on and everything was alright. But that's an example of what it was like. A traumatic experience like that and me just married! Then we went to Dundalk just for that night for our honeymoon. As we were driving down, we gave two girls hitching a lift a ride down to Newry. That was typical of Paddy. When his mind should have been full of a whole lot of other things he was thinking of others. He actually gave them a lift to their doors. Then we went down and had a night in Dundalk. That was our honeymoon and back the next morning.

Shortly after that, I was imprisoned for being involved in a protest. I didn't get out again until July. Then I found out I was pregnant with our Patricia. I came out of gaol on 14 July. We couldn't live together. When Paddy came to see me he always had a scout looking out for the Brits. Everything had to be safe for him. Paddy was on the run then. One time Paddy went to see his daddy in the house when his daddy was ill. Paddy loved and admired his daddy very much. He sneaked over the back and he was climbing over the yard wall when the Brits and peelers were coming up the entry. They saw him and shot at him. Lucky enough they missed. So even though we were married he couldn't live with me. He had to stay all over in safe houses and billets.

On 8 August Paddy and me went out to the Shamrock. Paddy had said, 'Look I'm fed up; come on, let's go out for a drink'. I was nervous the whole night we were there. When we came out I said to him, 'I'll walk you up' because I knew which billet he was in. But Paddy said, 'No, I want to be near you'. I was very pregnant by this stage. He was sleeping on the couch and I was in bed but he just wanted to be in the same house. At about 3.30 am or 4 am there was all this commotion. It was terrible. The whole area erupted with noise. There was screaming and shouting, whistles and bin lids. I ran out and I saw Mary Mullan from Jamaica Street. She said that they had brought internment in and they had raided the house where Paddy was supposed to have been staying. They had also lifted Paddy's daddy. He was in his sixties and he was very, very ill. He was dying from cancer. But they trailed him out with no shoes on. So I went round and woke Paddy up and told him what had happened. He said, 'I'll have to get out and start organising'. I said, 'Before you go I need to tell you something. But you have to promise me you'll keep your temper. Please don't be going out half shot'. And I told him about his daddy. That was the last time I saw him alive. The next thing I remember is when Gerry Graham came and took me round to the boys' school in Butler Street where they had laid Paddy out. Everybody was coming to pay respects to his body and he was just lying there with his brown suit on. His boots were underneath the table that they had laid him out on. He just looked like he was sleeping. I couldn't believe it because he had such a good sense of humour. I stood there and I thought he was going to jump up and say, 'That scared you, didn't it?' But he didn't. I don't know how long I stood there for.

After that, I came home I sat there with all these people coming in and out and telling me I would be alright. I couldn't feel anything. My doctor came round and he was absolutely fantastic. He told me that I had to be careful because the baby needed to be born and I had to stay healthy for the baby's sake. He gave me a week's load of tablets to dull the pain. But it didn't stop me from standing at the bottom of my mother's pad and looking up and saying, 'Please God, will you let me die now?' That was despite the fact that I had two children. It was not being selfish; it is because you are in grief. So what you think of is the person who is dead and that you want to be with. You don't think of anybody else. I was pregnant, I was having a baby, but I didn't even think of that baby. I just thought I wanted to be with Paddy and I couldn't be with him. Paddy got buried from his mother's house which was two doors below me. That was where he lay. On the day of his burial there were loyalists waiting with the intention of getting the coffin. So instead of the coffin being brought out in a hearse, it was taken in a van over to St Peter's and he was buried from there. Instead of being driven over in one of the funeral cars I had to be taken over in a wee red jalopy that belonged to John Kelly from Brompton Park. Even to this day, though, John is a gentleman and a gentle man. My mummy and me were driven up the Falls Road by John in that wee wreck of a car and all the men lining the Falls Road saluted and took off their caps. I felt so proud of Paddy. I had lost him and he was gone but he went with honour.

I had some problems afterwards. I remember when I went down to apply for the widow's pension in Corporation Street. They made me feel like I had just crawled out from underneath a stone. They kept me waiting 15 weeks. I would not have got through that time without the men that Paddy had worked with. He always worked full-time, even when he was on the run. Every morning he was smuggled out in a car. He was in the IRA, on the run and the whole of North Belfast was going crazy. But he was out doing a day's work because he thought about his responsibilities. The IRA did not keep him. They didn't pay him a wage. He didn't have any money; he needed money and he went out and he worked for it under very difficult circumstances. When he died, the men that he worked with collected every Friday when they got their wages and brought it up to me. That is how I survived and how my children were fed. Those people were very good to me and so were people in the IRA, like Martin Meehan. They bought me up clothes and things.

Paddy was my best friend. He had a wonderful sense of humour and people respected him. Even to this day, 30 years later, it is still exactly the same. Paddy McAdorey never shot or harmed an ordinary Protestant in his life. Never. He wasn't sectarian. He wanted this country to be united for all of us and he was no bigot. His contention was with the Brits, police and the loyalists, not Protestants. There is a difference between loyalists and Protestants. Paddy was a very strong character and a very politicised man. He didn't just go into the IRA to get a gun. It is men like Paddy, as well as men who are still alive, who brought this country to a point where you could get and negotiate a peace process. These men, going back 30 years, are men who are just as important as those who are trying to bring forward and negotiate this peace process today.

John Laverty
Killed by the British army,
Ballymurphy,
11 August 1971

> *There were 14 people killed in Ballymurphy between 9 and 11 August 1971. Our John was not a gunman and the paras murdered all those people.*

John Laverty was born at his father's family home in Brookfield Street on 3 April 1951. His parents, Mary (née Carty from Etna Drive) and Thomas, had married in Ardoyne chapel on 22 February 1943. John was the fourth of their eventual 10 children. Some of John's family had been affected by the north's political violence before. Thomas Laverty's sister Susie had been injured by a loyalist bomb thrown at her Mountwater Street home in the Short Strand as she was skipping in the street in the 1920s. Shortly after, the family were bombed out and moved to Ardoyne. John went to Holy Cross Boys school and St Gabriel's. This was despite the fact that the Laverty's had moved to Ballymurphy when John was only five. But they were Ardoyne people so all the children who had been born in the district travelled across the city to go to school. Even after his education was over John kept close connections to the area. Many of the friends he had grown up and gone to school with remained his friends. At the age of 15 he got his first job in the Flax Street mill. Two years later he began working for the Corporation at their yard in Beechmount. He was still working there at the time of his death. Known as 'Big John' because of his six-foot frame, he had grown up a gentle, quiet man, who liked a bet and kept pigeons and had no real interest in politics. But these were difficult times. Ballymurphy had seen some of the worst violence of the early years of conflict. That increased in intensity in the wake of the introduction of internment in August 1971. The Parachute Regiment was then stationed in the nearby Henry Taggart barracks. Between 9 and 11 August 1971 paras killed 14 people in and around the area. Six had been massacred in a single incident in Springfield on the night of 9 August. On the night of 10/11 August 1971 John Laverty was shot dead by members of the British Parachute Regiment. As in the cases of all those killed by the paras in Ballymurphy in those three days, no soldier was ever charged or convicted for John's death.

John's sisters

John was very close to his younger brother Terry and they spent a lot of time together. He used to like a wee bet on the horses and playing cards. John used to keep pigeons and he liked a bit of music too. He was a quiet big fella, very family-orientated and kind-hearted. He used to help out with our children, baby-sitting and that. Up until he died, he worked in the Corporation yard in Beechmount and every week when he got his wages he would buy a wee gift for our mummy. We were a very close family and our mummy kept us clannish. We were together no matter what. Every one knew John was a six foot, easy-going big fellow. He was known as 'Big John' because of his height. John liked to do nothing more than to stand in the street having a laugh and sometimes water fights with the fellas he grew up with. He went to mass every Sunday and would often accompany our mummy to the Novena in Clonard Monastery. It was terrible here after the introduction of internment on the 9 August 1971. Things were so bad that the priests in Corpus Christi were offering the last rites to the whole community. John went for it. Our mummy was a deeply religious woman; she was not political; and if our daddy had any views he did not speak of them to us.

Our brother was killed two days after the introduction of internment in 1971. On 9 August quite a few men were trailed from our street, being taken away and interned. It was just chaotic. There were six people shot dead that night, including our priest Fr. Mullan and one young fellow from our street called Noel Phillips. Mrs Connolly, Mr Taggart, Mr Murphy and Frank Quinn were also shot. They were all innocent people murdered by the paras. I remember John cutting the lining out of our sister Sue's coat to make a black flag for Noel's funeral. He said, 'Noel was not politically motivated. They are just shooting anybody!' By 10 August, people were fleeing south in cars and minibuses. John went across the street to a young woman who said she could not go down south as her washing was still on the line and her children were not ready. John took the clothes from the line and put them into a bag. Along with my older and younger sisters he walked us over to the community centre and we got on a minibus. John said, 'Cheerio, you will be ok' and we headed off to Kildare. That was the last time we saw our brother alive.

In the early morning of 11 August our mummy was over at Noel Phillips' wake. At about 3.30 am she started having this terrible feeling so she came home. She wasn't sitting at home long when the bin lids started to go. John and Terry awoke, got dressed and came downstairs. They were met at the bottom by our mummy. She told them they were not to go out especially after so many people had been killed. John said that he needed to go to the toilet. He climbed out of the bathroom window and Terry went out the back door. Our daddy stopped another brother from going out and our mummy was left banging on the bathroom door. But John had already gone to see what was going on in the area.

Terry heard shooting and decided to go home over Shepherds path, which is a short cut onto the Whiterock Road. Two paras called him over to where they were positioned at the Corporation yard. Subsequently, Terry was beaten and subjected to both mental and physical torture. During the torture a para said, 'I have shot one Irish bastard dead; another one won't make any difference'. This went on for a while. Terry was then handed over to the MPs and he was subjected to more of the same torture. They sliced his trousers and shirt with knives to humiliate him. Then they forced him to remove his shoes and socks and walk on shattered glass to a landrover in which he was taken to Girdwood barracks. On reaching Girdwood barracks he was taken out of the landrover to find the brits had formed two lines. They beat Terry and around 50 others as they passed between them. In Girdwood he was subjected to additional abuse. Following this they were all taken to Townsend Street barracks and put into cells.

Our mummy and daddy had been worried sick and tried to find out what had happened to John and Terry. Thirty-two hours later they were told that John was dead. They still did not know what had happened to Terry. My mummy thought that he was dead too. After 48 hours they found out that Terry had been arrested and would be up in court. Terry was taken to court on Friday 13 August where he was charged with riotous behaviour. Before Terry appeared in court a policeman gave him a pair of boots. A fellow gave him a coat to tie round the back of his trousers as they had been cut to shreds by the MPs. On his release (on bail), going up Castle Street my daddy told Terry of John's death. Terry was sentenced to six months imprisonment on December 1971.

To this day the family do not know exactly where John was killed. It is this that hurts the most. It is nearly 30 years later and we still don't know for sure where our brother met his death. The British army admitted shooting John but they didn't say they murdered him. John was shot twice. The first shot wouldn't have killed him as it was superficial. Mr Corr was also shot on 11 August and died in hospital on 27 August. The soldiers stuck to the same story, that they fired back at gunmen. However no weapons were ever found and there were no forensic traces to suggest that either John or Mr Corr had handled weapons. The whole process had a terrible impact on our family. The court was a farce. Our mummy said at the time, 'God knows my son is innocent'.

There were 14 people killed in Ballymurphy between 9 and 11 August 1971. Our John was not a gunman and the paras murdered all of those people. There was no justice in the courts but there was nowhere else to turn so the paras got away with murder. Our daddy was in the court and he was gutted. He shouted at the paras, 'May God forgive you; I hope you crawl the walls for what you have done'. They just laughed. Our mummy never got over John's death. One day we would like to find out what really happened. I would like the chance to come face to face with the soldier who killed him and ask, 'Why?' because our John was just a happy-go-lucky, good-natured fellow. He was very much loved and is still very much missed. We keep our cherished memories of him, like any family.

The soldier who actually shot him wrote a letter to my mother. It stated that he was basically fed up with getting hit with bits of bricks and he just decided to shoot somebody.

Michael McLarnon
Killed by the British army,
Etna Drive,
28 October 1971

Michael McLarnon's father, Joseph, was originally from the Markets area. His mother Bridget (née Butler) was from McMillens Place, a street in the Lower Falls later demolished to make way for the Divis Flats. They lived in West Belfast until World War II when their flat in Divis Street was bombed in an air raid. After that, they set up home in Northwick Drive. Then in 1944 that house was also bombed when German incendiaries fell on Ardoyne, leaving dozens of homes burnt out. As a result, Joseph and Bridget moved to Etna Drive where they would bring up their family of five boys and one girl (Lawrence, Jim, Joe, Matt, Mary, Michael and Paul). Two other children (Jack and Chris) succumbed to pneumonia before the age of two. Michael McLarnon was born the second youngest of the family in 1949. Michael (or Mickey as he was usually known) went to the Holy Cross school and St Gabriel's but left without any formal qualifications. Soon after, he went to work as an apprentice car sprayer on the Shankill Road. After a couple of years he got a job with a paper company in Ligoniel. Restless for something new, Michael then briefly joined the British army. He served for a while in the Parachute Regiment. But army life was not to Michael's liking. He soon returned to Belfast as a civilian and to the job he had left in Ligoniel. By late 1971 Ardoyne was the scene of regular rioting and gun battles. On the night of 28 October 1971 a small crowd had gathered in Etna Drive to throw stones at a patrol of the Green Howards regiment. The Green Howards were to be involved in the killing of a number of unarmed civilians in the district in the coming weeks. On that night one of the soldiers took aim, shot and killed Michael McLarnon.

Jim McLarnon (brother)

Mickey was a quiet, introverted sort of person, although he was outgoing with his own circle of friends. There was only a year of a difference between him and my younger brother Paul. They were very close and there was quite a crowd he knocked about with. A number of them were actually with him when he was shot dead. There was John McAllister, John Varndell, Brendan Clarke, Francie Fox and his brother, wee Bernard Fox [Bernard Fox, killed by the British army in Brompton Park, 4 December 1972]. Mickey's hobby was pulling cars and motor scooters to bits. He liked anything to do with engineering or electrics. I once bought an old car for £12.50, got fed up with it and sold it to Michael for £5. The car I bought next had the same engine and it blew up about a year later. I had to buy the engine out of the car I had sold Michael for £10. Then I had to give him another £10 to put it in for me! That was just about six months before he died.

I didn't see Michael on the day that he died. The last time I saw him he was fixing an old scooter out in the back in my father's shed. The day Michael was shot I was in Divis Flats with my own family. My father and my brother Matt came to the door at about 8 am as I was getting ready to go out to work. They told me that Michael had been shot and died at about 2 am that morning. My father and brother were so distressed that they asked me would I go down and identify his body with them. We went down to the mortuary and I couldn't believe it myself. It just wouldn't sink in, even when I saw Michael lying on the slab. I was hoping that when they pulled the sheet back it would be somebody else. I wasn't expecting it to be Michael because he was so quiet. I was thinking, 'It must be a mistake'. Rioting was occurring in Etna Drive on the night Michael was shot. He went out to the street at around 9 pm. The soldiers opened fire on the teenagers throwing stones down the street. They fired live bullets and Michael was hit. Then he ran up the street and straight into the house. He just collapsed on the floor in front of my mother and father and he said, 'Daddy, I've been hit with a rubber bullet'. My father looked and there was a big gaping hole in the back of his jacket. He knew it was obviously not a rubber bullet. Michael had gone out to the door about ten minutes prior to that, just to talk and stand at the door.

Afterwards you just couldn't get any answers from anybody. Long before the inquest I wrote a letter to the newspaper columnist Patrick Riddle and he invited me to meet him. He was a really fervent unionist. I told him the background to what had happened.

He thought I was in the IRA or something and was looking for propaganda. But he met my mother and father; they had dinner with him in his house on the Malone Road. They explained it all and he wrote an excellent column saying that you can't take the British army's word at face value. The British army said Michael was armed and that he was a gunman. But he was not. The soldier who actually shot him wrote a letter to my mother. He stated that he was basically fed up with getting hit with bits of bricks and he just decided to shoot somebody. Instead of shooting rubber bullets, he shot live bullets. My father submitted the soldier's letter to the inquest but the soldier denied that he had sent it. The letter wasn't signed. I think the guy had printed his name on it. But he just point-blank denied having sent the letter. The inquest held that it was, 'Death by misadventure' and didn't hold anyone to blame. There was no inquiry after that. Nobody was ever charged for the killing anyway. I don't believe that justice was achieved for my family. If somebody is throwing stones at you and you have rubber bullets, you shoot rubber bullets at them, not real live bullets. I don't think there is anything that can be done now in regards to it all. If you can get no justice for Bloody Sunday, which was just full-scale murder, you are not going to get justice for Michael.

Michael's death affected everybody quite badly but my mother and Paul were the two worst for it. Paul and him were very, very close and it hit Paul really, really hard. It just ruined my mother's life, it really did, ruined it completely. It was such a waste, a 22 year old guy getting shot dead for throwing stones. My mother was really inconsolable about him, but Mother Theresa actually came to visit us in our home and it really calmed her greatly. That was only about a week after Michael died, Mother Theresa came with a couple of other Sisters and it really calmed my mother down for days on end after it. The two of them were just sitting talking to each other in very, very low voices. I can remember looking at the wee woman and being amazed by her; it consoled me too. Mother Theresa had seen my mother on television, had a wee word with the nuns up at Ballymurphy and decided to come down.

There was no help given to my family at the time though. Even if there had been, my father was the type of person who wouldn't have taken help from anybody. My father applied for personal injury compensation on Michael's behalf and about four years later it came to court and they awarded my father £300. He told the judge to stick it. Those were his very words. I thought he was going to get arrested for contempt of court but the judge just shrugged his shoulders, walked out and that was it. But there were no organisations for counselling. Even if there had been at that time, in the 1970s, nobody would have gone near them or seen them as helpful. If I talked in close terms about Michael's death it was to my cousin Doreen Toolan. Her husband [Terry Toolan, killed by the British army in Eskdale Gardens, 14 July 1972] was shot dead just outside my mother's door about eight months later and she knows exactly how it feels. You don't really know how it feels until it happens to a person really, really close to you. You can't really explain it to anybody else that it hasn't happened to. The soldier who did it left the British army about two years afterwards. He became a Church of England minister. There was an article in the *Daily Mirror* about it. I thought that on reading the letter that my mother would forgive him. My mother is a very forgiving person. But she didn't.

She just said, 'No, he can rot in hell'. She just couldn't forgive him. I was very, very surprised at my mother saying that.

Matt McLarnon (brother)

Michael was 22 years old when he was shot dead. I saw Michael about three days before he was shot dead. My car had broken down in York Street and Michael came down in my daddy's car to tow me home. He towed me home and that was the last time I ever saw him alive. I found out that Michael was dead when my father came and told me he had been shot and killed by the British army. At that time there was a bit of rioting in the street. The British army admitted to killing Michael but they said that he was armed and that there was a gun battle going on. They said that is how he was shot. He apologised to my mother later on and my mother and father took him to court. He sent a letter of apology and my mother and father sent the letter to the *Sunday News* and they opened an inquiry into the murder. But the soldier involved didn't co-operate with the *Sunday News*. At the inquest the soldier was confronted about the murder of Michael. It turned out that this guy had actually shot seven people dead. The same soldier shot dead Johnny Copeland and a fella called Cassidy [Johnny Copeland, killed by the British army in Strathroy Park, 30 October 1971]. The soldier was quizzed as to whether he was in the right shooting our Michael, John Copeland and the rest of them. He said that he was and he was just doing his duty. They gave him the military cross. For every Catholic that they shoot they seem to decorate them and in this case it seems to be true. At the inquest it was an open verdict. To our family the soldier got off with the murder of Michael. There was no public inquiry into the murder of our Michael, nothing at all. I don't feel there was any justice done and I don't think that anything could be done now because it's a long time ago and too much water has gone under the bridge.

Brendan Clarke (friend)

Michael and me first met when we were children. He lived a few doors above me in 129 Etna Drive. We grew up together from childhood and the friendship carried on from there. Both of us went to St Gabriel's school together. It was a life-long friendship. We would have got into mischief at school, the usual boyish things. Michael always loved motor scooters and things like that. He was always working at old engines. When we left school we didn't get any qualifications; we just left with a basic education. I remember Michael went away and joined the British army and he was in it for a while. He liked it pretty well but I don't know the reason he packed it in. Maybe he was a bit homesick. We didn't really frequent clubs at that time. Michael was never really one for that. He was a bit quiet. I would have seen Michael nearly every day and I would have had a few words with him. He had an old shed out in his back garden and he spent most of his life there, fiddling with odds and ends. That was what kept Michael happy. There was a whole crowd of us that knocked about together. At that time you sort of made your own entertainment; there wasn't a lot happening. He was a quiet nice sort of guy, he never did anybody any harm. He was just one of those guys you just couldn't say anything bad about. He was decent lad.

I don't think I saw Michael on the day he died. I'm nearly sure the last time I saw him was the night the Saunders social club opened. Michael had just been scooting about the street. We all used to congregate at the corner of Eskdale Gardens/Etna Drive and he would have been about there. There was no rioting or anything that night. But that crowd of Brits were just out on a murder campaign. I didn't see Michael in the immediate period before he was shot dead. The shooting went on very close to my house and I went out into the street when I heard it. I was told that Michael had been shot and that the bullet went right through him. They [British soldiers] just opened up. Michael ran into his home and just collapsed on the floor. He was taken to hospital in the ambulance and died in hospital. He had no chance. He was never a member of any organisation or anything. He might have had republican sympathies but in a way I suppose we all had then. But it was just blatant murder. I always remember that for years Michael's father wore the coat that he had worn the night that he was shot dead. He wore it anytime he was going to work in his garage. You could see the hole in the back of it where the bullet had gone right through. I don't know why he wore it. It might have been in memory of Michael or to give him some sort of comfort. Maybe it made him feel that bit closer to him.

On the night of Michael McLarnon's murder something actually happened in my house. My wife Rosaleen and I heard a noise out in the back entry. As I went out the back, a patrol of Green Howard soldiers pushed their way into the yard. They pushed me into the house, came in and took over the house. They held us prisoner. Some of them stayed sitting in the living room. Others went upstairs to the front bedroom window. They were looking out onto the street. There were people at the bottom of Eskdale Gardens and Etna Drive. They picked on one of the people. I think it was Sean Montgomery; he came from Eskdale Gardens. They took aim and they fired trying to hit Sean. But they missed him and they hit a girl from Eskdale Gardens. She was Margaret Martin, I think. They deliberately opened fire. They didn't open the window but just shot through the glass. We were hostages in the house and we could not warn people. That British army patrol was just out for damage that night. They threatened to shoot me. They were making comments about the ones out in the street and laughing whenever they fired the bullets. It was great fun to them. The people hadn't a clue where the shooting was coming from. Then they came down and gave us a lot of verbal abuse. I remember they said, 'We are out to kill IRA men tonight'. But they were no more shooting at IRA men than the man in the moon. As soon as they left the house I ran out into the street and let the people know what had happened and where they had been shooting from. This all happened more or less straight after I heard about Michael. It would have been the same squad of soldiers. I think it was the same soldiers that actually shot John Copeland. He was shot the same night up on the Berwick Road. They were joking that there was, 'another fenian bastard killed tonight'. The regiment stayed in the area for a right while after that. They lost a few men themselves and there were a lot of them wounded. There was damage done to them.

Johnny Copeland
Killed by the British army,
Strathroy Park
30 October 1971

Officially, to this day, the British army say that Johnny was a gunman. But he wasn't. He was shot in the back for rioting. He was murdered for rioting.

Johnny Copeland's father Edward and mother Susan (née Moane) were both originally from the Short Strand. They also both moved to Ardoyne at an early age and brought up their family in Strathroy Park. Johnny was born in September 1949, the youngest of four boys (Eddie, Jimmy, Paddy and Johnny) and five girls (Kathleen, Evelyn, Ellen, Mary and Winnie). As most boys in Ardoyne did, Johnny attended first the Holy Cross school and then St Gabriel's. His nickname was 'snout' because, as his wife Carol puts it 'he had a long nose'. When he left school Johnny became an upholsterer, worked for a time as a bus conductor and later went on to become a male nurse. From an early age Johnny was a keen boxer and fought for the Holy Family boxing club. He was also a member of a weightlifting club in Butler Street and had played football for St Gabriel's. In addition Johnny was interested in Irish dancing. It was whilst travelling over to Irish dancing classes held in the Bone that Johnny met his future wife Carol when she was only 15. For a time they went to live in England, like so many Irish of their generation; they were both training to be nurses. The two returned home and were married in Ardoyne chapel in August 1968. After they were married, the couple lived for a time with Johnny's mother in Strathroy Park and started a family of their own. Linda was born in 1969, Eddie in 1970.

From its earliest days the conflict impacted close to home for Johnny Copeland. His best friend was Neil Somers, who lost a leg when he was run down by an RUC armoured car in early August 1969. Like so many others in the district Johnny would subsequently be active during the riots that characterised life in Ardoyne in the months and years to come. But Johnny was essentially a family man. He completed his training as a nurse in England in the early 1970s. By that time he had moved his young family first to Kerrera Street and then (in June 1971) into their home in Ladbrook Drive. But these were difficult days. The introduction of internment in August saw the Green Howards stationed in Ardoyne. On 28 October members of this regiment shot two unarmed Ardoyne men on the same night. One was Michael McLarnon, the other was Johnny Copeland. Johnny was 23-years-old when he died of his wounds two days later, leaving behind him a widow and two children under the age of two.

Eyewitness and neighbour

The night that Johnny was shot I was in my home in Strathroy Park and I heard a disturbance. Like everybody else, I went out to the door. There was rioting in Etna Drive. The army were down there and then up at the top of the street. I went up to Berwick Road at the top of the street. I was standing at the corner, like everybody else. There was rioting there and the soldiers were at the entry. They [rioters] were throwing stones and the next thing I saw a flash coming out of Strathroy and Northwick entry. I saw wee Johnny drop. Johnny was on the footpath on Strathroy side of the Berwick Road. The Brits were on that side too. He fell and I heard him shouting, 'I'm hit, I'm hit'. I thought he had been hit with a rubber bullet. I ran up toward him. Another fella came up behind me to give me a hand. Then we carried him down into Strathroy. Johnny could hardly walk. We were holding him up. I heard some fella saying that he hadn't been hit with a rubber bullet, that he had been hit with a bullet and that there was a hole in his back. He was shot once in the back because he had his back to the soldiers. I thought Johnny was going to be alright. I think he thought himself he had been hit with a rubber bullet. So a couple of people took him into Tucker Galway's. Then he was taken to the hospital from there in a taxi. He lived for two days after it.

Before Johnny was hit he was at the top of the street with us. He had come down the street earlier and my wife was talking to him at the gate. He owed his mother a couple of pound and he was over paying it. His mother just lived across the street from us. My wife saw him there. After that Johnny was further up the street when the rioting was going on. But there was no way he was a gunman like they [British army] said he was, no way. That's what their old war cry always was. I saw him fall, ran up and lifted him and he had nothing at all on him. My wife said he was wearing bedroom slippers. He'd been in his mother's house and probably heard the disturbance. Like everybody else he came out. I couldn't tell you whether or not Johnny was rioting, but there was no way he deserved to be shot.

At the inquest the soldier said that they were in the other entry, the Estoril and Cranbrook entry. He said Johnny was shot from there. But he wasn't. Then they turned round and said Johnny had knelt down and fired a gun, that the shot had gone over their heads. The judge turned round and said, 'Have you any evidence?' They [British soldiers] said they picked the bullets out of the wall and put them into a matchbox. The judge asked them where they [the bullets] were. They said they lost them. I told the inquest what happened. I thought at first that the court was going to come out in favour of Carol but the judge just turned it round. He said it was 'excusable homicide' because they [British soldiers] were under pressure. The British army still insisted at the inquest that they had shot a gunman, but there was no evidence. I couldn't understand it. There was no evidence relating to gunfire or anything like that.

Paddy Copeland (brother)

The Saunders was just opening the night Johnny was killed so there was supposed to be no shooting or anything. Johnny was going down to pay my ma a few bob that he owed her. He lived in Ladbrook [Drive] and my mummy lived in Strathroy [Park] and he came down in his bedroom slippers to pay my ma. He had just left and was going up Strathroy, heading toward Ladbrook to go home. Then a riot started. Somebody said Johnny threw a stone at a Brit. Then he turned to run away and they shot him in the back. This was at the top of the Strathroy, on the Berwick [Road]. He threw a stone and they shot him. Geordie Hagans and Gerry Quinn helped carry him down. They thought he had been hit with a plastic bullet. He was shot in the back. The Brits said that he was a gunman. I was living in Ballymurphy at the time Johnny was killed. I didn't find out until the next day that he had been shot the night before. I was in work in Goodyear's in Craigavon. Some guy said to me, 'Johnny Copeland's been shot dead in Ardoyne' and showed me the *Irish News*. I just got back on the train. I went back to Ardoyne, found out he had been shot and rushed down to the Mater Hospital. The cops and Brits were in the hospital when I got there. The Brits were fusiliers. They thought I was Eddie because me and Eddie were of similar build. So I got a bit of hassle. They stopped me going in and I told them I was Johnny's brother Patrick. They started asking me where Eddie was. It was only after that I got in to see Johnny. The whole family was there. Johnny was talking away. I didn't want to go in and see him; I'm not like that, I stood outside with the sisters. He died the next night. When he died he was pushed into a wee room. When they said they were taking the body out, the door jarred open and I saw them just throw him into an old body bag and cart him out. That got to me. Johnny just loved the craic like the rest of us.

Carol Copeland (Johnny's wife)

Johnny was never arrested or anything. He was a quiet fella, an awful nice fella. Johnny was a real family man. But where rioting was concerned he would have been out every night. The first I knew of that was when we lived in Kerrera Street, around 1970. Frankie Kane used to call for Johnny, and I used to say, 'Oh, there's something up'. They would have been running messages or whatever. We all used to run in and out of each other's houses. In June 1971 we moved into a house in Ladbrook Drive. We were only in it a few months before Johnny was killed.

Johnny was shot on the 28 October at exactly 9.05 pm. There was rioting going on. It wasn't really much of a riot. There were just a couple of bottles being thrown. Johnny went down to see what was going on; he was on his way down to his ma's. I had said to him, 'Let me go out' but he told me to stay in because we had been out vigilanting the night before till about six in the morning. So away he went. That was the last time I saw him, as he dandered down towards Strathroy Park. Now I don't know exactly what happened. If you are not there the truth of what happens never comes out. [What I have been told is] the Green Howards were coming up Strathroy entry. They were just at the first door when some fellas from Strathroy came running up the entry. There couldn't have been many of them. It was just a couple of kids throwing stones. Wee Geordie Hagans and Gerry Quinn were there and they wouldn't have got involved in anything. The Brits were sneaking up the entry and they just opened up. There were big hedges in the entry then so Johnny probably wouldn't even have seen the Brits. The fellas must have all run because Johnny got it in the back. He was shot once, right in the back. He must have slipped because there were big scrape marks on him. Geordie and Gerry lifted Johnny and carried him into Tucker's house in Strathroy and he lay there for a couple of hours. Eventually they got him to the Mater Hospital. But I think they should have brought him straight to hospital because they had to bring him anyway.

This is how I found out what had happened. I was up in the bathroom and there was a knock on the door. It was Josephine Short. She said she was looking for Johnny's sister Evelyn. But she would have known that Evelyn was at work. I knew there was something wrong by her voice. She didn't tell me what had happened. She ran out. She probably didn't want to tell me. But I had heard the banging. It didn't sound like shooting. It sounded more like rubber or plastic bullets. But the minute I heard the bang I thought 'that's him shot' because he was mad where rioting was concerned. Then Evelyn came running over. She just said, 'Josephine Short…' and I said, 'I knew it'. You should have heard the squeals of me. Johnny's brother came to the door and he just said, 'Why did you let him out?' Then I wasn't even allowed to go near the house. You would have thought it was a top IRA man that had been shot the way they were smuggling him out of the house. Michael McLarnon was shot the same night. He died right way. But it was two separate incidents. Margaret Martin was shot too that night; she was injured. After that I don't remember much. I do remember the hospital. Johnny lived for 58 hours. They [the British army] tried to get in to interview him. They said he was an IRA man. They wanted to get in to harass and torture him. But the nurses and the doctors wouldn't let them in. Johnny died in the Mater Hospital at 6.05 am on Saturday 30 October. It was a desperate end.

A couple of days later the Brits raided the house. The Brits admitted killing Johnny but they said he was a gunman. There was never any evidence to prove that. I was at the inquest. It happened a few years later. They passed an open verdict. There was a man called Sloan who owned the paper shop. He was on the jury. He told old ma Copeland that he was never on a jury like it in his life. He said it wasn't right. They had his clothes for years but there were no forensics. I didn't get Johnny's clothes back for another two years after the inquest. The Brit that shot Johnny was only 22. He actually appeared at the court. I think it was at the hearing for the compensation claim. I tried to hit the bastard but I got a big whack back. He [the British soldier] knew he was guilty. He stood up and said to the judge, 'Look, will you please compensate this woman?' But the judge said, 'You're not here to tell us what to do. Sit down'. But he [the British soldier] was still insisting that Johnny was an IRA gunman. He said that Johnny fired six shots at him. He said he dug the bullets out of the wall and kept them in a match box. But he said that he had lost them. So there was no evidence. I was going to take the case further but I went to see Gerry Fitt and he said that Johnny was a gunman. He said there would be no real point going on. Then somebody said to me that it was blood money. So I didn't bother with a claim after that. I got the children reared anyway. I didn't know much about anything to do with all that then. I had never had any dealings with solicitors before and you had nobody to help you.

I was wrecked and totally devastated by Johnny's death. We really had nothing. We were young and only married when the troubles started. The one thing that I will never, ever forget is being left with two wee kids. It was desperate. Basically I was left on my own with two kids. No government agency came near me. I never saw the social services. I was on a widow's pension and all I got was about £9 a week. You were left with nothing. It was terrible for about a year. I think I lost about a year or more. I can't remember now. I remember hitting the drink and I'd never drunk in my life. Our Maura was going to America about five months after Johnny was killed. Maura and a few others brought me out for a wee drink. I had two vodkas. I didn't even drink vodka then. So I started to get a wee quarter of vodka to make me sleep. I thought it was great because it knocked me out. It was like medicine. Before that I could never sleep because I cried myself to sleep at nights. Then Johnny's sister Ellen caught on to what was happening. I just stopped drinking like that then.

Officially, to this day, the British army say that Johnny was a gunman. But he wasn't. He was shot in the back for rioting. He was murdered for rioting. I don't know that there is anything that can be done in relation to the case now. Fair play to Sammy McLarnon for trying to get an inquiry into his father's killing. I would love something done about Johnny because the ones that did it got away with murder. They had to say that somebody opened up on them. They had to say it was Johnny and Michael [McLarnon] because that was who they shot. But they got away with it and there's nothing much you can do about it.

Joseph Parker
Killed by the British army,
Toby's Hall
12 December 1971

> *We knew there was never going to be anybody held accountable for it, no justice, nothing like that; it was just murder that was all.*

Joseph Parker was the son of Molly (née Cosgrove) and Joseph Parker senior. Molly was orginally from the New Lodge Road and later moved to 45 Northwick Drive, Ardoyne. Joseph was from Carrick Hill and he moved to the district in the 1940s. After the couple married in 1945, they set up home at 21 Eskdale Gardens where young Joseph and his sister Theresa were born. After leaving St Gabriel's School, young Joseph, or Jo Jo as his friends knew him, started working for Hugh and Dicks timber works. That was his first and only job. Jo Jo was well liked. He had a number of good friends, including Barney Bradley, Fra Cusack, Seamie McGrandles and Nicky Murphy; many of them he had kept in touch with from his school days. He liked a game of football, boxing and played for a local darts team; they named it the Parkerville Dart Team after his death. Jo Jo was regularly seen in the League social club playing a game of snooker with Patsy McAuley and friends. In general he was a quiet person and kept himself to himself. He married Dorothy, a girl from Ligoniel and they set up home there where they had one little girl called Joanna. Joseph was twenty-five years old when the British army killed him in Toby's Hall, December 1971. Carlene, their second child, was born shortly after her father was killed.

Jackie and Betty Haughey (eyewitnesses)

Jackie: Toby's Hall was a gathering place for all the young ones in the district. It was on every Friday night and was run by the republican movement. People couldn't get out of the district because of the conflict. There was a temporary bar in the Hall and every Friday night it was packed. Toby's Hall had been operating like this from about late 1971. There were usually a few hundred people at the event. The name of the group that played that night was the 'Circle'. One or two of them were injured that night.

The night young Joe Parker was shot dead I was working in the bar as usual and Betty and my daughter, Marie, were in the hall. The place was packed as usual. Then the Brits came to the door. This was about 9.00 pm. The crowd was already in the club dancing away and drinking. It was two senior members of the patrol that came to the door. They said, 'We know there are wanted men in here; we want to search the club'. So the local priest, I think it was Fr. Frank Goodall, said to the Brits, 'Look, there is no back door in here; there is only one way in and one way out. So let the people have their night out; let the people enjoy themselves. If you want, at the end of the night you can check people going out'. At that the Brits pushed the priest out of the road and Tom or Andy Goodall punched the Brit. The Brit's beret fell off and a shot went off in the air. One of the Brits fired his gun into the ceiling.

Betty: What I saw was the Brit with no beret kneeling down; he had blonde hair and he just riddled into the crowd of people in the club. He had an SLR. Then as he was firing into the crowd, the rest of the Brits outside began shooting into the club through the wooden panels and the windows. It was only a matter of seconds between the soldiers coming into the Hall in the first place to them opening fire on the crowd. I threw myself down and Patrick Kane came over and said, 'Get down, get down, 'cause they're real bullets'. I said to him, 'God, we are all going to die here tonight'. It seemed to go on for ages; then there was a lull. The poor wee fellow (Joe Parker) was lying there. He had been dancing with his sister Theresa. All his life was edging away from him. There were a lot of people wounded that night. Young Joe Parker had no cover when the shooting began. He was up dancing and would have been in the middle of the Hall. He didn't die instantly. When they lifted him he was still alive. He was still alive when they took him into the ambulance. But you could see he was losing the fight for his life. After the fear had gone and people realised what had happened, they were very angry. They ran out onto the street to confront the Brits, but they had got into their saracen and went to their barracks. I don't think they came out the next day either; no patrols or nothing came out.

When the first British soldiers came into the club and went out again, most people believed it was only a minor row. They didn't believe it was going to develop into anything and end up as it did. I think young Joseph was shot in the stomach. Immediately after the Brits stopped firing they all jumped into the waiting saracens and drove down to the barracks and never came near the district. They weren't seen for days after it. The bishop came the next morning along with the solicitor Oliver Kelly and there were a lot of photographers and journalists. The RUC came and marked all the bullet holes. I would say they counted up to two hundred bullet holes. The local people built an altar at the spot where he was killed in the Hall.

Theresa Watt (sister)

Jo Jo was my only brother. He didn't go out much. He was a very quiet person. I was with him the night he was killed. When my husband was killed [Barney Watt, killed by the British army in Chatham Street, 5 February 1971], Jo Jo used to take me to the disco in Toby's Hall. There was me, Joseph, our Francie, my aunt Sarah and Davy Richardson; it was a family thing every Friday night. We were up dancing on the floor and the place was packed. Two young lads ran in and the British army came in behind them. When the Brits came in, they got a bit of heckling from the crowd in the hall. The two soldiers that were inside got scared and shot up into the air. The Brits outside must have thought that they were getting shot; they came running in and opened up. When they opened up, everybody just went straight to the ground.

Jo Jo fell one way and I went down the other way. There was a Brit at the door; he got down on his knee and he opened up right round the hall. I was lying watching him. They stopped shooting and people got up. When I got up and turned round, Jo Jo was still lying on the floor. I said to him, 'Jo Jo, get up, it's over, they've stopped shooting', and he groaned. He didn't talk. A lot of people crowded round him. Somebody tried to get me away; somebody punched me to get me away. The Brits wouldn't let the ambulance in and they wouldn't let anybody in or out. I'd say we were a good half-hour or more in the hall and Jo Jo was still lying there. He was unconscious then; our Francie was talking to him, but he wasn't talking back. Somebody took me into a wee room; then they took him out. I got somebody to run me down to the Mater Hospital. When I went in, Jo Jo was getting wheeled out to theatre. But at this time he was sitting up on the trolley and he put his thumb up to me and said, 'I'm OK'. But he was dead when they got him to theatre. Patricia Hale was grazed in the head; she was in the Mater Hospital too when I got down. There were a few other people with minor injuries caused by the broken glass on the floor. Two people had been shot.

My daddy was in Long Kesh at the time and he heard it on the news that night. When my mummy was told Joseph was dead she just sat and cried, she was very quiet; she was like him. My daddy was released from Long Kesh for the funeral. The British army apologised; they said it was a mistake. There was no public statement. They came round to the house and apologised to my daddy. My daddy had been in the same regiment. I dare say they were the same soldiers that Jo Jo and myself baby-sat for in Germany. The British army tried to make out that they were opened up on inside Toby's Hall. But it wasn't true. It was the two soldiers that came in and opened up into the ceiling. They got afraid. At the inquest the British army said that their lives were in danger. They said that they were more or less under siege in the hall.

There was never any public inquiry. There was nothing ever done about it. You just depended on neighbours and family and that's how we got by, just day by day. There was only ten months between Jo Jo and my husband being killed. Barney, my husband, was shot dead by the British army in February and Joseph was shot dead in December. It was terrible for my ma; that was her only son. As the saying goes, they got away with it; it was just swept under the carpet as usual. There was never anybody charged with it and there never will be. You just had to grin and bear it; we knew there was never going to be anybody held accountable for it, no justice, nothing like that.

Joe Parker (father)

I was interned when my son was killed. I was interned on 10 August 1971. I found out about his death through a news flash. It came on the news that a young man had been shot dead in Ardoyne; it said his father was an ex-sergeant of the regiment that had shot him. At four o'clock in the morning one of the screws came in and said 'I've bad news for you', and I said, 'I know; it's my son'. It came on the news at twelve o'clock that night. The screw was an Indian and he said, 'Those b's wouldn't come up and tell you'. I said, 'Don't worry about it, son'.

The regiment that killed my son was the Queens Lancs. That's the regiment I was a member of. When I got out for the funeral the Colonel said he was sorry to hear about my son. I said, 'You're sorry; sure, it was one of your men that killed him'. I knew the soldier that killed my son. I never got out on parole right away. The prison administration sent for me and asked me to sign a piece of paper to get out. I said, 'No way; you put me in here, so you can put me out'. A priest came up and said, 'We'll sign for him and we'll bring him back'. I ended up getting a couple of hours parole. I had to be back for 4.00 pm on the day of the funeral.

All I know about the incident was that there was trouble with a British army patrol outside Toby's Hall. A lot of soldiers rushed into the hall and they started riddling all round them. There were 11 people injured that night and my son got shot in the stomach. Theresa, my daughter, was very lucky, they nearly killed her too; the bullets went right past her coat.

The British army version of events was that there were seven or eight shots fired at them from the hall. But I asked around and I was told categorically that there was no way any shots were fired at them from the hall. The British army admitted shooting my son. They didn't try to say he was a gunman. In fact one of the officers told me he was sorry my son got shot. I told him where to go. I never saw my son the whole time I was in prison. I said to my wife I didn't want her to bring him up. So the last time I saw him alive would have been before I went into gaol. I was in prison three or four days when he sent me a letter; that was the last I heard from him.

> *Billy and Catherine McCorry, devastated by the death of their daughter, said,*
> *'We will pray for the people who took her life'.*

Margaret McCorry
Killed by the IRA,
Crumlin Road,
20 December 1971

Margaret McCorry's father William and mother Catherine Nalty grew up in Chatham Street, Ardoyne. William's aunt, Cassie Myles, reared him. As teenagers, Catherine and William started courting and were married in Holy Cross chapel on 24 June 1945. They eventually had eight children: Francis, Fidelma, Danny, Margaret, Catherine, Anne, Damien and Laurence. Margaret was born on 23 October 1951. She attended Holy Cross Girls school and later progressed to Oranges Academy. She was a diligent student and left school with a number of qualifications. She worked as secretary in Brookfield Mill and as clerk in the Mater Hospital. While on a visit to Kerry, the year before she was killed, Margaret met her future fiancée, an American, Michael McCarthy. The couple started dating and made plans to marry the coming year. On 20 December 1971 the IRA accidentally killed Margaret when they opened fire on a British army convoy on the Crumlin Road. Margaret was 20 years old at the time of her death.

Frank/Catherine/Ann (sisters and brother)

Margaret's school friend was Cathy McCallum. They were both very close. Cathy lived in old Oakfield Street, just a street away from where we lived in Fairfield Street. Margaret was a very timid person, very quiet, but there were times when she was out going. She loved dressing up when we were younger and she had a lovely singing voice. We were all members of the Holy Cross choir and we were in a number of musicals organised by St Gabriel's youth club. Catherine and Margaret occasionally went to the Ulster Hall to hear bands like The Dubliners.

Margaret went to Kerry with my aunt Clarice. She stayed there for about three months and that's where she met Michael McCarthy, the fella she was engaged to. She was coming home to plan the wedding and to tell my parents. She wrote a letter to me beforehand and she asked me not to tell anyone until she came home. Michael had gone back to America and she was planning to follow. When she applied with her Irish passport, they wouldn't accept it. That's what happened; it just didn't work out. That's why she was applying for a job in Queen's University. She went for the interview that Monday morning in University Street. The professor that interviewed her actually came over after he heard about her death because he just couldn't believe it. He came over and spoke to my mum and dad. He said what a lovely girl she was and that he couldn't believe it. She had actually got the job.

Anne: The day that Margaret died was the 20th of December. It was quite a dark afternoon and I can remember Margaret and I walked up Butler Street together. That was our natural route. We met my aunt Francis at the top of the street and funny enough, I can remember her saying 'Be careful' and that's all I can remember. Margaret was going to visit my aunt Bridget who lived in Mountainview to tell her about the wedding arrangements. She walked up to the front of the Crumlin Road and I crossed over to the Ardoyne Hall to go to my dancing class. That was the last I saw her. I think we just said, 'I'll see you later'. The next thing I knew I was up on the stage dancing and shooting started. A little later I can remember my cousin coming up to the hall and I knew there was something wrong. I ran out of the hall and across the road. I remember seeing blood. I just ran down into Butler Street and I remember Fr. Fernando grabbing me as I went into the house. My mummy was sitting on the settee. I just fell at her knees and that was it. That's what I can remember of that day.

Catherine: I remember the day Margaret died; I worked in Holy Cross monastery and I heard shooting. Fr. Augustin came in and he said 'There has been shooting on the front of the road, stay in'. I don't know what made me feel I had to go out but I went to the gate of Holy Cross church. I heard somebody shouting, 'Somebody has been shot'. I looked over towards the bus stop and then I ran over. I did first aid so I thought at least I'd be able to help somebody or do something maybe. But then I realised it was Margaret; I recognised her scarf and her coat and she wasn't moving. I remember saying, 'She'll be alright, I hope she will be alright'. Then I was taken away and all of a sudden there were a lot of priests on the scene. I was brought back in to the monastery and then I had to go home. I couldn't stay, I had to get home. I went home and my mummy and the rest of the family were there just sitting.

Frank: I heard of Margaret's death very late on. I was on the buses at that particular time. I remember one of my last journeys, I was sitting in Castle Street. I don't know what happened but at 4.55 pm I wanted to go up to Ardoyne. Naturally people were trying to talk me out of it and I said, 'Look something has happened'. But nobody could find out what had happened. As the night went on, I had to go to different meetings and different things happened and nobody knew anything. My three uncles informed me at about half past ten that night. That's the only recollection I have. I had a feeling that something had happened to her or something had happened to someone in my family.

Margaret was killed in crossfire. There had been shots fired from a house at a passing British army convoy. How they were going to hit anybody was beyond me because the pillar was right in front of the window. My sister just happened to be on the wrong side of the pillar and that's what happened. We were told by my father that there was an apology sent to the family. My mother and father did not broadcast anything; they were very private. My father didn't mention any organisation. They should have given a written apology; that was the policy of the day and we never got one. I don't think if we got one now it would heal anything.

Frank/Catherine/Ann: The men that were in Long Kesh at the time sent us a cross and lovely handkerchiefs; they were fellas that knew Margaret. There were a lot of people that knew the family and they were stunned. I think the district was stunned, to be quite honest. It wasn't because of the way that it happened; it wouldn't have mattered who pulled the trigger in my opinion. But there were a lot of twists and a lot of things that had been said in Ardoyne afterwards. I remember Fr. Fernando saying, 'These people don't matter because they don't know the family; they don't know the roots that you come from so ignore them'. But sometimes it was hurtful because things were said that should never have been said. People were under the impression that the funeral was paid for by certain people and that did not happen. Things like that are hurtful to the family because my parents had never taken any money off anybody. The money that my parents got from the government was actually given over to my two younger brothers because it was classed as blood money.

My mum asked us all to forgive them because she forgave them, no matter who it was. It wouldn't have mattered who it was. That's what they couldn't understand about my mother and father: how could they forgive? They were brought up that way. It wouldn't have mattered who it was because it wouldn't have brought her back. I'm sure a lot of people think that way too about the deaths of their sons and daughters. It wasn't easy; it was my sister and it's an awful thing; it's the worst thing that can happen to you.

My mum told the newspapers, it was the *Irish News*, or the *Daily Mirror*, 'I'll pray for the people who killed my daughter. But I blame the people in Stormont who put the boys and the men onto the streets to defend the areas. They are the people that caused this. I am not the first mother nor will I be the last mother to lose a child'. The newspapers never printed a word of it. I'm very proud of my mother and father, great people and that's what really hurt because they were.

We were just devastated by Margaret's death, devastated, totally shocked, very hurt. It wasn't just a sister, it was the family circle shattered. Our family shattered after that;

my mummy died four years afterwards, well before her time. Then my aunt Eileen, my father's sister was killed by a British saracen tank on Black's Road three months after mummy died. So within four years we lost Margaret, mummy and my aunt Eileen. The only thing, I think, that kept mum and dad going was their faith. Our own children keep asking about their aunt Margaret, so there's always a constant reminder and having to explain what happened and the importance of the family staying together. The family circle is very, very important.

There was an inquest into the killing; my daddy went down but I don't know who went with him; I think it was my uncle Joe. I didn't go down, I couldn't. We didn't ask what the outcome of the inquest was. Those were questions you just didn't ask. Everybody just clammed up. My mother would never have uttered she wanted justice for what happened to Margaret. To me she would have said, and rightly so, that we'll pray to Margaret to help us and we'll just pray for the people who had taken her life. That to me is what we always did in our own different ways. Because we respected mum and dad, to us there was no other way because she was killed by mistake and it was accidental. Margaret was only 20 years old when she died.

I have fond memories of her; all I can say is we loved her. When we were children we used to go to all the weddings on a Saturday to collect the confetti. Then we always took turns at being the bride and we would have thrown the confetti over each other. The main thing was we were all together as a family growing up and we were very close. We mightn't have had an awful lot but we had a happy family; we had everything. We are not materialistic; we lived in number one Fairfield Street and we just had what we had. It was a happy family. I can look back on my childhood and say, 'Yes, we enjoyed it'. To me Margaret was always jolly. She had a favourite song and sometimes I get a wee bit emotional when I hear it. She sang it in the GAA club that Sunday night before she died. It was 'Four Green Fields'. Margaret went down to the GAA with a couple of others that Sunday night and thank God they did because when you look back on it, she left us with a smile and that was great.

Paul Di Lucia (eyewitness)

I knew Margaret to see but not personally. I knew the whole family; they are a fairly well-known family. They lived in the corner house in Fairfield Street. I can remember that day she was killed. It was a weekday and it was near Christmas. Myself and a couple of mates, including Sean McKee [killed by the British army in Fairfield Street, 18 May 1973] were going round to the League to have a game of snooker. We walked round past where the ex-prisoner's centre is today, at the top of Brompton Park; it was after 4.30 pm. It was dark because the lighting in the street then wouldn't have been great. As we got outside where the ex-prisoner's centre is now we heard a number of shots. It was a burst of gunfire and we stopped. We saw a British army lorry going up past the top of Brompton Park (up the Crumlin Road heading towards the Ligoniel direction) just before the shooting. The shooting stopped and cars started coming up the road. So we thought maybe it was safe to go on. We walked on and we came round the top of the Crumlin Road. I think there were two people at the bus stop. We saw someone lying on the ground. When we got up we realised it was a girl and I recognised her right away as one of the McCorrys. I didn't know if it was Margaret. There weren't many people about, maybe one or two when we got there. We were one of the first people on the scene.

At the time I was 14 years old and big Sean McKee was just going on 16 years old;,we didn't know what to do; shooting was all new to us then. I remember she had a wee mark on her forehead and there was no movement from her. It didn't look to us as if she was dead. But obviously she was; she was unconscious. At that, people started to come on the scene and the priest came from the chapel and sort of took over things. One of the priests said an ambulance was on its way. But there was no sign of the British army or RUC at the scene. The ambulance came and we left. We still weren't aware that she was dead because it didn't look serious at the time and then we heard on the news there had been a girl shot dead. We didn't go round to the family. We wouldn't have known what way to approach things or what to say; we were very young.

It was devastating to see a young girl lying shot on the ground. I would say she was only about 18 or 19 years old at the time. It was as if she was waiting on a bus, or else she was walking down the road. It was right at the bus stop she fell. There was a burst of gunfire and obviously she was hit. It looked to me like the British army patrol had been attacked, and it looked very like she was in the line of fire. I'm not sure if there was any return fire. But the shooting happened that quick, we stopped and life seemed to start going again; cars started moving and so we just went on round the corner and there was Margaret lying on the ground.

> *There was no trace of anything on him or on his clothes. So he was no threat to anybody; he wasn't doing anybody any harm. The British army just used the excuse that he was running away to shoot him.*

Gerard McDade
Killed by British army,
Brompton Park entry,
21 December 1971

Gerard McDade was born on the 22 November 1951. He was the fourth eldest of seven children born to Esther (née Duffy) and 'Tricky' McDade. Both parents were originally from Old Ardoyne and lived most of their married life in 17 Oakfield Street. Gerard attended Holy Cross Boys and St Gabriel's school. Like many other lads at that time Gerard didn't have a permanent job; he worked for a short spell in Lindsey's Mill and had a number of casual jobs. He had a wide circle of friends including Bobby Ewing [killed by loyalists in the Deerpark Road, 12 October 1981], Mickey McAuley, Frankie Kane, Dutch Doherty and his brother James [killed on active service in Coventry, 14 November 1974]. Gerard was a Celtic fanatic and a keen Boville player and supporter. He met his wife-to-be, Deirdre McGettigan, in the Saunders Club on its opening night and after a short courtship, they married on the 3 July 1971 in Corpus Christi chapel in Ballymurphy. After the wedding the couple moved in with Gerard's mother where they lived until his death less than six months later.

Gerard McDade was an IRA volunteer at the time of his death. He was shot dead by the British army on 21 December 1971, aged 20 years. Two weeks later his only son Gerard was born.

Isobel Lynch (eyewitness)

My mammy and Gerard's mammy were related and they were friends. We would have gone in and out of each other's house and that's how I knew him. Gerard's family lived in Oakfield Street. I knew the family well. The day Gerard was killed I had been up the road shopping. I called in to my mummy's house as I did every day. I don't know how long I stayed in her house but when I came out, I went down Kerrera Street and there was nothing going on. There were British soldiers in the entry at Brompton Park at the back of Bap Travers' house; I think it was the Green Howard regiment. Coming down Kerrera Street, just as I got to the row of houses, I heard shooting and I ran. I ran from Kerrera Street into Oakfield Street and I fell. By the time I got up and gathered myself together after the fall I saw my knees were bleeding; the two knees were skinned. When I looked across I saw Gerard, but I didn't know it was Gerard. I looked across and the fella was lying in the alleyway. To me he was trying to get into one of the houses – I think it was Lily McCoy's. But when I got down, Clarice Nulty was the only face I saw. She was praying in his ear. I don't know where Clarice came from that day; there were other people there but she was the only one that stood out. Then a crowd of people gathered. The soldiers just stood there and they didn't go near the body while I was there. When I looked up, all I could see in Brompton Park entry where the wee houses are was a black soldier. I don't know whether he was the one that shot Gerard or not; he was just standing where Maggie Matthews lived. He was just standing, leaning against the end house. As far as I could see Gerard had nothing on him at all. If he had had a weapon, sure it would have fallen; he had nothing.

I was there for maybe ten minutes and then I came round home. Everything else was a blank to me. Gerard lying there sticks in my mind and the soldier standing there. In my mind I thought this soldier shot him. But I don't know; he was just standing there. Nobody ever approached me regarding the circumstances of Gerard's death or regarding an inquest. To me Gerard McDade was just a guy running to get out of the road and the British army shot him as he ran.

'Micky' (friend)

I'll never forget our younger days. Jamesy and Gerard were two great friends of mine, lifelong friends. I didn't go to school with Gerard; he was two years younger than me but he still hung about with us. We all congregated at Reid's corner, a whole team of us, a span of different ages. It was just the place to be. Once he left school he just became companions with me, Cleeky, Dutch Doherty, the whole team of us. We all supported the Boville football team. Gerard's brother Thomas was the manager. He formed the team so naturally we all became supporters. The whole lot of us would go down to Moville or Buncrana or wherever they were playing. We had a great time. Gerard liked to gamble; he was a terrific gambler. Like myself, he gambled on the dogs.

Gerard had an unfortunate experience; he was along with Harry McAuley, Co-Co's brother, and they went down to Bray Street off-licence one Friday night to get a drink. Gerard was just turning 18. They bought the drink and they were walking back to Ardoyne when a crowd of Protestants started to give them a bit of grief. Harry McAuley hit one of them over the head with a bottle, a full bottle, a big bottle of Mundies wine. It ended up Harry and Gerard got three years each. They knew Gerard had no involvement in it but Gerard got three years because he was with him. We couldn't believe it: three years for hitting them! He did two and half years in Crumlin Road gaol; there was very little remission then.

The actions of the RUC and the 'B' Specials around August 14 and 15 had a huge impact on Gerard and me. We had had absolutely no interest in the Irish Republican Army, none whatsoever, or Sinn Féin or anything. When we saw what the RUC were capable of handing out, the beatings, then they started to shoot people. Gerard would have understood the Civil Rights when it came to the fore in 1967/68, but we weren't deeply involved in it. Gerard and me were of the same mind and so was Jamesy. Once we saw pictures, especially on television, of Catholics getting beaten, at Burntollet where they ambushed the Civil Rights march, it drove us nuts. The death of Sammy McLarnon shattered Gerard and me. Up to the time Sammy McLarnon got shot, we were not republican-minded. Then that night when Sammy got shot and we went into his house and we saw him lying dead and his family, all the children in distress – we didn't speak much in the house but when we got outside and back up to Butler Street, it was then we thought that stones and bottles weren't much good; they were not much protection. We decided to join the IRA if we could.

It was around the start of 1970 when we joined the Auxiliaries. We were both Auxiliaries at the time but Gerard for some reason was picked to join the IRA. He was a really, really dedicated volunteer, clean-living, no drinking, no womanising, no nothing. I honestly do think his whole motivation was built on what we had seen and what we'd witnessed. I believe what we had witnessed in 1969, our community coming under attack and actually being burnt to the ground, citizens being murdered – we were saying that we would never again let this happen. Me, Gerard and Jamesy McDade would never ever have been republicans; it was forced on us more or less. All we wanted to do was play football, gamble and have a drink at the weekends. It was forced upon us by the RUC and unionist politicians. Once we saw the way the British army were one-sided too, we couldn't believe it. So anything that me, Gerard or Jamesy ever did, that was their fault; they drew us into it and forced us into a situation that we didn't want to be in.

I was working the day Gerard was killed. When I came home from work my mother was waiting at the corner of the street and I said to myself, there must be something wrong. She said Gerard had been shot dead a couple of hours earlier. I couldn't believe it. I asked what happened and she said, 'He came out of the League in front of the foot patrol. He ran and they shot him at the top of Oakfield Street, just turning into the entry'. They shot him in the back. I don't know how many times he was shot. I was totally devastated. I couldn't believe it; my lifelong friend was dead.

Gerard was a great republican, a far better republican than I would ever have been. He loved the republican movement, he really did. He was a good bloke; he loved fun and he was well liked. He would have been alive today like many people in Ardoyne and the rest of the North, only for what was forced on them. That is my opinion; the war was forced on us. We didn't want it, we didn't ask for it, we were quite happy just living our normal lives.

Deirdre McGettigan (widow)

I met Gerard at the opening night of the Saunders Club; it would have been early in 1970. We married on the 3 July 1971. I was going with Gerard a year nearly before we got married. I'm from Ballymurphy; I was born and reared there. We started seeing each other and then we started going steady. I never knew that Gerard was involved in the republican movement. He never ever told me anything or said anything. Gerard was very quiet, very reserved and he kept himself to himself. He was very protective, especially of me. Gerard to me was unique. There were times at night, instead of staying in his mummy's where we lived, we had to go here and stay there. I never questioned him and he never told me why. I just went along with him. But it never ever dawned on me to ask him, to question him, because to me if my husband had wanted to tell me, he would have told me. As Gerard use to say, 'What you don't know you can't repeat'; maybe that's why he never told me anything.

I was pregnant when Gerard was shot dead; my son Gerard is now 28, and he was born two weeks after his daddy died. The actual day that Gerard died was 21 December 1971. We had stayed in my mummy's the night before in Ballymurphy Road. Gerard just said to me that we had to go away over the Christmas period, and I said to him, 'God, that will be the first time I've ever been away from my own family at Christmas'. I had got a maternity grant paid back to me and I said to Gerard, 'I'll go into town and get you clothes and I'll get a few wee vests and things for the baby when it's born'. So I arranged to meet him later in his mummy's house.

My friend Josie and me went shopping. I left Josie in Royal Avenue, where Debenhams is now, at the bus stop there. I was waiting on a No. 57 bus, the Ligoniel bus; it brought you up the Crumlin Road. I went on the bus and unknown to me Gerard was dead already by this time. I got off the bus at the top of Kerrera Street and as I was walking down the street a girl called me and told me to go over to Conrad's house. I said, 'Why should I go over to Conrad's?' When I went in, Kathleen Conrad was standing with her back to the fire and she was crying. I knew then that there was something wrong and I said, 'What's wrong?' Kathleen Conrad just kept crying and crying and I said, 'Somebody tell me please, what is wrong?' To me it was just like total confusion. Everybody seemed very reluctant to let me know actually what had happened. I think it was because of the condition that I was in. I said, 'There's something wrong; somebody please tell me. Has he been arrested?' At this stage I still wasn't aware that he was involved in anything. I said, 'There's something wrong. Will somebody please tell me what has happened?' By this time I was in hysterics. It was Aunt Maggie that came up and said, 'Come on down to our house', and I went two doors down into Esther's house. Just as I got sat down, my father and my brother Gerard came in. But they must have thought that I knew that Gerard was dead. But I didn't know. Our Gerard just hugged me and he said to me, 'I'm sorry, sis' and I said, 'What do you mean? Why? Where is Gerard? Where have they got him?' My daddy and our Gerard just looked at each other because they thought that I knew. It was my brother Gerard that said to me, 'I'm sorry; he's dead, Deirdre'. I couldn't believe it. My daddy and our Gerard brought me home to my mummy's and the next couple of days was just total confusion.

I buried Gerard from my mummy's house. The paratroopers had the whole place saturated; they were sitting in my mummy's coal shed and everywhere. Everybody that came in and out of the house were stopped and searched by the paratroopers. No matter who it was, they searched them; nobody got peace to come and pay their respects to Gerard. The soldiers crucified them; they were everywhere, in the garden, everywhere. If you opened the back door, the soldiers were standing there, it was the same with the front door; they were everywhere. The soldiers never left the three days that Gerard's body was here. No matter who came in and out of this house they were vetted. It was a republican funeral; he had a tricolour over his coffin and a guard of honour. At his funeral there was no confrontation with the British army. They were there but there were so many people at Gerard's funeral, I don't think it would have been in their interest to do anything. I buried Gerard on Christmas Eve. When I came back from the graveyard there wasn't a soldier to be seen; they had moved once he was buried.

People were telling me different stories about what happened and I never really knew anything until the inquest. The day of the inquest I went to the High Court on the Crumlin Road; it was six months after Gerard died, round about May or June 1972. At the inquest they kept referring to McDade, they never called him Gerard McDade; they just kept referring to McDade. I lost the head and I said, 'Excuse me, my husband has a name. You call him Gerard McDade'. All you got was 'soldiers A, B, C, D, E, and F'. At the inquest the soldiers' version of it was that Gerard and Eddie Larkin were coming out of the League and they were stopped and searched, and apparently up Oakfield Street there was a soldier A at one door, soldier B at another door, soldier C at another door. There were soldiers at different doors up Oakfield Street, along with the soldiers that were at the bottom. They searched Gerard and Eddie Larkin and they said to them, 'Go youse on'. But when they went to walk on they called Gerard back. Now this is the soldiers' version of it. Gerard ran up Oakfield Street and on the right hand side of Oakfield Street soldier A was there and he let him run past and soldier B said that when he got to him, he put his foot out and Gerard tripped, and Gerard got up and ran again. Soldier C said that he ran past him and he let him run past. It was soldier F at the bottom of Oakfield Street fired the shot. Gerard had just got to the top of Brompton Park entry when soldier F fired the shot and it hit Gerard. The death certificate said that the bullet hit Gerard on the hip and the bullet ricocheted through the hip and hit the main artery and hit his groin.

After he was shot, all that I can gather was that Gerard bled to death. This happened at 3 o'clock and Gerard didn't die until 4 o'clock. Gerard lay in the entry and he was bleeding to death. The soldiers wouldn't let anybody near him and there was a woman, Clarice Nulty, she broke the British army cordons and she said, 'I don't care, you can shoot me, but I'm going to see to that fella; he is lying there bleeding to death'. The priest, I can't remember his name, he went over and was able to give Gerard his last rites and Gerard was able to say his Act of Contrition to the priest. The soldiers made Clarice Nulty and the priest go away. It was nearly 4 o'clock before they would let the ambulance in. From what I can gather Gerard was still alive in the ambulance but what they said on the death certificate was dead on arrival. He had died actually just as he was going into the hospital.

There was only one bullet fired; when they shot him he was running away, up Oakfield Street. He was no threat to anybody. They had already searched him and told them to go on and then they called Gerard back. But he ran. At the inquest the coroner asked the forensic expert if there was any trace of explosives or guns. There was no trace of anything on him or on his clothes. So he was no threat to anybody, he wasn't doing anybody any harm. The British army just used the excuse that he was running away to shoot him. The British army never came to apologise; they just said he was running and that they shot him and he was a wanted man. They had ample opportunity to stop him. To me it seems like they deliberately allowed him to run so they could shoot him. It's not a capital offence to run.

Charles McCann
Killed on active service,
Lough Neagh,
5 February 1972

It was a terrible shock when Charles was blown up. I didn't know he was involved and there was no outward signs that he was a republican.
I would say he was an ideal IRA volunteer because he never gave anything away, even to his family.

Charles McCann was the second eldest of 12 children. Originally from Randalstown, in Co. Antrim the family moved to Twickenham Street on the Crumlin Road in the late 1940s before eventually moving to Northwick Drive in Ardoyne. Charles was first educated at St Kevin's primary school and then St Patrick's, Bearnageeha. He left school at 15 and served his time as a plasterer with his father James. Few, if anyone, knew that Charles was a member of the IRA; he was attached to the IRA's North Antrim Brigade. On 5 Februray 1972, while on active service, Charles and volunteer Phelim Grant were killed when an explosive device in their possession exploded prematurely. The incident took place on a barge moored on Lough Neagh at Ballyginniff, near Crumlin. The men are believed to have died when the door of the barge became jammed, trapping them both inside. After their deaths the IRA leadership issued a statement in Dublin saying the volunteers had died accidentally. Charles McCann and Phelim Grant are buried in the republican plot on the hillside above Cargin. Although 30 years since their deaths, many from Ardoyne still travel to Cargin every February to take part in a commemoration for Charles McCann and his friend Phelim Grant.

Colette Mc Cann (sister)

There were twelve in our family; my mummy reared six girls and six boys. She had fifteen children but three died in infancy. There was Brian, Charles, Rosemary,

Bernadette, Seamus, Angela, Pauline, Colette, Eugene, Sean, Gerard and Dolores. We didn't call my brother Charles or Charlie - we knew him as Charles (pronounced 'Charl-is'). Charles was born on 30 October 1943. He was 28 when he died. Growing up, my mother always believed in sending us to school with the nuns and the brothers. So the boys were all sent to the Christian Brothers and we were all sent to the Convent. My daddy came from Randalstown and my mummy was a Devlin from Toome. If anybody called to the door and asked for Charlie my mother used to say, 'There is no Charlie living in this house,' and closed the door. His friends all called him Charlie. Charles was a great singer; he would have sung anything. I always remember him and my daddy singing 'Danny Boy' in the house when they were drunk to see who could reach the highest notes. There was always lots of singing in our house. It was one of those houses where everyone seemed to be able to sing, except me. We had some really brilliant times in our house. Even though we didn't have much room, there was always singing and guitars and music. I have lots of really good memories.

At the time you never would have suspected Charles was in the IRA. But looking back now I remember him being arrested in Toome and being questioned in Gough Barracks. At the time I never took much heed of it. It was a terrible shock when Charles was blown up. I didn't know he was involved and there was no outward signs that he was a republican. I would say he was an ideal IRA volunteer because he never gave anything away, even to his family. Charles had been living in Toome with my uncle Henry at the time of his death. Uncle Henry lived there alone but he always had a lot of callers and still does.

The actual day that Charles died my uncle Brian and my aunt came unexpectedly to our house. We were sitting having our dinner. I remember them saying they had bad news. My mother collapsed. My daddy and my sister Bernadette and her husband Tony went to identify the body in Antrim. Charles and Phelim Grant had been killed planting a bomb on a barge in Lough Neagh. As far as I know they were inside the barge and had placed the bomb but the door jammed on them and they were trapped.

At the time I felt it more for my parents than for myself, but as time went on I thought about it more. As you get older and have your own kids you realise now just what your mother and father were suffering when Charles died. As time goes on you really miss him more. Charles and Phelim Grant were buried in the republican plot on the hillside above Cargin. There is a large Celtic Cross on the grave. Every year on their anniversary a bus leaves Ardoyne to go to the plot for a commemoration.

Pat Fennell, Pat Waring, Raymond Wilkinson (friends)

A group of us hung around together in Northwick Drive. There was Pat Waring, Pat Fennell, Raymond Wilkinson, Hughie Bradley, Willie Bradley, Anthony Woods, the Devlins, the McCrudden's and big Sean Doran and a few others. Charlie was a smart fella. His father was a plasterer and Charles took up the trade too. They were self-employed; they never lived off the social security. They worked all of their days. Charlie was a quiet guy; he liked a wee drink like everybody else. He used to drink pink gins. He worked all week and waited until the weekend to have a drink. He loved a game of snooker. He used to go down to the Oxford in Royal Avenue to play. He went with a girl from Holmdene Gardens. He went to the Plaza and Ardoyne Hall dance with the rest of us. He was a very nifty dresser. He wore the best of gear, smart clothes. He was always getting suits made in Burton's, sports coats as well.

His father had a plot over the Westland and we used to go to the plot every Sunday with Charles to dig up cabbage and spuds for the Sunday dinner. Charles loved to go to the dog races in Dunmore Park and he liked the odd bet too. He was quiet; sober or drunk, he wasn't a big talker. He was just a really nice lad. He kept himself to himself. He eventually ended up working in Toome and he moved into his uncle Henry's place. Charlie was a smashing singer, especially 'Danny Boy', he was brilliant at that; he had a lovely voice and was great at singing Irish ballads. He was like the street singer, Arthur Tracey. We all got together every Saturday night for a sing-a-long.

It was a real surprise to everybody to hear that Charlie had been in the IRA and died on active service. The troubles had affected everybody but Charlie had never mentioned anything. He would have been involved in the early riots with the loyalists, the RUC and the B Specials. But he was never arrested or charged with anything.

Charlie was killed on a barge in Lough Neagh. Apparently the barge tipped up and the doors locked and the bomb they were handling went off. There is a possibility that the barge wasn't the target itself; they may have been using it as a dump and they may have been moving the bomb to go somewhere. When things like this happen nobody really knows the details, which is probably the best way. We just couldn't believe what had happened. It was a very sad time for everybody. He really was a terrible nice fella.

Bernard Rice
Killed by loyalists,
Crumlin Road,
8 February 1972

He just happened to be in the wrong place. They knew he was a Catholic and that was enough.

Bernard 'Ernie' Rice was born in Elmfield Street in 1923. He was the youngest of three children (two boys and a girl). Having left the Holy Cross Boys school, Ernie joined the British army. He remained in the army for over 15 years, serving throughout the war. In 1945 he returned home and a year later married Lena Cassidy from Brookfield Street, where the couple also set up their home. They had one daughter, Mary, born in 1950. In 1968 the family moved to Mountainview Parade. As a one-time soldier Ernie was a member of the Catholic Ex-Servicemen's Association that used to meet in the Hibs club in Herbert Street. After the outbreak of the conflict, the training and expertise that these men had acquired ensured that the ex-servicemen were very much to the fore in the district's defence and welfare networks. On the evening of 8 February 1972 Ernie Rice had left work early so that he could attend a regular meeting of the ex-servicemen. He was walking by the Ardoyne shops on the Crumlin Road when he was shot dead by loyalist gunmen from a passing car. Ernie was one of the first victims of this sort of random drive by sectarian killings that would become all too familiar in the years that followed.

Elizabeth O'Connor (friend)

I first met Bernard when he started to go with Lena. That was it then. I was going with Jim (Elizabeth's husband). We didn't go out too much in those days, but when we were married, the four of us started to go out for a drink. We went on holiday together. We use to go to Blackrock. They had Mary and we had two and we went every year to Ivy House in Blackrock. Ernie was a great fella. He liked to go out on a Friday night for a drink on his own. That was his night and he loved that. He was always good fun, never a fighting man or argumentative. He was always slagging you and joking.

The last time I saw Ernie was the Sunday (6 February) before he was killed. I was waiting on a bus and Ernie was there with his wee grandson, Mary's son Ciaran. He asked me where I was going and after I told him he said, 'Come on down and get a cup of coffee and I'll run you down in the car'. So he gave me a lift to see my mother who was dying. She died at the end of the week. On the Tuesday, 8 February I went to bed when I came in because I was exhausted. Then my son came in and said, 'You know, there was a man shot up at the corner'. My husband Jimmy asked who it was and he said, 'Somebody called Bernard Rice'. Jimmy said, 'Do you know what you're saying Martin?' and shouted up to me. I couldn't go over so I rang. Lena just said, 'Lily, they shot him dead; Lily, they shot him dead'. We went to the funeral and Jimmy carried the coffin. I can see Ernie yet as he stood there on the Sunday at Delaney's waiting on his paper with Ciaran. Ernie took him everywhere. He adored Ciaran. Ernie was dead and buried the next time I saw him. It's just like yesterday; I can see him standing there. His death was terrible for the family. Lena was bad and Mary too. God help them, it was awful sad. It was hard for them.

Kevin McCarthy (eyewitness)

My friend Dennis McCann and me were up the road when Mr Rice was killed. We were approximately 15 years of age. We shouldn't have been on the road at the time because it was a no-go area. It was known that Catholics were being shot from passing cars. We were coming down the Crumlin Road as a bit of a dare. When we were coming towards old McCann's chippie and Armstrong butchers, we heard shots very, very close. We actually thought they were shooting at us. We sort of ran back up the road then stopped. We didn't know what to do or whether the shots were coming from behind us or in front of us. We stood in at the wall of McCann's chippie, very frightened. We actually ran up the road and ran back again. We didn't know what to do. Then it all went quiet and we were just about to run when we saw a man lying on the ground outside Boyd's chemist. There was another man running up the road towards the body. The body was lying on the ground. We didn't know if he was dead or not. But we didn't know if the man running up the road was a gunman or not so we started running again. Then we stopped when we saw the man was kneeling over the body and we went back down to see Mr Rice lying on the ground. Everything was quiet in the whole area for a change. Nothing happened that day at all. It could have been anybody; it could have been us. It was just that anybody on that side of the road had to be a Catholic. There is no question about it, it was just a random shooting at Catholics.

Mary Catney (daughter)

My father was a very quiet person, a real gentleman and very humorous in a quiet sort of way. The only interest he had was his wife and family. He only had a drink and a cigarette on a Friday night. He was so content with his own life. He always had a car and he never sat in the house at the weekend. We always went on holidays so many times in a year. We just drove about different places. He just had a real happy life. I had a very, very happy childhood and there was never any fights or arguments in the house. I just remember laughter all the time. Once he went, it was like a black cloud over us.

He was killed on a Tuesday night, 8 February 1971. My daddy worked a bit of overtime on a Tuesday night. But that particular Tuesday there was a meeting of the ex-servicemen's association so he got off work early. He was a member of the Catholic Ex-Servicemen's Association which was in Herbert Street. The ex-servicemen more or less started up the defence of the district. The fact that my daddy was an ex-soldier meant that he was a sort of coach along with a lot of other ex-servicemen about the area. He joined the club to help if anything was to go wrong. That night he first came in to the house and had his tea. He was joking with my mummy and me. I worked as the manager of ABC Credit Union and so I left the house before him. At about 7.30 pm everyone was coming in to the credit union saying that a man had been shot dead on the front of the road. There was trouble on the road every night and I remember thinking to myself, 'When I go home, I'll be able to tell my mummy and daddy about that'. There was nobody with my father when he was murdered. He was shot dead from a passing car. He had been shot with dum-dum bullets. The fire station was across the road and the men from the fire station came out. They washed what they could of the blood off the road. At the beginning we thought that he had been set up because nobody knew that he was getting out of work apart from the people that he worked with. My mummy was always under the opinion that it came from his work. But we found out later that was not the case. He just happened to be in the wrong place. They knew he was a Catholic and that was enough.

It was terrible coming into the house that night. The credit union closed at 9 pm and shortly after there were three priests at the door. I was behind the counter and as soon as I looked at the priests I knew. I just said, 'Was it my daddy?' One of the priests, Fr. Martin, nodded his head. I said, 'Is he dead?' He nodded again. I asked him, 'Does my mummy know?' He said, 'No, that's what we've come over to you for'. What had happened was my husband was in the bathroom and he heard shots. Then he came down and said to my mummy, 'There's some shooting up on the road'. About an hour later the front door bell rang and when my husband opened the door it was detectives. They said my father had just been shot dead. My husband went down to the chapel to get Fr. Fernando (who was related to my father) to tell my mummy. But Fr. Fernando wasn't there. So Fr. Martin and two other priests visiting from Clonard chapel came to get me to come to the house to tell my mummy what had happened. After that it was more or less a blur. I came into the house and my mummy was sitting dozing on the chair. Then I woke her to tell her. Afterwards doctors were brought to the house to sedate us.

We found out later that my daddy was shot through the neck. When he was lying in the coffin after he had been brought home the blood was still coming out of his mouth. He was so quiet and so good. He just idolised his grandchildren. My son was only seven at the time and he just adored his granda. My daughter was only about two. Every night she used to run out and get the paper that was delivered from the letterbox. Then she would bring it into her granda because he wouldn't let anyone else read the paper first. That night as he was lying in the coffin she ran out and got it and brought the paper over to him in the coffin. It was just natural for her to do that, to give the paper to her granda. My father was such a quiet man; he used to always say, 'When I die just bury me quietly. I don't want people coming over, looking at me and saying, "Oh, he was a good person".' I remember my mummy saying, 'He would never have wanted all this' when he was brought home and they came from everywhere. But everybody was just coming to show how sorry they were. He had a big funeral as well. Wreaths came from all over the world.

Nobody ever claimed responsibility for his death. But many years later the police came to the house and said they had somebody who had confessed to the murder and that they were in court the next day. We went down to the court and it turned out that it was somebody who had been lifted for breaking a window on the Shankill Road. Then as the police were letting him out, he confessed to the murder of a number of different people. It turned out they [loyalists] were just cruising on the road. When anybody walked on that side of the road then they knew they would be a Catholic. My daddy was just one of the ones that got it. The person who was convicted for it was Samuel Neil. But we always wanted to know who the driver of the car was. I don't believe justice was achieved because Samuel Neil only served a few years in prison. Then he was out again and that was that. It came out recently that it all more or less stemmed from Frankie Curry who was killed on the Shankill Road in 1999 [Frankie Curry, killed by loyalists in Malvern Way, 17 March 1999]. In 1972 he was the leader of the Red Hand Commandos. After Frankie Curry was buried, the police came to the house and said that he had been interviewed and had mentioned the people whose murders he had been involved in. That was an awful upset. Who else was in the car is not clear, whether it was Frankie Curry or whether it was somebody else from the gang. But I feel that it was Frankie Curry who was in the car along with them.

My daddy's death changed our lives. My mummy was never the same after my daddy was murdered. There was a dark cloud over the whole house. The changes were unbelievable. Our lives were just never the same. Part of us died along with my daddy. We just suffered; my mummy's health went down badly after that and the only thing that she lived for then were her grandchildren. That is what kept her alive. We just had this good bond that we learned to live with but we never, ever forgot. Nobody ever came and offered us help or support. But the neighbours were very good and we got letters from Catholic ex-servicemen associations all over the world. People wanted us to go to England or to America for holidays to try and relieve the grief. But you never took anything off people. The RUC came to the house after my daddy died but we had no dealings with them after that. It changed our lives dramatically and nobody was the same afterwards. If it hadn't affected my mother's health so much I believe she would have been alive today. I don't think counselling would be any use to me now. I haven't got over it, I've learned to live with it but counselling wouldn't help me at all, although perhaps it would work for other people.

David McAuley
Died as a result of
accidental discharge from
an IRA weapon,
Fairfield Street,
19 February 1972

Because he was so young he didn't have the chance to live his life or even begin to live his life. He was so young when the troubles started, that was it; he was just at that age...

David McAuley was the youngest of seven children. His father, Michael McAuley, was born in Fairfield Street and his mother Matilda, originally from Carrick Hill, moved to the street when she was fourteen years old. The couple met and married in the 1940s. After their wedding they set up home in Matilda's widowed mother's house, number five Fairfield Street. They lived in the same street for most of the sixty years of their marred life. The family did move briefly to Ballymurphy but returned to Ardoyne and bought a house in Farringdon Gardens where David was born. After only a few years the family moved back again to 5 Fairfield Street where David lived until his death in 1972. He attended Holy Cross Boys and later St Gabriel's school. David was a popular lad and well known for his devilment, always up to mischief with his mates Joey McArdle, Jamesy Toal, Joe Mallon and Michael Donnelly. He worked on the milk round and in the Saunders social club.

David died at the age of 15. He was in a house in Fairfield Street with IRA volunteers. There was an accidental discharge from an IRA weapon and David was shot in the side. He was taken to a hospital in Dundalk and later died from internal bleeding. He was OC of na Fianna Éireann (Cubs) at the time of his death.

Michael Donnelly (friend)

My earliest memory of David McAuley was actually growing up with him; we all lived in Fairfield Street and we grew up together. Fairfield Street was a very close-knit community and all our families were good friends. There was a wee gang of us at the time; there was myself, Davy, Micky Rice, Owney Rice, Joey McArdle; we all knocked about together. As kids we did all the normal things together, played football, went camping. I have no recollection of Davy ever being at school. He was full of mischief. He would get up early and do all the wee things on his own. I remember one morning he got up about six o'clock in the morning and stole a horse from the Travellers in Flax Street. He tied the horse to his ma's front door and they couldn't get it opened. What I remember of David was he was somebody who was always full of life, always getting up to stuff, full of devilment. But he never did anything really bad; it was just all a bit of fun. He would have got a battering off his daddy but it wouldn't have stopped him. That's my recollection of David just growing up together.

Davy came from a republican family; the whole family were republican. I always remember every time a foot patrol came down Fairfield Street they would always open their door and get the rebel songs on, and they never let a soldier light near the door. A lot of his family were connected. Davy was always surrounded by that. If there was a riot

Davy was at the front; he was a great rioter. He was always doing something, always around the IRA personnel at the time, always doing things for them, scouting or whatever. When we were trying to join the Fianna Davy was actually already in it. It came really as no surprise to us when we heard that he had been shot, or that he had been close to guns because he was always around IRA volunteers; that's the type of guy he was.

Davy was actually OC of the Fianna Cubs when he died, at that time I was adjutant. We were told that Davy had been shot in an accident but that he was all right. Just as quick we were told that he was dead. Davy's funeral was like a siege. I remember the coffin being set outside the house and we were all in the guard of honour uniforms. I remember the paratroopers trying to get closer. There was a lot of fear among the people because the paratroopers had a reputation at that time. I remember people saying, 'Don't break ranks, don't break ranks', and the Brits were getting closer and then the next thing pandemonium and the coffin was nearly knocked over and everybody was running. This was just as the funeral was about to begin; the coffin was still sitting on the pedestals. I don't think there had been any shots fired. I just remember the paras attacking the funeral and people running everywhere, trying to get out of the road. It was a military funeral and I think the paras were just hell-bent on disrupting it.

It was a terrible shock at that age. David was there one minute and the next minute he was gone. It was very, very hard to grasp. The family was devastated; David was the blue-eyed boy of the family and I remember the terrible state his people were in at the time. It was a terrible shock; I think David was one of the youngest people in Ardoyne at that time to have been killed.

Rita Alexander (sister)

David was born in December 1956. He was still at school when he was killed. David didn't have a favourite subject in school, he wasn't really interested; rioting would have been his interest. He would have started a riot in an empty house. I suppose that was a reflection of the era he grew up in. There was a lot of political unrest. He didn't have the chance to get a job but when he was younger he worked on a milk round and got a few shillings but he never kept it; mother got it, mother got everything. He also worked in the Saunders club. He never really got the opportunity to develop any hobbies or interests. He was so young when the troubles started, that was it; he was just at that age…

David joined the Fianna as a result of the troubles; it would have been about 1970. It was the events of 1969 that brought about his politics in terms of wanting Britain out of Ireland. Other than the Fianna he wasn't a member of any other clubs or organisations; that was his life, the Fianna. He had older brothers and you know what wee lads of that age are like, they try to act like their big brothers. He had a few girlfriends, Teresa Mullan and Geraldine Conrad. Teresa Mullan was his girlfriend at the time of his death. Because he was so young he didn't have the chance to live his life or even begin to live his life.

I saw him the night before he died. We were in the Saunders club; we weren't drinking because he was only 15 and I was only 17. He actually left me round home to my aunt's house in Velsheda Park. He went back and went to bed. The incident happened the next day. There were other people in the back of the house in Fairfield

Street. David wrote out his wee bet and he sent Rosaleen Larkin's young lad up to do the bet. He went into the working kitchen and the next thing was, he was shot. He came out and said to my mummy in the living room, 'I'm shot', and she didn't believe him because there was no blood. She said he was really, really white but he was still walking about the house. He went out to the toilet and coming out of the toilet, he collapsed, so they carried him in and at this point my mummy sent round to tell me to come round. When I got to the house David was already away. I said to my mummy, 'Well, if he was shot where is the blood?' and she said 'He wasn't bleeding'.

It was a wee while before we found out where he was because of all the confusion. The word came back that they had taken him to a hospital in Dundalk. Me and our Terence, Alex Conrad and Eamon Toner drove down to Dundalk. At the hospital I said, 'I'm looking for my brother, David McAuley' (they had given a false name). A nun said to me, 'We don't have any boy at 15 called David McAuley, but we have a boy here and he's dying; he was shot'. She brought me to see if it was David. Later that night after he had died, my mummy and daddy arrived. Mummy went in to see David but he was already dead. He had died on the Saturday night while I was there. A priest came to me in the hospital and said he had been talking to David earlier; he was unconscious at this point. He said that he just wanted to let me know that he heard his confession. He said David was very frightened. He was shot in the side with a bullet from a short.

The body came home next day. My family made the arrangements for the funeral and they were on their way to Belfast with the coffin when the British army stopped them in Newry. They wanted to search the coffin and there was a huge row because my daddy didn't want them to search the coffin. They had the coffin outside the barracks in a kind of courtyard. The peelers and the Brits opened the coffin and searched it and they still didn't release it because of the death certificate and other documents they had. It was the early hours of Monday morning about 6 o'clock before the coffin actually reached Ardoyne.

My cousin Charlie McArdle and Claris Nulty were with him when he was taken from Ardoyne to Dundalk. He drove the car and Claris Nulty, who was a first aid worker, went along with them. As far as I know they were the only three in the car. The family didn't make the decision for David to go to hospital in Dundalk; the family was in that much shock about David being shot that other people made the decisions as to what should happen. Apparently they brought him to the Mater Hospital and when they got there the hospital authorities told them they would have to inform the RUC. I don't know who made the decision not to let him go in to the Mater. Whoever brought him to the Mater Hospital made the decision to bring him to the Free State. But it wasn't the family.

There was chaos at the funeral; the British army were there and as soon as the volley of shots was fired they charged and they went berserk. The British army tried to get into our house a lot of times during the funeral and asked what route the funeral was taking. We wouldn't tell them and every time they came to the door there was murder again. They just continued to be provocative about the whole thing and after everything was finished and the funeral was over they still tortured my mother. The British army shouted in her door, 'Where's David now?' and other things. It got to the point where she asked Fr. Fernando to ring them to ask them to leave her alone. Her nerves were wrecked.

There are still a lot of unanswered questions regarding why a decision was made not to admit David to the Mater Hospital. Who was there and what way did that happen? And the actual incident itself; what exactly happened? What was going on? They are questions that I have.

Jackie (eyewitness and comrade)

It was a Saturday afternoon I think it was about 2.30 pm and there were weapons required for an operation, an ongoing operation. The weapons were brought to a house in Fairfield Street; there were four weapons. One of the weapons was a .38 Spanish Star Pistol and it was noticed right away by the quartermaster that there was no magazine with this weapon, so it was put to one side. The weapons were looked at and examined in the scullery of the house and the other three weapons were taken into another room. While the volunteers and the weapons were in another room a shot was heard and when we went into the scullery, we noticed young David was standing in the room; he was pure white but he was conscious. At that, he went outside to go to the toilet and when he came back in he collapsed. His wound was looked at and on the face of it, it didn't seem serious at all; there was no blood. The wound was in his right side and the first thought was that the hammer coming back of the recoil might have nicked his skin. The weapon wasn't even taken into consideration and at this time it was put to one side again. More concern was given to young David because he had turned very white. The decision was made to take him to the hospital. It was somebody who was dealing with the first-aid, somebody local that made the decision.

But we felt there was no great urgency because there was no blood from the wound. So David was taken to hospital. Whilst at the hospital one of the people that was with him approached the nurse in the accident and emergency and she warned them that if they were to admit David they would have to inform the RUC. A decision was made then, given the fact that the wound wasn't thought to be of a serious nature, David could be taken to Dundalk. It was felt that would be beneficial both to David and his family because there would be no RUC involvement. David was then taken to hospital in Dundalk. Now whilst this was happening the volunteers in the house were looking for strike marks and the spent shell casing from the .38 and none was to be found. It was only when the quartermaster examined the .38 that he discovered there was a .32 round jammed in its breech.

The conclusion that came from the IRA inquiry held after the incident, was that the .32 round had been jammed in the weapon prior to it being brought to the house, that it had been jammed in the breech. There was an accidental discharge from this weapon. It was a weapon that everyone thought was not capable of firing. The bullet actually entered David's side; we thought it had grazed him but it had actually gone into his side. We heard later that he had died from massive internal bleeding. This came as a deep shock. But we were told afterwards that even if he had been admitted to the Mater Hospital, the consequences probably would have been the same. As far as we were concerned the weapon was useless to us and it was no danger to anybody else because there was no magazine or no bullets. David didn't say he was shot. We didn't know what had happened. We thought that he had possibly nipped himself with the hammer and that's why we concerned ourselves with finding the strike mark where the round had hit, what furniture was hit and the shell. It was only when we couldn't find anything that the quartermaster examined the .38 more closely and then we discovered there was a .32 round jammed. David was away to Dundalk at this stage.

Later that evening, it was around 8 pm, we phoned a place in Dundalk to see if we could get any news about David. We were told to stay where we were and someone would get back to us shortly. About ten minutes later Martin Meehan phoned us and told us young David was dead. We just couldn't believe it. We were all totally devastated. I just couldn't understand how such a seemingly innocent incident had ended up in such a terrible tragedy. David's death had a powerful impact on me and I know everyone who was in the house that morning. He was a really likeable young lad, a desperate loss to his family. It was such a terrible, terrible tragedy. It just couldn't have been foreseen.

James O'Hanlon
Killed by the IRA,
Gracehill Street,
16 March 1972

> *The family were ecstatic that the inquiry had taken place.*
> *They had been given the official letter from the IRA*
> *exonerating their son and to me it had lifted this massive*
> *burden of pain from the whole family.*

Jimmy O'Hanlon's father James O'Hanlon was originally from Sailortown and his mother Bridget (née Hughes) was from Carrick Hill. Bridget and James were married in December 1950 and over the years they had five children: Robert, Mary, Theresa, James and Jackie. Like many of their generation, James and Bridget had to uproot their family and move to England in order to find work. James found work in the Vauxhall Motor Company in Luton and the family settled there for a number of years. In 1968 they returned to Ardoyne and set up home in Eskdale Gardens. Their son Jimmy was born on 6 January 1955. He was outstanding at sports and won a number of medals. When he left St Gabriel's school he worked as a dispatch clerk in the Beltex Mill. Influenced by the circumstances of the time Jimmy became a volunteer in the IRA.

On 16 March 1972 the IRA killed Jimmy O'Hanlon. His body was found in the Parochial Hall, Gracehill Street. He was 17 years old. The IRA later investigated the circumstances of Jimmy's death. A letter of apology from the leadership of the Irish Republican Army was sent to the O'Hanlon family completely exonerating James O'Hanlon as an informer. It further stated, 'Volunteer O'Hanlon stands now as always with his comrades in equality and credit'.

School friend

I first met Jimmy in St Gabriels school. We were in the same class for about three or four years. I got to know him very well through sports. Jimmy was very good at athletics. He was into basketball and so was I. He was exceptional at the high jump. The gym teacher, Mr Ramsey, took an interest in Jimmy because he was so good at sports; he thought Jimmy was something special. Jimmy was very friendly with Gerard Stitt [killed by loyalists on the Crumlin Road, 17 June 1976]. Jimmy was no quieter than any of the rest of us and he was no noisier. He never gave any bother to teachers; he just came and went like the rest of us.

When we left school around 1970 it was the height of the troubles. Once we left school that was more or less the end of my contact with Jimmy. He never mentioned politics; none of us were really interested in politics. Even at the start of the troubles we were all very naïve. I remember hearing about Jimmy's death and being told what happened. I'm not sure what happened and I don't even want to speculate. The IRA at the time claimed responsibility for killing him and as far as I know they later apologised and said it was a mistake.

As a friend of Jimmy's I was shocked at hearing the news about his death. There were a lot of allegations flying about at the time. After a while it came out that it was all a terrible mistake. I never knew he was in the republican movement and that was a big shock in itself. I am sure the family were devastated and still are. It is probably something they will never get over. Under the circumstances and the way it happened, I'm sure that added to their grief. Jimmy's death had an impact on me; you were saying to yourself, 'Jesus, did it really happen?' At that time there were a lot of deaths and it was just one tragedy after another. I think it's only now that people are reflecting.

Martin Meehan (friend)

I was in gaol at the time of James O' Hanlon's death. The whole community was absolutely devastated that this young lad had lost his life in the circumstances that he did. From initial reports coming in, it appeared to have been an accidental shooting and then somebody said he was an informer. There were a lot of conflicting stories coming into Long Kesh. The general opinion was that things had been handled in a very unsatisfactory way. The young lad lost his life and there were indications that he had not been treated properly. The family were totally devastated.

When I was released in October 1974 the family made contact with me. They asked me to try and get some sort of redress and to establish the truth about what had actually happened to their son. Between the death of their son in March 1972 and October 1974 no one had gone near the family whatsoever. They were just left in limbo. The O'Hanlon family were a republican family; their other son Rab had been in prison and the mother and father had been staunch republicans themselves.

I made inquiries to see if the family could get some sort of redress and to see what had happened to their son. I was only out for three weeks and nothing really came from that initial exchange. I was released from internment on 5 December 1975. Immediately on my release the family sent for me again and asked me if I would continue with the inquiries into their son's death. They wanted me to get official recognition from the republican movement that their son was not an informer. After some time word came back from the republican movement that they would set up an inquiry to investigate the circumstances of the death. This was the first inquiry held into the full circumstances of what happened. I was not involved in the inquiry. The family were very appreciative that something was being done to heal the pain that they had been going through since 1972.

The inquiry took place and after an extensive investigation, the family were given a letter from the leadership of the IRA at the time, apologising and exonerating their son from being an informer. The outcome was that their son had been accidentally shot; it was not a deliberate order from the republican movement to kill their son. Jimmy had been in the custody of the IRA; they had arrested him in relation to certain inquiries they were conducting and it was during the course of those inquiries that a gun went off accidentally and he was shot dead. I think they were trying to scare him and the gun went off accidentally.

The family were ecstatic that the inquiry had taken place. They had been given the official letter from the IRA exonerating their son and to me it had lifted this massive burden of pain from the whole family. I was thankful that I had been able to help in some way to relieve the pain that the family were going through. I thought it was a thing that had to be done. Basically, republicans should not be seen to be trying to cover anything like that up. They should be open and transparent. If a wrong is done I think we should be big enough and brave enough to admit it. And there was a wrong done with that young lad, no doubt about it.

As far as I know the statement from the republican movement was never made public; it was just a private letter for the family. Generally throughout the district it was known that James O'Hanlon had been exonerated. His name is among the republican dead, which is where it should be. The plaque in Brompton Park wasn't erected until 1976 and his name is on it; there was never any question that his name shouldn't be included as a volunteer.

The death of James O'Hanlon was a death that never should have happened. It was a tragic mistake in tragic circumstances and probably the people involved in it were devastated. It was a tragic mistake all round and given the circumstances at that particular time, it is inexcusable what happened.

The family of James O'Hanlon

There were five children in our family, two girls and three boys. James, or Jimmy as everybody knew him, was born in 29 Stratford Gardens on 6 January 1955. When Jimmy was still a baby, in order to escape the poverty and unemployment at the time, the family moved to Luton in England. Our father got a job in Vauxhall Motors and we stayed there for a number of years. Because of various circumstances the family returned to Belfast in 1968 and eventually bought a house in Eskdale Gardens. When we returned to Ardoyne Jimmy went to St Gabriel's school on the Crumlin Road. He was very keen on sports, especially running. He was a happy-go-lucky boy and very popular. When Jimmy left school he got a job as a Dispatch Clerk in the Beltex Mill. His time was occupied with sports, cars, motorbikes and his girlfriend. Like many young people in the area after the pogroms of 1969 he became involved in the republican movement.

A few days before he died, he was arrested and taken to Girdwood Barracks where he was held for a few days. On 16 March he was flooring the loft of the house when he was taken away by republicans. That evening my father was told by a friend that his son's body had been found in the Oldpark area with a bullet wound to the head.

Jimmy received a republican funeral and three death notices appeared in the *Irish News* from the Belfast Battalion of the IRA regretting his death. The family had to struggle for a long time with malicious allegations against Jimmy's name. Eventually the family received a letter from the leadership of the IRA at the time. The letter stated that Jimmy died as a 'result of an accidental discharge from a faulty weapon' and that there was 'no evidence to substantiate the allegations that Volunteer O'Hanlon was guilty of conspiracy against the ideals of the republican movement'. As far as we, the family, are concerned this letter totally exonerates our son. The IRA accepts his death was a mistake and they have apologised for it.

In 1989 the family were deeply hurt by an entry in the book *Lost Lives*. The authors of the book stated that Jimmy was 26 years old (which was incorrect) and that he had been killed because of his involvement with an older woman and other untrue allegations. Following complaints, the publisher wrote to the family and apologised for these errors.

> *Because the loyalists were on the roads we couldn't even bury our child in peace.*

Sean McConville
Killed by the UDA/UFF,
Crumlin Road,
15 April 1972

Sean McConville's mother, Kathleen (from the Falls Road) and his father Thomas were married in 1951. Three years later Sean was born in Crumlin Street, from where his father came. Shortly after the family moved to the Falls where Sean and his younger sister Mary and brother Danny were raised. In the early 1970s the family moved back into a house on the Crumlin Road. Sean loved football and was a member of the Celtic Supporters Club on the Falls. He also loved all types of music. When Sean left school, his father got him a start with the firm he worked for, as a mechanic fitting diesel pumps. Sean McConville was in the third year of his apprenticeship in 1972. On 15 April that year Sean was walking down the Crumlin Road with a friend. He was only a few yards from his front door when he was shot dead by loyalists. He was only 17 years old.

Jim Weir (friend)

There was a crowd of us who ran about together. On the day Sean was killed, about six of us met up at my flat down the New Lodge. We drank a couple of tins of beer and had a bit of craic in the house. Time went on and we all went our own way but arranged to meet later up in Ardoyne. So I met Sean and we went going up to Mountainview to see Sean's girlfriend. We were outside Boyd's chemists when a car pulled up. When I looked, there were three fellas in it. I was about eight or nine feet in front of Sean and I could hear them say something to him. Sean shouted, 'Jim' so I started walking back to him. He said the guys were looking for Brompton Park. Just as Sean was pointing down to Brompton Park, I saw two guns come up. One came out of the rear window and the other came out of the front window. But by the time I shouted it was too late. The shots had already rung out. I hit the ground and rolled over. The bullets missed me but they got Sean. Then the gunmen took off and went down Twaddell Avenue. I remember the Sunday night when Sean's body was coming home and his coffin was brought up the road. There was a crowd of loyalists down the road and they started to stone the coffin. At the time there was only about eight of us on the road. The Brits were all over the place. There was this man from down the road calling us all the names under the sun. One of the Brits said to us, 'Get stuck into them if you want. I wouldn't stand for that if it was me'. Within two minutes there was about 200 of us. It took that many to get Sean's body up the road. The cops were in touch with me a short time later and took me to do a photo-fit. They then asked me to identify the gun that had been used to kill Sean. They threw a gun down in front of me and I said, 'Yes, that was the gun'. It was an automatic. They then started to question me on how I knew what the gun was like. They asked me did I handle guns before. They made me feel as if I'd done something wrong. If I had known then what I know now about the RUC I wouldn't have gone. As of this day they have never got in touch with me again.

Mary McConville (sister)

When Sean was leaving the house the day he was killed I was walking up the road and he said to me, 'Where are you going, kid?' I just told him to mind his own business. You see, all we did was fight. I was only 15 and he was 17 so he was like the big brother trying to look out for me but at that age you didn't like it. Then I was standing at the bookies at the top of Brompton Park along with Phyllis Hawkins. Sean and Jim Weir went on walking up the road and just at that our Danny was coming across Twaddell. He was over on the Falls and came across on the bus. Me and Phyllis were talking away and the next thing was we heard cracks. We knew it was shooting and I pulled our Danny down along with us. But then I looked up the road and I could see Jim Weir standing but our Sean was lying on the road. I could also see another man and woman running over to him. I said to our Danny, 'Go and get my daddy' and I ran up the road. At first I thought Sean was only letting on. There was no blood or anything. He was just lying there. I said, 'Get up and stop acting the eejitt'. I was shaking and pushing him. Jimmy Weir knew at that stage that Sean was bad and he started to tell me that the ones in the car had called them. He said that they asked Sean and Jimmy for directions. Jimmy had noticed the gun first and was able to hide behind the car. He shouted out to Sean to get down but by that stage they had started to shoot Sean. Jimmy had shouted to him that the guns were out of the car and Sean was looking straight at them. It all happened very quickly. Sean got five bullets in him. Then the ambulance came and I went in it with Sean. As we drove down, I saw my daddy coming up the road and asked them to stop for him, which they did. I think they knew that Sean wasn't going to make it. Sean didn't lose any blood but his injuries were all internal. That is what killed him. We were only in the hospital for about half an hour when he was pronounced dead.

Somebody had just gone and got my mummy. The doctor had just told my daddy that Sean had died when my daddy had noticed my mummy coming in the hospital doors.

Thomas McConville (father)

Sean was a very quiet lad. He used to just do what any wee lad his age did. He liked to listen to music and follow football. The day he was murdered was Saturday 15 April 1972, at 6.45 pm. On that day there was only me and Sean in the house. His mummy was at work in the Royal Hospital. Early that evening I was sitting on the settee and Sean was in the kitchen getting ready to go out. He loved his hair; it was down on his shoulders and he always stood combing it. After 15 minutes he came out to me and put his coat on. He said to me, 'Daddy, I'm away up to see a friend and I'll not be long till I'm back'. That was the last I saw him until he was lying in the ambulance. We lived in 441 Crumlin Road, not far from where Sean was murdered. When I got into the ambulance I heard a wee groan from him. But all I could do was hold his hand tight. I told him to fight on. He died in the hospital. We had a lot of trouble at his funeral. Sean's funeral had to be directed away from the Crumlin Road. We had to take the long way, up Alliance Avenue, down the Cliftonville and then through the New Lodge. It seemed to take forever to get to Milltown cemetery. Because the loyalists were on the roads we couldn't even bury our child in peace.

In my heart I know that it was Sean's death that killed his mummy. You see, after about a year or so Kathleen went back to work and we were a bit happier. But it wasn't long after that when a loyalist hit squad broke into our home on the Crumlin Road. Kathleen was at work but our Danny was lying on the settee because he had a bad dose of the flu. A loyalist gunman came in and tried to fire two shots at him. Danny could do nothing but stare at him. Then the gunman tried to fire more shots but the gun jammed. He tried to clear it but, thank God, he didn't and walked out of the house. About two hours later they went to another house to try and shoot someone else but a woman hit them over the head with a milk bottle. After that our Mary had a wee boy and called him Sean, but he died five months later due to cot death. It was a couple of years after that when Kathleen died. She was only 49 years old. She developed brain tumours, but if you had seen Kathleen after Sean's death you would have known it was due to that. Sean's death is why she is where she is now. So really they murdered two people that day. We never knew who murdered Sean until Frankie Curry was shot dead [Frankie Curry, killed by loyalists in Malvern Way, 17 March 1999]. It was in the newspapers on the Sunday after, that Frankie Curry admitted being involved. That day I was getting ready to go to mass when the phone rang. It was my sister-in-law Eileen and she was in a terrible state. I thought that some of the family had died when I heard her crying down the phone. When she eventually told me what it said in the newspaper, I just dropped the phone. It was like a wake all over again. Within half an hour the house was packed and it was as if Sean had just been murdered, the feeling was that bad. What angered us most was the fact that the papers never notified us about the news reports. I ended up in hospital for four days that week with a heart attack. I couldn't have cared less if I'd died, that's just how low I was feeling.

Joseph Campbell
Killed on active service
by the British army,
Eskdale Gardens,
11 June 1972

> *He was sort of a big brother, always advising you, never neglecting people. He had a great respect for people and people's thoughts.*
> *That would be him, a brother.*

Joseph 'Josh' Campbell was born in July 1955 and was given his father's name. His mother Patricia was born in Edward Street, his father, was from Ardoyne and the two had married only three years before. Joseph went first to the Sacred Heart primary school and then St Gabriel's where he had many friends. He was always in the top stream in his classes. When he left school at the age of 15 Joseph attended Feldon House and qualified from there with a City and Guilds in mechanical engineering. After Joseph, his parents had two other children, Marion and Margaret. As is so often the case, the position of 'big brother' meant that, as the three were all growing up, Joseph often acted as a sort of referee between his two younger sisters. As a youngster Josh also enjoyed getting out of the city to stay with his grandparents on their farm near Lurgan. He would go there virtually every weekend, particularly in the summer. After the outbreak of the conflict Joseph was deeply affected by what was happening around him. As a result he joined the republican movement. On 11 June 1972 a fierce gun battle broke out in various parts of Ardoyne after loyalists shot dead Hugh Madden as he swept the street outside his greengrocer's shop on the Oldpark Road [Hugh Madden, killed by the UDA/UFF on the Oldpark Road, 11 June 1972]. Joseph Campbell was mobilised as a volunteer of na Fianna Éireann. He was still only 16 years old when he was shot dead by members of the British army whilst defending the district.

'Martin' (friend and comrade)

Joseph and I grew up together. He lived in one street, I in the other and our back doors led on to each other. We went through school together. He was always a thinker, he was very intelligent from a very young age, always wanted to be at the front of things and was good at organising. When we were kids, around 12 or 13, he would organise wee trips up round the caves on Cavehill, things like that. He had a great love for astronomy and talked a lot about the planets and the stars. He had his own telescope and would go and sit at night and watch the stars. He was very intelligent at school too, always in the 'A' classes. When he left he did a course in mechanics and after that was the only work I remember him doing. He was working when he was killed.

Joseph was very deep. He didn't browbeat people with his politics and didn't speak to everyone about ii, but when we had conversations it was clear he held the issue of Ireland very dear. He knew a lot about it because he read a lot of books. He was also very security conscious and was always aware. Joseph didn't go about telling people that he was involved. At that time it was very hard to hide, but he seemed to hide it from his family. He didn't want his family to be troubled through his involvement. He wanted to keep his family as far away from it as he could. His father was an old republican and Josh may have heard him talk about Irish politics down the years, but I wouldn't say that his father encouraged Josh to be involved. It was Josh who made the decision to join the republican movement. He held it very dear. I think he got involved shortly before or just after internment morning [9 August 1971] when everybody was at the barricades and the burning and rioting was going on. Not long after I also got involved in na Fianna Éireann through Josh.

As a comrade Joseph held the rank of an intelligence officer within na Fianna Éireann. That was no surprise because he had leadership quality. He was out and about, watching and taking note of things. He wouldn't let you do something that he wouldn't do himself. To me he seemed very protective towards the rest of the Fians. He was trying to shelter them and keep them away from as much danger as he possibly could. He was trying always to make sure that you were safe. I also found that on the day that he died. Na Fianna Éireann was a very active organisation. We firmly believed (and we were told so by the members of the Irish Republican Army) that we were their backbone; they couldn't operate without co-operation from the Fianna. Members of na Fianna Éireann would have carried out operations alongside the army and would have been involved in military operations on many occasions. At times some of the Fianna would have been just as active as some of the volunteers. Josh had an awful lot of contact because of his role as an intelligence officer. He found out from them [the IRA] what they wanted us to do and then he relayed it on. He told them about things that he had seen as regards the RUC and British army movements. He had us watching, timing, making notes and delivering them to him, then he would pass on the information that we gave him.

On the day of his death he was very active. It was the Sunday of the commemoration in Bodenstown, so a lot of people were away from Ardoyne that day. There was a gun battle taking place in Ardoyne and it was hot and heavy. The last time I spoke to Josh was in Etna Drive on that day. I think it would have been around 4 pm and I think he was killed around 6 pm. He was active that day and he was going to take a position in Eskdale Gardens to attack the British army. I asked to go with him and he refused. He told me to go back to another part of the area and just wait there until I was needed. I think it must have been about teatime that night that another Fian came round and told us that Josh had been shot dead at the corner of Eskdale Gardens and Berwick Road. That's how I got word to say that he was murdered. I was told that he had opened fire on the army with a shotgun. They [the British army] were around an entry on either Farringdon or Cranbrook when they shot him. He was hit in the head. I don't think there was a weapon recovered because I know that neighbours in the street went out and tried to move his body to take him to the side and see what help they could give him. I read in a book called *Lost Lives* that there were empty cartridges and live cartridges found in his pockets. I don't know if that was true. But it also said that they found documentation in his pocket and I find that hard to believe because I don't think Josh would have been the type to have something in his pocket, stating names, people's capabilities, that sort of thing.

Josh got a military funeral and I was part of his guard of honour. At first, I think the family did not want him to have a republican funeral. Because he had been so secretive, it was an added shock to Mrs Campbell, who is a lovely woman, to be told that her son was a member of the republican movement. When Josh died I actually thought that I had lost a brother, that's how close we were. His death had a big affect on me, even now. Even at such a young age I would speak to Josh in confidence knowing that he would never betray that trust. I tried to return that favour to him when he confided in me. Big Josh was very tall and would have done anything for anybody. He was sort of a big brother, always advising you, never neglecting people. He had a great respect for people and peoples thought's. That would be him, a brother.

'Bik' (republican activist and neighbour)

It was Bodenstown Sunday when thousands of republicans head off to Wolfe Tone's grave. So there was a lot of people away from areas across the city. Obviously, because of the time, things were very, very hot and heavy. There were a lot of IRA people and others on standby in Ardoyne that day in the event of any trouble or attacks. It had been quiet enough in the early part of the day until the loyalists opened fire on people on the Oldpark Road from Louisa Street at around 2 pm or 3 pm. A gun battle ensued over in the Oldpark and there was a man called Madden killed. [Hugh Madden, killed by the UDA.] Word quickly spread across to local units over in the Oldpark. The Brits in that big post down at the junction of the Oldpark Road, opposite Louisa Street were also aware. As the gun battle developed the Brits obviously didn't worry about tackling the loyalists, so local units came out and responded. This unit ended up under heavy fire from both the Brits and the loyalists and it gradually spread right across into Ardoyne. Then there was all sorts of activity. There were gun battles and people were coming out on to the streets. People were mobilised very, very quickly. This was 1972 and things happened very fast. So then a lot of units were mobilised. A crowd of guys went out to take on the loyalists who were attacking the area down at the bottom of Jamaica Street, Etna Drive and Alliance. That was a favourite spot for loyalists to shoot. By and large the Brits never really gave them much hassle if they were shooting from there. But this fighting spread and IRA units were out all over Ardoyne. They were out in Old Ardoyne, Glenard, up towards Farringdon, Duneden, Etna Drive, down at the bottom of Stratford and Eskdale. Then there were four-wheelers and six-wheelers coming in. Saracens were revving up and driving through. The boys [IRA] were cracking away at them and they [British soldiers] were firing back. Then one saracen came in right from Alliance and stopped at the bottom of Stratford. There was a bit of firing going on and then it just sort of ceased.

It was then that I spotted Josh Campbell down an alleyway as we ran into a house for cover. I can't remember the exact time, everything was happening so fast. That is when Josh got killed. It was unreal, tragic and very hard to take in. I can vividly remember that myself and a mate of mine came through the entry and into the house. Obviously they [the British soldiers in the saracen] spotted us moving. They drove in quickly and then they were only about 10 yards from the back door, so we decided to go out the front. Then we were in Eskdale Gardens and went up the left-hand side of the street, watching for them [British soldiers] coming up behind us. There was a unit [of the IRA] operating at the bottom of Farringdon Gardens. Half of it was a building site at the time, because of the renovations going on to the burnt-out houses, so there were a lot of bricks and mortar around. Somebody had built a big bunker with old water tanks full of bricks and sand to stop bullets coming through. There were also people operating from a big electrical transformer at the bottom of Farringdon Gardens.

We were making our way up Eskdale when we heard this unmerciful rattle of fire from the top of the street. Josh was with another young fella and they had a shotgun. Him and his mate were going up the far side of the street and I shouted over, 'I don't think it's a good idea to go up on that side of the road because there is no cover up there'. There were just hedges round the two houses at the top of Eskdale at that time. I was aware at this stage that he was going up to engage with the British army. They were going up to have a rattle at the Brits. I knew the Brits were at the corner of Berwick Road and Alliance. But I didn't know that by the time we had come out of the house and up the street the Brits had made a rush, got in to the top of Stratford and into the gardens at the bottom of Velsheda. With the boys operating from the good cover down at Farringdon, you're talking about people 50 yards away apart shooting at each other. So I said to Josh, 'I don't think you should go up there yet. Just stall a minute until we see what way this is going to be'. But he went up one side and we moved up a wee bit on the left-hand side. Him and the other boy got to the top before we did. I was about 50 yards from the top and I could see them on the other side at the hedges, just juking round the corner. There were just hedges and fences there, which is not solid cover. Josh shouted across the street for cartridges and a guy across in Farringdon tossed a couple across the road. The first thing that came into my head when I saw that was that the Brits were the same distance away from him the other way. So they would have seen that there is somebody at this corner as well as the other corner. Until then they had been concentrating on the guy at the other corner.

So his mate ran over and got the cartridges and brought them over to Josh. He was standing on the footpath and I saw him breaking the shotgun down to put a cartridge in. As he closed the shotgun up, he looked round the corner. Then I just heard a bang and saw him lifting off the corner right off the footpath and nearly onto the street. He was just lifted right back. We bolted for the top of the street and people came running out. There was a lot of people standing at their doorways watching all this and a couple of women and Michael Shevlin ran out and dragged him in a wee bit from the corner. As soon as I got up, I saw that it had hit him square in the face. There was no doubt in my mind that he wasn't going to survive that. Josh had shoulder-length hair; he was a big tall wiry lad with this mass of hair flicked back. His hair was totally matted in all this heavy, thick blood and you knew that this was going to be final. I was almost physically sick. Michael knelt down and myself and a woman were saying an act of contrition in Josh's ear. We were praying over him when the Brits tried to make a rush and the guy across the street walloped them a few times and kept them back. We were trying to get the road blocked to give us a bit more cover and somebody phoned for an ambulance. I have to say it was there pretty quickly in the midst of all that. The other young fella had just gone into shock. He was standing and staring and his eyes were wide. It scared the daylights clean out of me too; it frightened me to death. I grabbed the shotgun, gave it to him and said 'Get that out of here now and get into a house'. So he bolted down the street.

Those Brits were hitting anything that came round that corner. It wouldn't have mattered if you came walking round with your Sunday paper under your arm, you were going to get walloped at that corner. I had seen a lot of things before, people getting shot and the rest, but that scared the living daylights out of me. I started to be very fearful for myself. We stayed with Josh until the ambulance arrived. The Brits still couldn't get in. We managed to get Josh into the back of the ambulance but when you are hit with an SLR in the head it would take a miracle to save your life. But, there was no miracle for Josh. It was just tragic, a young man out defending his area, just snuffed out in a split second. But in a sense you say, that was what we were there for. Whether it was the Fianna or the IRA, they were the ones who dared to be the front line to defend your people and your area. They were the ones who tried to stop loyalists and Brits crucifying your people. To be involved as I was meant you had taken a decision and if you came to grief then that is something you had to accept. It was part and parcel of what you did in order to defend your area or to pursue the reunification of your country. I didn't know Josh's parents personally but I know that they didn't know that he was connected to the Fianna. I know that it was a deep, deep shock to his family. It was a bad, bad day for Ardoyne, a young lad like that. And for the Bone with Hugh Madden being killed. It was a tragic, sad day.

Patricia Campbell (mother)

Joseph was only 16 years old when he died. He would have been seventeen four or five weeks after he was killed. He was killed on a Sunday. He had been to mass, then came back again. Later that evening the shooting started. A man called Madden was shot on the Oldpark Road where he had a wee fruit shop. I think that there was shooting coming from Alliance Avenue right down into the district and there was crossfire. Joseph left the house to go to see a friend and he was trying to get across the Berwick Road when he was shot from Eskdale Gardens, as far as I know. Joseph was shot dead, they blew the back of his head off. It was about an hour or so after it that I got the word that something had happened. 'Stocky', the wee man who owned the shop, called me and said, 'Mrs Campbell, there is a wee boy shot'. I said, 'What wee boy, whose wee boy?' I ran up the street roaring and crying and my husband came running out. He got the hold of me and I said to him, 'Joseph has been shot'. Fr. Myles [local priest] was in a house in Havana Street. He came out and took my husband up to the presbytery to find out if it was Joseph. Then he took him down to the hospital and they told him that it was Joseph. Joseph's death left me in a bad state, they had to go and get the doctor the night that it happened and nurse Canning who lived up the street came down. The doctor told her to get me to bed, but I only went up the stairs and I just came down again. I just couldn't rest. I still didn't know at that stage that he was dead. Then it was confirmed to my husband. It was a terrible shock. Joseph's daddy was told everything [about his injuries] but he never told me because he didn't want to let me know how bad he was. He died from a laceration of the brain. Nobody ever came to offer me support. Neither the RUC nor the army ever came near the door, they never came near us at all. Nobody was ever charged for Joseph's murder, not as far as I know, and I don't think justice was achieved. Those who murdered Joseph should have been brought to justice the same as everyone else. I still can't take what happened to my Joseph. A part of me died with him that day and the void will still remain with me, as it did with my husband, until I die.

> *It didn't matter where it was or what the danger of the situation was, he was always prepared to put himself forward to defend the people of this area in whatever way he could.*

Terry Toolan
Killed on active service
by the British army,
Eskdale Gardens,
14 July 1972

Terence 'Terry' Toolan was born in May 1936, one of the 6 boys and 6 girls. His father Bernard was originally from Richhill, Co. Armagh. After moving to Ardoyne he worked as a boiler man in the British army's Girdwood barracks. Terry's mother Catherine 'Kitty' Malone was from St Joseph Street. The couple lost their eldest child in 1944. Terry's brother Patrick was also killed during World War II. At the time Patrick was the youngest captain in the British army. The family were brought up in Duneden Park and Terry attended Holy Cross Boys school. He then passed the 11+ and went on to St Malachy's College. Terry then spent most of his working life as a supervisor electrician. He met his wife-to-be Doreen Cairns at the Forum picture house on the Crumlin Road. Doreen had been born in England, but her family were originally from the Lower Falls. The two were married in England in April 1957. They would go on to have 6 children of their own. Before the outbreak of the conflict the family lived in Velsheda Park. Soon after Terry's father died and they moved into the original Toolan home in Ladbrook Drive. That was where most of their children were born. Terry was a GAA man and had played senior football and hurling for Ard-Eoin. He was also very active in defending the district during the upheavals and violence after 1969. Terry was one of those who took on the dangerous task of helping to move people out of other areas into the relative safety of Ardoyne, particularly in the wake of the introduction of internment. On the night of 13 July 1972 Terry Toolan was shot dead by British soldiers whilst he was helping to protect the district from loyalist gunmen. At the time of his death, Terry Toolan was a volunteer in the Ardoyne Defence.

Bik McFarlane (friend)

I first met Terry a long, long, time ago. I joined the GAA in the early '60s and Terry Toolan was one of the players at the time. He was a character, full of fun. Terry was a very witty person. He was a live-wire in GAA matches as well, Terry's fists would have been up as quick as the next man. I remember there was murder during one particular match played up in the country. Terry had this '50s hairstyle and somebody called him a teddy boy. There was murder. I wouldn't say Terry was a hard man but he wouldn't lie down. He was tough but he was a good character. He was very friendly and he always had time for us younger ones. He was a good, solid, sound fella. He was also a first class electrician, he used to inspect the work. We used to go in and out of Terry's house every day so we became good friends of Doreen, Terry and the kids. Terry was always with his kids and was great craic with them. It was a very young family of six children. There was always a good buzz and a welcome about the house. Terry loved a bit of music too. I played in a bit of a group around that time and Terry was learning the mandolin and the guitar. He always liked to chant as well. I used to go round and practice a few tunes. Every time I walked in, the mandolin was out and he would say, 'Right, let's try a tune'.

From the civil rights period on Terry was always available to help people. He was involved in the struggle himself in a variety of ways. He went into dangerous areas to bring people out who lost their houses. At the time of internment any Catholics living up around Tynedale were in fear of their lives because it was right next to Silverstream. The whole place came under attack and Terry Toolan led a squad of us to go up and help get people out. It didn't matter where it was or what the danger of the situation was, Terry was always prepared to put himself forward to defend the people of this area in whatever way he could. He didn't fear for himself. He was more concerned about helping people to get moved out. Terry played a very significant role in defending this district against loyalists, Brits and the cops right up until he was killed.

In the week that Terry was killed there was a tremendous amount of activity. This area was under massive attack and the IRA were at their peak in terms of military operations. I remember reading interviews with Brits talking about where they were serving. They used to panic when they were told they were going to Ardoyne. They preferred to go to other areas because they could not cope with the narrow streets round the old district, the wee alleyways and the big, long streets. They feared this place. Of course some of them (like the paras and the commandos) came in, went gung ho and shot a lot of innocent people to try and suppress resistance. There were all sorts of things going on. In the summer of 1972 you would be sitting in the house and the next thing you would hear a rattle of shots round the corner. About an hour and a half later you would hear another rattle at the top of the district. Then later on you would hear a grenade going off. There would have been three or four operations a day at that time. There was always sniping at posts and attacks on foot patrols and mobile patrols. In fact throughout July 1972 there was a massive gun battle going on in different parts of the district, it was ongoing every night. The loyalists would open fire from where there used to be a garage at the bottom of Alliance Avenue, just across from Jamaica Street. The Brits had a billet post. It was sand-bagged, breeze-blocked and camouflaged, so it was difficult to see in. They also had the adjoining house at the back with bricks out of the wall. There were derelict houses just behind that in Alliance and you never knew whether it was the loyalists or the Brits shooting. But people had tuned in on radio messages the night Terry was killed. That is how people know that the Brits had identified three or four loyalist gunmen at the back of the garage at the bottom of the Alliance. But the Brits in that post were told not to interfere with them [loyalists] until they flushed out the IRA boys. Then they [British soldiers] were told to do whatever they had to do.

The night Terry was shot there was a major gun battle going on around Eskdale Gardens. There was also a battle at the bottom of Farringdon, where the houses had been burnt. There was also shooting up towards the mill, another battle further up in the old district, this is all in the one night. It was going on non-stop from about 10.30 pm until about 4 am in the morning. They used to have this old saying about it, '20,000 rounds fired and who got hit?' But unfortunately that night there were two people killed in the area. Terry Toolan was one of them and Jim Reid was another [James Reid, killed by persons unknown in Eskdale Gardens, 14 July 1972]. There were also three people wounded. It all happened at the corner of Eskdale Gardens. It was believed that they were all hit by the Brits, including Terry. The loyalists had started the gun battle and then moved back. When the IRA returned fire, the Brits opened up. They fired in flares on parachutes to identify what positions the IRA were firing from. I remember I was lying in a garden and once the flares went up I just went to ground. Everything just lit up. That was between 12 pm and 1 am but it was so bright it was like the middle of the afternoon on a summer's day. When the flare went out people would start to try and move around. There were about 50 or 60 people trapped up in the old Highfield club because the loyalists were firing down the Highfield entry. Then, once the IRA started firing back, the Brits opened up. So anybody who wanted to get out of a club, cross a street or an alleyway had to cross a line of fire. But the Brits didn't care. They were firing at anyone who moved across an open patch. At this time I was actually further up towards Farringdon. But Larry Marley [killed by the UVF in Havana Gardens, 2 April 1987] told me a funny story. He was sent in to help to get people out of the Highfield. He said there was all these men hiding behind the door in the bar saying, 'You are the IRA; get you out there and attract their fire until we get out'. Larry said the women were all sitting with their glasses singing IRA songs. The boys were all hiding and the women were all saying 'Up the IRA'. But as people were coming out, I know that one guy got hit in the hip. It was difficult to get people out, you had to send somebody to rattle away at the Brits further up the road. Then, when the Brits concentrated on him, you moved people out of clubs across into the long streets like Eskdale, Strathroy and Northwick. It was in the midst of all this that Terry was shot.

I didn't actually see Terry being shot, I was up with another guy in Farringdon. Somebody came and told us that two or three people had been shot at the bottom of Eskdale Gardens. He said that a couple of people had been killed and that one of them was Terry Toolan. Me and my mate nearly dropped dead. We bolted down across the Berwick Road, the Brits were shooting up there but when our lads were firing, we made a break for it. Halfway down we ran into a couple of guys and they said that Terry was crossing the street at the bottom of Eskdale and Etna when he got hit. Jim Reid had also been shot. A mate of mine carried Terry into a house. Terry was coughing and choking and they couldn't find out where he was hit. My mate told me that it was heart-breaking. Those were his last words. A couple of guys got Terry and Jim into a taxi. John O'Connor (who is dead now) lived in Etna Drive and he came straight up in his taxi with bullets flying everywhere. Along with his daughter, he took the severely wounded and dying and put them in his black taxi (John's daughter was in the Knights of Malta) and he drove them to the Mater Hospital. But I think both of them were dead on arrival. Terry was hit under the arm, through the side. The bullet went through his body and came out the other side. It had punctured lungs and vital organs on the way through.

This all happened at about midnight or 1 am. Gun battles continued on till about 4 am. Everyone was wrecked but we got our heads together. We got some of the injured across the border and people were saying that we were going to have to inform the relatives. They sent for a priest, Father Augustine I think it was, and because we had been friends of Terry's, they asked me and Barney McKenna to go up to his house too. Seamus Clarke went along with me; Seamus was only about 15 at the time. He had actually pulled Terry in from the corner. Even though there were bullets flying everywhere, he grabbed Terry and pulled him in. He could easily have been killed himself. It was close to 5 am when I got to the gate of Terry's house. I remember it was incredibly bright and the sun was shining. I felt so tired and wrecked about the thing. We went up the pathway, rapped the door and went in. Barney went into the house along with one of the other lads and asked for Doreen. I heard this unmerciful scream from inside the house once she had been told; it was just a heart-rending scream of anguish and sadness. Then the kids came down the stairs. I just didn't know what to do. I stood in the pathway with Seamus and some other guy. You could hear the crying and the wailing. It was just unbelievable. Just after, a fella I knew came walking up the street and he said that his sister had been attacked earlier. The loyalists had broken into his sister's house [Mrs McClenaghan of Southport Street] over the Bone. They raped her and killed her son [David McClenaghan] who was 14 years old and mentally retarded. I just stood there and thought, 'Jesus, Mary and Joseph'. It was horrific and hard to take in. I told him Terry had been killed. We were standing in the middle of Ladbrook Drive at 5 am in the middle of the summer with the sun beating down and that was the conversation, it was unreal. I was a young man at the time, about 19 or 20, but we were growing up in an environment where we were seeing operations going on every day of the week. When you see people being killed, Brits getting killed, bombs going off and you are losing friends, you grow up very, very quickly and you become very hardened to the whole thing.

There was a massive turn-out for Terry's funeral. He was a very popular and well-known character in this district. It was a blistering hot, warm, sunny day in July and it was a very, very sad funeral. I felt numb. It was hard to take in that Terry was really gone. My thoughts were with Doreen. She was left on her own with six kids from 14 years old right down to nine months – though she did have a good, solid family with her. But it was a tragedy. It was a bad loss to the district to lose someone of the calibre of Terry Toolan. He was a conscientious, very loveable and likeable person. Terry was not just a man for the GAA and an electrician. He knew about politics and could see the shape of the way things were. Terry Toolan was a funny man, a very dedicated man, he was a great family man and his family wanted for nothing at all. He was and still is missed by all of us. We lost an exceptionally talented person in Terry, a good, solid Ardoyne man.

Gemma Di Lucia (daughter)

My father was a great Gaelic sportsman. Along with his brother Lawrence he was a member of the local Ard-Eoin GAA. They used to organise the club's children's Christmas party every year. He had played goalkeeper for the senior football team and had also played hurling. My father was also a great lover of music; he loved to play the guitar and the banjo. He was always telling stories and he was a great man for joking. My father and Bik would sometimes sit in our house playing music and telling old stories all night. He used to tell us a story or sing us a song when he was putting us to bed at night. He also loved to go fishing and he would take the family on trips to the Glens of Antrim for picnics or go down to Meath or Sligo. He was well-known in the area and had a lot of friends like Bik, Fred Heatley, Joe Lavery, Bill McCann, Barney McKenna and Martin Meehan, to name a few. Two or three weeks before he was murdered by the British army he had started to work from home. That was because he had been followed from his work on the Newtownards Road on a number of occasions. He always seemed to be working and was called all of the day and night. All the family were worried about his safety, so he decided to work from home. The situation in Belfast was getting worse. On the night of 13 July 1972, there was heavy shooting in Ardoyne. My father was shot at around midnight but was confirmed dead at 1 pm on 14 July. There were a lot of men out protecting the district from loyalist gunmen at that time. My father Terry was walking down Eskdale Gardens when he was shot from a British army post occupied by two British soldiers at the top of the old mill, where the GAA club is now. They shot two flares into the sky first. Anyone who was seen out at that time was obviously out protecting the area from the loyalist gunmen who were trying to invade the district. My father was shot in the right shoulder. It cut his spinal cord before exiting his body through his left shoulder. He was 36 years old when he as shot. Two weeks after Terry was killed a good friend of his and GAA member Frank Corr was found murdered in a car on the Cliftonville Road [Frank Corr, killed by the UFF in Landscape Terrace along with James McGerty, 26 July 1972]. Our family were devastated by the murder of such a good friend.

Doreen Toolan (wife)

When I was growing up we had a house up by the West Circular Road. But my mother got afraid and we had to move out because the 'Orangies' were breaking the windows and writing slogans on the walls. We moved down by Townsend Street, which was worse; we were nearly burnt out of there. So my mother took a swap and we ended up in Hooker Street. Then I worked in Kathleen McManus's hairdressers on the Crumlin Road from when I was nine years old. In the morning you would see the boys all passing going to school. Terry used to come down every morning and rap on the window when he was passing. Then we got talking. We were very young and still at school. We knew each other from when I was about 11. I never had any other boyfriend, we were childhood sweethearts. Later on, Terry's brother's wife moved to England for a job and she asked me to accompany her. I went over and lived with her mother. Three weeks later Terry and his brother Seamus appeared at the window. We were there about nine months and we decided to get married because we were kind of living together anyway. We married in St Barnabas' Cathedral, Nottingham, 27 April 1957. We couldn't even afford a good wedding ring. Terry gave me £10 to get a wedding ring but I got one for £1.50 in a pawnshop. But it is the only ring that has stayed on my finger and is not wearing away. We went to the pictures for our honeymoon that night and we watched a John Wayne film; Terry loved cowboy films.

A few months later I fell pregnant and decided not to have my child in England. So I came home in July on my own. Terry was learning to be an electrician and he wanted to serve his time. Terry came home before the baby was born because one of his friends wrote to him and told him they could give him a job here. We had Bernadette and then Gemma. We lived with his mother and father for a while, then moved to Velsheda Park, by that time Gerard had been born. Terry's father died after Paul was born, so his mother and brother bought the house in Ladbrook Drive. We sold our house in Velsheda and moved into Ladbrook. By then Terry was a supervisor electrician. We bothered with nobody or anything. We went out once a month because that was all we could afford. Terry would go to the GAA for hurling, football and to speak to the lads; that was the life we had. It was a happy, innocent life; Terry, me and the kids were alright. All Terry thought of was his garden and his work. We had 13 really wonderful years. I don't think we ever had a fight; there was too much love between us. The kids bonded us and kept us busy. It was the first time I ever knew how to truly love. Then all a sudden when the troubles started I lost him. It was just a living nightmare. It was just so unbelievable; Terry was a real family man and it is a big loss when someone so loving and caring about his wife and his family is gone. It leaves a big gap. I didn't think I could ever go through life without him. Some people say you that get over it but you never do, not even after 30 years.

By 1972 the situation had escalated; it had become dangerous for Terry because he was involved in the defence of the area. It just got to the stage that you couldn't go out of the district. Terry's work would phone him and let him know where he was to work because things had become so bad. He was followed twice and the Shankill Butchers would have been around at that time. I didn't really know just what danger he was in, though Terry did. He knew a lot of Protestants from working over in the Newtownards Road. So he could have been spotted anywhere. He was a sitting target. The year before he died we had decided to go to Canada. His brother Seamus was there and had a job set up for Terry. In the July week of 1972 we decided we weren't taking any holidays that year because we were waiting to get the money up to go to Canada. Then my grandmother took ill and died on 7 July. She loved Terry and he loved her. We were down in her house when she died. Then we were coming back home at about 3 am with the baby. We came through Cambrai Street [a Protestant area] and the car broke down. Some good person came and gave us a tow out to the Crumlin Road and we walked on down. But when we got into the house I think Terry was frightened too because he said to me, 'If anything ever happened me, you would never, ever marry again'. I looked at him real funny and said, 'Jesus, are you wise in the head talking like that? Is there something wrong with you? Are you going to die on me?'

Young McClenaghan was murdered on the night of 11/12 July, just before Terry was killed [Davey McClenaghan, killed by loyalists in Southport Street, Oldpark, 11/12 July 1972]. I was over in Ann Largey's all day on 13 July fixing her house. Davey was her nephew and was to be buried from her home. Terry was going up and down the street in the dumper to make a runway for the car. Later I went home and made a quick supper. Then somebody called for Terry. He went out but later he came back in. It was a mad, mad, bloody night, there were flares and shooting everywhere. Before Terry went out again he went up and brought the two girls down out of the attic. He put them in with the boys in the back for safety. Then he gave me a kiss on the cheek, went over and kissed the child and out he went. He just said, 'See you later, love'. But I never, ever saw him again. I just remember him walking through the door and he came back in a box. I have heard rumours that when he was shot he said: 'Tell Doreen and the kids I love them'. But I know from the way he died he couldn't possibly have spoken to anybody because he suffocated in his own blood. The flares that were going up in the air that night were atrocious. It was a roasting hot night but I had to come in and light my gas fire up because I was freezing; the sound of the bullets made me shiver. My husband must have got hit when I shivered because I could feel it. I felt it as if something had hit me and I froze. It was then that a fella came up and told me that Terry had been shot. I wanted to go and see but nobody would take me down.

When Terry's remains came home, we were harassed by the British army. In fact the house was raided even before his remains came home. They said they were looking for evidence and weapons. I went berserk. I said that they had done enough harm. My mother and brother-in-law had to restrain me. They [British soldiers] literally wrecked the house. They pulled electric fires out of the walls in the bedrooms and tore off the built-in wardrobe doors. They lifted nearly every floorboard in the house. My children were not used to that and it was very frightening for them. They were so young. The baby was only seven and a half weeks. I was feeling bad because my husband just been shot dead, then these bastards came round and raided me. It wasn't bad enough that they murdered him and just left me there like an old floor cloth, like I was nothing or nobody, and with six children to rear. They came back the next day when his remains were there. My brother-in-law told them to go and they went away. But they left instructions as to what we were supposed to do with the remains. Martin Meehan came in and he said that word had come from Dublin to give Terry an IRA funeral. But Terry's brother said, 'No' because he was not involved and had been policing the area. When Terry came home I just looked at him, I couldn't believe it was him lying in the coffin. I was sitting looking at him and I thought he was actually breathing. It was so depressing to think that the one I loved was lying there; I don't know what happened to me after that. All I remember is sitting in the chapel so close to the coffin that the smell of his remains was making me violently sick. Another thing that annoyed me was the way they did a post-mortem. It was a very, very hot summer and the remains were starting to smell badly. Fr. Myles said the mass. I vaguely remember Larry Toolan got up and gave a speech. I don't know how he did it. Terry's mother took me up for Holy Communion and I remember Fr. Myles putting his hand on my head. I don't remember anything after that because they had me drugged.

Afterward I became addicted to prescription drugs; I could not go through life without them. I didn't want to live; I just wanted to do myself in. I didn't consider my children or anyone else. I was being selfish and just wanted to be with Terry. As the years went on, it didn't get any easier. It actually got worse and I was hitting the drugs more and more. That went on until 1989. By then I was on 50 or 60 valium a day. My mother looked after my children and my sisters helped. I ended up having two nervous breakdowns and I had to go into Purdysburn [hospital] for a month to come off the tablets. I was locked up for a fortnight. They showed me a film of myself afterwards. I watched this woman in her pants and her bra in a padded cell on a mattress with foam flying out of her mouth. I couldn't believe it was me; it was like that scene in 'The Exorcist'. You had to see it to believe it. But that bucked me up a bit. I thought, 'If my children see me like that they will be frightened and they will run away. I will have to do something here'. So then I started corresponding with the children and I was allowed out to see them. Looking back now, I think about all that time that I could have had with my children. You wonder what life is all about.

In 1980 I had made a solicitor take me down to Crumlin Road court house and I made a settlement. But I didn't really want any money; I only wanted my husband. I was so full of drugs I didn't really know what was happening. I never received any help. In all those years I was never offered counselling. When my husband died I had to wait for the pension to come through and had to live on family allowance. My mother and my sisters kept me and my children. My sister went up to St Vincent de Paul in Ardoyne chapel for me. I didn't know anything about it. They gave me £2 a week for me and six children. But on the fifth week a man came round and rapped on the door. He said that the St Vincent de Paul were stopping the money because their funds were running low. So I just went to my purse grabbed £10 and threw it at him. But Fr. Augustine was a good friend and the only one from the church who stuck by me. He sent me £10 a week for about six years after Terry died; he never, ever forgot. He was based in Ardoyne and was here when Terry was shot. Him and Terry got on well. But it has been a hard life, a long hard struggle.

The only thing that I'm proud to say is my husband went the way he wanted to go. At least he was not butchered [killed by the Shankill Butchers] like other friends and people I have known. I feel sorry too for those people who have not got the remains of their loved ones. God help those people and the relations of people who were butchered. I lost a cousin too, young Michael [Michael McLarnon, killed by the British army in Etna Drive, 28 October 1971]. I always say to my kids, 'There is not a house in this place that death has not hit. Death comes to us all. But when there is the tragedy of a shooting or a blowing up then it is a nightmare. If you are going to die, die naturally. So don't get involved in anything and don't go out when there is trouble'. That is the fear in my life. I worry morning, noon and night; I never stop worrying. I have a lot of anger in me against the RUC and the British army. Although I have to say this, they are somebody's sons too. I mean that with my whole heart. I'm sitting here now and if there was one shot outside my door I suppose I would have to go out and help him, like I did for Mrs McGregor when she was shot [Elizabeth McGregor, killed by the British army in Highbury Gardens, 12 January 1973]. There is anger there but no bitterness. Anger and bitterness are two different things. I have forgiven so much, I have given into it so much. I can forgive the ones who shot Terry but not the ones that gave the orders. I hate the whole of the British government system. They came in and just shot around them that night; they didn't give a damn who they shot.

> *As he went out, he was joking to me that he was away to defend the district. That was the last I saw of him.*

James Reid
Killed on active service
by (persons unknown),
Eskdale Gardens,
14 July 1972

James 'Bimbo' Reid was born in May 1945 to his mother Rachel, a Gibbons from Brookfield Street and his father James, originally from Carrick Hill. He was the second eldest of four brothers and two sisters and attended the Holy Cross Boys school and then St Gabriel's. When they were growing up, the family home would sometimes be raided by the RUC and 'B' Specials because Jim's uncle, Steve Gibbons, was a known IRA man in the 1950s. His mother was a lifelong republican. Jim Reid became a labourer and from the age of 16 he worked on the sites in England. He had only been living back in Ardoyne for a few months when he was shot dead during a gun battle between the IRA and the British army in Eskdale Gardens. James Reid was a volunteer in the Auxiliaries, which was a section of the IRA. He was engaged in a gun battle with loyalists, who were shooting into the district, when he encountered a British army foot patrol. The British soldiers opened fire, killing Terence Toolan, a defence volunteer. Exactly who killed James is not clear, although at the time it was widely believed the British army was responsible. It now appears James may have been killed by an accidental round fired by republicans in the midst of a fierce and prolonged gun battle. Unfortunately the full circumstances surrounding James Reid's death may never be known. He was 26 years old at the time of his death.

Ann Reid (sister)

James was happy-go-lucky and took life as it came. He loved life. He was in England from when he was 16 and he only came home six months before he was shot. On the day that James was killed he moved me into a house in Havana Street. I was squatting and I wasn't long married. He was just joking, his normal self. He was always happy and always slagging. As he went out, he was joking to me that he was away to defend the district; that was the last I saw of him. I found out about James' death from my older brother Bobby. He came round to Havana Street and told me and my mummy who was with me at the time. From what we were told he was in a house in Eskdale, him and a couple of other ones; a shot came through the window and it ricocheted and hit Jim in the neck. It went through another fella first. He was wounded. Terry Toolan was shot outside the door at the same time; he was shot dead [Terry Toolan, killed by the British army in Eskdale Gardens, 14 July 1972]. There was no response at all from the RUC or the army at the time. They [British army] gave us a hard time. They completed ignored us; you didn't count; you were a nobody. It was believed at the time that the British army killed him; even they believed it. But we always knew the exact circumstances of his death were contentious. I don't think there was ever a proper investigation into his killing. The details of James' death were never really made known to us – just that he was shot in the middle of a very hectic night of shooting involving the British army, the loyalists and the IRA. That was it. The British media and British administration claimed our James was a 'terrorist', as they say. He wasn't. He was an IRA volunteer, but to them he was just a terrorist. We don't feel that justice was achieved. No matter who killed James or what organisation he belonged to, we feel the family is entitled to be informed of the exact circumstances surrounding his death. This has been denied us.

The death of my brother was very bad for the family. My mummy was never the same after it. There was a space that could never be filled. It was terrible, terrible emotional. Our older brother Bobby took it very bad, so did Frankie and Martin. Nobody ever offered counselling or help. The church did not treat us very well at the time, their reaction was that he was a volunteer so the church wouldn't let him inside the chapel with the tricolour. It had to come off the coffin before they said the mass. We were annoyed at that. Looking back after all these years, I don't think there is anything that could be done for me personally or for us as a family, it's been too long. There have been a couple round inviting me to go to the victim support group but I didn't bother. We just handled it ourselves.

Bobby Reid (brother)

He worked in England for a brave while. Our James worked with me on a couple of jobs but we were always moving about, the same company but different jobs. We went to England to work because there was no work here and we wanted to get away. He had a whole load of friends but he was younger and I was older. The thing I always remember about our Jim is that he had this wired sense of humour. Our James was a bloody nuisance at times but in other ways he was dead on. I mean, I loved him; he was my brother.

The day of our James' death the two of us were working over at the Royal. They were building a new wing and it was holiday time. So at about 10.30 pm that night he called in to my sister Ann to borrow £1.50. He wanted it to buy my young son Robert a dagger. Ann was moving from Havana Street to a new house, so Jim and all his friends were going to get a van to help her move to her new house. That was the last we saw of him. We found out our James was dead when his friend Larry Marley came to the door and said Jim was hit [Larry Marley, killed by the UVF in Havana Gardens, 2 April 1987]. I asked him how bad it was and he said he thought he was dead. So then I went round to Toby's Hall, they had a sort of wee hospital there. I was told they had brought our James round there but that he had been taken down to the Mater Hospital. Francie Markey brought me down to the hospital. There were Brits all over the place. I saw a doctor and asked him if my brother had been brought in. He said there were two people. He brought me into a cubicle and Terry Toolan was lying there. Then we went into the next one and there was my brother; he was dead. He was shot through the side of the neck and it came out the back. I was told that he was shot by the Brits, that was what everyone believed at the time.

There was no investigation into the killing. There was an inquest and I think it was an open verdict. I don't blame whoever shot him. Everyone was shooting everywhere at the time; there was a lot of confusion and panic I'm sure. But the thing that bugs me is that no one told me the truth. Maybe the truth was too difficult to establish at the time. But our James was a volunteer and he knew what he was doing, he was 26 and you couldn't say anything to him. He was a terrible loss to all in our family. We'll never forget him.

Willie (eyewitness and comrade)

To be honest with you, I didn't really know Jim. I knew he was a member of the republican movement, that he was a volunteer. That night he died I had time off as far as operations were concerned. You got one night off in a blue moon. So I decided that me and my wife would go out for the night and we went to the Highfield Club in Etna Drive. We were only there about an hour when a man came running in and said there was heavy gunfire. This was about 9 pm or 9.15 pm. So I went out of the club with the man and my wife. I told the man to stand and wait for me until I had taken my wife safely back to the house. But on the way down the street the Brits shot flares up and as they did, they opened fire from the Flax Street mill with heavy machine guns. Eventually I got my wife to the house then I made my way out the back and up to the man who I had left outside the Highfield. This man was armed although I wasn't armed at that moment in time.

There was a lot going on at the back end of Etna Drive. The British army were firing at us and the loyalists were there in big force at the back of Alliance Avenue. The volunteers were engaging the loyalists while the Brits were firing from the Flax Street mill onto their backs. Anyway, I took a gun from one of the volunteers and went up the entry and fired at them. But you would have been as well firing stones as firing the weapons we had. I went back down and gave the gun back to the volunteer and I said, 'Go see if you can get rounds for that'. So I left him and then me and two other men, 'Tommy' and 'Tony', got together. The gunfire was heavy and we had to wait until the flares went out before we could get across the road. So I ran first, 'Tommy' came next and then 'Tony'. We got into Katie Stone's garden at the corner of Eskdale Gardens and then we had to crawl on our mouth. I got over anyway and Terry Toolan was there with another volunteer. I was just passing the gate of Katie Stone's house and this guy called me and said, 'Willie, come here; I'm having trouble with this [weapon]'. He had a Lee Enfield rifle and it was jammed. So I went into the house and took the weapon into the corner. I turned the light on so that we could have a look at it. Jim Reid was in the house. I saw that the nut had seized up over the firing pin, it wasn't striking a round and I couldn't get it moved. I said to one of the volunteers, 'You may go and put that where you got it because it's no use to you now'. Then I gave him the weapon back. This other volunteer had the weapon although I am not sure if he was an auxiliary or what. Anyway, he didn't get that far and then blatter [gunfire]. I hit the wall and

Jim was hit in the top of the chest. The bullet went right down through him. Jim didn't actually drop. He spun round to me and anything he had in him was coming out of him. Then another couple of guys ran in. I was hit too, in the shoulder, and was lying in the corner. Before these guys ran in, I crawled over to Jim and tried to say an act of contrition in his ear. The gunfire that hit Jim appeared to come in through the window of the house. He definitely wasn't hit by anyone in the house because I don't think there was anybody else there that could have fired a weapon. Apart from Jim, the other volunteer and myself the only other person in the house (to the best of my knowledge) was the girl who owned the house. And she was pregnant. It has baffled me to this day, who fired the shot that killed Jim. You see, I was in the living room of the house the whole time. Jim and me were standing by the coal hole where you got into the meter box. I looked at the weapon, said I couldn't get it working and told the other fella to take it away. Then there was a burst of gunfire. When you are hit you don't hear it. So obviously the weapon we had could not have fired any rounds.

Jim died right away because what he had lost was enough for me to know he was dead. Then I took sick myself. I just fell back into the corner because the blood was like a fountain coming out of me. I was grabbing and squeezing to try and kill the pain that I had. I started boiling, then all of a sudden I went stone cold. I thought then that I was just sliding off. I said to the two guys who had come in, 'Lift Jim out of that mess, put his head up and set him on the chair because he's dead'. Then another fella ran in to the house and he was squealing that he had been shot in the back. You could see a groove in his back. It was basically a flesh wound but if it had been any deeper it would have taken his spine out. I think he was hit with the same gunfire that hit Jim. Then I was lifted out of the house by the two guys and we went down to the pad. It was dark, the lamps were out in the street, and the Brits opened up with heavy gunfire. They ushered me to into Varndale's mother's house across the street. By this stage I was like a wet rag then because I was losing a lot of blood. Then they put me up on a table or high chair. My head was lying on some girl's shoulder. I was near out and she was using a flannel and dabbing here and there. After that, a couple of my comrades came and shifted me in a car to another house where I lay for several hours. As I was lying there a foreign camera crew came in and tried to film me. But the camera men were stopped and put out. Then a doctor was brought in. He gave me an injection and put pads on the wound. I lay there for a couple of days in that house and then I was taken away down south.

It is difficult to say for certain who killed James Reid. I know it has always been believed that the British army killed him but of what I know of the situation the British army couldn't have fired the shots that killed him. It was physically impossible. There was a lot of panic and a lot of hype. I'm not sure that the confusion of that night will ever be sorted out. I really feel for the Reid family. As far as I know they have never been able to get to the truth. Unfortunately I'm not sure if they ever will.

I want to make it clear that I have no agenda here. It is possible that it was the loyalists who killed my father. There is a possibility that it was the IRA, though I don't believe that. But if it was them then, yes, I would like them to tell me and that would be another chapter in our lives closed.

Joseph (Giuseppe Antonio) Rosato
Killed by (unknown),
Deerpark Road
21 July 1972

Joseph Rosato's parents were Francesco and Beneditta. They were both Italian-born, from the village of Casalattico, halfway between Rome and Naples in the province of Frosinone. Migrants from that area tended to go to Philadelphia, Dublin or Belfast. Joseph's father travelled to Belfast and his young family followed him later. At first they lived in Nelson Street near the Docks, an area that used to be known as 'Little Italy'. It was here that Joseph was born in 1912. His elder sister Clara and brother Davy (Ottavio) had preceded him. He would be followed by Francesco (who died when he was 11 years old), Johnny (Giovanni) and the youngest sibling Angelo. The family moved once or twice more before setting up home in Springfield Avenue. That was after Joseph's mother died of pneumonia. Francesco found himself unable to deal with bringing up his young family and the grief of losing his young wife. As a result, Joseph and his brothers Angelo and Davy were brought up in Nazareth Lodge children's home. Joseph left at the age of 12 and started work selling ice cream with his brothers and father until the latter died in 1938. Just over a year later Joseph met his wife-to-be Sheila at the outbreak of World War II at a dance in a hall in Milford Street. Sheila was 21 at the time, and living in Albert Street, but she was a 'Falls Road woman' (her people being originally from Balaclava Street). In 1944 they married and soon had the first of their eight children. After living for a while with her mother in Albert Street, they set up home in the Deerpark Road on the edge of Ardoyne.

On the night of 21 July 1972 Joseph Rosato was at his home on the Deerpark Road. Earlier that day the IRA had detonated 20 explosive devices and killed nine people on what became known as 'Bloody Friday'. One of Joseph's sons had recently been arrested and was in Long Kesh in connection with 'Official' IRA activities. Another had been threatened by loyalists the week before and Joseph had reported this to the local RUC. There was also a feud developing between various sections of the 'Official' IRA and between them and the local IRA. At around 10 pm a car pulled up outside the Rosato home. Four men remained inside it whilst a fifth got out and knocked on the door. Joseph answered it and the person asked for Joseph's son Martin by name. Joseph and his son of the same name tried to slam the door shut. One of the men in the car got out and fired a single shot. The bullet went through the glass in the door and hit a main artery in Joseph's leg. He died shortly after of the wound. Afterward there was evidence that pointed towards the IRA being responsible for the shooting, although this has always been denied by the organisation. It remains unclear whether Joseph Rosato was killed by republicans, loyalists, or British security forces, intentionally or by accident. Indeed, the members of the Rosato family themselves are confused on this issue. What they all agree on is that they lost a loving family man, an 'ideal father'.

Kevin Rosato (son)

My father's mother died from pneumonia when my father was still very young and living in a little side street beside the Kitchen Bar. At that time my grandfather had an ice cream cart and he used to get the ice from an ice store in Great Victoria Street. But after my grandmother died my grandfather couldn't cope. The family was all still very young and he moved them up to Springfield Avenue. My grandfather was heartbroken. He and my grandmother had been very close, much like my father and mother were, and he half died when she did. He just couldn't cope. In the end my father's brother Johnny was raised by the Forte family and my uncles Davy and Angelo and my father went into Nazareth Lodge for several years. My grandfather died in 1938 but he was still alive when the boys went into Nazareth Lodge. My aunt Clare went to Springfield Avenue and then she got married. My father would only have been about five years old at the time all this happened. He never talked about those days but my uncle Davy has told me that they used to get hit for speaking Italian and they were separated from one another when they were in the home. So they had a hard time in there. Still, my father was on the committee of Nazareth Lodge right up until the day he died. They used to raise money for it and organise a trip to the Isle of Man every year. Anyway, my father got out of the home when he was about twelve and the brothers started selling ice cream from ice carts. They were also making plaster statues and selling them. They used to sell them on credit so people could afford them. For a while my father, my uncle Davy and my grandfather had an ice cream shop on the Lisburn Road. But they were put out of there, by loyalists, for opening on a Sunday. They were up by the Botanic Gardens so Sunday was a big day for them. They were put out one 12 July by the local Orangemen from Sandy Row. After that my uncle Davy had a place with my grandfather in Albert Street up until my grandfather died in 1938. That was around the time my father met my mother. They were in Coventry for a while working during the war. My daddy didn't like it because it was conscripted labour. He worked in a munitions factory for about a year. When they moved back to Belfast they got married. That was in 1944. At first they lived in my granny's house in Albert Street and they had Bernadette and Tony there. Then they got the house in Deerpark Road. It was there that Eamon, Marie, Martin, myself, Gerard and Joseph were all born. My daddy was a terrazzo worker, laying marble floors. That was his main job until he died.

My daddy didn't really have any hobbies, apart from my mammy! They did everything together. He didn't gamble, smoked about a packet of cigarettes a week and only drank at births, deaths and marriages. He might have gone up to the Horse Shoe about once a fortnight with my uncle Davy and that was it. He was a real family man. He always did the cooking because he was a far better cook than my mammy. I remember during the bread strike in the early 1960s he made homemade bread. He had no real education but he always had books in the house. My father was just a very warm family man. He was very emotional and he showed all of us that it was ok to show and express your feelings. As kids we would have done things around the house that would have been seen as women's work in other houses, but to us that was normal. We had a very happy family life. We just all gelled together. My daddy was close to the rest of his family too. My uncle Angelo died in about 1963 in his flat in England, he was a bit slow and hadn't been looking after himself very well. That was a sad thing. But my daddy would have been close to all his family, very close to my aunt Clare and very, very close to my uncle Davy. Both of their families have always been close too.

I had been arrested before my father's death, on 12 June 1972. That night a gun battle took place over in the Bone after Hugh Madden had been killed closing his shop on the Oldpark Road [Hugh Madden, killed by the UFF, 11 June 1972. Hugh's brother Thomas was killed two months later on the 13 August 1972. He had been stabbed over 100 times by the UFF and his body found in a doorway on the Oldpark Road.] The 'Official' IRA, 'Provisional' IRA and the Defence Committee were all out defending the area. In Ardoyne there was a lot of animosity and conflict between the 'Official' IRA and the 'Provisional' IRA; it got very nasty at times. People were beaten up and had loaded guns put down their throats. But where I was involved up in the Oldpark that wasn't really the case. Anyway, that night the British army surrounded the area and searched every house; I was one of four arrested. I was in Armagh gaol for two weeks and then all the republican prisoners were transferred to Long Kesh.

So I was in Long Kesh on the night my father was killed. On that evening, 21 July 1972, I had no knowledge of my father's death at all. I knew from listening to the radio about the various bombs that there were that day. Then it came out that there were people killed that had no connection with the bombs. But it wasn't until the next day that I found out my father had been shot. I was sitting at a table in Long Kesh making a Long Kesh hankie. You would write 'Long Kesh' on these hankies and the 'E' was made up of two chained up arms, signifying the need to free Irish people from British imperialism. Then I heard this announcement on Radio Ulster saying, 'Joseph Rosato, 103 Deerpark Road, was shot dead last night at 10.00 pm'. It was as simple as that. It was 12 hours later. My brother had been trying to get in to Long Kesh to tell me but they wouldn't let him. The screws, the prison authorities would have known but they didn't tell me. Straight after I went to see the republican OC of the compound, Seamie Connolly, and he got me some medication to dope me up. What do you do? You're in a prison compound with these massive long huts filled with people and you have just found out your father is dead. You have absolutely no control over the situation and no privacy. It wasn't until later that day that I saw one of my brothers but I was in the hut with forty other fellas for the next couple of days. That two-day period was one of the worst experiences of my life because I had no private space to grieve. Then on the Monday I made a court appearance and got bail. The funeral was on Tuesday and I only got to see my father in the chapel. It was sad. Immediately after I got out of gaol I thought my family was doping my food and drink to keep me from doing anything and getting involved in the feud going on at that time. That wasn't even on my mind but, to be honest, there were some strange circumstances surrounding my father's death that have never been resolved.

After being released from gaol I had to report to the cops daily for approximately one month. As far as I was concerned my father was dead and that was all I knew. Then at the inquest my brother Tony got very emotional and said that it was the IRA and not the loyalists who had killed my father. Within my family I was always the one who thought that it wasn't the IRA; I don't think there is any concrete proof. Apart from anything else, there would have had to have been a lot of people involved in organising all the bombings that day. There were a lot of Catholics assassinated that day and night by the loyalists as well, that tends to be forgotten. The media downplayed their deaths because it suited them to portray the IRA as the bad guys 'butchering' people on 'Bloody Friday' without talking about the Catholics killed. So it suited the authorities 'statistically' to claim that the IRA killed my father. It also suited them to try and stir up conflict between the IRA and the 'Official' IRA by suggesting my daddy was killed as part of a feud. But there were some strange circumstances. I have been told by some people that it was a named UVF man who did it but I don't know if that is true. The problem I always had with the loyalist theory was to do with the car that was used. The car had been stolen in Galway and then the number plates had been changed. But if it was loyalists why would they have stolen a car in Galway? The 'Official' IRA had a transport section at that time that used to steal cars in the South. There was a lot of conflict within the 'Official' IRA at that time. Some people were leaving to form an organisation that would later become the INLA, some were going over to the IRA. I know the hierarchy of the 'Official' IRA did not trust my family. But then again, the RUC might have gotten hold of an 'Official' IRA car and handed it over to the loyalists. The details about the car did not come out in the court but only afterwards. It was the police that told our Tony about the car. But you can end up going round and round with conspiracy theories.

Afterwards we did try and piece together what had happened that day. My father had been out that day in the vegetable plots in Westland Road. He brought over some vegetables to some Protestant neighbours then came home and made the dinner. Just a normal day. There had been various police patrols around that day. Where we were was close to a Protestant area, Alliance Crescent, and the Deerpark would have been about two-thirds Protestant then. But then, who knows if there was any connection to any patrols or road blocks? It is so difficult to put the jigsaw of what happened back together after thirty years. About a week before, some Protestants in Alliance had also said something to my brother Martin. My da was naïve enough to go up to the RUC and report it. He went up because he was a good citizen and didn't think that people should be allowed to say sectarian things to his son. I don't know if that has any bearing on things.

All I know is that at about 9.50 pm someone came and knocked at the door. One guy put his foot in the door and my daddy tried to close it. Then someone else shot at him from the footpath. As far as I heard there were two guns but only one shot was fired through the door. Was it an accident? I mean, I never knew republicans to fire one shot like that. If it was loyalists is it just a case of firing a shot at a fenian and running off? I don't know. I don't know who did it or whether it was intentional or accidental. Firing from 15 feet away through a door, it is hard to know. There were rumours it was a guy with ginger hair and that made our Tony think it was a particular fella in Ardoyne who had ginger hair. But I think it is unfair to draw a conclusion on the basis of someone's hair colour. My mother and Joseph were in the house when my daddy was shot and then about an hour or so after the event Tony and Martin went over to see people connected with the 'Official' IRA in Ardoyne. As they made their way over Tony was almost killed. A bullet fired by loyalists from Alliance went through his hair. Loyalists were shooting at Catholics all over the city that night. At the same time some neighbours came over the road just after my daddy was shot and they would have been Protestants. They were all shocked as well. Then Tony had to go and identify my father's body and the cops showed him pictures of his injuries. They gave him a pound note that had been in my daddy's pocket. It had my daddy's blood on it. Tony gave it to me, I still have it upstairs. Sometimes I wonder if I should burn it but it's something to have.

Nobody ever admitted killing my father. There was a coroner's inquiry but you have to remember the context of the times. There was over 400 people killed in 1972; some days there were four or five people killed. The verdict was death by misadventure. After my father's death I was never back in the Deerpark Road. It would only have been a matter of time for us to be targeted, particularly with me being in Long Kesh. In hindsight a Catholic family with members involved in republican politics or military activity should have got out if it lived in a mixed area but that did not happen in those days. But afterward, we all moved out of the house. In some respects I believe that my father sacrificed his life for us. Some other members of our family were going to be killed in that house at some point.

My father's death impacted on the whole family but probably worst on my younger brother Joseph. At that time there was just myself and my brothers Martin and Joseph still living at home. Joseph ended up going to live in Dublin with my brother Eamon. In many respects I think it had the longest and deepest-lasting effect on Joseph. A few years ago he had a mental breakdown. There were a number of things involved in it but to me it was a lot to do with when my father was killed. Joseph was only 16 at the time and I think it left him with long-term emotional hurt. My mammy was 53 when my father was killed and she half died after it. I think her life was shortened by my daddy's death. The only support network we had was our own but I think that was sufficient. I am not sure I rate counselling as that important. I think some of the ways that they are doing things is demoralising and insulting. Am I supposed to apply to the memorial fund for a grant for a computer or something because my father was killed 28 years ago? I think that sort of thing is ridiculous and insulting. I think if the conflict is finally over they need to build a big monument to all the people who were killed. They should get guns from the Brits, the loyalists and the IRA, cut them up and melt them in a big pot. Then make a big sculpture out of that. Don't put any name on it; just make it a monument to everyone.

People talk about justice but what is justice? There were so many people who were killed and had to move here in North Belfast because of the conflict. Justice cannot be about vengeance; bitterness can destroy what is inside you. There were a lot of people involved in the 'Official' IRA and the 'Provisional' IRA at the time who were very young. There were a lot then who had little in the way of a political thought in their head. Many of them have matured now and see the need for politics. But there were a lot of stupid things done at that time, a lot of mistakes made within the whole republican family. People in the 'Officials' did nasty things to people in the 'Provisionals' and vice versa. There were people hurt, mistakes made. There were people shot as informers who were not informers and afterwards apologies were made. In any conflict that is going to happen. In any conflict it is the innocent who suffer. I would have to put it like this. If someone could explain what happened so I could understand the circumstances that would not make me sad.

Martin Rosato (son)

My father was born in 'Little Italy', Belfast. There used to be a lot of Italian families that lived around the Docks area, in Nelson Street. At home they would have spoken Italian. I know Italian families who still do to this day. My father was a terrazzo worker most of his life. There were a lot of the Italians that used to work at that. It was a bit of a family tradition but it was hard work; there was no romance in it. I remember as a child going out with my father on jobs and it was hard work. But a lot of my father's time was taken up with us children as we were growing up. My father didn't drink very often and he spent a lot of the time around the house when he wasn't working. He had plenty of friends that would be round to visit but for my father the family was the most important thing. Maybe it is to do with Italian tradition. He spent a lot of time with us. I remember he used to take us for long walks up the Cave Hill and Ligoniel Park. He loved cooking and that rubbed off on all of us children. He would make various Italian dishes, meats, pastas and other things too. He made lovely Spanish omelettes. He was always doing DIY round the place as well. When I think of my father I can never once remember a harsh word between him and my mother. That has always stuck in my mind. He was a very caring person, not selfish in any way. Maybe it was to do with their experiences growing up that our parents brought us up as best they could – although my father never had a chip on his shoulder about being in the home after his mother died. To me my daddy was the ideal father.

In the period around the death of my father loyalist groups were carrying out a lot of sectarian killings. Catholics were being kidnapped at random on their way to and from work and being killed. I knew quite a few people, friends I went to school with and people connected with the GAA in Ardoyne, that were kidnapped and butchered by loyalists. There was a young fella called Charlie Watson who I went to school with. He was pulled out of a taxi just below the Bone on the Oldpark Road and murdered the next morning. That was just over a week before my father was killed [Charlie Watson, killed by the UDA, July 11 1972]. There was Frank Corr, a well-known guy in the GAA. He was murdered shortly after my father [Frank Corr, killed along with James McGerty on his way to work, 26 July 1972. A few years after, Ciaran Murphy was killed and I knew his brother really well [Ciaran Murphy, killed by the UVF, 13 October 1974]. Those sorts of things all stick in your mind. The day my father died always stays in people's memories as 'Bloody Friday'. Of course I remember it because of my father but not just that. I also remember watching the early evening news and the graphic, horrible pictures of people blown up and being shovelled into plastic bags. A lot of horrible things have happened but it was one of the days of the troubles that stays in your mind. One thing that always got up my nose though was that things were always reported with an anti-republican bias in the press and the papers. There was always a lot made of whatever the IRA did but not so much when it was loyalists. They would be referred to as 'terrorists' rather than by the name of the group. So people from outside could think that those deaths were down to the IRA too. It was like the press in the 1920s, the blame for things was always put on Catholics/nationalists.

At the time my father died I had a temporary job with the civil service. On that day, 21 July 1972, I had been sent over to East Belfast. It was terrible going through the city at that time, the UDA had roadblocks everywhere. They used to get on the bus intimidating people, selling you their papers. You were afraid to look sideways at them. So when I got into town I went up to my brother Tony's place near the university because I heard there had been bombs everywhere. It was there that I remember watching the news of all the bombs and the people killed. Later that evening we went out for a walk in the university area, had a couple of bottles of Guinness, then went back to his house to watch a late night movie. Then there was a knock at the door. Tony was always very security conscious and made sure before he opened the door who was there. It was the Catholic chaplain from the university. He came in and told us there had been a shooting incident involving our father. We were confused and thought at first he had been one of the people caught up in the bombings. He did not tell us at that stage that our father was dead. So we got into Tony's car with his wife and a friend and drove up to the Deerpark Road.

When we got to the house there were two soldiers outside. We told them we were sons of the man shot and one of them just said, 'Oh, the man's dead' – just so matter of fact. So that was how we found out; it was a brutal way to be told. The way the rest of the family found out was hard too. Kevin was in Long Kesh and heard it on the radio, another brother living in Dundalk found out the same way. My brother Gerard was on a bus from Galway back to Belfast and a friend of his had bought a copy of the *Belfast Telegraph*. By the time Tony and I got to the house there was no one there. My mother and Joseph had gone to my older sister in Kilcoo, Ballysillan. We decided to drive to my sister's house but were diverted from the Cavehill Road into the Sunningdale estate by the British army at a roadblock. UDA men came out with hoods over their heads and stopped the car. My brother Tony's friend who was with us had Irish parents but was brought up in London so he talked to them. They must have thought we were soldiers or something because they just pulled the hoods off and directed us back onto the Cavehill Road. After spending some time with my mother we went back down to Jamaica Street in Ardoyne. There had been some shooting going on there and a shot was fired by a British soldier at my brother Tony. You could pick up army messages on the television and we heard them say just after that they had shot a gunman in Jamaica Street. That just shows what happens. The poison had already been set in and the media would have taken up their version. If our Tony had been shot dead then they would have had him down as 'just another gunman'.

We found out later about the circumstances of the shooting of my father. Apparently there had been a road block a short distance from the house up until about a half hour before the shooting. My mother told me that a car had driven up and down the street several times. She was upstairs when a knock came at the door. She looked out the window and shouted out, 'Don't open the door'; but sometimes my father was a little hard of hearing and he may not have heard her properly. He may have then opened the door a bit and somebody tried to force their way into the house. I have been told that whoever it was asked for me by name. When he realised something was wrong my father tried to get the door closed. My brother Joseph came running out from the backroom and between them I think they got the door closed. I have been told that there were five of these men altogether; one was at the door and the other four were in the car. One of those got out of the car and stood at the fence at the bottom of the garden. It was only a small garden so he was no more that about ten metres away. Then he fired one shot, it went through the glass panel of the door and hit my father in the leg. As a result he bled to death because the bullet hit a main artery. The shot might have been fired randomly or it might have only intended to frighten. After asking for me by name, I don't know if it was their intention to shoot me, kidnap me or what. It is all water under the bridge now.

As far as who was responsible for my father's death I personally have no agenda in saying that it was this group or that group. In a book by Martin Dillon, *Political Murders in Northern Ireland*, he doesn't get his facts right and does not give a reasonable account of the incident. For example, he says there was a volley of shots fired at my father when in fact only one shot was fired. He said my father was a restaurant owner when he was always a terrazzo worker. He also made completely unsubstantiated and wrong accusations against my older brother. What he said is just not reliable. Cheap journalism has always helped the state by muddying the waters. I think the media have used the stories of the bereaved when it has suited them and not bothered with others because they happened in dubious circumstances. It is as if a family like ours, that had people involved in the republican movement, doesn't have the same rights as everyone else. Our family have been given assurances by different people living locally that it was a particular loyalist from Glenbryn that was responsible. Anyway, I am not seeking vengeance because we are supposed to be going through a peace process and reconciliation. For my own satisfaction I might want to know who did it but I am not interested in names or anything like that. Personally I never believed it was the IRA who were responsible for my father's death. My brother Tony did stand up at the inquest and blamed members of a rival republican group. That's why the media latched on to that version of events, for their own agenda.

There are a number of reasons why I don't think that is so. As the troubles were getting bad, and particularly after Kevin was arrested, we had pleaded with father to move out of there because it was in a hot spot. That is why I wasn't actually living in the house at the time. If it was people looking for me then anyone who knew me would have known that I wasn't in the house then. I usually stayed over where it was safer, either in Glenard or in the university area. The night before I had been in a club in Ardoyne, so if someone had wanted to get me why didn't they do it then? In addition, after the bombings that had happened that day, it doesn't make sense that the IRA would have gone out that night to shoot or kidnap someone. They would have been lying low and not risking weapons. As far as the evidence about the car is concerned, I got a letter from a friend of mine shortly after with the registration number in it. I was in Dublin then because after my father's funeral my mummy wanted me to get out of Belfast. The first thing you think is that because it was stolen in the Free State that it was down to some republican group. But things are not that simple. There is a lot of skulduggery involved with people (paramilitary and otherwise) robbing cars, bringing them over the border and re-selling them. So we just don't know. No one admitted killing my father. The IRA issued statements at the time to the local papers specifically denying it. No one has ever admitted it and no one has ever been charged. Nobody from the authorities has come to either me or anyone in my family in relation to any investigation. I don't think justice was done because I think it suited the authorities after the suggestion was made that my father had died because of a feud to just let sleeping dogs lie.

As far as threats from loyalists against us went, all the Rosatos would have been well-known around Ardoyne, the Bone and Cliftonville. But we would also have been well-known in the Protestant areas of Glenbryn and Alliance as well. We lived right on the edge of Alliance. I was threatened by a bunch of loyalists walking past me in the street one time in 1970. That was after I appeared on TV at a picket outside the American consulate. On another occasion some of them shouted at me from a passing car while I was heading up toward my parents house on the Deerpark. I told my father and he went up and gave the details of what had happened to the RUC at the Oldpark station. I have always had a lingering doubt that maybe a rogue cop went back to the local loyalists and told them that some of them could be pinpointed. Maybe it was that simple, that they came to get me because of that. They wouldn't have had intelligence on me so would have thought that I was still in the house. Local IRA personnel would have done their homework beforehand. For those reasons I don't think it was the IRA.

Still, it doesn't surprise me that there were so many unsolved murders at that time. If we are talking about truth and justice now what we need is a level playing field. I have no doubt that a lot of the murders have a very sinister side. There were people from different factions of the security and military establishments with different agendas. There were plain-clothed soldiers going out and murdering people because it suited them to keep the pot boiling. It is important to know if there has been collusion because the state authorities are supposed to be the ones who are the guardians of law and order. The key thing is accountability. But in the case of my father's death the RUC never approached us and asked us for a statement. But someone once said to me that if they gave me a gun and told me who shot my father could I shoot them; I said 'no'. I'm not trying to paint myself as a saint but what good would it do? It just leads to a vicious spiral of vendetta and vengeance and that doesn't get any of us anywhere. I want to make it clear that I have no agenda here. It is possible that it was the loyalists who killed my father. There is a possibility that it was the IRA, though I don't believe that. But if it was them then, yes, I would like them to tell me and that would be another chapter in our lives closed.

Patrick O'Neill
Killed by loyalists,
Forthriver Drive,
22 July 1972

Paddy was one of a kind, a real super lad who can never be replaced. Not only was Jamaica Street affected by his death, the whole of Ardoyne was.

Patrick O'Neill's parents were Rose (née Doherty) and Hugh O'Neill. They married, had Patrick and lived in Jamaica Street. Both had children from previous marriages. Hugh was a furniture dealer and Rose had a stall in the market. Patrick went to Holy Cross Boys and St Gabriel's school. His work and hobbies revolved around cars. Patrick loved traditional Irish music and travelled regularly to fleadhs throughout Ireland. He didn't smoke or drink but enjoyed socialising with his mates in the Wheatfield Bar. His friends describe him as a very generous, happy-go-lucky person. On 22 July 1972 after a night out in Kelly's Cellars Bar Patrick and his friend Rose McCartney (from Iris Drive), were abducted and killed by the UDA/UFF in a brutal sectarian attack. Their bodies were found dumped in a car in the Glencairn estate. Both had been shot several times and Patrick's body showed signs of having been beaten. Patrick was 23 years old at the time of his death.

Martin McIlroy (cousin)

Hugh, Paddy's father was married to my great aunt Rose Doherty. Rose died about 1967. Hugh died about two years after that. I stood for Paddy when he was confirmed. Paddy was a good kid who was really into cars. He could take a car apart and put it back together. His passion was driving. He never smoked, drank or gambled. If he went to the bar with his mates he drank a glass of lemonade. He was full of life but quiet in his own way. I never ever saw him getting into a fight. He used to drive the lorry for his daddy and they did the markets together. His daddy was known as big Clute O'Neill and he was a dealer in furniture. Paddy was an all-round good guy who liked a bit of a laugh and joke. Driving was his love and driving was his sport. I was only in London about a week and I got a telephone call that Paddy had been murdered. I jumped straight on a plane and came back home for the funeral. Paddy was waked from his sister's house in Havana Street. When I was told of Paddy's death I was in total shock and just couldn't believe it. Paddy was one of the closest people to me murdered during the troubles. He was really well-liked by everyone and all who knew him sorely miss him.

Anthony Keenan (friend)

Paddy O'Neill came from the same street as myself, Jamaica Street. Jamaica Street was full of great people. It was a street of champions, there were footballers and boxers and there was hurling too; the Maguire brothers Tommy and Harry were County Antrim players. So many great people came from Jamaica Street and Paddy was certainly one of the champions. Paddy's father was called Hugh and he was a dealer in furniture and antiques. He went to markets all over the country and Paddy went with him. Paddy's parents were very quiet, respectable people and very well-liked. They kept themselves to themselves. He was very close to his family, his mother, father and sisters. In particular he was very close to his father and went everywhere with him. His father got the nickname Clute O'Neill. Paddy was the darling of his mother and father and they loved him to bits.

Paddy was a quiet lad when he was young. My memory of him was that he was full of life and he loved life. He had a heart of gold. Paddy loved cars; in fact that was Paddy's life, cars. He was always fixing them up; he was an expert in my opinion and would have made a brilliant mechanic. He was a man who bought a car one day and sold it the next. After a day's work Paddy would come home and say, 'Right lads, where are we going?' He bought us to places like Carrick or Larne for a drive. Paddy was the first to buy the fish and chips you didn't have to ask twice. He was a giver, never a taker. This was in the early 60s and not a lot of people had money and there weren't many cars in Jamaica Street. Every time you saw him he had a smile on his face. He was always happy, just a happy go-lucky type of chap.

Paddy loved folk music. He was coming from Kelly's Cellars the night he was killed. He was a good-looking fella and a real lady's man. He went with some good-looking girls. Paddy never drank; if he sold a car he used to take the lads out for a drink and he drank Coke. He took us to the Wheatfield, that was our old local then. There was me and my brother Billy and Willie Mallaghan, John Mulgrave, old Hugh Murphy and a few others from Jamaica Street.

The troubles of 1969 had an effect on Paddy just like it did on the rest of us. Paddy had no fear and you never had to ask him to do a thing twice. He loved the people of Ardoyne and would have done anything for them. He helped Catholic families who were intimidated out of their homes by loyalists. We all went with him and helped move their furniture. It was dangerous; we had to go into loyalist areas like Ballysillan. This was round the 1969, '70 and '71 period and Paddy had the big van. He was always ready and willing to help someone out, even if it threatened his own safety. Ardoyne then was totally under siege and people were going through real rough times from every angle. Ardoyne has always been the kind of community where everyone sticks together and people generally get along.

The actual night he died he was with a girl called Rose McCartney, but I didn't know her. They had been drinking in Kelly's Cellars; there was a folk session on that night. He was brutally murdered. It was a terrible shock for all of us who knew him. I couldn't believe it and I just couldn't get over the way he was brutally murdered. All I could think of was his lovely smiling face in front of me. I was totally shocked. Everybody was shocked. Paddy still lived in Jamaica Street right up until his death but was waked in his sister's house in Havana Street. He was buried from Ardoyne chapel and crowds of people attended his funeral. It was a very sad occasion; people were just breaking down in tears all around you. In fact I think it really affected the whole community. The turn-out for his funeral was great, which he really deserved. Paddy was one of a kind, a real super lad who can never be replaced. Paddy was very witty and funny. The only way I could describe him is he was the most loving generous person I have ever met.

Sadie Grieve (friend)

I came to know Patrick through the Ardoyne Relief Committee centre, which was based in Toby's Hall in Butler Street. We first met when the men were interned because Paddy drove the Long Kesh bus. We decided to try and buy a bus to go up to Long Kesh. At that time it was dangerous going up and down to the Kesh. Paddy and Vera McKenna and I went to see a man called Phil Curran, a member of the Ex-servicemen's Association. We went to see if we could get a donation. By the time we came out of his house he had given us the money to buy a bus. Paddy talked him round. First we were getting a couple of hundred and the next thing we got, I think, around five hundred pounds to buy a bus. The bus needed a lot of work done to it but Paddy knew people that could fix it. The bus was on the road about three or four weeks later. It took all the internees' wives and families to the Kesh. Then Paddy took us on trips to Dublin to collect clothes that were donated from the United States for prisoners' families. He was that type of a character. Many a night we were up to all hours separating clothes in the wee shop in Butler Street. He was with us the first time nationalist people were in the city centre blocking the traffic and protesting. We went down Leeson Street, cut round by the Tech and we ended up in Royal Avenue and that was the first time nationalist people were in the centre protesting. There was Kathleen Carmichael, Vera McKenna, Pat Fox and Betty Haughey. At that time Paddy was always there for us.

I was down South when he was murdered. He didn't deserve the death that he got; it was terrible. The Shankill Butchers were blamed for it but nobody was ever charged with it. A very bitter feeling was left behind. His whole family went to pieces over his death. He was with a young girl called Rose McCartney; the loyalists killed them both. God help her family too.

Charles McNeill
Killed by (unknown),
Brompton Park,
14 August 1972

He was a great man ... he wouldn't have hurt a fly. The British soldiers shot him; that's all I know. If you'd met him, you would have just loved him. Everybody liked him...

Charles McNeill's parents were John McNeill from North Queen Street and Mary (née O'Connell), originally from County Mayo. The couple had six children: Charles, John, Francie, Jimmy, Mary Catherine and Margaret. Charles attended St Columban's school in the Bone. He met his wife-to-be Kathleen late in life; they married in Holy Cross chapel and set up home in Brompton Park. They had no children. For most of his adult life Charles was a docker. He was a quiet man and kept himself very much to himself. By all accounts he was a good neighbour, well respected and liked by everyone.

On 14 August 1972 there had been a gun battle between the IRA and British army. Charles, who was partially deaf, came to his front door. Several shots rang out. Charles was shot twice and killed. The IRA issued a statement the next day denying the killing of Charles McNeill. Although no one has ever admitted killing Charles

McNeill some members of his family believe the British army killed him. To this day his family do not know the exact circumstances of his death and who was responsible for his killing. Charles was 68 at the time of his death. On the previous day, loyalists killed a very close friend of Charles, Thomas Madden. He had been stabbed 110 times. His badly mutilated body was found dumped in a doorway on the Oldpark Road.

Family members

Charlie was a very quiet man; he enjoyed walking, watching football and indulged in a drink once in a while. He married Kathleen; she died before him and they didn't have any children. He attended mass regularly; he wasn't involved in politics and was not one for expressing his beliefs.

On the day Charlie was killed he was sitting at home. From his window he saw a young nephew and he went out to the front door to give him a candy rock that he had brought back from holidays. He went outside to find a gun battle going on; shots were fired from the direction of Etna Drive. A British soldier who was in the garden of 168 Brompton Park was shot. There was another soldier several doors up on the opposite side of the street that opened fire while running to the injured soldier. Charles was shot at this point. Another burst of gunfire followed from Etna Drive and the soldier who was in the garden of 168 returned fire.

The family believe that the IRA did not kill Charlie. We believe that the British soldier shot him before the IRA opened fire again. The ambulance arrived within five minutes and attended to Charlie after the soldier. There was a small piece reported in the *Irish News*. We were not aware of any inquest and believe that the killing was brushed aside. The truth was never fully established and the killing was not fully investigated. No one has ever been brought to justice for the murder of an innocent pensioner.

The family took the IRA's statement after the killing that it was not responsible in good faith and we still believe it to this day. The family have one question they would like answered: if the inquest was carried out fully and properly, why was the calibre of bullet used to kill Charlie not discovered? Surely there were spent bullet cartridges lying on the ground that would have determined if they belonged to the British army or the IRA.

Mrs Hunter (relative)

Charles came home from Bray that Saturday. There was trouble in Ardoyne and he went out to give the child a rock and the British soldiers shot him. He was over sixty and he couldn't see a finger in front of him; he wore double-rimmed glasses. You would have been dying about him, he was a great man. He was easily frightened. The least wee thing would have scared him. You could have told him anything and he would have more or less believed it. There was one time one of my nephews dressed up in old people's clothes and rapped the door and we were saying, 'Oh Charlie, who's that, who's that Charlie?' and he said, 'Oh, I'm not going to the door'. God help him, he nearly went into convulsions; he was really frightened. He was that type of person; he wouldn't have hurt a fly.

The British soldiers shot him; that's all I know. He was like a big soft child, that's just what he was. If you'd met him, you would have just loved him. He never really bothered much with anyone apart from his own relations. He always came over to my husband's mother's house; they kept very great. He had three brothers – Francie, John and Jimmy – and two sisters – Mary Catherine and Margaret. They are all dead now, so really he has no immediate family living. He was married late in life and he didn't have any children. He was like a big, quiet child, that's what he was. Everybody liked him; he didn't bother with one. Charlie would have been the last person to join up in anything. For years in and years out he worked down in the docks. The whole immediate family is now deceased.

Due to the difficulties in getting interviews regarding the death of Charles McNeill we have included extracts form statements of three British soldiers who were on duty the day he was killed. The statements are taken from Public Record Office files. It is clear from the statements that there are a number of inaccuracies in their version of events.

Corporal John Michael Nicholls (British soldier, 1st Light Infantry)

On 14 August 1972, about 17.20 hours, I was on duty in Brompton Park, as part of a routine patrol proceeding in the direction of Flax Street. A woman came up towards us; as she passed me she put a paper to her mouth and said that 'they' were waiting for us. She was about 60 years old, wearing a grey coat. Just after she said this I heard two rounds of high velocity fire. Pte. Haig of my unit called me over to him; he was in Brompton Park, outside No.1 Etna Drive. I went over to him and then heard a burst of automatic fire, 8-10 rounds, coming from the waste ground in Flax Street, apparently at the main body of our patrol. Haig told me that he had seen a man in No. 5 Etna Drive. I took two men and went to the rear of this house. Six or seven children of about six to eight years came out of the house and one of them said, 'The bastard nearly had me in the head'. I saw about 20 to 30 men standing on the corner of Brompton Park and Jamaica Street,; they were laughing. I stayed in position at the rear of the house while 34A joined us. They searched the house with negative results. In between the two shots and the automatic fire I heard one round of high velocity fire from the direction of Etna Drive.

Lance Corporal Martin Sidney Vigus (British soldier, 1st Light Infantry).

On 14 August 1972, about 17.20 hours, I was on duty in Brompton Park, Belfast, as third man on the left side of a routine patrol going down Brompton Park towards Flax Street. I heard one round of high velocity fire which came from Etna Drive. There was an elderly man in the garden of 170 Brompton Park; he was directly opposite me when he was hit by the round that I had heard. I saw blood going through the air and heard a woman shout, 'He's hit'. I took cover in the garden of 168 and then heard two shots from behind me. These must have been the ones fired by Pte. Finn of my unit. About ten seconds later I heard another round of high velocity and someone shouted that my tail-end Charlie had been hit. That was Pte. Finn. I attempted to go to his aid but a Thompson, or some automatic weapon, began firing in my direction, forcing me back into cover. The fire came from waste ground in Flax Street. A civilian ambulance took the wounded civilian away.

Sergeant John Thomas Reah (British soldier, 1st Light Infantry)

On 14 August, about 17.10 hours, I was the commander of a 13-man foot patrol. I was armed with an SLR and a magazine of 20 rounds. We were mobile along Brompton Park heading towards the junction of Havana Street and Jamaica Street. I was in the lead position on the left hand side and Pte. Finn was in the rear left hand side position. There were six men on the left and seven men on the right. I took up position in the front garden of No. 172 Brompton Park; the remainder of the patrol were in the process of deploying themselves on both sides of the road. I was in this position for about 60 seconds covering the area of Etna Drive and the waste ground of Havana Street, when I heard three high velocity rounds being fired from the direction of junction between Berwick Road and Brompton Park. Every member of the patrol automatically took cover. At the time of the first shooting there was a total of about 100 women and children standing in the immediate area. After the shots they were all running and shouting and taking cover. I tried to locate the gunman at our rear but could not. It was at this time the second burst of gunfire was directed at our position. It was fired from the direction of the waste ground at the bottom of Havana Street. It was a burst of automatic low velocity fire which I believe to be a Thompson sub-machine gun. I think it was a total of five rounds which I believe all struck the centre of Brompton Park. I tried to locate this gunman but could not. I enquired as to whether any of my men were injured. Pte. Haig, who was on the opposite side of the street, informed me that Finn had been hit. Pte. Finn was located in the front garden of No. 160 Brompton Park. I attempted to get to Finn's position by running up the garden path of 172 Brompton Park. As I got to my feet and started to run up the path I came under fire from the direction of Etna Drive; it was a total of three low velocity rounds, again fired by an automatic weapon, which I believe to be a Thompson sub-machine gun. The three rounds missed me but two of them hit a civilian male aged between 50 and 60 who was standing on the front door step of No. 170 Brompton Park. I jumped the garden hedge into No. 170 Brompton Park and I saw the male civilian lying in the doorway bleeding from the upper part of the body. As I cleared the hedge, three more high velocity rounds were fired from the area of Berwick Road and Brompton Park. I do not know where the rounds struck but they were close. Simultaneously a further burst of automatic fire came from the area of No.5 Etna Drive. This was a burst of about eight rounds of again Thompson sub-machine gun. I could not see where the rounds struck. By the time the last burst had ceased I had reached Pte. Finn's position. Pte. Chapman was already in attendance. I could see Finn had been hit in the region of the base of his spine. I did not attempt to dress his wound because it was too serious for an unqualified person to attempt. The radio operator had in the meantime radioed for an ambulance. The ambulance, which was an APC, arrived two minutes later. The RMO, Capt. Cried, was in attendance and conveyed Pte. Finn to the R.V.H. After the wounded had left the scene Cpl. Tabuvaka of my unit arrived and carried out a search of No. 5 Etna Drive which was believed to be the location of one of the gunmen. Nothing was found in the house. The patrol then regrouped and we returned to our HQ.

Joseph McComiskey
Killed on active service
by the British army,
Flax Street,
20 September 1972

Joseph McComiskey's father Joe was originally from Mayo and a soldier in the Irish army. He left the army, married Bridget (née Hutchie) and set up home in Ardoyne. The couple had five children Joseph, Jim, Martin, Paul and Mary. Joseph was the eldest son, born September 12, 1954. He attended Bearnageeha School on the Antrim Road and like most of his peers left without qualifications. He was a keen footballer, played handball and was a member of the Ardoyne Accordion Band. He was close to his brothers and sister and was always one for playing pranks. Joseph was popularly known as Josie.

On 20 September 1972 Joseph was accompanying a female comrade who was carrying a concealed weapon under her coat. The gun was not assembled, nor it was ready for use. It was when they crossed the brickyard that Joseph was shot and killed by the British army. Joseph was a member of na Fianna Éireann. He was 18 years old at the time of his death.

Ray McCann (friend)

Joseph was just like any other normal kid. As far as I can gather Joseph was down at the bottom of Brompton Park at the old Shamrock Club when he was killed. In those days there used to be a little bridge there and the Shamrock Club was a small green hut. Joseph was shot once and he fell down. He tried to get up again and he was shot in the head the second time. I think his brother Jim was there at the time. Somebody ran up to Mrs McComiskey and told her that her son had been shot. A few people ran down to the scene. Jim lifted him up but he was already dead. The British army killed him. I think basically that it tore the family apart. His father hit the drink and got a bit difficult with his family. I don't know what influence it might have had on the other younger brothers and sister. His younger brother committed suicide. I know that that was in relation to his girlfriend but Joseph's death probably had some sort of effect on him. I think that for a while Jim, Martin and Mary lost all interest in life. That's what it seemed like to me. I think they have had one tragedy after another and they just lost that drive for life.

Joe Stewart (eyewitness)

There was a crowd of us standing outside the laundrette at the bottom of Brompton Park. There was about ten of us. Josie McComiskey was shot on the waste ground facing us. It was before the new houses were built. I heard shots being fired and I saw the young lad falling. People were frightened to run over because he was shot from the observation post at the mill in Flax Street. I was one of the first persons to run over to Josie and he was already dead when I reached him. I took my jean jacket off and put it over him. It took a long time for the ambulance to arrive and the Brits didn't arrive on the scene until about half an hour after the shooting. The British observation post looks over Ardoyne and it was obvious that the shots came from the post.

The British army claimed that he was armed. There was no gun visible at the scene, no gun whatsoever. I found out later that the girl Josie was with had a weapon concealed up her coat. I did not see this weapon at the time. But eve so, it was not a threat, and certainly young Josie wasn't. Earlier that day there was a shooting incident in the direction of the Bone. There may have been a gun battle between British soldiers and the IRA. Something definitely happened. I witnessed Josie coming from the direction of the Bone towards Ardoyne along with a girl. Suddenly shots rang out. That was it. Josie fell. The British army claimed he had a gun but I was one of the first ones on the scene. He had no gun.

Jim McComiskey (brother)

Joseph was just a typical wee boy. He would have gone to the dances and he had a couple of girlfriends. He was a lively wee lad and would have done anything for fun.

On the day of Joseph's death he was walking past the mill. The British soldier in the observation post opened fire and shot him. He shot him in the face. Joseph got up and was shot in the back of the head. I saw him and ran up and told my mother. There were a lot of people around that day and I don't think there was any rioting. There were people standing at the corners; it was just a normal day for Ardoyne. A policewoman came and informed the family of Joseph's death. They didn't give us any problems. But my mother wouldn't let them in; that's Bridget for you. A lot of people came to the house after his death.

Joseph's death had a very bad impact on the family. He was the oldest in the house and it hit us hard. We found it hard to cope with. I always think the soldier that killed Joseph got to go home but Joseph is dead. There was no justice done. Nobody came and offered us any support after Joseph's death. In a way it ruined my own life. It was hard for my mummy. Then our Paul committed suicide and that devastated my mummy.

> *The only good thing was that our Gerry didn't know what happened to him when he was shot. That night when we went into the morgue and they took the sheet back, his eyes were still open as if he was staring up the road.*

Gerry Gearon
Killed by the UFF,
Crumlin Road,
30 November 1972

Gerry Gearon was from Glenbryn Park. Born in 1950, he was the second youngest of eight children, with five brothers and two sisters. Gerard's mother, Lily, was a McLaughlin from Elmfield Street. His father Tommy was from Mayfair Street in the Oldpark. They set up home first in Brompton Park and then in Glenbryn Park where the family was to live for 36 years. That ended when they were put out of their home by loyalists during the violence that erupted when internment was introduced on 9 August 1971. By then Gerry had already finished his education at the Holy Cross Boys school and St Gabriel's. At the age of 15 he went to work as a barman in McGlade's Bar in Donegall Street. He briefly worked in Peter's Bar in Gresham Street, and for a time he moved away to a job in Dublin. Hobby-wise Gerry liked to go to the pictures or swimming. He was also active as a youth worker. Gerry loved a game of snooker too. That is what he had been doing on the night he was shot dead. Homesick, Gerard had come back to Belfast after only a few months in Dublin. The manager of McGlade's offered him his old job back and he started on the evening of Wednesday 30 November 1972. After his shift, Gerry went off to play snooker at the 'Hibs' club. Then he went to get a taxi from Arkle Taxis at the bottom of Clifton Street. Gerry got into a taxi with two other men. They were both members of the UFF. As the taxi passed the Mater Hospital, one of the men feigned illness. The two gunmen then got out and shot into the taxi wounding the driver and killing Gerard. It was a nakedly sectarian attack. Gerry Gearon was only 22 years old. He was killed simply because he was a Catholic.

Philip Gearon (brother)

Gerry was only a year or so older than myself, so we grew up together. As two brothers Gerard and me had our ups and downs but there was never a real argument between us. There was one time he came in drunk, when we were still living in Glenbryn. I was sitting sober and I said, 'If you don't sit down, I'm knocking you down'. Then I did. He was still lying there the next morning! We were close because of our age and our Gerry had a fantastic personality. He could get on and work with anyone, except me! Gerard was very, very popular. He had the sort of personality that nobody could dislike. If you fell out with Gerry, half an hour later it was over and things were great again. He was very witty. Gerry used to run about with Fr. Ailbe and Fr. Marcellus, they used to go for a drink together. One night they were sitting in our Noel's [brother] house in Herbert Street. Gerry fell asleep and Fr. Marcellus got soot from the chimney and put big strokes of it on Gerry's face. Fr. Marcellus had to say 7.30 am mass so they woke Gerry up and all headed off to the chapel together. Gerry was sitting there with big black marks on his face as Fr. Marcellus was saying the mass. He could hardly keep his face straight. But Gerry loved my mummy and was very close to her. When he had a drink on him he used to sit on her knee, kissing, hugging and torturing her! They were very close. By 1972 my mummy and daddy were living in Cranbrook. We had been put out of Glenbryn in 1971. It had been a case of 'get out or be burnt out', so the whole Catholic population left. They actually moved in with me at first because I was just getting married in 1971. Gerard was my best man. His speech was very simple because Gerry was quiet. He was jolly but he had a quiet nature. He was always the one way, friendly and jolly.

He liked playing snooker when he started working in town. He used to knock about with a lot of the fellas who worked as barmen in the town. They would have been his friends. Gerry was a barman all his life. Me and Gerard worked together in McGlades but I was off the night he was murdered. He had come back from Dublin just before that night. That was because he had a girlfriend and he was missing her. The last time I saw Gerard was a couple of days before he died. It was me that told him that Paddy Cullen [the bar manager] wanted him back and that was the last time I saw him. I found out Gerard was dead when Joe Shepherd [the owner of Arkle Taxis] came to my door. They thought that it was actually me who had been shot. This was about 1.30 am, 30 November 1972. I was the first of the family to know Gerry was shot. Then I went up to get my daddy and brother Noel in Cranbrook.

What happened to Gerard was this. He had been working up in McGlade's and at closing time he went to a wee club next door, the City Hibs Club, for a drink and a game of snooker. When he left there, he walked up to Arkle Taxis in Clifton Street, just above North Queen Street. As usual he walked in and said to the girl that worked in the office, 'Right Mary, a taxi for Ardoyne'. Mary said that a taxi was coming. There were two fellas sitting there and they said to Gerard, 'Would you mind us sharing your taxi?' Now normally Gerard would have said no. But apparently that night he said, 'Go ahead; if you're going up to Ligoniel I can get out first'. So they drove off up the Crumlin Road. Outside where Ewart's House used to be, just down by Sugarfield Street, one of these fellas said that he had to be sick. The taxi driver pulled over and they started to get out. The taxi driver was just turning when he saw a gun getting pulled out and then they fired. The taxi driver told us later that Gerry just turned, looked at him, and slumped over. The taxi driver was hit too, but he managed to turn the car round in the middle of the road and get back down to Arkle Taxis.

The authorities didn't come out and notify me or my mother about Gerry being shot. The RUC never came out to the house then or later. They never told us anything about the investigation. They never came near the house. It was Joe Sheppard [owner of Arkle Taxis] who came and told us what had happened that night. Then he drove us down to the Royal Hospital. The doctors and nurses there told us that there was nothing that could be done for Gerard. We had to go to the Laganbank morgue. But when we got there and rang the bell there was nobody to let us in. So then we had to go round to Musgrave Street and the police brought us back round to identify the body. The inquest later said that the shot that killed Gerard had severed the main trunk of the arteries of the body and that he had drowned in his own blood. It delivered an open verdict: killed by person or persons unknown.

Nobody ever admitted responsibility for killing Gerard. A while later two gunmen went into that same taxi depot and shot dead Mary and another man [Mary Sheppard and William Hutton, killed by UFF in Arkle Taxis office, 23 November 1974]. Mary was the only one who could have identified the ones who killed Gerard and they went in and murdered her. Apparently one of the fellas who eventually did time for Mary's murder went to Scotland, came back a 'born again' Christian and gave himself up. He was charged with Mary's murder but not with Gerard's. Nobody was ever charged for Gerard's death. The family was never offered any support or counselling. Those were the worst times for assassinations but nobody ever got any support then. But I don't think it would have helped my brothers and sisters or my mother and father. After Gerry was killed that night they killed my mother as well. She took it very badly. A couple of years later she suffered a stroke and never smiled again. At the time we were all devastated and angry, though as time went on it sort of healed. It did split the family a bit. It made our Noel very bitter. He worked with Protestants for the Corporation but it made him very hard about things. Noel named his son Gerard after his brother. Within the community as a whole there was a sense of revulsion. Gerry's funeral was massive. I had never seen such a big funeral out of Ardoyne chapel. Because Gerry worked in McGlade's he knew all the English and Belfast press men and politicians. People went out of their way to do things for us at the time. All the neighbours rallied round, even people you did not know. The only good thing was that our Gerry didn't know what happened to him when he was shot. That night when we went into the morgue and they took the sheet back, his eyes were still open as if he was staring up the road.

Patricia Gearon (sister in law)

I was the last person in the family to see Gerard alive. He was standing at the bus stop that morning and he just waved across to me. He was happy, his usual self. He was only just back from Dublin. I remember Gerry's mother saying that when she was lying in her bed, the morning that Gerard was killed, she felt somebody pulling at her. This was before she heard he was shot. After Phil and Gerard's daddy went up to the morgue the doctor came round to the house at about 6.30 am. At this point we still thought that Gerry was just injured. When the doctor came to the door, his mummy started to scream and I could hear Irene [Gerard's sister] screaming too. That is how I knew that he was dead.

Irene Gearon (sister)

Our Gerry was a very happy-go-lucky fella. He loved kids; it was always him who played with the nephews and nieces. He was also very sentimental. He would always say to me, 'What's going to happen to mummy if I get married or anything?' He really did always worry about mum and dad. I often just said, 'Sure she'd get on with life, the same way she did when we all got married'. He would have even cried and would say, 'If anything ever happened to mummy or daddy what would I do?' Gerry loved going swimming and going to the pictures. He worked with young people along with Fr. Tony and young Fr. Marcellus. They worked with the youth in St Gabriel's school.

Gerard worked in McGlade's Bar, then in Peter's Bar, went back to McGlade's and then he went to Dublin. I think he only stayed there for a few months. When he went to Dublin he stayed with our Jimmy. He went on that much to Jimmy about how much he hated Dublin that Jimmy ended up saying to him to go home. To this day Jimmy blames himself for Gerry being murdered. Gerry came back home in November and the manager of McGlade's came up for him to see if he would go back to work in McGlade's again. He came back from Dublin on the Friday and the manager came up the following Tuesday. I remember everything so clearly because Gerry met me that Tuesday to say he would be starting work tomorrow and he gave me my Tracy's [Gerard's niece] birthday present as her birthday was the next day. He started back to work that Wednesday and was killed the same night.

Mummy always said to Gerry to let her know when he was staying out of the district. The night he was killed, daddy had said he was going to bed early as he had a bit of a cold on him. The next thing there was a knock on the door at 2 am. It was to say Gerry had been shot. We thought he had been shot in the leg or something. Our own doctor, who was very friendly with my daddy, came to the house shortly afterwards and it was him who broke the news to us. No one was ever charged with our Gerry's murder. There was another sad twist and we connected it with Gerry's death. The girl who was on the desk that night in the taxi depot [Mary Sheppard] gave a good description of the two fellas. Well, she was shot dead in the depot along with an old man from the Shankill around 18 months later. The only good thing was that our Gerry didn't know what happened to him when he was shot. He always had a terrible fear of dying like if the Shankill Butchers had got him. I know he would have cried for my mummy. That was just our Gerry.

Seamus Regan (friend)

I knew Gerry all my life, but I really got to know him through the youth scheme at St Gabriel's. We worked a lot with the kids and we became really close friends. He met Geraldine Hogg the same night I met my wife and as they were both very good friends, anytime we went out we went as a foursome. I was the only son in my family and Gerry just lived up the street from me. He came in and out of my house everyday. My mummy looked on him as one of her own. I'll never forget the morning I heard that he was murdered. You see, he went away to Dublin to work and I didn't know that he had come back a couple of days previous. So I was going out to work that morning and Bernadette Stafford stopped me to say that Gerry had been murdered. Our whole family took it very bad. It was like losing a brother. I still think of Gerry and the good fun and times we shared. You could not fall out with him; if any kind of argument ever did occur a few minutes later Gerry would simply have forgotten about it, so you had to do the same.

> *1972 was a very bad year, particularly for the Fianna in Ardoyne. We lost four members during this period, probably the biggest loss in the Fianna in the North at that time.*

Bernard Fox
Killed on active service
by the British army,
Brompton Park,
4 December 1972

Bernard 'Bocky' Fox was born in January 1956. His steeplejack father Francis (originally from Carrick Hill) had come to Ardoyne in 1934, when his family moved into Jamaica Street. His mother, Elizabeth, was a McCormack from the Short Strand. In 1945 they married and raised their eight children (four boys and four girls) in their home in Etna Drive. Bernard left St Gabriel's school in 1972 at the age of 16. He was a keen footballer and a regular snooker player at the Ardoyne working men's club. His early death would ensure that he never had the chance of a career. Like many others, Bernard Fox joined na Fianna Éireann in the early years of the conflict. Bernard was a month short of his 17th birthday when he was shot dead by the British army while on active service in late 1972.

Margaret Fox (sister)

My mummy was in O'Neill's shop in Etna Drive when she heard the shots. She didn't know that our Bernard was involved but she said, 'God, I hope that no one was injured or hurt'. Bernard was shot dead by the British army on 4 December 1972 at the top of

Brompton Park, where the bookies is today. The whole family were shocked and devastated when we heard the news. Bernard was so quiet. We had no idea that he was involved with the republican movement until after we were approached and asked if we wanted a military funeral for Bernard. Five months after Bernard was killed another member of the family, Gerard, was shot in the arm while in the Stewart's house at the bottom of Northwick Drive. Gerard had just got up to get a glass of milk in the kitchen when two bullets came through the window. The family thought it was the British army. They denied any involvement and said it was loyalists who had shot down Etna Drive.

Bernard Glennon (friend)

I can't really remember when I first met Bernard Fox. I grew up with him. It was as if he was always there. There was a gang of us who went around together. There was Bernard Fox, Gerard Fox (his brother), Geordie Thompson, James Cardy, Seamus Clarke, and Gerard Clarke, Jim and Denis Coleman, Albert McKeown, myself, Mickey, Gerry and Francie Glennon. The gang were always playing games like 'rally-oh' and 'cribby' and handball growing up in Ardoyne. We used to play cards on the street corners trying to copy the big fellas. And, of course, we played street football. When the troubles arrived, we also played 'snatch squads'. There were two sides. One took on the role of rioters and the others were the Brit snatch squad. We were sort of preparing for the riots that were then becoming a constant feature of Ardoyne. Bernard was a couple of years older than me and he always excelled in whatever sport we happened to be playing. He was a particularly gifted footballer. Everybody wanted to be on his team. At handball he was unbeatable. He was fiercely competitive, but in a fair way. He was a natural leader. Whenever the gang would meet, Bernard took the lead. He made the decisions. Bernard was looked upon as a guiding light of the group. He was wise beyond his years. They were wonderful and happy times. Bernard, of course, was always organising and in the thick of things. Everybody had nicknames. Bernard had the name of BOC. Others later called him 'Bocky'. He had a quiet calm nature but was also very determined in whatever he did. He was not a bragger or a show-off and he rarely lost his temper. Bernard was also very patient and quick to help others when they needed it. By the time Bernard was about 14 years old he became quite serious about politics and the constant British army harassment of the Ardoyne people. It was around then that he joined the na Fianna Éireann and became an extremely active member. Bernard was never far from the action. In the early 1970s, Ardoyne was a constant battleground between the people and the British army. All too often the district was also under loyalist attack. Bernard was often on 'standby', keeping watch for any loyalist attacks on the area. In those days the Fianna played an extremely active role in the republican struggle. Indeed, after internment day in 1971 some areas were so depleted of IRA volunteers that it was Fianna volunteers that kept the struggle alive.

I have never forgotten the day that Bernard was killed in action. I was staying in my aunt and uncle's house in Etna Drive. I was in bed at around 10:40 pm when I heard SLR fire. I think there were about three or four cracks. I never thought any more of it. In those days shootings in the area were almost a daily occurrence. However, about midnight, my cousin, Mickey Savage came in and said, 'Wee Gerard Fox has been shot'. My mind ticked over, and I thought, 'It must be Bernard!' It was impossible to sleep that night as my mind just jumbled over the news. I prayed and prayed. Eventually I drifted off to sleep. In the morning I had to get up for school. By then the news was clear that Bernard Fox had been shot and killed. I was too numbed and too shocked to do anything except go to school. On my way to St Gabriel's I walked up Brompton Park and stopped at the spot where poor Bernard had been killed. I started thinking about Bernard, and about his family, and how they must be feeling. Bernard's death shattered me. It must be remembered that the Ardoyne Fianna unit had lost four members inside a year. Bernard knew all the other Fianna members who were killed. Bernard Fox was a remarkable person. At the time of his death he was the OC of the local slua of the Fianna in Ardoyne. When it is considered that at that time the Fianna ranks had numerous volunteers, it is a glowing testimony to his leadership abilities. He had a full Fianna guard of honour. Bernard had been part of the guard of honour at the funeral of Joseph McComiskey when he was killed in September [Joseph McComiskey, killed by the British army near Flax Street, 20 September 1972]. His death left me without one of my oldest and best friends. We lost our carefree days when Bernard was gone. Bernard's family were totally devastated by his death. His mother Lizzie in particular never really got over his untimely death.

'Dutch' (friend and comrade)

I knew Bocky from school though not very well. We played football together. I got to know him a lot better in 1971 when I joined na Fianna Éireann, Bernard was already a member. Around then there was an election to choose our own staff. We would all talk between ourselves about who should be OC and it was clear to everyone that Bernard was the best person for this position. Bernard was a very good motivator. I suppose he was my first inspiration within the movement. He was a happy-go-lucky lad and had a nice way about himself. He was very popular with everyone. We asked Bernard to become OC but when the time came to elect the staff, Bernard told the lads to vote for another person as he was happy with the position he held as adjutant. In the not-too-distant future, though, Bernard would become OC of the Fianna in Ardoyne. 1972 was a very bad year, particularly for na Fianna in Ardoyne. We lost four members during this period, probably the biggest loss in na Fianna in the North at that time. David McAuley, Josh Campbell and Joseph McComiskey had all been killed [David McAuley, killed accidentally in Fairfield Street, 19 February 1972; Josh Campbell, killed by the British army in Eskdale Gardens, 11 June 1972]. What you have to remember is that some members of the Fianna would have been as active as some IRA volunteers in those days. Bernard would have been OC for most of this period. 1972 was a very traumatic year for everyone in the area but especially for the Fianna. Because of these three deaths, the IRA within the area were very reluctant to let the Fianna have any major input into IRA military operations. Some members of the Fianna were very angry at this decision and argued that they should be permitted to do more in the struggle. Bernard and myself, along with many other Fianna members, would have adopted the position that we were capable and willing enough to have a more direct military input. We didn't view ourselves as 'young boys' or not mature enough. We just saw that there was a job to be done and were committed enough to fulfil any task required.

On the particular night in question, 4 December 1972, we made our way to the point where the military operation was to take place. The three members of the Fianna were standing together at the top of Brompton Park where there used to be 'dragon's teeth' across the road. The IRA volunteer was on the other side of the street. After a number of shots were fired, I knew something was seriously wrong. What had happened was that the British army came up the Woodvale Road in a saracen. They had taken up position in the empty house. They would have been able to see everything as they were only about 20 or 30 yards away from us. I was in the middle, Bernard was to my right and the other Fianna member was on my left. When the shooting started, I looked to my right and saw Bernard fall. I remember looking at him. He was silent. I immediately wanted to help him and instinctively began to reach out to him. But I knew he was dead. I was completely shattered. My closest friend and comrade was shot dead right beside me. When I realised that there was no sense trying to move Bocky I turned to get out of the way of the ongoing British fire. Everything was happening so quickly. It was then that I heard the other Fianna member shout out, 'Don't leave me, don't leave me'. Unknown to me he had been shot and was lying unable to move. I could hear the bullets hitting the ground and the 'dragon's teeth'. So as I ducked down to run, I grabbed my comrade, dragged him down to the first door I saw open and told the woman to call an ambulance. To me what is amazing is that they did not shoot us all and to this day I still think their intention was to kill us all. Bernard was dead, another volunteer was hit in the leg and I was lucky to get away along with the other IRA volunteer. Bernard's death had a powerful impact on me. He was the first real close friend that I lost during the conflict. His family were also shattered. I suppose the pain and agony they went through is indescribable. How do you ever come to terms with something like that? Bernard was a big loss to everybody who knew him, especially his family. I was on the Fianna Éireann guard of honour at Bernard's funeral. It was a fitting tribute to a young man who loved his country but who unfortunately didn't live long enough to fulfil the massive potential he undoubtedly had.

Seamus Clarke (friend and comrade)

I grew up with Bernard; we were near enough brothers. We lived in the same street and his mother and mine were very close. We made our communions together, went to the same schools and knocked about with his cousin Patrick McAuley and Billy Cairns. Bernard was always a very good-natured fella and was very good to his mother, though, like the rest of us he always wanted to stay out during the troubles. We used to just hang around Glenard but Bernard started going round to old Ardoyne. Most of the 'stickies' ['Official' IRA) came from Glenard then but around 1971 I found out Bernard had joined the Fianna of the 'Provisionals'. I couldn't believe it at first because there used to be a bit of a grudge thing between Glenard and old Ardoyne. Obviously everything that had happened after 1969 had a big impact on Bernard. That is why he started going round to the old district and why he joined the Fianna. His family would not have known he had at first because he very much kept it a secret. Within the movement Bernard had a very strict attitude. He would tell you what to do but he always wanted to do it himself as well and do it right. He was always straight up and would be the first one out on the street if something needed to be done. I think one of the main reasons he was shot dead was because he always wanted to be there to do whatever was expected.

Bocky was not really interested in anything else apart from the Fianna and the 'RA. When we were asked who we wanted to take over as OC of the Fianna, we all said there was nobody else but Bocky because he was always fair with people.

The Fianna of 1971 and 1972 were just as active as IRA volunteers. The 'RA couldn't move in Ardoyne without the Fianna. They would be scouting, standing beside the volunteer if shells had to be lifted or involved in providing cover. Whenever there was a job to be done Bernard would be there. Through the Defence group, Fianna boys also started handling weapons. The Defence would have been more flexible than the 'RA in working with the Fianna. People may say that having young ones handling weapons was wrong but it was a fact of life in those days. We had to just learn things on the street. There were a lot of people being arrested and shot so the Fianna boys were the ones who were there. So before his death Bocky would have had experience with weapons and learnt from the older ones he was working and knocking about with. The IRA got to trust and like him. I ended up leaving the Fianna for the IRA before Bocky because the IRA wanted him to go on as OC. They wanted him to stay because the role he and the Fianna were playing was so important.

The night Bernard was killed, myself and Rusty had just left him and few other members of the movement down at the old Shamrock. Bernard was that tight that you had a sense that something was going on, although he would not have said anything. I noticed he had one of the old Parka coats with the hoods on. So I knew he must have been on standby. So myself and Rusty headed home and that was the last time I saw Bernard alive. The next thing I knew was when Rusty came in to tell me that Bernard had been shot. I ran out of the house and up to Brompton Park. On the way some people told me that Bernard was badly wounded and was in an ambulance. When I got to the top of Brompton Park they were closing the ambulance doors so I did not get to see him. There was a big commotion because another Fianna boy had been hit and he was still down in a house in Brompton Park. I ran round to the Saunders club to let everyone know what was happening. Then all hell broke loose. There was even more of a reaction because a Fian had been killed. He was the fourth Fianna boy to be killed in Ardoyne that year so we were hit really badly.

Bernard's death hit his family very hard. When his mother died, she died of a broken heart. She just went downhill after Bernard's death because they were very close. The whole family were. I remember Bernard's funeral very well. Everyone wanted to be involved in the guard of honour and in the end it was a mix of Fianna boys and members of the Cumann na gCailíní [junior wing of Cumann na mBan) The funeral itself was really massive and was a real tribute to Bernard. The impact Bernard's death had on me was shattering. But it also made me more determined as a member of the 'RA to do as much as I could to help. I was always the one to volunteer for things after that. I just wanted to be continuously operating. When you lose four Fianna boys in an area like Ardoyne it affects the community as a whole. Bernard was only 16 years old when he was murdered so he never had the opportunity to grow old like the rest of us. I often wonder what kind of a man he would be now. I have talked to his family about that and have come to the conclusion that he would have ended up in the leadership of the army. He just had the right sort of leadership qualities. Bernard was a huge loss and he is sadly missed. His family all stayed close and I have stayed close to them ever since. I am treated like one of the family still although I have been away nearly 20 years. It is as if it was 1972 again when I see them. We have the same conversations about Bocky when we meet, 30 years on and he is still fresh in all of our minds as if the incident happened yesterday. When I went on the run years later I took the name Bernard Fox. I know his family still really miss him.

Hugh Martin
Killed by the UVF
outside the Tip-Top bakery,
East Belfast,
30 December 1972

> *The gunmen may have believed they had just killed a Catholic but they killed my best friend in life. He was a man devoted to his wife and children. We were all he cared for because he had been an orphan and had no other family.*

Hugh Martin was born in a workhouse in Ballymena on 14 April 1916, just a week before the Easter Rising. His mother had to give him up for adoption when Hugh was only six months old and he was taken into Nazareth Lodge, Belfast. However, just a year later Hugh was adopted by the Molloy family from Brompton Park. During World War II Hugh served with the British army in North Africa. He was captured by the Germans and eventually served three years in a prisoner-of-war camp. After the war (in 1945) Hugh met and married 17-year-old Margaret McCool from Whiterock. The two eventually set up home in Eskdale Gardens and would have five children together (Margaret, Sally, Patrick, Kathleen and Gerard). Hugh was always a quiet, devoted family man. His spare time was spent with his family or tending to the roses in his garden. Hugh worked for more than 20 years as a baker in the Tip-Top bakery in East Belfast. In the early 1970s that meant that he had to travel into what had become dangerous territory for Catholics. He had always been a cheerful and well-liked workmate. On the morning of 30 December 1972 Hugh had just finished a night shift and was leaving work as usual. He had just got into his car when two UVF gunmen shot him twice in the arm and once in the neck. Beforehand Hugh's killers had ensured he could not escape by letting down the tyres on his car. It was a blatantly sectarian attack.

Kathleen Russell (daughter)

My father worked as a baker's labourer in a bakery in East Belfast. I remember when I was seven years old he got me a birthday cake in the shape of the figure seven. That memory always stuck in my head. When we were growing up my father was a very good father. He never smacked us, he just had to tell you off and that was you in tears. We were his whole life because he had been adopted. He just did everything for us. My father never went out much because he was a night worker. He would come home in the early hours of the morning, go to bed and get up in the afternoon. Then that was him away to work again. He never went out to clubs or pubs. He loved watching wrestling on the TV, especially Mick McManus. He loved his garden too, he was always out tending to his roses. After the troubles started we were concerned for my father's safety.

I don't know if he ever felt threatened in any way and 1969 never really impacted upon him because he just went on going to work and coming home again. He used to just joke that he was sticking it out for his gold watch. My father was never politically minded. He got on with anyone and had friends from both religions.

I can remember every second of the day that my father died. My husband and myself were lying in bed. It was the early hours of the morning. I was living in Eskdale Gardens at the time and my brother Patrick lived in the street as well. I heard the door getting rapped and I looked out the window and saw Patrick's house all lit up. I thought he had been raided. My husband went to see what was wrong. But a couple of minutes later he came back and said, 'Kathleen, your daddy's dead'. My first words were, 'Well I hope he died of a heart attack', because it was always in the back of my mind that something would happen to him. My husband didn't say anything to me because I was four months pregnant with my second child. I was on my way to my mother's house when my brother Patrick stopped me and I asked him how my daddy died. 'The bastards shot him', he said. Then my brother Patrick and brother-in-law Seamy identified the body.

We found out later what happened. My father had finished work. I think it was 4.20 in the morning when he was shot. That was the time he finished; that was his routine. The papers said the car engine was going and two men came out of an alley with bush hats on them and started shooting. He was in the car by himself. I knew my daddy's routine. He started his car up and lit a cigarette and sat there for a minute and then he took off. This was in my mind as I was reading the newspapers. They made sure he didn't get away because they let the tyres of his car down. The UVF claimed responsibility for my daddy's death. They didn't state why they killed him. But we all know it was because he was a Catholic. The RUC never came out to explain to my family the circumstances of my father's death. The first one to come out was the priest. My mummy said all along that it was somebody in work that set him up and it was. Later somebody who worked along with my father was arrested and charged with setting my father up. We never knew him.

My mother was totally devastated after my father was killed. Thankfully we were all close at hand. We knew our father was murdered solely because he was a Catholic. We knew because it was happening all around us and it was happening to a lot of other families. We were just hoping it wouldn't happen to him, though we were worried because of where he worked. I loved my father and I wanted him to die naturally if he was going to die at all – not somebody else take his life. My daddy was a really brilliant father and a brilliant husband. He was a real family man and we wanted for nothing. I loved him. He just lived for his family. I named my second son after him. I was four months pregnant with him at the time his grandad was killed. That's what I hate most about the whole thing. He missed out on so much. Those people robbed us of everything. He was that type of father who just loved doing wee things for you. He thought it was great that we were all living round him in the same street. We were always a close family.

Margaret McGrandles (daughter)

After the Christmas holidays in 1972 my daddy returned to work. His routine was that once he finished his shift at 6.15 am, he gave a workmate a lift to the train station and then went straight home. On that Saturday morning he finished work two hours earlier.

His workmate insisted that he shouldn't wait for him. He said he'd make his own way to the station. After a while my daddy decided to go on home and got into his car. He'd only switched on the ignition when someone ran out of an entry and fired through the car window. He died instantly, slumping over into the passenger seat. A British army patrol which was in the next street heard the shots and ran round. Whatever there was to indicate that my daddy was a Catholic prompted one of the British soldiers to get a priest from the local chapel. That priest wrote to us after the funeral and assured us that he had administered the last rites and that my daddy's death had been instant. A year and a day after my daddy's death one of his workmates at the bakery was charged with helping to plan the murder. At the trial it emerged he was to have been murdered before the Christmas holidays but he had been off work due to sickness.

Margaret Martin (wife)

My husband was one of the best. He was all for his family and he loved to help out. At Christmas he took the old-age pensioners in his car up for their Christmas dinner. He loved to help others. He was a true gentleman. The gunmen may have believed they had just killed a Catholic but they killed my best friend in life. He was a man devoted to his wife and children. We were all he cared for because he had been an orphan and had no other family. You can't understand just how much he cared and loved us all. I really miss him even to this day.

Elizabeth McGregor
Killed by the British army,
Highbury Gardens,
12 January 1973

My mother was very angry and said to them,
'What was she going to do, shoot them with a bit of bread?'

Elizabeth McGregor was given her mother's name when she was born, the eldest of three daughters, in 1897. Like her mother, Elizabeth's father, William Murray, was from North Thomas Street. The family lived at the bottom, Catholic end. William Murray was a trade union and socialist activist, a founding member of the ITGWU in the city and a follower of James Connolly in the ILP during his years in Belfast. In the family memory Elizabeth herself, when a girl, met Connolly numerous times when paying in her father's union dues. In the 1920s the Murray family house was raided, an RIC man was shot dead in their backyard and William Murray was targeted for attack because of his trade union activities. At the same time Elizabeth was attending Earl Street school. She did so (as was the norm for so many in those days) as a 'half-timer', working half the week until the age of 14 when she left school altogether. Elizabeth worked all her life, mostly in flax mills. She married a seaman, Jimmy McGregor, who was often absent. The couple had just one child, Barney, who died when only two years old. After that, despite the fact that all her family lived in and around North Thomas Street, Elizabeth set up a home for herself and Jimmy in Highbury Gardens in

Ardoyne in 1950. When her husband died, Elizabeth took in a girl not of her own family who would herself later marry and whose children would always know Elizabeth simply as 'granny'. Elizabeth McGregor was 76 years old when she was shot dead by the British army whilst walking back from the shops at just after 11 o'clock in the morning.

Anthony Fogarty (nephew)

My mother [Elizabeth's sister] used to tell us that in the 1920s men came into their house searching for my grandfather and other men in the area to kill them. They were well-dressed men with bowler hats on and they were apologising while they were smashing up all the statues and things in the house. She used to tell us about the big barricades being up at Nelson Street and how the ITGWU men were trying to get down to work at the deep water end of the docks. They used to go into the first Catholic house, went up the stairs and through the attic walls the whole way down to the bottom end of the street until they were safe. That's part of what made me mad when she was killed – the thought that my aunt went through all that. She was a very, very big-hearted person. She was the type of person who couldn't see wrong in anybody. If she could do you a good turn then she would. My mother and father were the same and brought us up that way too. To me she was the greatest aunt in the world. She was the sort of person who kept to herself; she never stuck her nose into other people's business, but if she could help you she would. She looked after us and made sure we got anything we wanted. Her family were her friends. The only hobby Elizabeth and my mother had was having a wee bet on the horses. They weren't gamblers or anything; it was just the way of life in them days. She never went out dancing and she never met anybody after her husband died. My mother and the family she lived with were her life. She used to work in the Royal Hotel as a dishwasher. This was when she was 50 or 60. She worked all her life. Just before she was shot, we were laughing because she was looking for a job for herself. She was 76 years old.

At the time my aunt was killed I had just come back to live in Ardoyne. I had been put out of my workplace in Carrickfergus because of my religion. I found out Elizabeth was dead through my mother. She got a phone call to say that my aunt had been shot. My aunt was in the Royal Hospital and she died two hours after my mother got there. Then my mother got in touch with me and I went up. During the wake some of the neighbours came in and told my mother the story of how it happened. Their version was that my aunt had been up to put on a bet. Then she went to the baker's and bought a Vienna roll. After that she was coming down home with a newspaper and the bread in her hand. She stopped to speak to someone in the street. The neighbours all agreed that there was no shooting and no gunmen in the area whatsoever. They said that a soldier must have seen her head bobbing behind the hedge and fired from an army observation post. He hit her in the head and she spun round. Then they fired another shot at her which hit her in the body. When the soldiers realised it was a woman they had hit, they sent up one of their first-aiders. But he said he could do nothing for her and to phone for an ambulance to get her away.

The British army didn't give any version of the events to my mother at all. They just said that they thought she was a gunman. My mother was very angry and said to them, 'What was she going to do, shoot them with a bit of bread?' The British army did not come to the house to say this. My mother got a letter from the commanding officer of that section saying that he was very sorry that it happened but they thought she was a gunman. They never mentioned who shot her. They just said it was one of the snipers. That was all my mother got. She put it into the hands of a solicitor and he got no satisfaction either. He was told the same thing. They never made a public apology. Anything they said was in the letter. My mother wanted justice because they had gone through so much in the '20s. My mother wanted to find out who did it and why. But she was told nothing. My aunt was shot dead and buried and that was it. It was put down that she was killed during a battle with gunmen but there were no gunmen. They were just covering themselves.

Betty McKinney (family friend)

Elizabeth was a great, hard-working wee woman who just liked a wee bet. It was a Friday the day she was murdered. My mummy came home from work at the mill for her lunch. I was in the house that morning. Elizabeth went up the road to get something from the shops around 11 am. Then she was just coming home. They [British army] said that they had seen gunmen and they shot from the post up at the Oldpark. Doreen Toolan went out to Elizabeth that morning. I found out when somebody came to the door and said, 'Your granny is lying at the top of the street'. But by the time I got up the ambulance had taken her. She died in hospital. Someone then went for my mummy. She went up to the hospital but Elizabeth was dead when my mummy got there. The British army said they spotted gunmen. They eventually admitted killing her but they tried to say that they were firing at gunmen. The British army never came to the house.

Doreen Toolan (neighbour and eyewitness)

I knew Elizabeth McGregor very well. She lived at the bottom of Highbury Gardens. She always said good morning every day going to 10 am mass. I lived in Ladbrook Drive so she would walk straight up Highbury and up Ladbrook going to the chapel. She was a very quiet woman and kept to herself. I'll never forget the day she was murdered. I was out brushing the path and I had the baby sitting out. It was just about 10.40 am. Mrs McGregor had come out of mass and was coming down the street. She said, 'I said that wee prayer for you Doreen'. I said, 'God love you, Mrs McGregor'. Elizabeth had her wee bag with her and a scarf on. She was wearing a longish dark coat and wee granny boots. She had her wee shopping bag on her arm. I shouted to her, 'Did you do your wee bet this morning?' She used to go to the bookies every day. If she got a wee tip she would say, 'Doreen, I've a good wee runner the day'.

I had just brushed the path and went to leave the brush in. I got to the front door of my house when I heard the shooting. I heard three high velocity shots. When she was shot, Mrs McGregor was actually on the verge of Highbury Gardens. She was very friendly with the people that lived in the first house there so she might have been talking to them if they were standing at their door. She was on the right hand side going down Highbury because she lived on that side. She was only about six foot on the footpath when she was shot. You would have said that she was shot from the Bone Hills, but yet it was the back of her head that got it. There were also Brits in the entry coming into Brompton Park from Herbert Street. So I don't know if it was the ones up on the Bone Hills or those in the entry. At the inquest they said it was the ones on the Hill that did it. When I heard the shots I dropped the brush and ran to the gate. It was then that I saw Mrs McGregor lying on the ground. That was before she got into Highbury Gardens. So I just ran and left everything. In the meantime, as I passing Berwick Road, all the Scotchies [Scottish soldiers] were in the entry at Herbert Street at the gap. They were shooting like mad. Somebody shouted to me that I would be shot dead. I told them I didn't care that I was going down to Mrs McGregor. The entry was crammed and the Scotch soldiers were shooting up the Berwick Road. This was after Mrs McGregor was shot. I stated that at the inquest and there was never any explanation given for it. There wasn't a sinner on that Berwick Road. I was wishing there had been because everybody's door just seemed to be closed. I ran over to Mrs McGregor without thinking because I saw her lying there and her hand was up. Then there was no movement from her. So I went over and whispered the act of contrition into her ear because I felt her pulse and knew she was dead. She didn't live long.

A few seconds after that, the army came and I sent somebody up to my house to phone the priest and the ambulance. This British soldier said 'Oh my God'. They thought she was a gunman. I said, 'Aye, a gunman'. In the meantime some fella had come on the scene and he went to lift her up a bit to put a cushion under her head. I said, 'Don't move her' because I noticed the blood coming from the back of the head. It was the back of the head that was blown off. The priest came and loosened her scarf. Her wee scarf fell off. The priest was lovely. He anointed her, loosened the scarf and whispered a prayer over her. Then the ambulance came. Then we were surrounded by the army and that was it. The army accepted the fact that they shot her. They didn't say anything when her body was there but the one that came on the scene said it was sad to see an old woman like that being shot. He said it was unfortunate, but he didn't give an explanation. Then her nephew asked me to go to the inquest, so I went. The prosecutor tried to say that she was an IRA gunman. They stated that the British army thought she was an IRA gunman so they were going to say that it was 'death by misadventure'. Then I got up and raised riots in the court. They emptied the court house for a while, then brought us back in again. The judge asked me to get up on the stand and I gave my version of what had happened. There were some photos showing the view from the Oldpark lookout post on Ladbrook. They were very clear, so how they could have mistaken her for a gunman? It is unbelievable that they tried to make out she was a man shooting a gun. They were going to give a verdict of death by misadventure but I caused an upheaval at that. I said, 'No, it was definitely murder'. So they put it down as 'mistaken identity' and an open verdict. Her grandson came over and thanked me and I never heard anything else. The paper had it down that they thought she was a binman with a brush in her hand. But there were no binmen in the area at the time. It was just a wee woman who came out of the chapel, into the bookies and was walking down the street. They just tried to cover it all up.

Pat Crossan
Killed by the UVF,
Woodvale Road,
2 March 1973

Most of them got on great with him but you had that element, you get it everywhere, and that's how Paddy lost his life. I think Paddy was set up to be killed.

Pat Crossan was born on 5 June 1938. His mother Catherine was originally from Ballynahinch and was the second wife of his father, Stafford Crossan, who was from Crumlin. As a child Pat was brought up with his three brothers and sister in Ladbrooke Drive in Ardoyne. He attended the Holy Cross Boys school. When he left, he got a job as a delivery driver for Kennedy's Bakery. Then he became a bus driver for the Corporation. As a young man Pat Crossan loved to go to céilís. They were often held in Ardoyne Hall, with which Pat would become very much involved through much of his life. It was at one such dance that he met his future wife Maureen. They married in August 1962 and together raised two daughters, Roisin and Bernadette. Pat was a man who devoted himself to family, community and chapel. A member of the Ardoyne Hall committee Pat organised dances and concerts for many years. As someone very active on behalf of the church in the area he also ran trips to Lourdes.

At work Pat was known as someone who liked to joke and banter. He made light of the sectarian divisions that could be found in the bus depot as in the world outside. For some people, however, such comments were enough to make him a target for the very sectarian hatred that he ridiculed. On 2 March 1973 Paddy Crossan stopped his bus to pick up passengers on the Woodvale Road. Two loyalist gunmen shot him as he sat in his cab and killed him. Far from being a random attack, Pat had been specifically targeted. To add obscene insult to grievous injury in the weeks that followed his death, his widow received hate mail from people claiming to have been involved in his murder. One of the few people Maureen and the girls could rely on for support in these difficult times was Pat's brother Frankie. In November 1975 Frankie Crossan was making his way to his home in West Belfast from Ardoyne when he was picked up and brutally killed by members of the notorious UVF Shankill Butchers gang [Frankie Crossan, killed by the UVF near Tennent Street, 25 November 1975].

Artie McAlea (friend)

I knew Pat from when we were both in our early teens. We would go to céilís up in Ardoyne Hall, Toby's Hall and over to the Falls. Pat always loved céilí dancing. We were always great friends from then right up until the time of his death. Pat was a great fella. You never saw him getting into a bad temper. He would have always argued his point but he was never abusive in any way. He was a tireless worker for the chapel and for anyone in the district. He was one of the top ten gentlemen to come from Ardoyne, a gentleman in every respect. You never even heard him swear. Anyone that came into contact with Pat Crossan always left in a good mood and a sense of being a friend of his. Every time you were with Pat it was fun. When we were all going to the céilís there was never any badness. I believe that if Pat had lived he would have been one of the main people working in and for this district. He was that kind of fella. Pat devoted his life to his work and to Maureen and his family. When they were happy he was happy, that was the type of him. I just remember him with such fondness. It was a terrible tragedy for our district when he was taken away from it. When I found out that Pat had been murdered I was absolutely devastated. I couldn't believe that a fella such as that could be taken down by the likes of those that did it. It was a terrible tragedy and there was a massive funeral for him. People came from all over the place because he was very well liked.

Tommy Donnelly (friend and workmate)

I remember Patrick from when he started on the buses. He was the sort of guy that everyone got on with him. He was always bantering with people from the Protestant side of the community. Most people were grand with it. He used to banter about the Orangemen, the parades, little things that happened. He would say, 'Are you marching next week then?' That sort of thing. People would be all 'lovey-dovey' all year but when it came round to July, Paddy was one of those who would say, 'Have you stopped talking to us now the marching season is coming up?' He was just a character and didn't care. Paddy was just a very jolly person, good-natured. He was a good character, a nice guy. Both communities had some great times in the depot with Catholics and Protestants getting together. We used to go down to Dublin and play football against the fellas from CIE. They would come up here too. Paddy was among the characters that would have gone down to enjoy himself. So it was a myth that built up about Paddy. Somebody picked it up wrong, probably didn't like him and picked him out. That's the sort of thing that was happening then. If you were a character and spoke out, even if it was only banter, then you were highlighted and picked out. They used to have a Radio Shankill and Paddy's name was mentioned on it. There was some character saying, 'Now watch out Paddy Crossan'. It was a warning. We were getting it very hard then on both sides. If a Protestant person went up the Falls he was afraid and any Catholic who went up the Shankill or Glencairn was afraid. That was the way things were then. It was really bad. Most people on the Protestant side were brilliant. They are good people. But there was always that element of people who take things differently. Paddy was also a great church man and he did a lot for the Holy Cross chapel. He used to wear the badge of the chapel. Maybe that annoyed some people on the Shankill Road too. Most of them got on great with him but you had that element. You get it everywhere. That's how Paddy lost his life. I think Paddy was set up to be killed. The people that killed him must have picked him out further down the road. When he got up to Woodvale Avenue there was a guy waiting on the platform just outside the bus. Another one stoned the front of the windscreen. They [the loyalists] knew who they were after. They went in and shot Paddy from both the windscreen and the platform. We couldn't believe it when Paddy was killed. That it could happen to him was terrible because he wasn't bitter. Paddy had no bitterness in him, not an ounce; he just liked to banter. He would never have done anybody any harm. But, there was just a certain someone that maybe didn't like him. That is what killed Paddy, the hatred.

Maureen (wife)

Patrick was a very outgoing person. He really was very jolly and full of life. The only thing he was interested in was Ardoyne Hall. He ran concerts. He was so well-liked that he was able to bring in big names, like Bridie Gallagher, Eileen Donaghy. I think he achieved an awful lot for the community through what he did for the church. He used to run trips to Lourdes as well. My last moment with Patrick was when I said good morning to him as I was going to work on the day he was killed. Pat was working up at the bus depot which was just up at the corner. So he would have been in and out of the house throughout the day. I came in from work later that day and was cleaning my bedroom windows when I saw a crowd of people outside. I heard somebody shouting, 'A bus man has been shot'. But I tried to put it out of my head and think that it was not connected with me. A lot of our neighbours were all out and I saw a couple of them looking across at my house. I had a funny feeling but I just went on working. The next thing, a couple of neighbours came up and told me what had happened. The first thing I did was to run across to the chapel.

What I have been told is that Pat had stopped at a bus stop on the Woodvale Road. It was around 3 pm in the afternoon. He had started to drive off but two or three fellas flagged him down and he stopped the bus to let them on. But they were not passengers. They had flagged him down to shoot him. Nobody admitted to killing Patrick and nobody was ever caught or charged either. I don't believe justice was achieved. A few weeks after the funeral I had a letter sent to me; I can't remember exactly when because I was numb for months. I was on a lot of medication. But one morning a letter came here. I only read the first couple of lines then I ran across the street and gave it to my neighbour. They took it to the police. The letter said that it came from the ones who had killed Pat. I didn't read it all because the first few lines were just revolting. It said that they had got another fenian 'so and so', something to that effect. They went on to say that they had gotten away with it and would not be caught. Then the week after that another letter came. I didn't even open the second one. I ran across the street again to a friend and neighbour who had been on the Ardoyne Hall committee with Pat. As far as I know he took it to the police but I have never heard anything. I couldn't even tell you if there was an investigation into his murder because neither the RUC nor anybody else ever came near me to tell me. The details of the killing were not made clear to me by anybody. He was just shot and that was it. After that you were just left.

I always say that for anybody who had somebody killed in the early troubles it is as if they were just forgotten. If it hadn't been for the like of Father Fernando I don't know how I would have gotten through it. Nobody ever came to help. Once the funeral was over you were on your own. I had to go to the Corporation solicitors by myself. It was an awful experience, they asked terrible things. It was degrading and at the end of the day all you got was a pittance. There was no community or other platforms of support available at the time except for parish priests. You were just left to take tablets and that was it. Anybody who has had someone killed definitely needs someone to come and advise them about what to do and where to go. I got through it but to be honest I had to counsel myself. After a time I joined a bereavement group which was started up by a woman whose son was murdered. We used to go up to Corrymeela. We still meet once a month in each others' houses. We just have a wee cup of tea, go out for dinners and go on holidays together. That was the way we got through it, by ourselves.

Pat's brother Frankie came here every night after Pat was murdered. He used to look in on my girls because they were only seven and nine at the time. Frankie would put the girls to bed. They wouldn't go up to bed unless he carried them up. As soon as he saw that they were alright he would call into the Ardoyne Hall for a drink or whatever. But he always walked down the road. We were always shouting at him about it. Then one night he was picked up [by the Shankill Butchers] and he was found butchered in one of the entries. They mutilated his body so much that we couldn't open the coffin. He was married with two children as well, a boy and a girl. Frankie's wife more or less died when he did. That girl never got over what happened to Frankie.

> *My father was an innocent victim. The people who killed him didn't care how innocent he was because the belief among those people is, if you are a Catholic you are not innocent.*

David Glennon
Killed by loyalists,
Summer Street,
7 March 1973

The Glennon family were originally Markets people; most of them were traders and dealers. David Glennon was born on 7 April 1922 in Riley Street. The family had a long tradition of basket-making which David took on after leaving school. He had three brothers and four sisters: Paddy, Barney, Jimmy, Alice, Lily, Mary and Ann. The family moved to Ardoyne and that's where David was reared. He married Maureen Quinn from Stratford Gardens in Holy Cross chapel. They lived in a room in 39 Stratford Gardens and eventually had six children: Davy, Theresa, Francie, Martin, Maureen and Geraldine. In 1968 the family moved to 36 Divismore Crescent, Ballymurphy.

In 1973 David Glennon was abducted and killed by loyalists in a brutal sectarian attack. His mutilated body was found in the boot of a car, hooded, with his feet bound and shot in the head. Although no one has ever claimed responsibility, the killing is attributed to the Shankill Butchers.

Francie Glennon (son)

My father's mother and father came from Eskdale Gardens in Ardoyne. In 1968 he and his sister, my aunt Alice, moved from Ardoyne to Ballymurphy because there was a new estate built there. My daddy still frequented Ardoyne regularly and knocked about with my uncle Barney, Dan McGaughey and Neilly Shevlin from Holmdene. He drank in the old Shamrock club, which was then at the bottom of Jamaica Street. My daddy was a very quiet man, but he was also a very strict man. He used to tell us that he was in the old IRA, and one day he said, 'Son, don't you be turning to those Provos. There is only one IRA and that is the Official IRA'. He told me about doing time in the Curragh; he was interned, and I think he got sentenced during the 1956 - 62 campaign. My daddy was an old republican; he still had his connections. One day, after he had moved to Ballymurphy, he saw a wee man getting beaten by the paras and he ran out of the house and got into them. He had mates from the Murf, like Billy Weir, Mr Black, Frankie Donnan, Tommy Reid and Billy McElwaine. They all came out and backed him up and they all ended up getting into the paras in a big field on the front of the road. My daddy read books on republicanism and he was aware of civil rights issues and discussed politics. He tried to teach us what to do and what not to do, but I never listened to him. I just went and did my own thing. If I had listened to my daddy I think I would have been more aware of the conflict. He taught me one thing for sure: you keep your mouth shut when you get into the barracks and say nothing. My daddy was on the committee of the Ballymurphy Defence Association in the early stages of the conflict.

The day my daddy was murdered I was hiding in a house; I had done an armed robbery of an old bakery to get a few quid and I got away with it. I was hiding in my daddy's mate's house when my mummy came up and said that my daddy had not come home. I told her not to be worrying about him as I thought he was probably somewhere in Ardoyne. She told me that a body had been found on the Oldpark Road. She had big bags of washing; she was going to the laundrette. We helped her with the bags and went back down to my mate's house. The next minute she came running down, squealing, 'It's him, it's him'. She said they described his shoes; 'His shoes have a wee buckle on the slip'. We went into the house and her neighbour Bella McElwaine came over and sat with her. Eventually, the cops came and took her to identify the body. I was waiting for a couple of hours looking out the window and I saw the saracen coming down the street. It pulled up at our door and the door flew open; I thought it was a raid coming up. I saw Bella McElwaine come up the path first, and then I saw my mummy stumble out, crying. I ran down the stairs to my mummy and a British soldier grabbed me and said, 'Francie Glennon, you are under arrest'. I whacked him, but the major came over and said, 'Come here, son, it wasn't us who killed your father. We are going to have to arrest you'. I got charged with robbery of the bakery, which had happened a few weeks earlier. I eventually got bail because my daddy had been killed.

The day he was murdered he was in McGlade's Bar with what he had left from his bru. He had a couple of pints with his mates. People say he left and went to see his sister Alice between 6.00 pm and 7.30 pm in the evening. He was picked up in the vicinity of the Oldpark area. My daddy was found on Summer Street in the boot of a car. I don't know how long they had him before they killed him. The cops said he had been tortured and that he must have put up one hell of a fight; he didn't go down easy. They tied his feet, his neck, his hands and his testicles with barbed wire, and they shot him three times. They killed my daddy because he was a Catholic. It was Bella McElwaine who identified his body; my mother was too distressed. Bella was a tower of strength and a great help to my mother. What happened was a fella and a girl were walking down Summer Street to work and they saw blood running down the street; they noticed it was coming from the boot of a car. The Brits were sent for and they thought it was booby-trapped so they blew the car boot open and dragged my father's body out with a rope. No one ever claimed responsibility for his killing because of the way he was tortured and the way his privates were tied with wire; it was widely associated with the Shankill Butchers. My daddy's cousins are the McCartans from the Markets and between the McCartans and the Glennons there have been 17 people killed as a direct result of the conflict.

Davey Glennon (son)

We lived in one room in a house in Stratford Gardens. I can remember the room; in it were beds, wardrobes and clothes everywhere. When I was a kid growing up, I used to try and pick a friend who had a TV and when there was a programme I wanted to watch we just headed up to whoever's house had the TV. My mummy and daddy then decided to move to Ballymurphy; it was a breath of fresh air for nationalists because it was an estate where they had their own house and a garden. I think if the house had been in Timbuktu they would have gone because you just can't rear a family in one room. My parents had six children. The house in Ballymurphy was like a mansion after living in Ardoyne in one wee room.

When I was 14 I ran away to London. I fell in with a couple of other Irish people. It was coming to the end of the 'flower power', the dope, the long hair and all. We lived in a squat; it was a real 'chill den'. Eventually, at the end of all of this, I finished up in jail. The only contact I had with home was when I sent a postcard after a couple of years saying that I was okay. I think I was actually away so long I was terrified of going home. I wish now, when I look back, that someone had caught me and brought me home. A week went into two months and it got really hard to go back and then it went into a year and it just kept getting harder and harder. Deep inside I wanted to go home, I wanted to be back with my family, but I was afraid. I was about 14 or 15 years old, so the years just went on and I didn't go home. When I came home I asked if anyone remembered ever getting a card but nobody could ever remember a card landing in the house.

I finished up in prison doing a six months sentence for stealing a car and driving without insurance. I was actually a wee lad in a man's gaol. The gaol was for over-18s, but I wasn't even 18 at the time. One day a fella from Ballymurphy came in and he said to me, 'That was terrible about your daddy. I am sorry to hear about him'. I asked him, 'What do you mean? What about my daddy?' He said to me, 'Your da was murdered; the loyalists killed him'. When I think back I remember that I walked away from him, and I don't think it sunk in at the time. It didn't register. I was sort of in a trance about it. Two days later, just by the biggest of coincidence, I was reading the Sunday paper in my cell and one of the stories was, 'Heartbroken grandmother dies'. The story was about Mrs McCartan, old granny McCartan, who died from a broken heart after seeing so many of her family murdered. It listed all her family who were murdered and one of her family members was my father, David Glennon. I think this happened roughly a year after my father died. That is when it hit me. I can always remember that it was as if the curtains had been pulled back and everything was out in the open and I realised that he was dead.

I was emotionally devastated and was crying in my cell. I hadn't seen my father since I had run away; I didn't have the time to tell him anything and I was full of guilt. I went to the doctor the next day. He was standing with an M.O at each side of him and he didn't even look at me; he was just writing something and he said, 'What do you want?' or 'What is wrong with you?' I said that I had received a bit of bad news and that I was having trouble sleeping and asked could he give me something to help me sleep. He said, 'Well, what bad news did you get?' and I said to him, 'My father died' but I never told him in what circumstances. He just looked at me and put his head down again and said, 'Sure, they have all to die sometime'. I just flipped; I must have been emotionally stressed out. I can remember landing on him over the table and punching him and the M.O.s pulling me off. I remember getting dragged out of the office and I was taken to the hospital cells where you get fed through a trap door and there were grills on the door. I was in there for about seven days and they were giving me a heavy sedative. I was roaming about the cell doped up. I remember getting in touch with a priest and I told him who I was and what age I was and I explained to him that I had found out that my father had been murdered back home in Ireland. The priest then got in touch with a priest back home and they got in touch with my mother. My mother and younger sister, Maureen, came over to visit me; I was just out of the hospital. This was the first time I had seen my mother since I had run away from home. I can remember going into the visiting area and seeing my mummy and my sister and my mummy was crying. I just went over and hugged her and that was us back in contact again as a family.

My daddy always went to Ardoyne because his family was there, his brothers and sisters. He always brought us to visit them. From the time my daddy was killed our family was never really the same; my mummy went heavy on the drink and she changed drastically. The day my daddy was murdered he was in town like any ordinary person and wherever he was, he didn't do anybody any harm. He was an innocent victim. The people who killed him didn't care how innocent he was because the belief among those people is, if you are a Catholic you are not innocent. There was a photograph of my father published in the paper; it was of the car he was dumped in and it showed his bound body and all... That photograph brought much heartache to my mother because in the aftermath of my father's death, she had all of the newspaper cuttings of all the different angles of the scene of the crime and newspaper cuttings of the stories about it. Every now and again she took them out until she drove herself absolutely mental. She turned into a very heavy drinker and those photographs didn't help. Not only did his death affect everybody in the family but the photographs of his death haunted the family for years after it. Those photos only got destroyed when my family decided enough was enough and they took the photos from my mother and burnt them.

Later, when I was in gaol doing time for political activity, I did a bit of self-education. The situation here put me in mind of countries likes El Salvador where the regime there was involved in just lifting people of the streets and killing them. The situation in El Salvador is similar to here in that it was done to terrorise people. In the north it was kill Catholics and hopefully it will instil so much terror into us as nationalists that we wouldn't either fight the regime that was in Ireland, or the IRA would collapse round it. They had this thing in their head that, if we kill Catholics we will defeat the IRA and that was utter madness. For years I was just an ordinary Catholic, just a nationalist youth or boy; I never had any concept of politics in Ireland. When I was in gaol, I realised how little I knew and how little time I actually spent thinking about things. I can look at things now with a clear head, and I can say loyalism, by its very nature, is always going to turn on the innocent Catholic. It is because they are the easiest targets. It is a warped sense of politics and strategy, but it still hasn't changed from the seventies until now; they still have that same mentality. There have been hundreds of pipe bombs thrown into Catholic homes within the last two years and the thinking behind the pipe bombs is no different from the thinking behind the sectarian murders of the seventies.

My father was just a hard-working, honest man who genuinely liked people. The thing that I always remember and the thing that I will always hold dear to me is that he was genuinely liked and that he was a likeable character. Anytime I talk to anybody about him, they all have had a good word to say about him, though very few people speak ill of the dead. But there is genuineness among people when they say that he was a nice fella. I have met thousands and thousands of people and there are very few who have the quality of being liked by most people or near enough everybody. My father's death was a terrible loss for all of our family.

Come on to see the moon.

Eddie Sharpe
Killed by the British army,
Cranbrook Gardens,
12 March 1973

Eddie Sharpe (or 'Big Sharpe' as everybody knew him) was brought up in Fairfield Street and was one of seven children. Eddie was the fifth child and youngest boy, born in 1943. His father Edward was a Protestant from Carnan Street in the Shankill and worked laying tarmac. He married Eddie's mother Elizabeth in the 1920s. Elizabeth was one of the McAuleys from Fairfield Street and so Eddie grew up alongside his McAuley cousins, particularly Mickey and 'Thunder'. Eddie went to Holy Cross Boys School and St Gabriel's and left the latter in 1958. At first he got a job in Lyndsey's Mill where his mother already worked. But regular employment was not an easy thing to come by. For a while this led Eddie and Mickey McAuley to join the Territorial Army, though both left after about a year. After that Eddie went to England to try and find work. He stayed in Dorset for two years before returning to Ardoyne. It was then that he met his wife to be, Alice Magee. The two married in 1965 and began to raise a family. They eventually had four children; Paul, Audrey, Alison and Edward (who died at birth). At first they lived in Hooker Street. However, when the conflict broke out in 1969 they had to move and went to live in Turf Lodge. This was after a member of the RUC beat Alice at her door. It was an attack that led her to lose the child with which she was then pregnant. Eddie was also attacked by loyalists making his way home from Ardoyne to Turf Lodge in 1971. His assailants cut a cross with razor blades into his head because he was a Catholic.

Eddie and Alice tried to get on with living their lives and bringing up their young family. Eddie did a number of jobs. He laboured in a quarry for a time and worked on the houses in Farringdon Gardens. He then took up what was as much his hobby as his job of work, fixing peoples TVs, fridges and radios. Eddie was also a 'Hibs' man, and could be seen either there or in the League [social clubs] with his mates Jim Magee and 'Tucker' and 'Coco' McAuley. Just four months before his death Eddie and Alice moved once more, to Cranbrook Gardens. Cranbrook Gardens had been one of those burnt out by loyalists following the introduction of internment in 1971. On the night of 12 March 1973 Eddie Sharpe was standing at the front door of his home taking in the night air and looking at the sky. Alice was inside making a cup of tea for the two of them. A British soldier stationed at a nearby observation post shot Eddie dead. The British army later alleged that Eddie was a gunman. He was not. No charges were ever brought against his killer. Eddie Sharpe was 30 years old at the time of his death.

May Flood (sister)

Our Eddie was a big, easygoing fella. He was a big soft-hearted lad and he would have given his last up for you. My da loved him and we were a very close family. Even after he married and moved round to Hooker Street he was still always coming round to the house. That was after he had been working in England and had come back and married Alice. They got the house in Hooker Street and were there when the troubles got bad in 1969. The loyalists came in and burned Brookfield Street at that time. The loyalists attacked Eddie in Twaddell Avenue in 1971. I think he was living in Turf Lodge at the time. He was walking home through the Woodvale area after visiting my mum and dad. The loyalists would have known he was a Catholic because of the road he was walking. They used razor blades on Eddie and cut a big cross on his poor head. He ended up getting a claim for it but it didn't come through until after he was murdered. That was after Eddie and Alice had moved up to that hell-hole, Cranbrook, where the paras had an army post at the top of the street. Four weeks prior to Eddie's death he was in our roof space in Jamaica Street to fix an aerial. He came back down the stairs and asked for something to pick bullets out of our rafters. They had been fired down from Alliance Road by the loyalists and the British army. He said to us, 'Why don't you come up to Cranbrook and stay with me? The British Army will protect you'.

My father died in January 1973, just seven weeks before Eddie. The night Eddie was killed was the 12 March 1973. He was just standing outside his door looking at the stars and the paras blew his head off. I was living at the top of Jamaica Street at the time and was just sitting looking at my dad's memory card. My mum came up and was banging on the window saying, 'Eddie's dead'. I flew up the road to the house. By the time I got there our Eddie's body had already been taken away, but his brains were everywhere. I actually lifted up our Eddie's brains and had them in my hands. It was then that everyone started to assemble up at the army post. People were mad. The army tried to say that the IRA were operating from the garden and that Eddie was shooting. But there was no truth in it at all. There was a big distance from there to the door where Eddie was shot and there was no shooting that night anyway. It was just lies. It was a great big March night; there was a big moon and our Eddie loved the stars.

We never went to the inquest. In those days you didn't know what to do and we were very quiet. The inquest gave an open verdict. Every family got hit by things but our Eddie was just as innocent as the people who died on Bloody Sunday. A few years ago someone with an English accent phoned through to the Jamaica Inn asking if someone knew where the Sharpes lived. He said he had something important to tell us relating to Eddie's death. But we never heard from him again. I think it might have been the one who killed Eddie. But whoever it was that murdered my brother they got away with it. Our Eddie was just a big soft fella. If your TV broke you went to Eddie. He was a very kind-hearted, big softie and he is sadly missed.

Alice Sharpe (wife)

Eddie was murdered on 12 March at 11.55 pm. He had been in the house all day. I heard the whistles going earlier and I told Eddie I was going to the shops. I ran round and the paratroopers were raiding Ladbrook Drive. This was about 3 pm. So I came back in after the riot was over and Eddie said to me, 'You're going to be shot some day, wee girl'. That night I was in the house and our youngest Alison was lying on the settee sleeping. The two other wee ones were up in bed. Eddie was standing at the door and I was making his tea before we went to bed. He shouted into me, 'Alice, come on to see the moon'. It was right and big that night. It was a big, big thing. I said, 'Hold on a wee minute'. I was just setting his tea down to go out and then I heard the shot. I thought he was down at the gate and he couldn't get up again. I called his name out three times and there was no answer. I said to myself, 'He doesn't hear me'. So I went out and he was lying there. His head and half his body were in the path and his legs were on the steps. His hands were still in his pockets. Eddie was only standing at the door about five or ten minutes.

The paratroopers shot him from a lookout post at the old bus depot. The first statement that the Brits put out was that Eddie was shot dead climbing over a yard wall. Then they must have realised that they'd got their stories mixed up. The next statement said that he was a gunman standing pointing a rifle at them from his garden. At the inquest they admitted that he wasn't a gunman and he shouldn't have been killed. The verdict was a 'tragic mistake'. But they never apologised. In fact they tortured me after it. My house had never been raided before this incident. But the Brits tortured me for a whole year maybe. They raided the house and every time they passed me in the streets they were stopping me and searching me. If I didn't let them search me they were sending saracens to come and that. They were singing, 'Where's your daddy gone?' and things like that to the kids.

Eddie was a great person. He was a very generous person where old people were concerned. He would fix their TVs and wouldn't charge them. He was good to the kids. He was a gentleman. Eddie was as innocent as they come. I've never ever come into contact with the person who killed Eddie – not at the inquest, never, and I don't think I'd like to.

Sean Murphy (neighbour)

It was a Monday night and Monday is a members' night in the Shamrock. I left the club about 11.45/11.50 pm. I always remember I got a sausage supper on the way home. The paras were in Ardoyne at the time. That's why I brought the car down to the club. You hated walking anywhere because the paras were lying in the gardens. You just couldn't walk anywhere without getting battered. Just as I parked my car outside my front door I heard a shot. So I ducked down in the car. I heard the screams straight across the street, from Eddie Sharpe's house. So I just automatically ran over and Eddie was lying there with the head blown off him. Apparently the bullet had ricocheted off the wall and took the whole back of his head off. Alice was standing screaming over the top of him and

I pulled her into the house. I couldn't believe it. Then Eric McCullough (he was the next door neighbour) came out. We just said an act of contrition into Eddie's ear.

Then I cracked up. I ran up to the barracks and kicked the big steel gates. The Brits opened the gates and let me in up at the bus depot. There was about 20 or 30 Scots soldiers all standing in the yard. I called them all sorts or murdering bastards. Then an officer came out. I always remember his name, Major Benjamin, with his Oxford voice. He said two of his men had observed a gunman and shot him. I called him a lying bastard and asked him to bring the two soldiers down to me, which he wouldn't do. So at that a lot of neighbours started gathering. They were worried about me being inside the place so they kicked on the gates. So my wife and a couple of neighbours came in and took me down to the house. Then the ambulance came and took Eddie away.

In the next couple of days, a detective sergeant interviewed me along with Fr. Myles up at the depot. I told him that Eddie was a completely innocent man who had been murdered. He took my statement. There was no question Eddie was an innocent man and everybody knew it. He was actually lying on the ground with his hands still in his pockets. There had been no activity in Ardoyne that night, nothing at all. The British army said that they had observed a gunman through a telescope. One Brit said to the other Brit, 'Have a look at that; isn't that a gunman?' The other Brit said, 'Yes that's a gunman'. Then there was just the one shot.

About four weeks after Eddie was murdered the paratroopers raided the Shamrock club. They took me away and kept me for three days in Castlereagh. One of the main interrogators was the same detective sergeant who had taken my statement about Eddie being shot. He knew I wasn't in the IRA or anything political like that. They never mentioned Eddie during the interrogation – just asked the usual: did I know anyone in the IRA, etc. It was a long three days. They screwed my hands up my back and gave me a couple of slaps around the head. But it was nothing too bad. It was a Sunday when I got out and on the Friday night there was a 'do' in the Shamrock. We were carrying a woman out of the club and we were at the corner of Etna Drive and Brompton Park. One car drove round first and I thought it was a bit suspicious; it was a Volkswagen. Then a Ford Cortina came round with the back window open. I just remember sparks flying everywhere. I was shot in the leg and Jimmy O'Hanlon was shot. Fr. Myles came up to see me in hospital and said we weren't going ahead with the public inquiry. He feared that it was me they were after and that they were trying to bump me off. Whether or not that was true or not I don't know. But we weren't taking any chances. Fr. Myles called off the public inquiry.

Fr. Myles (local priest)

I remember Eddie Sharpe's case because it was through it that I nearly got poor Sean Murphy killed. The day after Eddie was killed the paras announced that he was armed. The reason I decided to hold a civil investigation into the circumstances surrounding the death of Eddie Sharpe was because it was pretty blatant what had happened. I got John D. Stewart (a journalist) and a man called 'Red' McCaughey who was a lecturer in law at Queens University to conduct the investigation. They were both Protestants. The first day they came into the area to begin their investigation I brought them to the scene of Eddie's killing. Immediately we were confronted by the local British army regiment who killed Eddie. The head of the patrol, a Colonel Lorimer, came up to us and asked what we were doing. I told him who everybody was and that we hoped to get the truth surrounding Eddie Sharpe's killing. Colonel Lorimer approached me and reminded me that we were surrounded on all sides!

The civil investigation was out to establish two things: to check out the British army statements on the killing of Eddie Sharpe and to check out the witnesses to the incident. The inquiry concluded that the British army statement, that Eddie was a gunman about to open fire on the British army, was physically impossible. We decided that Sean Murphy should go to the RUC and make a statement as to what happened. I said I would go along with Sean to meet the RUC up at the bus depot at the top of Cranbrook Gardens. Sean made a statement. Shortly afterwards Sean was arrested and taken to Castlereagh. Whilst in Castlereagh Sean was interrogated by the same RUC man to whom he had given the statement in relation to Eddie's killing. This proved to us that the RUC and the British army were pretty anxious about our investigation. Sean wasn't out long when he was shot by a passing car at the junction of Etna Drive and Brompton Park. I believe it was the paras. The next time I saw Sean he was lying in the Mater Hospital. It struck me he was a married man with a young family. I said, 'Sean, I don't think I've any right to put you in this situation. We are taking on the full power of the state, the police and the military. I don't think we have any mission'. I told him the only thing we could now do was to call off the inquiry. So I contacted John D. Stewart and 'Red' McCaughey and told then it was all off. The state was not amenable. They agreed that if witnesses were going to be shot then it couldn't go on.

As we were driving up Estoril Park we were stopped by the paras. They surrounded the car, aiming their weapons at us and screaming at us to get out of the car.
I was in the back seat with Pat lying across me; he was badly wounded. His head was on my lap and I did my best to comfort him. I shouted at the Brits to let us get to the hospital. I knew Pat was dying.

Pat McCabe
Killed on active service
by the British army,
Holmdene Gardens,
27 March 1973

Pat McCabe's mother Bridget O'Reilly was originally from Pilot Street in Sailortown. His father William was an Ardoyne man, born and reared in Crumlin Street. For most of his life William worked as a docker. He met Bridget at the daily mass held for dockers in St Joseph's chapel Sailor Town. Both were devout Catholics. Bridget was an active Sinn Féin member. After a few years courtship the couple married in St Joseph's chapel. The day after the wedding they were fortunate to move into 105 Duneden Park. This became the family home where they reared their seven children, Marian, Pat, Theresa, Christine, Geraldine and Gerard (Pat's twin brother died at birth). Pat was the second child, born on 17 May 1956. He attended Holy Cross Boys school and studied at Crossgar seminary for the priesthood. Pat eventually decided against the priesthood and finished the remainder of his education at St Gabriel's school. Pat was a quiet fellow. He had very strong convictions and was a committed republican. Pat was always protective over his family, particularly his younger brother Gerard. After his mother's death he was devoted to their welfare. He was, according to his older sister Marian, 'a tower of strength'. Shortly before his death Pat and his girlfriend Geraldine McGrandles got engaged, to the delight of both their families.

On 27 March 1973, the British army killed Pat McCabe while he was on active service At the time of his death Pat was an IRA volunteer. The Parachute Regiment had arrived in Ardoyne on 9 March and within a matter of weeks five people, including Pat, had been killed in controversial circumstances (Eddie Sharpe, Brian Smyth, Anthony McDowell and Sid McKee). There is evidence of a shoot-to-kill policy in a number of the cases. Pat McCabe was 17 years old at the time of his death.

'Jamesy' (comrade)

I remember Pat long before the war actually started. We were altar boys and it even struck me then that he was not the type to do anybody any harm. He wasn't an altar boy because his peers were altar boys. I think he was an altar boy because he wanted to be one. When he approached me years later to join the Fianna I was really, really surprised – not sceptical but surprised. His family were all very quiet. We went to the same schools and joined the Fianna together. I progressed into Oglaigh na hÉrieann, into the army. About a year later Pat became an IRA volunteer. In those days a year on the street was a long, long time.

The day of the shooting, this is something his family might wonder about even to this day. It was the first time I had been out on an IRA operation with Pat. He had a .38 automatic and I was carrying a AR18 fold down butt. I don't know how Pat came to be on that particular operation but I was told he was going to do cover with the pistol. The two of us proceeded along Etna Drive on the left-hand side heading towards Alliance Avenue. We were intending to go up to Alliance Avenue where there was a British army post. There was just the two of us, no scouts. This was the first opportunity I had to talk to Pat as a volunteer; that stands out in my mind. I've had years to think about this. I suppose it hit me that Pat McCabe the altar boy was now Pat McCabe the Irish Republican Army volunteer. Strangely enough the responsibility was on my mind. Pat was such a lovely fella and when I say that word lovely, I mean he was a really decent fella.

It was roughly 3.30 pm in the afternoon. It wasn't dark; it was what you would call a nice afternoon. There were kids running about in the street. I remember specifically when we got to between Highbury and Holmdene Gardens there were a lot of kids running about and I was worried in case anybody noticed we were carrying weapons. I remember saying to Pat words to the effect, 'Are you OK? Have you got that hidden enough?' We proceeded on and we hadn't really got any worries. We were coming from Brompton Park towards Alliance Avenue with our backs to Brompton Park. Pat was on the outside and I was on the inside nearest to the railings on the left hand side going up. Coming past Highbury Gardens we checked around to make sure there were no foot patrols or anything around us. But foot patrols weren't a big thing in those days; in those days there were the 'whippets' (British army armoured vehicles) and they used to suddenly appear from nowhere. We got to Holmdene Gardens, went down the crib path, walked across the road and the incident happened.

I had the weapon down the leg of my trousers. Putting my own memory together with what I recall from the inquest a year later this is what happened. The NCO was in the lookout post on the top of the mill at Flax Street. That evidence came out in the inquest. Shots came from the Flax Street mill observation post. The British soldier said that he had been watching and observing two men moving along Etna Drive, one that he knew as a well-known IRA man and the other whom he later knew to be Patrick McCabe. He said, 'I took sights on Jamsey, knowing he was armed'. It was physically impossible for the soldier in the mill observation post to see any weapon that we were carrying, especially from behind. The weapon was completely concealed; it was a fold down butt AR18 and it was concealed up my coat and down the front of my trousers; no part of the weapon was exposed. And as I say, the view from the observation post was from behind. It would have been a physical impossibility for the British soldier to have seen that weapon. It would also have been physically impossible for him to have seen a short down the front of Pat's trousers. If the observation post had been in Etna Drive, yes it is conceivable that he might have seen a bump or something but from behind; no, it is physically impossible.

Returning to outside Holmdene Gardens I sort of skipped slightly up the step. This is where God or whoever it was intervened. I went half a pace in front of Pat and a shot rang out. I saw the bullet physically hit the railings; it was Tank Turley's railings, and they were old brown picket fence railings. I saw the bullet hit the railings. My brain told me that the shot had come down from Etna Drive, the top of Etna Drive. I instinctively turned and went round the corner, thinking Pat was with me. I went two or three paces up and took the weapon out in full view of the lookout post because my brain told me that that was where the shot came from. He could have fired again and it would have hit me but there were no other shots. After maybe two or three seconds or slightly longer I had the weapon out in my hand. I went round the corner aware of watching up towards Etna Drive. Pat was lying on the ground. He was clutching his stomach, not physically saying anything but definitely still alive. I gripped him by the top of the coat; it was like an old, soft, zip-up coat. The NCO admitted that he took target on me and when I half skipped up the step Patrick moved slightly into line and it hit him. One single shot was fired. It hit Pat in the back. I found out at the inquest that it hit him in the spine.

Within seconds I think it was Joanie Clarke and Owney Whelan were there and another male. They suddenly appeared from nowhere. A car suddenly appeared and they shouted to me to get out of the road. I heard the 'whippets' coming up Etna Drive from Brompton Park direction. At this time I'm not sure but I think a civilian got Pat's short out of the road. I ran round into Holmdene Gardens and my eyes scanned for an open door; there were no open doors. I ran up to the third or fourth house and I banged at the door; they wouldn't let me in. Then a man on up the street called me; I ran up and got into his house.

I had been arrested after Pat's death for another IRA operation. I was brought from the Kesh in handcuffs to Pat's inquest. They brought me presumably because I had been involved in the incident. At the inquest the British army kept sticking to the story that they'd taken sights on me, a well-known IRA man. They cited my full name. To my knowledge at the inquest the British soldier never said that he saw a weapon. But it was years later when we were talking in gaol and I remember saying, 'The shoot-to-kill policy isn't a recent thing; it's been here for a long, long time'. It was one of the only incidents that I know of when they actually admitted that they took sights on a person and fired to kill. They never at any time said that Pat was armed; they were totally unaware that Pat was armed. The verdict at the inquest was death by misadventure. It was just straight in and straight out whitewash. I got the impression, I could be wrong, that the British soldier was railed over the coals for it and that there was a clumsy cover-up that he was meant to shoot-to-kill. It was years ago and we were all kids and I wouldn't have known then to say that it was a physical impossibility for someone to see through my back to see a weapon. There was no cross-examination. But at that particular time my head was away. I think it was a case of straight in, a verdict of death by misadventure and straight out. It didn't warrant any high profile. I was surprised that I actually got called to the inquest.

I liked Pat, I liked him an awful, awful lot. If Pat hadn't been shot dead and he had stayed in the IRA he would have been what you probably would call a career army man, moving on politically. It was just one of those things that happened. He was a very nice person. He probably would have gone on to be a great army man and maybe a strategist of some sort.

Joanie Clarke (eyewitness)

Pat and a friend of his had been walking along Etna Drive towards Alliance Avenue and they had just got to the junction of Holmdene Gardens when a shot was fired. When we saw Pat fall, my brother and I ran towards him; it looked like he had been shot in the stomach. People were hysterical. Mr O'Connor who lived in Etna Drive ran out of his house to help. He ran back to his house and got a cloth to stem the bleeding from Pat's wound. He handed me a towel, which I held against Pat and I started to yell for someone to get a car. Gerard Comerford ran down to Owney Whelan's house. I can remember clearly Owney reversing his car up Etna Drive and with the help of Mr Galway we got Pat into the car to go to the Mater Hospital. As we were driving up Estoril Park we were stopped by the paras. They surrounded the car, aiming their weapons at us and screaming at us to get out of the car. I was in the back seat with Pat lying across me; his head was on my lap. He was badly wounded and I did my best to comfort him. I shouted at the Brits to let us get to the hospital. I knew Pat was dying. Owney was eventually allowed to get back into the car and the paras followed us down to the Mater Hospital.

Owney and the other man were immediately arrested. I was determined to stay with Pat. After being in hospital a matter of minutes Pat died. I stayed with him. The senior nurse who had seen the British army activity was worried that I was going to be arrested. She made me wash the blood from my hands and she then hid me. She thought if I stayed long enough the Brits would be pre-occupied with other things and would forget about me. I stayed in the Mater for two maybe three hours. As soon as I put my foot outside the door I was arrested and taken to Tennent Street RUC Station. From there I was taken to Castlereagh

Interrogation Centre and held for something like ten to twelve hours. I was the last to be released, probably because I was arrested three hours after Owney and Mr Galway.

My interrogators in Castlereagh tortured me the whole time about the shooting and said things like the para who shot Pat would get a medal for it and 'another Provo gunman out of the way'. Pat was murdered because he was a republican. I was one of the first at his side when he was shot. While in Castlereagh I asked for a cigarette. A box of Park Drive cigarettes were thrown onto the table; they were soaked in blood. Along with the cigarettes, eight pence was thrown onto the table as well. Before any of the Special Branch spoke I knew these were Pat's belongings. The Special Branch were sadistic. I tried to ignore the taunts about Pat and I refused to allow myself to respond. It was very hard not to respond. I kept wondering about what was happening in Ardoyne. I knew what I had done wasn't a crime; I comforted a teenager who had been shot. The Special Branch and Brits knew I'd committed no crime. I'll never forget what happened that day nor can I forget an 'open verdict' was returned at his inquest. Pat McCabe was cut down in cold blood like many others before and after him.

Marian Mailey (Pat's sister)

My mother gave birth to twin boys on 17 May 1956 in 105 Duneden Park. One twin died at birth (Gerard) and the other baby, called Pat, survived. Pat was the second child in the family. My mother died when Pat was only 16 years old. He was a tower of strength to the rest of the family. Pat was very close to Theresa (sister) and he was forever teasing her. Pat was a very active member of St Gabriel's Youth Club and was passionate about judo. Among his close friends were Patsy McKinney, Raymond Mullan and Sean McKee (killed on active service by the British army, Fairfield Street, 18 May 1973). Their friendships lasted through school and into their teens. From a young age Pat liked to be around people connected to the republican movement. As a teenage he was eager to play a role in the conflict. Like many of the young lads in the district then he was constantly being harassed and arrested. It seemed to be nearly every other night my mum and me were down in Tennent Street RUC station bringing him home. My father tried to curb his enthusiasm by sending him up to his room. But once in his room Pat was away out the window and down the drainpipe. He loved cars and at the time of his death he was training to be a mechanic in a garage on the Antrim Road. He had applied for a job in Burton's Tailors in Royal Avenue and the date for his interview was March 27, 1973, the day of his death. On that morning before he left home he went to my father, put his hands on his face and said, 'Daddy, you know that I love you'. None of us knew that before the day was out Pat would be dead.

When my mother died in April 1972 I took over the responsibility of rearing the children. I was working in Rosebank. That day I just knew something had happened to one of the family. But I never expected to hear that the British army had killed Pat. Rose Craig and Kate Carmichael came and told me that Pat had been shot. Later Joanie Clarke was able to tell us that she had cradled Pat on his way to hospital and that she comforted him. Pat was shot from the lookout post at the top of the mill in Flax Street.

Pat was going out with Geraldine McClenaghan (nee McGrandles) from Northwick Drive at the time of his death. They had been going out with each other for about two and a half years and they had got engaged on Geraldine's birthday in April 1972. Pat was very fond of Geraldine's parents, Jimmy and Mary and both of them loved him to call to the house. Geraldine married Martin McClenaghan, who was a friend of Pat's. A photo of Pat, along with other family photos, has always been on show in their home. Their five sons grew up and referred to him as 'our uncle Pat'. Their youngest son Pádraig is named after Pat.

After the death of our mother my father was devastated. Pat, even though he was only sixteen, was always there to depend on and he helped me to manage all the family matters. My brother Gerard was ten years old when my mother died and Pat was very protective of his one and only brother. Pat was just a lovely person and he had a great sense of humour. He was mature for his age and he was very attentive to my mum while she was ill. My father died four years after Pat was killed. He never really got over it. He grieved terribly and existed more than lived.

Gerard McCabe (brother)

Pat was the second eldest child in our family. He was my big brother. I have a daughter who is actually older than Pat was when he was shot dead. When I look at her she is a child but whenever I looked at Pat I thought he was a big mountain of a man. Pat may have only been seventeen years old but he was mature for his age. He had his direction in life worked out.

When Pat was younger he was an altar boy in Holy Cross chapel. He actually went into the Monastery in Crossgar to study to become a priest. I remember him actually going away to be a priest. I was about six years old and he was about 13. He used to come home at the weekends from Crossgar. My parents used to hide me out of the road when he was going back to Crossgar because I used to run after Pat when he was going for his bus and he would chase me home. I remember the day he told my daddy he was giving up the priesthood. The priest was in the house sitting on the arm of the chair towering over Pat, intimidating him. The priest said to my da, 'Pat wants to leave the priesthood'. I remember thinking, 'You are in for it here, boy'. My mother and father were very religious people; they would have gone to mass every day if they could and they said the rosary regularly. My da said to the priest, 'Well, if that is what he wants, that's fair enough'. I couldn't believe it. My mother took the same attitude. Up until that point as far as Pat or my parents were concerned, his destiny was to be a priest. I used to blame my parents for letting my big brother go away. I remember being in total shock and saying, 'I don't believe this, they are not saying anything to him'. Pat never talked about the reasons why he made that decision but I think that Pat's convictions would have been very, very strong. If he took something on board, he took it on board and that would have been it. I reckon if he had become a priest he would have probably gone off to the missions in the Third World, which would have been typical of him.

I think Pat's greatest love was the Irish Republican Army. The two biggest parts of his life for me anyway were his priesthood and the Irish Republican Army. The family were not conscious that Pat was in the IRA, not right away. I think that Theresa would have known for obvious reasons. Apart from that I probably would have been the first one to know that he was involved in the IRA. My mother took really ill and she died just before Pat became deeply involved. Pat always was the figurehead for me but after my mother's death he became the figurehead for all of us. When he worked he always gave Marian money for the housekeeping and made sure we had what we needed. After my mother died Pat actually told me that I had nothing to worry about and that he would look after me. I thought happy days, I'm as sound as a pound here, that is when Pat really started bonding with me. After my mother's death Pat became more heavily involved in the IRA and my da was wrestling with that. He used to lock Pat in the house and Pat used to climb out the bathroom window and do what he had to do and come back in through the window. I think my da was a bit of a pacifist but he was a nationalist, a republican. Pat decided that the military way was the way to do it and my da didn't.

The day Pat died I came back from school and was playing in the street. This was about 3 pm. To hear shooting in Ardoyne then wasn't a strange thing; you had to try and judge where it was coming from and you tried to get out of that direction. We were messing about in the street just outside our door and there was one single shot and everybody kind of a way just stood and looked to see what was going on. Within split seconds there was a crowd gathered at the bottom of Holmdene Gardens. Two of my mates started to run down and asked me to join them. I was a kid like everybody else; I was inquisitive and wanted to be in the middle of it but for some reason or other I didn't go down. I don't know why to this day but I didn't go down. I saw the crowd gathering and all of the commotion. I saw the car drive away from the scene. The car came right up Holmdene and it drove straight up our street right by me. I remember looking at the car and it was like an inner something was telling you that there was something wrong, it was really, really weird. Then a mate of mine came up and kids being kids, he said to me, 'That was your brother that was shot dead'. I think at that stage I went into shock. Pat had actually been in that car that drove by me.

I was taken into a neighbour's house for a while. Then I walked into the house and just got myself together. It was only eleven months from my mummy died and so the whole house was back to that again. I remember thinking to myself I have to get away from this. I went upstairs. I remember and when I came down that is when I started to find out that Pat was dead. Marian told me Pat was dead. It was as if I was up in the corner of the room looking down at this. The IRA came and told my da that Pat was an IRA volunteer. They wanted to give Pat a military funeral. My daddy said, 'That is what he died for; give him what he died for'. Then everything was organised by the republican movement, literally from bringing sandwiches into the house right up until buying a drink in the Star after the funeral. It was like that security was back again, the security I had with Pat; they brought it back in again. Whatever we needed was there. I always remember the republican movement for years and years after Pat's death helping us out in different ways. I realised when I got married, after we had our Catrina, how much you actually relied on the republican movement for that cushion to get you through.

Pat was the person first and foremost that gave me my direction and conviction. He gave me convictions in life that I'll take to my grave with me. All that I can say is that I have two sons and if they have the values that Pat had in life I'll be proud.

Anthony McDowell
Killed by the British army,
Etna Drive,
19 April 1973

He sort of looked round at me and he said, 'Uncle Michael, I'm hit, I'm hit' and I said, 'Don't be silly, son' and then he said, 'No, no, get my mummy, get my mummy'; that's all he said.

Anthony was born to Con McDowell and Marie (née Allen) on the 13th June 1960. He was the eldest in a family of four but since his death the family has extended to four sisters – Annemarie, Samantha, Hannah and Sarah – and six brothers – Con, Gabriel, Alan, Michael, Mark and Robert. His grandparents Sadie and Bobby McDowell reared him at their home in Duneden Park. Like most boys in the area he went to Holy Cross Boys School and did all the normal things young lads do. He was a good child and never caused any trouble for the family. He was a cadet in the Knights of Malta and played in his school football team. On 19 April 1973, as he and his uncle Michael drove back into Ardoyne after spending a weekend in Craigavon, the British army shot and fatally wounded Tony. He was only twelve years old when he died.

Patsy McArdle (friend and neighbour)

I knew Tony McDowell well because he lived next door to me with his grandparents. I never had any children of my own so Tony would come to my house regularly and do messages for me. His mother and father are Marie and Con McDowell; his grandparents were Sadie and Bobby McDowell who reared him. He had just joined the Knights of Malta a few weeks before he was killed. He was a wee boy who kept very much to himself. To be honest, he was always afraid of the British army. He was afraid to be anywhere near where they were. I don't know why; I only know if there was a foot patrol he would run to get out of the way. I was in the Knights of Malta; that was reason enough for Tony to join as he went everywhere with me.

The night Tony was shot dead I was actually looking for him at about 6.30 pm to go to Davidson's shop for me. His granda came to my door to tell me he was away for the weekend to Craigavon with his uncle Michael. The next thing, the soldiers came running down our street and I went out to see what was going on. Someone shouted, 'There's a child shot'. I grabbed my first-aid bag and when I was running down the street, somebody said to me, 'It's Tony McDowell'. That was as good as telling me it was my own son. I ran round the corner; the place was thronged with people. I just kept shouting, 'Where is he?' A car stopped and I remember well, it was Paul Shevlin. He got out of the car. He said to me, 'Patsy, if you are looking for young McDowell, he's dead'. I said, 'Where is he?' and he said, 'Round in Stratford Gardens'. Well, with that all hell broke loose and I never got anywhere near the child. But I do know that two of my first-aid workers went to him, Kay and Frankie Boyle.

Later I spoke to his uncle Michael; apparently what happened was they were driving down Alliance Avenue and instead of the British army stopping them and telling them there was shooting ahead, they were allowed to go on. As they got to between Jamaica Street and Etna Drive Tony said to Michael, 'I've been hit' and Michael said to him, 'Stop acting the eejit'; but he looked at Tony and saw the blood draining from him. He drove into Etna Drive and up Stratford Gardens; he jumped out of the car and ran round to the passenger door. There was a bullet hole in it and he then realised Tony had been shot. He opened the door to lift him and the only words Tony spoke were, 'Where's my mammy and where's Patsy?'

Later on that night, I know the British army came in full force to his grandmother's house, next door. They arrested Pascal O'Hare, the solicitor. They opened fire with rubber bullets and shot Tony's uncle Joe on the wrist. His watch was nearly burnt into his arm. I think Joe and Michael were arrested that night too. There was hand-to-hand fighting with soldiers in the street. I was literally fighting myself. As I said before, it might as well have been my own child that was killed. Everybody was so angry because the talk was the British army were saying, 'We got the wee one anyway'. Knowing Tony the way I did, like a son, there is no way he would ever be involved in anything, no way. As far as I can remember, they were trying to imply that the shooting was coming from the car, but believe me it wasn't. As far as I remember, there was shooting that day. The British army should have stopped cars driving into the area, but they allowed Michael to drive into an ambush or crossfire.

I don't know whether the British army ever admitted shooting Tony; I don't honestly think they did. When Tony's granny was told she passed out. Marie, Tony's mother, came in to my house. As quick as my house filled it just as quickly emptied, leaving Marie, Rose Craig and myself. Rose asked should she make tea and I said, 'Yes'. As Rose was making the tea Marie asked me who was shot. It suddenly hit me, 'She doesn't know'. I got up and put my arms around her and said, 'Marie, do you not know? It's your Tony'. She started crying. I think Fr. Fernando then came in and tried to console her.

I remember quite vividly things about Tony because he was like my child too. He lived next door and came in and out of my house. His granny and granda never got over it.

Joe McDowell (uncle)

Tony lived with his grandparents Sarah and Bobby McDowell. He was always a good child and never caused any trouble for the family. He was a cadet in the Knights of Malta along with one of his grandparents' neighbours, Patsy McArdle. He always said Patsy could make him better if he ever hurt himself. His Knights of Malta meetings were held weekly in Ardoyne Hall and Patsy and Tony would be seen going up the street each week to attend their meeting. Patsy's knowledge of first-aid throughout the early years of the troubles was of tremendous help to the people of Ardoyne and they always encouraged all age groups to join the Knights of Malta.

On 19 April 1973, Holy Thursday, Tony had been visiting his uncle Michael. His uncle Michael had been forced out of Rosapenna Street and had moved down to Craigavon. Earlier that day there had been some shooting in Ardoyne. Michael drove Tony home; they drove into Etna Drive from Alliance Avenue and were turning up to go into Stratford Gardens. There was a British army patrol at the top of Jamaica Street. The Brits opened up and a bullet went through the passenger door and hit Tony in the back. Michael stopped the car outside Sean McFarland's house and got out. A few people had run to the car and someone sent for an ambulance. Tony kept asking Michael to get his mammy and Patsy. Michael left to get his parents but he only got a short distance to Estoril Park when the Brits (paras) pulled him into a side garden and started to beat him. At this point the ambulance had taken Tony to hospital. The Brits let Michael go. He ran towards the family home and met his sister-in-law Joanie and told her what had happened. They went to get the rest of the family. Tony's uncle Tommy and Michael got into the car to follow Tony to hospital. They got as far as Flax Street and they were stopped outside the Brit post. They were arrested and taken to Tennent Street. Even though the Brits knew they were heading to hospital they were held for a few hours. During this time word had filtered around Ardoyne about Tony and fierce rioting had broken out. Michael and Tommy were released and went straight to hospital. Tony was already dead when they arrived.

Throughout the night rioting continued and at one point the Brits tried to enter the wake house, claiming the IRA had been seen entering it. Scuffles broke out as the family refused to allow them in. Tony's uncle Joe was shot with a rubber bullet; his aunt Joanie was threatened that she would also be shot. Tony's body was brought home on Good Friday and his funeral took place on Easter Monday. A close family friend, Elizabeth Williams, was being married on the same day; she was totally devastated as Tony's coffin passed her home. She was preparing to get ready to be married and guests of the wedding were attending the funeral. It took a lot of persuasion from Tony's family and her own not to call off her wedding.

Hundreds attended Tony's funeral. He had the Knights of Malta flag and his cadet beret on his coffin. All his school friends and practically the entire community of Ardoyne walked behind his coffin. The IRA met Tony's family and gave their condolences to them. No one was ever charged with Tony's murder. His family were granted £700 compensation, which they immediately refused. The British army insisted it was an IRA bullet that killed Tony but Michael and Tony's family know the bullet was fired from the British army post at the top of Jamaica Street.

Michael McDowell (uncle)

Tony was a gem. He was just a kid that was so, so, innocent. He never got into mischief. He got a Grifter bike from my mummy and I think that was his life. He just loved that bike. He was totally unreliable; anything you sent him for it took him an hour doing it. Patsy and Paddy McArdle just loved him. I think everybody loved Tony. We were living in Craigavon at the time and Tony had been down with us. On the way home I left my wife off at her mother's in Gracehill Street and went on down to leave Tony over to my mother's. On the way across there was shooting. We came down Deerpark Road. The British army said they stopped me. But they definitely didn't stop me; they definitely didn't, no way. If they had stopped me, I wouldn't have gone any further; but they didn't stop me. I drove on down and as we got to Jamaica Street to turn down Etna Drive, bullets were fired from my right, from an old billet where the soldiers were billeted. I wanted to get into Ardoyne very quickly. So I just turned the corner and that's when Tony was hit, on the corner turning into Etna Drive, just on the bend. He started to cry beside me and I just turned in and went up Stratford Gardens. He didn't even jump; he sort of looked round at me and he said to me, 'Uncle Michael, I'm hit, I'm hit' and I said, 'Don't be silly, son' and then he said, 'No, no, get my mummy, get my mummy'. That was all he said. Then I turned into the street and I got out of my side of the car and whenever I put my hand round his back, I felt the blood and I shouted. People came out and sat with Tony. I never ever got their names. I ran to get my mother because I thought he was just wounded. But apparently he died after I left him.

The paras were at Estoril and they pulled me over the first wall. I kept telling them that a child had been shot and I wanted to get my mother for him. They were questioning me. But the women came out and in the commotion I got up and ran off again to get my mother, to bring her round, because he just adored my mother. Whenever I got up to the house I told my brother Tommy and he said, 'Don't be telling mummy; I'll go round and see'. But by the time he got round apparently Tony was already in an ambulance and on his way to hospital. He brought the car back round to my mummy's and me and him and somebody else got into the car. We only got as far as Flax Street, coming down the Crumlin Road and we were stopped by the paras because they saw the blood on the seat of the car and they took us out and put us against the wall. They arrested us and then took us to Tennent Street for questioning. One of the things I always remember in Tennent Street was they said, they shot the wee bastard who was shooting out of the car and now they had got the other fucker, meaning me. We were separated then; I was questioned in one place and Tommy was questioned in another. I just gave the statement as it is. The next thing the three of us were taken in a car, hours later and thrown back into Ardoyne. We walked down to the house and that's when we found out Tony was dead and he was in the morgue. Tommy my brother went and identified his body and I'm not sure whether Con went or not.

There was an inquest and we all went. But at the inquest they said they stopped us and it was death by misadventure because the uncle drove on. Who drives on past the paras, let's face it? As I said, if they had stopped us, I would have stopped. I have a book somewhere in the roof space, *Contact* you call it; it's written by a para, a colonel. I actually have the words underlined, it mentions Tony being shot and he says something like the silly little bastard was in the wrong place at the wrong time. He was put out of the paras for writing the book but he was actually in command of the post at the time Tony was killed.

Tony was just an innocent wee child; he was no more. But as I said, they kept on saying that they knew there was gunfire coming from the car, which is a load of rubbish. Because whenever they did the forensics, there was nothing ever found in the car. There was never anything found on Tony and there was nothing found on me. But at the end they still said that it was death by misadventure. They said there was an IRA man at the bottom of Jamaica Street. They said that he could have fired the shot and he was using the same type of weapon as the British army, an SLR. This was said at the inquest. This was their explanation and washing their hands of it. I would love to see justice done. I don't accept the verdict of the inquest. I never did accept it. I categorically stated that I was never stopped, never, ever stopped.

He was a fantastic kid. He was just like any other kid; he hated going to school. The Knights of Malta did a wee guard of honour at the funeral. I never saw as many children crying in my life; it was sad, truthfully. All the kids from the district were there. I think every one of us kept something belonging to him; we have a wee coat of his, wee odds and ends and his wee purple shirt and his jeans. We were all like brothers. We all still think of him as a brother rather than a nephew; he is a brother to me.

Sean McKee
Killed on active service
by the British army,
Fairfield Street,
18 May 1973

> *Well, he did have a rifle but he was murdered;*
> *he was murdered.*

Sean 'Sid' McKee's mother and father both moved to Ardoyne from other parts of Belfast. His mother Alice was originally a Murray from Nelson Street by the Docks; his father Bobby came from the Lower Falls. Sean had one older sister, Maureen, and he himself was born in Ardoyne in January 1956. Throughout his life the family lived in Ladbrook Drive. Like almost all the boys of the district Sid went to the Holy Cross Boys school and St Gabriel's, leaving the latter in 1971. He worked first at the Rosebank Mill but by 1973 he was asphalting roofs. A few months beforehand Sean had also joined the IRA. On the afternoon of 18 May 1973 Sean was setting out on an operation, preparing to attack an army post. He was leaving a safe house when he was spotted and shot by members of the Parachute Regiment. Sid McKee was only 17-years-old at the time he was killed.

Paul (friend)

Sean and me were brought up together because he only lived seven doors away from me in Ladbrook Drive. He was about 18 months older and my earliest memory of him is from when we were playing in the street when we about three or four years of age. We grew up best friends and did everything together. There was a crowd of us who went about together but me and Sean were very close. He loved football. He was a Tottenham Hotspurs fan, then he changed to Chelsea. He loved the 1970 Brazil World Cup team as well. He was a big, well-built lad and he used to play football for a couple of teams too. He played for St Michael's and the Star of the Sea in the Down and Connor league. He liked a bit of snooker and he was good at handball as well. He used to beat fellas years older than him. Sean was a quiet big lad but joined in the fun. He was good craic and he was well-reared. He wouldn't have bullied people even though he had the height and the build to do it. He never did. In those days there was more life at the corner for 16 and 17 year olds than there would have been in bars. We used to drink up the entry and play cards at the corner. Sean never had a steady girlfriend but he would have got the odd lumber [kiss] up the entry. We used to go the discos in Toby's Hall, Ardoyne Hall and the Saunders. At that time everybody was wearing tartan scarves and crombies. Sean did too along with ox blood boots. Really, he was just a young fella starting to enjoy life. He didn't show any interest in politics; he was too young. There was no republican element in Sean's house, although his family were not anti-republican either. They were just ordinary people. He was rioting like everybody else. We all came home from school and were straight into rioting. But that was the norm in the area. Everybody did that. Like the rest of us he didn't like the British army. There was a lot of hate there. So from that Sean was keen to join the movement. He was in the Fianna, but I think his mother may have put pressure on him and he left for a while. In early 1973 he went back in and got involved in the more senior part of the movement, the auxiliaries and then into the IRA.

I knew he was a volunteer. He didn't talk about the danger of it but he was aware of it. It wasn't as if he was just given a gun and he was running around looking for somebody. He knew what he was doing. Sean was an intelligent person and he knew what he was about. Unfortunately the day he died it was in a new type of thing. The paratroopers were hiding in boarded-up houses. Anyone would have fallen for that at the time. Sean was in a house and he just came out with an armalite up his coat. There was no way he could have fired it and they just cut him down. He was only a wee lad and the gun he had never fired any shots. He had a green parka jacket on and the gun was up inside it. He would have had it upside down so there was no way the rifle was in a position to fire. I think a British soldier could have walked up to him, hit him a slap on the head and took the rifle away. They knew what he was at and that their lives were in no danger at that particular time. Nobody's life was in danger. Sean was shot dead on Friday 18 May 1973. The night before there was a similar operation carried out. The Brits came on the scene, there was a scattering match and he got away. I think they [British army] put two and two together and waited for him. When they took him away, Sean was lying on the ground. Afterwards people who had been there told me that they [British soldiers] just trailed him and threw him in the back of a saracen. There was no ambulance or first-aid. As the Brits were closing the doors, apparently you could see Sean's hands gripping the outside. He wasn't dead and people could see him just getting pulled in. That was the last anybody saw him alive, with his hands gripping at the doors. It's a brave way to go. They [British army] had control of the whole area so they could have sent for an ambulance and tried to give him treatment. But they didn't. It was just pure murder.

I was coming back from work when I heard about Sean's death. I got off a bus outside the chapel at about quarter past five. I met Anthony McBride and he said, 'That was terrible about your big mate'. I was shocked. I went home and my father and sister were there and they told me what had happened. I remember being in the house at the time of the funeral. When he was laid out, there was no trappings or anything. Sean's mother didn't know what her son was involved in and so she never believed that he had a rifle when he was killed. Well, he did have a rifle but he was murdered; he was murdered. He had a gun but it was impossible for him to fire it wrapped up in his coat. It would have taken a minute or 90 seconds to take it out, assemble the butt, cock it and get it ready to fire. Sean could have been arrested. His family were totally devastated by Sean's death. His mother took it to her grave that he wasn't involved in anything and his father never said much about it. His father was a happy-go-lucky fella. But when you saw him in the street afterwards you could see in him that he missed his son. But he never complained or said anything about Sean's birthday or anniversary. He just never spoke about it. Sean was one of the best fellas you could ever meet. I'm sorry I never had later years with him. It was an awful waste of life because he was just one really good fella.

'Tommy' (comrade)

I got to know Sean 'Sid' McKee through the movement. I would have been a close friend. He was one of the best blokes I ever met in my life. His heart was in the right place and he was a brilliant bloke. He was not in the movement very long. He was probably in the IRA for only five or six months. He was a quiet fella, very deep. He was just somebody you could take to easily. He was also determined to do what he wanted to do. We all knocked about and socialised together. We were close, like a family. Sid was always interested in the political situation; by that time we were volunteers. Becoming a volunteer was not as if you were led into it by anyone, not by a long shot. But Sean always wanted to know the ins and outs. At the time a lot of his friends were in the movement who would explain things to him. Sid believed in what he did and there was no going back for him. At the end of the day he did what he meant to do.

The day he was killed I called round to his house and we went to this house in Fairfield Street. A weapon was being brought round and the person that brought it said, 'Watch yourself because that's not working'. Sid jammed a round up into the breech but there was a round already there. So Sid beat it out. He was determined to do it. Then he was walking away and I said, 'Don't you put your hand or your finger near that'. We were going down to Fairfield Street corner. The operation was to fire at the Brits at Toby's Hall. A foot patrol was going up Butler Street. Sid was in the hall of the house and I was going up to check on where the Brits were. I walked down to the corner. There was a brick knocked out so you didn't have to walk round to look down the street without showing yourself. By that time the foot patrol was there. I wasn't armed and was just looking down the street when I heard a shot. I turned round and then everything felt as if it was in slow motion. Then I saw Sid falling out of the door. I was running up Fairfield Street and the Brits fired around nine shots at me and hit me in the foot. The Brits were in a derelict house in Butler Street/Fairfield Street. Some of them were standing in the yard and firing across the road. I think the man who fired the shot that killed Sean was shooting from the back bedroom window where Joe Hughes' old house was. There was a girl who tried to run over and help Sid but the paras put a gun to her head and said, 'Don't'.

By this time I had got into a house so I could see what was happening. Then they [British soldiers] were going to fire in through the door of the house I was in. I saw one para lift his rifle and I knew he was on the verge of firing. Then he fired through the door. I pushed this woman who was standing at the fireplace out of the way. It would have blown her head off. I tried to get out the back but the Brits were all over the place. The people of the house put me up the coalhole. By that time my foot was killing me. The woman gave me a bit of stick to bite on because of the pain. It was like something from a cowboy film when they have to take the bullet out. After that the Brits jumped all over Sid in the saracen once they got him. A woman said that a priest was running after the saracen asking if he could give Sid the last rites. The Brits more or less told him to 'fuck off'. Sid's mother always blamed me for what happened and said it was my fault. There was one time when I was up in the graveyard that she turned round and said, 'My son wouldn't be lying here if it hadn't been for you'. I didn't have an answer for the woman. All I could do was cry. I said to her, 'I'm sorry; it's your only son. I wish it had have been me'.

'Gunther' (cousin)

I came home from Australia on Good Friday 1972 and my mother and father moved to Glengormley. I wanted to stay in Ardoyne because that was where I came from. So I lived in Sean's house until I was arrested in the beginning of March 1973. At that time he was like a brother to me. Sean was a lovely kid. He was a big lad, only 17 when he was killed but already six foot two inches tall. But he was a gentle giant and always had a big smile on his face. He was so young. If he had lived in a normal society he would have had a million normal interests. He was just a real good, happy-go-lucky guy. I was interned in Cage 5 in the Kesh at the time Sean was killed. The first I heard of it was through a report on the news. It said that a gunman had been killed by the British army in North Belfast. Then it said it happened in Oldpark. When I went to bed everyone in the Kesh was wondering who it was. When I got up the next day everyone was talking about how someone from Ardoyne was dead and it was probably going to be someone we knew well. I used to have a visit from a girl every Saturday. Then when I went into the yard to see her, a fella came over to me and said, 'Do you know a guy from Ardoyne called Sean McKee?' I said I did and that he was my cousin. Then he told me that Sean had been shot dead. That is how I got found out about it. I was devastated. I didn't even know that Sean was connected. It was like a bolt out of the blue, totally unexpected. The only inclination I had that Sean was connected was when he had been on the scene the time that Bernard Fox was killed [Bernard Fox, killed by the British army in Brompton Park, 4 December 1972]. He had just been at the top of Brompton Park with a couple of mates and probably didn't know what was going on at the time. But that may have influenced him to become involved.

Internment morning 9 August 1971. Loyalists abandon their homes in Cranbook Gardens (shown above), Farringdon Gardens and Velsheda Park, burning the houses as they go.

Lena Hughes and young family in their Butler Street home, early 1970s, following a British army raid

Women on hunger protest in solidarity with POWs, old Ardoyne early 1970s. Among those present: Libby Murphy, Teassie Corrigan, Margaret Scullion, Marion Regan, Ann Davidson, Mary Mallon and Mrs Carson (looking on).

3

1974-76
'Murder Mile' – Truces and Terror Campaigns

T he mid-1970s witnessed some of the darkest days and nights of the thirty-year conflict. Mass shootings, pub bombings and 'random' sectarian killings left deep social and psychic scars in communities throughout the North. Political initiatives failed to achieve any meaningful breakthrough and a frightening logic of attrition began to take hold: that the imposition of ever greater violence could, in and of itself, produce a desired end. Certainly this was a key element of the thinking of loyalist paramilitary groups in this period. Targeting Catholics for assassination, whether or not they had any political or military involvement, became a stock in trade of loyalist actions. This was not, of course, entirely new. Abductions and drive-by shootings in particular had already proven to be a threat realised against nationalist communities in the previous few years. The deaths of Bernard Rice, Sean McConville, Patrick O'Neill, Gerard Gearon and Hugh Martin all showed that. For the people of Ardoyne there was also the memory of such killings from previous generations (most notably during the pogroms of the early 1920s). However, the fear instilled by loyalist gangs in the mid-1970s reached new heights both because of the level and the nature of the violence that certain groups were willing to employ. In terms of the number of victims, 1974 to 1976 was the most offensive period for loyalist paramilitaries. As a matter of strategy some loyalists saw the killing of innocent Catholics in as brutal a manner as possible as the best way to sap the support of the Catholic community for the IRA. It was also testament to how deep-seated and pervasive was the culture of sectarianism.

Nowhere did this loyalist campaign impact more that in North Belfast. The sectarian geography of that part of the city is such that many Catholic and Protestant areas sit cheek by jowl. In many places the two communites are separated by mere yards. Increasingly walls and fences also marked these divisions. The intimidation and evacuations of people during the previous few years had also ensured that there were virtually no mixed areas left. Ardoyne was therefore one of a small number of enclave Catholic districts that were all but surrounded by loyalist estates during the 1970s and 1980s. While, by and large, this continues to be true up to the present day the situation was far more acute (and far more dangerous) in this earlier period. This meant, for example, that there was no entirely safe route through Catholic areas from Ardoyne into the city centre. One outcome was that many people seldom (if ever) went out of the district. People shopped, socialised and essentially lived in what was both a relatively small and overcrowded area. Apart from anything else, this contributed greatly to the intense sense of belonging and loyalty to the district and its community that is characteristic of many Ardoyne people. It also meant that people were acutely aware of when and where it was more or less dangerous to be, particularly on the district's boundaries. Fear was never very far away, especially at night. Countless people from the area have stories of diving into doorways and hedges when an unrecognised car passed by. Pat Murphy lost his brother Ciaran in a brutal sectarian attack in October 1974 and describes the atmosphere at that time [Ciaran Murphy, killed by the UVF in Hightown Road, 13 October 1974].

> The worst period for sectarian killings was from about September 1974 to September 1975. It was a terrible time and was particularly bad in North Belfast which is something of a cockpit for sectarian attacks. My brother Ciaran was killed in October 1974 and he was the third nationalist from around the area to be shot by loyalists in a four day period. That gives an indication of how unrelenting the attacks were. It also created a terrific pressure on republicans locally to hit back. People in the district were demanding that they give like for like. That did happen for a brief period, solely due to the pressure for action from the community and it was very much resisted by the IRA. If republicans had taken the same attitude as the loyalists and carried out a wholesale campaign of random attacks on Protestants then there would have been a complete bloodbath. The difference is the way in which loyalists view the Catholic community. For loyalists everyone in a nationalist area is 'guilty' and therefore a 'legitimate target'. They don't differentiate between different shades of green. It is a perverse logic that allows them to de-humanise nationalists to the point where they can do unspeakable things to them. Nothing else can explain what the Shankill Butchers did to their victims.
>
> That attitude was born out of the sectarianism that defined life in North Belfast long before the troubles started. Sectarianism was something that you were simply always aware of. It was just a part of your life and you had to take precautions as a result. Ardoyne was like Noah's Ark because you always had to travel around in pairs! There was also a lot of very personal animosity because people often knew exactly who those involved in doing things on the other side were. That made it all the more vicious. But it just got crazy in the mid-1970s. The district was so demonised, marginalised and hemmed in. The area was very tightly defined and the boundaries ran from the Cliftonville Road, by Alliance Avenue, Ardoyne Road, Crumlin Road and down to the Bone on the Oldpark Road. You just spent as little time as possible on the fringes of the area. You would walk miles out of your way to avoid certain places. If you were walking down the road you watched cars all the time and always walked into oncoming traffic. I moved to Dublin in 1975 and on one occasion as I was walking home a motorbike pulled up behind me to ask for directions. I jumped over the wall of a garden because I thought I was going to be killed. It was only afterward that I remembered I was in Dublin. That was reactions that you had to develop. It was what the fear of sectarian killings bred in you. (Pat Murphy, Ardoyne resident and brother of Ardoyne victim Ciaran Murphy)

In every home in the district people would always check first before answering a knock at the door, particularly at night. Amongst others the deaths of Geraldine McKeown [killed by the UVF in her home in Moutainview Gardens, 8 December 1976] and Larry Marley [killed by the UVF in his home in Havana Gardens, 2 April 1987] illustrate why. If Ardoyne people tried to take great care about where they went, when and how, then there was good reason for such caution. Loyalist groups often looked to those nationalist areas that were closest to their own heartlands to find their victims as this gave them ease of access and escape. Given its proximity to loyalist North and West Belfast, Ardoyne was an obvious choice for their deadly attention. So pronounced was the degree of sectarian segregation in that part of the city that loyalists could also be more or less sure that someone walking down a certain street, at a certain time and in a certain direction was a Catholic. It is because of this (and the large number of people who were abducted and killed there) that the Cliftonville Road became known as 'murder mile'. It was one of the favourite 'hunting grounds' of various loyalist groups. This was particularly so for the most notorious and brutal of them all, the UVF gang that came to be known as the 'Shankill Butchers'. A number of the Shankill Butchers' victims were from Ardoyne.

The loyalist killing campaign came against a backdrop of political and constitutional crisis. It was clear from early 1974 onward that both loyalists and right-wing unionists were intent on bringing down the power-sharing executive set up in December 1973. The new executive came into power that January but quickly found itself in trouble. There were acute internal divisions between the new power-sharing partners in the SDLP and UUP. On 4 January the Ulster Unionist Council rejected the deal leaving Brian Faulkner isolated in his own party. It was against this background that Terry McCafferty became the first Ardoyne victim of 1974. Terry had grown up in Ardoyne. At the time of his death he was living in Ligoniel Road. He was also a well-known boxing trainer at the Ligoniel amateur boxing club. On 21 January Terry was working alongside James McCloskey in Woodland Close in Whiteabbey. The two men were laying cables for the Northern Ireland Electricty Service. Two UDA gunmen first robbed Terry and James of their wages and then shot them dead.

A general election took place on 28 February with 30,000 British troops on duty. Various anti-Sunningdale unionists combined to win 11 of the 12 parliamentary seats. The new Labour administration in London soon had to contend with a more direct challenge to their policies in the North (now in the hands of Merlyn Rees). In late March the recently formed Ulster Workers' Council (UWC) announced its intent to bring down the Executive. On 15 May the UWC called a general strike and set up a co-ordinating committee under the leadership of Glenn Barr and including Ian Paisley (DUP), William Craig (Vanguard), Andy Tyrie (UDA) and Ken Gibson (UVF). Support for the strike amongst Protestant workers was initially limited. However, because of paramilitary intimidation and a lack of action on the part of the British army, the strike soon began to have an effect. It exacerbated the conditions of day-to-day living that were already extremely difficult. Marian Kane was a young mother at the time and she describes the circumstances that she and other women in Ardoyne had to face.

Sometimes trouble would break out, the shops would all close and you would be left with babies to feed. Then you would hear that the Ardoyne Relief Committee or whoever were giving nappies, bread and milk out down at the school. So you would get down there as quickly as you could before everything was gone. To some people it felt like begging but you had no choice. Things just closed down and you had to feed your children. People used to try and keep a stock of things in as well if they could. That was not easy because people couldn't afford to stock food. They were just existing. But you always had to try and buy an extra tin of something to have a wee store up on one side. You always had a tin of Marvel, dried milk and some tea bags. You would always have a tin of corned beef or soup so you could at least boil that up. And you always had some candles. I used to have a few things up in the attic for when things got bad. You were basically just existing from day to day. You never stopped worrying. When your kids went out in the morning to school and your husband to work you started to worry. As soon as you closed the door you just prayed until they came home safe again. You were not thinking, 'It can't happen to me'; you were thinking, 'When will it happen to me'. If your husband was 10 or 15 minutes late coming in from work you started saying to yourself, 'Where am I going to put the coffin? I will have to move that chair to get it in'. You were always listening to the news waiting to see if someone you knew had been killed. (Marian Kane, Ardoyne resident and community worker)

In Ardoyne, as elsewhere, the UWC strike brought the practical problems and discomfort that resulted from cuts to electricity and water supplies. But the crisis also brought the prospect of a more immediate threat to the district. Deaths, injuries and arrests had ensured that the local IRA was at a relatively low ebb. Ardoyne republicans had hit both loyalists and (even more so) the British army hard in those years, killing many and wounding more in gun and bomb attacks. They had equally had their own ranks whittled down by the sustained impact of conflict and internment. There were contingencies put in place, however, should the district come under wholesale attack. Dozens of Ardoyne men and women who were not active members of the IRA were recruited into a defence organisation. This was to be mobilised if and when attacks on the area looked imminent. Once again, it was this localised reality that was uppermost in the minds of people in Ardoyne. Continued confrontations with the British army added to this greater sense of vulnerability.

The capability of loyalists to inflict great loss of life was emphasised two days after the start of the UWC strike. On 17 May loyalists planted several bombs in Dublin and Monaghan, killing a total of 33 people. Allegations of involvement of British intelligence agents in this action would surface soon after. This highlighted the role that collusion between the British state forces and loyalist paramilitaries had during the conflict. Certainly many people in Ardoyne believe that, even in these early days of the conflict, the RUC and British army colluded (either directly or by omission) in a number of the killings of local people by loyalists. Suspicion still lingers that loyalists and British soldiers co-ordinated with one another during gun battles. At the very least, it was clear that the British army did not see loyalists as either a threat or a target for their fire during such encounters. British soldiers certainly appeared to be anything but impartial. Collusion was, however, to be more of an issue in later years when the counter-insurgency 'dirty war' tactics of British intelligence and special forces came more to the fore.

By the end of May the UWC strike had brought down the power-sharing executive. Faulkner resigned on 28 May and the Northern Ireland Assembly was prorogued on 30

May. Direct Rule returned. This was seen positively by many republicans. They felt that Britain would soon tire of the situation and begin to look to withdraw from the North. It was within this context that talks between the IRA and the British government began toward the end of 1974. However, the IRA also stepped up its bombing campaign, particularly in Britain. In October and November bombs were planted in pubs in Guildford, Woolwich and then Birmingham; 19 died in Birmingham. Pub bombings had in fact already become a terrifying feature of the war in the North. Throughout 1974 and 1975 several were detonated by both republicans and loyalists. For example, on 16 July the UVF planted a bomb in the Sunflower Bar in Corporation Street. Before the start of the conflict there had been 30 pubs within a mile of the Sunflower bar. By the time it was blown up only 7 remained. Over a dozen people had died in these various blasts. One of those killed in the Sunflower was Thomas Braniff. Thomas was a Protestant from Great George's Street who had married an Ardoyne Catholic woman and then lived in Brookfield Street. His brother was seriously injured in the same explosion.

The first half of the year had, however, seen a relative lull in the numbers killed in Ardoyne. Then, on 5 August Martha Lavery was shot dead by the British army. Martha was in her son's house in Jamaica Street when a gun battle broke out between British soldiers and local members of the 'Official' IRA. On 10 October, just 5 days after the Guildford bombings, Harold Wilson was returned as Prime Minister with a narrow majority. On the same day Bertie Lutton from Stratford Gardens was visiting his Protestant girlfriend in Newtownabbey. Bertie was sitting in her living room when loyalist gunmen came in and shot him dead. Bertie's death was claimed by the 'Protestant Action Force', a cover name for the UVF. Three days later 17-year-old Ciaran Murphy from Strathroy Park was killed. Ciaran was coming from a Chinese restaurant up the Cliftonville Road when he was abducted by members of the UVF. He was badly beaten and shot six times. Ciaran's body was then left on the northern outskirts of the city. It was an ominous sign of what was to become all too familiar in the weeks and months to come.

Then on 14 November Volunteer Jamesy McDade from Oakfield Street was killed when a bomb he was planting exploded prematurely in Coventry. His body was flown back to Ireland for the funeral several days later. However, this was only after the cortege was attacked in England and British Airways had refused to handle his remains. The doors of churches and funeral parlours in Belfast were also closed in the face of Jamesy's family. In the meantime, on 21 November, the Birmingham pub bombings had occurred. Five of the 'Birmingham Six' were subsequently arrested and charged with causing these explosions as they boarded a ferry for Belfast. They were returning home to attend the funeral of Jamesy, who had been a popular figure within the West Midlands Irish community. The Birmingham Six would subsequently spend sixteen and a half years in prison for something they did not do. James McDade's funeral eventually took place in Milltown cemetery on 23 November. Later that same night Mary Shepherd (who had given evidence in the case of the UDA killing of Gerard Gearon from Strathroy Park two years before) was shot dead along with another man as she was working in a taxi office in Clifton Street. All in all three Protestants and four Catholics were shot dead in Belfast over the same weekend. Amongst these victims was Michael Hanratty, killed by the UDA at the social club he managed in the Bone.

In the charged (not to say hysterical) atmosphere that ensued in the wake of the Birmingham pub bombings the British government rushed the long-prepared Prevention of Terrorism Act (PTA) through parliament in less than twenty four hours. As self-confessed 'draconian' legislation it was argued that the PTA was only a 'temporary' measure to deal with a specific 'emergency'. It has remained in place ever since. On 30 January the Gardiner report recommended the ending of Special Category Status. This was not entirely unexpected and at first seemed to some to be a positive step. It promised the end of internment and a return to 'normal' legal procedures. However, somewhat more ominously, Merlyn Rees announced the construction of the H-Blocks less than a week later. Britain was putting in place the measues needed to conduct more easily a counter-insurgency campaign.

At the same time Britain was making overtures to republicans. This led to the declaration of an IRA ceasefire in December. Talks between the British government and the IRA were then held. Little progress was made and the ceasefire was called off on 17 January 1975. However, it was re-instated for an indefinite period on 9 February. The truce between the IRA and the British that then came into effect lasted through most of the year. However, it would be broken on numerous occasions and tensions on the ground were never entirely subdued. Incident centres were established throughout the North in potential flashpoint areas and were the cornerstone on which the truce was built. To all intents and purposes there was a tacit agreement reached that republicans were more or less left to control their own areas. In Ardoyne the incident centre was set up at the bottom of Brompton Park and through much of the period there was a relative lull in confrontations between the British army and the Ardoyne population. A suspension of hostilities was undoubtedly welcome to all. However, for many of the young people of the district the conflict had become 'normal', as Brendan Whiteway explains:

> We used to joke that you could always spot a tourist in Ardoyne. Growing up in the conflict you would be playing football in the street or whatever, and you might hear a rattle of gun fire from the corner. The IRA might be opening up on the RUC and you could hear it but we would just carry on playing or even run over toward it. Sometimes you would see someone diving over a wall going 'oh God, oh God' and you thought 'spot the tourist', you know. We grew up in it, we were used to it. If we heard a bomb blast going off we would actually run toward it like we were scared of missing something. That was the sort of world we knew. You were a bit wary of gunfire but at the same time you didn't want to miss anything and you loved to be one of the first ones on the scene. There was actually excitement growing up in the midst of the troubles. People get the wrong idea if you say that the troubles were fun but when you were a kid growing up, there were things that were fun. If the RUC or the Brits came in with plastic or rubber bullets during a riot you used to try to be the first one to pick one up to show it off. When your ma and da weren't looking you might grab an old bottle and throw it over the back wall. It was like, 'Here come the Brits; let's throw an old bottle and run'. But it was more to try and get a bit of chase going, looking for a bit of excitement than anything else. None of us at the time were really interested in politics; it was never really mentioned. We were just growing up and having as much fun as possible. (Brendan Whiteway, Ardoyne resident who grew up in the district in the 1970s and 1980s)

The existence of a truce seemed to offer the nationalist minority the prospect of meaningful political progress and a lessening of a threat from the British military. It impacted very differently on the loyalist community. For loyalists the truce suggested that a possible British withdrawal was being considered. At the very least republicans were being invited to take part in political decision-making in the future. As a direct consequence the diminution of IRA activity led not to less loyalist violence but to a very significant increase. This ran directly contrary to the 'tit-for-tat' rationale so often offered as the explanation for loyalist paramilitary violence. An unprecedented campaign of killing Catholics got under way that was specifically intended to provoke an end to the truce and to frighten the nationalist community into submission. The representation of such sectarian assassinations as 'random' and 'mindless' is therefore not only misleading but positively disingenuous. This was a campaign designed to create terror and fear within the Catholic community. It was intended to evince, in the coarsest and most brutal terms, loyalist determination to oppose all and any political change.

By early April the truce was already under considerable pressure. The level of violence, which had abated briefly, began to intensify once more. This had an almost inevitable effect on people in Ardoyne. On 5 April the UVF planted a bomb in McLaughlin's pub on the New Lodge Road. Two Catholics were killed. Less than three hours later the Mountainview Tavern on the Shankill Road was bombed and five Protestants were killed. As news reached Ardoyne of these events people began to make their way home fearing further attacks. Thomas Robinson and his wife were amongst them. They left the Highfield Club and were nearing their home in Stratford Gardens when Thomas was shot dead by the UVF. On 19 June Francis Bradley from Northwick Drive was killed in a UVF bomb attack at the Shamrock Filling Station on Corporation Street. An oil can had been booby-trapped and left sitting on the forecourt of the garage. When Francis got out of the car he had driven up in with four friends the device exploded. Through the summer the pace of loyalist killings intensified and certain attacks would live long in the memory. One such was the shooting dead of three members of the popular Miami Showband on 31 July. Two members of the UVF gang that carried out this attack also blew themselves up as they tried to make it appear that the band had been carrying explosives. With the truce increasingly in tatters the IRA in Ardoyne was also increasingly meeting like with like. This was in large part because they were coming under pressure from the community to respond to ongoing loyalist attacks. By the anniversary of the introduction of internment the truce was close to collapse after tensions led to severe rioting and gun battles in West Belfast.

Loyalist attacks against Ardoyne continued. On the morning of 21 August John Finlay from Duncairn Gardens was making his way to work along Brougham Street when members of the UFF shot him twice in the head. As John lay injured on the ground, a loyalist gunman stood over him and shot him three more times. The very next day William Daniels from the Crumlin Road was sitting with his girlfriend outside his home. He had survived an attempt on his life only 11 days before. A bomb attached to a lorry in which he had been travelling fell off before it exploded. William was not so fortunate a second time. Two UVF gunmen shot him dead. In October a newly installed UVF leadership signalled their intent to launch a new phase of the conflict. On 2 October the UVF planted a total of

13 bombs and carried out attacks that led to the deaths of 12 people. One of these was Thomas Murphy from Stratford Gardens. Thomas was at work in his photographic shop at Carlisle Circus on the Antrim Road when a group of UVF gunmen shot him dead and then blew up the building. On the following day the UVF was re-proscribed having been legalised as part of a conciliatory package the year before.

This period also saw violent feuds rip through communities in many parts of the North. First the IRSP and the 'Officials', then the UDA and the UVF, and finally the 'Officials' and the IRA were all involved in internecine struggles. Fuelled by the activities of British intelligence these splits and divisions contributed greatly to the overall atmosphere of tension. People in Ardoyne also suffered directly as a consequence. The numbers of those killed from such feuds was less than in other areas but they still very much left their mark. Over the decades of conflict fighting between republicans would leave at least four local men dead [Seamus McCusker killed by the 'Officials' in the New Lodge, 31 October 1975; Trevor McNulty killed by the IRA in the New Lodge, 27 July 1977; John Fennell killed by the INLA in Bundoran, 6 March 1996; Fra Shannon killed by the INLA in Turf Lodge, 9 June 1996]. As the truce disintegrated the tensions within as well as between communities also heightened. On 31 October IRA Volunteer Seamus McCusker from Strathroy Park was working at a Sinn Féin Incident Centre on the New Lodge Road. A dispute had developed within the local community arising from the recent split between the 'Officials' and the INLA. Seamus had been asked to investigate a particular incident. He went to some nearby flats. As he did so he was shot dead by members of the 'Official' IRA. By this time the truce had become all but non-existent. On 10 November the IRA in Derry indicated as much when they blew up the incident centre in the Bogside. Two days later the remaining incident centres were all closed down. There was to be one other Ardoyne victim killed by republicans before the end of the year. The circumstances of the death of Christine Hughes were, however, to be very different to those of Seamus McCusker. Nor did they have anything to do with any feud. Christine was a mother of eight. On 21 December 1975 she was in her home in Mountainview Parade with four of her children. Members of the IRA came into the house, believing it to belong to a member of the British Security forces. They then shot Christine dead.

By the time of Christine's death there had also been more loyalist killings of Ardoyne people. On 25 November Frankie Crossan, a 34-year-old father of two, spent the evening at the Holy Cross Bowling Club held in the Ardoyne Hall. Frankie was originally from Ardoyne but had moved his family across the city to West Belfast a few years before. However, he was in the district virtually every day, often to see the family of his dead brother Paddy. Paddy Crossan had been shot dead by the UVF just over two years before [Paddy Crossan, killed in the Woodvale Road by the UVF, 2 March 1974]. That evening he was with Paddy's widow. At around midnight Frankie was making his way home down the Crumlin Road toward a taxi rank in the centre of the city. He was hit from behind and bundled into a taxi that drove off to the Shankill Road area. Frankie was then tortured and severely beaten before his throat was cut by a man wielding a large butcher's knife. His body was then left in an entry off Tennent Street where it was found the next day. The man who wielded the knife that killed Frankie was Lenny Murphy, leader of the Shankill Butchers. It was not the first gruesome attack that Murphy had been involved in. As early as August 1972 Murphy was one of those responsible for the killing of Tom Madden from Cliftonpark Avenue. When Tom's body had been found, it had over 100 cut and stab wounds. He had been hung from a beam in a lock-up garage off the Oldpark Road and subjected to systematic torture over several hours. He eventually died from slow strangulation. Only two months earlier his brother Hugh had been shot dead by loyalist gunmen. The Shankill Butchers took both anti-Catholic hatred and the terrible logic of the 'next worst atrocity' to new depths. Their macabre means of inflicting death were designed to cast a cloud of fear over Catholics. The 'cut-throat' method first used to kill Frankie Crossan was thus intentionally gruesome. It was those in enclave areas like Ardoyne for whom this frightening message was most obviously intended. On 10 January 1976 the Butchers struck again. Ted McQuaid (who was originally from Ardoyne but was then living in Andersonstown) was shot dead on the Cliftonville Road as he and his wife made their way home after a night out. Lenny Murphy and his cohorts had been cruising the area in a taxi for hours looking for a 'suitable' victim: a Catholic.

But the Butchers were not the only loyalist group operating in and around the district at that time. Everyone in Ardoyne had to live with the threat of loyalist attack. Alongside those who died as a result of such terrifying incidents there were many others who survived. On 3 June 1976 Marie Fusco and her family were the targets of a loyalist gun attack. She describes what happened and the long-term impact it had upon her.

We used to live in Mountainview, which was a mixed middle class residential area on the fringes of Ardoyne. In early June 1976 I had been travelling over to England for a christening. I was stopped on the way over, arrested, strip searched and questioned for about eight hours by Special Branch. I then flew back over to Belfast and arrived back up in Ardoyne on the evening of 3 June. Nobody else knew that I was coming home and it always seemed too much of a coincidence to me that Special Branch were the only ones aware of my travel arrangements. At about 8.10 am the next morning there was a knock at our front door. My father asked who it was and a voice said it was the postman. When my father opened the door a gunman came in and put a gun to his head. Luckily the gun jammed and my father ran upstairs as they fired a shot at him. He ran into his bedroom, never dreaming that they would go after anyone else. I was still lying asleep in bed and woke up to find this man standing at the bottom of the bed. I remember he had blond hair and was wearing a checked sports jacket, a shirt and tie and white gloves. He pointed the gun at the bed and I just hid under the bedclothes. I curled up into a ball and put my hands over my head. Then he opened fire. I don't remember hearing the shots or feeling any pain. I just felt myself bouncing on the bed. After the fourth shot I lay pretending to be dead. I didn't breathe or anything. All told, he fired six bullets and put ten holes in me. My two young sisters were lying in a bed next to me and he shot at them too. One of them, Conchetta, was shot in an arm; she had been lying over the front of my other sister Jacquelyn. If it had not been for Conchetta's arm then Jacquelyn would have been killed. My mummy and daddy tried to stop the gunmen as they ran out but couldn't. Neighbours said they saw the gunmen driving out of the street laughing and joking. Afterward the loyalists tried to claim that my father and I were in the IRA but that was completely untrue. My family moved out of that street after the attack and got a house in Ardoyne itself. I survived the shooting but it completely changed my whole personality. Before I was outgoing and bubbly but was much more quiet and withdrawn afterward. It took me years to get over the bitterness too. I still find it very difficult going into a predominantly Protestant area. I am on tenterhooks all the time if I do and would never dream of going on a bus. (Marie Fusco, Ardoyne resident and victim of a sectarian attack)

Shots had been fired into the chip shop owned by the Fuscos (situated on the front of the Crumlin Road) on a number of occasions in the past. This was the way in which the intensity of the conflict could impact on the lives of an ordinary family in Ardoyne in this period. Two days after the Fusco family home was attacked, the Butchers' gang were involved in the mass shooting of five men in the Chorlane bar in Smithfield. Two days later, on 7 June, loyalists struck in Ardoyne again. Members of the UFF came into the area and shot Paul McNally from Estoril Park. At the time Paul was standing outside the Fuscos' other premises (a sweet shop) at the top of Brompton Park. Paul McNally was not as 'lucky' as the Fuscos. He died from his wounds two days later. On 17 June the UFF hit Ardoyne once more. Gerard Stitt from Highbury Gardens and Patrick Meehan from Duneden Park had both separately boarded a bus in Ardoyne that was travelling from Ligoniel into the city. Two members of the UFF were already on the bus. They then shot the two men dead and made their escape into the area of the Shankill Road.

Ardoyne deaths from loyalist attacks continued toward the end of the year. John Maguire from Ashgrove Park drove a van delivering copies of the *Belfast Telegraph*. Charlie Corbett from Holmdene Gardens worked with him. Charlie was a 'little slow' and John had taken him under his wing. On 30 October the two were also accompanied on their round by John's nine-year-old son Michael. As they pulled in to make a drop off at Greggs newsagents on the Crumlin Road, a group of UVF gunmen jumped into the van. They forced John and Charlie into the back of the van with Michael and drove round into Leggan Street. There they shot both men dead and left the boy severely wounded. Then on 6 December two members of the UVF went to the home of Geraldine McKeown in Mountainview Gardens. They knocked at the door. As she always did Geraldine juked her head through the venetian blinds to see who it was. The gunmen opened fire and Geraldine died of the wounds she received two days later. She was 14-years-old.

1975 and 1976 had been years of awful carnage for Ardoyne. They were also years that saw important shifts in the political environment and the direction of British state policy. A Constitutional Convention elected in May 1975 had been dominated by an anti-power-sharing unionist majority. When it supported a report calling for a return to simple majority rule in November it was clear that political compromise was unobtainable. The Convention was formally dissolved in March the following year. On the other hand the truce between British forces and the republican movement had also not led to a major political breakthrough. Republicans initially thought that the truce and the Convention were part of a British strategy to extricate itself from the North without losing face. As time went on it became clear that this was an unfounded belief. Whether or not the British intended from the outset to use the period of the truce to build up its counter-insurgency capacity and undermine the position of the IRA is not entirely clear. What is apparent is that measures for a new phase in the British approach to the conflict were being put into place through this period.

By the mid-1970s the consequences of using regular British troops as the 'blunt instrument' to re-establish state control were proving to be deeply problematic for the British government. The state's aims were clearly not being delivered. The number of non-combatant Catholics killed by the state and the level of casualities suffered by the British army were (in different ways) causing the British government problems. Far from ending resistance the state killings in nationalist areas had hardened people's resolve to continue it. That so many British soldiers had died led to negative political fallout that the death of people from the North seldom caused. The level and nature of militarisation was also an issue. Despite the demonisation of communities like Ardoyne through 'black propaganda', international opinion still tended to view the conflict as a war. The image of well-armed British troops occupying ordinary working class estates was very much a key factor in this.

However, if the British authorities had concerns about their image it did not lead to a decrease in the the day-to-day use of military force in Ardoyne. Far from it. Nor did it mean that the British army had stopped killing people in the district. On 18 December 17-year-old John Savage from Velsheda Park was shot dead. A British army foot patrol opened fire on a hi-jacked car in which John and others were travelling. Over the years some dozen or more 'joyriders' would be shot dead by the British army. Seemingly, for both the RUC and the British army driving through a checkpoint was an offence often meriting a death sentence. Patrols, spot checks, arrests and mass searches continued. House searches were a regular feature of life for many families. The recently deceased Mrs Mulvenna (from the Bone), whose son Jim was shot dead in an SAS shoot-to-kill operation in 1978, explained what such searches involved [Jim Mulvenna, killed by the SAS in the Ballysillan Road, 21 June 1978].

There was one weekend in the mid-1970s when our house was raided 30 times. There were 30 raids inside three days. I was raided Friday, Saturday and Sunday. It was unbelievable. They would search the place, then the saracens would just drive round the corner, come back round and then they started again. They were just in and out all the time. It was continuous. It got to the stage that I said to them coming in, 'Evidently this house is not mine' and I handed them the keys. The week before a group of British soldiers came into the house with picks and shovels on their shoulders. They were all singing 'Hi Ho, Hi Ho, it's off to work we go, we work all day and get no pay' as they came in. They went out to the backyard and dug every inch of it up. It had been a cement yard but they left me a garden where I hadn't had one before! We ended up with no toilet, no yard and no doors, just an open space. I went up to the barracks to complain and they sent some engineers down to fix it and gave me a new toilet. So I always say, at least I got a good new yard out of them! But it is hard to take people coming into your home singing and treating it as if it is not yours. They acted as if it was not my home. I remember one time one of them just went to put the teapot on himself. Then I went in the other room and some of them were sat there using our polish to blacken their boots. They just did what they wanted; your house was not your own. You were always waiting for a raid. For a long time I went to bed in my clothes.

There was only once that they came into my bedroom when I was wearing my nightdress and I swore it would never happen again. So after that I went to bed fully clothed. You wouldn't want anybody to go through what we went through. (Mrs Mulvenna, Bone resident and mother of victim Jim Mulvenna)

It was against this backdrop that the British state began to establish what would emerge as the 'containment' strategy of the late 1970s and early 1980s. This was more clearly to follow the guidelines laid down by Kitson and others for how a 'low intensity' war should be fought. On 5 December 1975 internment was finally ended. In all 1,981 men and women had been interned. Only 107 of them had been loyalists. At the time the ending of internment was regarded by many as a positive step toward the phasing out of 'abnormal' legal powers. However, the Special Courts were to remain and from March the PTA was to come into force in the North alongside the EPA. In November 1975 the British government had also announced that Special Category Status would no longer apply to anyone convicted for 'scheduled offences' committed after 1 March 1976. The policy of 'Criminalisation' was getting under way. There is ample evidence to suggest that the SAS had been operating in the North for quite some time. However, in January 1976 they were officially deployed. On 25 March Merlyn Rees announced the policy of 'police primacy' in the House of Commons. By July a package of measures was put in place that would lead to the militarisation of the RUC and the creation of special units. Another strand of the counter-insurgency approach was being put in place. On 10 September Roy Mason became Northern Ireland Secretary. The days of seeking a political solution, or a rapprochement with republicans were gone. Mason's remit was to look for a military solution by defeating the IRA in any way he could. Five days later Ciaran Nugent became the first IRA prisoner to be convicted of a 'scheduled offence' since the removal of Special Category Status. When he was taken to the H-blocks he refused to don the prison uniform given to him. As a result he wrapped himself in the only thing available – a blanket. A new phase of the conflict had begun. What would happen within the prison walls over the next few years would have profound implications for what also happened beyond them – nowhere more so than in Ardoyne.

He was just an ordinary guy out doing a day's work and was murdered for nothing, other than the fact he was a Catholic.

Terry McCafferty grew up in Highbury Gardens with his two brothers and sister. Educated at St Patrick's in Donegall Street and then Holy Cross Boys on the Crumlin Road, he first worked in the mills where he met his future wife Eileen. The couple moved to Ligoniel and had five children, three girls and two boys. Both boys died at birth. Although a keen golfer and darts player, it was boxing which was Terry's main pastime after his family. He was a founder member of Ligoniel amateur boxing club and was a lifelong friend of Freddie Gilroy. At the time he was killed he was working for Northern Ireland Electricity.

Terry McCafferty
Killed by loyalists,
Rush Park estate,
31 January 1974

The father of three was murdered by the UFF on 31 January 1974, as he sat with his workmates during lunchtime at the Rush Park housing estate in Whiteabbey. The men had been laying electricity cables for the new housing development. Two masked UFF men entered the workman's hut and forced Terry McCafferty to collect the wage packets. The Protestant workers were then ordered onto their knees while the Catholics were ordered to the back of the hut. The gunmen then opened fire on the Catholic workmen. Terry McCafferty and James McCloskey were killed outright and three others were seriously injured.

Eileen McCafferty (widow)

Terry and I met in Ewarts Mill in 1955. He was a rove drawer and I was a doffer. Terry loved the greyhounds and we use to go to Dunmore Park to watch the races. I lived in Ligoniel then and he lived in Highbury Gardens. We married in December 1958 at Ligoniel chapel. We had three girls – Margaret, Denise and Terri – and two boys, but both the boys died at birth. After we married we settled in Ligoniel. Terry loved golfing and darts but his biggest love was boxing. He was one of the founders of Ligoniel amateur boxing club. Terry lived for that boxing club. We went to all of Freddie Gilroy's fights; he and Terry were very close friends and we travelled everywhere to watch him.

Terry never had any interest in politics. He travelled everywhere with the boxing club. I remember once he went to the Shankill and I said to him, 'You want to be very careful where you are going, not only for your own sake but for the sake of those kids', but he said, 'In boxing it doesn't matter'. They went to the boxing club that night somewhere off Agnes Street and the kids all got watches for winning their fights; he came home as happy as Larry.

I can remember the day Terry died like it was yesterday. I put Terry's dinner on and it was steak, onions and potatoes; my sister-in-law came in and said there had been a shooting and that it had been electricity workers. She went away and came back about a half an hour later. I put the news on but there was nothing on it about the shooting. She said, 'Eileen, get your coat; we are going over to the hospital'. I asked her what was wrong and it still never dawned on me; she said to me, 'Well, it's electricity workers and apparently it is Jimmy Lynch's squad'; he was the foreman that Terry worked with. We went to the Royal Victoria Hospital. A nurse took me into a small room and a doctor asked me my husband's name. I gave the doctor his full name, Terence Patrick McCafferty; there were two Terry McCaffertys in the squad. He asked if he was wearing anything that could identify him. I told him that Terry was wearing a silver chain and there were three medals on it. He said to me, 'I am sorry to tell you that your husband is one of the men who didn't make it'. I came home; I never got to see Terry in the hospital.

Apparently what happened was the UFF came into the hut at lunchtime and the men were playing cards. They asked the Catholics to go to the back of the hut and the Protestants to move forward. They told Terry to collect all the wage packets because it was a Thursday. Terry said to them, 'Why, what is wrong? Why are you putting us to the back and the others to the front? We have all worked together and we are all only out doing a day's work'. Terry collected the wages and gave it to them and they made him go to the back of the hut too. They brought the Protestant workers forward and they just opened up at random on the Catholic workers at the back. They weren't actually singling anyone out; they were just shooting at them all, knowing they were Catholics. There were two shot dead that day and two others badly injured. After the shooting the gunmen took the wages and left.

The UFF later claimed responsibility under the name of Captain Black; they never stated why they did it. The RUC or British army never called to my door after Terry was murdered, no one did. We stayed in 221 Ligoniel Road until the Housing Executive built new houses and I was moved from there to where I live now. Terry was definitely one in a million. The kids and myself wanted for nothing. What he had, he gave to us. My kids missed their daddy; when they were getting married there was no one there to give them away. A father's role is in the home, and I am going by my father, I worshipped the ground that he walked on; my kids never really got that chance with their daddy.

Larry McCafferty (brother)

My mother's maiden name was Jane Dunseith; my dad's name was Lawrence McCafferty. They met in York Street mill where they both worked. My mother was a Protestant and my father was a Catholic, so when they were married it was a pretty quiet wedding because my mother's family didn't approve. They were married in St Patrick's chapel in Donegall Street. Their first home was with my father's parents. My parents moved into Highbury Gardens when it was built. They had been living in York Street but when trouble started there they moved to Ardoyne. There was myself Larry, Terry, Paddy and Lilly. Terry married Eileen Griffin and moved to Ligoniel.

Terry used to go about with Freddie Gilroy the boxer, and Terence Toolan [killed by the British army, in Eskdale Gardens, 14 July 1972]. Terry never boxed himself but he went to all of Freddie's fights. He wasn't overly religious but he went to chapel every Sunday and he made sure his kids went as well. Terry was in no way political. He mixed with both Protestants and Catholics. He was shop steward and looked after the union.

The day Terry was killed, I was working in the town centre and I was called home from work. On my way home on the bus two women sitting in front of me were talking about workmen being shot earlier that day. But I never thought anything of it. I got home and everything was okay; my mummy was making the dinner. Then my uncle Peter called to the house and told me Terry had been killed. I was totally dumbstruck. My mother was still making the dinner and when I told her, she totally broke down. What really hurt me was that Terry and me had had some stupid argument beforehand and we hadn't spoken for about a month. That's what hurt me most because I knew that I would never be speaking to him again. Terry was buried from Ligoniel chapel. I never saw a funeral like it in my life. Ligoniel just stopped that day; it was a massive crowd of people. It stuck in my mind for a long time after it because I was hurting at that time, but to see so many people come to pay their respects to Terry was unbelievable. Terry had never received a threat in his life. He was just an ordinary guy out doing a day's work and was murdered for nothing, other than the fact he was a Catholic.

I don't feel that justice was achieved. The soldier got off scot-free. I think he should have been sentenced for carelessness. I don't believe there was a sniper in Jamaica Street that night. I don't believe it. The shooting only came afterwards. I don't think there will ever be anything done.

Martha Lavery
Killed by British army,
Jamaica Street,
5 August 1974

Martha Lavery was born in 1907. Her family, originally from Cushendall, moved from the Markets to Ardoyne in 1937. She was the eldest of six children: Alex, Dan, John, Eddie, Martha and Grace. Martha had only one child, Joseph. When his wife Kathleen died in 1965 Martha reared their six children: Ann, Lily, Joseph, Mary, Danny and Gerard. Martha lived all of her days in Jamaica Street and was well-liked and respected by her neighbours. Her brother Alex lived next door and her son's house was just across the street. Martha went to bingo once or twice a week and enjoyed the odd flutter on the horses. In her spare time she made beautiful quilts for her family and friends. Essentially Martha was a private person and kept herself to herself. In addition to looking after her grandchildren, she worked as a stitcher for Douglas and Green's in Lower Donegall Street.

On 5 August 1974 Martha was shot and killed by the British army while she sat watching television with her son and grandchildren. It is unclear when the gun-battle started that night between the 'Official' IRA and British army. The 'Official' IRA denied responsibility for her killing. During the inquest the RUC stated that the fatal round was 'probably a British army bullet'. An open verdict was recorded. A large number of open verdicts have been recorded at inquests when an agent of the British state caused the death. Martha was 67 years old at the time of her death.

Mrs Kane (neighbour)

I moved to Jamaica Street from the Sacred Heart parish when I was sixteen years of age. I lived there for 61 years, so that's how long I knew Martha Lavery and her mother and father. Martha just kept herself to herself. She only really bothered with her son Joe. Joe's wife Kathleen died very young.

It was a Tuesday night when Martha was murdered. She was at bingo that night and I was at bingo that night too. She loved bingo like myself. When I heard that Martha had been shot dead I couldn't believe it. She had just come from bingo and was sitting in her son Joe's house when a bullet hit her where she was sitting. There had been shooting at the top of Jamaica Street at Alliance Avenue. That's what I remember about Martha's death.

She loved a laugh and a joke. Her parents were country people from Cushendall. I only ever knew Martha's mother as Mrs Lavery. Her father was a seaman. They were quiet people and kept themselves to themselves. They would have bid you the time of day but they never bothered much. Martha had two brothers; one was called Dan and the other Alex. Alex lived next door and Joe her son lived across the street from her. Martha lived at 146 Jamaica Street. Martha would have spoken to you and had a wee yarn. She always bid you the time of day. Martha was a quiet person; she never bothered with anyone or was never in any sort of trouble. She loved bingo and had her daily routine. She was good-living and I think she went to mass every morning. The family kept themselves to themselves. They were just lovely people.

Gerard Lavery (grandson)

Martha Lavery was my grandmother. We called her Martha. She loved bingo and she went to it every week. On the night she was killed, she arrived home from bingo around 10.30 pm and she called to our house. There was no sign of rioting or any disturbance, although earlier that day there had been a lot of British army activity in and around the Belmore factory that was close to her house. Martha was sitting in our house, in the living room, watching TV. She called to our house most nights. Her own home was just across the street. I'm not sure of the exact time Martha was shot but I think it was about 11.20-11.30 pm. When the shooting started my daddy shouted to get down on the floor. Most of the grandchildren were in the house at the time. Martha got on her hands and knees and the next thing was she said, 'I'm hit', and she fell flat on the floor. The family all started screaming and pulled my granny into the middle of the floor. We could still hear shooting. Some of the family ran out onto the street screaming that Martha had been shot; they banged on neighbours' doors to get help.

The Brits started to run down the street and made their way into our house. I tried to get out of the house. As I got to the hall there was a Brit and he was hysterical. He started to shoot towards the other side of the street. I was only a child at the time and I was pleading with him to stop. The Brit kept shouting, 'They are in that house', pointing towards Christie's house. There was no return fire from that house. My sister Ann managed to run down to Eileen Kelly's house and phoned an ambulance. As far as I can remember no Brit even attempted to give medical assistance to my granny while they were in the house. My daddy went in the ambulance with Martha and the neighbours took us, the children, into their houses. Martha was dead on arrival at the hospital. When my daddy got home he collected all of us and told us the news that Martha had died. We did not go back to our own house that night but stayed in my granny's house instead. In fact we never entered our house again except to empty it. We lived in Martha's house until we all grew up and got married.

Martha was buried from Ardoyne chapel. At the inquest into her death the coroner stated it was an 'open verdict'. No one has ever been charged with her murder. The family has never challenged anyone over her death. Not one penny of compensation was awarded.

Martha was a great person. She helped my daddy to raise us because my mother died during a difficult pregnancy. The youngest child was aged five. Our family looked on Martha as more of a mother. She was a humorous, no-nonsense type of person who led a very simple life. She loved going to bingo. She was totally committed to rearing us. At the time of her death she had a total of three grandsons, three granddaughters and two great grandchildren.

Lily Jackson (granddaughter)

Martha was great at making patchwork quilts. She loved bingo and doing the odd wee bet on the horses. Martha went to bingo in Ardoyne Hall and the old Star club in Butler Street. She made sure she went to bingo once a week and if she could afford it, she went twice a week. She went to the bookies at the bottom of Brompton Park and she would say to me, 'Now, you wait outside there. I'll be out in a minute'. You didn't question her. You just knew that she always said, 'Women didn't go into the bookies', but she did. Martha only had one child, my daddy, and his name is Joseph. She loved a wee yarn with her neighbours across the road, Mrs White and Mrs Kane. She reared us. My mummy died when I was only 11 years old and there were six of us. She was a mother to us.

The day of her death I remember going round to visit her. I lived in Etna Drive and I had two young children aged three and four. I remember going round to ask her if she wanted anything from the shop. She was just picking up after an illness. I went to the post office and got her a few things. That morning I helped her light the fire and I asked her if she wanted to go to bingo that night and did she feel up to it. Well, she hesitated and then said, 'I don't feel too bad. I think I'll go'. I told her I would call round for her later that night. I think I called for her about 7.30 pm and she was just putting on her coat and her scarf. I remember the very coat she was wearing that night; it was a red, burgundy coat and away we went.

There had been trouble the night before and there were a few barricades at the bottom of Jamaica Street. As we were walking down the street that night she was a bit sort of iffy; her mood was a wee bit weary. She said, 'I have an awful feeling that something is going to happen tonight'. Of course I tried to shrug it off and said, 'Sure, this is an every-night occurrence. Why worry about tonight?' Then she said out of the blue, 'Lily, I don't mind dying. I am not afraid of dying but I don't want to die by the bullet'. I said,

'Don't talk nonsense. Come on or we are going to be late'. We made our way up the hill and into the hall. Of course all of her friends were shouting, 'How are you doing? Are you keeping alright? Are you feeling better? I'm glad to see you back at the bingo again'. She was all delighted everybody was asking how she was. Bell Burns was there, Mrs White was there, Mrs Whelan, wee Jimmy Weir shouted over at her and her brother Alex was there too. She didn't win that night. She won once in a blue moon. When she did win you would have thought she got the lotto but it was very rare.

That night when we left bingo we went to Martha's own house. She pulled her blinds down and she put her light on, which was normal routine. I said, 'Now, are you alright tonight? Are you going to go to bed or what are you doing?' She said, 'No, I think I will go across the road to your daddy's and watch the film'. He lived in 135, straight across the road. I left her across the road and then I went home to Etna Drive. I said 'Good night', and she said, 'Good night, love' and 'I'll see you in the morning'. That was the last time I saw her.

The next morning I was getting up to put my husband out to work and the radio was on. The news was on; it must have been the 7 am news. It said that a woman had been shot dead in Ardoyne and I said to my husband before he went out the door, 'God, I wonder who that was'. It never struck me that it was anybody belonging to me. My husband went out to work but he only got round the corner when one of the Christies told him Martha had been killed. He came back and told me. Of course I couldn't believe it. I couldn't accept it. Danny, my younger brother, was sleeping upstairs; he was only about 14. I just remember running up the stairs and standing at the bottom of his bed and saying 'Danny, get up son, get up. Martha's dead'. He never even asked for an answer or explanation or nothing. He just up and ran and made his way over to my daddy's house to find out what had happened. We all did. Neighbours met us and told us we couldn't go into the house. We found my daddy; he was over in 146, in Martha's own house. I went over and asked my daddy what had happened and he told me.

My daddy's recollection was they had sat down to watch the film. In my daddy's house the door was to your left and the sofa was alongside it. Everybody else was sitting on chairs over the other side of the living room. Martha always sat on the edge of the chair; she never ever sat back. If she had been sitting back the bullet probably would have passed her. But she wasn't; she was sitting out on the edge of the settee. When my daddy heard the first shot he said 'Get down on the floor', which was normal routine in those days. When you heard shooting everybody would have said get down on the floor in case a bullet came through the window. My daddy said they all got down on the floor but Martha hit the floor with a thump. He said whatever way he looked at her she was on her knees and she said, 'Jesus, Joe I think I am hit'. She just fell down on the floor and my daddy trailed her across to the other side of the living room floor and he saw where the bullet had come through the door.

He said to Ann, my younger sister (she is in Australia now) to get an ambulance and there were more shots fired. There was a gun battle after that. Ann didn't care; she ran out and down to the bottom of the street to Mrs Kelly's house. That was the only woman she knew had a phone. She just ran down the street squealing, 'Martha has been shot, Martha has been shot'. We always called her Martha because she always said 'I am too young to be called granny', so we always called her Martha. It took the ambulance quite a while to come and by the time the ambulance came, the police and the British army were all over the place.

I think the RUC went into the house that night to look for the bullet or whatever they could find. They wouldn't let my daddy back into the house. They wouldn't let anybody in the house. The police were the only ones allowed in the house. The whole next day the police were in the house and the bullet that killed her was lying on the sofa beside where she was sitting with not a mark on it. As she was sitting forward on the sofa the bullet had hit her under the arm, went right through her whole body and came out through her other shoulder. But it was lying on the sofa beside her; that's where they found the bullet, a big SLR bullet. The next day they told my daddy he could go back in to the house. They had the bullet and told my daddy it was an SLR bullet that killed her.

A long time after that my daddy had to face the inquest. My younger sister went with him. My daddy had to stand in court and listen to the evidence of the soldier that shot her. The soldier was only about 17 years of age. He was a young Scottish soldier that shot her. Their story was they had spotted a gunman in the street and fired at him. They said the gunman fired at them first and they returned fire. But my daddy said that wasn't the case. My daddy said as soon as he heard the first shot he told the family to get down onto the floor. It was the first bullet that hit her. There was no shooting before she fell onto the floor. The bullet went straight through the hall door, the living room door and straight into Martha. It's hard to believe. There was only one bullet that came through the door that night. There was other shooting after that because my sister ran down the street and the shots were going over her head. But she didn't meet anybody on the way down the street.

At the inquest they said there was a gun battle that night. They said they had spied a gunman in the street and fired at him. But there was no gun battle going on when Martha was shot. When the first shot was fired my granny hit the floor with the bullet in her. There was no other investigation other than the inquest and nobody came back and asked my daddy any questions. The only question they asked him that night was, 'Was your front door open or closed?' I remember my father using the word, 'The door was ajar'. We were watching the film and we knew my granny had to go home across the road. So the front door was half opened and half closed. They never said anything else; no other questions were asked, none.

I don't feel that justice was achieved. The soldier got off scot-free. I think he should have been sentenced for carelessness. I don't believe there was a sniper in Jamaica Street that night. I don't believe it. The shooting only came afterwards. I don't think there will ever be anything done. My father got no compensation, nothing, when my granny was killed. They said it was because she had no dependant children, although she reared us and Gerard was only 12. My daddy tried to fight the case and they said if Gerard had been younger than 12, you might have had a case for compensation but because there were no dependant children under 12, you have no case.

The next day when my granny was lying in the living room in her coffin in her own house, the British soldiers came up the street. They came up the street the way they did every day, maybe half dozen times a day. My daddy had his house locked up. The door was closed and locked up because daddy wouldn't go back into that house again and never did; he stayed and lived in my granny's house after it happened. You could see the bullet hole in the front door. A soldier stopped and put his finger in the bullet hole and turned to the rest of his mates and laughed, 'That's another one for us' he said. I remember that because I was standing at my granny's gate. The house was full of people and that was while the wake was going on. So to me they didn't care; it didn't mean anything to them, it was just another notch on the belt.

She was buried from Holy Cross chapel and then she was buried in Milltown cemetery. I didn't go to the graveyard. I stayed at home with my children and the neighbours and the older ones. I can remember the newspaper headlines were 'Grandma Courage'. That was the big headline in the *Irish News* and it just told you how it happened. It told you every detail: that she had come home from bingo with me, went over to her son's to watch the film and the bullet came through the door and killed her.

When my mummy died in 1965 Martha was mother to us. She helped out and reared us. There were six of us and it was tough enough in those days. I never ever remember her going to the doctor's but she had been ill about five months before she was killed and in hospital. She was just picking up again and getting back to her normal self and going to bingo again when her life was taken away from her. I don't think anybody came and offered support after she was killed. The only people that were good to my daddy were the neighbours, the Christie's, Mrs Kane and Bell Burns. They were the people that were there for my daddy when he needed them.

Thomas Braniff
Killed by loyalists,
Sunflower Bar, Corporation
Street, 16 July 1974

Thomas Braniff's parents were originally from the Docks area of Belfast. His father Thomas was born in Great Georges Street and his mother Elizabeth came from Dock Street. It was a mixed marriage; Thomas was a Catholic and Elizabeth a Protestant. The couple brought up their eight children in the Protestant faith. Thomas was their second youngest child. He attended Mount Collier Street school and left with no qualifications. He was a quiet, hard-working fella who enjoyed a pint with his family and friends and did the odd bet at the weekend. He worked in Cooks Scrap Yard where he met and became a close friend of the Foster family from Ardoyne. In 1970 he married Margaret Foster in Holy Cross chapel and they eventually had two children, Thomas and Annmarie. The young couple lived in several temporary homes before eventually settling in number 76 Brookfield

Street. They spent a short spell in England and returned home in 1974. Just a few months after returning from England, Thomas was killed in the Sunflower Bar on 16 July 1974 in a no-warning loyalist bomb attack. The tiny bar, packed on a Saturday evening with regulars, was wrecked in the UVF bomb. Thomas Braniff was killed and several others, including his brother Jimmy, were seriously injured in the carnage.

Albert Lutton
Killed by loyalists,
Ballyduff estate,
10 October 1974

Albert Greer Lutton, son of Wright and Mary Lutton, was born and reared in 68 Stratford Gardens, Ardoyne. Bert, as he was commonly known, had one younger brother called Raymond. Growing up in Ardoyne meant that Bert went to the Holy Cross Boys school and St Gabriel's. Amongst his friends were 'Bap' Matthews and Paddy Joe Hill (later to become one of the Birmingham Six). He was also a good friend of Michael Lynch, one of the first people from Ardoyne killed in the conflict in August 1969 [Michael Lynch, killed by the RUC in Butler Street, 15 August 1969]. Everyone remembers Bert as a quiet, likeable young man who kept himself to himself. He was a member of no political organisation. Indeed the only person in his family who joined any group as a result of the conflict was his mother, Mary. She was a member of the Women Together Peace Movement. On 10 October 1974 the then Labour government was returned to power with a narrow majority in a British general election. In the north of Ireland the election took place in a charged and tense atmosphere. This was heightened by a wave of loyalist killings. In a frenzied four-day period loyalist gangs killed four Catholics, two of whom were from Ardoyne. The first of these was Bertie Lutton [the other person from Ardoyne was Ciaran Murphy, killed by the UVF in Hightown Road, 13 October 1974]. At around 9 pm on 10 October a taxi was hijacked in Sydney Street West, near the Crumlin Road. Just over an hour later the taxi was used to bring two loyalist gunmen to a house in Ballyfore Park in the Ballyduff estate. It was the home of Bert Lutton's girlfriend and the couple were sitting in the living room. The loyalist gunmen knocked the door and it was answered by Bert's female companion. The gunmen then pushed past her, wearing coats over their heads, and went into the living room. They then fired at least three times and shot Bert dead as he sat in the chair. He died almost immediately. Bert Lutton's death was later claimed by an organisation calling itself the Protestant Action Group (later known as Protestant Action Force). It was a cover name for extreme elements within the UVF who were disgruntled with that organisation's then ceasefire. Bert Lutton was the first person killed by the Protestant Action Force. He was clearly the victim of a sectarian attack. His killers knew that he was a Catholic and probably that he was from Ardoyne. Bert was 30 years old at the time of his death.

Ciaran Murphy
Killed by loyalists,
Hightown Road,
13 October 1974

> *He was held and tortured for three or four hours and then taken to Hightown Road were he was tortured again and then shot eight or nine times by a loyalist gang. He was just 17 years of age.*

Ciaran's father John Murphy was from Berry Street. John's family moved to the Barrack Wall in the New Lodge area, were he lived until he married his wife, Kathleen Hannaway, from the Falls Road. The couple moved to Ardoyne in 1941/42 and lived with John's sister Catherine Lavery until they got their own home at 59 Strathroy Park. Ciaran was born there on 19 July 1957 and was the youngest of six children: Anne, Sean, Kathleen, Eithne and Patrick. Ciaran attended Holy Cross Boys school and St Gabriel's Secondary school and when he finished his education he worked at installing electrical heating. It was during his schooldays that his father John died, in 1967, aged 48. Ciaran was a very popular lad; he had a wide circle of friends and at six foot one, with an Afro-hairstyle, he was easily recognisable. Like other members of his family, he was a GAA man, played hurling for the Ardoyne club and by all accounts was a brilliant player. After a night out with his mates, Ciaran was abducted by a loyalist gang and in scenes reminiscent of the Shankill Butchers, he was brutally tortured, murdered and his body dumped on the Hightown Road on 13 October 1974.

Pat Murphy (brother)

Our parents moved to Ardoyne around about 1941/42. Both were from a republican and socialist background. My father had been interned in Crumlin Road gaol in 1943-1945; my mother was eight months pregnant with my older brother Sean at the time. He was the second of six children, of which Ciaran was the youngest child. Anne, the oldest sister, and Eithne, the youngest, both now live in America. Kate, my middle sister, and my brother Sean both still live in Belfast. Ciaran and my mother went to America to live in 1972 but they couldn't settle to the fast pace of life and came back home.

Ciaran was 17 at the time of his death and he had been going with Kay Lundy, a girl from Ballymurphy. Kay was working in England at the time of Ciaran's murder. He had left St Gabriel's Secondary school and was working for a firm putting electrical heating into offices and homes. He had lots of friends and was well-liked in the area. Ciaran was older looking than 17 and could have passed as my twin brother, though not an identical one. He hung about with myself, Brendan McFarlane, Jim McCullough as well as his own mates, Seamus Larkin and Paddy Mulholland and that crowd. He used to steal my clothes; I would have been coming down the street and seen him disappearing out of my house with one of my suits on. He was a good looking kid and he used to get slagged about looking like Gilbert O'Sullivan, though when he needed a hair cut, he looked more like Jimi Hendrix. He was very popular with the girls. On top of that he was totally great craic for an evening out. There was only three and a half years between us and he would have tagged along with me to Kelly's Cellars and the traditional music sessions. Even though he was only 17 he was already a character. He had joined the GAA at a very young age and he would have been more of a hurler than a footballer. Having said that, he was a fair footballer and played in goals for the Holy Cross Boys' team that won the '68 primary schools Gaelic Football League. He was quite famous round the district for giving people 'lifts'. He drove an old white van for the central heating crowd he worked for and if he had seen anyone from the district at a bus stop he would have piled them into it – which when you think about it was a much safer way to travel into Ardoyne than a Corporation bus. People met him and remembered him.

On Saturday 12 October, the night of his death, Ciaran was out with Seamus Larkin and Paddy Mulholland in the Saunders Club. After a good night's entertainment they drove down to Provie Charlie's Chinese, as it was then, on the Antrim Road. While they were in the Chinese a bit of a nark rose between the lads about the car they had come down in and Ciaran walked out of the Chinese and set off on his own up the Cliftonville Road to Ardoyne. Now it was about 1.30 in the morning and any person at this time of the night on the Cliftonville Road would have been a Catholic and would have been easy pickings for any loyalist gangs operating in the area. That was exactly what happened to Ciaran. He was picked up round Manor Street by a loyalist gang operating out of the Silverstream area. He was taken to a community centre in the Ballysillan area and he was held and tortured there for three or four hours. He was then taken to the Hightown Road where he was beaten and shot eight or nine times by the gang. Forensics showed he had been shot with four or five different handguns.

Later on Sunday my mother called up to my house. When she had come home from mass she had gone in to Ciaran's bedroom to waken him and realised his bed hadn't been slept in. She asked me to go and check if he had been arrested; she was distracted because he hadn't been home. I came out of the house and met big Bik who was just heading down the street to call for me for a match we had in Hightown that day. I said to him, 'Come on down to the mill with me. Ciaran hasn't been home; hopefully the Brits have scooped him or something'. I always remember as we came out of the path onto the street in Cranbrook, Frances Waring, a neighbour, came over to me and she said 'Pat, I don't want to alarm you; they have been giving out a description of a fella, of a body they've found murdered and it sounds like your Ciaran'. She told me the description they had given out and the only thing was they had said the body was 5'8" and in his late twenties or early thirties, so I thought, 'Good, maybe it isn't him' – although I think I knew he was dead from the time my mother called to the house.

We went down to Flax Street Mill where the Brits were stationed and they told us they had arrested nobody the night before, but that we should go to Musgrave Street police station as the description we had given them of Ciaran matched the body that had been found on the Hightown Road. You see Ciaran's body had been stripped of all ID. His pockets were emptied and they'd robbed his watch and ring as well. Bik and I went to the Club and Gerry McGivern ran us to Musgrave Street. The police then took us to Laganbank morgue. When they brought us into the room where Ciaran's body was I saw his hair sticking out from under the sheet they had covered him with and knew right away, even before the cop pulled the sheet down, that it was Ciaran. It was plain that he had been badly beaten; there were stab wounds to his face, chest, right shoulder and arm. The police brought us back to Musgrave Street where Gerry was waiting for us and they took me into an interview room. I think Brendan was still with me, though I'm not sure; I was badly shocked at this stage. They began interviewing me. They asked me who he had been drinking with. I told them that I didn't know but I knew he had been in the Saunders Club. Their questioning then went along the lines of, 'Would he have been drinking with republicans? Would the republican movement have shot him?' – all that type of shit they were asking me. I pointed out to them that unless they were as stupid as they looked they would know who had killed Ciaran. I don't know how long this went on for; it seemed like half or three quarters of an hour. Eventually I asked them if they had me under arrest and they said, 'No, we're just asking you and trying to get the background'. So I then said, 'I have to go and let my mother and the rest of the family know that my brother has been murdered, so if I'm not under arrest, I'm out of here'. Gerry ran Bik and myself back to the district. I got him to drop me at my sister Kate's house. I told her and then walked round to my Ma's. Bik went down to the Club with Gerry and broke the news to the boys in the GAA.

It was just total devastation. It hit the family very hard, particularly my uncle Liam; my father and he have been more like brothers than brothers-in-law. The Hannaways and my father were life-long republicans going back on the Hannaway side to the Fenian Rising. There was also a big tradition of socialism and trade unionism in the family. I remember my sister Kate telling me about going into Ciaran's room later that Sunday night and finding Liam there; he was breaking his heart. She couldn't believe it, seeing my uncle Liam crying. He said to her, 'I feel like going and getting something and taking out four or five of those bastards, but I'm sitting here thinking what would the "Big man" do (that was my father Johnny) and it wouldn't have been his way, or the republican way, to retaliate like that'. So there was that sort of duality about it. There was this massive anger about the manner in which he had been killed and the desire to strike out but it was contrary to all his beliefs to act in that manner.

It's 28 years later and I still feel exactly the same way, so 'closure' is really just a word the Americans invented.

There was a massive turn-out for Ciaran's funeral. The area was a lot tighter then; it hadn't expanded to the extent it has now. As the funeral came down and crossed where the Ardoyne Road hits the Crumlin Road, there were a couple of Shankill Road black taxis coming from the Woodvale Road direction. They must have known whose funeral it was and as they passed the cortege they began sounding their horns. The women that were with the funeral blocked the top of the Woodvale Road standing with their backs to it to prevent a repetition. This caused a tailback of cars with taxis in among them. Just as the hearse was turning into the chapel gates the horn blowing started again. About half the funeral crowd ran over and there were various cars wrecked and heads punched. It would have been a lot worse only for the likes of Barney McKenna and other senior republicans in the area at the time who calmed the crowd down and got it broken up. The whole district at that stage was just about to boil over due to the hammering it had taken. At that time in 1974 Ciaran was actually the third guy from Ardoyne and the Bone to be killed in something like four days, shot in different incidents.

The GAA Club was great, from senior members right down. The likes of Jimmy Lynch, Jimmy Fennell and Frank McCallan had seen our Sean join the Club, then me, followed by Ciaran as a very young kid; they would have seen him grow up. It was as if the Club was big family. Unfortunately it's a thing we have seen too many times over the years. Funnily enough, Ciaran's murder is one that seems to stick in people's heads. It must have been the age of him and probably because, as I have said, he was so well-known round the district as a young lad. It's amazing how many babies in the next couple of years were called Ciaran after him. He is buried in Milltown with my father.

There's a guy called Aubrey Tarr, he was the only one ever charged with Ciaran's murder. He got life; he did about 12 years. It never ceases to amaze me when I hear unionist politicians complaining about the early release scheme under the Good Friday Agreement because when you think about it, there's been one going on for loyalist prisoners for years.

Father Myles, Father Fernando and Father Ailbe were of great support and comfort to my mother after Ciaran's death. We weren't offered support of any description from any government organisation. The only support the family got was from friends and the broader community. In fact my mother is still waiting on contact of any sort from the RUC to tell her; 1. that he was murdered and; 2. that they were going to charge anybody with it. The biggest slap in the face for the family from an official source came from the Northern Ireland Office. About January 1975 they used a black and white image of Ciaran lying under a blanket on the Hightown Road in an advertisement for the police confidential telephone line. They did that without consulting my family. They ran the advertisement in the local press and on TV. It was done like a negative but you could see it was Ciaran. I complained about it to the NIO and they said that their solicitors felt it was a generic image and that you couldn't identify anybody from it. I pointed out to them that I, my family and large numbers of friends had identified him from it. I asked them if they could tell me that it wasn't him but they came back with the same answer. They at no stage denied that it was him. They never asked for permission or consulted with the family at any stage; they just printed it.

Ciaran was a one off. He was either going to end up a millionaire or as a qualified spark hanging round Ardoyne but whatever way, he would have had plenty of mates around him. When we were kids he was an absolute pest. I had to trail him everywhere with me but we became best mates as well as being brothers. I still miss him.

Seamus Larkin (friend)

I first met Ciaran in the early '60s when we moved from Old Ardoyne to Glenard. Ciaran was two years younger than me. We went to primary school together but at secondary level he went to St Gabriel's and I went to St Malachy's. So I have known him a very long time. There was myself, Ciaran, Paddy Mullholland, Eamon McAreavey, Terry Smiley and Bill Reid. We all ran about together. Ciaran had massive frizzy afro-style hair. One week we would go to the Highfield Club and the next week we would go to the Saunders. We had a lot of good times together.

The night Ciaran was killed we were in the Saunders, myself, Ciaran and Paddy Mullholland. We decided to go for a drive. We ended up having a few words … it wasn't a fall out between the three of us but Ciaran sort of took the huff. Paddy and I went looking for him but we couldn't find him. Paddy then drove me home.

The next morning I remember well. My mother came up to me before 12 o'clock. I was still lying in bed and she said, 'Seamus, do you know where Ciaran is? He hasn't been home'. And I said, 'He was with us last night but he took the huff and walked off and we couldn't find him'. I said to my mammy, 'He's probably at a party or whatever'. Then I got up and was sitting in the living room; my ma was in the kitchen listening to the news on the radio. They said that a body had been found up in the Hightown Road, a male, about mid to late '20s, with afro-style hair cut and they described what he was wearing. I said, 'Mammy, that's Ciaran'. We went up to see his brother Pat and he had heard the news as well. Pat went round everybody to see if anyone had seen Ciaran. Mid-afternoon we were in the house and my ma saw Pat coming up the street. I went out and said, 'Pat is it?' and he just nodded. I had been with Ciaran most of that day.

Myself and Paddy, Pat and Fr. Fernando went to the trial. Fr. Fernando went with us for moral support. It was hard on Pat of course, no doubt about that. It was a very serious day; I will always remember it. It was 1978, four years after his murder.

Ciaran had everything going for him, he really had. He was a good guy, good craic, had a heart of gold and was a very good friend. He's sadly missed. Ciaran would have been 43 now, if he'd still been alive.

James McDade
Killed on active service,
Salt Lane, Greyfriars,
Coventry,
14 November 1974

> *Jamesy completely changed when his brother Gerard was killed. It had an awful effect on him. He came back from the funeral and you could see the change in him. He was very down and very, very angry.*

James ('Jamesy') McDade was the third of five boys (Thomas, Peter, Francie, Jamesy, Gerard) and two girls (Ann, Mary) in the family of Esther 'Acey' (née Duffy) and Joseph 'Tricky' McDade. Jamesy grew up in Oakfield Street in Old Ardoyne and went to the Holy Cross Boys school and St Gabriel's. When he left school Jamesy got a job for a time in one of the nearby flax mills. But just after the outbreak of the conflict he moved to Birmingham to find work. He soon became very well-known and much liked within the large Irish community in the city. Those were difficult times to be Irish in Britain, so bars and clubs were important places for the tight-knit Birmingham Irish. For Jamesy they were also where his talents as a singer would make him a very popular figure. It was a popularity that would mean that on his death a large number of friends would travel back to Belfast for his funeral, with dire consequences for some. While in England Jamesy had also met and married a local girl, Jackie Mountjoy, and the couple soon had two young sons, Gerard and Anthony. Jamesy did have clear political views and was active in raising money for the Green Cross and Prisoners Defence Fund. However, it was probably the death of his brother that would lead him to see the need for more drastic action. On 21 December 1971 Gerard McDade was shot dead by British soldiers near the family home in Ardoyne [Gerard McDade, killed by the British army in Brompton Park, 21 December 1971]. Gerard had been a member of the IRA's 3rd Battalion. The death of his brother had a devastating effect on Jamesy. Certainly he was soon to become active as a member of the IRA himself. On 14 November 1974 Jamesy McDade was on active service when he and another volunteer were carrying a bomb in order to blow up a telephone exchange in Coventry. The bomb exploded prematurely and killed Jamesy.

Following his death, the family were at first prevented from taking Jamesy's body home because they had to await a decision by the coroner's court. In the meantime (on 21 November 1974) two pubs in Birmingham were blown up leaving 21 people dead. A wave of anti-Irish hysteria ensued and the Prevention of Terrorism Act was rapidly rushed through British parliament. The impact for Jamesy's family and friends was more immediate. Mourners were attacked by the National Front as they made there way with Jamesy's coffin from the morgue to Birmingham airport. Then British Airways refused to handle the body. Eventually Aer Lingus agreed to fly the coffin to Dublin but the problems did not end there. The Bishop of Birmingham, George Patrick Dwyer, had refused the family permission to take the body into a chapel in his city and in Belfast the local church hierarchy would not allow the Ardoyne chapel or others to be used for the funeral. Eventually Jamesy was buried in the republican plot in Milltown cemetery on 23 November. His coffin was draped with the flag that had previously been used in the funerals of the hunger strikers Michael Gaughan [died in Parkhurst prison, 3 June 1974] and Terence MacSweeney in 1920. Veteran republican Liam Hannaway gave the oration at the graveside. Five of Jamesy's Irish friends travelling back to Belfast for his funeral were stopped and arrested by the British police for allegedly planting the Birmingham pub bombs. They were beaten and false confessions were extracted from a number of them. Along with one other man they became known as the 'Birmingham Six' and would eventually serve almost 17 years in prison for 'being Irish in the wrong place and at the wrong time'. Jamesy McDade was 26 years old when he died and left a wife and two young sons behind him. His mother gave a statement to the *Republican News* at the time saying, 'I am proud of both of them, Gerard and James. They were doing what they believed in and died for their country. I think James deserves a hero's burial. After all, he gave his life for his country'.

Sean Doherty (cousin and friend)

James and I were second cousins. His mother and my granda were brother and sister. We were virtually born together; there was just a year or so between us. We also lived in the next street to each another. When we left school we used to go to the League [social club] for a game of snooker and to the 'hop' at St Gabriel's or Ardoyne Hall. There was a group of us from the top of the 'Pad' who ran around together. There was Jamesy, me, Bobby Ewing [killed by the UFF in the Deerpark Road, 12 October 1981], 'Thunder' and Mickey McAuley, Roy McCallum and a load of others. We all ran around together. There is a brave few dead now. Jamesy was a quiet sort of bloke. We all took a wee drink, but not that much. We couldn't afford it! We used to go down to 'Kills', Logues or the Wheatfield [bars]. They were all bars that got burnt down in 1969. Sometimes we would go down to the Plaza for a dance. Jamesy liked a dance. But what he was known for most was singing. Jamesy was a brilliant singer. He would have got up on stage to sing and if there was a singsong on, then people would always look to him. When all the clubs in the district started up after 1969 he was always being called up to give a song but his local club was always the League.

Jamesy worked in one of the mills in Flax Street. That is what people did in those days because there was nothing else. Then he went over to Birmingham in England. There was a lot of Irish in Birmingham then. I think he went to get work as a painter. When he was there he ran into Robbie McLaughlin and was with him and the rest of the lads. He was in England at the time Gerard was shot. I remember when his brother Gerard was killed because he came back over and I had a drink with him. That was the last time I ever saw him. Jamesy, me, Eddie Donnelly and Bobby Ewing were in the Shamrock on the night before Gerard was buried. It was just some huts then. Gerard's death had a terrible impact on Jamesy because they were very close and next to each other in the line of the family.

I was in the League when I heard that Jamesy was dead. Jim Mailey got a phone call from England telling him what had happened. I was totally shocked when I heard that Jamesy was dead. It was not the fact that he was in the IRA but with the way he died. I told my ma about Jamesy's death and she went round and told his mother and father. No one was quite sure when he was going to get buried because British Airways refused to take the body from Birmingham. My Ma, Tory and 'Snooker' McDade [all cousins], they all went over to England to try to get the body. Jamesy's remains ended up being flown back through Dublin because the staff at Aldergrove refused to handle the coffin. In the end Jamesy was buried from the Falls and not from Ardoyne a week or so after he was killed. But I missed his funeral. On the morning of the funeral the British army stopped me walking down the street toward my ma's house. They held me for two hours so I missed the funeral.

Mary McLaughlin (friend and neighbour)

Jamesy came over to us in Birmingham to find work. My husband and Jamesy were cousins and so he was living with us when he first came over. He was single then but met his wife in England, Jackie Mountjoy. He was about 20 or 21 when he got married and they were still living with us at that time. They had two boys, Gerard and Anthony. Anthony was just a baby when his father died. Jamesy was just an ordinary fella but he was a great singer. He had a brilliant voice. He was well known in the Irish community because of that and he had a lot of friends from the old district. He used to go about with all the ones who became the Birmingham Six. Billy Power and Gerard Hunter would have been good friends of Jamesy's. It was just Irish people going about together. They would do collections for the prisoners and Jamesy would sing. But Jamesy completely changed when his brother Gerard was killed. It had an awful effect on him. He came back from the funeral and you could see the change in him. He was very down and very, very angry. He would talk about the political situation and about Gerard after that. He felt things were unjust and he was angry about Gerard.

I think it was a Thursday, 14 November 1974, when Jamesy died. I heard when a news flash came on the TV to say that there had been an explosion and that a man had been badly hurt. It said later that he was dead. Jamesy died carrying a bomb that blew up and the fella who was with him, Raymond McLaughlin, was caught. I think Raymond did about 12 years, although he is dead now. As far as I know they were going to blow up a telephone exchange or an electrical tower. Jamesy had left our house earlier and I still have the coat in my wardrobe that he had on him and left behind. I remember as he went out he just had a couple of words with my husband then shouted in, 'See you later' to me. That was the afternoon he was killed.

Afterwards Jamesy's wife and children were arrested. Jackie ended up going over to her mother's. But the mother started getting threats so Jackie came with the two children and stayed with us. She got a lot of hassle, particularly from the media. But she had to remain in England until the coroner's court could take place in Coventry. It wasn't until about eight or nine days later that we were able to go to Coventry to try and bring the body home. When we got there the National Front were outside the court. When we were in the morgue in Coventry on Thursday 21 November two priests came and gave a 20-minute Catholic service. Jackie was there with her wee son Gerard. So were John Gaughan [brother of Michael Gaughan who died earlier that year in an English prison on hunger strike] and Veronica Phillips [sister of Frank Stagg who died on hunger strike 15 months later in an English prison]. I remember there was a piper playing as we moved toward the cars outside. There were republicans, mostly from Birmingham, outside lined along the main exit roads as a tribute to James. On top of his coffin there was a white carnation, a gold chrysanthemum and a green ribbon. But outside a big crowd of anti-republican demonstrators had gathered. It was awful. They were National Front supporters. They were throwing bottles, paint and flour at the mourners and hearse. They were shouting all sorts of abuse. It was really frightening.

Eventually we got to the airport and we were put in a room along with some Sinn Féin people who had come up from London. But British Airways refused point blank to take the body. Apparently the airport workers at Aldergrove said they would refuse to unload the plane if it went to Belfast. The workers around the place were doing anything they could to make it clear to us that we were not welcome. Then we were told that the coffin would be put on an Aer Lingus flight but that we couldn't go to Belfast because there was a crowd waiting at Aldergrove. Eventually we had to fly to Dublin. There was the family and about 30 members of Sinn Féin who accompanied the body on the plane. We arrived with James' body in Dublin at about 10.00 pm that night [21 November]. We went straight to Dundalk that night. The coffin was draped in the same tricolour that had covered Michael Gaughan's coffin. The whole way we were flanked by Free State Special Branch and car loads of journalists. The original intention had been to bury James from Holy Cross chapel in Ardoyne but because of the delays at the airports, the hassle and intimidation, it just wasn't possible. But there was a requiem mass celebrated for James at Holy Cross that Friday morning. When the cortege crossed the border the RUC stopped a lot of the cars. They arrested a number of the mourners who were taken to Castlereagh. I think they were held for about three days. Even James' two-year-old son was taken into custody! He was held at the RUC station in Lisburn. When we eventually got to Belfast, James body remained overnight in an undertaker's funeral parlour. Jamesy was buried the next day. The funeral set off from Clonard Street and the IRA provided the guard of honour and a volley of shots fired over the coffin. It was a really terrible day, raining really heavily. But there was still a large turnout for the funeral. After everything that had happened it was such a relief to see James buried with dignity. The whole thing was just horrendous for his family.

Louis Chapman (friend)

Jamesy and I grew up in the same area and went to school together. He was from Oakfield Street and I was from Chatham Street. We were both in the same class in St Gabriel's. He used to knock about with 'Dutch' Doherty, Toner and 'Cleakey' Clarke. There was a whole gang of them went about together. I didn't really see Jamesy again until we met in Birmingham. I had gone over to England in 1968 and Jamesy came over when he was about 19 or 20 in 1969. I was in London at first but my brother-in-law lived up in Birmingham and I decided to try it out. Jamesy just went over for the work, to get a good job with decent money. He was a good spender and good craic. We got into a brave few escapades together. We used to get our wages and head off down to London on a coach for the craic. We were both painting and we worked all over, in Wales, in Somerset, anywhere. I remember we painted a cider farm in Somerset. We did a lot of work together. Jamesy was a good worker and good craic as well. As he got older he got more and more popular. When he was young he had been quite small, then he just seemed to sprout up and came into his own. He was a brilliant singer and so anywhere we went people always used to get him up singing. Jamesy was lovely to listen to. His voice was really polished and wherever he was, he was asked to sing. Jamesy was just a social drinker, not really a heavy drinker, and it never put him off his work. We were in our prime then. Jamesy used to love talking about Ardoyne, particularly if there were any Bone men in the company, to get the slagging going!

There were a lot of Dublin and Belfast people in Birmingham at the time and there were like two cliques. We all got on well enough together but we tended to have our own clubs. The Belfast ones used to drink in the Eagle in Park Lane and the Malt Shovel. There was a very big Belfast community in Birmingham and that included Gerry Hunter and Billy Power. Them and Hugh Callaghan would have been good friends of Jamesy. They were some of the Birmingham Six and we all knew each other because we all used to knock about together. In fact I had come over to Belfast a few weeks before Gerry Hunter and the others were arrested. I was actually staying in his house in Birmingham before I came home to Belfast. But for the grace of God it could have been the Birmingham Seven because I had stayed on in Belfast. If I hadn't I would have been travelling back for Jamesy's funeral with the rest of them.

When Jamesy was killed I was in Belfast. I was totally devastated. I was in the League [social club] and it just came on the news. Apparently he had been involved trying to plant a bomb to blow up the telephone exchange in Coventry. It exploded prematurely and Jamesy was killed instantly. The other fella with him ended up being caught. After Jamesy was killed they had real problems trying to get the body back to Belfast. There were a lot of hold-ups. In between Jamesy's death and the body leaving England the Birmingham bombs went off. There was a lot of bad feeling in England at the time. They wouldn't allow Jamesy's body into St Chad's in Birmingham because the bishop of Birmingham refused to have it there. The National Front attacked the coffin. Then British Airways weren't willing to bring the body home. Aer Lingus eventually agreed to take it to Dublin. The coffin was to go to the Saunders club in Ardoyne. They had it all laid out and ready but the delays prevented that.

In the end he was just taken straight to the Falls Road. I was in Belfast but I never got to the funeral. Nobody was sure when (or if) it would happen. I stayed in my cousin's in Cranbrook Gardens so I would be handy in Ardoyne for it. The district was black with people just waiting around to see when the funeral would happen. That lasted for three days. In the end we just heard that the coffin was buried from the Falls. He was never brought back to Ardoyne. There probably would have been bad rioting if they had buried him from home because the loyalists were threatening to stop the funeral. There was massive tension coming from the loyalists, the British army and the RUC. I never went back to Birmingham after that. Jamesy's wife came and lived in Belfast for a while after the funeral. Then she moved south but she is back now living in Belfast. My daughter Kimberley married Jamesy's cousin and he's called James McDade.

Thomas Robinson was born in Ardglass on 11 July 1914. He had four brothers, Paddy, Willie, Joe and his step-brother Tony. When still a young man he moved to Glenbryn near Ardoyne. Around the same time he met and married Eleanor (Nellie) Chew. It was a mixed marriage. He was an ex-serviceman and was later a member of the Catholic Ex-Servicemen's Association. Thomas and Nellie soon had two daughters themselves, Doreen and Ann. Ann would die from cancer at the young age of 28 leaving her own two girls (Linda and Annette) to be brought up by their grandparents. By then, in 1960, the family had moved to their home in Stratford Gardens. For a time he also worked as a bus driver and later as a civil service messenger based in Corporation Street. He had retired just six days before he was killed. On the night of 5 April 1975 Thomas and Nellie went for a night out to the Highfield social club in Etna Drive. Earlier on the same evening two Catholics were killed in McLaughlin's pub on the New Lodge Road when a UVF

Thomas Robinson
Killed by loyalists,
Etna Drive,
5 April 1975

bomb left in the front porch exploded without warning. Shortly afterwards five Protestants died in the Mountainview tavern when the IRA launched a gun and bomb attack. When news of what had happened in the Mountainview reached Ardoyne Thomas and Nellie decided to make their way home. When they reached the house they realised that their granddaughters were at a friend's nearby. As they were walking down Etna Drive at around 11.50 pm two loyalist gunmen approached. One of them shot Thomas dead. A British soldier was stationed at an observation post in Flax Street mill that night. He gave evidence to the inquest that he had seen the gunmen entering the area shortly before but that he lost sight of them seconds before the shooting. It was a circumstance that, for some, raised suspicions about possible collusion in Thomas' death. Thomas Robinson was 60 years old when he was killed in a blatantly sectarian attack. No group ever claimed responsibility for his death.

Eleanor Robinson (wife)

(This testimony is based upon extracts taken from evidence given to the coroner's court)

I am the wife of the late Thomas Robinson. On the evening of 5 April 1975 at 10 pm, my husband and I went down to the Highfield Club in Etna Drive. When in the club we heard about the explosion at the Mountainview Tavern on the Shankill Road and I suggested we go home early in case there would be trouble. Sometime after 11 pm we left the club and walked up home to 62 Stratford Gardens. When we got home our granddaughters were out and we realised we had no keys to get in. We knew the girls were at a friend's house in Alliance Avenue and decided to walk round there to get the keys. We walked down Stratford Gardens and turned left into Etna Drive. We were walking on the footpath. When we turned the corner into Etna Drive and walked about half way up towards the entry I saw two young men walking towards us from the direction of the butcher's shop at the corner of Alliance Avenue, Etna Drive. There were no other people about at the time. These men walked towards us casually and when they were right up against us I saw at least one of them had a hand gun. I saw him take the gun from either his pocket or waistband. I said to my husband, 'There's two very strange looking fellows and they don't look right'. He said to me, 'Take it easy'. That is the last words he spoke to me. The man with the gun fired four shots at us from the front and my husband slumped onto the ground. I also fell onto the ground but was not struck by any of the bullets. I received injuries to my right knee and left hip. The gunmen were young, well-dressed, low-set and about 18 years of age. These men were at the top of the entry when they fired the shots. I screamed and they ran up the entry which runs between the houses in Stratford Gardens and Alliance Avenue.

Francis Bradley
Killed by loyalists,
Corporation Street,
19 June 1975

I asked the guy why the loyalist left a booby trap there. He said Catholics owned the garage, Catholics frequented it and it was all Catholics who worked in it.
So the loyalists knew if the bomb was going to kill anybody it would more than likely be a Catholic.

Francis Bradley was born in May 1958. His father was John Bradley from the New Lodge Road and his mother was Bessie Boyd originally from the Newtownards Road. The couple had sight impairments and met each other through attending workshops for 'the blind'. Bessie was a Protestant and John was a Catholic. The couple married in 1937 in St Patrick's chapel and eventually had fourteen children. Their first house was in North Queen Street but they later moved to Ardoyne, first to Jamaica Street and then to Etna Drive. During the Second World War a bomb landed in their garden; it wrecked the bottom of Etna Drive, Highbury Gardens, Holmdene Gardens and part of Strathroy Park. John and Bessie then moved to 52 Northwick Drive where they lived until they died.

Francis was the youngest of fourteen children. There were nine boys – John, Davie, Willie, Hughie, Barney, Tommy, Gerard, Brendan and Francis – and five girls – Mary, Patricia, Isabel, Angela and Elizabeth (who died shortly after birth). He went to Holy Cross Boys and progressed to St Gabriel's school. His first job was as a cloth cutter in Rosebank Mill. Francis was a quiet, happy-go-lucky lad. He had great respect for his parents and his only vice was smoking. He had a small close circle of friends that included Sean Grant, Kevin Wylie, Joe Quigley, Billy Cairns and James Carty.

On 19 June 1975 Francis went for a jaunt with his mates in their newly purchased 'collective' car. They stopped at the Shamrock garage in Corporation Street to pick up a tyre and get petrol. Francis was killed when he lifted a booby trap bomb, concealed in a tin can, planted by loyalists. The intended target was any innocent Catholic that happened to stumble on the device. Later that evening the Protestant Action Force claimed responsibility for the sectarian attack. Three other members of the Bradley family have been killed during the conflict [Isabel Leyland, killed by IRA in Flax Street, 21 August 1992; Martin Bradley, killed by loyalists on the Crumlin Road, 12 May 1994 and Fra Shannon, killed by INLA in Turf Lodge, 9 June 1996].

Sean Grant (friend)

I went to school with Francie and we lived in the same street. There was only a year of difference between us. Francie was hardly ever at school. Joe Quigley and myself were Francie's best mates. I started knocking about with him around 1970. He was a happy-go-lucky type character who would do anything for a laugh. There was a squad of us that worked as the Highfield Club 'security team'. There was me, Francie, Joe Quigley and Billy Cairns; we saved up and bought a car. The car was a Vauxhall four door; Billy Cairns was the driver. He painted it canary yellow. The week before Francie was killed, Billy, myself, Joe and Francie all went to Bundoran. It was the first time we had been 'on holiday' together. We went on a Saturday and came back on Sunday. The craic was great so we decided to plan another trip. That Tuesday, after the trip to Bundoran, Billy left one of the car tyres in to the Shamrock garage, Corporation Street to get fixed. On Thursday, the day of the explosion, 19 June 1975, we had planned to go to the pictures. One of the lads didn't turn up so we decided to go for a drive. We left Ardoyne and made our way to the Shamrock garage to collect the tyre. Billy Cairns, me, Francie, James Carty and Joe Quigley were in the car. On the way to the garage we were having great craic. We were talking enthusiastically about the trip to Bundoran and were planning the next excursion.

We pulled into the Shamrock garage and got out of the car. Seconds later I heard an explosion and Francie shouting, 'Joey, help me'. Francie just collapsed. He looked like he was unconscious and I thought he was dead. James Carty was injured in the leg with shrapnel as well. The petrol attendant phoned an ambulance. Shortly afterwards I heard a second explosion. I think there was a bomb somewhere nearby and a doorman was killed. A short time later an ambulance came on the scene but it rushed by us to the scene of the second explosion. It seemed an awful long time before the ambulance and the RUC finally arrived on the scene. Everyone in the car was arrested and taken to Townhall Street. The RUC put bags over our hands and took swabs. They were really aggressive. We were kept in Townhall Street from around 7.30 pm until about 1.00 am. During that period we were questioned by the RUC about the explosion. The RUC told us they suspected us of being on a bombing mission and that Francie was hiding the bomb up his coat. Later an RUC man came in and said, 'Your friend Francie the bomber just died in hospital'. The RUC were adamant that Francie was a bomber.

The RUC continued to aggressively interrogate us and continued to accuse us of the bombing. The Protestant Action Force (PAF) claimed responsibility for the killing later that evening. At that stage we were all released. I believe if the PAF hadn't claimed responsibility we would have been kept in RUC custody much longer and possibly charged. I'm not sure if James Carty was brought first to hospital and then to Townhall Street, but he was with us when they we were released. After we were released we went straight to the Bradley family. The whole street was out. The rumours had been flying about and people thought that two of us had been killed. There was confusion over the second explosion in which one person also died. Francie's parents were totally devastated.

Months later I was travelling to England with my uncle Martin and we were stopped and arrested at Liverpool Docks. We were held from Saturday until the following Thursday. The British police told me that the RUC told them that they knew Francie and the occupants of the car had been on a bombing mission. They constantly referred to the explosion when they were interrogating me. It was an experience I will never forget. The British police gave me a real hard time.

Brendan Bradley (brother)

Francis's nickname was 'the bone' because of his slight frame. He could eat twice as much as everybody else but never seemed to put any weight on. He was about 5 foot 8 and very, very thin. I was in Long Kesh when Francis was killed. I was in Cage 13. It was after lock-up time, about 9 pm or maybe 10 pm. The guy I was standing beside got up suddenly and walked away very, very quickly to the toilet. The governor and a couple of screws came over to me and asked me had I got any brothers; I told him I'd a load of brothers. They asked had I one called Francis; I said I had. They said, 'Well he was killed in an explosion'. That was it; they walked away. I asked the guy why he had walked away. He said he knew someone was getting bad news. It was usually after lock-up that the screws came to tell you someone was dead. That was 19 June 1975. There were five of my family in gaol at the time. Tommy and Willie were interned, Gerard was sentenced, as was John. The other four got out on parole for the funeral. I was on remand. I didn't get released for the funeral. I went to court for compassionate bail and I remember the RUC detective getting up and saying he believed that Francis was carrying the bomb when it exploded, this was the day after Francis was killed. At that stage I knew nothing about the circumstances surrounding his death but I remember the media saying things like, 'guy blows himself up'. I was eventually released on 6 August 1975; the Crown dropped the charges.

I tried to find out what happened but I only got snippets of what actually occurred. But about three years ago I was standing in the Jamaica Inn and this guy came over and said to me, 'I've always wanted to tell you this. I was there the night your brother was killed in the Shamrock filling station, Corporation Street'. This person was the petrol-pump attendant. He said Francis and the lads had come to put petrol in the car but the petrol gauge hadn't been working in the car and one of the lads had asked was there a petrol can so they could put 50p worth of petrol in it. The guy told them there were empty petrol cans in the corner. So Francis went over and lifted one of the cans and it exploded. I asked the guy, 'Why did the loyalist leave a booby-trapped can there?' He said Catholics owned the garage, Catholics frequented it and it was all Catholics who worked in it. So the loyalists knew if the bomb was going to kill anybody, it would more than likely be a Catholic.

Francis lived for about two hours after the explosion. They brought him to the Mater Hospital and then to the morgue. All the occupants of the car were arrested. The RUC initially believed it was an IRA bomb. The Protestant Action Force claimed responsibility and at the coroner's court it was revealed the detonator was a type the loyalists had been using. Nobody was ever convicted for the killing. But some years later an RUC man came to my brother Hughie and said they had arrested somebody for Francis's murder. They said he had confessed to it but nobody was ever charged. They told Hughie this person would be appearing in court but nothing ever came of it. Maybe he decided to work for the RUC and they never went ahead with the charge.

Francis was the first member of our family to die during the conflict. I don't know how I felt but it was like a role-play. I broke down and cried but I didn't know how to react or how to feel. It was only at the bail hearing I realised that I wasn't getting out for the funeral. The devastating thing was my mother. Francis was her youngest son. I remember in the High Court that I was going to bash a screw with the handcuffs over the head because he was pulling me away when I wanted to talk to my mother. They gave me a couple of minutes with her afterwards.

There was only a year between me and Francis and we did everything together. I went to work in Rosebank Mill; he left school and went to work in Rosebank. I helped the lemonade man; he helped the lemonade man. He wouldn't have looked up to me; I wasn't really his big brother, Tommy was more his big brother. Francis tried never to do anybody any harm. He was quiet in his manner, respected his parents, never had any vices other than smoking. He didn't make a big splash in life, nothing outstanding; he didn't get the chance. He was a good kid basically; nothing really extraordinary about him except that he was caught up in extraordinary circumstances that killed him.

John Finlay
Killed by loyalists,
Brougham Street,
21 August 1975

They didn't only kill John; they killed my mother and my brother. They wrecked our whole family, that is what they did.

John Finlay was born in Gamble Street in 1939. The family home was bombed during World War II and they moved to Strathroy Park. John Finlay was the youngest in a family of six. He was educated at Sacred Heart Boys and later went on to St Gabriel's. John married a Protestant girl called Ann Long and they had a son called Paul. On several occasions the family were intimidated by loyalists and were forced to leave their home.

John was shot dead on the morning of 21 August 1975 as he walked from his Duncairn Gardens home to work in a nearby timber yard. The UFF gunmen who carried out the killing either knew the victim personally or knew his daily routine. As he made his way along Brougham Street shortly after 8.00 am he was approached by two UFF men and shot twice in the head. As he lay helpless on the ground, the gunmen stood over him, firing another three shots into his body. They then got into a car and drove off towards York Street. The car had been stolen in the nearby loyalist Tigers Bay district. John Finlay was the second employee of the timber yard to be killed by loyalists.

Malachy Smyth (friend)

John was my next-door neighbour in Strathroy Park. They were marvellous neighbours and every time one of the Finlays grew a bit, I got their clothes. We were poor, but so was everybody else so you never noticed. John loved to sing; he sang like Dean Martin and he was great at imitating people. I remember John married a Protestant girl from Tigers Bay in the late sixties and lived down there. They were a mixed marriage and John always said they were caught between the devil and the deep blue sea. In the end it was probably the fact that he was a Catholic married to a Protestant that got him killed. They just couldn't tolerate mixed marriages.

Mary McGarry (sister)

I am an O'Neill. My mother was originally married to Patrick O'Neill before she married Hugh Finlay. My mother's 19 year-old brother Robbie Lynch was murdered by the Black and Tans in Townsend Street in the 1920s. The Tans came and shouted that they were giving them five minutes to get off the street. But they didn't give them five minutes and they killed her young brother and another man. In those days there was five of us. My sister Bernadette died when she was two years of age and my father died three months later. He was 30 years old and my

mother was left a widow with four children. Then my mother met big Hugh
Finlay from Sussex Street. As the family got bigger we moved to Gamble Street;
that was where John was born. The family was known as the Finlays and the
O'Neills. We eventually moved to 78 Strathroy Park in Ardoyne in 1943. In the
early years John knocked about with boys from Etna Drive and in those days I
used to love to hear them sing at the street corners. John had a beautiful voice and
Dean Martin was his favourite. Every time there was a new Dean Martin record
he bought it. He used to stand and sing along with the records in the house.

John worked at McHugh and Dick's timber yard in the Docks but the
intimidation got to him. He was frightened; he knew he was being watched; he
knew he was going to be killed. One man used to leave some of the Catholic lads
home from the timber yard in his car. He left everyone off one night and had just
got out of the car when it exploded. On another occasion the loyalists opened up
on a lorry full of Catholic men from the yard. They killed a young fella and
injured another man in that attack. John would have been on that lorry only that
day he was visiting Ann in hospital.

The morning it happened, John got up and Ann wasn't well. He made her a cup
of tea and told her to go back to bed. He had just crossed over into Brougham
Street when he was killed. Ann heard the shooting. She never knew it was John.
John's body was taken to the Mater Hospital and then home to Duncairn Gardens.
Two days before John was killed we were bombed out of our house in
Mountainview. The loyalists drove a car bomb in and blew up the street. We were
sleeping in St Vincent's school on the morning John was killed.

I always knew they would shoot John and they did. I went down to tell my
mother and as soon as the soldiers came to the door to tell her officially, my
mother knew John was dead. She just knew; they tortured John. I went over to the
Ormeau Road to tell my sister Peggy and as soon as she opened the door she
looked at me and said, 'It's our John; they've murdered our John this morning,
haven't they?' Everybody knew that they would eventually kill him. The worst
thing about it is there was no reason for it. They killed John because he was a
Catholic and because he was married to a Protestant.

No one will ever know the devastating effect John's death had on the family.
Hugo loved John. John's death killed both Hugo and our mother. She died in 1982
and he died eight months after her. It left a terrible mark on them all; it was awful.
After he died I went to confession and I asked the priest to pray for him and I was
shocked when he said no. He told me, 'You don't pray for him; you pray to him,
because John died for his faith, because he was a Catholic, nothing else'. When
they killed my brother, they killed a good kid who hurt nobody. Whoever they
are, I don't know whether they are living or dead, they have an awful sin to
answer for. They didn't only kill John, they killed my mother and my other
brother. They wrecked our whole family; that is what they did.

William Daniels
Killed by the UVF,
Glenbank Place,
22 August 1975

> *William was always very careful and ever since the bomb in his lorry on 5 August 1975 he was extra careful. He never told me if he had been threatened and never spoke of having enemies. I know for certain he was not a member of any organisation.*

William Daniels was the son of William (senior) and Jean Daniels who lived in Brompton Park. William (junior) was born in 1948 and grew up to be a motor mechanic. By 1975 he was living on the Crumlin Road with his girlfriend Eileen Boyer and her four year-old daughter. William was a Catholic and Eileen was a Protestant. On 5 August of that year William had survived an attempt on his life. A bomb had been attached to the underside of a lorry he was driving. Fortunately it fell off onto the road before it exploded. At just before 1 am on 16 August 1975 William had just got back with Eileen from a night out in town. He was sitting and locking his car outside their home as Eileen stood waiting for him. Then two UVF gunmen fired three shots at him, hitting William in the head and shoulder. He was taken to the Mater Hospital shortly after and survived without regaining consciousness for a further 6 days. However, he died from the gunshot wound to his head at around 3.50 pm on 22 August 1975. His 68 year-old father had to go to identify his body. An open verdict was subsequently recorded by the coroner. William Daniels was 27 years old at the time of his death. William's sister's husband, William Rankin, was killed by the IRA in his home on 19 June 1976. They suspected him of being a member of the UDA although. William Daniels' family and friends also denied that he had any link to any political organisation.

Eileen Boyer (friend)

(This testimony is based upon extracts taken from evidence given to the coroner's court)

I have known William James Daniels for about two and a half years. I went to live with him along with my four year old daughter, just before Easter 1975, at 801 Crumlin Road. I am a Protestant and William was R.C [Catholic]. At approximately 9.45 pm on Friday 15 August 1975, William and I left 801 Crumlin Road to go out for the evening. We had been home all day since he came home from work at 3.30 pm. We took the child with us and left her with my mother. After leaving my mother's house at Downview Gardens, we drove to the Albert Clock where William parked the car. We were in his car, which was a yellow Ford Cortina. We walked round to the Royal Avenue Hotel and went into the Lounge Bar. We were there a few minutes when we were joined by a man who lives two doors from the garage on the left hand side of the Antrim Road. They talked about cars and had about three drinks. He left us and we left and went to the Starlight Ballroom in Cornmarket. It was then about 11.30 pm. We stayed about an hour but we didn't dance. William spoke to the manager as he knew him. It was just a friendly conversation. About 12.30 am on 16 August 1975 we left the Starlight. We walked back to the car. William was driving. We went up Great George's Street, up York Street, then Limestone

Road onto the Antrim Road. We stopped at the Chinese Restaurant on the Antrim Road near the top of the Limestone Road. William went up and got chips for me. We then went along the Antrim Road to the North Circular Road and over the Ballysillan Road to the Crumlin Road. We turned right on the Crumlin Road to our own house which is on the corner of Crumlin Road and Glenbank Place. Then we turned just into Glenbank place and stopped on the right hand corner of Glenbank Place at the side gable of our house. It was then about 12.50 am. There was no one at all about Glenbank Place. When William stopped I opened the passenger door which was nearest the roadway and stepped out onto the road. William was slower than me because he had to put the chain on the steering wheel. As I stepped out of the car I saw two young men come from the left hand side further up Glenbank Place and cross the road towards the front passenger door which I was just about to close. One of them pulled the door open from my hand. Both of them had handguns. The other one fired two shots in through the open door at William. Then the one who had pulled the door open also fired. I don't know if it was one shot or two. Neither of them spoke. They both ran off up Glenbank Place way from the Crumlin Road. Two other chaps came round from the Crumlin Road and tried to help William who was lying half in and half out of the driver's door onto the footpath. These two fellows took him out, then they tried to start the car to go after the two boys. They couldn't get it started. I was then taken into 805 Crumlin Road. William was always very careful and ever since the bomb in his lorry on 5 August 1975 he was extra careful. He never told me if he had been threatened and never spoke of having enemies. I know for certain he was not a member of any organisation.

John Butler (eyewitness)

(This testimony is based upon extracts taken from evidence given to the coroner's court)

At 7.45 on 15 August 1975 I left my lodgings in Glenbank Place with two others, one of whom was David Armstrong, and went to the loyalist social club for a drink. The other man with us left at about 10 pm and I left at around 12 pm, leaving Armstrong on his own. I got a taxi on the Shankill Road which took me to the corner of Crumlin Road and Glenbank Place. I was back at my lodgings in Glenbank Place for about three-quarters of an hour when Armstrong arrived back. A few minutes later a few shots were heard nearby. The landlady and I ran to the front door. I ran down towards Crumlin Road and David Armstrong followed me. I saw a car parked in Glenbank Place near the junction of Crumlin Road. A woman was standing in the middle of the road opposite the car and she was screaming. The driver's door was open and a man was lying out the door with his foot jammed between the seat and the door. I put the car out of gear and pushed it forward to release his foot. I then put my hand into his mouth and pulled his tongue out for safety in case he would choke. A crowd then gathered and shortly after this the army arrived. They gave the injured man medical assistance. Shortly after this the police and ambulance arrived. Armstrong and I both went with this man to the Mater Hospital.

Thomas Murphy
Killed by loyalists,
Antrim Road,
2 October 1975

I would describe Tommy Murphy's murder as the slaughter of the innocent.

Thomas Murphy was born and reared in Brookfield Street. He attended Holy Cross Boys and St Gabriel's school. At the age of 14 he went to Crossgar to join the priesthood. After two years he left and then trained as a photographer. He met Patricia in 1967 and three years later they got married. Thomas was regarded in Ardoyne as a quiet family man, who lived for nothing but his wife and his passion for photography. On the afternoon of 2 October 1975 he was working as usual in his photographer's shop on the Antrim Road. He had just returned from having lunch with his wife when two loyalist gunmen entered the premises and shot him dead. Before the killers made their escape, they left a twenty-pound bomb inside the shop. The UVF later claimed responsibility for the murder. Eleven other people were killed on the same day, including two Catholic sisters. Despite the fact that an off-duty RUC man had seen the killers enter and leave the shop, no one was ever arrested, questioned or convicted of Thomas Murphy's murder. A week before Thomas Murphy's murder the couple received notification that they could adopt a child.

Patricia King (widow)

I met Tommy through the Legion of Mary. Men and women had separate meetings but one night a week, men and women would get together for a chat. That's how we met. I started to go out with Tommy in 1967 and three years later we were married. His hobby was taking photographs; he got a job in a photographer's and they trained him professionally. He really loved that. We had no children. We were burnt out of our house in Farringdon Gardens on internment morning in 1971 and eventually moved to Stratford Gardens. Tommy started his own photography business in 1973. His first shop was in Brompton Park. He wasn't in it a year and a bomb went off in the bookies and nearly demolished the building. So he had to start all over again. He eventually got premises on the Antrim Road and set his business up there. That was about March or April and he was killed in October. We both worked in the shop together at that stage.

The day he was murdered he didn't have very much work on. He told me if I wanted, I could have the day off and he left me into town. When I came home I went to my sister's in Velsheda Park. Tommy came home for lunch and we heard the one o'clock news. It reported that the Casey sisters had been murdered in the wine company facing Millfield Tech. They were tied to chairs and shot dead by the UVF. The day that Tommy was killed there were eleven people murdered. As we were listening to the news Tommy and I talked about how terrible the killings were.

He left the house about 1.55 pm that afternoon and told me he would be home about 5.30 pm. He was killed about 2.45 pm. I heard the bomb but I didn't really think anything of it; it was the '70s and there were bombs going off all the time. The next thing, a couple of friends came by thinking that I already knew. Then the house was packed with people and I still didn't know. Fr. Myles came down; I was told afterwards that he knew by looking at me that I didn't know but he couldn't bring himself to tell me. He told me that Tommy had been in an accident and he was in hospital. I assumed it had been a car accident. Still no one could tell me that Tommy had been shot dead. It was actually 5.30 pm - 5.45 pm when Tommy's cousin told me the circumstances of his death.

The shop that Tommy owned had three floors and he used the third floor as the darkroom. He was in the darkroom or one of the studios upstairs when he was shot. At the inquest an off-duty policeman said that he had seen two youths getting out of a car outside the shop and going into the premises. What he thought strange was the back door passenger's side was left open. He thought they were going to rob the shop and then said to himself, 'Why would you rob a photographers? It wouldn't have a big turnover of money'. He said that thought had just crossed his mind when the bomb went off. The gunmen had gone upstairs, found Tommy, shot him at point-blank range and on the way out put a twenty-pound bomb on the counter. The owner's wife of the shop across the street lost her leg in the explosion. She was standing at the door when the bomb went off. A lot of other people were hurt as well. The UVF later claimed responsibility.

After Tommy's death my life was just turned totally upside down. Someone just comes along and says, 'This is what we think of your life; it's worthless'. I just wanted to die. I felt I should have been with Tommy. I always felt he died alone, killed by two strangers. On the other hand, in comparison to other people he was lucky that they didn't take him away; it was during the time of the Shankill Butchers. It sounds a really ironic thing to say, he wasn't lucky, he didn't deserve to be killed, but he was lucky it was quick, in comparison to how other people had been killed.

I was never officially informed that Tommy had been killed. I was never questioned, which in any society is strange because I worked with him. I was never asked anything. The RUC never asked if we had ever been threatened. Had we ever got threatening phone calls? The inquest only dealt with the circumstances of the death. It was an open verdict because no one was ever arrested and charged with his murder. The awful thing is, it is left like an open book. It's something that's never closed because there has been no justice. I need to know who did it. Where are they now? I feel that justice has never been achieved and that applies to everybody. You ask yourself if anybody cares and at the end of the day when things happen you don't really care, because it's somebody else that it's happened to.

Tommy McAuley (brother-in-law)

After Tommy and Patricia got married we all socialised together. My wife Ann and Patricia were very close sisters and Tommy and I were always close because of the two of them. His only interest was the family. He was an Irishman and a nationalist and that was it. He was a quiet fella; he never drank and was very religious. Tommy was able to provide slides of the original stain glass windows in Ardoyne chapel after they had been destroyed in a bomb. The priests were able to reproduce the stain glass windows of the 'St Paul of the Cross' chapel. When the houses were burned on internment morning Tommy got in touch with the bishop and told him to get off his butt and come over and help the people of Ardoyne. The bishop told him to pray and I remember Tommy bringing the phone outside and saying, 'Listen, our houses are burning'. I was shot in 1972 and Tommy used to say he didn't know how I went out to work again. He always watched what he did and watched where he was going. He was a careful sort of a guy.

The day Tommy was killed he was at work. You had to know the lay out of the place to know where to find him. Tommy was the only person in the building. Seemingly they went upstairs, shot Tommy with one bullet, put the bomb down and ran out. The building just collapsed like a deck of cards.

Tommy was a good fella who worked for his family. They had put in for adoption and it was confirmed they could adopt just before Tommy's death.

Fr. Kenneth Brady (friend)

Tommy Murphy and I were students in Crossgar. We went there in 1960 and ended up in the same class. We became good friends. When we were home on holidays I would go to his house in Brookfield Street and he would come over to see me and my folks. Tommy was a much more religious person than me. He was extremely conscientious. He always kept in touch; he did some of my family's wedding photographs. I was ordained in 1972 and after that I went away for a number of years. When I came back to Belfast I was in and out of Ardoyne practically every week. I used to call to his house in Stratford Gardens. At that time the British army were on the streets and trying to get in and out of Ardoyne was a major feat. I always remember Tommy was very conscientious about getting me out of the area at night.

I remember particularly well the day Tommy died. I had called to my mother's in Linden Street, West Belfast. My younger brother Pat came in and told me someone had been killed in the Antrim Road. I had been planning to go over to North Belfast but then decided to go back to Crossgar. That night I got a phone call from Fr. Fernando to tell me that Tommy Murphy had been shot dead. I was really stunned. It was sadly ironic that the guy who took such care to make sure that I was safe getting out of Ardoyne ended up being shot dead himself. I would describe Tommy Murphy's murder as the slaughter of the innocent.

Seamus McCusker
Killed by the 'Official' IRA,
New Lodge Road,
31 October 1975

Seamus was someone that had true ideals, a very genuine person and he very quietly worked away at what he believed in.

Seamus McCusker was born 16 March 1935 in Belfast and moved to Ballinagh, Co. Cavan at an early age. His mother was Bridget Brady and his father James McCusker; James played Gaelic for Co. Antrim. Seamus moved back to Belfast and lived in St Matthew's parish, the Doagh Road and Divis Flats before settling in Ardoyne in 1971. He was an electrician by trade and worked for the Water Service Agency. He married Betty McGoran from Divis Flats and they had three children: Gregory, Myles and Felicity. Gregory was killed in a tragic road accident. Seamus was interned in October 1971 and released in November 1972. He became the director of the Sinn Féin Incident Centre in the New Lodge and through his dedication and diligent management soon earned the respect of the local community. Friends describe him as unassuming, thoughtful and mild mannered. He was one of life's gentlemen.

Seamus McCusker was an IRA volunteer. On 31 October 1975, a member of the 'Official' IRA killed him. During this period there was a feud between different sections of the republican movement. Seamus was buried from St Peter's chapel; a volley of shots was fired over his coffin. Malachy Foots, Ard Comhairle Sinn Féin member, gave the graveside oration at Milltown cemetery.

His wife Betty (deceased) gave this account of Seamus to a local newspaper; 'Seamus was an idealist who suffered for his ideals. He was an intellectual, not a man of action. He was so dedicated to his ideals that he worked in the incident centre round the clock. He hadn't been able to get home since Tuesday. The last time I spoke to him was at 12 today, 31 October, when he phoned me. Two hours later he was dead.'

Bobby Lavery (friend)

Seamus and his wife Betty lived in Strathroy Park, Ardoyne. His wife is now dead. I think she was originally from West Belfast; her mother and sister lived in Divis Flats. Seamus was born in Belfast but lived much of his life in Co. Cavan. My first memory of Seamus was when I was a prisoner in Long Kesh. We were watching TV and Seamus was the Sinn Féin spokesperson. When I got released, my next meeting with Seamus was when I made a complaint at the incident centre where he worked. Seamus was very personable and managed to sort the problem out. My young son Sean was with me and he was running about pulling things out. I said, 'Sean, will you please stop?' I was trying to talk to Seamus. I remember this clearly, Seamus said, 'Bobby, never stop a child's sense of adventure, it's their best learning'. I remember thinking that's really profound. It's really strange that should have had such an impact on me, something so simple as that. I have actually used that several times myself and people think I'm dead clever, but it's not me; it's Seamus McCusker talking.

The truce was called in 1975 and Seamus was appointed head of what they called the truce incident centre on the New Lodge. They had a hot line to Stormont that was used from time to time.

He practically lived in the centre. He had a camp bed there. You know Alan Lundy – Seamus was that type of person. He was just one of life's nice people. He wasn't shy, far from it, but he wasn't aggressive either. He was just a nice, pleasant person. I love to remember people as a whole person and remember the bad things too. It's important not to remember them as some kind of saint. But where Seamus is concerned, either he didn't have a bad side or I didn't know him long enough to see it.

At the time of his death there was a feud between the 'Official' IRA, INLA and IRSP. This was late October 1975. A number of women were beaten up and they made a complaint to the incident centre. Seamus McCusker and Sally Morgan, another member of Sinn Féin, went down to get the details. They came out and were walking along Artillery Flats. Members of the 'Official' IRA were standing at the bottom of the alley that leads up to where their drinking club was, off North Queen Street. One of them ran up and shot Seamus in the back of the head. There was someone arrested and served time for his killing. I remember distinctly that I was sitting in Lynch's Bar and somebody came in and said, 'They have just shot Seamus. I think he's dead'. At first I thought they were talking about my brother Seamus. Then I was told it was Seamus McCusker.

People like Seamus, decent, good people, are a small minority. Seamus McCusker was one of life's gentlemen. His killing was really, really horrendous. The following year the feud was off. I wrote a poem about his death in our local bulletin, The Campaign. It was devastating, especially for people that knew him in North Belfast.

I remember the day of his funeral… He was buried from St Peter's on the Falls Road. Ruairí Ó Bradaigh, then president of Sinn Féin, and Maire Drumm, then vice-president of Sinn Féin, were at the funeral. There was a tricolour over the coffin and it was flanked by a colour party of Cumann na mBan. There were two women pipers ahead of the hearse. At the graveside I remember Malachy Foots giving the oration; he talked of Seamus devoting his full time to the republican movement and how he was an inspiration and a daily source of strength for many people in the struggle. It was a very moving occasion. Seamus was really well respected. On reflection, I think Seamus would have been a vital part of the republican leadership today. I think he would have been a leading strategist behind today's process.

Sally Morgan (friend)

Seamus came to run the incident centre on the New Lodge Road. That was the first I met him. Seamus practically lived in the centre. He was there 24 hours a day. There was a cease-fire in 1975 and the incident centre was set up as a result. We monitored any incidents with the British army or RUC that could have jeopardised the cease-fire. The centre had a direct phone line to Stormont. There was a special code word and there was a contact at the other end of the line; everything was written down and reported. It was the same for the Brits. If they had anything to complain about, if somebody did something, they would phone us. On the rare occasions when Seamus took time off, Tom Fleming or myself covered for him.

Seamus was a gentleman and a very educated person. He was the type of person that thought things out. If you went and asked him 'What do you think about this?', Seamus would have thought it through. He used to scratch his beard, thought for a wee minute and then gave you the answer. That was his mannerism. He was very mild-mannered, quiet and calm. He was well respected; a lot of people would have sought Seamus out when they wanted advice. We had set up the centre and all of a sudden people looked to him for advice. Within quite a short while he had built up a reputation for himself in the New Lodge area.

Betty, Myles and Felicity would call some days to the centre. Betty was from Divis Flats, her mum and sister lived there. I went over to visit Betty a number of times when she was dying. She died of cancer in 1979. Seamus was the type that kept himself very much to himself. He didn't talk a lot; he didn't divulge a lot about his private business.

There was a feud between the various factions of the republican movement and a few people had been beaten up. Seamus was taking statements about what had happened. It was Halloween, 1975. I wasn't actually in the centre that day because Paddy, my husband was working the 3-11 shift. I said to him, 'Before you go to work I'm going to run up and get an apple cake for Halloween'. Seamus was at the door of the centre and asked me for directions to Alexander Flats. I explained where it was. The bottom of the New Lodge Road would have been very much 'Officials' territory. I decided to take him down. People said to me afterwards, 'You and him walked down there'. But that was the type of Seamus; he didn't feel that he was in any danger and he certainly didn't feel that I was in any danger or he would not have let me go with him.

We went down the road and walked into the Barrack to the seventh floor in Alexander Flats. The person Seamus wanted to interview wasn't at home. He wrote a note and left it for him. We walked down the Barrack towards North Queen Street. As we turned into North Queen Street, I felt uneasy. I turned round and saw a guy coming towards us with a gun and his hood up. He fired three or four shots at Seamus. It just happened so quickly. Seamus was hit and sort of fell against me. I threw myself on the ground on my hands and knees and crawled round to the flats. Seamus didn't stand a chance; he just hadn't a chance. The gunman shot Seamus in the head. I didn't realise at the time that Seamus was dead because I had kept crawling. It was fear I suppose. It was only when people started coming running that I actually got up. It was all sort of hazy after that. Somebody came and said TV cameras were up in the centre and would I come up. But I couldn't; I didn't go near the place. I went over to Divis to visit Betty. She was devastated; I found out later at that time she was already quite ill. Seamus had a military funeral and was buried in Milltown.

He was such an easy target for them. I remember thinking at the time there wasn't one of them fit to even lick his boots. Seamus was someone with true ideals. He was a very genuine person. He quietly worked away at what he believed in. He was intelligent. Seamus was a friend; I suppose he was more than a friend, he was like a teacher to us. We learnt an awful lot from him. I think Seamus could have gone far. Things could have been an awful lot different if he had been around to support and guide us. His death has left a great void in the New Lodge area.

> *The Shankill Butchers were picking up anybody. Frankie was killed simply because he was a Catholic … to them it wasn't Frankie Crossan; he was just another Catholic and that was good enough. Their aim was to murder any Catholic. Frankie was easy prey.*

Francis Crossan
Killed by loyalists,
Shankill Road,
25 November 1975

Frank Crossan was born 2 May 1941. His mother Catherine (née Nevin) was originally from Ballynahinch and was the second wife of his father, Stafford Crossan, who was from Crumlin. As a child, Frank was brought up with three brothers, Desmond, Pat and Matt, and sister Margaret in Ladbrook Drive, Ardoyne. He attended Holy Cross Boys school and worked in a number of shops, including Lipton's supermarket on the Crumlin Road, before working on the buses as a conductor. He married Mary Rafferty from Butler Street in 1961 and they eventually moved to Glenveagh Drive in Suffolk where they brought up their two children, Tony and Margaret. Frankie was a generous, obliging fella. He was a nice guy to know. He was involved in community work and helped organise cross-community holidays for young people.

On 25 November 1975 Frankie Crossan was making his way home after a night out in Ardoyne when he was abducted and brutally killed by members of the notorious UVF Shankill Butchers gang. His badly beaten and mutilated body was found in an entry off Tennent Street in the Shankill Road; his throat had been cut. One of the UVF gang said in a statement that they had been drinking in a bar and decided to 'pick up a Taig [Catholic] and do him in'. Two members of the Shankill Butchers were sentenced to life for Frankie Crossan's murder. Frankie was 34 years old at the time of his death. Two years earlier (2 March 1973) his brother Pat was killed by the UVF in a sectarian attack.

Susan McCormick (sister-in-law)

I met Frankie when we were quite young; we played together in school. I didn't know Frankie's mother because she died when Frankie was born and their father reared them. Frankie married my sister in 1961 in Holy Cross chapel. They had a boy called Tony and a girl called Margaret. When they first got married they moved into a flat over the Antrim Road and then they got a house on the Glen Road.

Frankie mostly worked in shops; he worked in Lipton's on the Crumlin Road. Then he went to work on the buses. His brother Pat was on the buses as well, as a driver. Frankie always suffered from very bad migraines; they were very severe. It got that it was difficult for him to work on the buses, so he left.

Frankie was killed by the Shankill Butchers. I remember when I found out about it I was in a terrible state. It had a terrible impact on us. I think Mary died never having forgiven the people who did it. It would be a hard thing to forgive. Mary wanted Frankie to go to the doctor's with her the morning he was killed; my sister had angina. But Frankie said he hadn't time to wait and she never saw him again. I don't think she ever really got over that; she never said goodbye to him properly.

Mary said Frankie went out and she got the kids off to school. She said the soldiers were hovering about outside where she lived. She saw them talking to her next-door neighbour. Then the soldier came up the path, rapped the door and asked if she knew Frank Crossan. Then he started to question her, 'When did you last see him?' Mary said that she had seen him yesterday morning. Frankie's father was not well and Mary never thought much of him not coming home; she thought he was with his father. The soldier said to her, 'Could you tell me what he was wearing the last time you saw him?' Our Mary was able to reel off everything. He then asked her had she anybody with her and it was then that she saw her neighbour coming in. The soldiers had brought her neighbour in. Mary couldn't remember much more after that; she just couldn't believe what had happened to him.

Frankie had great hands; he could have made a cabinet. He was a good painter and decorator as well. As a brother-in-law he was a good lad. He was very much into the community. When I used to chum about with him I never imagined he would have done as well as he did; you wouldn't have thought he had it in him to do all of those things. Mary used to say, 'He just paddles about there and does this and that because he can't work'. If my mummy needed her front room decorated Frankie would have done it. He helped everybody out.

Frankie always kept contact with Ardoyne after he moved; he was in Ardoyne nearly every day of the week. Frankie's brother Pat had been shot dead by the UVF. His wife

Maureen lived in Ardoyne. Maureen just didn't want to go on living after Pat was killed, so Frankie was over at Maureen's regularly trying to help her get over Pat. Mary said he used to say to Maureen, 'Come on, Maureen, you have to get through this. Why don't you take up driving?' Frankie pushed her to take lessons. Maureen then had her own independence and got a wee car and she could take the kids out.

After Frankie was murdered our Mary was very, very bitter. It nearly killed her and I don't know how she survived for so long. She died two years ago. I was talking to Tony, her son, two years ago and he still feels the same way, bitter that his father was taken away from him. It was bad enough for him, but wee Margaret didn't even get to see her father. It's bad enough to lose your father but the actual nature of his death is a horrifying image to have in your mind. We were all worried about young Tony. But he coped with it very well at that particular time. We always worried that he would look for revenge. But he never did. It must have just been his upbringing. Frankie was a very good dad but very strict; Tony did what his daddy said. There was no counselling or anything like that provided for the family. Thank God they have done all right. Margaret is a teacher and Tony took up the plumbing trade. Tony is the picture of his daddy; the absolute spit. If Frankie had lived he would have been very proud of them. Frankie Crossan was a good man; all the Crossans are. Frankie never did anybody any harm. He did what he could to help other people.

Maureen Crossan (sister-in-law) and **Margaret** (niece)

Margaret: Frank's father was my grandfather and he was from Crumlin. My grandmother, Catherine, was from Ballynahinch. My grandfather, Stafford, worked for Mc Allister of Kenbann Cottages. My grandparents got married in 1934 in the Holy Rosary chapel on the Ormeau Road. I don't know how they ended up in Ardoyne. Maybe it was the availability of the new houses being built in Glenard at the time. Frankie was born on 2 May 1941 and he was the youngest of the family. There was no connection to Ardoyne; they had no one in Ardoyne. They set up home in number 39 Highbury Gardens and had five children: Desmond, Margaret, Pat, Matt and Frankie. During the Second World War I think the houses at the bottom of Highbury Gardens were hit by a bomb. So the family moved to number 68 Ladbrook Drive and that became the new family home. The children all went to the local schools. Frankie was only ten months old when his mother died.

Frankie was married in 1961. I don't know how Frankie and Mary met. They were married in Holy Cross chapel and then my mum brought them over to the house for a meal. Away back then in the sixties that was how it was done. Frankie and Mary lived in Glandore Gardens, off the Antrim Road, in a flat at first. They left there and went to live in Benview Park. But loyalists put them out of their house. Frankie then went to live in West Belfast and that became their family home. They had two children, Tony and Margaret. Frankie never played sports. He liked music and he liked to socialise. He didn't go to the clubs. He went to the Ardoyne Hall. Both Frank and Pat socialised in Ardoyne, because that is where they had grown up. Frankie wasn't a heavy drinker but he did like to have a wee drink. He enjoyed mostly traditional Irish music. He was great at making things. He made carvings and other things for the house. Frankie's best friends were Paddy Largey and the Keenans from Ladbrook Drive. Frankie was a very quiet person but he liked to go out. He was a religious person and would have gone to mass on a regular basis. He wouldn't have had much interest in politics.

Maureen: My husband Pat was killed in 1973 and Frank was killed in 1975. From the time Pat died Frankie sort of took over Pat's role here at home. He came here every day to see that we were all right because my two girls were very young. Frankie would have put them up to bed and the kids got used to him coming. No matter where he was he always called. He used to do a bit of painting and decorating houses for people and on his way back he would have called here before he went home. The night he was killed he had called here and then went to Ardoyne Hall for a couple of drinks. He was walking down the Crumlin Road when he was picked up by loyalists. That would have been routine for Frankie to call into the Hall just for a pint before he went home. Frankie always walked home and I was always at him to take a taxi but he always walked home. He walked everywhere. If I said it was too dangerous to walk he just brushed it aside and said, 'I am all right; nobody would touch me'. I was told after he was killed that he had been followed one night before and that he had run down Tennent Street and into the RUC barracks.

The night he was killed he left Ardoyne Hall and walked down the Crumlin Road. I would say he would have been going into the town to get a black taxi up the Shaw's Road. That was Frankie's route, down the Crumlin and towards Millfield to Castle Street. I don't know where on the Crumlin Road he was picked up but he was found in an entry off the Shankill Road. It was the Shankill Butchers who got him. Frankie was one of the first to be murdered by them. Frankie was buried from his father's house in Ladbrook Drive; his father brought him home to Ardoyne. They couldn't open the coffin because he was that badly mutilated. The impact on the family was one of sheer devastation. It was only two years before that my husband Pat was killed. They had another brother Desmond killed in a car accident – that was three brothers killed. His sister Margaret and brother Matt are now both in America. Frankie's wife died a couple of years ago.

My husband Pat's death had a terrible impact on Frankie; they were always very close and Frankie was always in and out of the house with Pat. They socialised together. I think Frankie looked more on Pat as his big brother. When Pat was killed, Frankie took it really, really bad and I think that is one of the reasons why he took over Pat's role here, to check on us everyday to see if we were all right. If there was anything needed he was there to do it and he used to say to me, ' I will always be here for you and the kids' and he was. He never missed coming over. My two girls were absolutely devastated when he was killed. They lost their father and then they lost Frankie as well. They clung to him like a father figure. I think Frankie was at the wrong place at the wrong time. The Shankill Butchers were picking up anybody. Frankie was simply killed because he was a Catholic and they knew he was a Catholic; to them it wasn't Frankie Crossan, he was just another Catholic and that was good enough. Their aim was to murder any Catholic at that time. Frankie was easy prey. Frankie was a real gentleman, a real gentle person who wouldn't have harmed anybody. He would have done anybody a good turn. The whole Crossan family are like that. Frankie was a harmless soul and a very kind person.

Paddy Largey (friend)

I lived in 58 Ladbrook Drive and Frankie was born and reared in 68 Ladbrook Drive. We were all reared in the street together; we all ran around together. Frankie was a right lad, adventurous you know. He went to Holy Cross Boys school; there was no St Gabriel's in those days; you just did primary school and you left when you were 14. Frankie had his own wee group of guys he ran around with. He did all the things young lads do.

He was on the buses for years. He was a bus conductor. But he suffered from migraines and different illnesses. Eventually he was discharged because of ill health; that would have been in the late '60s. He wasn't working at the time he was murdered, and as a matter of fact, his wife said that the judge said, 'Mrs. Crossan, you seem to be better off now financially than you were beforehand' as regards money. But it seems you always hear these things afterwards. Frank had got involved with cross-community holiday schemes, taking kids to America and all different places. He got a trip himself out to America and was able to see his brother and his sister.

Frankie was a generous fella, an obliging fella and a nice guy to know. Every Christmas we arranged to meet up and had our day out. That was tradition for a number of years. Either I would go to his house or we would meet in the town and have a beer. Nine times out of ten I spent it in his house. It was terrible when he died, terrible, terrible, terrible. I just couldn't get over it.

I was angry that nobody came to see me but I just put it completely out of my mind. That was twenty years ago and I have never, ever talked about it until this day.

Christine Hughes
Killed by the IRA,
Mountainview Parade,
21 December 1975

Christine Hughes was born to Mary and Jim Magee of Hillman Street in the New Lodge on 21 July 1932. She was the ninth of 11 children and the youngest of three daughters. One of her brothers was later killed during World War II fighting in France. Christine went to Newington Primary school, down by the York Street spinning mill. In 1950 she met Freddie Hughes from Brookfield Street at an Irish dancing night in Toby's Hall, Butler Street. The pair started to see each other and were married on 26 September 1953. At first the newly weds lived in rooms over a shop in Hillman Street. Then they got a house after about a year in Greenisland, County Antrim. They stayed there until 1974 when they were intimidated out of the area by loyalists. Anti-Catholic slogans were daubed on their walls and windows and their home was attacked with bricks over a period of several months. So the family moved and made a new home for themselves in Mountainview Parade where Christine and Freddie continued to raise their own family of four boys and four girls. 'Tina' (as Christine was usually called) was a quiet woman who lived mostly for her family. She had little enough spare time for hobbies and outside interests and what she did have was usually spent making clothes for her children. She was a good neighbour, a good friend and lived her life according to a deeply held religious faith.

On Sunday 21 December 1975 Christine was at home with four of her children, painting a door in the hallway and making preparations for Christmas. Her husband Freddie was at work as a manager of the Star Social Club in Ardoyne. Members of the IRA entered the family home, assuming it was the house of their intended target (a member of the British security forces who apparently lived nearby). They shot and killed Christine in a case of mistaken identity.

Margaret Mervyn (friend)

Christine and I worked together in Rosebank factory when she lived in Hillman Street and I lived up in Strathroy Park. She was about 18 when we met and I was about 15. We used to walk home for lunch together because she used to go to her sister Molly in Holmdene Gardens. I found her a very nice girl, a nice person and we just struck up a wee friendship. We would go to her house, listen to records and go for walks. She had a record player. I thought she was rich! We would sit in her parlour all night listening to Frankie Lane, Dicky Valentine and the like. We really enjoyed doing that. They were happy times, innocent times. I thought an awful lot of her. My very first impression of Christine was how family-orientated she was. She was very, very much a family person. She loved her mother and father and had a great love of her whole family. She adored her sister Molly and took all Molly's religious principles and lived her life by them. Family-orientated and great faith, that was Christine that I knew. Chris was always a really generous person and my memory of her is of a very innocent, very naïve girl. I always felt that I was in good company when I was with Chris.

Chris was like me and was happy enough going out to dances in our own areas. So she started coming up and going out around the places in Ardoyne. We would go to a dance in Toby's Hall on a Sunday night, sometimes on a Wednesday. It was there that she met Freddie [her husband-to-be]. It was me who introduced them. I knew Freddie from way back. Freddie and Chris just clicked; they were just an absolute match in my eyes. She loved him and he loved her from day one. She would have been about 19. I started to go out with my husband, a good friend of Freddie's, about that time. The four of us had a lot of good times going out together. We used to go on bus runs, to Buncrana, Bangor, places like that. We really had nothing to spend but we just made the best of it.

Then Freddie and Christine got married. It was a lovely wedding. Then a neighbour offered them rooms over an alleyway in Hillman Street. That was their first home. My boyfriend and I used to go down on Saturday night and Chris and I would sit in. The fellas would go to the pub for a wee drink and we would have a wee cup of tea. I used to look forward to that. Then she had her first wee boy. He was gorgeous. I was always a good knitter and I taught Christine to knit the wee baby matinee coats. I would go down and bring the wool and we would knit for the baby coming. She had the baby at home. Nobody went into the hospital unless you had to in those days. We had a great celebration. Then Christine and Freddie moved out to Greenisland and they lived there for years. I would mostly hear about Chris from her sister Molly and met Freddie sometimes because he worked in the Star [social club]. So we sort of lost touch. Both of us were raising families and I went to America to live for a time. I don't think I even met her during that whole time until about 1975.

I met her again at a 'do' in 1975 in the Ardoyne Hall. I couldn't believe it; she hadn't changed one bit. We just kissed and hugged. She was in Mountainview by then and I was in Alliance Avenue, so we started seeing each other again. I was going to move to stay for a while with my brother in Canada. I had lost my home through the troubles, a member of our family had been killed and my own wee boy was caught in a bomb. It was all getting on top of me and I was getting run down. So it was great that we met up again, though she had a lot on bringing up her wee family too. We promised each other to keep in touch no matter what. So I went away to Canada at the beginning of November 1975. I wrote Chris a letter with a Christmas card and posted it. Three days later I got one back and thought, 'Boy that was quick'. I thought it was from Chris because her address was on the back. But when I opened the letter it was from a person writing on behalf of Freddie to tell me of her death. I just couldn't believe it. I was absolutely devastated and destroyed. I immediately saw her as a saint in heaven. My whole heart and soul went out to Freddie and their children. I think for the very first time (and hopefully the last time in my life) I questioned God. I really did. I couldn't make sense of it. I have come to accept it and I just feel proud that I have a saint in heaven as a friend. I believe I was in the best of company when she was my friend. God was looking after me by putting Chris in my way. That's the best thing I can say about her. We lost a good person when we lost Chris Hughes. She would have been embarrassed to be talked of like that but I held her in great esteem. I loved her for her sense of family and for her faith, her great faith; she was very proud to be a Catholic and she made me proud of my faith.

Freddie Hughes (husband)

I met Christine at a dance in Toby's Hall in 1950. It was Irish dancing that particular night. We were going with each other two to three years before we got married on 26 September 1953. Christine was quiet, a very quiet person, very much family-orientated. She enjoyed herself when she was out amongst company. She had a few good friends. She had a good personality and was well liked by all the neighbours and got on very well with them. That's the way I would sum her up really, a quiet, good woman.

Christine was killed on a Sunday night [21 December 1975]. I had left the house at about 6 pm that day to go to my work at the Star [social club]. At about 8 pm the door of our home was bust in. Christine was painting the wee door in the hall. Apparently when the door was pushed in she ran into the sitting room. It was there she was shot, just standing at the fireplace. I think there was only one shot fired and there wasn't anything said that I was told. My children never said that there was ever any words spoken. My daughter ran out of the house and right across the road. I was at work in the office of the Star club. It was a quiet night and I was more or less finishing up because I had said to Christine that I would be home early. So my daughter came flying in roaring and crying that her mother was shot. I ran out and by the time I was going across Mountainview the ambulance was coming out of it. When I got to the house Fr. Fernando was there and he just shook his head. Then I was brought down to the Mater Hospital. The doctors were with her and within about ten minutes they came out and said that she had passed away. Nobody claimed responsibility for her death. It is a very sore point with me, that particular situation. I can only go by what other people have told me and they said that it was the IRA that did it. Certain names went about. The police came and said they had two people who they were questioning but it never went any further. There was no reason given for why they did, none whatsoever. I was never involved in any confrontation or anything at any time, never in anything. I don't know why they came to my door or targeted my wife. There had been some incident involving the Crumlin Star committee and local republicans in the past but that was nothing to do with me. To this day I just don't know why Christine was shot. Nobody has ever come to tell me.

I could get a wee bit out of hand for about six years afterwards. That was when I had a few drinks in me. In the end a couple of people came round to see me about it. But I told them the truth, that for six years I had not slept one night in my bed because I was worrying about the kids and things like that. So I said there would be no more 'acrobating'. But it wasn't so much 'acrobating'. I was angry that nobody came to see me. So I told them that I would not be acting that way again and I just put it completely out of my mind. That was 27 years ago and I have never, ever talked about it until this day. Christine's death should never have happened. But it did happen and there is nothing I can do about it. The way I see it two wrongs never make a right. That's the way I am and always will be. I just want to get on with my life. I think now I would rather just let it rest. I think I would probably prefer not to know [who killed Christine]; it might leave me feeling bitter if names were mentioned. I don't want that so I think, 'No, leave it'.

Ted McQuaid
Killed by loyalists,
Cliftonville Road,
10 January 1976

Ted and Deirdre were walking down the Cliftonville Road ...
A fella got out of the taxi, crossed the road and when he got
up close to them, he started shooting.
Ted went down after the first shot.

Ted McQuaid's mother's maiden name was Julia McNeill, from Crumlin Road and his father, Ted, was a bookkeeper from Derry. Ted's grandfather was a publican but was burnt out of his Louisa Street pub in 1922. Ted senior and Julia were married in Holy Cross chapel and lived all of their married life in 439 Crumlin Road. They reared six children: four girls – Ann, Julie, Maureen, Chris – and two boys – Ted and Brian.

Ted was the second youngest. He left St Mary's school well-qualified and worked for the Health and Social Services Department until his death. From an early age, Ted was a member of the Ardoyne GAA club. He was a keen hurler and played for the club at both junior and senior level. He became chairperson of the club, probably the youngest in its history. In August 1974 he married Deirdre Hyland from Andersonstown and they set up home in Ladybrook Crescent, Finaghy Road North. They had no children. On 10 January 1976, after leaving a party on the Cliftonville Road with his wife Deirdre, Ted was shot and killed in a loyalist sectarian attack. He was 25 years old at the time of his death.

Brian McQuaid (brother)

Ted was born at home at 439 Crumlin Road. He was my big brother and I really looked up to him. For all the boys the GAA Club was the focal point. Charlie Toner was his best friend, as were all the lads from the GAA. I was a member as well. He was club chairman, probably the youngest chairman ever. He joined the club in the early '60s. Like any guy at that age he trained two, three nights a week at the club. That's how we grew up.

In January 1976 Ted and Deirdre lived in Ladybrook and mum and myself lived in the Crumlin Road. Anne and Chris lived in London, Maureen was in Andersonstown and Julie was in Ballymena. I was nineteen at the time. He was shot on the night of 9th/10th January; that was a Friday night/Saturday morning. That week was a particularly bad week in the country. There were a number of killings in South Armagh; the Reavey brothers, O'Dowd brothers, and then at Kingsmills the men in the minibus were lined up and shot. This all happened within a week. It was a desperate time. It was very evident to everybody that the Kingsmills killings weren't going to be the end of it. There was a view that something was going to happen. I thought Ted was safe living in Ladybrook. While Andersonstown was volatile they didn't have the same level of sectarian murders as we experienced in the north of the city.

I remember speaking to Ted a week before he was shot and he said to me, 'Just watch yourself; don't be staying too late. Try not to leave mum on her own'. That has really haunted me. I was in the house when the word came that Ted had been shot and I went down to the hospital. I always think if I'd stayed over in my girlfriend's house my mother would have been on her own in the house and what would she have done hearing that terrible news on her own. That had a huge effect on me and it still does. It was like somebody was looking over me saying, 'You be in the right place if bad news comes'.

We weren't out with Ted that night. Deirdre and him were at a party with work mates on the Cliftonville Road. The unfortunate thing was his car had broken down; he had only bought the car about a week before. Because the car had broken down, they had to get a taxi. Like many others murdered he was in the wrong place at the wrong time.

I heard the news from Ted's father-in-law, John Hyland, who was the chief fire officer in Ardoyne fire station. I was in bed; it was the early hours of Saturday morning and I heard the knock on the door. Living on the Crumlin Road in 1976 when you heard a knock at the door 3 o'clock in the morning you panicked a bit. The Crumlin Road was a dangerous place. The doors were locked, and double locked, so I looked out my mum's bedroom window and I could see a car outside. I looked down and I could see the uniform. I didn't know who it was, but I thought it was the RUC. I went downstairs and one of my memories of looking out was seeing the row of silver buttons through the window and thinking, 'That's not a policeman'. I went into the parlour and looked out again and saw Mr Hyland in his fireman's uniform. I thought to myself, 'What's he doing here at this time?' I went out and he was obviously fairly stony-faced and he said that Ted had been shot and was fighting for his life. He said Ted had been at a party on the Cliftonville Road and that Ted and Deirdre were walking home and a car stopped, a boy jumped out and shot at them. I said, 'John, are you sure it's him? I was talking to him a few nights earlier and there was no mention of a party. Are you sure it's him?' That was the thing that kept coming into my mind: what would Ted be doing on the Cliftonville Road without me knowing about it? But as I said, it turned out it was a works party. So John said, 'No it's definitely him. I have been told'.

I went down to the Mater Hospital and to this day, every time I drive past the Mater Hospital there is a silence; people know not to talk because I can still see that wee room. I went in and it was a wee side room just at the left of the gate. I went in and Deirdre was there; she had been with him and was in hysterics. The police came over and asked had I any idea what happened. Of course I had no idea, no knowledge of what happened at all. John Hyland, Deirdre's father, was sitting with me and the two of us were just sitting waiting. All I could think was, 'What am I going to tell my mum? All I could see were the nurses running in and out with towels. I don't know how long it was; it could have been two minutes, it could have been an hour. The doctor came out and he just shook his head, and he said, 'Sorry, there is nothing we could do', and that was it. We were just sitting there and Deirdre and myself just went berserk. Then a few people started to filter in; I can't even remember who they were. But I know the big worry I had was how I was going to tell my mum that news. I still think of that to this day. I was nineteen. How could I tell my mum her son had been murdered, but I had to. A nineteen year old shouldn't have to do that.

The police brought me home and then they were going to contact my sisters, but I wanted to do that. I ran down to Mallon's house; they lived two doors down from us. I got Martin out of bed and his sister, Susan, and they came up to the house with me. By this stage my mum knew there was something wrong but obviously didn't know what I was going to tell her. After that, it's all a bit of a blur.

Nobody ever claimed responsibility. But they were caught. It was the Shankill Butchers; Lenny Murphy was the gunman. The book, The Shankill Butchers, gives a fairly good description of what happened. Nobody claimed responsibility but it was quite obvious to us that it was a sectarian murder. I didn't go to the court and I didn't go to the inquest either. I have to say I didn't know if I would have been able to control myself. I think for the sake of my mum I decided not to.

I lost it the night the remains were brought to the chapel. That's my memory. My brothers-in-law were there and had their arms round me and I was just gone. I hardly remember anything. I certainly don't remember the mass. I remember walking the coffin up the Falls Road past Maguire's garage and then at the graveside. I do remember I never carried the coffin. My four sisters were distraught. One of my biggest memories is just looking out from my mum's bedroom window at the flowers down on the pavement. I don't know how many wreaths there were; they seemed to stretch the whole way to Kerrera Street.

The clergy were very helpful and the neighbours were great. The Mallons and Charlie Toner were a tremendous help. I always remember Frank Clarke who owned the shop at the top of the road coming down to the house with groceries just to take the strain off us. The GAA was a huge support too. I don't know what I would have done without them. The GAA was like a big family. The reaction in the club was total devastation. Charlie Toner made a statement; he said, 'If they had known him, they wouldn't have shot him', and I'll never forget that. That was 27 years ago and that's still in my head. At that time I was engaged to my wife-to-be, Terri Watts, and I don't know what I would have done without her and her family.

Charlie (friend)

The first time I ever met Ted was when I joined Ardoyne Gaelic Club in 1963. I was only 11 years old at the time. Ted was about two years older than me. The other connection between us was we both went to St Mary's school in Barrack Street. When I joined the GAA, Ted and I got really friendly. We played in the same team. A whole lot of us came together at that time and remained great friends: Brendan McFarlane, Micky Coleman, Danny Clarke, Paul Shevlin, Paddy McAleer, Denis McMullan, Fred Heatley and Pat Murphy. But Ted and I in particular became really friendly and we were right up until his death.

He was a gentleman, a great man and a tremendous friend. I can remember my 14th birthday. I was a Manchester United fanatic and Dennis Law was my hero. I remember Ted coming up beside me and saying to me, 'That's for your birthday'. Lads didn't buy each other birthday presents but he had bought me Dennis Law's life story. I always remember that. That was the sort of person he was, very thoughtful. He couldn't have done enough for you.

He was the youngest chairman the club ever had. I was vice chairman. It was at the height of the troubles. We had to try and keep the club going. I remember in 1975, just before his death and he was chairman; we won club of the year in Antrim, basically because we had managed to keep the club going in desperate times. He married a lovely girl, Deirdre Hyland from Andersonstown. He lived in Ladybrook at the time of his death. I always think back, if he had been over this side of town they would have stayed in our house. Things were that dangerous at that time and you wouldn't have risked travelling, unless you knew who you were travelling with. To take a taxi was a big risk and especially to cross over the other side of town. The weekend before that they had stayed in our house. The day before he was killed I rang him at work to see what he was doing. We were trying to find out where he was going that night so that we could meet up and go out for the night. If we had gone to the party with him he would have come back and stayed in our house instead of trying to make his way home. I wouldn't have let him. You have to put it into the context of what was going on at the time. There was an awful sectarian murder campaign going on in north Belfast. It was very, very rough. As it turned out, Ted and Deirdre went to a party on the Cliftonville Road and decided to make their own way home.

The background to Ted's killing was and it comes out in that book The Shankill Butchers, the people that killed Ted were in a club that night and they decided they were going to kill a taig (Catholic). They took a gun from an off-duty UDR man in the toilets of the bar. The UDR man reported it immediately to Tennent Street RUC station and he actually told who stole his gun. After the shooting, they threw the gun into a hedge and the police found it. But they had it for ages in Oldpark police station before they actually connected it to the UDR man in Tennent Street.

Ted's death was awful shock; I couldn't believe it. It was the worst tragedy that ever happened me because we were like brothers. It was a tremendous loss to his family and the Ardoyne GAA. It broke his mother's heart. He was a tremendous fella and an ordinary fella at the same time. He was a very intelligent lad, good craic and he enjoyed life. He was the best friend I ever could have wanted.

Deirdre McQuaid (widow)

[This testimony is based upon extracts taken from evidence given to the Coroner's Court]

I remember Friday 9 January 1976. I arranged to go to a party with my husband Ted. There were quite a number of people at the party when we arrived. Ted and I were dancing, having an odd drink and chatting to people at the party. Ted knew most of the people there as quite a lot of them worked with him at the Ministry of Health and Social Services building in Frederick Street. At about 3.30 - 3.45 am Ted and I decided to go home. I left Ted to get his coat and I walked slowly down the stairs and out onto the footpath at the front of the house. At this time, I noticed a black taxi driving slowly up past on the opposite side of the road from me. It turned left into a side street and disappeared from view then re-appeared from a street opposite where I was standing; it turned right and drove down the Cliftonville Road. Ted arrived and he and I started walking down the Cliftonville Road towards the Antrim Road. The taxi suddenly drove up the road from the Antrim Road. I told Ted I thought it strange as this taxi had driven up the road a short time previously. We were still walking on down the road. Suddenly the taxi drove past us going in the same direction as us and I saw it stop a short distance in front of us. I said to Ted again about the taxi but he didn't seem to be alarmed. Ted was between the taxi and me. The door of the taxi opened and a youth got out of the taxi and started walking towards us; he was swaying about as if he was drunk and I said to Ted, 'It's okay, he is drunk'. Suddenly he put his left hand inside his jacket and pulled out a small gun. He pointed it at Ted and started shooting. He never looked at me; he just kept shooting at Ted. Ted fell to the ground but the young fellow just kept shooting. I threw my bag but the youth jumped into the taxi and the taxi drove off, did a 'U' turn and drove off at speed up the Cliftonville Road towards the country. I went to Ted and he said, 'Deirdre'. I started screaming and left and I ran back into the flat we had just left to get help.

> *Paul was able to talk to me and he knew he was dying,*
> *which was bad at the time. He asked me would I find out*
> *who the people were that did this to him.*
> *That has always been a big thing with me.*

Paul McNally was the youngest of the eight children born to Tommy and Rachel McNally of Strathroy Park. Tommy was originally from Ballyclare and Rachel was from Antrim. They moved into Ardoyne when Tommy opened his barber shop in Durham Street, and later moved to the Shore Road. Paul attended Holy Cross Boys school and St Gabriel's before beginning work as a plumbing and heating engineer. In 1969, when Paul was 18 years old, he met his future wife, Hazel. They were married two years later in the Holy Cross chapel by Father Aquinas. They lived in Estoril Park where they raised three children, Karen, Pauline and Damien. A member of the League [social club], Paul was a quiet, good-natured man whose main hobbies were football and darts. On the afternoon of Saturday 5 June 1976 Paul was standing at the junction of Brompton Park and the Crumlin Road, when two loyalist gunmen shot him. He died two days later.

Paul McNally
Killed by loyalists,
Brompton Park,
7 June 1976

Kevin Fusco (eyewitness and neighbour)

On the day Paul was killed I was in my father's shop at the top corner of Brompton Park. It was a lovely day, a Saturday. People were just going about their own business, doing their shopping. It was just like any ordinary day. Then all of a sudden there was shooting, which was not uncommon then. It was really loud so I knew it was happening near by. When I heard the shots, I ran to the side window of my father's shop and looked out. So I saw everything that was happening. I saw two fellas lying on the ground and everybody was running about panicking. There were these guys standing with suits on. Then I heard revs and saw an army jeep driving up Brompton Park. Then the soldiers in the jeep started to shoot. The jeep swung round at my daddy's shop and one of the soldiers jumped out of it. He ran over to the side of the wall at my daddy's shop and starting firing at these guys. It seemed to me that one of them got shot because his arm just swung in the air and the gun went flying. When I was looking out the window I could see the bullets bouncing off everything. Then the guy darted down the hole in the wall at Chatham Street. After that there was just pandemonium. The soldiers and people were all running about. So I just ran outside and one of the fellas was just lying there. He was lifeless and they were rolling him over like a rag doll. This soldier was trying to give first-aid. The other fella was moaning. I sort of backed off and then went back into the shop. People's messages [shopping] were all over the street where people had just panicked and dropped everything. They all just ran when they heard shots so close.

Geraldine and Margaret Brown (eyewitnesses and neighbours)

It was a good day until the shooting. We heard the shooting because we lived in the middle of Chatham Street. We were going from home up to my mummy's brother's who lived at the top of Chatham Street when these two guys came running down. These two men were armed. We automatically assumed they were republicans in danger of being arrested by the British army. So we offered them into the house out of harm's way. But they said, 'No' and ran on down. They turned into Butler Street which led them out to the Crumlin Road and that's the last we heard. There was just total madness that day. It was a couple of hours later we found out that the two men we saw were not republicans but were actually members of the loyalist murder gang who had just shot Paul McNally. But nobody ever came and asked us about it, never.

Hazel McNally (wife)

I remember clearly the day Paul was shot. He had been ill because of problems with an ulcer and had been off work for four weeks. We had been financially 'tight' for a while, but Paul had received a tax rebate that morning and was in a very good mood. He wanted to take me out for a drink that night. I was reluctant to leave our son Damien with someone unfamiliar as he was only four months old. Then a friend offered to baby-sit for us. Paul always went out about 1 pm on a Saturday afternoon but he left a little later than usual that day. My friend and I were talking at the garden gate when we heard the shots. We hid in my house in case the shooting came near to us. Then I saw one of Mrs McKenna's sons going into Paul's mother's house. Then he and Paul's sister, Veronica came over to tell me that Paul had been shot. Veronica was in a terrible state. Paul had been injured, but no one knew to what extent. The British army came round the corner from the shops where Paul had been shot. They managed to shoot one of the men in the leg whilst they were making their getaway. Some people in the area told me that it was the IRA who had carried out the shooting (although shortly afterwards I found out that it was loyalists) and that someone had helped them to get away through a house. I still don't know if the latter was true or not. Joe Murphy was shot at the same time as Paul. He was shot in the arm as he was hiding under a car.

I was taken to the Mater Hospital, where a junior doctor informed me that Paul had been shot six times and that his legs had been broken. But they thought he would be all right. That good news brought me round and calmed me down. I had waited a few hours while Paul underwent surgery. Then the surgeon came out to inform me that a bullet had gone through his liver. He gave his apologies, but said that nothing could be done about it. It was an awful shock because I had been expecting to be told that he was all right. I stayed in the hospital for two days with Rachel (Paul's mother) from 3.30 pm on Saturday until 2.30 am on Monday. No one came to talk to us, help us or console us. We sat in a room praying. Paul was able to talk to me and he was very aware that he was dying, which was hard to cope with at the time. He asked me to find out who the people were that shot him, and that has always remained with me. It was terrible when he died. His mother was strong but she just stopped talking. I needed to cry and release the pain and anger. It was very hard to cope on your own with two young children to look after. I was very angry because I had grown up without a father and I knew that my children would never see their daddy again.

No one was ever charged with Paul's murder. Shortly after the shooting, word came through that the killers were hiding out in the Crumlin Road picture house, which was derelict. The police cordoned that off, but no one was caught. There was a detective who contacted my father-in-law and informed us that the killers were now in Scotland in a safe house. That was the end of the investigation. I don't know how the police operated behind the scenes, but with regards to my family as Paul's next of kin, the incident was not handled correctly. I think they should have given me any information they had, kept in touch and reassured me that they were going to continue the investigation until they caught someone. I believe that because Paul was a working class, Catholic man his death didn't matter to them. There was an inquest into the killing. But unfortunately I wasn't informed about it or any of the details surrounding the killing. At the time my father-in-law didn't think I was emotionally fit enough to attend the inquest. He was probably right, but I would have very much liked to have gone to it. I have always regretted not having been present at the inquest. No one has ever claimed responsibility for the murder, not to my knowledge. Neither the RUC nor the British army have ever come to me to tell me what happened on the day of the shooting, or what happened after it. I didn't think that the press stressed enough that he was an innocent victim, and there were various discrepancies in the description of him, such as his age.

Justice for the murder of my husband was never achieved. A large part of the pain that I and my family feel comes from the fact that no one has ever spoken to us of the events surrounding his shooting, I feel as if no one cares. After Paul's death nobody came to offer moral support. Once an Anglican sister came to visit whilst I was out. She left a bunch of flowers at the door of my house. She did call back and we spoke about Paul. But other than her, nobody came. I don't think that there is anything that can be done to make up for the lack of support. It feels like such a long ago time that it all happened. I have moved on with my life but I found it very hard to come to terms with the way in which Paul's life was ended. I still get very angry at times. I believe that if I had received counselling at the time, it would have helped enormously and I'm glad that people can receive this help nowadays. Something that angers me is how people outside my own community perceived me when I moved out to Antrim. If I or someone else mentioned what had happened to Paul I was viewed with suspicion. I was working at the Holywell Hospital and was very friendly with a girl. She was a lovely person and was from London. When someone told her about Paul she just stopped talking to me. My next door neighbour who was from the Irish Republic, actually said to me, 'I'm sure he wasn't killed for nothing'. It was traumatic enough to have to go through the death of my husband, without having to defend him for having been killed in the manner that he was. It made me very, very, angry and upset and I moved back to Belfast again.

Paul was a very quiet, good-natured, unassuming man. He was the last person you would have expected to be shot. He was a very placid man and it was just so sad that he had to die in such a violent way. I found it devastating at the time of his death because I had no family living near to support me. Two of my close friends and my mother-in-law were always there, but it was a great responsibility to have two young children. To be truthful, those first few years without Paul were a nightmare. I would never like to go through something like that again on my own. The children always miss Paul. Damien is very bitter about not ever having his father around. I would just like to add a tribute to my mother-in-law, Rachael, who passed away in January 2000, for all the emotional and financial support that she gave me throughout the years, right up until her death. There are not too many people left who would do that.

Damien McNally (son)

I always find it difficult to say how I feel about not having a father. It has just been something that I have been used to. I am lucky in that I was not old enough to realise what was happening at the time and how terrible it was for my mum to have lost a daughter and her husband, all at the age of 23. I am also lucky to have had a close family, especially my grandmother who died just recently. I will always be proud of my father for the things he did and the way he made mum happy. I don't feel any anger towards anybody but just think it's very sad that I never knew him. Somebody decided to go out one day and shoot a Catholic and was never brought to justice. They affected my family's life forever. I don't really know at the moment how I am supposed to feel about that. I am 24 and now realise how tragically short my dad's life was because he was only 26 when he was killed. Somebody else took his life away. I don't think I will ever know how difficult it was for my mum losing two people like that at such a young age. I may only know when I have children of my own. But I also know that mum was lucky to have met her fiancé Leo. It is doubtful that there are many people who would settle down with a person whose husband has been shot dead and has two young children.

I cannot think of any word to express my feelings other than sad. I'm sad that we never knew each other. I'm sad that I have to hear everything about him second hand and that a part of me will always be missing. I just feel confused a lot of the time. I know that none of my friends or girlfriend will ever understand how it feels, but of course I don't expect them to. I am more apprehensive about things and in many ways insecure because something so important was taken away without anything being done. It is totally outside your control. But life goes on and I am fully aware of how lucky I am. I now have a university education behind me and have been blessed by such a close and loving family, especially mum and sister Karen. They have always done everything possible to look after me and provide me with the best opportunities in life. I hope someday that I will be able to give my mum something back as she had little or no financial support and had to work herself into the ground. I am proud of my family and know that my father would be very proud of myself and Karen. I am the only one now who can carry on the McNally name.

> *Then hatred must have overtaken the pain. You just feel the hatred growing in you, like a flower growing up from the field. Everybody was all round you but at the end of the day there is nobody with you; you have only got yourselves. We just felt totally on our own. We were lost for a very long time.*

Patrick Meehan
Killed by loyalists,
Crumlin Road,
17 June 1976

Patrick Meehan's people all came from the Lower Falls. Patrick himself was born in Cyprus Street and went to school at St Paul's. He had five brothers and two sisters, all of whom lived in the west of the city. Paddy came to Ardoyne after meeting his future wife, Maureen Toolan from Hooker Street, at a dance in the Falls. They married in the Holy Cross chapel and set up home in Duneden Park where they reared four children, Helen, Jackie, Maureen and Patrick. Paddy had gone into Andrew's flour mill from school and worked there for many years before moving to a job with the Gas Board. Apart from work, Paddy's life revolved around his family and the Star social club. Paddy was a founder member of the Star, was on the committee and so most of his circle of friends were, as a result, 'Star men' too. He played a bit of golf, draughts, and liked arithmetic and doing puzzles. He was also an avid Celtic fan and made regular trips to Glasgow to see them play.

On 17 June 1976 Patrick left his home in Duneden Park at the usual time to clock in at the Gasworks. He got on his usual bus and sat down on the upper deck. Two members of the UFF who were already on the bus shot Patrick and Gerard Stitt dead for no other reason than that they were Catholics. Patrick's wife Maureen had died just over a year before so his death left their four children parentless.

Maureen Meehan (daughter)

> The day my father died was just like any other normal day. My daddy was fixing people's gas meters in Ardoyne at the time, but I remember he came in during the morning for egg and toast. I was rushing though because I was training at the time to be a barmaid in the Star. I think I just said 'Good morning'. I went to work and at about 4.45 pm I was sent to have a cup of tea, which was an unusual time because of the way the shifts worked. It didn't make sense. I went round to McErlean's bakery to get something for my tea and I noticed that people were looking at me. I was thinking, 'What's everybody looking at?' Obviously, I didn't know what had happened but I'm sure other people knew. I'm sure they were saying 'God help her, she doesn't know'. I just got what I wanted from the bakery and went back to work in the Star. I was only in it a couple of minutes when my brother walked in and when I looked at his face I could tell there was something wrong. He just said, 'Maureen, come on'. So I knew there was something wrong but I didn't know what it was. At that time people's houses

got raided, people got arrested, things like that were happening on a regular basis, so I just thought that maybe the house was getting raided, someone had been arrested or something like that had happened. Then he took me down the entry because he didn't want anybody to tell me in the street and I really started to panic. I said, 'What's wrong? Tell me what is wrong?' When we walked in our back door, my uncle Seamus had found out and he just said to my brother, 'Is it right about your daddy?'

The next thing I remember was getting a slap in the face. Apparently, I was in hysterics, but I can't remember. I must have just flipped. I just knew my daddy was dead; I didn't know how and it didn't really seem to matter. Then I remember people coming to the house, trying to humour you. Because my daddy went to the Star it was mostly men came to the house and we didn't really have many relatives living in Ardoyne. That's the way men are. My sister was living down South and I was the only girl in the house so I sort of felt lost then. My mate came and she took me up to her house. The 10 o'clock news came on and her mummy turned it off. But at the time I wanted to know, I wanted to see the news, I wanted to know what happened. It is something I have thought about; they didn't want me to see what happened but what people don't realise is that you couldn't be more upset and you have to know what happened. Did he know he was going to die? Where was it? Who was it? Did they get them? Did he die right away? All these things are important to you but nobody wants to tell you. People don't know what to say.

The Crumlin Star social club were very good to us. Freddie Hughes came down with a blank cheque because he knew we had no money. My brother wasn't working at the time; he had been shot years earlier and he wasn't very well, so there wasn't a wage coming in to the house. In the end we didn't use the cheque because places like the Spar on the Crumlin Road sent down a massive box of groceries, shops in the area sent cigarettes, people just couldn't do enough for us. People made a pot of stew or sandwiches and brought it round to the house. You didn't feel on your own and I think it was important because of our young age. There were people there for us if we needed. It was a comfort.

I have one memory that will stick with me until the day I die. The police brought my daddy's personal effects home in a black bag and gave them to my brother Jackie. He told me not to look at what was in it. Of course, being human, if somebody tells you don't look, you want to look and later I opened the bag. I never knew what people's brains looked like but I saw them; they were all over the back of the coat. I just remember looking at it and saying, 'This time yesterday that was my daddy's thoughts and feelings. Everybody he ever knew or anything that had ever happened to him was in that part of him and look at it now, look where it is and it doesn't mean anything now'. I felt sick but I couldn't be sick. That will stay with me always.

I felt for a long time that justice was achieved until the person that murdered my daddy took part in a Channel 4 programme. He got out on early release because he was so young when the murder happened. I always comforted myself with the idea that he was young and didn't really realise the impact of what he was doing. I felt that he had probably grown up and regretted what he had done. That sort of helped me come to terms with it. Not that you expected people to go out and murder people but, considering the political situation that was here then, it was something that just happened and you accepted it. I mean, I knew people from Ardoyne who were arrested and went to gaol for murder. It was like a mirror image. People on our side had their grievances; they were raided, they were arrested and interned without trial. There was anger in the Catholic communities. I think with the loyalists it was more a fear of losing what they had. I was shocked by what the person who murdered my daddy had to say on that programme … it was as if somebody was just murdering my daddy all over again. He said he knew who he was shooting, that he associated him with someone well-known at the time. But that is just a lie. I want him to know that he didn't shoot who he thought he was shooting. He just said that to make himself look good. He had no remorse whatsoever and that he would do the same thing again but had now left it to younger ones. He was arrested a few years later for armed robbery and went back to gaol. I was angry about that. I just want people from his area to know that he's not the big loyalist freedom fighter. He's a thug. He is just a common criminal in my opinion.

Patrick Meehan (son)

I was fifteen when my father died. That morning my daddy got me up for school. He used to get you up and always made a boiled egg in a cup with butter. He used to drown it with salt. I hated salt but you had to eat it. But that was a holy day and we were off school; he said 'Go you on back to bed'. That was the last I time I saw him ever again. Later on that day he called to the house for a cup of tea but I wasn't there. I remember the news coming on at around half or quarter past four. Everybody used to be glued to news at that time because things were hot and heavy. Me and my older brother Jackie were in the house and we heard that two men had been shot on a bus on the Crumlin Road. I don't know what it is, you just get a feeling that there is something wrong, but you tell yourself it's not. My father usually came back home for work about half four. Then at about quarter to five I saw his mate Robbie who he worked with in the gas works. He came to the house and told my older brother, without me knowing, that my father hadn't clocked into work. I knew it was probably the same bus. My father got that bus every day at the exact same time to get him into work to leave the money and the books in and then back home again.

It wasn't really that long before I saw two policemen coming up the path and Jackie told me to go to the shop and get him cigarettes. But I knew as soon as I saw the cops. I ran round to Davidson's as fast as I'd ever run in my life to get there and back again to see what was going on. I remember coming back up the street and everybody was saying 'Your da's dead, your da's been shot dead'. But you tell yourself that they have picked it up wrong. When I got into the house, Jackie said, 'Listen, I've got something to tell you; that was daddy on the bus'. I only cried for about a minute, no big major outburst of tears. I think it was shock. Then a thing of hatred must have overtaken the pain. You just feel the hatred growing in you, just like a flower growing up from the field. As I said I was only fifteen and I think Jackie was twenty-one and we actually didn't know what to do. We had nobody; we hadn't got a penny, not a penny. My mother had died a year and four months previous to that, so we were on our own.

After the funeral we all went to the wake in the Star. I can remember coming into the house on my own after and there was nobody in the house whatsoever and I said to myself, 'This is it'. It was a terrible feeling, and it stuck in my mind that everybody was all round you but at the end of the day there is nobody with you; you have only got yourselves. Everybody has to get on with their own life.

The family were devastated after the death of my father. Although my father had plenty of family we never really had much contact with them because they lived over the Falls. We just felt totally on our own; we didn't know where to turn for any help or anything. We were lost for a very long time. Nobody ever came and offered us counselling or help. Nobody from the Catholic church came round either. There was a benefit night in the Crumlin Star because my father was a committee man but that was it. I was going to St Gabriel's then, in my fifth year. They brought this new rule out that for the first time you had to have a uniform to get into school. There was a lot of protest about it because we had to walk up the Crumlin Road past Protestant schools and you were easily identified because of the uniform. We had no money to buy a school uniform. I was expelled from school for not having a uniform. I asked them, 'Who is going to buy me a uniform?' It was just totally ignored. We didn't know anything about benefits and there was nobody there to tell us what we were entitled to. I returned to school eventually and was helped out by Mrs McKeown and Margaret (the dinner lady) who let me slip through the line without a dinner ticket; I didn't even know I was entitled to free dinners or how to apply.

I didn't have much contact with the British army or the RUC. I never had any information passed on about the investigations. They might have contacted my older brother once to say that they were pursuing the investigation and they knew who it was but they hadn't got the evidence. Then two men were charged with my father's murder. I think they got 25 years because they had also done other murders. My brother was at the court case and any information that was given out in the court was relayed to us through him; he wouldn't let us go. My older sister was only sixteen or seventeen at the time so we were fairly young and he didn't want us hearing first-hand. Even to this day I think he might have softened it a wee bit so that it wasn't so hard on us.

I can remember about six months after my father was murdered I was up the stairs in the back room. I came across a brown bag, opened it and found my father's clothes from the day he was murdered. I remember taking the coat and the clothes out of the bag and they were hard with blood; they were saturated in it. Also in the bag I found a copy of the *Belfast Telegraph* and when I opened it up there, on the front page, was a photograph of my daddy on the bus shot dead, full-face. The *Belfast Telegraph* printed that, not giving two hoots about our family. That was a big shock and it really hurt me big time again. Then I was listening to the TV years later and the editor of the *Belfast Telegraph* was talking about Diana's car crash and these 'vultures' taking photographs of her in the car. But he printed my father's photograph. Why? – because we were poor people from Ardoyne who couldn't have challenged him. That really hurt. I'm very bitter about that to this day.

What is justice? I'm very confused about my idea of justice. One minute I would say 'There is a war going on' but at the same time, you have lost somebody in your own family and you tend to think 'an eye for an eye'. It's very confusing. One week you feel that the killers have done their time and there was a war going on. Then there are other weeks when you think, 'I wish they would shoot the bastard or hang him'. I think that you have to fully accept that there was a war going on here. If people accept that there was, they might be able to deal with it a wee bit better.

But I think something needs to be done now. I think the families and friends that have lost someone need to express what happened to them. We are often too quiet. In those days you were expected to just go into your house and deal with it and that was it. That was people's way of dealing with it, but they didn't actually deal with it; they buried it and forgot about it. But it is still in there and they need to bring it out. I will always be grateful to Doreen Toolan, the wife of my mother's cousin, who helped us through with the practical things that had to be done and kept an eye on us for years after. I mean, sometimes counselling can come from a good friend and they don't even know they are being a counsellor, just somebody to listen to you now and again. I have my wife; she is my counsellor. I have her head put away. But there needs to be somewhere for people to go. I think that Victims of Trauma Group are doing a lot of good work but it's just getting the message to the people. People still feel a wee bit apprehensive about going to places like that. But I think if they realised that the people they are going to are people who have experienced the same thing as them it might work a lot better than, say, an outsider coming in.

About six months after the loyalist ceasefire of 1994 the man who murdered my father was released and he was on a Channel 4 programme. I had to watch it, to see what this man was about. In the back of mind I was hoping to see someone who was remorseful. Instead I got the bitterest bastard you could ever have got. He was actually turning the screw on me again. It was just so hurtful for the family; it catapulted us back twenty years. Here he was, thinking he was a big hard man from the Ballysillan Road. But, to be quite honest with you, he was just getting on that bus to shoot the first two Catholics that got on. He was trying to make out that he was this big macho hero, an army against another army, but at the end of the day he was shooting unarmed people going to work. Not long after that I was going to work in Antrim and I was driving up over the Ballysillan when I saw him coming out in a car. I actually bumped into the man that had murdered my father and I didn't know what to do. I tried following him but I lost him. I came back to the house and I felt a wee bit ashamed. I was thinking, 'Why did I not do this and why did I not do that?' I was totally confused and it was totally unexpected. But at the end of the day I have my own family now. I have a grand daughter, and I have to think of them. It's hard, but in the end I don't want my kids to grow up the way I grew up.

Gerard Stitt
Killed by loyalists,
the Crumlin Road,
17 June 1976

From what we were told, it appeared that Gerard was murdered because he was a Catholic… He got on the bus at a certain stop. They [the loyalists] were already on the bus just waiting for any Catholic to get on. Mr Meehan got on at the bus stop down below him and the two of them never got off.

G erry Stitt's father, Thomas, met his mother Rose Ann Trainor (as she then was) at a wake in the Markets. Rose Ann was originally from John Street on the Falls Road but Thomas was a Markets man. The two eventually had a family of thirteen children (although one child died at birth), including Gerard who was born on 27 September 1954. The Stitt children were all brought up in Highbury Gardens and Gerard went to the Holy Cross Boys school and then St Gabriel's. Gerard left with no formal qualifications and so did not always find work easily. He took labouring jobs whenever he could. Gerard also had a wide circle of friends in the district. It was through his friends that Gerard met Gemma McAuley. The two were always together and were engaged until shortly before Gerard's death. Gemma left Belfast for England just after Gerard was killed and has lived there ever since. Gerard was an honest, carefree young man, with no interest in politics but whose abiding concern was rather with the then very popular kung fu and kick-boxing. He used to train in a club in Herbert Street and ran a class to teach the smaller children such skills. Many of them were to soon attend his funeral.

On the afternoon of 17 June 1976 Gerard Stitt boarded a bus travelling from Ligoniel at Ardoyne to go into the Belfast town centre. He was on his way to give blood to the blood transfusion unit. A stop later Paddy Meehan (also from Ardoyne) got onto the bus [Paddy Meehan, killed by loyalists in the Crumlin Road, 17 June 1976]. The two sat separately on the upper deck. Two loyalist gunmen who were already on board then shot and killed them both. The loyalists would later try to suggest that Gerard was an 'IRA man'. A photograph of him was found in a search of the house of one of his killers. However, Gerard was a member of no political group. It is clear that Gerard Stitt, and Patrick Meehan, were killed in a purely sectarian attack. They were regarded by loyalists as legitimate targets simply because they were Catholics from Ardoyne.

Henry McErlean (friend)

Gerard came from Highbury Gardens and I came from the next street, Holmdene. There was a big group of us that all went around together. There was Gerard, myself, the McAuleys, Arter Magee, Jean Murphy and Elizabeth Mahoney. It was through that group that he and I became very good friends. Gerard was very interested in a girl from further up his street, Gemma McAuley. At first she didn't realise it but Gerard was absolutely head over heels in love with her. I remember that they started to see each other after a bus trip we all went on. That was their first date. Gerard only had eyes for Gemma after that. They were always together. Gerard used to wait for her coming home from work. They used to go the mass together. They just did everything together. He really, really loved her.

Gerard was really into Bruce Lee films as well. Through that he took up kick-boxing. He and I started to go down to a club in Herbert Street to train, which Gerard took very seriously. Gerard was physically very, very strong. He took after his father in that way. We used to wrestle and mess around, the way that young fellas do. But I could never find a weakness in him. He would never give in, that was just the sort of fella he was. I remember a couple of times that people tried to bully him but Gerard would have none of it. There was one occasion at school [St Gabriel's] when this older fella tried to bully him in front of the masters. Gerard just floored him. The masters all shook his hand afterward because this guy was always picking on boys younger and smaller than himself. On another occasion about 12 fellas tried to bully Gerard. But he just stood there and laughed at them. He would never back down. That is something else he got from his father. Gerard was a brave, fearless fella. He also never told a lie. Gerard always said things the way he saw them. To me, you don't get many friends in life and I would have regarded Gerard Stitt as a very loyal and true friend. There wasn't a political bone in Gerard's body. He never took any interest in politics at all. I remember that he was working in town a year or so before his death and he told me that some of the people in his workplace had accused him of taking part in an IRA march. But Gerard just laughed it off. He was just not a political person; he was only interested in life.

The week that he died I remember Gerard calling around to my house in Alliance Avenue to tell me that he and Gemma were not going to be seeing each other anymore. I couldn't believe it because if you saw one of them, you saw the other. That was just a couple of days before he died. When I found out he was killed I just felt a sense of total and complete shock. I remember that I found out when I was lying on the settee in my house. My wife Ann came in and told me. All I remember is going into shock, running out of the house down to Highbury Gardens leaving the door wide open. I just couldn't believe it.

Theresa Stitt (sister)

Our Gerard was full of life, a fun-loving person. He had a lot of friends: Gerard Magee, Henry McErlean, Michael and Joseph McAuley, Peter and John Osborne. But he was really a home bird. He was very good and kind. He could be a bit of a devil sometimes, very mischievous and full of pranks. He was just a typical wee boy really. I remember one time our Gerard coming down the stairs in the morning, clean as a shining star, just out of the bath and with a white shirt on. I asked him what he was doing and he said he was going to clean the chimney and that he wouldn't get dirt anywhere. The next thing was there was soot everywhere, all over him and us as well. Gerard's real interest was in kung fu. There used to be a youth club down in Herbert Street. It was there for kids to go to rather than running around on the street. Gerard used to go down and help out teaching the little ones.

The last time I saw Gerard was on the morning of his death. I was going to out work and went in to tell Gerard to get up out of bed. It was 17 June, the feast of Corpus Christi. So on my way back from work I got off the bus and went to mass in the Holy Cross at 6 o'clock. But I didn't stay long. I just had a strange feeling that something was wrong. I was coming down old Kerrera Street and there was a lady talking to a girl across the street. She turned round and said, 'Do you know who it was that was shot?' The girl said, 'No'. The woman said, 'That was Tommy Stitt's young son'. That was how I found out about Gerard being shot.

From what we were told it appeared that Gerard was murdered because he was a Catholic. But eventually it turned out it wasn't just that. He got on the bus at a certain stop. They [the loyalists] were already on the bus, just waiting for any Catholic to get on. Mr Meehan got on at the bus stop down below him and the two of them never got off. We weren't really treated fairly by the army or the RUC. As far as I could see they were just insensitive and unconcerned. To them it was another Catholic who had been shot dead – although I have to admit that the soldiers who told my mummy and daddy were very good to them. The police were more insensitive. They just sort of shrugged their shoulders over it all. I thought the press were quite insensitive as well. A journalist came from the *Belfast Telegraph* the next day. He just wouldn't leave us alone even though we were really in shock and didn't want to have anything to do with him. They just wanted to get a photograph of Gerard and wouldn't go away until they had one.

Gerard's death had a terrible impact. We all felt such a sense of disbelief, such a sense of loss. It was just shattering. My mummy and daddy took it very hard. My mummy was devastated but she kept it all inside and closed it in. The rest of us in the family all felt numb and in shock. There was also anger and pure hatred at times to be quite truthful. My brother Thomas had to go with my daddy to the hospital to identify Gerard and he was devastated afterward. He just couldn't take it in. There was an investigation into his death but we didn't know anything about it until it was all over. My daddy found out what had happened by accident. He was angry and annoyed about that because we believed that the police were supposed to inform us. Maybe it was better that we did not know all the details, but I know that my daddy did want to know. We didn't really hear anything until the night of Gerard's birthday the following year. The RUC came and told my daddy that they had arrested two suspects. That was the only time we were ever really told anything.

The trial was a few months later. Two of them were charged and convicted. During the trial one of the accused gave us the finger. He was a small, tiny insignificant thing with tatoos all round his back. We had to hold Thomas back because he tried to jump and get him. This guy was so proud of himself. He just stood there with a look of sarcasm on his face. It was like he was saying they were doing time but it was just another fenian. They even tried to say that Gerard was an IRA man. Of course that was completely untrue. It came out in the papers that one of them had a picture of Gerard and they were trying to suggest that he was a 'suspected IRA man'. I think that the only way they could have got a photograph of Gerard was from the RUC. They used to come around the district in the 'pigs' and jeeps and take photographs of people out through the back. Anyway, the two of them were convicted for murdering Gerard and got life sentences. But I don't know if justice was achieved. They got out early for good behaviour.

There was never any support or help offered to us after Gerard's death. There was so much tragedy in the district at that time. The neighbours were good. They were brilliant. But there was no outside help. I am not sure that there is anything that could help now. Even though it happened 25 years ago it just seems like yesterday. But I think you just learn to live with it. It all stays hidden except for certain occasions, like birthdays and family gatherings. Sometimes people like to grieve on their own and find it hard to open up. Maybe if there was a support group or something there... You can't make people go but just let them know that it is there.

Rose Ann Stitt (mother)

I never had any trouble at all with Gerard from when he was born onward. He was always a good child, one of the best. Gerard died on 17 June 1976. The last time I spoke to him was earlier that day. I asked him where he was going because there was a wee bit of bother going on and I was a little concerned. Gerard said that he was just going out to give blood. Then out he went. He was a terrible character, always full of life, always joking. But there was never any trouble with him at all. Later on in the day Tommy, his father, and I were here in the house just about to have our dinner. Tommy asked me where Gerard had gone and I told him that he had gone to give blood. At about 6.00 pm British soldiers came and told us that Gerard had met with an accident. But they did not say that he was dead. So Tommy and our eldest son Thomas went down to the Mater Hospital and discovered that he was dead.

There has been a lot of tragedy in our family. My brother's son, Jim Trainor, was shot dead at the top of the Falls Road [Jim was a mechanic killed at his workplace by the UFF, 29 January 1973]. Larry Brennan from the Markets, he was Tommy's sister's son. Larry was shot dead [a taxi depot manager, Larry was killed by the UFF whilst outside the depot on 19 January 1998]. My other sister's son was going to midnight mass one Christmas in a car with a couple of other fellas and girls. He was killed in a crash and died on Christmas day and he was only eighteen. Gerard was only 21 when he died. We found out that Gerard and Mr Meehan were sitting on the top of a bus going into town when two young fellas came on and first shot Mr Meehan and then Gerard. Some boy from the Shankill got fourteen or fifteen years for murdering Gerard. I was never offered and didn't get any support after his death. I'm not sure anything would help now.

Paul Marlow
Killed on active service,
Ormeau Road Gasworks,
16 October 1976

Paul was a great person. I'm proud to say I got to know him for the short time I did. He had a big influence on me and I'm sure on everyone who knew him. His premature death was a tragedy not only for his wife and kids but for his comrades as well. He was well-respected and I'm sure all his loved ones have a sense of pride amidst their terrible loss.

Paul Marlow grew up in Duneden Park in the 1950s. His father drove a lorry for Harkins on the Shore Road. Paul was the youngest of three children. He had a brother Con and a sister Margaret. As a child he went first to Holy Cross Boys school and later to Wheatfield House and finally St Gabriel's. Like many other young Catholic men at that time he saw his only chance out of long-term employment was a career in the British army. As a British soldier his capabilities were spotted at an early stage and he served time with the Parachute Regiment and SAS in Malaysia and Eden.

Paul married Annette and they had three children. He returned home at the beginning of the conflict and joined the IRA, where he quickly went up through the ranks. As a key member of the Belfast Brigade Paul Marlow was instrumental in restructuring the IRA's training methods. He is also credited with being the first person to use Claymore mines in Belfast. Paul was interned without trial for a short period.

On 16 October 1976 Paul Marlow led an IRA unit into the Gasworks on the Ormeau Road to attack a British army post within the site. What happened next has never been satisfactorily clarified. The official account claims that the bomb the three IRA volunteers were carrying exploded prematurely. Many believe that the British army lay in wait for Paul Marlow, Frank Fitzsimmons and Joey Surgenor and set off the bomb after the three IRA volunteers had already been shot dead.

Joe McDowell (friend)

As kids we were always messing around with fireworks and blowing things up, the way young lads do. Then we joined the Air Training Core. We were corporals together. We went shooting every week on the B Specials range at Divis Mountain and to Bishopscourt every week to do gliding courses. Every month we got a flight on a Chipmunk at the RAF base in Sydenham. We used to go to summer camps and RAF camps across the water. We visited fighter stations and coastal command stations. If it was a coastal command station you often got a trip in a big Shacklelton bomber. They used to bring us away in the middle of the night on manoeuvres. They gave us a map and dropped us off in some place in the English countryside. You had map references and had to make your own way back. We were 13 years old at the time.

Paul joined the British army when he was 16. The next and last time I saw Paul was during internment and we were stuck in small cubicles in the Grand Central Hotel and Paul was shouting, 'Tell the bastards nothing; say nothing'. I always wondered what happened to him. I never knew he was involved. Then I heard he was dead. Although we had grown apart over the years Paul's death had a devastating affect on me. A good kid, someone who once you met him you would never forget him.

Danny Morgan (comrade)

I met Paul just after the pogroms in Belfast in 1970. Paul had been working for a specialist unit in Malaysia. As far as I know when he left Malaysia he went back to England and bought himself out of the British army and moved back to Belfast with his wife. They ended up on Finaghy Road North.

Paul joined the 'Provisional' IRA at the very start of the conflict. We got to know his capabilities straight away and he moved up the ranks very quickly as he had all the experience and training from his time in the British army. Paul was very politically aware but he had no time for politicians. His idea was to get the war finished first and keep as many volunteers alive as possible. There would be time for politics after that. Paul was such a good operator that he was quickly promoted up to Brigade status within the IRA which covered the whole of Belfast. He joined the IRA's 3rd Battalion, which would have then covered Ardoyne, Ligoniel, the Bone, Unity Flats, Newington, Bawnmore, the New Lodge, the Markets and Short Strand.

I first heard about Paul's death on the news. The target that night was the Gasworks. But it was a very costly operation. Three IRA volunteers, Paul, Frank Fitzsimmons and Joey Surgenor, ended up dying. To me Paul's death was a very big personal loss because he taught me to understand the complexities of war. Paul was a deep thinker and he was a terrible loss to the republican movement. If we had another half dozen Paul Marlow's we would have been further on with the war a lot quicker. As a friend he was a great bloke. As a volunteer he was a close comrade and was sorely missed. The IRA lost a good soldier the day Paul Marlow died.

John O'Caroll (comrade)

Paul had originally joined the Irish Guards then moved on to the Parachute Regiment, where he was part of a crack squad that was sent into Aden and Borneo. He also served with the SAS. He was kicked out of the SAS for an incident that occurred. He came out of the jungle mucked to the eyeballs and tried to get into the officers' mess. They wouldn't let him in, so he threw smoke grenades and then fired shots at them as they scrambled out. He was sent back to the Irish Guards, so he finished out his time and came home. He left the British army in 1968 and moved home to Ardoyne. Then he moved with his wife Annette to the Finaghy Road.

I first met Paul in Andersonstown around 1969. He came into the IRA's 1st Battalion 'A' Company. 'A' Coy was probably the only company at that time in the first battalion because it was the start, more or less, of the 'Provisional' IRA in Andersonstown. When Paul joined the IRA nobody knew him and even the guys from Ardoyne didn't know him because he had left there as a teenager. That is the way Paul operated. He was a loner and preferred it that way. That was part of his tactic to keep himself alive.

I remember one day I was with Paul and the SAS pulled up in a car and began speaking to him. I didn't know who the SAS were and Paul said to me, 'That's the SAS;

that's the squad I was with in Malaysia.' I was surprised at them being in Belfast, because it was 1969. I remember Paul saying, 'That's the SAS and they're here for something.' They were on first name terms with him.

When Paul joined 'A' Coy he started to train guys the way he was trained in the SAS. He put people through SAS assault courses. He taught them tactics, ambushes, sniping and counter-intelligence. Everything the SAS taught him, he taught us. He always said if you know your enemy then you can always use their tactics against them. Paul was responsible for a lot of developments that happened in the IRA. The first Claymore mines that were used outside of Vietnam were used in Andersonstown. It was Paul who designed them and showed the engineers how to use them. In Belfast alone Paul would have put 200 volunteers through an SAS-type training course. I remember in early 1970 he was asked to go to Angola as a mercenary and offered big money. Paul was unemployed at the time and he hadn't a light, as the saying goes. He was offered four hundred pound a month, which was big money then. He refused to go.

Paul was interned for a short period of time in the Cages of Long Kesh. I can never remember Paul being arrested again after internment because he moved around all the time. He went from Andersonstown to the Lower Falls, to the Short Strand and Ardoyne. He was on the border for a while and would have been doing things outside of Belfast from time to time.

I remember a friend, Henry Smith, came and told me Paul was dead, that he had been blown up in the Ormeau Road Gasworks with two other volunteers. Henry went down and identified Paul's body. To be honest Paul's death hit me pretty hard because I was with him maybe three nights before it happened. You just think that someone like that is invincible. Paul double-checked everything; he was so precise and disciplined about everything he did.

Paul had actually brought the volunteers on three dry runs into the Gasworks before the operation that night. He had brought them through the actual plan and brought them into where the bomb was going to be placed against the military billet in the Gasworks. Nobody knows exactly what happened that night. The bomb is supposed to have exploded prematurely. Other people say that the Brits caught the lads and set the bomb off on them. I suppose we'll never know.

Paul's death was a big loss to us all because in 1976 we were just starting to use mortars and rocket launchers. The training of volunteers was the highest priority to Paul. With Paul volunteers were actually getting trained properly. For the first time they weren't being sent out with weapons that were inferior to what they were going to come up against. Paul's motto was to give you the same chance as the enemy you were fighting. That's why Paul's training was vital. He didn't only teach you how to use a weapon, he taught you why you were using it.

Annette was totally gutted when Paul was killed. She thought he was just part of the ex-servicemen's group which would have done patrols to protect the area. I will never forget her face whenever the flag was handed over to her at the funeral and the guard of honour at the house. She allowed it because she felt that was what he would have wanted. After Paul's death Annette left and joined the Quakers working in Long Kesh visitors' area.

I'll never forget the night of Paul's wake. Myself, Martin Meehan, Fra Fox and a couple of others were sitting at the wake. There was a full guard of honour at the coffin and the door knocked and the next thing Paul's brother-in-law, who was a leading loyalist, wanted to come in and pay his respects to Paul. We didn't know what to do. He said, 'Look, I am not going to look at any faces. I just want to come and pay respects to the man who was good to my sister. My sister loved him and he loved her and he was a soldier and I want to pay my respects to a soldier'. The guy came in, said a couple of prayers and came out and asked what would happen to him now. Martin said there were two guys who would make sure he got home safely and that was it. That was the sort of influence Paul had on people. Even though he would have been hated by his enemies there was a respect.

Paul was a great person. I'm proud to say I got to know him for the short time I did. He had a big influence on me and I'm sure on everyone who knew him. His premature death was a tragedy not only for his wife and kids but for his comrades as well. He was well-respected and I'm sure all his loved ones have a sense of pride amidst their terrible loss.

Basically Charles was just a very, very innocent person, just a big child. There was no reason for him to be killed, they can't bring up a reason for that; he was just pure innocent.

Charles Corbett
Killed by loyalists,
Leggan Street,
30 October 1976

Charles Corbett was the third of four boys (Tony, John, Charles and Paul) and four girls (Catherine, Ann, Mary and Colette). He was born on 1 June 1955, to Charles and Ellen Teresa who were married in Holy Cross Ardoyne Chapel in 1947. Ellen was originally a Gault from Whiteabbey but her family had moved into Ardoyne due to the conflict in the '20s. Charles senior was brought up in Carrick Hill. He spent a number of years in the Royal Navy and then worked as a bus conductor for the Corporation. After Ellen died from heart trouble in 1969, he brought up the children by himself. The young family first lived with relatives in Jamaica Street, moved to Alliance Road and then a few years later set up home in Holmdene Gardens. Like his brothers, young Charles went to the Holy Cross Boys and then went on to St Gabriel's school. Shortly after leaving school he got a job as a van boy with the *Belfast Telegraph.*

Charles Corbett was only 21 years old in October 1976 when he was killed along with John Maguire as they delivered the Belfast Telegraph on the Crumlin Road. Charles, John Maguire and his son had gone to a shop to deliver newspapers as usual. They were hi-jacked, hoods put over their heads and forced into the back of a van where Charles and Mr Maguire were shot dead by the UVF. The van was abandoned in Glencairn. Passersby heard banging from inside the van and went to investigate. They found Charles and John Maguire dead and his young son alive but seriously wounded.

Bernadette McCann (neighbour)

Charles Corbett didn't bother with anybody; he was in a world of his own. I knew him from he was a child and he was the most inoffensive creature that God ever put on earth. He just loved to go his own way and do his own thing. He was very highly intelligent in school, but the brain, whatever way it worked, there was something not right, some wee thing just out of place. He was a very nice boy, but you knew there was a wee deficiency.

I was distracted when Charles was murdered. Of all the ones to pick on, that poor boy wouldn't have harmed a mouse. I was in the house and somebody came and said, 'Do you know who was shot dead in the van? It was poor Charlie shot dead'. I said, 'God, why did they pick on Charles? Is that who they are going to pick on, the innocent people of the world?' His father was in an awful bad state and I don't think that he did well after it. It just broke his heart because everybody loved Charles. He was a loveable person. The most inoffensive person I ever came across, a child running about; never was in any trouble or anything like that, not even with a neighbour, not even with one of his mates.

Mary, Colette and Ann Corbett (aisters)

The *Belfast Telegraph* was Charles' first and only job. He was about 16 or 17 when he started it. Astronomy was his hobby; he loved the 'Sky at Night' and he loved to talk about the stars and science fiction. He supported Leeds United Football team. He was a bit slow for his age and a bit of a loner. He loved to go for long walks and he loved adventure. He was always getting lost, even when he was a kid; everybody used to be out looking for him. The police got to know him well and would buy him sweets and drinks. We sometimes thought he got lost deliberately to get brought home in a police car. I remember he had this old bike and Charles decided to go for a ride. It wasn't really safe as the brakes were faulty and you couldn't really go out of the estate. Charles however decided to go to my aunt Mary's in Ballymurphy. On the way home he crashed into a road sign and broke his collar bone. A motorist brought him home and explained what had happened. Instead of being worried about Charles I wanted to know where the bike was.

Charles had a birthmark on the back of his head. It was shaped like a shamrock. Because of this he got taunted and called names. We were very protective of Charles. We got into many fights over people calling him names.

After Charles' murder dad's health deteriorated. He assumed he would always have Charles to look after, a companion for life. This is what kept him going after the death of our mum. Life changed for the whole family in different ways.

Ann: I was in London when I heard on the news that someone who worked for the *Belfast Telegraph* had been shot. Then my brother Tony phoned to tell me (Charles had been killed) and then I went to tell my brother John. By the time I got to John's the police had already contacted him. We flew home the next day.

Mary: The night it happened I was at Gerard's mum's home (my mother-in-law). His mum came in and said somebody delivering newspapers had been shot dead. I didn't take much notice. I went on watching a film and fell asleep. The next thing, Gerard's mum woke me to say that my dad and my cousin were there; then I knew. I just said to him 'Don't tell me, don't tell me. I don't want to know'.

Colette: A friend Vincy Mulholland owned the local shop and when the Telegraphs were not delivered, he phoned the offices to see why. He was told of the hi-jacking. Knowing my brother usually delivered his papers, he came for my dad. They both went out to find out what happened. Myself and my younger brother Paul waited at home. We put the TV on to listen to the news. That's when we heard about the shootings. It said two men had been shot dead and a youth who was also in the van was fine. I thought that Charles was fine as I classed him as a youth, not a man. When my cousin Phil and his wife Anne came in to take us to their house I knew then that Charles was dead. Everything after that seemed unreal.

Tony Corbett (brother)

At the time Charles was killed he was 21 years of age, but he was still a big innocent child. His only treat was a packet of five cigarettes. He used to love getting the cigarettes; he would come and ask you for money to buy them. He had no other vices in life; he didn't drink and he didn't cause trouble. He watched TV in the house and that was it. He had his job as a van boy with the Telegraph and he enjoyed that job. He worked with John Maguire who was killed at the same time. Charles was quite happy to just lead his life and bother no one. He didn't really understand what was happening in the area. He had been warned not to go back into that particular area and he was killed there. That's the sort of person he was; he held no offence against anybody and had no concept of what was going on.

As far as I know his last delivery was at the top of Ligoniel and that was part of their regular tour. They were stopped and killed. There were three of them in the van, Charles, Mr Maguire and his son. Charles and Mr Maguire were killed and the kid was left. On the day Charles died I was sitting at home with my wife and we were listening to the news. There was talk about two people being killed but the details didn't click. Then I received a phone call from my friend Vincy Mulholland from across the street. He said, 'Tony, you better go over to Tennent Street police station; your father needs you'. So my wife drove me across to the station and when I got there, my father told me what had happened. I just couldn't believe it. My father said that Charles had been murdered, but he didn't know the actual details. The body had been taken to the morgue so I didn't see Charles until he came home two days later, just before the funeral. Charles was buried from home. He went from Holmdene Gardens to Holy Cross chapel and then to Milltown where he was buried in my mother's grave.

Mr Maguire's son identified the people who did it; it was the UVF. He was only about nine at the time and he got up in court. I think that cut everybody up. I don't think they (loyalists) claimed responsibility for it right away but they were charged and sentenced and I think they got 25 years. I don't remember who they were; I didn't want to know. I went to the court case but I wasn't really interested; I just wanted to see the trial over with. My father wanted to go to the trial and I went along with him.

We were treated okay at the time by the British army and the police. I take it from their point of view they were seeing so much of it, violence. They just told you what happened. They weren't abusive or unhelpful; they just did their job and let you get on with your grief. The press came and got the initial facts and then disappeared. They weren't really interested; it was just another three short lines on the page for them. The Telegraph was very helpful and supportive; they contacted us and asked if there was anything they could do for us at the time. In those days there was no other kind of support except from your own priest. I think you were left to get on with it yourself; there was no victim support.

At the time you were thinking 'Give me a gun and I'll give them justice' but it solves nothing for anybody. I just left it to the state to get on with it and they did. At the time I thought they would never get anybody but they did so. Is justice just locking four guys up for 25 years? Does it really solve anything? .

John Maguire
Killed by the UVF,
Glenbank Place,
30 October 1976

Before he died, his daddy had said to Michael that he had been shot. Then he said, 'May God save you, son'. And God did save him. But his daddy was close to God. I don't think John ever did hurt to anyone in his life.

John Maguire's mother had been born in the United States of America but had grown up in Ireland. His father was a Belfast man, although he died when John was still young. John himself was born on 18 August 1920, the young brother to his two sisters Bridget and Maggie. The family grew up in Lady Street, just off Albert Street. John went on to St Mary's College after school. Then he began to train as a printer's compositor. As a young man John became involved with republicanism and was interned in 1940. He would spend the next seven years of his life in Crumlin Road gaol. He did, though, become a fluent Irish speaker while imprisoned. A few years after he was released John met Lillian Nugent from Stratford Gardens at a dance. Lillian was a very keen dancer and John was an avid follower of traditional music. He also played the accordion. The two married in July 1953 and set up home in Alliance Avenue where they had four of their five children. John was not a great one for socialising in the clubs and pubs of the area. He was a Pioneer most of his life. But he spent the majority of his time with his family, fixing up old cars and looking after the dogs that he loved. In 1968 the Maguires moved to Ashgrove Park. By then John had been working on the buses for almost a quarter of a century. However, as times got more dangerous he left the buses and ultimately got work driving a van delivering newspapers for the *Belfast Telegraph*. In the early 1970s delivering newspapers in the wrong areas could also prove to be a dangerous job. So it proved for John. On 30 October 1976 John was delivering newspapers to Gregg's newsagents on the Crumlin Road. He was accompanied by Charlie Corbett from Holmdene Gardens [Charles Corbett, killed by the UVF in Glenbank Place, 30 October 1976] and his own ten-year-old son Michael. Three loyalist gunmen got into the van and forced John, Charlie and Michael into the back. As they drove the van into Glenbank Place they robbed John of his money and then shot him and Charlie Corbett dead. They also shot young Michael in the leg. Both John and Charlie were killed in a deliberate sectarian attack. Two years later the gunmen were convicted for their killing.

Lillian Maguire (wife)

John was a quiet, unassuming person. He was quite shy and very respectful to women. We met at a dance in 1949. I always loved Irish dancing, céilí dancing and old-time dancing. John wasn't a bad dancer but he loved music. He loved playing the accordion and he had a great feel for music. It always made a great impression on him. John had been interned in 1940. He had been training as a printer but had got involved with a group over in the Falls Road. He spent seven years in Crumlin Road gaol. He learnt Irish when he was inside and had a fainne. I have been told that he actually taught Irish during his time in prison. But those were his young, valuable years and he came out a bit disillusioned. He still loved Ireland but he didn't want to be involved in anything after that. A month before he died he said that what was really important was where you stood with God. He was religious but not 'holier-than-thou'. John was a man with very strong principles who you could trust implicitly. He wasn't an angel and had his faults, like all men. But he held women in great respect. He was a very intelligent man and would have talked about a lot of different things.

Because he couldn't go back to printing, John worked at asphalting. It was very heavy work. Then he started working on the buses. He was working on the buses for about 25 years. But after the troubles started that got very dangerous because of some of the routes he was working. He went from there to a security job at Aldergrove and then on to the Telegraph as a delivery and salesman. That was in about 1969. After we got married we had a house in Alliance Avenue. It was very mixed in those days. We lived at the top end where there were only about five Catholic families. But there were no problems then. They were a decent lot. We had four children who were born in Alliance [John, Christine, Paul and Michael,] then Gerard, the youngest, was born after we moved to Ashgrove Park in early 1968. This was before the conflict started but I felt something in my bones that I wanted to move. Different things happened there after that proved it was a dangerous spot.

John always liked playing the accordion but that was mostly in the house. He wasn't one for socialising in the clubs or anything like that. It was noisy in a small house and he would take himself off up the stairs to play. He used to do it when he was supposed to be looking after the dinner if I wasn't back from work. My daughter Christine used to laugh that you would always end up with the food burnt because of it. Christine was always very fond of her daddy. I honestly don't believe she ever got over her daddy's death. Charlie Corbett used to come to our house for dinner sometimes too. John was very good to him. Charlie worked with John as a helper and he was a bit slow. About a fortnight before they were both shot, John bought Charlie a book about astronomy. Charlie was interested in the stars. I doubt he ever got a chance to read it. John always said that if he didn't look after Charlie then no one else was going to go out working with him. John sort of took him under his wing. In the early 1970s John would have been very conscious of what was happening around him. It was a dangerous time and he was going into dangerous areas. He knew that he wasn't even safe in the Telegraph. I think he had been threatened before too. I remember the Sunday before he was killed he showed me how to lock the door on the car. He said it with this voice of authority. He never explained why and it didn't really register with me at the time. I think he had been threatened but wouldn't tell me. That was the Sunday and the next Saturday he was murdered.

My husband John was murdered on Saturday 30 October 1976. It was the day the clocks went forward so it was darker earlier. It was also the last time that route was to be followed. I don't know whether John had asked for the route to be changed but it had become too dangerous and was going to be changed to another route on the Monday after. Catholics had been brought in to work for the Telegraph in some areas where Protestants felt unsafe. I mean loyalist areas; they didn't feel safe working in their own areas. But that was the last chance for them to have killed John because on the Monday he was being moved on to the Ligoniel route. John had been working all that day. He went out about 9.30 am that morning. I remember he shouted up that the dog wasn't talking to him. We had an old lassie dog that John loved. He loved animals. I said if it did speak he would get a bit of a shock and he went out laughing. That was the last time I heard him. Then John went down to the *Belfast Telegraph* office. Our son Michael was in the van on the night his father was murdered because he used to help him. Michael was very bright and would have been counting the papers and getting them ready as they were going round on the deliveries. Michael was very curious about everything then. He was always asking questions and had a very inquiring mind. He is not like that now. Michael changed completely after his father was murdered. He had his hair washed that night and it was still wet when he went out. I told him he couldn't go with his hair wet but Michael went anyway. Michael knew where his daddy would have been driving past so he went up there. His daddy just said to him, 'Alright, get in'. Charlie was in the van when Michael got in and they headed over the Ballysillan Road. An odd thing happened when they were on the round. John hit a rabbit with the van on the road up by Ligoniel. He asked Michael to go and look at it. That was not like him. He would usually never have asked a child to do that.

They were making a delivery to Craig's shop in Glenbank Place, on the corner of Ligoniel Road. They [loyalists] got into the van as Michael and Charlie came out of the shop. The people who murdered my husband got in and forced John to drive down into Glenbank Place. There were five of them [loyalists]. There was one doing lookout, one took the guns away and there were three who got into the van. They made John stop and then they shot them in the van. John must have put up a fight because his knuckles were all skinned. The gunmen called them 'fenian bastards' and all the usual, then shot them. They took John's money too, his private money and the Telegraph money. They shot wee Michael in the leg as well. Then Michael kept his eyes closed and they thought he was dead. They would have wanted to shoot him because he was an eyewitness. As it turned out, he was a very good witness. But it was a terrible ordeal for a child. Before he died his daddy had said to Michael that he had been shot. Then he said, 'May God save you, son'. And God did save him. But his daddy was close to God. I don't think John ever did hurt to anyone in his life.

My sister told me that my husband had been shot. She had got a phone call from Irene Mallon who knew there had been a shooting and thought that it might have been John. My sister went up to the Tennent Street police station to see if they would come out and tell me what had happened. But they wouldn't come out. So my sister came to tell me. She said there had been an accident. I asked her if he was hurt. No answer. Then I asked if he was dead. She just nodded. I asked her about Michael and she said he was hurt and in the hospital so I went up there. After my husband was murdered, there were people who got into the van to try to help. One odd thing is that there was one woman who was a nurse who came to help. One of the men's sons who had been involved in the murder had been married but had left his wife. It was his wife that got into the van to try to help. They took Michael out and into a woman's house in Glenbryn Crescent. I went round later to tell her that Michael survived and she thanked me for that because she had been worrying about him. They took Michael to the hospital with what turned out to be a flesh wound to his leg. I was really worried that he needed to be home when his daddy's body was there, otherwise he wouldn't realise that his daddy was dead. I nearly went insane thinking about that. He asked me that night how his daddy was but I couldn't tell him. But he said he just knew his daddy was dead. He never, ever got over it. It did terrible harm to him psychologically. Michael never got over his father's death. He is making a life for himself but I doubt that he will ever get the event out of his mind. He doesn't like talking about his daddy. In fact, none of the boys do.

I have learnt to live with what happened; you have to. John and I had talked a month or so before he was killed about what would happen if I died. That was because I had heart trouble for years. I told him that if anything happened he would have to go on because the children were his responsibility. The night John was killed I could hear his voice in my brain saying, 'They are your responsibility'. That is what kept me sane. John had a big funeral and there were a lot of our neighbours from Alliance Avenue there. There was one Orangeman who had lived across the street from us who told me later that he came into the chapel. He just wanted to let me know that. People thought a lot of John.

Michael has told me so much about what happened that I imagine that I was in the van. I can see the expressions on both their faces. I couldn't get the scene out of my mind for a whole year. It would involuntarily just flash into my mind. I also made a note of anything that seemed odd – like the shop where they were making the delivery when they were killed. Usually there was a crowd outside it but that night there was no one about. I would ring the police for months after with anything I could think of like that. I wanted these people caught, not for revenge but just to know that there was some justice in this place. Even getting the people who did it would not bring John back but I wanted these people found. I wouldn't leave it alone. Eventually they did get them because one of them squealed on the others.

I have had ongoing arguments with different people who believe that if you were murdered then you must have been involved in terrorism. John would have loved to see

Ireland united but not at the cost of all that has happened. He didn't think that so many deaths were worth it. John was a person I could trust. My own life had not been that happy when I was younger so I knew that there were periods in your life when things could go wrong. Unless a person has stamina and strong morals they can fall down. I knew that John was someone who could be trusted from the moment I met him and I never changed my view of him. He didn't lie and if he said he would do something, he would do it. He spent too much money on cars but when it came to the important things in life he was what you would have wanted. John and I had a trust between the two of us and we could talk to each other as friends. John was a good person and I would say that he was ready to meet God.

Michael Maguire (son)

(This testimony was compiled from an interview with Michael and extracts taken from the evidence he gave to the Coroner's Court)

I am a schoolboy. On Saturday evening 30 October 1976 I was helping my father and Charlie Corbett deliver papers. My daddy was employed by the *Belfast Telegraph* and he drove the van. At about 7.20 pm my daddy stopped the van outside Gregg's newsagency shop at the top of the Crumlin Road to deliver newspapers. He reversed the Ford transit van toward the front of the shop. I was in the back of the van and Charlie Corbett was in the front passenger seat. Charlie took the papers and went towards the shop. While he was away, daddy turned the van to face away from the shop. Charlie was only away about a minute and then he got back into the front seat. We were about to drive off again to go back to the *Belfast Telegraph* depot when three men wearing hoods over their heads and all carrying guns jumped into the van. One of them jumped onto the doorstep on my daddy's side of the van and two others jumped onto the doorstep on Charlie's side. They told Charlie to get to the back of the van. They also wanted my daddy to get into the back. My daddy asked the fella at his door what was up and he tried to push him off. The fellow at his door got into my daddy's seat. He switched off the light in the van. One of the fellows who was standing at Charlie's door told us clearly to get into the back of the van. My daddy and Charlie did. The same man came into the back of the van carrying a gun. The fellow with him got into the front passenger seat. The fella in the driver's seat had his gun resting across his knee and he turned the van to face back up the Crumlin Road. The fella in the back of the van said, 'Empty out your pockets, you bastards'. My daddy took out his wallet and the man took about £40 in notes and stuffed them in his jacket pocket. Charlie was still standing up in the van and the fella sitting in his seat said, 'Get fucking down on the floor'. My daddy got on the floor and so did I. The fella in the back of the van gave Charlie a kick in the stomach and Charlie fell down. They spoke no more. I just thought that these men were going to take the money from my daddy. Just before the shooting my daddy said to me, 'God save you'. As we were turning off the Crumlin Road the man in the back of the van (who had kept his gun pointed at my daddy from when the van started off) fired at my daddy, who was lying crouched. I closed my eyes. I don't know how many shots there were.

When the van started to slow down I opened my eyes. The man in the front passenger seat jumped out while the van was still moving. The fella in the back who was shooting squeezed out of the van. Then the driver stopped the van. I got up on my knees in the back of the van and asked my daddy, 'What will I do?' My daddy said nothing. I got up and ran out of the van. I was in a street. I saw a woman come out of a house. I ran over to her and told her my daddy was dead. She didn't believe me at first. She brought me into the house and she went to look in the van. I heard a scream and then she came back. She told me my daddy was alright. I saw blood on my trousers and I felt my leg was sore. Another woman rang the police. I was taken in an ambulance to the Royal Victoria Hospital. Then my leg was treated.

The next day my mother asked the doctor to let me home. She felt very strongly that I should see my father's dead body in the coffin and attend the funeral. The doctor agreed and I attended the Royal Victoria Hospital as an outpatient for a number of weeks. The ambulance took me there and back home.

> *She used to say that she couldn't wait until she was old enough to go and listen to music in those clubs. But, God love her, she never got to that age.*

Geraldine McKeown
Killed by loyalists,
Mountainview Gardens,
8 December 1976

Geraldine McKeown was born in 1962, the youngest and only girl of the four children born to Patrick and Patricia McKeown. Patrick was originally from Fairfield Street. He saw service abroad during the war with the RAF and returned shortly after to marry Patricia Lavery from Butler Street. In the years to come the family moved around as Patrick was stationed in various air force bases. After his discharge in the early 1960s they settled in Crumlin Street. In 1967 they moved again to an estate on the outskirts of Rathcoole. However, at the outbreak of the conflict they were forced to move because of the threat of sectarian intimidation. As refugees in 1969 the family lived in other people's houses until they were rehoused in Mountainview Gardens. Dena (as Geraldine was usually known) was by then attending the Holy Cross school. Then she went on to Our Lady of Mercy on the Ballysillan Road. In late 1976 her brother was arrested and was being held on remand in Crumlin Road gaol. On 6 December 1976 two gunmen came to the door of the family home. Dena was waiting for a friend to call to the house. The gunmen shot Dena as she looked through the window to see who was there. She died two days later. Dena was only 14-years-old at the time of her death.

Kate McCurdy (friend)

I met Geraldine at Ardoyne Youth Club and we went down to a house to play records. That was it then; we became friends. Dena would have been about thirteen so it was roughly about a year before she died. We didn't go to school together because she went to Our Lady's and I went to St Gemma's. We knocked about together after school. We would go on up to Mountainview to sit and play records because there wasn't really that many discos about. She was game and would do anything for a joke. She wasn't malicious or a fighter or anything like that – just wee mischievous things that all kids get up to at that age. She was a beautiful wee girl. All we ever talked about was getting married and having kids; I think at that age you go through that stage. Dena was lovely, a lovely wee girl. She wasn't cheeky, just a lovely wee girl, dead bubbly, dead friendly and she went anywhere for you. If you said to her, 'Dena, jump through that hoop' she would have jumped through it for you. She was a really, really beautiful wee girl.

Dena was mad on music and we spent most of our time sitting in Dena's room playing records. She loved Abba and the Eagles. She used to get the tennis racket and pretend she was playing the guitar while I sang into the hairbrush. All my memories are centred around records because me and her just really loved music. Like most people with records, they conjure up memories. Dena had a wee portable record player that ran on batteries and we brought it out one day and had it on at the street corner. We were playing 'Dancing Queen' by Abba. It started to rain so she ran up to the house and got a bit of cardboard and an umbrella. She set the record player on top of the cardboard and put the umbrella over it. Then me and her stood dancing with it raining like we were two eejits. Every time I hear 'Dancing Queen' I think of her; I can just see her. I would stay in her house on a Friday night and she would stay in my house on a Saturday night. When we were passing the Shamrock [club] we use to stand outside and listen to the groups because we were too young to go in. She used to say that she couldn't wait until she was old enough to go and listen to music in those clubs. But, God love her, she never got to that age.

Dena knew what was going on around her, with her brother being inside and that. That affected her. She was afraid of something happening. I remember after she died, I slept in her house for a couple of nights over the wake. I was up in her bedroom crying. I found these letters of Geraldine's saying, 'I am afraid to die. I'm afraid'. She used to say that she heard her mummy and daddy talking about the threatening letters and phone calls [the family were receiving from loyalists]. Her parents tried to keep it from Dena because we would have talked about it and had it all around the district. But she obviously heard wee snippets to have written something like that. She told me her mummy and daddy were a bit afraid living in Mountainview because it was so open. So many people were killed in that wee area alone. I think she was aware of something. One time she thought that someone was following her. Whether it was true or she was just being paranoid I don't know. I think when you are frightened like that you can't really think straight. The last time I saw her was a couple of days before she was killed. We were up in my house in Oldpark Avenue because I was grounded. We watched that Paul Newman boxing film, 'Someone up there likes me'. We were on our knees with our fists saying 'go on' and all that crack. We planned to meet up on the Monday. I said on her way out that if I wasn't grounded I would be over to her about 7.15 and she said, 'Right, so if you're not up for 7.15, I'll know'.

The circumstances of her death were terrible. I was down in our Gerard's when I found out about what happened. My brother was getting married on 18 December and I was to go down and help with wedding presents and stuff like that. I phoned to Dena's to get her to come down too. Denise Murray who lived a couple of doors down lifted the phone. I thought it was Dena. She used to put on a deep voice and let on you had got the wrong number. She was a terrible wee girl for that sort of thing. But Denise said, 'It's not Dena; this is Denise. Dena has been shot'. That was 6 December. It was the Monday night that I had told her I would be over at 7.15 pm if I was allowed out. I finally realised it wasn't Dena; it wasn't a joke. So I ran up to the house and told mummy. I thought Dena was shot in the leg or something. When I went up there was a terrible mess in the house Her mummy and daddy were away to the hospital but there were neighbours. That is when I was told that she had been shot in the head. I found out that it was just shortly after 7 pm when she was shot. Her mummy and daddy said later that when the door rapped she said, 'That's Kate'. She thought it was me. She always lifted the venetian blinds to see who was there. That is what she did that night. Dena died at 12 o'clock on Wednesday afternoon. She lived for two days. I went up to see her when she was on a life support machine. She was unconscious but if you held her hand she would squeeze back faintly. She was in a coma so her mummy and the nurses said to me to talk to her because there was a good chance she would hear what was being said. So that night I sat talking to her. I don't know whether she heard me or not.

Ciaran McKeown (brother)

I only found out later what actually happened to Geraldine. They [loyalist gunmen] called at the house and they rapped the window; it was about at teatime, about 6.30 pm. Geraldine had a terrible habit that if anybody rapped the door, she would look through the venetian blinds. That's exactly what she did. The fellas saw the blinds opening and they just fired through the window. It could have been anybody. They didn't try and kick the door in or get access to the house or anything. They fired a lot more than two shots. One of them had some sort of sub-machine gun and they just fired through the windows. My daddy was actually lying down on the settee and my mother was in the kitchen. Dena was only hit twice but both times was in the head. Then the gunmen got into a car and drove away. The car was found up in Sommerdale in the alleyway that leads down into Glencairn. I think it had been hijacked in the Woodvale.

I actually heard the shots. I was in Crumlin Road gaol at the time, on remand. But nobody told me that Geraldine had been shot until the following day. The screws or the prison chaplain never came near me before that. There was something on the news that someone in Mountainview had been shot. It went through my head that it might be somebody belonging to me because we had been threatened that much, especially with me going into gaol. The phone calls and threatening letters had gathered momentum so I was always very, very wary. I was being arrested on a regular basis before that. When I was in the family house there were phone calls every night of the week. I imagine when I wasn't there they got worse if anything. People were phoning to say that they were coming up to shoot me. But I knew nothing until the next morning because you were locked up at night. Then I got a visit from my mother, father and a priest first thing in the morning.

As soon as I knew I was getting a special visit so early in the morning it more or less clicked right away that it was something to do with the family. I knew there was something wrong. So on the way down I had more or less accepted that somebody out of the family had been shot. My ma was in some state and my da could hardly talk. The priest was from Ardoyne and he did most of the talking. You can imagine what it was like. Geraldine was shot in front of them and they had just come from the hospital. At this stage Geraldine was still alive and nobody really knew how bad she was. But she was shot twice in the head so there wasn't a great hope.

After the visit I went back to the wing. I knew she was still alive and in a critical condition. My solicitor, Paddy McGrory, came up and wanted me to apply for compassionate bail. But the governor didn't want anything to do with it. So we let it go and I applied for a visit to go to the hospital to see her. But they refused to let me go and they wouldn't give me any more visits with the family. I was just banged up. Geraldine died on 8 December and they allowed me just one special visit the day before with my mother, father and an aunt. I asked the governor again for a compassionate visit so that I could go and see her before they turned the machine off. They allowed me to go handcuffed to two screws. They wanted me to stay and watch the machine being turned off. I couldn't do it. So they just allowed me five minutes to see her. I wasn't allowed to touch her or do anything because I was handcuffed at both sides. That was the only time I saw her before she died that morning. I applied for bail for the funeral but they wouldn't let me out. The RUC and crown prosecution objected because I was on remand for a political offence at the time. The governor said he would allow me to go to the funeral but that I had to be handcuffed at all times to a couple of volunteer screws. None of them would do it so bail was refused. I watched the funeral on the TV in the canteen. We were segregated then and the loyalists were shouting at me to rub it in when I was in the exercise yard.

No one admitted the murder. The cops said that they arrested people but nobody was ever charged. They were probably just saying that anyway. I think the reason that nobody claimed it was because she was only a kid. Nothing really came out of the inquest. The weapons that were used were tested by ballistics. They turned out to be UDA weapons that had been used before in other attacks. I can only imagine how my family coped because I was inside. I don't think anyone approached them offering help or support, apart from family and friends. My mother and father were never the same afterwards. I was in gaol, my brother Vincent was in Canada, the other brother Colm was in England. Dena had been the last one living in the house. You can imagine the effect it had watching your child being shot dead. They were never the same after it.

Dena was like all kids. Being a wee girl she was into clothes and going to wee dances. She was a typical teenager, into dancing, into clothes, full of life. She was always happy. She never reached adulthood so she never really had responsibilities to weigh on her. That's the way I remember her. She was just a great kid, friendly, lively, chatty and with loads of friends; Kate [McCurdy] and Geraldine [Close] were her closest friends, but she had loads of other friends. She had a friend in Newington who was shot dead only weeks before under almost the exact same circumstances. She was also only fourteen too. It was a coincidence.

Today you could take some kind of court case against them but in those days you knew nothing. They murdered John and there was nothing we could do about it.

John Savage
Killed by the British army,
Springfield Road,
18 December 1976

John Savage's parents were Frankie Savage from Glenview Street and Alice (née Glennon) from Eskdale Gardens. They had nine children, four boys (Francis, Martin, Michael and John) and five girls (Alice, Kathleen, Ann-Marie, Bernadette and Rosaleen). John was the third eldest, born 31 January 1959. After living in West Belfast for a period, the Savage family moved to Ardoyne in the late 1960s. John went to St Aidan's school on the Somerton Road and then served his time as a painter and decorator in Feldon House.

John Savage was travelling in a stolen car with two other teenagers along the Springfield Road when the British paratroopers opened fire on the car. The vehicle was sprayed with gunfire and crashed. John Savage and Mickey Mooney [killed by Direct Action Against Drugs, 25 April 1995] managed to get out of the car while the other teenager James Smyth, was too seriously injured to move. An eyewitness recalls John Savage shouting that he was unarmed before he emerged from the car. The teenager was shot in the face as he stumbled from the vehicle. None of the paratroopers turned up at the inquest nor was the eyewitness ever questioned or asked to give evidence. The British soldiers claimed that they had opened fire on the car because they thought they had seen a weapon. No gun was ever found at the scene of the killing.

Michael Savage (brother)

My parents met in the early 1950s. My mother's family owned Glennon's Bag Stores. They got married in 1952 in Holy Cross chapel and lived with my grandparents in Eskdale Gardens. They eventually got a place of their own in Longsdale Street but that went on fire and we lived in Ballymurphy for a while. We eventually moved back to Ardoyne in the late 1960s. As a child John was hospitalised after he ate poisonous blackberries. He was in hospital for about a year. Because so much time was taken off school he had to go to St Aidan's special school on the Somerton Road. On internment morning he was shot in the shoulder by loyalists as he walked up Estoril Park. Leo McGuigan, a young lad from the Bone, was killed and Tommy Gillespie lost a finger after being shot in the same incident.

John came to me the night before he was killed and asked me to give him a lift to his friend's house. His friend wasn't in so I left him into town. His last words to me were, 'I have eight quid here Mickey. Do you want four quid of it?' That was the last time I saw him. We were in the city centre the next morning when we heard that John had been killed. One of my cousins told us the bad news. I identified John's body; once I saw the snorkel jacket I knew it was John. The paratroopers tried to say they had shouted warnings. They said they thought they saw a rifle. There was no rifle; they just shot him dead. John was shot in the face. The two other young lads in the car were also shot several times. They justified killing John and shooting the other two young lads by giving them nearly ten years.

I met one of the young lads who was in the car a number of years ago and he told me that the first thing they knew was when the bullets came through the windscreen and the car went out of control. There was no attempt to stop the car. None of the paratroopers were at the inquest. The simple truth is that there was no gun in the car. Today you could take a court case against them but in those days you knew nothing. They murdered John and there was nothing we could do about it. Our family was devastated and still are. My father doesn't even talk about it to this day. None of us ever got over John's death.

James Smyth (eyewitness)

[This testimony is based upon extracts taken from evidence given to the Coroner's Court]

I was in the town centre with John Savage and Mickey Mooney. We hung about Castle Street until midnight and got a black taxi up to Turf Lodge. We walked down to the infants' school at the Holy Trinity chapel. The back door is always open; we went in and slept on the chairs until the next morning. I think it was about 9.00 am, we woke up and walked up the Hannahstown Road. We took a car and the three of us drove off. As we drove down the Springfield Road Mickey Mooney shouted that a soldier was coming out of the Henry Taggart barracks. I then put my head down. I saw soldiers in front of me and I didn't know what to do. I was nervous. The next thing, I heard bangs and something came all over my face and the car turned into the Springmartin side of the road and hit a fence or pole.

I couldn't get out of the car, as my arm was caught in the steering wheel. Mickey Mooney and John Savage got out of the car. I can't say how they got out; all I could hear was Mickey and John shouting, 'I'm hit, I'm hit'. I then put my head up and the shooting started, and my right ear was grazed. I put my head down and couldn't see anything. After the shooting stopped the soldiers came down to the car and took me out of it and sat me on the footpath beside the car. Later an ambulance came and took me to hospital. I was shot in the right arm and lost the top of my right index finger. Also the bones in my right arm were shattered. At no time were there any mention of guns in the car and I didn't see anyone pointing a gun from the car at the soldiers.

Tommy Maguire (eyewitness)

I knew the Savages, including John, very well. They came into my shop on a regular basis. On the day John was killed I was driving down the Springfield Road at the Henry Taggart Memorial Hall when a car came past me travelling very fast. The next thing, I saw British soldiers coming out of Springfield Park, just down from the Henry Taggart, and they were shooting at the car. The stolen car John was in mounted the footpath and tumbled over. I had my car windows open and heard a voice from the stolen car. I don't know what he was shouting but when the young lad emerged from the car they just shot him dead. To me it was murder.

After the shooting we were ordered to drive on but when I drove past the body on the ground I could see that he had been shot with his hands above his head. I only discovered that it was John Savage when his mother came to see me later. There must have been at least seven paratroopers shooting at the car. Every one of them fired at the car and young John as he got out of it. He didn't stand a chance.

No one ever approached me about a statement or asked me to attend the inquest. I firmly believe that John Savage was murdered. There was no way those soldiers were going to let anyone out of that car alive. In my opinion they tried their best to kill everyone in the car. They just shot John dead and waved us on as if nothing had happened. I think to them he was just another Catholic and they could do what they wanted.

Highfield Social Club, early 1970s. First Green Cross/PDF meeting. Among those present: Tom Fleming, Maggie Clarke, Lily Largey, Arder Corbett, Lily McCleneghan

4

1976-1983
'The Long War' – Containment, Criminalisation and Resistance

In the early years of the conflict people of various political persuasions believed that it was going to be a brief (if all too bloody) affair. By the late 1970s such a view was already a fast fading and forlorn hope. That this was to be a 'long', and increasingly 'dirty' war was becoming more and more evident. The British state decided that it would not embark on another failed political initiative. Instead it set its sights on conducting a counter-insurgency war of attrition. The aim would be (in Roy Mason's words) to 'squeeze the IRA like toothpaste'. The strategy of 'containment' was to be the means of pursuing this goal. Containment involved a wide range of both tactical and policy initiatives. But its core aim was to undermine both the will and the ability to continue resistance. This was to be achieved not only by breaking the organisation of opposition but also by sapping the collective morale and solidarity that made resistance possible. The effects of this strategy would be deeply damaging and long-lasting. Certainly this was to prove the case in Ardoyne. The most obvious effects of 'criminalisation' were the 'blanket' and 'no-wash' protests that took place within the prisons. They were struggles that came to define this period. The battle for 'hearts and minds' was fought out on this terrain. Ultimately the 'containment years' would climax in the events of the 1981 republican hunger strike. The legacy of the hunger strike was to be long and far-reaching.

This 'battle for hearts and minds' took place in an atmosphere darkened by the ferocity of what had already taken place. By the start of 1977 almost 1,900 people had lost their lives as a result of the conflict. 56 people from Ardoyne had already been killed. This was over half of the total who would lose their lives during three decades of conflict. War weariness had already fed the emergence of the 'Peace People' in the summer of 1976. The Peace People gained little tangible support within Ardoyne. This was mainly due to their unwillingness to criticise the violence of the British army and the RUC and the suspicion that they were serving a state agenda. However, there were very real tensions about the direction to be taken in the future. These tended to revolve around a struggle for leadership within the community between local republicans and the Catholic church. The tenor of that division was evidenced in September 1976. A priest from the Holy Cross monastery, Fr. Aquinas, issued a call through the *Belfast Telegraph* for people in the district to 'turn in' IRA activists. This marked a new and embittered low in relations between 'parish' and 'community'. The struggle for community leadership would not only centre on attitudes toward the conflict. Of equal importance was the growing emphasis upon the need for social and economic development.

Certainly Ardoyne faced massive social and economic problems. Recent years had, though, seen substantial re-development of the area's housing stock. From 1975 onward the physical landscape of Ardoyne began to change dramatically. This was a process which accelerated in the late 1970s and continued through until the mid-1980s. 'Old Ardoyne', the cockpit of the conflict, all but disappeared. Its poor, rundown and ageing back-to-back houses were pulled down. Or, to be more exact, streets were demolished that had not already been reduced to wastelands of rubble and ash by the burnings and battles of earlier years. Streets synonymous not only with the dark memories of 1969 but also with a dogged pride were relegated to the realm of memory. Hooker Street and Brookfield Street became names of the past. But even more important were some of the social repercussions that re-development brought with it. The prospect of new housing provided an impetus for the creation of various campaign groups. A redevelopment committee was established to liase with the Housing Executive. A number of tenants associations, such as the Ardoyne Housing Association, began to appear. As in other parts of the North a nebulous form of street politics based on social issues was beginning to take more definite shape. As elsewhere too both secular and clerical figures were to the fore in these groups. For example, the Flax Trust was established under the chairmanship of local priest Fr. Myles Kavanagh (another priest from the Holy Cross monastery) in 1976. The declared aim of the Trust was the promotion of economic regeneration to overcome the area's social ills. Such problems were often felt most acutely by the women of the area. To offer some relief to women in the district a Family Centre had already been established by the church in 1974. Marion Kane (who would herself become a community worker in the area) describes how the Family Centre came about and what it did.

> At that time there was nothing for women to do or anywhere to go. A lot of them were living on their nerves and on valium. You didn't really have a proper life. That was when the Family Centre was started up by Sister Joan. She was a nun who came up from Drogheda. She had specifically requested to be sent to the North where she felt she could do some good. She established the Family Centre in an old school building beside the Holy Cross chapel. It wasn't really very fancy or organised at first. It was just somewhere to go and get a cup of tea while someone minded the kids for an hour or so. Sister Joan asked the women what they wanted and it was the women then who said that they wanted classes in this and that. Women didn't really have much then. You went to work, then you got married. If you wanted a career you just didn't get married. That is the way it was then. When they started off the classes would have been in the usual things: cookery, arts and crafts, dressmaking, knitting – just the basic things women would have been involved in. Then after a few years they introduced classes in English, maths, sociology. It was as much about companionship and support as anything else. We started a wee 'nearly new' shop to help pay for things. Mrs Wilson ran that for years. She loved it. We just went round people's doors to get them involved. Then people would come in to buy something and just sit and have a wee cup of tea in the kitchen. It was having company that mattered. Then the NSPCC got

involved and they set up a crèche. Later there was a Family and Home Programme, and an Outreach Programme. It was voluntary work that got things going. It all had to be done in the area because people were terrified to go outside the area. That is why the black taxis started. It was just ordinary people getting involved because they felt intimidated and under threat. Most people had some experience of having their house raided, losing their home, something having happened to someone in their family or losing a loved one. It wasn't politics then. It was just survival. People were looking for leadership and sometimes they didn't get it. I am a very strong Catholic but for a time I didn't go to mass because I thought that the church needed to speak out more on things like internment. There were good priests. But I thought there was a need to highlight injustice. I have a good relationship with the church now but that was how I felt. People in Ardoyne had to be self-sufficient and I got involved in things through the Family Centre. (Marion Kane, Ardoyne resident and community worker)

Certainly the area was faring badly by virtually any indicator of social and economic deprivation. A study published in 1982 found that 35 per cent of houses lacked basic amenities. 28 per cent of dwellings in the district were still classed as being overcrowded. Indeed the conflict had increased the level of overcrowding. People had flooded into the area and stayed there (despite its problems), as it was one of the few in North Belfast where people felt relatively safe. Ardoyne bulged at the seams of the cramped confines imposed upon it by the city's sectarianised geography and the threat of loyalist violence. At a time when the average unemployment rate for the North was roughly 25 per cent that of Ardoyne was more than twice that figure. For young men it was a staggering 60 per cent. Even amongst those in work 95 per cent were in manual trades and virtually all earned less than the average wage. Poverty and the traumatic effects of the conflict also left their mark on people's health. As the chairman of the Flax Trust, Fr. Myles Kavanagh was deeply involved in community development. He describes what Ardoyne was like in those days, the relationship between church and community and what the Flax Trust set out to achieve.

Ardoyne is like a village. It may be one of the last villages left in the city. It is a very tight-knit community with very close inter-relationships. It takes its identity from the spires of the Holy Cross chapel. Whether people are churchgoers or not, the identity of Ardoyne comes out of a relationship with the church spires and with the monastery. They can't identify with the state or with the whole of Ireland. So the only identity available to the people of Ardoyne is a local identity. For good or ill that is with the monastery. It has also been a distinctive relationship because Ardoyne was cut off from the main Catholic community in West Belfast. This was an island community. However, I think that the close relationship and degree of dependence on the church did change with '69. That was the beginning of people saying 'no' to state and church. There was a change in values, not necessarily of the whole community but a significant element. It was not necessarily a bad thing.

But there was still an identity with the church. For example, when the monastery was attacked from the Woodvale Road there was an instantaneous response from the community to defend it. It was like people were saying, 'This monastery is ours. Whatever you fellas [priests] think about violence, this is our territory and we are going to defend it'. I think that is an indication of the bonds rather than the division that was there. Although there were divisions too. I think that the church's attitude to violence was always going to mean that there were going to be serious tension between it and the IRA. That is still a reality. They [republicans] have a mindset that they have the right to confront injustice with violence. My view is that violence begets violence. It was important to resist injustice and to encourage people to say 'no' to injustice. But there are other ways of doing that than violence. If the church was remiss for many years it was in not confronting injustice and promoting a mindset that if you had been treated badly you should 'offer it up'. But I have no doubt that confrontation with injustice should take place. The way to do that was to make people accountable. Whether it was the IRA, the British army or the British government, the thing to do was to make them accountable.

One of the things we organised in the early 1970s was the 'People's Assembly'. It had various committees, including an economic committee. Even after the Assembly fell into disuse other issues were taken on, like the housing problem. You had the setting-up of the Ardoyne Housing Association, for example. A lot of that then became part and parcel of the Flax Trust which was set up in 1976. The aim of the Trust was to promote reconciliation through economic development and enrichment through respect for difference. It saw unemployment or bad housing not just as consequences of violence but as root causes. There was a consciousness that if you developed the community in social and economic terms then that could break down isolation and create dignity. So over the next few years we sought to make the British government accountable by setting up Flax Trust America and using the influence of the US lobby. We got the housing issue addressed, developed a shopping centre and set up employment and training schemes. The big battles to develop those sorts of things happened here and we had to fight tooth and nail. I am fully convinced that the government did not have a conscious strategy toward community development. They absolutely took it for granted that any money coming into a project in this area would end up in IRA hands so the government were very unwilling to engage. (Fr. Myles Kavanagh, Ardoyne Priest and Chairperson of the Flax Trust)

However, community development issues could not be divorced from the wider political environment. Often rancorous divisions within the district opened up as a result. On the one hand local republicans felt they were deliberately excluded from many community groups and forums. They also increasingly viewed the channelling of public funding through such organisations as part of a British state 'pacification' strategy. On the other hand, non-republican and (in the main) church-led bodies were suspicious of republican intent. They were similarly opposed to much republican activity and argued (as Fr. Myles' view well illustrates) that much needed resources should be welcomed rather than be treated as a conduit of counter-insurgency. The depth of anger generated in these disagreements was shaped by the 'battle for hearts and minds' between 'chapel' and 'cumann' within the community. It was also testament to the tension that the heavily militarised condition of Ardoyne brought in its wake and the effect that the containment strategy had. Gerard McGuigan became the first Sinn Féin city councillor for the area during the mid-1980s. He argues that the counter-insurgency context is central to understanding the debate over community development.

Roy Mason came seeking a military victory. He had no conception of a political solution. Mason let loose the dogs of war. It was all morale sapping. I don't think anyone could think about anything else. There were no old slogans about a quick victory, 'Victory in '72, Victory in '73', that all went out the window. Everybody realised this was going to be a long, hard, brutal slog. Part of that was the terror that took place in Castlereagh. That was designed to induce people to say whatever it was they wanted them to say. But Mason's Ulsterisation policy came in many guises. They had a pacification programme as well, building leisure centres and the like. The church became part of that policy and that led to a very poor relationship between church and people. I think that sections of the church started to realise that they were out of touch and moved to fill the gap. In doing that they became a focal point for manipulation by the Brits, certainly by the 1980s. The Brits decided to isolate this community and starve it of resources. But when they had to provide resources they decided to do it through channels they chose. That was through certain senior Catholics. The Catholic church always worked with handpicked committees and selected people who they thought would best serve the interests of the church. That became more and more evident as the '70s went into the '80s and they started talking about community development. But I think they overstretched themselves. They were quite proud of the fact that they had every senior British Tory minister into their places at a time when people were on protest in the Blocks. That may have been acceptable to the 'parish' but not to the broader community. People saw it as giving succour to the those who were oppressing this community. I don't think they [church people] were evil in doing it, just wrong. But it left a very sour taste that never really went away. It was because that was happening when so much else was going on. (Gerard McGuigan, Ardoyne resident and ex-city councillor)

By 1977 the criminal justice system had been turned into a 'conveyor belt'. Arrest for 'scheduled offences' was followed by interrogation in one of the newly established (and euphemistically named) 'holding centres', such as Castlereagh. Allegations soon emerged of severe brutality being practiced in these interrogation centres. These allegations were confirmed by a report published by Amnesty International in 1978. The purpose of the centres was to elicit a confession in order to secure a conviction in the non-jury Diplock courts. A study carried out in 1979 found that over 90 per cent of those who appeared before a Diplock Court were found guilty. More than 80 per cent were convicted on the strength of (usually uncorroborated) confessions. From 1975 onward large numbers of young men and women from Ardoyne found themselves going through this process. At any one time there were between 50 and 100 political prisoners from the district in gaol. Up until 1976 gaol meant the 'cages' of Long Kesh and the relative benefits of Special Category Status. When he was first imprisoned Bik McFarlane (a leading Ardoyne republican) was sent to the cages, although he was transferred to the H-Blocks after an attempted escape in 1978. Bik's testimony gives a sense of what life in the 'cages' was like. It was an experience he shared with scores (if not hundreds) of people from Ardoyne of his generation.

I was originally imprisoned in the Cages in Long Kesh in 1976 before the ending of special category status. We had almost complete control over our daily activities in the Cages and it was a critical learning experience for me. I was in Cage 11 with Gerry Adams and others and I learnt more about politics in six months than I had in my whole life up till then. I was working with Adams when he was producing pamphlets. It meant I had to read about socialism, capitalism, foreign struggles, the nature of British strategy, past and present, everything. It was as if somebody just opened my head up and shovelled masses of vital information in. I had an extraordinary political education through that process. Cage 11 was a hotbed of education and analysis. A lot of us were studying things like Kitson's *Low Intensity Operations* which had been smuggled into the Cages. That helped us develop our understanding of what was taking shape and it was increasingly clear that this was going to be a very long-term struggle. That was becoming even clearer as the Brits introduced 'criminalisation' and began constructing the H-Blocks. The 'conveyor belt system' they put in place was designed to undermine the whole struggle by breaking the prisoners. That was the Brits' intent. They started rounding up huge numbers of people and holding them on remand. There were dozens and dozens of people from Ardoyne who came in at that time and who ended up on the blanket protest. Most of them were very young, usually between 16-20 years old. A lot of them were given massive sentences. Many of them ended up spending the formative years of their lives in gaol. I think the impact of that has still not been fully seen. I had tried to escape from the Cages a number of times. When me and others did so again in April 1978 we were transferred to the Blocks. That was how I ended up on the blanket. There were a lot of other fellas from Ardoyne on the protest. We tended to be quite popular with the other prisoners because they thought we were all off our heads! There were a number of Ardoyne men who played important roles during the blanket protest, the hunger strikes and afterward. (Bik McFarlane, Ardoyne republican and OC in the H-Blocks during the1981 Hunger Strike)

By late 1976 those from Ardoyne being convicted found themselves thrust into the maelstrom of the H-Blocks with ever heavier sentences. Following the example of Ciaran Nugent many also joined the growing protest against the attempt to 'criminalise' what they had done. The stage was being set for one of the most pivotal events of the long war, the republican Hunger Strike of 1981. Gerard McGuigan again helps provide an insight into the impact these British counter-insurgency policies were having outside the prisons.

The significance of the removal of political status did not sink in for the broader community for several years. However, it was a giant nightmare for the families involved. The average age of the young men and women getting lifted was about 18 or 19, then they were getting sentenced to 12 or 15 years. You can imagine how that was for the parents. It was parents who put together the Relatives Action Committee that led the Anti-H-Block campaign. With the ones on the blanket, isolation was a problem as well because they were not allowed visits. It was like a member of your family disappeared off the earth, the anxiety for parents must have been terrible. It was a very, very bleak period. But they [the state] had no idea what was going on. It is a tired old slogan but repression does breed resistance and people did resist. It affected people who had not been part of the struggle. Because of the brutal treatment being dished out to their loved ones, a family became politicised. The Relatives Action Committees began to grow and grow. It was very much the families of the people who were in the Blocks who got things going with marches and pickets. I remember that Larry Kennedy was very affected by it. Larry contested and won a council seat as an Anti-H-Block candidate. But just as important were all the other wee things that he was doing then. There were lots of things done to build up a support base around the prisoners' issue, for example, they built a mock cell outside the Shamrock [social club] and had a seven day fast to try to build support. Larry was the man behind that. The issue just started to draw people in. There wasn't really a tightly organised formal group, it was more that people began to get involved through the Shamrock and the other clubs in the area. (Gerard McGuigan, Ardoyne resident and ex-city councillor)

An infrastructure of advice and support on prison issues had first been set up for the relatives of prisoners and internees in the early 1970s. It was still very active and continued to offer vital practical help to people often encountering courts and prisons for the first time. Initially, however, the momentous nature of the struggle taking shape within the prisons was far from clear. The conditions being endured by the (usually very young) protesting prisoners only slowly came to light. But for the young men and women charged after the cut-off date for 'Special Category Status' the impact was immediate. One of the first IRA political prisoners to be convicted at this time was 17-year-old Paddy McGrandles. Paddy describes what happened to him after his arrest.

I was moved to the H-Blocks from Crumlin Road gaol in September 1976 when I was still on remand. The verbal and physical abuse I had received in Crumlin Road continued in H2. There was a lot of talk amongst the remands about Ciaran Nugent and the blanket protest. We never saw Ciaran though. He was being held in isolation over in H1. I knew that my turn to make my mind up about whether or not to join the protest was not far away. I was sentenced in December and received seven years for hijacking a car that was used in an attack on a screw. My co-defendant, 15-year-old Perry McLarnon, and I were assaulted as soon as we reached the tunnel that ran under the Crumlin Road from the courthouse to the gaol. The assaults continued as we were brought in through the reception area to the cells where we were once again separated.

The next day after dark I was moved to the H-Blocks. I was handed a prison uniform and brought to H1. I was stripped of my own clothes, battered and thrown into a cell naked. For the next few weeks I was the only blanket protestor on the wing. The screws kept up the abuse, threats and insults. I had late night searches accompanied by beatings. One screw seemed to take particular delight in beating me at every opportunity he could. The worst thing, though, was that three times a day the screws would open the door and I'd have to walk to the canteen naked. There were ordinary prisoners on the wing, dressed in prison uniforms. Sometimes there would be members of the Board of Visitors, including women. I would have to line up in the canteen to get my food and all the time I was subject to a stream of verbal abuse. It was really degrading and I grew to hate those short trips out of the cell. I was feeling really down around Christmas and to be honest I prayed for the strength to stay on the blanket. I had no visitors or contact with my family at all. I felt like I was totally alone. I didn't know how I was going to cope but hoped that I could make it through. At Christmas I was offered an hour's exercise in the yard. It was snowing and I walked out naked. The screws thought I was mad, I probably was. I was walking around freezing but enjoying the feel of the snow beneath my feet. I also felt like I was sending a message to the screws that they would not break me. Bobby Sands had told me on remand that we needed a structure in the Blocks but it was almost impossible in the early days of the protest because we were so scattered. Séanna Breathnach came into the Blocks in 1977 and started organising us. He had been in the Cages and knew the system. We began to take visits with our families and 11 months after I had started my protest I saw my family for the first time. On those visits I told my family that I was OK. I told them nothing about the brutality of life on the blanket. I knew it was really hard for my mother and father as they could see how badly we all looked but I didn't want to worry them anymore than they were already. (Paddy McGrandles, Ardoyne resident and blanketman)

Paddy McGrandles became one of the first 'blanketmen' and the first man from Ardoyne to join the protest. He would spend the entire five years of his sentence 'on the blanket'. Criminalisation was designed to undermine the will to struggle both within and outside of the prison walls. However, there was a growing realisation of what was at stake. Even more importantly there was an awareness of what the loved ones of prisoners were having to go through. Again, criminalisation would have the opposite effect to what was intended. Criminalisation and the blanket protest engendered politicisation rather than diminishing it. The local branch of the Relatives Action Committees became the focus for a popular political campaign not seen since the start of the conflict. Paddy McGrandle's mother May was one of those active in the Relatives Action Committee. She describes her family's experiences and the role the Relatives Action Committee played.

My husband Paddy had just got out of Long Kesh after doing two years and my 15-year-old boy Billy had just been cleared of a murder charge when my younger son Paddy was imprisoned. They were very hard and difficult times. Paddy was the second or third person to go on the blanket protest and the first fella from Ardoyne to do so. He was only 17 at the time and the screws really tried to make an example of him. He got it hard from the minute he was taken to the barracks in Queen Street. While he was there they stripped him naked and humiliated and insulted him in front of a group of women. Then when he was on remand in the Crumlin Road gaol he got a lot of terrible beatings. On one occasion the screws came down at four in the morning and took Paddy out. They hung a rope with a noose from pipes on the ceiling and placed it around Paddy's neck. Then they kept threatening to hang him. Paddy just got whatever was going: spitting, kickings, beatings. He would try to tell us that everything was ok when we visited him but I could see that wasn't true. A mother knows her own.

After he was sent to the Blocks and joined the blanket protest we were not allowed to see Paddy for over a year. Paddy was sentenced in December 1976. As far as the treatment he got it was the same story as before. The screws targeted the younger ones to try and break the blanket protest; Paddy was beaten all the time. He has never been able to talk to us about it all; I know what happened to him from other blanketmen. They all had it hard but the screws never let up on Paddy. They really tried to break him with the beatings. But they didn't break him. Paddy did tell me about one screw who always gave him a hammering. After months of these beatings there was a day when this screw took him down to the punishment cell. Paddy was lying on the concrete bench that jutted out of the wall. He had just a towel around him but he had his hands behind his head and was singing away to himself. This screw sat down on the end of the bench and started crying and asking Paddy to stop the protest. Instead of breaking Paddy, he broke them. He was determined never to come off the blanket protest and the beatings only made him more determined. Paddy came out in 1982 and was on the blanket throughout.

If it had not been for Relatives Action Committee I don't know how I would have made it through that whole period. The Committee gave me somewhere to go where I could talk to people who understood what was going on and who would really listen to me. It was also very important in mobilising people behind the prison struggle, particularly as it became more and more clear what was going on inside the Blocks. The campaign really began to build up from around 1979 onward. There was about 25 or 30 people in Ardoyne who were very active in the Relatives Action Committee. It was all women really, women were not only the backbone of it, they basically were the Committee. It was mainly women who had a husband, son, daughter, brother or sister inside. We were involved in all manner of protests and fundraising activities. We organised collections in the clubs and we held a regular 'mothers' night'. For those we used to make sandwiches for people coming in, even though there were times when we could barely feed our own children. It was all done to boost the funds of the Action Committee. We had a small shop too in Brompton Park. A fella from Kilburn in London used to send containers of clothes over for prisoners' families. Whatever was left over we used to sell to raise money for campaign work. I was also involved in campaign tours to Britain and Europe. A load of us from Ardoyne, the Falls, Turf Lodge and elsewhere went over to London. We held pickets and some of the women chained themselves to railings in Downing Street. There was also a tour to different parts of Europe to raise awareness about the prison issue organised by women from Derry. I went on that too and it was a fantastic experience. I was really surprised that there were so many people in all those countries who were ready to stand up for us. It really opened my eyes. (May McGrandles, Ardoyne resident and mother of blanketman Paddy McGrandles)

The H-Block issue developed as the conflict outside went on. Lives in Ardoyne continued to be lost. John Lee from Mountainview Gardens had served a total of 15 years in the British Parachute Regiment. He left the British army in 1975 and had only recently returned to the district. Republicans in the area regarded him with a great deal of suspicion because of this life history. On 27 February 1977 John Lee was shot dead by the IRA. On 17 March Danny Carville from Jamaica Street was driving down Cambrai Street with his young son. They were going to visit friends. Loyalist gunmen shot him four times as Danny shielded his son from their fire. One of those later convicted for killing Danny was the loyalist Kenny McClinton. McClinton later became a community worker, pastor and close friend and confidante of LVF leader Billy 'King Rat' Wright. Exactly one month later, on 17 April, Volunteer Trevor McKibbin from Etna Drive was shot dead by British soldiers. Three days later the UVF exploded a car bomb as mourners at his funeral waited in Etna Drive for the cortege to depart. It was the first and only time any funeral was bombed during the three decades of conflict. It could easily have left dozens of people dead. As it was the blast killed two of the mourners, 19-year-old Sean Campbell from the Bone and 18-year-old Sean McBride from Flax Street. Eleven years later Sean's brother Paul would also be killed when UVF gunmen shot indiscriminately into the Avenue Bar in Union Street [Paul McBride, killed by the UVF in Avenue Bar, 15 May 1988]. Sean McBride's brother Henry, was standing close to him when the bomb in Etna Drive exploded. Henry describes the indiscriminate carnage he witnessed.

> I will never forget the scenes I saw that day. If anybody had told me beforehand that such a thing could happen I would have said they were disturbed. I saw a programme a short while ago about the bomb in Omagh [August 1998] and it was like re-living the whole thing that happened in Etna Drive. The way it was described and what I watched, the gusts of smoke, for a moment I was back in Etna Drive. I remember I was standing about 12 feet away from my brother Sean when the bomb went off. I was pushed back into a hedge by the blast. As I was falling backwards I remember seeing Leonard Stewart as he was blown toward me. It was the force of him being thrown into the air that blew me into the hedge. Leonard died about a year later from cancer but he was hurt that day and that had a lot to do with his death. As I was falling backwards I remember looking up to the sky and watching as scalding pieces of metal were flying around me. Red roaring hot metal was being thrown up and falling down everywhere. I woke up in Sean McGeough's mother's house and at first I thought my leg had been blown off. I was just lying there and looked over to see a blanket being placed over my brother Sean. I thought I saw his hand move and said, 'He is not dead; his hand is moving'. My other brother Seamus then took his hand. I can't remember anything after that. (Henry McBride, Ardoyne resident and brother of Ardoyne victim Sean McBride)

If death from loyalist attacks went on so too did those inflicted by the British army. The decision to 'officially' introduce the SAS into the North had been taken two years before. It formed part of the murkier, dark and 'dirty war' aspect of the 'normalisation' policy. The sight of swathes of battle-dressed British troops invading communities and killing large numbers of civilians had created a great deal of international political embarrassment for the British government. The introduction of 'police primacy' had been the result. However, that went hand-in-hand with a fiercer prosecution of the state's counter-insurgency campaign. It was to be largely fought in the shadows beyond the light of legality. Groups like the SAS were increasingly involved in a 'shoot-to-kill' policy. In the early hours of 21 June 1978 an IRA active service unit were planting a bomb at a telecommunications pylon in Ballysillan. They were ambushed by an SAS unit accompanied by members of the RUC. The SAS unit had been lying in wait at this spot for several days. Three IRA volunteers were shot dead. They were Jackie Mailey and Dinny Brown from Ardoyne and Jim Mulvenna from the Bone. All three were unarmed and trying to surrender when they were killed. They were also shot repeatedly, even when on the ground and with their hands in clear view. This was a 'shoot-to-kill' policy in action.

These were also years when feuds between the 'Officials' and the IRA could also break out with little or no warning. Ardoyne-born Trevor McNulty was a member of the 'Officials' and a leading figure in their republican clubs. In the early hours of the morning of 27 July 1977 Trevor was shot dead by the IRA at flats in the New Lodge Road. He was one of four people killed in a five-hour period. The local IRA itself suffered two further casualties in early 1979. On the morning of 5 January Frankie Donnelly and Lawrence Montgomery were on active service, loading explosives into a car in Northwick Drive. The device exploded prematurely, killing them both.

Loyalist violence diminished in most parts of the North in the late 1970s. Many members of the Shankill Butchers were behind bars by the end of the decade. However, the threat from that quarter still remained as far as Ardoyne was concerned. On 4 January 1980, Alex Reid from Jamaica Street was returning with a friend from an evening in the city centre in a black cab. The taxi stopped outside a loyalist bar on the Shankill Road. The driver went inside and re-emerged a few moments later with a mob. Whilst Alex's companion was able to make his escape Alex was not so lucky. In these horrific circumstances he was beaten to death with a breeze block. On 27 March 1981 26-year-old Paul Blake from Jamaica Street was walking along the Berwick Road when a car stopped beside him and the occupants asked for directions. They were members of the UFF. One of them then shot Paul from inside the car. Paul was shot again as he lay on the ground. Jim Craig, leader of the UDA in the Shankill Road, later gave one of these gunmen £2, and another £5 for their part in the murder.

As the deaths of Jackie Mailey, Dinny Brown and Jim Mulvenna had shown, the character of the conflict between the British state and the IRA was changing. Britain was becoming more selective in its use of violence and employed their intelligence networks in covert operations far more regularly than operations involving mass troop numbers. One consequence was a fall in the number of civilians killed by 'ordinary' British state security forces as compared to the early 1970s. However, militarisation was far from diminished and a large British army and RUC presence continued to be the norm in Ardoyne. This brought with it the potential of gun battles and (as a consequence) of further civilian casualties in the area. Such was the case on the night of 17 August 1980. On that evening Colette Meek was standing with a group of neighbours outside her home in Alliance Avenue. A unit of the IRA killed Colette when they opened fire on an RUC landrover and a bullet ricocheted and struck her. Nor did the shooting dead of unarmed civilians by the British army become a thing of the past. On the evening of 9 July 1981 15-year-old Danny Barrett was sitting on the front wall of the garden of his home in Havana Court. A British soldier opened fire from an observation post in Flax Street and shot Danny dead. In order to defuse any possible political fallout from Danny's death the British army spread disinformation suggesting that he had been armed. He was not.

Young Danny Barrett was killed when the 1981 Hunger Strike was at its height. By then the prison struggle had become the central focus of events in the North. This is not what any of the main parties to the conflict had intended. In the late 1970s the IRA had shifted to a 'cell system' and 'long war' strategy as more and more of its volunteers were either killed or imprisoned. At the same time a new generation of leaders within the republican movement was emerging. Calls for a more conscious political struggle to win 'hearts and minds' were increasingly heard from this quarter. However, events within the prisons themselves dictated actions to the republican movement rather than the other way round. That the prisons became so important was in part because it was a battleground chosen by the British state. In 1979 a Conservative government was elected under the leadership of Margaret Thatcher. Her close adviser and shadow Northern Ireland minister Airey Neave had promised an intensification of the containment strategy when they came to office. It was not a policy Neave himself was able to put into action. In mid-March 1979 Neave was blown up in a car bomb by the INLA. His approach was, however, to be wholeheartedly endorsed by Thatcher herself.

It was within this context (and after years of the blanket and 'no-wash' protests) that things came to a head within the H-Blocks in 1980 and 1981. Despite opposition from the republican leadership outside the prison, the blanketmen decided to embark upon a mass hunger strike in late 1980. Indeed, Ardoyne republican Martin Meehan had only recently conducted a hunger strike of his own in protest against his conviction on the evidence of a paid informer. His fast had lasted 66 days. Then on 26 October 7 blanketmen began a hunger strike in pursuit of political status. By 18 December a number of the hunger strikers were reaching a critical condition. Then a deal appeared to have been struck with the British administration. To all intents it appeared to grant the 'five demands' being asked for by the protesting prisoners.

However, the British authorities soon reneged upon the deal. Preparations began for a second hunger strike. This time it was to be led by the Officer Commanding (OC) within the Blocks, Bobby Sands. On 1 March 1981 Bobby Sands began his fast. He would die on the 66th day of his protest. Before that, however, he had been elected by more than 30,000 people as the MP for Fermanagh and South Tyrone on 9 April. His funeral was attended by over 100,000. It was the largest single demonstration by northern nationalists in history. It was also the most public rejection imaginable of the attempt to depoliticise the conflict, the British state's key objective for criminalisation. Over the summer and into the autumn of 1981 nine more Republican prisoners would die in the struggle for political status. Bik McFarlane was closer than almost anyone to the events of the hunger strike.

[…] Throughout the whole period there was also a sense of how important this struggle was and that, no matter what happened, we were not going to be defeated. That was an intense feeling that everyone had too. It is almost impossible to describe how it felt when Bobby got elected. To see people mobilised and galvanised in that way was incredible. To have 30,000 people voting for him smashed through the barrier of criminalisation. 30,000 people don't support a criminal. 100,000 people don't go to the funeral of a gangster. The whole world does not send messages of support to a non-political person. Losing Bobby was a terrible loss for all of us but the effect it had, politically and historically, was extraordinary. When we brought the hunger strike to an end I was actually with the remaining hunger strikers in the hospital. There was an intense sense of relief; you could almost touch it. There was also an intense sense of anger that we had lost ten close friends and comrades. But there was a determination that the battle the hunger strike had begun would never fade away. There was an absolute determination as people came off the protest that the struggle went on, that control was never going to be yielded to the administration. Building the next stage of the struggle for the five demands began the day the doors of the cells opened. The mass escape of 1983 and developing educational and other programmes through the following years were all part of the same struggle that the hunger strike set in motion. We simply were never going to accept defeat. (Bik McFarlane, Ardoyne republican and OC in the H-Blocks during the1981 Hunger Strike)

In Ardoyne, as in other nationalist working class areas of the North, the hunger strike period would prove to be one of the most traumatic, exhausting and politicising events of the conflict. Dozens of young men from the district had been (or still were) on the blanket. Many women from the area were also on protest in Armagh. That helped galvanise a local campaign of support that was in full flow by the start of the hunger strikes. A loose group of prisoners' relatives and others (often working through the area's social clubs) held numerous events to raise both awareness and finance for the campaign. People organised all sorts of demonstrations. They blocked roads, formed pickets and were involved in all manner of protests. It was the greatest popular mobilisation of nationalist opinion since the early 1970s.

Women were very much to the fore in these actions, many the wives and mothers of blanketmen and protesting women prisoners. Working class women (like Ardoyne's May McGrandles) who had no previous political involvement became the driving force behind the Relatives Action Committees. Suddenly they found themselves doing press conferences, going on public platforms and undertaking speaking tours through Europe and the US. May McGrandles explains the impact the hunger strikes had upon those relatives campaigning outside the prison walls.

Everything came to a head with the hunger strikes in 1980 and 1981. Outside the prison there was a lot of mixed emotions about the hunger strike but I think those boys took it all on themselves because they knew something had to be done. It was all really terrifying too because as each of the hunger strikers died you knew someone had to take his place and you did not know who it would be. If our Paddy had gone on hunger strike I don't think I could have taken him off it because I know that is not what he would have wanted. But I also know that deep in my heart I would have wanted to stop it. It was all so frightening. It was bad enough when they were on the blanket but once the hunger strike began it was absolutely terrifying. But what the hunger strikers did was the ultimate, the most extraordinary thing anyone can do. As the saying goes, there is nothing greater than to lay down your life for your friends. That is what they did. There was a lot of relief but a lot of disappointment too when the hunger strike was over. Some people condemned those mothers who took their sons off the strike. But I would never do that because in the end you have to do what your conscience tells you. It is hard to watch your son die. There was a lot of doom and gloom at the end of it all. But we survived, that's the main thing. I would never want to have to go through it all again. (May McGrandles, Ardoyne resident, mother of a Blanketman and leading member of the Relatives Action Committee)

In May 1981 the district council elections were looming. Larry Kennedy decided to stand in Ardoyne for the Belfast city council as an Anti-H-Block and community worker candidate. Larry's campaign provided an additional focal point for the activities of the local Relatives Action Committee. Always an 'ideas man' as well as a 'doer', Larry 'the Brain' was himself a mainstay of the popular agitation that characterised the campaign. In what was a watershed event Larry Kennedy won the election. He therefore took his fight for both prisoners and the Ardoyne community into the unwelcoming territory of Belfast city hall.

As the long summer drew on and one by one the hunger strikers died, the impact was devastating. The investment of emotional as well as practical commitment that people gave to the campaign was great. The apparent failure to achieve the five demands by the autumn was grievously and personally felt by many. Support for the hunger strike could also have fatal consequences for those outside the prison walls. On the night of 15/16 May (exactly one week after the death of Bobby Sands) Patrick Martin arrived home in the early hours of the morning. He had just finished working a shift at the Star Social Club. UFF gunmen cut the telephone wires to the home and then came inside. They shot Patrick six times as he lay in his bed. His killers claimed that Patrick was targeted because he had been at the funeral of the MP for Fermanagh and South Tyrone. Newspapers initially reported that the IRA had shot Patrick, it was suggested he had been killed for not closing his shop as a mark of respect when the second hunger striker Francis Hughes had died on 15 May. In fact, Patrick had closed his premises that day. As has been mentioned, young Danny Barrett was killed on 9 July by the British army. Danny's death also came amidst the charged atmosphere of the hunger strike period.

On 3 October the remaining hunger strikers called off the protest. While the five demands were more or less granted in the months to come there was initially a sense of defeat. Many people both within and outside the prison walls were deeply demoralised. Such a feeling was accentuated locally with the killing of Larry Kennedy only five days after the end of the hunger strike for which he had been such a vigorous campaigner. On the evening of Thursday 8 October Larry briefly dropped into the Shamrock social club. Fearing sectarian attack, youngsters from Ardoyne could not use the leisure centre in Ballysillan. As a result they had to be bussed up to Andersonstown in the west of the city if they wanted to go swimming. Larry organised the bus. On that night he was in checking to make sure that everything was in place for the regular Friday night trip. As Larry left the club UFF gunmen shot him dead. They then entered the bar and opened fire at the people inside. Three days later there was a massive turnout for Larry's funeral. Bobby Ewing was sitting watching television coverage of the funeral in his home in the Deerpark Road. As he did so members of the UFF burst into his living room and shot him dead.

Coming in the wake of the hunger strike such events cast a pall of unease, insecurity and despondency within the district. This gloom was to be further deepened in the coming months and years when the area was hit by the Christopher Black supergrass trial. This signalled a new turn in British policy. Supergrasses were essentially informers who gave evidence against others on behalf of the state. Britain had long used informers as part of its counter-insurgency campaign. There were a number of reasons for this. Most obviously, informers provided the British state with much-needed information. This then allowed them to conduct covert operations, make arrests, gain convictions or (as was increasingly the case) to carry out a shoot-to-kill policy. However, informers also undermined trust and solidarity within an area. This was particularly important in a close-knit community like Ardoyne. It formed a key part of the psychological battle that was such an important dimension of the conflict. Indeed, the issue of informers had already had a direct impact on the district in this period. On 20 January 1981 Maurice Gilvary from Butler Street was found dead on a border road in South Armagh. He had been shot as an informer by the IRA, of which he had been a member. Then on 27 September 1981 the body of Anthony Braniff from Jamaica Street was found in an entry in West Belfast. He too had been shot by the IRA as an alleged informer, although the circumstances in the two cases were completely different. His family strenuously denied the allegations made against Anthony both at the time and up to the present day.

Supergrass trials were also not entirely new. There had been at least four of them during the 1970s. One of these involved Billy Bates from Ardoyne whose evidence led to the imprisonment of six people. However, the supergrass strategy as it emerged in the early 1980s was a new departure. It formed a cornerstone of a coherent counter-insurgency approach. The aim was to mould the criminal justice system to fit the purposes of the British state. That purpose was to destroy the cohesion not only of various organisations but also the communities from which they came. The result was a series of trials that took place in a two-year period from November 1981 onward. In all there were a total of 25 supergrasses. Their evidence produced ten trials with charges being laid against some 600 people.

The supergrass era was signalled by the Christopher Black trial. Black was from Ardoyne. He had previously served a prison sentence as a member of the IRA. On 21 November 1981 he was arrested after taking part in an IRA road block. Three days later he was granted immunity because he agreed to give evidence for the British state. The trial of those he accused ran from December 1982 until August 1983. A total of 38 people (from Ardoyne, the Bone and the New Lodge) were charged and held on remand throughout that period. All but three were eventually found guilty. Roisin Loughlin's husband Gerald was one of them. Before Gerald was arrested what was uppermost in Roisin's mind was the second child the couple were expecting. Roisin had lost a baby during pregnancy less than a year before so she feared the prospect of a worrying time ahead. She had no idea how difficult things were to become.

My husband Gerald was getting our three year old girl ready for nursery school when we heard jeeps and saracens pulling up outside. The house was raided and Gerald was taken to Castlereagh for 7 days. The headlines in the paper that night said that 30 or so men from West and North Belfast were being charged on the word of a supergrass, or paid perjurer as I would call him. He was called Christopher Black; I had never even heard of him. When the evidence started to come out it became clear just how unjust and unbelievable it all was. A few of us relatives, almost all women, got together and decided we had to start doing something. We started to have a few meetings; most of them happened in my house because I had just given birth to a baby boy born with pneumonia. But it was difficult to get people mobilised. This was just after the hunger strike and even though people were angry they were just exhausted. Initially we did not do much because the evidence was so ludicrous we were being assured the men would not be sentenced. My husband's case was a prime example. Black got his name and address wrong and on some of the dates when he was supposed to be committing offences he was charged with he was actually out of the country on holiday. But then Black changed his evidence on advice from the RUC.

The courtroom was very intimidating. Before you went in you were searched and had to give your name to the RUC. Then you were searched again. There were 38 defendants and they were all sat along one side of the courtroom with screws lined up behind them. There were dozens of screws and a number of armed RUC. The relatives were all up in the gallery so the room was very packed. I gave evidence. I took my deceased granny's rosary beads with me and when the prosecution lawyer started asking me questions I just held on to them, stared into his eyes and tried to blot everyone else out. It was very scary but I had the strength to do it because I knew I was not telling any lies. But the men were all convicted and my husband got a life sentence. The evidence was just not there but it was a political decision and that really frightened me too. It was only really then that it all hit me. People were shocked, some despaired and I was absolutely devastated. I had two young children, one of whom was ill in hospital a lot of the time and I knew that I was going to be without the husband I loved for years for things he did not do. That was when about eight of us decided to keep going with the campaign. Even if we were up against a brick wall we were going to keep banging our heads against it. I was very lucky in that my husband's barrister, Eilish Kelly, was brilliant. She had leaflets printed up and arranged for civil liberties lawyers from England, America and elsewhere to come over. We held a big meeting in the Felons Club to highlight the case. We also used to hold a weekly picket outside Crumlin Road courthouse with a banner saying 'Stop the Show Trials'. We held protests in Dublin and other places. After about a year there was an appeal and that lasted for another eight months. At the time I really hated Christopher Black for doing what he did but now I don't feel any animosity for him. In the long run he was as much a victim as those he accused. At the end of the day it was the British government that was responsible for it all. (Roisin Loughlin, member of the Anti-Show Trials Campaign)

Throughout the trial the 38 defendants sat in rows around three sides of the courtroom guarded by over a dozen RUC and prison officers, many of them heavily armed. The majority of the 45 separate incidents involved took place during the period of the hunger strike. Only in one instance did it relate to activity that had led to someone being killed. The vast majority of the accused were charged with relatively few and minor offences. The purpose was, in other words, to effect a climate of suspicion and instil a fear of aiding republican activists in anyway. For the first time, for example, people were charged who had merely had republicans sitting in their homes. It was precisely to attack the idea that 'every door was open' in Ardoyne that such action was aimed. Certainly the Christopher Black affair had a massive effect on the district, even though almost all the accused were released on appeal by 1986. To have so many people from such a small area imprisoned in one fell swoop created difficulties enough. However, it was by engendering a suspicion of neighbours, friends and comrades that the impact of Christopher Black was most devastatingly felt. In a wider sense, that was the real social and psychological cost of the 'containment' years.

> *Jackie was born and reared in Ardoyne.*
> *The only reason he joined the British army was because he*
> *had a wife and children and responsibilities.*
> *Jackie was not a diehard soldier; he just saw his role in the*
> *British army as economics.*

John Lee
Killed by the IRA,
Balholm Drive,
27 February 1977

John Lee's mother was Mary Megahey, originally from Parkview Street in the Bone. His father, Thomas Francis Lee, was from Brookfield Street, Ardoyne. In the early 1930s the couple were married in Holy Cross chapel. For the first few years of married life they lived in Butler Street, in a room in 'Frank the Barber's' house. Like many men of this time Mr Lee went to find work in England. After living in Birmingham for a number of years the couple returned home and moved into 40 Chatham Street. They had thirteen children but only seven survived: Tom, Joe, Jackie, Eileen, Mary, Jean and Margaret. The third child was John, better known as Jackie. When Jackie left St Gabriel's school he worked as a messenger in McCaufield's butchers on the Crumlin Road. He married Mary Wade from lower Chatham Street and they had three boys: Patrick, Joe and Jim. Jackie was a member of the Ardoyne Cycling Club and in his spare time was a keen fisherman. He joined the British army in the 1960s and served in the Parachute Regiment. On 27 February 1977, while walking home with his wife from the Star social club, the IRA killed Jackie Lee.

Jean Martin (sister)

We were brought up to work; you didn't laze about. My daddy actually packed my older brother off to England to an uncle because there was no work for him here. Two of my brothers went to England to work and they settled there. That's the way it was. My great, great-grandfather, originally from the south of Ireland, had been in the British army. My uncle still has the bright red uniform. My daddy's brother was in the RAF and my mammy's uncle also served in the British army during the First World War. But my daddy's uncle was taken out of his house by the Black and Tans, brought up to where the Mercy Primary school is now, was tied to a tree and killed.

Leading up to the 1969 situation Jackie was still in the British army. The night that Constable Arbuckle was killed on the Shankill Road, October 1969, there were riots. Jackie's regiment was put on 24-hour stand-by and eventually flown to Belfast. He belonged to the first battalion parachute regiment. Once the trouble stopped on the Shankill they were pulled out. That was the only time he served in the north. Jackie left the army a year or two later. They bought a house in Holmdene Gardens and Jackie worked for the Post Office. But because of the trouble he didn't want the kids being affected and he went back to the army a year later. He did not go back into the first battalion; he went back to a brigade in the parachute regiment, which meant he would not, or could not, be sent here to serve. That is the only way he would go back because he didn't want to serve here. They lived in an RAF base in Abingdon; he worked in the stores.

Jackie left the army after he finished his reserve time in Abingdon and came home here. That was the year before he died, which was 1976. Jackie had no fear about moving back into an area where he was born and reared. If he did fear anything he didn't let you know. Jackie was a confident person; he wouldn't have shown fear. He was in the Saunders club one Sunday having a drink and the IRA pulled him in, hooded him, and questioned him. Then they told him he was safe, that nothing would happen to him. That happened about nine months before he died. After they let him go he went back in to the Saunders to finish his pint. That was just the way Jackie was. If anything, the experience made him more determined; he wasn't doing anybody any harm. The only reason he joined the British army was because he didn't want to end up hanging about the corners because that was not the way we were brought up. Jackie had a wife, he had children and he had responsibilities. It was a good life; the money was good and you got married quarters. Jackie was not a diehard soldier; he just saw his role in the British army as economics.

Jackie would have liked to see a free Ireland but he didn't like the way they were trying to achieve it. If asked what his politics were, I would have said he was a socialist. He was very, very clever. I know he was asked to join the IRA after he left the army and he refused – not because of their beliefs but because of the way they were going about it. Jackie was more into politics.

The night Jackie was killed him and Mary had gone to the Star to celebrate their wedding anniversary. Jackie saw fellas looking at him and decided to go home. They were walking home and Jackie heard footsteps behind him. He told Mary to go on. He said, 'If they are going to get me they are not going to shoot me in the back' and he turned round and faced them; they killed him.

The IRA claimed responsibility for Jackie's death. They said he was a member of the SAS under cover. The truth for the family is he was an ex- British soldier who had come home, was living here for almost a year. As far as the family were concerned there was no truth whatsoever in the IRA statement. No one from the IRA ever approached the family to explain why. We never approached them because we didn't see why; we knew the truth. What good would it do going to them? Afterwards I felt bitter but that doesn't do any good because you are only hurting yourself. Whoever did it has it on their conscience and they will have to deal with it. They may have had their reasons and thought that their reasons were good enough for doing it. We know different and they will have to live with that.

After his death the family were shattered. My mother never ever got over it. My father-in-law had been murdered, Hugh Martin [killed by loyalists in East Belfast, 30 December 1972]. Paddy my husband had to identify his father; he had to identify Jackie as well. Jackie was fun -loving and brilliant company to be with. He had a brilliant sense of humour. He was a good father; he was very fair but strict with the boys. The year that I went to the Gaeltacht, he sent me the money to go. Only for him sending the money I wouldn't have been able to attend. He was that sort of big brother, always looking after you.

Joe Lee (son)

My father joined the British army in the 1960s. He left the army and came home in 1970. He was a postman for a short while but he got fed up with that and rejoined the British army for another couple of years. We moved to a place called Abingdon in Oxford, England. My father joined the army to see the world; a lot of people in Ardoyne at that stage joined the forces. There was no real trouble back then and people joined because there was no work. He was in the parachute regiment on both occasions. I think he rejoined just to get us out of here. At that time there was shooting every night. I think he thought, 'Get the kids out of here'. The second time my father didn't serve in the Six Counties; he did his time in a British army camp in England. He had no interest in politics, none at all. For him it was just a job.

When we came home in 1975 we lived in Bangor for a number of months. It felt like ten years... I went through a bad time in Bangor. He got a job with the DOE. We had to move out of Bangor because of intimidation, loyalists terrorised us. Me and my brother got beaten up regularly. We lived in an area that was mainly Protestant. They stoned us every day coming from school; we went to a mixed-religion school. Flute bands regularly came and played outside our house. I remember my mother pulling down the blinds; I was upstairs blasting rebel music and a full flute band was playing outside our back door. I was about thirteen years of age. I got so fed up getting beaten up that one day I pulled a tricolour out of my school bag and ran through the estate with half the school after me. We got badly beaten that day. My daddy wasn't too pleased. What we went through in Bangor was unbelievable. When we left Bangor in 1976 we moved to Mountainview Gardens. I don't think my father ever felt under threat when he returned home because he was born and reared in Chatham Street and he had family all over Belfast.

After my father's funeral the IRA released a public statement saying that they had killed Jackie Lee. People initially thought it was the UVF, a sectarian killing. It really had a devastating effect on me that people within my own community had killed him. I had to go to school with all my mates and the majority of them were supporters of the republican movement at the time. People that knew me treated me the same; I never got any harassment from anyone. My mates came to the funeral and were supportive of me. My mother was totally devastated and it will live with her until the day she dies. We don't really speak about it.

There is one issue that I have; it is the memorial in Brompton Park. It was erected for people from Ardoyne who were killed during the troubles. That is what it says. To be snubbed and left off the memorial is not a snub to him; it's a snub to his family. That's the way I see it. Another issue for me is when my daddy was taken out of the Saunders Club by the IRA and given assurances that he would be safe. When we moved to Mountainview I said to myself, 'Thank God we are home, we are safe, we are among our own'.

I would describe my father as a bit of a 'cool hand Luke', a practical joker. He didn't like to be told what to do. He definitely put his family first. We left Bangor because he didn't want to put his kids through torment. He was a loving father who was always full of surprises. To me his killing was wrong but I suppose with everybody there was a wrong; there have been three thousand or more.

Danny Carville
Killed by the UDA,
Cambrai Street,
17 March 1977

> *That memorial in Ardoyne was always special to Danny.*
> *When he got a few drinks in him he'd say,*
> *'Come on up and see my Cross'.*
> *It was a very special thing to the people of Ardoyne and he*
> *was that proud that he was the one that put it up. He loved it.*

Danny Carville's parents were Martha and Robert Carville. Martha came from the Bone, Robert was a Falls Road man. They were married in Ardoyne chapel on Christmas day 1940. They eventually set up home at 89 Jamaica Street in Ardoyne and had seven children; Robert, Danny, Jackie, Ann, Margaret, Brian and Mary. Danny was the second eldest, born on 10 September 1943. He lived almost his entire life in Jamaica Street. Danny went to the Sacred Heart school until he was 11 and then moved up to St Gabriel's. When he was 22 he married Sheila Gray and they had six children, four boys and two girls, although tragically one of the girls was to die at an early age. When Danny left St Gabriel's he got a job and eventually went to work on the cranes, where he worked until he was shot dead. A couple of weeks before Danny was killed he assisted in erecting the memorial which is presently situated at the corner of Brompton Park and the Berwick Road. Danny went down to Wilton's funeral parlour on the Crumlin Road and helped move a concrete Celtic cross up to Ardoyne. Ironically Danny Carville's name was the next name added to that list of dead on the Ardoyne memorial. Danny was killed by loyalists. Exactly why he was targeted is not clear. Perhaps his was just one of the many random sectarian killings of Ardoyne residents. Alternatively, he may have been deliberately selected because he was identified as one of the people seen collecting the Celtic cross outside Wilton's funeral parlour.

Gerry Hamill (friend)

Danny and myself knew each other from when we were children. He was born at 89 Jamaica Street and I was born at 105 Jamaica Street. We went around together all of our lives. When we were kids we would have played a lot of handball and knocked about in a wee gang. There was me and Danny, John Murphy, my brother Frankie (who is dead now) and wee Fart McAllister. We used to go camping up to Carrs Glen every Sunday. We brought bread and beans with us and we'd stay there all day! We hated school so we did an awful lot of mitching. We used to get crabs and put them upside down on the lines waiting for the trains to crush them. We used to do the same up at the top of the Oldpark Road and the Crumlin Road when the trams were running. Once we got into our teenage years we started drinking on a Friday night and then we would head up to Freddy Fusco's chippy. That is were the women were! We used to go to the Wheatfield. In the late 1960s we used to drink down in a bar called Ernie McLean's, down among the Protestants, everybody did it. There was a time when you could have gone anywhere. I even drank on the Shankill Road. But the oul' troubles put the stoppers on that. Danny was just a social drinker. We ran around together for years and never fell out. Danny was a real good kind of bloke. We had some good craic and good oul' times together. The rest of us would have been wilder than Danny because he was so easygoing. Danny was a quiet sort of bloke. He wouldn't have bothered anybody and I never remember Danny ever being involved in rows. Then Danny met his wife, Sheila Gray. She was from Colinward Street on the Springfield Road. Me and Danny met her and another girl called Margaret one night up in Freddy Fusco's. We just got talking to the two of them and then Danny started going out with Sheila. The next thing was they were married and they moved into a house over the Bone. Then he sold that house and bought a house down below his mother's house in Ardoyne. He was there until he was murdered. Danny had no interest in politics whatsoever. When he was killed he was a very easy target because he drove the same route down Cambrai Street with his son every day. His eldest son Frankie was only a kid at the time. The guy who shot Danny was going to shoot the wee lad as well. When Danny saw the gunman coming he threw himself across the wee lad. I found out what had happened to Danny when I was at home. I heard all this commotion and I ran out and I looked down the street. Danny's brother Brian was trying to pull the rifle off a peeler. The peelers had come up to tell the family what had happened to Danny and Brian went into a panic. He was trying to get the gun to run down to the Shankill Road. I ran down and said, 'What is going on?' Brian turned round and said to me, 'Gerly, it's Danny'. I went up to the Royal Victoria Hospital with Brian and he went in to see the doctor. Then he came out crying. He said to me, 'Danny is dead'. I just couldn't believe it, for such a thing to happen to such a quiet fella. In those days you wouldn't have thought about going back and forward across these routes. It just was a case of whatever was handy.

Martha Carville (mother)

Danny had plenty of friends, but he chummed with Gerly Hamill most of all. Danny was a lovely son and very pleasant. He was very easy to please. He loved music and he was mad about Elvis. He thought he looked like Elvis; he cut his hair like him. The day my son was murdered, I looked out the door and there was a jeep at Danny's door. I thought it was a raid. I shouted in to Brian, 'They are raiding Danny's house; there is a jeep at his door'. Then two policemen came up. They said that there had been an accident. I don't remember much after that. They all went to the hospital and I went down to his house and stayed with the wee ones. My husband was only dead 15 months at the time of Danny's killing. It is a terrible thing to happen, but you just have to live with it and you never forget it.

Brian Carville (brother)

Danny was 11 years older than me so he was the big older brother. I didn't really get to know him until I started socialising myself. Danny was quiet and easygoing about the house. He had his own views and he did his own thing. He was the type of fella who felt that if you believe in something you shouldn't let anybody else tell you that you are wrong. By the time I got to really know Danny his main interest would have been his work. Danny had grown up with a number of blokes who he had seen getting killed. It really got to him. Paddy McAdorey was a close friend of Danny's and Danny's house was directly facing where Paddy got shot [Paddy McAdorey, killed by the British army in Jamaica Street, 9 August 1971]. He was looking out the window and he actually saw Paddy get shot dead. Danny's best mate ever was big Gerry Hamill from the street. Danny was killed on St Patrick's day 1977. About a fortnight before he was killed a few fellas down in the club asked him if he would collect the cross out of Wilton's funeral parlour for the Ardoyne memorial because Danny had a mobile crane. Danny, Martin Meehan and Coco McAuley went down with the crane to collect the cross. I remember CoCo saying that there were a couple of people watching them while they they were there. One of them actually wrote down the registration number of the crane. I think it took them until about 3 am to get the cross erected and centred. That is the memorial that is presently there now at Brompton Park. Ironically Danny's name was the next to go on it. Each year Paul Shevlin did the oration at the memorial and he always mentioned that it was Danny who erected the cross.

The day Danny was killed was the first St Patrick's Day they got off work in Danny's place. The fella who owned the Bunch of Grapes, Liam Mc Mahon, had a special do on for them. They had all gone to mass earlier that morning wearing their shamrocks. They were in the Bunch of Grapes until about 3 pm and then they went on to the Shamrock. Danny had to collect our youngest sister Mary because everybody was going out that night. Sheila told me to go down and get Mary because Danny had taken a couple of drinks. I went upstairs to get washed but when I looked out the door Danny was away with his son Frank. That was the last I saw of my brother. About five minutes after he left the street, my mother told me that the peelers were at Danny's door. It all happened very quickly. Danny was actually shot at 5.55 pm and the peelers were at Sheila's door at 6 pm. His son Frankie told us afterwards what had happened. He said that when they left Flax Street there was a car sitting at the top of Leopold Street, facing down the Crumlin. When they turned into Cambrai Street they noticed that the car was coming down the wrong side of the road and onto Cambrai Street after him but staying a distance behind him. When they got half-way down, Danny said to Frankie, 'Get down on the floor' because he had seen your man flashing the lights. The driver was actually flashing the lights at Kenny McClinton who was in the phone box at the bottom of Cambrai Street. That was his signal that there was a car coming from Ardoyne. When they went over the ramp Danny dived over the top of Frankie to protect him. Danny had seen a man pulling the gun out, so his first reaction was to throw himself over his wee 10-year-old lad. Frankie can still remember McClinton standing at the front of the car. He shot at the front and then moved round to the side. Young Frankie was grazed on the leg by one of the bullets that went through Danny. Frankie said that he heard your man saying, 'Come on, that's enough' and another fella said, 'No, finish off the two of them'.

McClinton was not by himself. There was a second gunman called Sammy McGaw. He was a UFF commander who was hated and feared on the Shankill. The guy who drove the car was Arty Bettice. It came out after Danny's death that Bettice was an RUC informer. We still don't know if he knew Danny. I was actually lifted on the night that Bettice was shot. The RUC came for me at about 5 am and took me to Tennent Street. I found out later that Bettice had been shot dead at 4.30 am [Arthur Bettice, killed by the UFF in Silvio Street, 4 November 1981]. The RUC obviously thought that I had the motive and the means for killing him. Then the UFF admitted murdering him, saying that he was a paid informer and the third man in Kenny McClinton's cell. About a fortnight before that McGaw, McClinton and Bettice had been arrested, but only Bettice was released. McClinton and McGaw were charged with the murder of Danny. I think that is when the UFF tippled that he was touting. I was at the first day of the trial of McClinton and McGaw. I was actually warned by a peeler not to attend the second day because there were UFF men from the Shankill sitting behind me. Bettice's name was never mentioned at the trial. He was only referred to as 'the driver'. McClinton and McGaw were found guilty and got life because the RUC had the forensics on them. They found the guns in McGaw's aunt's house when he was arrested. McClinton became a 'born again' Christian when he was inside. He admitted to murdering another five Catholics, but he was never charged or gave their names. Then he even admitted to burying bodies of his own ones on the Shankill and he was never charged. McClinton ended up marrying the widow of an RUC man. She appealed to us to forgive him to get him released. McClinton doesn't know it himself, but because of his high profile, Danny's name keeps coming up, which is a good thing. He is not just another forgotten statistic.

Death didn't really shock you then in Ardoyne. You expected there was a good possibility you were going to be killed yourself. You just lived in hope that you weren't next. There was always that chance that when you were going out, you weren't coming back home again. There was always that fear in you. Still, losing a brother is a big blow. You don't realise how much you miss someone until they are away. It really hit me when the ceasefire was declared. You can't walk up to the graveyard, blow the horn and say 'Come on lads, it is all over; everybody out'. That memorial in Ardoyne was always special to Danny, and when he got a few drinks in him he'd say, 'Come on up and see my cross.' It was a very special thing to the people of Ardoyne and he was that proud that he was the one that put it up. He loved it. My mother has yet to see it. She won't go near the memorial at Brompton Park. She says that it was his downfall because he was spotted that night with the crane. Danny's son Frankie did not speak about his father's murder for years. But he is starting to open up now. Frankie's memories of his da are vague because he was only ten. I am glad this book is being printed. It is about time that people remembered those who have been murdered here. It gives families a wee bit of comfort knowing that somebody actually cares. It is nice to know that people remember our dead relatives and that they don't have to have been connected or on active service. They were all victims of the conflict. Everyone of those people who were murdered in Ardoyne would probably have gone on to live a normal, natural life if it had not been for the conflict.

Trevor McKibbin
Killed on active service
by the British army,
Flax Street,
17 April 1977

> *Trevor was a lovely person. Nobody and I mean nobody could have said a thing about our Trevor.*

Trevor's mother, Colette (née Short), was originally from Stanhope Street and his father, James, was from the Newtownards Road. They were married in Holy Cross chapel and had five children: Paul, Trevor, Hazel, David and Gerard. Trevor was the second child, born on 26 September 1957. Like most of the young men in the district he attended Holy Cross Boys school and St Gabriel's. On leaving school he worked as a bricklayer with Enterprise Ulster. Trevor was a keen footballer and like the rest of his family, supported Manchester United. He was a quiet, good-natured, unassuming lad. Trevor McKibbin was a member of na Fianna Éireann. At the age of 19 he was shot and killed by the British army in Flax Street.

Colette McKibbin (mother)

I used to go to 7 o'clock mass on a Sunday night. That particular day, the day Trevor was killed, I went to 1 o'clock mass, which I've always regretted. When I came home I was getting the dinner ready. I heard the shooting and I ran down the street. A woman was walking up the street and she said to me, 'It's your Trevor', so I ran round the corner. I saw him lying there (shot), soldier came over to stop me going to Trevor; I lifted my arm and I hit the soldier. I lifted Trevor and put him into the ambulance. I went to get into the ambulance myself but the next thing I remember was falling back out again; I don't know what happened. Before they would let Trevor go straight to the hospital the British army took him into the Flax Street Mill; that's where the British army were based in Ardoyne. I think he should have been taken straight to the hospital. This was around 2 o'clock. The incident happened at the back of Tommy Maguire's shop. They murdered him. He was cut down very, very brutally. I had a very bad breakdown over his death and was hospitalised.

I went to the inquest with Tommy Short. A detective said to me, 'Rub your hand down this' (the gun Trevor was carrying when he was killed). Tommy said to him, 'Don't ask her to do that'. I rubbed my hand down the gun and it was an old rough thing. The detective held the gun up and broke it into two halves. He said to me, 'That's what your son died for, an old broken air rifle; it wouldn't have killed a bird'. It was an open verdict. The British soldier said, as he was fixing his tie, 'It was just one of those things'. He was very cocky about it: 'just one of those things'.

Trevor was a lovely person. Nobody and I mean nobody could have said a thing about our Trevor. When Trevor died, they came from everywhere to his funeral. When he came home at night he would say, 'Mammy I'm home; don't be worrying about me, I'm home'. I don't know what it was about him, I just never wanted to let him out of my sight, even when his daddy went to work in the mornings; as long as my Trevor had gone to work and he was safe, I was all right. The priest asked me one day, 'Why were you clinging so much to Trevor?' I said, 'I don't know. I just couldn't let go of him'.

'John' (comrade)

The first time I met Trevor he approached me to join the Auxiliaries. This was about six months before he was killed in late 1976. For a number of reasons Trevor didn't become a member of our organisation and shortly after he joined na Fianna Éireann. Because of the lack of weaponry available at that time it became normal and natural for the Auxlliaries and Fianna to use the same weapons for G.L (gun lecture) purposes. We had a particular weapon that was good for gun lectures. You couldn't have fired this weapon, or used it for any other purpose than giving a gun lecture. It was basically used for showing people the rudimentary of what a weapon is, how to hold it, how to fire it. It was basically useless for any other function. There was no danger at G.L's because after young Davy McAuley was killed in Fairfield Street, there were no bullets allowed at G.L's.

Trevor approached me on behalf of the Fianna for the loan of a weapon to carry out a G.L. This was normal procedure. We agreed that on Sunday 17 April Trevor would pick up the weapon. This had been done many times before, usually on a Sunday morning. The area was a bit quieter then, especially early in the morning. On Sunday morning Trevor was given the weapon from a female member of the movement from a 'dump' in Etna Drive entry. We weren't expecting the weapon back until perhaps Tuesday when the Fianna had finished with it. That was the end of our role in this operation. Trevor's role was to bring the weapon from there to the old district. That's where the G.L was taking place. Trevor was given the weapon early on the morning of Sunday; there was a gap of a few hours until the time he was actually shot.

Trevor had been walking with the weapon from Etna Drive to behind Tommy Maguire's shop on the waste ground. It's possible he was spotted with the weapon from the British army observation post at the top of Flax Street, who may have radioed through to the foot patrol. Apparently he was challenged by the foot patrol. He ran and the Brit shot him.

As I've said, the weapon was only used for G.L's. Trevor was fully aware of the state of the weapon; he knew its limitations. I heard from someone who was on the scene later that one of the soldiers who actually shot Trevor broke down when he saw the state of the weapon; he obviously realised the weapon was harmless.

'Odd Job' (friend)

I used to live in Etna Drive and I got to know Trevor when he joined the Fianna. To look at him you would have thought he was a nervous type of person but that just was his nature. I got on with him very, very well. Anything he had to do he did it well. He never drank in the clubs. He may have had the odd pint because he was a wee bit older than we were. He seemed to be a very happy fella. He was never in bad form. He was very quiet in his own way.

Years ago the comradeship was unbelievable. Even though we were young, everybody watched everybody else's back. Trevor wasn't one of those ones that advertised himself. People didn't know he was involved with the republican movement. His family didn't know he joined; they didn't know he was involved at all. He didn't want his family to worry about him.

The day he died was a Sunday. I was walking down Etna Drive when I heard about it. I didn't hear the shooting. Someone approached me and told me he was dead. The gun he had when he was shot was an old broken thing; that's all it was. I don't know whether he knew it was broken but everybody else knew it was at that time. As far as I know he was crossing the waste ground and the British security forces challenged him. He ran, as far as I know, to the wall of the school and that's where he was hit. He tried to jump the wee wall and that is where he got hit. I felt really sorry because he was a nice fella; it was the sorriest thing. It was sad the way it happened.

He got a military funeral and guard of honour. Loyalists planted a bomb at Trevor's funeral. We were walking down Etna Drive and the bomb went off. After that, it was bedlam; there were people lying injured all over the place. I'll never forget what happened that morning. Sean McBride was blown up at Trevor's funeral. He was a good friend of Trevor. I was very shocked about his death. Personally I think he shouldn't have died the way he died. We've talked about this and cried over it … it was the thought of him getting killed the way he did. He was a good guy.

Thomas (workmate)

I first met Trevor McKibbin while working for Enterprise Ulster. It was a scheme funded by the government and at that time rather than being out of work, I joined. We all called him 'Trebor' just because of his name being Trevor. He had a good sense of humour; he was just like the rest of us. We were working out at Whitehead at the time of his death, just doing general labouring. I only knew Trevor for the short space of time that we worked together before his death. I knew him to be happy-go-lucky and quite funny at times. He would have told us jokes on our journey from Belfast to Whitehead and it made the journey that wee bit shorter. We all enjoyed his craic. He was a young fella without malice and he enjoyed working with the whole crowd of us.

When I heard about Trevor's death I was shocked because he wouldn't have gone out of his way to cause anybody harm. I remember going to his house the day of his funeral. I had it in my head what I wanted to say to his mother but I just dried up because I saw the heartache the family was going through. I told his mother how much the lads in work would all miss him. If he were alive today he would have been a bonus to society; he would have worked his way through life because he wasn't afraid of a bit of hard graft.

> *My ma and me were shouting to each other and the child was squealing the whole time. There was total chaos. People were running all over the place. There were people screaming. And I'll never forget the smoke. There was smoke everywhere. There were so many injured.*

Sean Campbell
Killed by the UVF,
Etna Drive,
20 April 1977

Sean Campbell's mother Annie was from Grovesnor Place on the Falls Road and his father John was from Springhill Avenue. They first lived in Turf Lodge, then Ballymurphy and the Antrim Road. For a while Annie lived in England with the children before, in 1962, the family finally settled in Parkview Street in the Bone. Sean was by then four years old, having been born on 12 February 1958. He was the sixth in line of seven children in the family coming after Jim, Tony, Martin and Bobby and followed by Kathleen and Michael. Sean's nickname was 'Binlid'. He struggled at school and had problems with his basic education. As a result he was educated at St Aloysius. If Sean had difficulties at school, his talents lay elsewhere. He was extremely musical, playing the mouth organ, drums, pipes and the banjo. He soon joined the Sacred Heart Band run by Martin Lavery [killed by the UVF at his home in the Crumlin Road, 20 December 1992]. When he finished school, Sean went to work at a brewery in Derriaghy. A short while later he also started seeing a girl. He was a young man starting out in life. On the morning of 20 April 1977 he went ahead of his sister and mother to the funeral of Trevor McKibbin. Trevor McKibbin was a volunteer in na Fianna Éireann from Etna Drive. Like most people from the district Sean and his family were going to the funeral as a gesture of respect to the McKibbin family and in memory of Trevor. Sean was standing beside Sean McBride as the funeral cortege waited outside the McKibbin home. They were both close to a car inside which the UVF had planted a 100-pound bomb. When it exploded, Sean died instantly. Sean McBride died the next day and dozens of people were badly injured [Sean McBride, killed by the UVF in Etna Drive, 22 April 1977]. It was the first such attack on a funeral. Sean Campbell was only 19 years old.

Kathleen and Michael Campbell (sister and brother)

Sean was born on 12 February 1958. Growing up, Sean always had the nickname 'Binlid' because he was so 'wired up'. He got the name because he used to dress our dog Bruno up in a tricolour. Then he would go out in the street with a big drum marching up and down early in the morning. He couldn't read and write very well but he was great with the mouth organ, drums and the spoons. He was brilliant at all kinds of music. He used to play the big drum for the Sacred Heart band that was run by Martin Lavery. He used to play up in the ex-servicemen's club as well. There was one time they got him to go and play the mouth organ on the stage for a couple of hours because the group hadn't turned up. He was very good. Sean started playing the mouth organ after a load of us had gone up to the Oldpark playing fields to play a bit of football. All of a sudden Sean pulls out this mouth organ. Nobody knew where he got it from. He must have swiped it! When we got home we said that he should give our mum and dad a tune. It was the first time he had put a mouth organ to his mouth and he just started playing it. My dad was a good old chanter and was well into his music. He couldn't believe that our Sean could just pick this instrument up and start playing. He became really great at folk and traditional music.

Sean would have played a bit of football too and he was a mad Celtic fan. He also was a great handball player. He used to knock about with a squad of fellas. There was Martin McCromish, Jim Donnelly, Peter Morgan and Paddy Fennell. Because of his difficulties with reading and writing Sean ended up going on to a special school, St Aloysius, after he left the Sacred Heart primary school. He had never really been given a chance to learn anything there so that was why he went to St Aloysius. He wasn't stupid; he was just a bit slow. There was one time our mum caught him lying sunbathing when he was supposed to be at school. He was just lying in the park with his eyes closed and he used to say that he just felt a shadow pass over the sun. Then he opened his eyes and nearly passed out when he realised it was our mum standing there. He could be an eejit at times! In August we would all have been out collecting wood for the bonfires. We were always fighting with the Ardoyne ones because we were the 'Bone Hoppers' and they were the 'Sewer Rats'. Sean was always a leader of the gang in those situations.

The day he left school he went to work in a brewery in Derriaghy and he worked there right up until just before he was killed. He had a girlfriend by then too. They had been going together a while and were engaged at the time of his death. Her name was Theresa Toal and she was from Havana Street. They moved to the Free State after Sean was killed. He wasn't quiet but he wasn't a big drinker or anything either. He used to help the nuns in St Gemma's a lot and he used to go up to the chapel just to give a hand or to talk to the priests. He would have given anybody a hand. But the thing is, Sean died so young we didn't really get a chance to get to know him properly.

Sean wasn't really republican or politically minded. I remember one time at the start of the troubles he got into a fight and blattered three Orangemen with a hurley bat just by Hale's fruit shop at the top of Glenview Street. But he was never arrested for anything. He used to get hassle from the cops when he was coming to and from work. But even though he was into the bands he wasn't that republican-minded because he was a bit slow. The day Sean was killed there was a lot of anxiety in the area; people were just a bit worried about something happening during Trevor's funeral. Sean knew Trevor McKibbin but only because Sean's girlfriend lived in Havana Street just round the corner from Trevor's and she knew Trevor's sister Hazel.

Kathleen: The morning that Sean died my mum and myself were babysitting one of my nieces. Sean came in and took out the clothes horse and threw his trousers over it. Him and me were fighting and I was telling him to take himself round to my mum's house because I was trying to tidy the place. The two of us were arguing and I said to him, 'Get out and don't come back'. Those were the last words I said to him. He went round to my mum's and told her about me throwing him out. Then he headed round to the funeral. As he left the house, he said he was meeting up with Booster, Seanie Bateson and a few others. My mum and me were going round with the child as well but Sean ran on ahead. He had one arm in his coat and was trying to get the other in as he ran over the brickyard. Sean knew there were going to be cameras and he loved to get to the front of the crowd so as to be in the limelight. My mum and me had just got to the bookies beside where the old Shamrock used to be when the bomb went off. That was just before 1 pm on Wednesday, 20 April 1977. Then we just heard squealing and panic. We came round and saw people injured. There was blood gushing out of them. My mum and me were shouting to each other and the child was squealing the whole time. There was total chaos. People were running all over the place. There were people screaming. And I'll never forget the smoke, there was smoke everywhere. There were so many injured. Then the chaos began to settle down and Trevor McKibbin's funeral started to go ahead. The coffin had still been in the house up until then. We still didn't have a clue that our Sean was killed. My other brother Martin and me were standing in Etna Drive for the funeral and right beside us was our Sean's body. But we didn't know it was him because someone had put a canvas sheet over his head. I remember Marie Fusco pushing me out of the road and I remember wondering why people were kicking back whatever it was that was under the canvas. You see, other people knew it was Sean even though we didn't.

We still didn't know Sean had been killed and me, my mum and a few others were heading back home across the brickyard. We didn't go up to the mass but just waited till the funeral had gone out of Brompton Park. It was then that Margaret Townsend came up to me and my mum and said, 'God, Annie, I'm sorry to hear about your Sean'. We asked what was going on but nobody wanted to tell us. It was actually Nan Saunders who asked me what Sean had been wearing. I told her and she said, 'Well, that was your Sean who was killed in the bomb blast'. When my mum heard me squealing she knew right away what had happened. That was how we found out Sean was dead. Right up until this day the police have never come near us to tell us that Sean was killed in the bomb. We had to run around the hospitals ourselves that day to make sure that it was definitely Sean. The police never came near our door from that day to this. As far as I know Sean wasn't standing beside the car for that long a period. When the bomb exploded Sean got the full blast because he was leaning on the roof of the car. Apparently the car ended up in bits, it was demolished. It had been parked next door to Trevor McKibbin's house on the same side of the street. Sean died instantly. He was just by Shorty's house; it was Shorty who told us what had happened. Our Sean had actually asked him for a glass of water and the bomb went off when he came out with it. Shorty said that young Sean McBride had been leaning on the bonnet of the car as well. He died the next day.

Michael: Some people have said that they were actually standing talking to one another. They were the only two that died but there were a lot of people injured. I was actually over on the Falls Road waiting for the funeral with a crowd of people over there. I went into my aunt's house and she told me there had been an explosion. So we got a taxi over. Booster Hughes was standing with a fella called Brendy McClenaghan at the bottom of

Etna Drive and I heard him say that our Sean had been killed. Booster turned round to me as much as to say, 'That's his brother'. Brendy just looked at me and said, 'Michael, I'm sorry. I didn't know he was your brother'. It was a bad way to find out but it was just the way it happened; it wasn't intentional or anything. By then the funeral was away but the scene was chaotic; people were running around in a daze. Then my da and me had to go up to the barracks to identify Sean's body. The cops asked us what he was wearing and then said that they were not sure if it was our Sean or not. We had to go up to the morgue. I said I would go in but the cop said I was too young. My dad went in and came out with Sean's watch in his hand.

Kathleen: They identified Sean from a scar on his leg that he had got when he was young. My dad told me after that Sean had been completely decapitated. The two CID men that went in with my dad collapsed when they saw him. He said that all there was of his head was a wee string of hair under the skin at the back of his neck.

Michael: I can't remember if anyone claimed responsibility for the bombing but it was the UVF who did it. A guy called James 'Tonto' Watts was convicted for it and he is UVF. He was from Ballysillan. His dad used to be the park ranger up on the Bone hills playing fields. Before the troubles Sean would have played football up on those playing fields with this guy's older brothers. When he was inside Tonto Watts tried to claim that it was a military attack because the target was the guard of honour for Trevor McKibbin's funeral. But there was always going to be innocent people, women and kids there. I think it was the start of the attacks on funerals. No matter what side people are on there should be an honouring of them burying their dead. But you got what Michael Stone did later in Milltown cemetery in 1988. A lot of the time the loyalists didn't have to attack funerals; the RUC and Brits did it for them.

Kathleen: I am 100 per cent sure it was the first attack on a funeral. At Sean's funeral his band formed a guard of honour. The cops lifted a couple of fellas coming out of the graveyard. They didn't give any reason, just lifted them. We protested for a couple of hours until they got out. One other thing I remember is that the media never came out to my mother to do an interview or anything. It wasn't until the late 1980s that anyone came to interview her. That was because they were doing something on the people that my mummy and her sister Alice had lost. My aunt Alice lost a son, Patrick, who was the first child killed in the troubles [Patrick Rooney, killed by the RUC in his Divis Flats home aged nine, 14 August 1969]. My mummy had lost our Sean and they had both lost a sister, Mary Sheppard [Mary Sheppard, killed by the UFF, Arkle taxi office, Clifton Street, 23 November 1974 along with William Hutton. Mary Sheppard had also given eyewitness evidence at the inquest of Gerard Gearon, killed by the UFF, Crumlin Road, 29 November 1972]. Mary had been shot by the UFF in the taxi office where she worked along with another fella from the Shankill Road. He got up to help Mary and they shot him. They just assumed he was a Catholic. After Sean's death the community and our neighbours rallied round and that is where we got help from. There was no help from outsiders. The death grant was £30, I still have the cheque. My mum didn't want compensation because she said it wouldn't bring Sean back and it was blood money.

Michael: I am really sorry I never got the opportunity to know our Sean. He was so young and his death so sudden; it was a real tragedy. He was killed because he was a Catholic attending the funeral of a republican. Everyone who was near the McKibbin home that day was a target. They didn't care who got killed or who was injured. It was a totally indiscriminate bombing aimed at the whole community, men, women and children. We all really miss Sean, just as much today as 25 years ago when it happened.

> *People were saying that he was dead but I went over anyway.*
> *I just felt that I wanted to lift him up, to do something.*
> *Maybe I just didn't want to leave him there lying in the*
> *street. I wanted to say, 'Someone cares for you'.*

Sean McBride's father James was born in the New Lodge but moved to Etna Drive when he was still young. His mother Mary (née Gillen) was from Hooker Street. After they were married the couple moved into 54 Hooker Street. The two-bedroomed home was close to Gillen's shop, owned and run by Mary's aunt. Sean's granny was Mary Ann Gillen who used to be the midwife for the area and who washed the dead. Sean and Mary eventually had 11 children: Anthony, Seamus, Patrick, Sean, Paul, Henry, Gabriel, Joseph, Marie, Kathleen and Martine. Sean was the fourth eldest, born on 8 January 1959. Sean (or 'Skin' as he was usually

Sean McBride
Killed by the UVF,
Etna Drive,
21 April 1977

known) went to the Holy Cross Boys school and St Gabriel's. He left the latter when he was 15 in 1974. After a while he got work in a bookies in Brompton Park. By then he was seeing a girl in the area, playing a bit of handball and football, going to local discos – just a young fella growing up. On 20 April 1977 Sean was going over to the family home from his work. He was also going to pay his last respects amongst the crowd beginning to gather for the funeral of Trevor McKibbin [Trevor McKibbin, killed by the British army in Brompton Park/Flax Street entry, 17 April 1977]. He walked up Brompton Park and into Etna Drive where a car bomb planted by the UVF exploded. The bomb killed Sean Campbell instantly [Sean Campbell, killed by the UVF in Etna Drive, 20 April 1977]. Sean was also caught in the blast; glass punctured his lungs and he died in hospital early the next day. Sean's younger brother Paul was killed in a UVF gun attack 11 years later [Paul McBride, killed by the UVF in the Avenue bar in Union Street, 15 May 1988]. This was a blatant sectarian attack on a nationalist community mourning the tragic death of a local young man. It was the first time a funeral had been attacked. It was an atrocity. Sean was 18 years old when he was killed.

Patrick 'Hockey' McBride (brother)

There were 13 in our family including my mother and father. When we were kids in Hooker Street we all lived in a two-bedroomed house. One bed was just shoved up against another and there was no bathroom, just a big, blazing fire and a big bath in front of it. My da worked away a lot so my ma was left to rear us on her own. Like all of us, Sean went to Holy Cross Boys school and St Gabriel's before leaving school in 1974. He didn't have any qualifications. Sean used to knock about with a whole lot of fellas. There was Robbie Gillen, Sean Cairns, Tucker Foster, to name but a few. Sean was wiry and good with his hands. He was a good handball player. He liked a bit of snooker and would have played football up on the old Bone pitch. Before he died Sean was seeing a wee girl called Eileen for about 18 months. Sean was full of life. He was very outgoing and happy-go-lucky. He got up to a bit of mischief but nothing serious. He was never in trouble with the authorities or anything. He used to go up to the Deanby dance. Sean and all his mates were skins and there were also mods up there. There were 'sticks' and 'provos' too. There would have been a fight of rival gangs and Sean would have had a go with the rest of the boys. After he left school Sean had got a few wee jobs, then he got work in Sean Graham's bookies. It used to be beside the old Shamrock at the bottom of Brompton Park, he was happy enough in there. The morning he was killed he was coming from the bookies round to give me my wages. He was making his way over to the house when the bomb went off and he was thrown to the ground. It was the day of Trevor McKibbin's funeral, 20 April 1977. He knew Trevor very, very well. Sean was caught at Brompton Park entry, he was only about 10 or 12 yards away from the bomb. He was killed along with the wee lad Sean Campbell who was decapitated. It was terrible. There wasn't a mark on our Sean, but the doctor said that glass went down his throat and wrecked his lungs. Our Sean lived until the next day. He died at about 3.10 am the next morning in the Mater Hospital. He was only 18 years old.

When the bomb went off I was down the town with my wife Elizabeth. A fella told me that there had been a bomb in Ardoyne and that a wee lad from the Bone had been killed. That was Sean Campbell. When we got back there was a big crowd around my mother's door. I asked what was wrong and was told that Sean had been hurt. My ma said he wasn't too bad but somebody else shook their head to me. To be honest I just broke down; I went out into the yard and started beating the walls. Then I went straight down to the hospital. A nurse told me that Sean would be ok. He had internal injuries so they were not sure how bad he was. They said they would have to remove one of his lungs. They operated on him for several hours. They were running back and forth with bags and bags of blood. Then Fr. Fernando came out and told my father he had given Sean the last rites. They let us in to see him. I looked at Sean and walked out. I couldn't hack staying there and went home to my ma. That was at about 2.20 am. There was just me and my ma sitting in the house when another of the brothers came to the door. He said to my ma, 'Mary, your son's away'. We were never officially notified about Sean's death by the RUC. I don't even know if there was an inquest, to be honest. People in the area were very good to my mother and father afterwards. They didn't have much and people really helped us out. But it hit my father hard. Before that he was a social drinker. Then he drank himself to death. He had been a big strong man and I can tell you it was a broken heart that did it to him. This was after Paul was dead too. When we were sitting by my father's bedside he said, 'I'd be better off dead and with my two sons'. My mother took it awful bad. She was really bad, came round a bit and then when Paul died, she went straight downhill. I think it is too late for counselling; we have helped ourselves through being together. We are a big family and we may never get over it but we came together. We will never forget but time heals. But when I say we came together I mean the area, Ardoyne, not just the family. Everybody in Ardoyne has been touched by the troubles.

Seamus and Henry McBride (brothers)

Seamus: We all lived in Hooker Street when we were kids. One end of it was mainly Catholic, the other mainly Protestant. As it came up to July we would all have been out collecting wood for the bonfires. It was coming up to August then too so the ones from Brookfield Street would come round to try and steal the wood. Life was completely different then. As kids we just played out on the streets, not like now. I suppose, looking back you would call them the good old days. Sean was just a good honest kid. He could have taken a bike apart and put it back together again. He loved music. He was into Gary Glitter and he used to wear an oule trench coat. He was one of the 'glitter gang' as they used to call themselves. There was a load of them all from the same year at school in it. When Sean was growing up he was seeing a girl from the Falls Road. Eileen Connolly was her name. Sean was talking about getting engaged the week before he died. He was just turned 18. He had been working painting gates on the Woodvale Road but my mother had got him to stop because she thought it was too dangerous. He tried to get a transfer but couldn't. So he had to just leave it.

Henry: On the day Sean died my da was actually with him in the bookies. My da would mark the boards if there was no ashphalting work to be had. He handed Sean some money and Sean told him he was just going round to pay his respects and goodbyes to Trevor [McKibbin]. He was only supposed to be half an hour. My da sent me round to find him. I was just calling to him when the bomb went off. Our Sean and a young lad from the Bone called Sean Campbell were killed – just two young fellas saying their last farewell to a fella from their school. Our Sean was standing beside Sean Campbell when the bomb went off. I had just called to Sean and he was coming across the road; He had just reached the footpath when the bomb exploded. I will never forget the scenes I saw that day. If anybody had told me beforehand that such a thing could happen I would have said they were disturbed. I saw a programme a short while ago about the bomb in Omagh [August 1998] and it was like re-living the whole thing that happened in Etna Drive. The way it was described and what I watched, the gusts of smoke, for a moment I was back in Etna Drive. I remember I was standing about 12 feet away from my brother Sean when the bomb went off. I was pushed back into a hedge by the blast. As I was falling backwards I remember seeing Leonard Stewart as he was blown toward me. It was the force of him being thrown into the air that blew me into the hedge. Leonard died about a year later from cancer but he was hurt that day and that had a lot to do with his death. As I was falling backwards I remember looking up to the sky and watching as scalding pieces of metal were flying around me. Red, roaring, hot metal was being thrown up and falling down everywhere. I woke up in Sean McGeough's mother's house and at first I thought my leg had been blown off. I was just lying there and looked over to see a blanket being placed over my brother Sean. I thought I saw his hand move and said, 'He is not dead; his hand is moving'. My other brother Seamus then took his hand. I can't remember anything after that.

Seamus: Apparently Sean Campbell had been standing with his back to the bomb; he had his head blown off. Our Sean was facing the bomb and he swallowed the blast as it came toward him. I was just walking down Butler Street as the bomb went off. I had just met my uncle John Toal. I thought the explosion came from the Oldpark. Then I saw the smoke rising and thought it was round near the bookies. We ran down and as we got to the bottom of Brompton Park my daddy was coming round the corner. He said that he thought Sean was dead. He went round to see my mummy and I went up to Etna Drive. When I got there the Knights of Malta had placed two sheets over the two lads. Then Sean moved and someone shouted, 'Sean McBride is still alive'. We got him into the ambulance. Sean was conscious by this time and asked me what had happened; I told him he would be alright and patted him on the back. I didn't know his whole back had been blown away. When I took my hand away it was covered in blood. It was crazy on the road and we couldn't get the ambulance out. I was kicking people out of the way and screaming at them that we had to get the ambulance through. By the time we got to the Mater Hospital it was pandemonium. People were panicking and running around. There were people coming up and trying to find out if their relatives were there. After a few hours I got to speak to the doctor and he explained that it was unlikely Sean would pull through. So I had to go up to the house to explain the situation to my parents. When I got into the house everyone was there. My mummy was crying and asking me how Sean was. I couldn't just blurt it out. I took my daddy into the kitchen and told him to get to the hospital because Sean only had a few hours to live. He told my mother. My mummy just started squealing and then she fainted. Everyone was crying; they were totally devastated. Sean died about 12 hours later. People in Ardoyne really rallied round afterward. Lizzie Whelan and another woman got up a collection for the funeral because they knew that because of the size of the family we could not afford it. Lizzie had a heart of gold. My daddy put a thank you notice into the *Irish News* afterwards to the people of Ardoyne. Our Patrick in particular took it real bad; he just couldn't come to terms with what had happened. He couldn't forgive these people for what they had done to our family and at times his anger just spilled over. At the funeral itself I thought that my mother and father were going to die of broken hearts. The family all rallied round and helped each other.

Henry: Sean's funeral was massive. The cortege ran the whole length of Brompton Park. As Sean was being brought up to the mass that night the place was black with people. There was a load of cops there and they were all standing to attention. Most cops gloated when Catholics were killed because they were bigoted bastards. So that was very rare. It lifted my da a bit and restored some of his faith in human nature.

Seamus: About four weeks after the burial my father was asked to go down to Tennent Street police station. The cop on the desk treated my daddy very badly and abruptly even though he explained why he was there. Then the detective my daddy was there to meet came out. He told the desk cop that he would deal with him later. My daddy had no love for the RUC but he said he had to respect that detective because he gave my daddy respect. The detective told my daddy that they knew who made the bomb and who planted it. They knew who killed Sean. He said they had evidence but these guys had alibis. Eventually a young fella who had hijacked the car squealed on them and they all got time. Tonto Watt was one of them. He was in the UVF and it was the UVF that claimed it. We were just awarded the cost of Sean's burial by the court. My daddy didn't want to take any money. The judge said that because Sean was not the breadwinner then the family was not entitled to anything else. After Paul died this was mentioned to the judge in that case and he said that no judge should have said that. He said it was a disgrace to say such a thing to a family who had just lost their son.

Henry: I had to go to the court too. I was put on the stand. I was only 15 at the time the bomb went off so my father had to come with me. The court case was just about a year later. The judge asked me if I was on medication and how many tablets I was taking a day. He said it in such a way that it confused me. At the end of it they gave me three times more than what they had said my brother who died was worth. That was typical of them. It was a joke.

Seamus: I went to the doctor's with my nerves after the bomb and was put on anti-depressants. I went to see a psychiatrist as well. He tried to get me to go into a hospital but I didn't want to. He told me to go home and come back a week later. I said to my wife afterwards that it made me feel worse. So the next week I just said I was fine and I was in and out in five minutes. I told my wife that I would rather we worked it all out ourselves. It took a long time to come to terms with it. One morning I woke up to find my knuckles all bleeding and my wife sitting shouting at me with a pillow in front of her. I had put my hand through the wardrobe door; I had been killing people in my sleep. After that, I came off the medication and I put every tablet down the toilet. It took me about two years to come to terms with things. I think it is a good thing now if people can turn to counsellors because it is important if people can talk to others who have been in the same spot as them.

Our Sean was just like any lad of his age. He liked to go to discos. He had a girlfriend to whom he was planning to get engaged. He was madly in love with this wee girl and would ask me how much an engagement ring would cost. Sean would never have made any trouble for anyone. He was just a normal, happy-go-lucky fella. The trouble was going on around him but he wasn't politically aware of it. He didn't want to get involved. He was a bit of a joker and loved a laugh, just a kid who loved life and dreamed about what he might do. When Sean died a mate of my daddy's from the Shankill Road, a fella he worked with, sent my father a letter. This guy would have loved to come up to see my father but because he was from the Shankill he was afraid. He just wanted to explain the grief he felt and that his thoughts were with my father. I thought that was a lovely gesture and my daddy always held onto that letter. It just goes to show that despite everything that has happened not everyone is bitter. Not everyone is bitter enough to plant a bomb.

Thomas (eyewitness)

I was attending the funeral of Trevor McKibbin on 20 April 1977. Me and Trevor (or 'Trebor' as everyone knew him) had worked together in Enterprise Ulster. As everyone knows, Trevor was shot dead by the British army. I took the day off work to go and bring a wreath up to his mother. Everything seemed to be going alright. There was a lot of sadness and tension but everybody was just going about things quietly. There were things going off in other parts of the town so the funeral directors got to the house late. The funeral was to have left at 1 pm but the undertakers didn't get there until about 1.15 pm. That's probably what saved a lot of people's lives. If the funeral had left on time the bomb would have killed all the people walking behind the hearse. Whoever planted the bomb intended to kill a lot more people. There were a lot of people going to the funeral because Trevor was a likeable lad and everyone seemed to know him.

My friend Sean and me went up to the McKibbin family house to pay our respects to Trevor's mother. Then we just hung about for a while. We decided to walk up to my aunt Sarah's in Brompton Park while we were waiting. I remember that there wasn't a British army or RUC patrol around. That was surprising. I didn't find it strange at the time but looking back, it seems odd. I remember walking past the car that turned out to contain the bomb. It was a silver, mark two Cortina; I remember thinking it was a lovely motor. It was parked with its rear end at an angle sticking out into the road. It was only later we realised that was to maximise the impact of the blast into where the funeral cortege was supposed to be. We had just walked up past it when there was a massive explosion. You could say that we were lucky because we had just passed the car. The next thing I remember was coming round. There was smoke coming out of Etna Drive. There were bits of stuff in the air and there was that funny smell that you associate with bombs going off. We ran around with everybody else to see if we could help. I can remember looking up Etna Drive as clear as day. I could see different people aged from 14 to 70 lying over hedges or dazed in the road. There were old people that looked like they had taken a heart attack with the shock of it. There were people moaning and groaning. I remember running up and down looking at people, checking them out. I was dusting people's clothes down as they had blood coming out of them.

Then I saw this young lad lying further up Etna Drive toward Alliance Avenue. He was lying in the middle of the street dressed in a suit. He looked as if he had decided to lie down and go to sleep; there wasn't a mark on him. All you could see was that there was blood coming out of his ears. People were saying that he was dead but I went over anyway. I just felt that I wanted to lift him up, to do something. Maybe I just didn't want to leave him there lying in the street. I wanted to say, 'Someone cares for you'. I don't know what was going through my mind. I'm sure a lot of other people were thinking the same. Then I saw that his eyes were flickering so I thought, 'I am just going to stay here'. A woman came out and I shouted to her for a pair of rosary beads. I am not that religious but it was the only thing I could think of. So I wrapped the rosary beads around his hands and said an act of contrition. I didn't do the wee lad any good but it made me feel better for saying it. I thought he had died there and I didn't realise until afterwards that he died in hospital. It was only later that I knew it was Sean McBride.

We covered Sean up and the next thing was a jeep pulled up with Brits in it. I think they had green berets on. There was two in the back and two in the front. They had their SLRs strapped to their arms so they couldn't lose them but the crowd attacked them and started rocking the jeep. I could hear these guys squealing inside but, to be honest, I had no sympathy for them. As I have heard people say, 'Why do they always arrive after something happens?' That was the general feeling of the crowd. Then a fella (I think he was well up in the republican movement) came out and said a few words to the crowd to stop. He said that this was neither the time nor the place for that because we had to have dignity for the people who were dead and the McKibbin family. Those Brits can count themselves extremely lucky because otherwise they would have been torn asunder. People were getting really angry at the Brits coming in. I remember one of the funeral directors telling one Brit to 'fuck off'. But there was a sense that we had to keep our dignity and not let any animal instinct take over. There was a great feeling of, 'We'll look after our own. We don't need the cops, we don't need the Brits because they had probably set it up anyway'.

You don't feel things at a time like that because your mind is racing ahead of itself. You are in a daze. You run around trying to help people because there is nothing wrong with you and you feel that you should be doing something to help. It wasn't until later that evening that a sense of sadness and depression set in. I went to bed early but just lay there thinking. I thought about how lucky I was and about people coming to pay their last respects and some of them being killed. The wee lad Trevor McKibbin was a good, funny kid. I thought about the people injured and older people who I am sure probably died afterwards from the shock of it. And I thought about the two wee lads that died. I thought about the wee lad McBride lying there looking as if he was sleeping except for the fact that he was a whiter shade of pale. He went to pay his last respects to Trevor McKibbin and ends up being murdered.

> *I think it was one of the biggest tragedies of the whole troubles, republicans killing each other when there was so much to be done both politically and in other ways. To me it could have been, and should have been, avoided.*

Trevor McNulty
Killed by the IRA,
Alexander Flats,
27 July 1977

Trevor McNulty was from a mixed marriage. His mother May Grayson was a Protestant from Bray Street off the Crumlin Road and his father, Charles, was a Catholic from Carrick Hill. Despite strong objections from her family the couple got married and set up home in Lawnbrook Drive off the Woodvale Road. During the 1930s they were intimidated out of their home by loyalists. The couple then moved to Brompton Park, Ardoyne. They had four children: Brian, Trevor, Thelma and Ethna. Trevor was born on 17 June 1948. He attended Holy Cross Boys and St Gabriel's secondary school. His first job was with his father in Martin Baker's Aircraft Factory where he served his time as an engineer. A number of years later he worked as a technician in Bearnageeha school. Trevor married Margaret McNulty from the New Lodge Road on 14 June 1971. They had two children, Sean, and Trevor who was born several months after his father was killed. Trevor was a very political person. He was a socialist and heavily involved in the Civil Rights Movement, Republican Clubs and Workers' Party. At the time of his death he was a member of the 'Official' IRA. On the 27 July 1977, the IRA killed Trevor McNulty.

Brian McNulty (brother)

When Trevor was younger, he knocked about with the kids in our street. We were very clannish in those days. Trevor played football a lot and he joined the Cadets. He supported Spurs and Cliftonville; they were his favourite football teams. As Trevor got older he got more interested in music; he played the drums for a while and that was his main interest. He didn't play in a group; he just played in the house. I played too. My father was a drummer as well; he played in a band with his five brothers from Carrick Hill. They were called the McNulty's and they played in all the dance halls.

Trevor got married in the early seventies to Margaret McNulty from the New Lodge Road. At the start of the troubles Trevor was heavily into politics. He started off as a member of the Republican Clubs and he went from that into the Workers' Party. His wife was heavily involved in politics at the time as well. It was the Civil Rights Movement that brought Trevor into politics. We both went on many civil rights marches together. He was interned in 1971 on the Maidstone internment ship and then in Magilligan prison. He was interned in the 'Official' IRA section. He was only in for about six months. It was a shock to the family but at that time everybody was sort of up in arms.

He got married in St Patrick's chapel in Donegall Street. Bobby Lavery was at the wedding; they were good mates. That was another tragedy of the split between the 'Provisional' and 'Official' IRA. It split friends and families. I joined Sinn Féin and there was a rift over it in the family, just one of the tragic rifts of the whole troubles. Family and friends both religiously and politically were torn apart, some with animosity and some without. When my brother was killed, a feud had started in Bawnmore between the 'Provisional' and 'Official' IRA. I had a building firm at the time and we were working in Newtownabbey. We had the radio on and the news reported that there had been a man shot in the New Lodge Road but I never thought anything of it. Then later when I was driving into Ardoyne, a friend stopped the lorry and said that Trevor had been shot dead. Trevor always maintained that when he died it wouldn't be the loyalists or the British army that would kill him. He always said that it would be republicans that would shoot him. Some of the feuds were very vicious at that time. He always thought that his life was in danger from the 'Provisionals' for some reason. He might have been in the 'Official' IRA but I wouldn't have known.

Trevor was always a very hard-working guy. He was a good lad and he was good craic to be with. Trevor ended up very heavily into politics. The conversation always came round to politics and the likes of James Connolly. I think it was one of the biggest tragedies of the whole troubles, republicans killing each other when there was so much to be done both politically and in other ways. To me it could have been and should have been avoided. It could have been avoided through dialogue and talking to each other. A lot of people would still be alive and there would not have been as many feuds and bad blood. That is the legacy you are left with.

Margaret Smith (widow)

I first met Trevor when I was fourteen years old; that was about 1965. It was through friends of mine that we met. His friends were John Hennessy, Bobby Lavery, Joe Austin and the Creighs. I think the main attraction between us was the fact that we had the same surname. We got engaged on 10 July 1969. I was 20 and Trevor was 23. We got married on 14 June 1971. John Hennessy was the best man. I was married five years before I had my first child Sean. He was a year old, and I was three months pregnant, when Trevor was shot dead. Our second child was a boy and I named him Trevor.

Trevor was a member of the Republican Clubs and he was also a member of the National Executive of the Civil Rights Movement. Trevor was always very politically minded. I knew of his involvement in the trade unions and his interest in politics. He was a socialist and very much up on current affairs. He was always reading about current affairs and about Connolly and the history of Ireland and the struggles of other countries. Trevor was involved in politics before 1969; he was involved in the Civil Rights Movement and would have been on civil rights marches in Newry and other places. Trevor was a very serious person and a very deep person. People found that they could confide in him. People would have come to him with their marriage problems and different problems. He seemed to have the knack of talking to people and discussing things and settling rows. He wasn't a violent person; he was more of a talker.

A couple of days before Trevor's death there had been trouble between the 'Provos' and the 'Sticks' and that happened quite often. Trevor had been away that weekend and came home on Sunday night because I wasn't well; I was pregnant at the time. That night we were rapped up because a few people had been given a hiding by the 'Provos'. One of them was my brother-in-law and a friend of Trevor's. Things developed and there were negotiations. Everything was supposed to be settled between the two republican groups. As far as Trevor was concerned everything was settled.

The day Trevor was killed I had been at the Royal Hospital with my sister who was pregnant and had been having labour pains. Once my sister got settled in the hospital we got a taxi home. We were coming along North Queen Street; it was after three o'clock and a fella that we knew ran round the corner and he shouted something like, 'Quick, they are after opening up on me and Trevor'. I ran up and Trevor was lying there; he had been shot and so had my brother-in-law, Joe Flood. I knew by looking at Trevor he was dead. My brother-in-law was shot two or three times as well. Trevor and Joe had been in Alexander Flats – that's where we lived – waiting on the lift and a gunmen came out of the stairway and shot them. Obviously Trevor and Joe turned to run. Trevor was lying at the door in the foetal position with his face out because that must have been where he fell. There was just a trickle of blood out of the side of Trevor's mouth but with my brother-in-law there was a massive pool of deep red blood around him. Trevor had been shot three times in the back and when he was on the ground they put one behind his ear and one in the nape of his neck.

I saw my husband lying dying. Everybody reacts differently to the sort of situation I was in; you just don't want to accept it and admit that it was happening. The ambulance came and took him to the hospital. Joe Flood was okay; he survived. Trevor was dead. I knew Trevor was dead when I saw him lying there. It is still hard thinking about it to this day. But I have used what happened to me in a positive manner. I have worked with the Workers' Party and worked in advice centres across Belfast. When I became a widow it was difficult dealing with things as a lone parent and I depended on support from my friends and family, especially my own family. I don't know what I would have done without them. At that particular time I was just in a daze.

I was politically active before Trevor was killed and his politics would have been my politics; I was also a member of the Republican Clubs. Trevor was not given a military funeral and he was not claimed as being a member of the 'Official' IRA for various reasons. Trevor was a member of the 'Official' IRA. He always said he knew he was going to die. He said that if he did die he didn't want a tricolour on his coffin; he wanted the Starry Plough and that is what he got.

You may think it strange when I say that I have no issues outstanding, looking back on what happened, because you have to be in my position and be involved. I know it was wrong; he never should have been shot dead, for whatever reason. I mean, one Irishman shooting another one dead... It could have been down to personality reasons because as far as Trevor was concerned the feud was settled. There was a report in the *Republican News* that there was going to be an inquiry but to the best of my knowledge there was never anything done about it. I didn't see it as a feud because there was no feud at that time. Others would see it as a feud. I think the dirt was done on Trevor because as far as he was concerned it was all settled. Basically at the end of the day they shot him in the back. The IRA claimed that they killed a member of the 'Official' IRA; they didn't give a reason. They said it was being looked into. There was a lot of retaliatory shooting after Trevor was shot. It happened across the city; it happened in Unity Walk, in West Belfast and other places.

As far as I am concerned it's the people left behind who actually suffer quite a lot and have to deal with it and live with it. The most horrible part of all, just after it happens, is going to bed at night. Your mind is in turmoil because you are going through their last minutes of life, wondering what state they were in; that is one of the worst parts of it all. I think the women here in Northern Ireland have bore the biggest brunt of all of this, more than anyone else. When husbands are shot dead women have to carry on looking after their kids and raising them as best they can. When you think about it, at the end of the day, the burden always falls on women, the mother, the wife or partner.

Trevor was my first love, the first boyfriend that I ever had. He was a very good friend and a very good partner; he was very understanding. Trevor lived for life and believed in equality for everybody; to me that was what his aim in life was. I think Trevor's death was a terrible waste. It was a terrible denial to my children who never got to know their father. One of my children was only a year old and the other wasn't even born when their father was killed. They never knew what it was like to have a father and there are loads of kids out there like that and that is the real pathetic part of it all.

> *The family know that those who killed Dinny will never be prosecuted. We just want them to stand up and say that they were murdered in cold blood. Even though they were IRA volunteers at the time..*

Dennis (Dinny) Brown
Killed on active service
by the British army,
Ballysillan Road,
21 June 1978

Dinny Brown was born 13 May 1950. He was the eldest of five children; Dinny, Pat, Margaret, Geraldine and Roisin, born to Dennis and Margaret (née Foster). Dinny attended Holy Cross Boys school and then St Gabriel's. His younger brothers and sisters and his young nephew Paul regarded Dinny as the big brother figure. On leaving school he worked in the Franklin Laundry on the Springfield Road, then in Menzies paper distributors and eventually as a barman in McLaughlin's Bar on Hallidays Road. On 22 August 1970 Dinny married Rosaleen Rooney from the Bone in Sacred Heart chapel. The couple had three children: Mark, Bronagh and Damien.

Dinny Brown was an IRA volunteer. On 21 June 1978 Dinny and two comrades, Jim Mulvenna and Jackie Mailey, were killed while on active service. In one of the earliest cases of 'shoot-to-kill', four IRA volunteers, while attempting to blow up Ballysillan Post Office Telecommunications Depot, were ambushed by the SAS and RUC who were acting on information received. The SAS and RUC had staked out the area at least 24 hours in advance and were lying in wait. The fourth IRA volunteer escaped. A Protestant passer-by, William Hanna, was killed and a friend accompanying him home was wounded in the attack. The inquest papers reveal that all three IRA volunteers could have been arrested. They were unarmed, surrounded, had their hands behind their backs and were lying face down on the ground when they were shot and killed. At least two of the victims were shot repeatedly while lying wounded on the ground. The SAS and RUC fired over one hundred rounds of ammunition. A key eyewitness has stated that he heard no warning shouts before the gunfire.

The extent of Dinny, Jackie and Jim's injuries, evident in the inquest papers, reveals that excessive force was used. It is also clear from the inquest papers the killings were subsequently not adequately investigated by the British authorities. The Brown family, along with the Mailey and Mulvenna families, have launched a campaign to reopen the cases of their loved ones in an effort to establish 'the truth' after twenty-three years of cover-ups and silence.

Mrs Brown (mother)

In the late 1960s Dinny, Hugh Hughes, big Lu Lu and a few others had convinced themselves that they could make their fortune elsewhere. They went to England and survived for about five days. They had no jobs and nowhere to live. Being Irish meant that they drew the attention of the cops and they were arrested. They weren't charged thanks to the intervention of a cousin of Dinny's father who pleaded their case. As soon as they got released, they wasted no time and returned back home to Belfast.

Dinny was a bit shy. Before he would leave the house to go out on his date he'd get me to juke up and down Chatham Street, not to check for Brits but to make sure not too many people were about to see him all dressed up going out on his date. It was an ordeal for him to be seen wearing anything other than his wranglers and jean jacket. He wasted no time getting from our house to Saunderson Street in the Bone to see Rosaleen Rooney who was his girlfriend. They got married in Sacred Heart chapel on 22 August 1970. Uncle Francie ('Hitler') Foster was chauffeur for the day of the wedding and Teddy Foster was their best man. The reception was held in what was then the Crumlin Star. The Star then was nothing more than a tin hut at the junction of Flax Street and Butler Street. It was a great day. Dinny and Rosaleen's first house was in Brookfield Street and then they moved over to Ballynure Street in the Bone. They had three lovely children: Mark, Bronagh and Damien. Dinny was a really devoted father and husband.

Dinny was dedicated to the cause of republicanism. I've never got over his death and neither have the rest of the family. We visit Milltown cemetery weekly but it is one place Dinny's father couldn't go. Dinny's father suffered so much grief when Dinny died it had a huge impact on his health. There's not a day in my life when I don't think of my son and what helps me cope is the great unshakeable belief I have in the power of prayer.

Rosaleen Rooney (widow)

Dinny and I met when we were about 15 years old. My friend and I would go to Ardoyne every night. We met Dinny and his friends at the shops on the Ardoyne Road and we had great fun. Dinny was a joker; he and his friends would ask us to buy cigarettes for them and if we didn't have any money, they would steal our shoes and hang them on the handlebars of the old street lamps.

Dinny and I got our first house in Brookfield Street, just a few houses away from his granny Foster. We would sit in at night at the front of the fire and plan getting married and how many children we would have. We got married when I was 21 in the Sacred Heart chapel. Teddy Foster, Dinny's uncle, was our best man as Pat, Dinny's brother, was in Australia at the time. Mr. Brown had our reception in the old Star club, which then was at the bottom of Butler Street. Mr. Brown, who was also called Dinny, was a member of the Star. We didn't have a honeymoon; we just went home and partied all night.

We had three great children whom Dinny loved. At night when we would be watching television, Dinny would get a water pistol and soak the children and me and just keep us going with his fooling around. Dinny was a very loving and caring person. I asked him once why he joined the Irish Republican Army and he said he wanted a better country for his children to live in. I just hope by losing him it will bring peace and happiness to all in Ireland.

Pat 'Aldo' and Geraldine Brown (brother & sister)

Pat 'Aldo' Brown: My mother was born and reared in Brookfield Street and her maiden name was Foster. My grandparents adopted my father, the Pattersons. He married my mother in 1950 and he took his own name, which was Brown. They had two sons and three daughters. Dennis was the oldest. When my parent's got married they settled in number 45

Chatham Street and that's where we were born and reared. That was the family home. It was my grandparents' house; they lived in the back room and my mother and father and all of the kids lived in the front room. You had nothing then; there was a big tin bath and you brought it in and had your bath on a Saturday night. Most of Ardoyne was reared that way.

I left for Australia in October 1969 and I came back in December of 1971, I was away just over two years. I knew before I came home Dinny was well involved with the republican movement. I saw a powerful change in him when I came back. He had no interest in what was going on before I left; it was just him and his girlfriend. When I came back from Australia it didn't take long until I was sworn in to the IRA in a house in Fairfield Street. Dinny came to me later and said, 'You've gone about this the wrong way. You should have waited and got involved in what I'm involved in; it's called the 'Unknowns'. They aren't out in the front; they do other work in the town and outside the district.' I told him I hadn't known any different.

Dinny was interned in 1973 and then got sentenced to nine months for trying to escape. He started off in Cage 5, hut 28. He was a totally different fella from what I'd seen. Dinny was politicised; he was in tune with what was happening; he was educated to a certain degree. He was very radical but a very straight person. If Dinny didn't like what you said, no matter who you were or what you were, he would let you know his views. He was always straight to the point and there was never any backstabbing. When he got released, he went back to the Bone again. He reported back to the IRA and that was 1975. He didn't go back into jail after that. Then the structure of the IRA was moving into cells, four and five people keeping things tight. He teamed up with Jackie Mailey and Jim Mulvenna and I am not too sure of the others. They ran a tight ship.

The day Dinny was killed, I wasn't actually living in the district. I was living in Ballymurphy Road. I was working in the district in Velsheda Court and I called to my ma's in the mornings, got changed into my work clothes and went straight down to work. I was hudding with Paul Kane and we were talking about the shooting that previous night. Nobody had come to say Dinny had been killed. I said to Paul, 'That was bad last night,' and Paul, being the quiet fella that he is said, ' I think that was your kid'. So I ran from Velsheda right down to Etna Drive entry; obviously on the way down my heart was jumping into my mouth hoping it wasn't the truth. When I got to the entry and saw all of the men standing I knew then it was true. All that I asked was, 'Who was the third man?' and they told me it was Jim Mulvenna. I just turned and walked out of the entry; I didn't know where I was walking but I just walked out of the entry. I walked up Brompton Park and was coming through the gap and at this stage my family didn't know anything about what had happened. I met Dickie Martin outside Lily Davidson's shop and Dickie came over to me and said, ' Aldo, I'm terribly sorry'. I said, 'How am I going to tell my ma and da?' That's all I could think about.

Geraldine Brown: I worked in Stewart's supermarket on the Crumlin Road and I was on my way to work when I saw Pat going into the house; I knew something was wrong. I went back to the house and he was out in the yard squealing and he still didn't tell my ma. My mummy was standing plaiting Roisin's hair for school; and God help my daddy, he was in bed. Aldo was out screaming in the yard and my mummy was saying, ' Pat, what is wrong, what is wrong?' and he said, 'It was Dinny last night.' Everything then just went berserk after that. Jackie Mailey lived at the top of Chatham Street at the time and somebody went up to tell Agnes Mailey. So it was left to the families to tell, well our family anyway. Apparently somebody was sent over to tell Rosaleen and they sat on her wall from 7 o'clock that morning; they just couldn't tell her. Rosaleen said she had woken up about 3 am and had taken the rosary beads down and started saying the rosary. She said she knew.

Pat 'Aldo' Brown: Neither the British army, nor the RUC, came to inform our family. There was no contact at all. They never came near the door to say, 'Your son has been shot dead', or whatever; they just didn't inform anybody. We found out through the grapevine in the area. I went down to identify my brother's body. I was taken into a room and the first body they pulled out was Jackie Mailey. I looked at the body, fully-clothed, full of blood as you could imagine. I was still in shock at this stage and he said, 'Is that your brother?' I said, 'No.' I knew what was going on. So they pulled another body out and it was Jim Mulvenna. He said, ' Is that your brother?' I looked at him and I said, ' No, it is not.' So the third one he pulled out was my brother. He pulled the sheet half way down. I went over and lifted the body. I was feeling round his head and I said, 'Pull the sheet back I want to identify the body properly'. Dinny's body was fully clothed. The guy who worked in the morgue stopped me and said, 'Look, for your own good don't go any further; if that is your brother please identify him.' I said, 'Yes, it is my brother.' He just put the sheet over him again and put him back.

On the way out I stopped at the desk; the RUC man had a form and he said, 'Now this is only formality, we want to know all of your brother's details: your brother's name, where he lived, the last time you saw him, if he was in good health, who his doctor is, how many kids he had.' But I noticed on the form he had written Dennis, in brackets Aldo, and then Brown. I said, 'What's this?' And he said, 'That's nothing; it's a mistake,' and he scribbled Aldo out. I said, 'If you want to know his right name I will tell you his right name; it was Dennis Emanuel Brown.'

Geraldine and Pat 'Aldo' Brown: The impact on the family was devastating, particularly the way it happened and the circumstances surrounding it. Dinny was the oldest and we were, and still are, a very close-knit family. Dinny and Pat worked on the building site in Ardoyne and that meant they came to my mammy's every dinner hour. On Saturdays and Sundays Dinny was over with the kids and if he missed one day out of the week, my mummy knew he was arrested.

The family believe that Dinny should have been, and could have been, arrested. To us it was premeditated. The SAS knew that the operation was taking place; they could have taken them prisoner and intercepted at any time. We believe they knew they weren't armed. They had the area staked out for two days. There was an RUC man along with the SAS. None of the SAS were at the inquest; there was a guy representing the MOD. The RUC man said, 'I emptied my sub-machine gun and then reloaded again'. He talked about a gun battle. But there were no guns found on my brother and the others. The British army released a statement the next day saying there was a gun battle between IRA volunteers and the British army. It then transpired that the volunteers had no guns and that all they had was incendiary bombs. The SAS fired 171 rounds that night and a passer-by called Hanna was shot dead too. His brother actually stated in one of the newspapers that he was going for an inquiry into his brother's death. The whole cover-up of the circumstances is an issue for all of our families and the way we were treated by the British security forces. We want to know why the SAS fired so many rounds; the lads were obviously unarmed when they were killed. The British security forces never admitted that there had been no gun battle, so officially they are still saying that there was a gun battle even though there were no weapons found on the bodies. There was no forensics connecting them to weapons.

The family know that those who killed Dinny will never be prosecuted. We just want them to stand up and say that they were murdered in cold blood. Even though they were IRA volunteers at the time, the European Court of Human Rights has stated clearly, you have a right to life. It is a human right. This was declared recently in the case of the Loughgall Inquiry, that everyone has the right to life. Dinny was denied that right and was so viciously killed.

Dinny was a very sound person. He had loads of friends. A straighter fella you wouldn't have met in your life. Anytime you were in trouble he was always there to help you. He was a good family man; he had three lovely kids and wife and they all think very highly of him. Dinny is sadly missed and the families will never get over it. Our mother had to get on with things because there were other kids in the family. My daddy was never the same after it. My daddy died eleven years after Dinny and he never accepted his death; he never came to terms with it. He was a quiet man and would never speak about it. We used to go up to the graveyard every Sunday and my daddy actually parked the car and sat outside the graveyard. He borrowed the car off his mate to take us to the graveyard and he used to say that he couldn't leave the car unattended. He just said that; he couldn't face the graveyard. He just never got over it.

> *The saddest day of my life was the day my son Jim was buried. They had murdered him and I was burying him. My daughter and son had been released on compassionate parole for the funeral. Then they came and they took my daughter Patricia back to Armagh jail. Then they came and they took my son Paul back to Long Kesh. But for once I had them all together after all the years they were separated. Then I stood at the door and watched the three of them go again. I wouldn't want anybody to go through that day.*

Jim Mulvenna
Killed on active service
by the British army,
Ballysillan Road,
21 June 1978

Jim Mulvenna was born on 26 January 1950. His parents were Agnes (née Mulholland) from Islandbawn Street, Falls Road and Patrick Mulvenna, originally from Mayfair Street in the Bone. When Agnes was 14 years old her family moved to Brompton Park, Ardoyne. She met and later married Patrick in Holy Cross chapel. Due to the dire housing shortage in Catholic North Belfast, the newlyweds moved in with Patrick's mother to number 15 Mayfair Street. A few years later they bought a house in Ladbrook Drive but moved back to Mayfair Street where they reared their seven children: Jim, Philomena, Mary, Patricia, Paul, Loretta and Anthony.

Jim was the eldest of the seven children. He attended Holy Cross Boys school, went to St Gabriel's for a few years and finished his education at the Christian Brothers. His first job was in Mackie's where he trained as an engineer. In a familiar story of religious discrimination, despite being better qualified than many of his Protestant work mates, Jim was one of the first to be paid-off when work became slack. He then took up employment as a rent collector and for a while worked in the construction business in Derry. According to his family and friends Jim was a bit of a loner; he was very deep, 'a thinker' and an avid reader. Foremost he was a dedicated republican and an idealist. He was close to his family and in particular his sisters whom he was protective of. The other side to Jim was his mischievous nature; he was well-known in Long Kesh for the pranks that he played. But by all accounts he was a 'very cool', level-headed and steadfast person.

Jim Mulvenna was an IRA volunteer. On 21 June 1978 Jim and two comrades, Dinny Brown and Jackie Mailey, were killed while on active service. In one of the earliest cases of 'shoot-to-kill' four IRA volunteers, while attempting to blow up Ballysillan Post Office Telecommunications Depot, were ambushed by the SAS and RUC who were acting on information received (see Dinny Brown case for details of the incident). The Mulvenna family, along with the Mailey and Brown families, have launched a campaign to reopen the cases of their loved ones in an effort to establish 'the truth' after twenty-three years of cover-ups and silence.

Agnes Mulvenna and Philomena Baker (mother & sister)

Jim was born in Paddy's mother's house in Gracehill Street. His first job was in Mackie's doing engineering. He earned a small wage of £4. When he turned eighteen, and he got his City and Guilds, his money went up to £8. I was delighted when he got his City and Guilds; I thought he was flying doing engineering. He lost his job in Mackie's because he was a Catholic. He found out later that a Protestant boy took his place. There was real, real discrimination going back into the 1950s and '60s; it was bad. That was a terrible thing to happen to him; it deprived him of doing the job that he wanted. He got a job with Montague, the rent people and he collected rents in Ardoyne. But that didn't suit him. Mrs Brown said to him one day when he came for the rent, 'Jim, the rent is spent, son', and he killed himself laughing, and he said, 'Did you enjoy your dinner?'

Jim was a loner to be quite honest. He was very politically aware and he joined the republican movement. He was up in Ligoniel on an IRA operation and the British forces ambushed and shot him. He had nine bullets in him. They took him to Musgrave Park Hospital and when I got there, they said there was nothing they could do for him. But the doctor came out and he said 'Ach heck', that's the way he said it to me; 'Ach heck, I may as well take a chance and operate because he is only lying there anyway'. Jim was shot in the back, shot in the gut, shot in the two legs and shot in the arm. They operated on him and after a lot of hours, they told me he had a 50/50 chance of surviving. But he was brave. He was only over the operations in February and on the 18 April he jumped two storeys and got away in his pyjamas. But he was caught in the Bog Meadows the day that Joe McCann was buried. The funeral was going on and he was lying in the ditch. His father and I heard that he had escaped and we went in the car looking for him. We drove down Broadway and a cousin of my husband ran out and shouted, 'You're too late; they have got him already'. We drove to Musgrave Park Hospital and they had him lying on the floor. I'll always remember it. I said, 'Jim, why didn't you tell me? Sure, I would have got one hundred cars for you'. Then he was brought to court and sentenced to seven years; that was in 1971. He served four and a half years in Long Kesh. He was released on the 1st June 1976 and he was shot dead in June 1978. About three or four months before he was killed his daughter Ciara was born. A beautiful girl she is. Her mother Kathleen and Jim had a life together for about a year and a half; they lived together in Ballycastle Street.

When he came out of the Kesh he would not draw the dole; he was that type. That's the kind of person he was; he was an idealist, he really was. He used to say to me, 'Mother, always remember to thine own self be true', and I said, 'You've been reading again'. He was a great reader. I depended on him an awful lot; he was like a father figure. He would have listened to your problems. He was a calm person; maybe he thought too much. He would have sat and planned things out. I used to say, 'I have six jewels and one gem'. He was my gem. It's just that he was hurt so badly and for him to have come through what he did and then to start doing a sentence... To me seven years was terrible.

I have a daughter Patricia and she got nine years and another son who got eight years. Patricia was released in 1979, the year after Jim died. Paul got released in 1980. I had three children in at the same time. It was touch and go running from one prison to another. The British army raided my house thirty times in one weekend alone. In the end I said, 'Evidently this is your house not mine'; I handed them the key. They raided me Friday, Saturday, right through into Sunday. The saracens just drove round the corner and drove back and stopped. I can honestly say that I never got into bed unless I was fully-clothed. That's the way I went to bed, whatever I had on me, in and out again; that went on for a long time. God, you wouldn't want anybody to go through what we have gone through!

When Jim was murdered, the RUC never came to say he was shot dead; nobody came to tell me anything. At that time Paddy was doing taxi-ing in Ardoyne and some fella stopped him and said, 'I think Jim is one of the fellas shot up in Ballysillan'. Nobody ever came to tell me. That fella told Paddy and he came over and told me. Jim knew he was going to die; he told me and Philomena. About two months before he was killed, he got down on his knee and he said, 'Mammy, you know I'm going to die', and I said, 'Don't be talking like that', but he knew it himself. Then the night before he died, he said a similar thing to Philomena. Jim and Philomena were very close; he called to her the night before he died and he said to her, 'Mena, I'm never going to live to see my daughter Ciara grow up'. He had been that badly shot the first time I thought it would never happen again. Well, given the law of averages, it should never have happened again. But he was a dedicated republican; there was nothing that would have swayed him.

In my opinion Jim, Dinny and Jackie were murdered. They really were. I knew from the day and hour they were shot that they were deliberately murdered because they didn't have any guns. The Protestant people up in Ballysillan said that the British army had surveillance in the area 24-48 hours beforehand. They knew that there was something going to happen. They were definitely informed on. They could have been arrested; they were entitled to that. They were entitled to their life. We are bringing the case to the European Court. I would like to see us getting justice but I have no doubt we will not get it. But if we are bringing the Brits through the courts that will be good enough and hopefully the truth will come out, but to be honest I don't expect to get that either.

Jim was a great person and I'm not just saying that because he was ours, but he was. He had great character. The saddest day of my life was the day Jim was buried, 1978. They had murdered Jim and I was burying him and then they came and they took my daughter Patricia back to Armagh prison. Then they came and they took my son Paul back to Long Kesh. But for once I had them all together after all the years they were separated. Then I stood at the door and watched the three of them go again. I wouldn't want anybody to go through that day.

Kathleen Doran (partner)

I met Jim while I was working in the Glenpark as a waitress. The Glenpark was his local club. We had known each other from away back, just as friends. We got chatting as you do and he left me home one night. Then we started going out together. We mostly socialised in the district; that's where Jim felt happiest. I think we ventured into the town once and we had a drink or two in the Bodega. We started living together and we had a house in Ballycastle Street, number 25. I became pregnant which Jim was over the moon about. We didn't have a very lush life; we just had the basics. We were quite content to be at home getting prepared for the baby's arrival. At that stage Jim knocked about with Dinny Brown and Jackie Mailey. They, and their wives, were good friends of both of us. We all socialised together. The six of us were great friends. I give birth to our daughter on 30 January 1978 and we named her Ciara. That was just the start of a whole new thing because there was now three of us and he was just delighted.

We got a lot of harassment from the British army. They regularly raided the house. I knew that Jim was in the IRA; there was no secret that he was involved. I would have worried when he was leaving the house. He had served a lot of time and I don't think it ever crossed his mind that it might happen again. But Jim kept himself to himself and never discussed what he was doing.

The night Jim and his two friends, Jackie and Dinny, were shot dead, I think everybody must have heard the shooting except me. I remember round the time they were being shot I was sitting at the side of the bed feeding the baby. I heard nothing, no gunfire. The next morning I still didn't know he had been shot dead. My door knocked and Jim's brother-in-law Sammy Baker was at the door. My first reaction was they had been arrested. I really thought he was going to say they had been arrested. I did not expect him to say they were dead. It was raining that morning and I remember going upstairs and lifting the child out of her cot and walking out into the rain. I didn't even have a coat on. I just kept walking aimlessly. This lady stopped me and brought me into her house. Someone phoned my parents and they arrived. I didn't know where I was going and what I was doing. I was in a state of total shock. I'll never forget the feeling that I had that morning.

We had problems trying to find out where they had taken their bodies. Jim's body was taken to Forster Green. My father and brother drove me there to identify him. We got to Forster Green and they just left us in a room; there was no trace of manners about them at all. They left us in the room until the Special Branch arrived and then they brought us to identify the body. Jim was there by himself. There was eight or nine of them standing round us. I can remember putting my hands on Jim and he was soaking wet. I happened to say to my daddy, 'He's soaking wet', and one of the Special Branch said, 'You would be soaking wet if you were lying in a field all night'. I remember my father saying to them, 'You couldn't lick that man's boots'. We just walked out. Jim's body was brought home to his mummy's house and that is where he was buried from.

Ciara is now 23 and I think she has felt cheated over the years. I had to wait until she was a bit older to tell her about what happened to her father. But sometimes other people get to your child before you do. She came into me one day and she said, 'My daddy was shot dead'. She was three, going on four at the time. I had to sit her down and explain everything to her but I couldn't explain everything to her. She couldn't really understand what I was talking about. As time went on I kept all of the newspapers of the time and I was able to produce the newspapers and let her read for herself. She was horrified when she heard the way that they were slaughtered; there was no necessity for that amount of ammunition to be used on unarmed men. Ciara has accepted it now. She has a wee boy of her own now; he is four years old. But we will wait until he gets much older before we tell him what happened.

Jim was a fun man but he was also a deep man. He served a lot of time. He had done a lot for his country without any qualms about it. This country needed men like the three volunteers. It was a sin the way they were killed. It was a sin because he was looking forward to his daughter growing up and she lost out, he lost out and I lost out. Jim was just doing what was necessary for his country. When I think back about the age he would be now and what could have happened and it didn't. Jim had been through an awful lot and he was a very strong man, very strong in his mind yet very gentle. He was very loving and very caring towards me. It was just a terrible loss for myself, for our baby and his family. It was a tragedy.

Jackie Mailey
Killed on active service
by the British army,
Ballysillan Road,
21 June 1978

If Jackie had been arrested, he would have done his time. He would have been out long, long ago and back with his family. That is the hardest part to grasp – because we believe they were brutally murdered and they could have been arrested. We have launched a campaign and I just want to get the truth about what really happened that night. I know we'll never get justice; we all know that. But there are so many questions to be answered.

Jackie Mailey, better known as 'Jake', was born 17 September 1947. His parents were William Mailey from Elmfield Street, Ardoyne and Sarah (née Lambe), originally from Ballymoney Street. The couple were married in Holy Cross chapel in 1946 and eventually had thirteen children, including triplets. Four of the thirteen children died and nine survived: Patrick, Jackie, Jim, Tom, Anne, Carol, Linda, Noel and Sharon. The young couple lived for the first five years of their married life, and reared four children, in the upstairs room of William's Aunt Minnie's house in Elmfield Street. In 1952 they moved a few doors down to 5 Elmfield Street and this became the family home.

Like most young lads in the district Jackie went to Holy Cross Boys school and then on to St Gabriel's. He finished his education at 15, became an apprentice tiler and later worked in Hicks and Bullocks. Jackie was always very protective of his younger brothers and sisters. He was a fairly deep person and a modest fella by all accounts. In 1971 he married an Ardoyne girl, Agnes Mullan from Chatham Street. They had three sons: Sean, Seamus and Niall. Niall was only three weeks old when his father was killed. At the time of his death Jackie Mailey was an IRA volunteer. On 21 June 1978 Jackie and two comrades, Dinny Brown and Jim Mulvenna, were killed while on active service. In one of the earliest cases of 'shoot-to-kill'. Four IRA volunteers, while attempting to blow up Ballysillan Post Office Telecommunications Depot, were ambushed by the SAS and RUC who were lying in wait. The fourth IRA volunteer escaped (see Dinny Brown case for details of the ambush). The Mailey family, along with the Brown and Mulvenna families, have launched a campaign to reopen the cases of their loved ones in an effort to establish 'the truth' after twenty-three years of cover-ups and silence.

Patrick Mailey (brother)

Most of Jackie's friends knew him as Jake. He was an excellent snooker player. Any spare time he had he would have spent up in the League playing snooker with his brothers and cousins. He wasn't interested in any other sports and he loved to get out with his mates for a few drinks and a bit of craic. Jake was a very independent person; when he got something into his head there was no shifting him. He just wouldn't back down for anyone; he was so stubborn when I think about it now.

I was interned and so was Jake. I was released before Christmas 1973 and Jake in late 1974. I suspected that Jake was already involved in the republican movement before he was interned. I know he rejoined the IRA after his release from the Kesh. Our mother and father would not have known about his involvement in the movement. Our home was raided before we were interned, during and after internment. The RUC and British army had no respect for our property or our family. They would leave our home in a total mess. But in saying that, most families in the area would have experienced the same as our family.

The day that Jake and his two comrades, Dinny and Jim, were shot I was talking to him. It was only for a few minutes; I was on my way to work. But I remember that he was in good form. The three of them were in the League that day and had a game of snooker with my cousin Michael. It wasn't until the next morning that I heard the news that Jake, Dinny and Jim had been killed. I didn't believe it at the start; I was working away when Jackie Donnelly, who was on his way to work, pulled up in his car and said, 'Patrick, Jake and the boys, they were shot dead last night'. I couldn't believe it was true. On the way round to tell my mother and father the bad news I had to keep saying to myself, 'For God sake Patrick, pull yourself together'. As I approached the house, a neighbour told me that they already knew. It wasn't from the RUC or the British army that my parents found out. No one ever called to inform the family about the death of my brother; we had to find out for ourselves. My mother told me later that Jake had called to see them the night before he was shot; he kissed my mother and father and said good night before leaving.

Jake and his comrades were murdered by the SAS on Wednesday morning, 21 June 1978. They were unarmed, trying to plant a bomb at Ballysillan Post Office Telecommunications Depot in Belfast. SAS men were waiting in ambush for them and surrounded them. They then opened fire on them, mercilessly cutting them down; two innocent victims were also shot as they walked home. The British army admitted later to firing over one hundred rounds. People said to me that they had heard the shooting that night. I was in my mother and father's house in Elmfield Street that night and we didn't hear any shooting, thank God.

Myles O'Kane drove me and Aldo (Dinny's brother) and young Alex Trainor to Tennent Street RUC barracks. The RUC told us to follow them to the morgue. I went into the morgue on my own. The RUC pulled something like a big slab out and there was Jim Mulvenna. The RUC man said, 'Do you know him?' I said, 'No'. I wasn't telling them anything. He pulled the next one out and it was Dinny. 'Do you know him?' 'No', I said. By this time it was starting to get to me and obviously Jake was next. He said, 'Do you know him?' I just lost it at that point. It wasn't until months later when I settled down that I thought about what had happened in the morgue. I believe the RUC deliberately showed me the three bodies. I'm sure that some of the families of the two other lads murdered along with my brother had to go through the same ordeal. I'm sure the RUC would have kept their loved one to the last also.

While I was in the morgue there was a young fella there. He was younger than me; he was about 22 or 23 and he was crying. I found out later that he was a young Protestant lad. A member of his family was also shot dead as he walked home that night. Maybe he had seen what happened, the SAS executing my brother and his two comrades and they shot him. Another Protestant man was also shot and wounded and was lucky to survive. I believe that Jackie and his comrades were captured and had their hands up. They were unarmed and of no danger to anyone when they were executed by the SAS. The two Protestant men I think witnessed what had happened and were both shot.

Jake was the best man at my wedding; we were very close, being the two oldest in the family. I feel very bitter about the total cover-up of the circumstances. We would like to know what really happened that morning; the truth is all we ask. I still can't get over it. The family has never received any official notification from the RUC, British army or the British government about the circumstances surrounding the death of Jake. All we want is to know the truth about what really happened.

Ann Stewart (sister)

My earliest memories of Jackie are that he was always very protective towards us. He always worried about us and he was very, very close to us. My father wasn't well for a number of years and Jackie took on the father figure role for his younger brothers and sisters. When we were in our teens we had to be in for a certain time or Jackie was out round the district looking for us and sent you home no matter who you were with. He was that type of person; he looked after you and he expected you to do what you were told as a teenager growing up. In the house he was just a messer, always up to something. He came in one Friday and just said to my parents that he was getting married to Agnes (Mullan) the next Friday. All the older ones in the family went to the wedding; it was too short notice for my mother to get the younger ones sorted. The reception was held in Agnes's mother's house. Everybody had a great day and Jackie seemed very happy. They had three sons, Sean, Seamus and Niall. His son Niall was only three weeks old when Jackie was murdered. I remember he was just so happy when Niall was born. Little did you know he was only going to see the child for three weeks and the child would never know him. Jackie loved his children. Had he lived I think he would have had many more children. It really is so sad because his sons would have had such a wonderful relationship with their father and he would be a grandfather now.

I knew about Jackie's involvement in the movement but didn't know the extent of his involvement. My husband Joe and I heard the shooting that night; we where in bed in our house in Strathroy Park. The next morning I got up and didn't even hear the news. I went on to work in Gallaher's in York Street. Then I was sent for. The Protestant fella, William Hanna, who was shot with my brother, his sister worked on the floor below me. She was a stranger to me. When I went down to the medical office I noticed a girl sitting crying and they were giving her a sedative. It was William Hanna's sister. I didn't realise her brother had been shot dead with my brother. I was just told that there had been an accident and I had to go home. There were two taxis waiting outside, one for me and one for William Hanna's sister.

The taxi took me straight up to my mother's house. When I arrived, my father and brother-in-law were sitting there and they just said, 'Jackie has been murdered' and that was just the beginning. It was sheer agony, that is the only way I can describe it. I looked especially at the faces of my mother and father; I was in agony and I knew that Jackie was their son first and foremost. At Jackie's funeral I looked at my father's face as he was carrying the coffin; he seemed to have aged ten years over night, he really, really did. He got very ill afterwards.

My mother and father found out about Jackie's death when a young lad, Sammy Toaster, came up to our house and he said, 'Sadie, your Jackie was killed last night; your Jackie was shot dead last night'. That's how my mother found out. My mother and sister Carol automatically ran up to Jackie's house and my mother asked his wife Agnes where Jackie was. My mother always says that her heart was thumping and she was saying to herself, 'Please, please don't let him have stayed out'. Agnes told her Jackie hadn't come home the previous night. After that my mother knew it was true. It was just devastation after that. Agnes was very distraught at the time as well; she just started screaming and screaming, then neighbours came running in.

I think the whole community was really hurt; three men murdered was a terrible loss for the community. They were three good men, three very good volunteers. Jackie was a very, very loyal person. It came out in the way he looked after his family and I know he would have been like that as a republican, as a member of the IRA. It was a hard loss for everybody. I don't think any of the families have ever got over it.

It was a massive funeral; there were thousands at it. Barney McKenna took an awful lot to do with the funeral. Some things you can remember but others things you can't, you were too distressed. The RUC never came to the house to explain and nobody ever came to the house to offer us counselling. After the funeral, the feeling in the area was very, very tense. But to be honest the family were completely devastated because it's after the funeral that the real nightmare kicks in. I can honestly say for two solid years after Jackie's death it got harder and harder; it went to a certain peak where it couldn't get any harder and then you started to learn to live with your heartache.

My brother Pat went to the inquest. Pat took it really, desperately bad as well. Pat just told us it was an open verdict. I think he didn't tell us details about the inquest because he didn't want us to suffer any more than we already had. He just didn't want us to be hurt any more by going into details about what happened, what really happened. I have only found out recently, in the last few months, when I read the inquest papers the extent of injuries and what happened to my brother. Going through the inquest papers I realised that Jackie was still alive and lying on the ground wounded when he was shot. I just really couldn't believe what I was reading. I really honestly couldn't. I can't emphasise that enough, the cruelty. You see people on TV saying, 'I forgive them, I forgive them'. I just can't; I'm not strong enough maybe. I have good enough faith but I don't think I could ever forgive. When I read the inquest papers and saw the extent of Jackie's injuries I was shocked. I could never forgive them because when I look at the devastation they've caused my family and the other two families, they didn't care about us or our loved ones.

We have launched a campaign and I just want to get the truth about what really happened that night. I know we'll never get justice; we all know that. There are so many questions to be answered and when you read the inquest papers there are so many contradictions the whole way through. Soldier A, B, C – they just literally murdered them and got away with it. I know they will get away with it but it's important even to have them stand and admit what they did like in so many other cases. I find as the months go on you get more determined. I think reading the inquest papers it hurt you so much but it gave you an inner strength to say, right, let's try and do something about it. After all this time the hurt doesn't go away. The rest of the family are all one hundred percent behind the campaign; the three families are, and we'll just do what we can. We are getting plenty of support from the community and from different groups.

As a family we are very close. I always say your family is your blood and to me when Jackie was murdered we lost blood as well; that's the way I feel about it. You do go on with your life because you have to get on with things, rear your family, but there's not a day that goes past that you don't miss him out of your life. If he had been arrested he would have done his time. He would have been out long, long ago and back with his family. That is the hardest part to grasp. Because you know they were brutally murdered and they could have been arrested. It should never have happened.

Jackie was a very strong, loyal person. In many ways he was a very modest person. He was a very loving son to my parents and he was a very, very good brother. He is dearly missed. There is not a day goes by that I don't think of Jackie and say a prayer. I don't think there ever will be; he is just so deeply missed.

Frankie Donnelly
Killed on active service,
Northwick Drive,
5 January 1979

> *The real sad part is Frankie never got to see his daughter Frances and she never got to see him. Frankie was killed in January and Frances was born in July.*

Frankie Donnelly's father, Frank, was born and reared in Chatham Street, Ardoyne. His mother Mary (née Doherty) was originally from Vere Street in Sailortown. The couple married in 1950 and had three children, Betty, Jackie and Frankie. Frankie was the youngest child, born 26 August 1954. He attended Holy Cross Boys and then St Gabriel's Secondary school. He initially worked as a welder and then took up employment as a labourer. Although Frankie was quiet, he was a very sociable person. Throughout his life he had a number of close friends, including Marty Devlin, John McGurk and Kevin McGarry. Frankie was interned from May 1974 to November 1975. In 1978 he married Rosemary Foster in Holy Cross chapel. They had saved for years to furnish their new home and were looking forward to married life. As his brother Jackie said, 'Rosemary was Frankie's whole life'.

Frankie Donnelly was an IRA volunteer. On 5 January 1979 while on active service Frankie and his comrade Lawrence Montgomery were killed. They were moving incendiary bombs when the devices exploded prematurely, killing both volunteers. Frankie was aged 24 at the time of his death. Several months later his wife Rosemary gave birth to their only child Frances.

Rosemary Donnelly (widow)

When Frankie and I were going together, I guessed he was a member of the Fianna although he never actually told me. We went together for six years and finally married on 26 August 1978; this was an extra special date as it was also Frankie's birthday. Throughout the six years Frankie kept up his involvement in the republican movement and became a member of the IRA. I accepted Frankie's commitment and knew he would always be connected, although how deeply I never really knew.

On 4 January 1979, the day before his death, Frankie came home from work late; it was about 9 pm. We just sat talking that night about plans for the baby. I was a few weeks pregnant. Next morning I got up as usual and got ready to go to work. Frankie at this stage had already left the house. I called to my mother's house and heard an explosion. Unaware that Frankie had been injured in the explosion, I left my mother's to go to work. On the way up the Crumlin Road a friend said to me, 'Wasn't it awful about the explosion?' and she went on to say that the work boots of a man could be clearly seen in the wreckage. I knew Frankie was wearing work boots so alarm bells were triggered but I tried to put my fears in perspective. The area was swamped with the British army. The next thing I remember was my aunt arrived at work to bring me home. On the way down I saw some of Frankie's friends that were connected and I started to scream at them, 'What is going on?' I knew then that the explosion had killed Frankie. From then on, everything is practically a dream to me.

Hundreds came to pay their respects at the house. The following Monday Frankie was buried from Holy Cross chapel along with Lawrence Montgomery who was killed in the explosion. By the time their cortege got to the Falls Road a few thousand people were following it.

Frankie had been interned in Long Kesh from May 1974 until November 1975. I still have every letter he ever wrote to me. We wrote to each other every single day. I know Frankie took a lot of stick about this from the rest of the lads in his hut. Frankie was a very tactful person and he had time for anyone. No matter how big or small their problems, he would always try and help. I gave birth to our daughter Frances on 24 July 1979. Frances has developed into a lovely young woman and I think she has inherited a lot of her daddy's personality.

Jackie Donnelly (brother)

My parents were married in 1950 in Holy Cross chapel. My mother and father got married, for those days, fairly late in life. My father was 29 and my mother was a few years older. My father had been interned for about six years and was released in 1947. That might account for them marrying late in life. He was a republican right up until his death. He got an IRA guard of honour at his funeral. We were born in 60 Highbury Gardens. That was always the family home. My grandfather, aunt Betty, mother, father and the three children lived there. Frankie was just an ordinary fella. His friends didn't change over the years. But he got very friendly with Lawrence Montgomery, the fella he was killed with. He loved a bet, but he wasn't a heavy gambler. His nickname was

'Fungus' but I don't know where it came from; I have no idea. I think it was one of those boy things, something that came out of school. Frankie was very quiet and easy going but a good mixer. He was the type of fella that didn't offend anybody, therefore people naturally liked him. He kept himself very much to himself. I didn't even know that he was connected with the movement until he was interned and joined me in the Cages. He was interned in 1974 and I was already in.

He left school in 1969. He didn't have a steady job in his early life; he worked for a while at welding and then took whatever work came his way. Later in life he worked steady as a labourer on the building sites in Ardoyne. Then he started going out with Rosemary. I didn't know Rosemary until he introduced me to her. What actually happened was we were both interned and we used to get double visits. My father had cancer and the double visits made it easier for him to visit us. My father couldn't make one of the visits and Rosemary came up. He was already going with Rosemary. That's when I met her. They got married in 1978. He did what he had to do for the IRA; the rest of his life was Rosemary and trying to get a house sorted out, making sure he had work and that was basically it. His whole life was Rosemary. They had just started off their lives as a married couple and Rosemary had just found out she was pregnant.

The morning he died was a Friday morning; I can remember it exactly. I lived in the bottom end of Etna Drive and I was awoken by the sound of explosions. I knew it was in close proximity. It was about 7 am. I got dressed and walked up the street. I could see the ambulance driving off. Crowds of people were in Eddie Donnelly's house in Etna Drive and I went in. I remember everybody who was there. I could see the car burnt out and I said, 'What's happened?' Everybody said, 'I don't know'. It really annoyed me at the time. I'm still annoyed about it now when I think about it. I sat in that house for a good half-hour. I was still saying, 'Who do you reckon did it? Do you reckon it was the loyalists?' People kept saying, 'I don't know'. I didn't know the people in the car were dead. I was told they were taken to the hospital. But I didn't know who it was. I had no idea and that is what annoyed me. I walked out of the house and as I walked down Etna Drive Jim Truick stopped me and said, 'You don't know, do you?' I said, 'Know what?' He said, 'That was your kid'. And that was the first I knew about it. What annoyed me was the boys in the house knew but they didn't say for whatever reason. They probably did it for the best of reasons but that really did have an affect on me. I said to Jim, 'Does Rosemary know? Does Betty know'? He said 'Jackie, we thought you knew'.

My aunt Betty took it really bad. My sister Betty couldn't even get home for the funeral. She was living in England and the weather was so bad she couldn't get a flight. At about 10 o'clock the RUC pulled up to the family house in Highbury Gardens. They wanted me to identify the body. The RUC man said, 'You're Frankie Donnelly's brother? Come with us; you have to identify the body'. I said, 'I'm not identifying any body'. The RUC man said, 'I'll arrest you', and I said, 'Do whatever the fuck you want but I'm not identifying any body'. It was obvious what they were up to. Jackie Doherty, a cousin, who was in the house at the time, agreed to identify the body. That was a Friday and they were the longest days of my life until he got buried. I got arrested the day after the funeral and held for three days. The Special Branch taunted me about Frankie's death. But they couldn't have made me feel any worse than I was already feeling.

Frankie was a volunteer in the IRA; he knew exactly what was happening and what could happen. Unfortunately the bomb detonated for whatever reason but that came with the territory. Obviously Rosemary would find that difficult to accept but I accept it and would have no grievances about it with anyone. It was just a very sad thing that happened. Frankie and Lawrence got a military funeral and they are buried together. We had to take the tricolour off the coffin outside the church and then put it back on again outside. On an individual level, I have no complaints whatsoever about the church. Fr. Fernando was very, very, helpful. He did what he was expected to do and he was very, very kind towards Rosemary and the rest of the family. I think he genuinely grieved with the family.

The real sad part is Frankie never got to see his daughter Frances and she never got to see him. Frances was born after his death. Frankie was killed in January and Frances was born in July. Frankie knew Rosemary was pregnant and they were really delighted. That's the real sad part. The nice part of it is you would swear blind that he spat Frances out of his mouth; she's his double.

Betty Doherty (aunt)

Frankie's mother Mary died of cancer on 28 February 1970. Jackie was 17, Frankie was 15 and Betty had just gone 18. Frankie stayed with me after his mummy died. His closest friends were Marty 'Duck' Devlin, Davy Glennon and John McGurk. They were the three musketeers. The first time I knew Frankie was involved with the republican movement was when I saw him doing guard of honour at Jim Reid's funeral. He idolised Jackie, his big brother; he used to copy him in many ways. When he was young and his mummy was working the night shift I used to put him up to bed and teach him his prayers. He went everywhere with me. I got him his first communion and confirmation clothes. I was very protective of him. Then Frankie met Rosemary and they got engaged while he was interned.

My house was continually raided. The Brits tortured me; they wrecked my house many, many times. They planted bullets in my yard once during a raid. It was the early hours of the morning when they raided. The Scottish soldier went out to the yard and the next thing he said, ' Get your boys up; get them up. Wait till you see what I have found.' Frankie, Jackie and Gunther lived in my house at the time. Out of nowhere the Brit produced six bullets. He had planted them in the grate. The boys were arrested and taken to Castlereagh. My sister and myself had to report to Tennent Street RUC station that night. It ended up they let the boys out and there was nobody charged. But that was the type of thing the British army did.

I remember the morning Frankie died, the funny thing was I didn't hear the explosion. I went round and opened the shop. The next thing one of the lads came and asked me had I seen Jackie. An awful dread came over me and I said to myself, 'Sacred heart of Jesus, I wonder if our Jackie has been involved in that explosion.' Not for one minute did I dream it was Frankie. The next thing, Jackie walked into the shop and told me Frankie had been in the explosion. I went into hysterics. I wanted to go to the hospital but Jackie advised me not to. They had to get Tommy Maguire to bring me round home. The next thing I saw Mary McGuigan coming up my path. I knew right away Frankie was dead. The next thing I saw Rosemary nearly getting carried down the street.

When Frankie was killed I went off the rails, to be honest. I couldn't sleep. I was working in the Highfield at the time. I took two or three drinks while I was working and would have taken another three or four at the end of the night. This was to try and get me to sleep. I didn't realise at the time that I was doing myself more harm than good. I used to go over to Northwick Drive where they were killed and I prayed to Our Lady to let me see him. I was always crying. It really hit me hard. But when Frances was born that really brought me round. With all of the stress I didn't think Rosemary was going to carry the child; it was a miracle.

Frankie was buried from my house; he was born here, made his first communion, confirmation, was married and buried from here. Rosemary wanted that; it was her husband and her decision and she came to me and said, 'Betty, will you bury Frankie?' I said, 'It would be an honour, Rosemary.' I have a great memory but with Frankie's death I blanked an awful lot of that out of my mind. His daughter, Frances, is very like her daddy. In her he was born again. She is like him in every way. She is very close to me too as he was. When he was young he was my right hand. Frankie was my blue eye. He was genuine in every way. What he believed in was genuine too. He is still sorely missed.

Lawrence Montgomery
Killed on active service,
Northwick Drive,
5 January 1979

He was just a good, ordinary bloke, no different to anybody else, very warm, always had plenty of time for you.

Lawrence Montgomery was born on 12 June 1954. His mother Veronica died of cancer when he was only 18 months old. His aunt Patricia, whom he called his mother, reared him. Lawrence came fourth in a large family of six sisters – Eilis, Veronica, Christina, Ann, Pat, Deirdre – and two brothers – Sean and Robin. He attended Sacred Heart school and went on to St Gabriel's. After leaving school he was a 'jack of all trades' and worked, amongst other things, as barman in the Highfield social club and for a time with Ardoyne Taxis. Lawrence married Maureen when they were both very young and they had two children, Laura and Ciaran. He was a great provider and devoted to his family. He was a very private person, quiet and well-liked.

Lawrence Montgomery was an IRA volunteer. On 5 January 1979, while on active service, Lawrence and his comrade Frankie Donnelly were killed when the incendiary bombs they were moving exploded prematurely. Lawrence was twenty-three years old at the time of his death.

Maureen (widow)

Lawrence was a very easygoing person and very private. He loved his children deeply and was not only a husband but also a great friend to me. He was a great believer in saving and never borrowed. If we needed anything, he worked and saved the money before he would borrow it. He was a great friend of Pat McCabe. Pat was a fellow volunteer; he was shot dead in Etna Drive by the British army. His other mates were Paul Murphy and Martin Reid. I knew Lawrence was involved in the IRA, although how deeply I wasn't sure because he kept that to himself. He never spent time in jail and to the best of my knowledge he was never arrested.

The day before Lawrence died I had a feeling something was going down; not that Lawrence said anything; it was just that he seemed very busy. I had fallen asleep on the settee; it was around 7.15-7.30 am when there was a loud explosion and I awoke. My stomach was in knots. I had a gut feeling that told me something bad had happened. Neighbours in the street had come out. I asked Ann Toner to keep an eye on the two kids who were still in bed until I ran to the shop. The shop was in Alliance Avenue; the bomb had gone off close by in Northwick Drive. I looked down the street and I could see a mangled car and the smoke. An elderly lady was standing beside me and I said to her, 'I'm sure somebody has been killed' and I remember she said, 'Aye, somebody's son'. The Brits and peelers started to arrive so I went home to the children and the area was sealed off. I got home and Mary McGuigan and a man were waiting on me. Mary told me Lawrence was involved in the explosion along with Frankie Donnelly; they said Frankie was dead. My first reaction was concern about Rosemary (Frankie's wife); they told me Lawrence was in a bad way. Lawrence's family started to arrive at the house, including Patricia (Lawrence's aunt who reared him). Everyone was hysterical; the children were taken into the houses of neighbours. My mother, Mrs O'Reilly, arrived about 9.30 am; they put the radio on to hear the news. It reported that a second person was now confirmed dead in the bomb. The next thing I remember is a doctor arriving and he gave me some tablets; the rest of the day is a haze to me.

The next day I found out that my sister-in-law Eilis, her husband Michael and Tom Fleming had identified Lawrence. The wake was like a dream to me, I was in such a state of shock. The night before he was buried, in the early hours of the morning, the street was invaded with Brits, cops and plain-clothed cops. One of the plain-clothed cops rapped my door and tried to offer condolences. He told me he had a document to give me; this was to advise on the route the cortege was to take. The morning Lawrence was taken for burial I remember hundreds upon hundreds of people outside the chapel, and the Falls Road was black with people waiting on the funerals. I will never forget the support Lawrence's family gave to me during this time and right up until the present time.

Pat McAfee (sister)

I remember Lawrence as being just an ordinary guy, just absolutely your typical brother. I remember him as always being there. I remember the funny things he used to do. He loved driving; every time my mummy turned her head, the car would have been away from the door. Lawrence would have just lifted the keys and away he went. He always stood with his bum to the fire and the clock was knocked back on the mantle piece. That's how we knew he had been in the house. I use to torture him to take me everywhere with him. He was just a good, ordinary bloke, no different to anybody else, very warm, always had plenty of time for you.

I was 12 when Lawrence got married. I don't remember how he met his wife but I remember they were both very young. I remember him bringing his wife Maureen to the door and she was a lovely girl. They were very, very, happy. They got married in Holy Cross chapel and the reception was in Maureen's sister's house in Chatham Street. It was great; there was drink for the older ones and a lot of sweets and food. Their wedding cake was lovely and the music and craic was great for everybody. I just remember it being a really good day.

The morning he died I was lying in bed and I heard a bomb go off. I jumped out of bed; the whole family, the whole district I think jumped out of bed. It was about 7.30 am. I remember running down and mummy being very shocked; everybody was. It was a very loud bang and everybody knew that something drastic had happened. I put slippers and a coat on and ran out. Everyone was running and I followed the crowd to see what had actually happened. I got up to near the bottom of Northwick Drive and my brother-in-law John came and asked me where I was going. I said I was going to see what had happened. He told me that somebody had been hurt in the bomb and made me go back down Etna Drive; he would not allow me to go any further. He did not say anything to me. I said, 'What's wrong?' and he said 'Pat, I don't know who it is'. I know now that he did know and that's why he wouldn't let me go any further. I stayed there for a while, and then went back home to go to work.

I went home, got ready and went to work. I wasn't in work that long whenever Veronica and Christina my sisters came and all I remember is the manager coming to me and saying that I was wanted at the door. When I went to the door and I saw Veronica and Christina standing there, I just knew; they didn't have to tell me. I said, 'It's our Lawrence; he's dead'. It's just one of those things; I don't know how I knew, just looking at their faces. Before that I always had my doubts that maybe Lawrence was involved. I think deep down everybody maybe knew that he could have been involved but he never, ever said anything. My mummy used to say to him, 'If I find out you're involved, I'll kill you. Is it not enough that I have one lying up in Long Kesh without another one?' But nobody knew – well obviously only people that had to know knew.

I went to Lawrence's house and mummy was there. They were devastated, absolutely, totally and utterly devastated, her and Maureen and the family, just total and utter shock. Mummy took it awful, awful bad but then everybody takes it bad when such a tragedy occurs. When Lawrence died they said his body had to be identified and his body was not really identifiable. Both Eilis and Michael wouldn't let mummy and Maureen go to identify Lawrence. They thought they could deal with it better. So mummy and Maureen agreed that Eilis and Michael would go and identify Lawrence's body. He was identified by a scar on his hand; from then Michael was never the same person.

Lawrence was buried from his own house. He went to Holy Cross chapel. Both Lawrence and Frankie Donnelly had the same funeral mass and it was just the one funeral. It left the chapel and went down Brompton Park across the Berwick Road and into Northwick Drive. It passed where Lawrence and Frankie had been killed. I remember thinking it was very morbid but looking back on it I think it was nice. The funeral passed off quite peacefully. Lawrence and Frankie were buried in the republican plot in Milltown.

I think that at the time he was an ordinary young fella caught up in something that he believed was right. When you have lived in a place like Ardoyne ... young fellas just thought they had to go out and do something. Nothing was right; the way people were treated wasn't right; you were obviously treated as a second-class citizen. You can't say they were right and you can't say they were wrong for getting involved; they were doing what they believed was the right thing to do and that's the way I look at it.

Paul Murphy (friend)

I would say Lawrence and I first got to know each other at the age of 11 or 12. There was Lawrence, John McCann, Martin Reid and myself. We started secondary school together. Lawrence's nickname was 'Monty'. He played handball and we all played football just round the streets. He was a great person to know; he was a very adventurous kind of a guy. After school I would have gone straight home but Lawrence and the other boys would have gone up to the forest to do a bit of exploring. He just had to get out and do things. We used to do the milk rounds while we were supposed to be at school. As we got a bit older, we always went out and had a few beers. He met Maureen his wife when he was very young; I think he was only about 14.

The last time I remember speaking to Lawrence was in the Shamrock club. It was a good while since I had seen him. I introduced him to my girlfriend; we were married in 1979. I think that was the last time I actually spoke to Lawrence. I was working in Littlewoods at the time he was killed; somebody phoned me to work and told me Lawrence Montgomery was dead. I couldn't believe it; I was totally shocked. I didn't even know that Lawrence was involved. I went straight to his house that night. It was very, very sad. Everybody was absolutely devastated.

I was born in the same street as Lawrence, Jamaica Street. In these days we saw the things the Brits and cops were doing to us. They were coming into your house every other night, wrecking your house, pulling up floor boards; my mother was a nervous wreck. Cops, you just had no time for them at all. You saw what they did in 1969, and everybody knows that, it's a fact of life. Lawrence was a very genuine fella; we were very, very close friends. We had a happy childhood, fantastic, absolutely; we used to run about the streets and just did what wee boys do.

Alex Reid
Killed by loyalists,
Shankill Road,
3 January 1980

The taxi driver stopped the taxi and got out and went and got a couple of friends. They came out and pulled the two of them out of the taxi. The body wasn't found until about 1 am.

'Speedy' Reid was a bit of a character. He was one of those guys that everybody wanted to knock around with. He was born in 1959, the third son of Bertha and Sammy Reid. Sammy went to Manchester in search of work and that's where he met Bertha. The couple got married in England and moved to Ardoyne in 1947. They lived in a room in Sammy's aunt Eileen's house where three of their six children were born. Seven years later they moved to 62 Jamaica Street, which became the family home. Alex attended Holy Cross Boys and St Gabriel's school. Typical of that generation, he left school with no qualifications. According to his friends 'Speedy' was a 'live wire', full of life and keen for adventure, just like the cartoon character 'Speedy Gonzales' he was affectionately nicknamed after. He had a penchant for unusual hats, loved rock and roll music and was an Elvis Presley fan. Above all 'Speedy' was a 'free spirit'.

On 3 January 1980 'Speedy' and a friend boarded a black taxi outside the City Hall. The taxi went up the Shankill Road and stopped outside a loyalist bar. The driver entered the bar and publicly announced he had two Taigs (Catholics) in his car. Minutes later a gang dragged Alex and his friend from the taxi. His friend managed to escape but 'Speedy' was beaten to death with a breeze block in a vicious sectarian attack. His body was dumped in a derelict building off the Shankill Road. A woman heard his moans and called the RUC. 'Speedy' was twenty years old at the time of his death.

'Jap' McWilliams (friend)

I came from the same street as 'Speedy'. He was a bit of a character in the street so more or less everyone knew him. Everybody seemed to want to knock around with him; he was that type of person. 'Speedy' was always trying to make money. He also liked the odd gamble. This was when he was around 15 or 16. He also played cards for money and did very well. He liked to keep fit and turned his loft into his own wee private gym. He had this fashion thing for hats. He also carried a walking stick, which added to his character. A lot of girls liked him. They liked his character and good humour. He started to go out with a Protestant girl from Glenbryn. Her name was Ann. They met on holidays in the South. This would have been around 1977. I actually did a tattoo for him with a Celtic Cross and her name below it. We were caught once in the Deerpark area robbing apple trees. The guy that caught us found out where we lived and reported us to our parents. It turned out he was a community RUC man and his form of punishment was we were sent away on holidays. This was around 1977, we couldn't believe our luck. We had robbed the right tree. We were sent to Skerries, down South for a two-week holiday. This was organised through the Community Shop and the Community Centre in Alliance Avenue. We really enjoyed this because we ended up doing things that we had never done before: canoeing and climbing, etc. We had never been out of the district, we didn't even know that things like that were going on. So we ended up doing a bit of work for the Community Shop, doing DJ and looking after younger ones and bringing them to the swimmers and that. In the end we were rewarded with another holiday to Guildford in Surrey. This kept us out of trouble too, which I suppose was the whole idea. 'Speedy' was a bit of a free spirit. He would just make his mind up about something and went and done it. He would go missing for days and would have gone to Dublin to see his cousin Tommy or even as far away as England.

I was on my way to work on the Friday, 4 January 1980 and I heard on the news that a body had been found in a derelict building in Berlin Street off the Shankill Road. The first thing sprang to my mind was, 'some poor Catholic'. I just went on to work. I heard the news throughout the day but there was no description given. When I left work I went to my girlfriend's house in the Falls. I was eventually told it was 'Speedy'. This was around 5.00-5.30 pm that evening. Three members of the UDA were convicted for the murder of Alex: Calderwood (he used the breeze block) and Smith (he drove the taxi) and Ferguson (he took Alex from the taxi) – he got six years for G.B.H.

Martin Reid (brother)

Alex was born on 12 July 1959. Jap McWilliams and 'Spike' Milligan knocked about with him. His aunt Sadie gave him the nickname 'Speedy' because he was a wee bit hyper when he was a kid; it just stuck with him. The night that Alex was killed I was working in the egg factory. I went to work the next day, Friday, and Charlie, a friend of mine, said, 'I see someone was found dead over in the Shankill'. I had a terrible premonition about our Alex. He hadn't come home that night. Charlie said, 'Forget about it because this guy had red hair'. But apparently they thought he had red hair because of the blood. Around 10 o'clock I went over to our Kathleen's house and told her I was worried about Alex. I think it was about 12 o'clock and I saw two cops coming in to the factory. They looked at me and said, 'We're afraid we've a bit or bad news for you'. The cops had come up to ask me to identify the body. The cops went on and the boss brought me down to the mortuary to identify Alex's body. I still wasn't too sure if it was Alex. In fact it was a bit of a shock. It didn't look like him. I always imagined that within the next couple of days I'd find out I'd identified the wrong person. I was hoping that was the case.

Apparently Alex had been out drinking with his friend. Then they were driving up through the Shankill in a taxi and they must have been talking. The taxi driver stopped the taxi and got out and went and got a couple of friends. They came out and pulled Alex and his friend out of the taxi. I think three people were charged with his murder but only one got convicted with the killing. The other two were convicted of GBH.

I can't remember seeing Alex that Thursday at all, then that night he didn't come in. I just got up the next morning and put the news on at 9 am and heard that a body had been found. Apparently his friend had given a loyalist address and a different name when they pulled Alex out of the taxi. I heard they gave him a slap on the back of the head. I'm not too sure if he did report the incident that night or the next morning. People said to me if he had reported the incident that night they might have had a chance of saving Alex. I never really bothered with him after that. I couldn't look at him. I think it was just caught in the wrong place at the wrong time.

Alex was a wee bit of a rascal, but he was a good kid. He would have done anything for me. He was just like all the other kids in the district, nothing out of the ordinary.

James Loughran (friend and eyewitness)

[This testimoty is based upon extracts from evidence given to the Coroner's Court]

It was about 10 pm. We had been drinking in a number of bars; we were both pretty drunk by this time. We decided to go home. We walked up to North Street to get a black taxi up the Shankill Road. Both of us got into the front seat of the taxi beside the driver. There were a number of other people in the back of the taxi but I can't remember much about them. I told the taxi driver to drop us off at Twaddell Avenue. On the way up the road me and Alex were talking but I can't remember what it was about. When we reached the library on the Shankill Road the taxi driver stopped, got out of the taxi and went over to talk to a number of men who were standing at the corner. Either the driver or one of the other men, I am not sure which, came over to the taxi, opened the door and told us to get out. Alex and I both got out. The men put the both of us up against the wall. They started to ask us questions about who we were and where we lived and things like that. It was at this point Alex made a run for it. He ran away down the Shankill Road. I think it was two of the men ran after him. I stayed where I was and the men kept asking me questions. One kept hitting me on the face and body and knocking my head against the wall. I told them I was from Carrick and I was just down visiting friends in Belfast. Someone searched me and found my Giro card in my pocket. It had an Ardoyne address on it. When they found this they started to ask me about the Provos and who I knew and things like that. I told them I knew nothing about that sort of thing. I started to cry and told them I had a wife and family and had never done anyone any harm in my life. One of them then walked me down the street. I started to plead with him not to shoot me. He told me that no one was going to shoot me and he told me to go on home. I walked up home by myself. I never saw Alex again.

> *I never got to know my mummy. I was deprived of her when I was growing up. That infuriates and saddens me. I never got the chance to have friendly mother and daughter discussions and that really upsets me. They just shouldn't have done it.*

Colette Meek
Killed by the IRA,
Alliance Avenue,
17 August 1980

Colette Meek's maiden name was Toner. She was originally from Baker Street on the Falls Road and the middle child in a family of six. Her husband Bobby Meek was originally from East Belfast. In 1955 the couple were married in St Peter's Cathedral, Falls Road. They had four daughters: Louise, Angela, Pauline and Claire. In 1973 loyalists intimidated the family out of their home in Hesketh Park. They were re-housed in Alliance Avenue, which became the family home. Colette was a quiet, friendly, happy person who lived for her family.

On 16 August 1980, while standing in her driveway, Colette Meek was accidentally shot and fatally wounded by the IRA during an ambush on the RUC. The IRA later apologised and stated that their intended target was the RUC. Colette Meek was 47 years old at the time of her death.

Claire Meek (daughter)

There are four girls in my family; I am the youngest. My mummy worked for the NSPCC and then in Deanby Gardens Nursery. At the time of my mummy's death I was only 11 years old. I always remember her laughing a lot. She was always a happy person. I don't know if she was a political person; politics was something that was never discussed in our house. She supported the Peace People and she went to some of their rallies. She liked reading and in particular Agatha Christie books. My mummy was a religious person, never missed mass and attending novenas.

I remember the day she died. She was shot on Saturday 16 August but actually died on the 17th. As a treat, my sister Pauline and I had been allowed to stay up late to watch a film. It was Saturday evening. A neighbour a couple of doors down had a brick thrown through her window and everybody had gone out to the street. So there were quite a few people standing round talking. Someone had called the RUC and they arrived. My sister and I were still inside the house. It was around 10.30 pm or 11 pm. The people that threw the brick through the window were obviously trying to lure the police to the area because, as soon as they arrived, we heard shots. We were always told if you hear shots to stay away from the windows. But my sister and I being curious sneaked into mummy and daddy's bedroom and looked out. We didn't see anything apart from people. Then my daddy came in to get a blanket and we asked what was wrong; he said that mummy had been shot. A neighbour across the road, Jimmy Burns, had also been shot in the foot. His daughter came over and brought us to their house. We weren't allowed to go down the pathway; we had to go through a hole in the hedge and down our neighbour's path.

We sat in our neighbour's house while my daddy went to the hospital. My other sister had been at a friend's house. I don't think they knew who had been shot. But when they came running down the Deerpark Road they saw the police and people standing around. Louise, my eldest sister was in hospital at the time. We waited for a while in a friend's house and then went back to our own house with a neighbour. A couple of hours later my daddy came back with Louise and a priest. He sat us on his knee and told us mummy had died. I think this was about 1 am or 2 am. I don't think I understood at the time. I just assumed that she would come back from hospital.

My mummy was shot once with a ricochet bullet. At the time there were about six or seven people standing around in the street. The RUC obviously stopped where the people were and as soon as they got out of their vehicle, they were shot at. The only two people that were hit were my mother and Jimmy Burns.

There was a terrible emptiness after her death. It wasn't quite real; you were still always expecting her to come back in the door for a long time after it. I know we all dreamt about her coming back. It was hard waking up the next day and knowing that wasn't going to happen. I was only 11 years old and it was hard to take in; she was my mummy. My other sisters were 13, 19 and 21 years old. My sister Louise took on some of the responsibilities of the mother role.

The IRA claimed responsibility. They said they were sorry and that it wasn't their intended target. Their target was the RUC. It makes me angry because there were six or seven civilians and two policemen; what are the odds that you're going to hit a civilian? It shouldn't have happened.

I never got to know my mummy; I was deprived of her when I was growing up. That infuriates and saddens me. When people tell me about things they did with their mummy it really makes me sad. I know I shouldn't let it affect me so much but it does. I never got the chance to do that and to have friendly mother and daughter discussions. What I remember of my mother is that she was great. But I'm biased; she was my mother. She always had time for us. I remember when we were sick and off school she would make up games for us to play. She was the best in the world; she was my mummy. There was and still is for all of us a great sense of loss and a great sadness. That is something that will never go away.

Billy Christie (neighbour)

Colette lived in number 51 and I lived in 46 Alliance Avenue. Colette and Bobby were a quiet couple, kept themselves to themselves. I remember the day Colette was killed. We came home from a wedding in the Star social club around 7.00 pm. We were sitting watching TV. I went upstairs. I heard a thud and looked out the window. I saw two boys standing at the hedge and they threw a brick. They missed Miss Taylor's window and hit the wall. I saw the other boy throw a brick right through Tony Kelly's window and they ran off down Jamaica Street. I ran down the stairs. By that time John Kelly and his wife had come out to the street. Then Tony went and rang the police.

By this stage Bobby and Colette Meek had come out and Jimmy Burns and his wife. We were all standing at number 55 out on the footpath. The next thing a jeep came round the corner and we were in its headlights. The policewoman jumped out of the jeep and suddenly shots were fired. About four bullets hit the jeep door as she got out and bullets were bouncing round. A couple hit below Tony Kelly's window; we ran up the path. Mrs Meek was at her own house. Jimmy Burns, who was standing with us, got shot in the foot. The bullets actually hit number 42 where Jimmy lived; you can still see the bullet holes. A policeman was lying at the bottom of my driveway and he didn't return fire; he was afraid to put his head out. There seemed to be two gunmen involved and they were firing from different points. It was a good night; they couldn't have missed that we were civilians. They actually had to watch for the jeep to arrive. When all the commotion was over we realised that Mrs Meek had been shot.

I ran to help Jimmy Burns and Tony Kelly and a few others ran to help Mrs Meek. Mrs Meek wasn't actually out in the street. She was in her own path; she was about 25 yards behind the jeep. Her husband wasn't with her; he was down with us. That's how I didn't realise she was hit until after it was all over. The ambulance was sent for and they were rushed off to hospital. It was all over in a matter of seconds.

I called to Bobby the next morning and asked how Mrs Meek was. He told me she was dead. Mr Meek was clearly shocked that it happened. With so many civilians about they shouldn't have opened fired. Any one of us could have been hit. I would say about 30 shots were fired and that is a low estimate. They were using automatic weapons. It never should have happened but it did. Mrs Meek was a family woman. Her personality was outgoing and she was chatty; she had time to speak to you. She went to chapel every week, so did the girls. They were good neighbours. It was an awful, awful tragedy.

Maurice Edward Gilvary was born in 1957. His father Maurice (senior) was from Havana Street. His mother Teresa was originally a Reid and came from Elmfield Street. Maurice senior was a sheet metal worker but his real passion was Gaelic games. He was a keen GAA activist, and a member of the local Ardoyne Kickhams. He was also a member of the Shamrock social club. Maurice senior and Teresa had a family of five boys and four girls (Lorraine, Eamon, Annette, Brendan, Frances, Maurice and the triplets, Gemma, Dermot and Damien). Maurice was the second eldest in the family. His mother Teresa worked in the family shop at the corner of Elmfield Street and Butler Street. Known locally simply as 'Reid's shop' it was something of a landmark of Old Ardoyne. The shop was owned by Teresa's mother Jane and was part of the Reid family home. It was here, in his granny's home, that Maurice lived most of his young life. Maurice attended Holy Cross Boys school in Butler Street and later went to St Gabriel's. When

Maurice Gilvary
Killed by the IRA,
near Jonesboro, S. Armagh,
19 January 1981

he left school, Maurice worked on various building sites in Ardoyne. He was known as a very good footballer, even though he wore glasses during the game. He enjoyed music and was a big fan of the pop group 'Queen'. He frequented most of the local clubs in the area but particularly the Saunders and the Star. His nickname was 'Isaac'.

Like many young people in the area Maurice joined the republican movement at a very early age. Initially he was a member of na Fianna Éireann and later progressed to the IRA. Maurice had been arrested a number of times by the British security forces during his short life. He spent a few months on remand in Crumlin Road gaol, and then was interned between 1974 and 1975. On Monday 19 January 1981 the IRA killed Maurice Gilvary. Maurice's body was left on a border road near Jonesboro, in South Armagh. He had been shot a number of times. In a released statement the IRA noted that Maurice was one of their volunteers and had been, 'executed for endangering the republican army and undermining the struggle'. The statement went on to say, 'We are extremely reluctant to execute volunteers, realizing the methods and duress, the physical and psychological pressures, used by the RUC to solicit information'. However, the Gilvary family have never accepted the statement or the actions taken by the IRA. A short time later the Gilvary family suffered another bereavement when their mother Teresa, who had been in ill-health, died. The family believe her death was accelerated by Maurice's killing.

Paul Blake
Killed by the UFF,
Berwick Road,
27 March 1981

They just came into Ardoyne with the attitude that 'any Catholic will do'.
Paul was just the unfortunate one that night.

Paul Blake was born on 29 October 1954 to his father Barney and mother Mary Ellen. He was the sixth child of their six girls and five boys. His mother was originally from Jamaica Street in Ardoyne but Paul was actually born in Ballymurphy. That is why he was educated at St Kevin's primary school on the Falls Road and St Thomas' secondary school on the Whiterock Road. But Paul's family connections with Ardoyne were always strong. From around the time of the introduction of internment he spent almost every weekend in the district, enjoying the social life of the clubs in the area. By the mid-1970s he was a member and regular of the Shamrock. Like most of his family, Paul always saw Ardoyne as home and by the late 1970s the Blake household had moved into Jamaica Street. By then Paul was working as a labourer and dump-truck driver. He was rarely out of work. When he wasn't labouring he was usually out having the craic. A big Manchester United fan, snooker player and follower of horse racing, Paul looked forward in particular to his Saturday nights. He was often to be found in the Shamrock with his cousin Jim Dickson and friends Martin Kane and Hughie Burns. Paul was also known for his ability to doze off virtually anywhere after a few pints. That earned him his nickname, 'The Big Sleep'. At about 9.30 pm on Friday 27 March 1981 Paul left a hunger strikers' support function at the League social club and was walking up the Berwick Road toward his girlfriend's in Velsheda Park. A car pulled up beside him. It contained members of the UFF who had been sent out by Jim Craig, a leading Shankill Road loyalist, to 'avenge' the death of loyalist councillor Sammy Millar. Any Catholic, it would seem, would do. One gunman shot at Paul from the car and another got out and fired at him from behind. They then sped off leaving Paul dead on the ground. Paul's killers were later given a couple of pounds apiece for their day's work. Paul Blake was a member of no political group or organisation and was 26 years old when he was killed.

Jim Dickson (cousin)

Paul was a bit of a character. He started coming over to Ardoyne when he was still living in Ballymurphy. He used to come over at the time of internment, during the rioting. He was only about 15 then. He used to stay in our house in Jamaica Street. After that he was over every other weekend. He came over to the Shamrock [social club] and was a member from the mid-1970s on. Like most of his family Paul always harped on about moving to Ardoyne and eventually his mother relented and they moved to Jamaica Street. That was the very street where his mother grew up and where the family always spent time with relatives and friends. Paul liked a drink and was into 'chasing the girls' but he was a good guy. He loved following the horses and having a wee bet. I remember the time that Steve Cauthen, the American jockey, came over. We all put money on him to win, me, Paul and Martin. When he came in we were all up singing 'God save America!' Paul loved life and enjoying himself. He loved the weekend and a good Saturday night disco. He liked a bit of craic. The only thing I didn't like about him was that Paul was a Manchester United supporter. He loved them. I remember the time Man United played Arsenal in the cup final. We were all in the big room in the Shamrock. Paul just put his head down at the end of it when Arsenal won 3-2 and went to sleep. He loved snooker too and he wasn't a bad player. He was a guy who just liked a bit of craic and a bit of banter. He wasn't nasty, never fought and I don't think anyone disliked him. Paul wasn't interested or involved in politics. He would have talked about the conflict like all of us but he wasn't involved or into it in any big way.

I saw Paul on the day he was shot. It was a Friday, 27 March 1981. Paul was shot on our Michael's birthday. Michael was only three at the time and Paul had been up to give him a couple of bob earlier in the day. I remember it rained all day. Paul came into our house at about 4.30 pm. He had been driving a dumper-truck all day and was standing in a big duffle coat and boots. He said he was going down to the League that night because there was a do on for the hunger strikers. Then he headed off down the Pad and that was the last I saw of him. I was in the GAA [social club] that night when I heard Paul had been shot. Some fella came in and said that Paul Blake had been shot on the Berwick Road. This would have been around 9.30 pm. I headed up the road but they already had it sealed off. He was actually shot just up at the gable wall at the corner of Cranbrook Gardens. He had been dandering along up there. He was just coming away from the League [social club] going down to see Jimmy Farrell's sister in Velsheda Park. He had only started going out with her. Apparently he had been walking along and this car pulled up to ask directions. The guy in the car shot him and the bullet went through the neck and straight out. It didn't kill him. But this other guy got out, walked up behind him and shot Paul while he was lying on the ground. He hit him on the shoulder; it hit the bone and went down through Paul's body and came out the other side. That was the shot that killed him. If they had left him after the first bullet he would have lived. The two younger fellas who did it got time but there was an older fella as well and he didn't. For the young guys that was the first kill they had been on. Jimmy Craig [Shankill UDA leader] was implicated in it. He sent them out but nothing ever happened to him over it. He gave them a couple of pounds for it and a pat on the back. Later he got shot by his own [Jim Craig was shot dead by the UFF over a racketeering dispute on 15 October 1988]. After we heard Paul was dead Kathleen [Jim's wife] and me went down to Mary Ellen's. His mummy had actually been walking from Alliance Avenue when it happened. She heard the shooting and came down to see Paul being put into the ambulance. She recognised his boots so she knew it was him. Barney and Mary Ellen [Paul's father and mother] were in the house when we went down. There was a lot of confusion. Barney had to go down to identify him.

Paul's death had a very bad impact on the family. His mother Mary Ellen never got over it. Paul was always mummy's 'blue-eyed' boy. Bernie [Paul's sister] was very badly affected by it too. They were very, very close. He was actually buried from Bernie's house. His brother Martin became a Hare Krishna afterwards and I think that had a lot to do with Paul's death. It hit us all bad. We used to all get together in the house before and have the craic, all the lads together there. But a lot of the fun went out of that house. Mary Ellen moved out of that house not long after. Paul's death hurt me bad because he was a good bloke and my closest friend and relative. It hit everyone in the club as well. Paul was one of those fellas who, when he walked in, everyone would be shouting over 'alright mate' to him. He had time for everyone, just a regular bloke.

Michael Blake (brother)

Although he was one of 11 children, our Paul was always mummy's 'blue-eyed' boy. Like most of the family Paul always harped on about moving back to Ardoyne area. Eventually our mother relented and moved to Jamaica Street in the mid-1970s. It was the very street where our mother grew up and where the family spent a lot of time at granny's house. Paul very quickly settled into the Ardoyne 'way of life'. He was always very popular. Saturday was our Paul's big day and he was usually in the Shamrock right through until the small hours of Sunday! He always loved the cabaret and dance on a Saturday night, though, more often than not, the 'big sleep' would end up lying asleep on a chair balanced on two legs. But he would never spill a drop even then! That was Paul. He loved the football and was a big fan of George Best. He also loved snooker and idolised that other great wayward Irishman, Alex Higgins. Basically Paul loved life and certainly knew how to live it to the full. He had no real political aspirations at all. That sort of makes it worse that people who knew nothing of or about him saw fit to end his life at the tender age of 26.

Bernie Reid (sister)

Our Paul knocked about with his brothers most. Tommy and Paul were very close. Even while the family were still in Ballymurphy, Paul was always over in Ardoyne. I remember my mummy once blaming herself for Paul's death because they had moved into Ardoyne.

But that was simply not true. He was always here anyway. He used to come over for the clubs. Paul played snooker for the League and he was a member of the Shamrock. He loved playing snooker. When Alex Higgins was playing he always went to see him. He was supposed to go to see Higgins play a couple of nights after he was killed. Someone must have told Alex Higgins' mother because she sent a lovely mass card for Paul. Paul was a really lovely person. There was never any bother with him.

My brother was murdered on a Friday night. He had been in the League [social club] and was walking up the Berwick Road towards his girlfriend's house. A car pulled up beside him and the people inside called him over and asked for directions. Paul put his head in and saw the gun. He tried to turn and they [loyalists] shot him in the neck. They say that if they had left him after that Paul would have lived. But they got out as he fell on the footpath and shot him again. Just afterwards my mummy was coming from a friend's house in Alliance Avenue. She was walking along the Berwick Road when she saw an ambulance. She asked someone what was wrong and they told her that, 'Some wee lad called Blake has been shot dead'. This was just after Paul had been shot. My mummy has always said that she can't remember how she made her way home. All she remembers is screaming. My aunt Amy saw my mummy coming along Etna Drive just afterwards. She saw my mummy throwing herself on top of a car. The car was still moving and had to make an emergency stop. My mummy just threw herself on the car because she was completely devastated.

A few minutes later I was in my house in Havana Way with my daddy when there was a big bang at the door. My sister Ann came in and she screamed, 'Quick, Paul has been shot'. This was at about 9.40 pm or 9.45 pm. Paul had been shot at 9.35 pm. We ran up to my mummy's house but she had been taken into a house in Jamaica Street. I ran up to where my mummy was in Jamaica Street. It was then that the woman of that house told me that Paul was dead. My mummy was in a terrible state so I stayed with her rather than go up to the Berwick Road. I know that by this stage there were crowds of people around. The ambulance crew tried to treat Paul on the road but he had died. My daddy had to go up to identify the body. Tommy Dickson a relative went in with him because if my daddy had gone in by himself, he wouldn't have been able to come out again. The police came to the house about two hours after Paul was killed to officially tell us that he was dead. They eventually got two UFF fellas called Calderwood and Moore for Paul's murder. There was a man called Jim Craig who had paid one of them £5 and the other £2 for killing Paul. It was like my brother's life was worth £7 to them. They came into Ardoyne with the attitude that 'any Catholic will do'. Paul was just the unfortunate one that night. In the court the only thing that annoyed me was the way that the families of the two who were convicted behaved. When they were sentenced, one of the women of the Calderwood family got up and shouted 'No Surrender'. The cheek of it! Her son had killed my brother and had left my family broken. These two are probably still running about now. They did eight years in prison and they were only about 18 or 19 at the time they killed Paul.

Paul's death had a terrible impact on my family because we are very, very close. My mummy was never the same woman afterwards. My daddy died six years after Paul and he was totally heartbroken. I don't think families are ever the same again, mentally and physically. The family unit is just broken and is never the same again. My brother Tommy took Paul's death particularly badly because they were very close. My two brothers Martin and Patrick joined the Hare Krishnas after Paul's death and I think it was as a direct result of it. Paul was a great brother and a very, very good and generous person. He was good to my mummy and she was good to him. He never got into rows or anything, just a really nice person. What made the whole thing so hard was that he was totally innocent. If he had been involved in something you would have been almost expecting it, but Paul was totally innocent.

Patsy Martin
Killed by loyalists,
Abbeydale Parade,
16 May 1981

Even now, none of us know why Patsy was killed, but the fact that the telephone wires were cut, the break-in the couple of weeks before, the fact that they took the glass out of the back window and the fact that the shooting was done by using silencers has always haunted me. It was no random shooting; it was carried out by a professional.
Even at the time people were talking about collusion and to tell you the truth, in those days you thought that people were making it up, but now it isn't so bizarre.

Patsy Martin was born in Eskdale Gardens. He had four sisters and three brothers. Upon leaving St Gabriel's in the late 1950s Patsy served his apprenticeship in Mawhinney's Butchers in Ligoniel. In 1966 he married his childhood sweetheart, Roisin McLoughlin and the next year they had a baby girl, Elaine. Patsy and his brother-in-law Bobby ran successful butchers' shops, one on the Falls and the other on the Crumlin Road.

On 17 May 1981 Patsy Martin was found shot dead in bed at his Abbeydale Parade home. Unusually his killers had gone to extraordinary lengths to carry out the killing. Telephone wires along the Crumlin Road had been cut earlier in the night. A small pane of glass was removed from the kitchen window to gain entrance to the house, before the victim was shot three or four times as he lay asleep in bed. Neither the victim's family nor neighbours were alerted to the shooting due to the fact that the weapons used in the killing had been fitted with silencers. In a second unusual twist the killers are thought to have left the house through the front door, rather than retracing their steps back through the kitchen.

Although one of the weapons was subsequently recovered in Silverstream a number of years later, the RUC made no effort to inform the Martin family of any new evidence in the case. Patsy Martin's widow Roisin was the only person ever questioned about the murder. It is widely believed that Roisin Martin was arrested solely in an effort to force her to abandon a legal challenge against the NIO's refusal to provide any compensation to the victim's family. The circumstances of his death have never been explained. No one has ever been charged with Patsy Martin's killing.

Roisin Martin (widow)

Myself and Patsy met as teenagers; we were about 14 or 15 years-old and we fancied each other like mad. We went together for about six years before we got married in August 1966. Our daughter Elaine was born the next year. We eventually bought a house in Abbeydale Parade. The street where we lived was a mainly Protestant street with the odd Catholic family in it. By that stage Patsy and his brother-in-law Bobby were in partnership with a butcher's shop. They got a shop in Carrickfergus initially, but it was blown up. With the insurance money they opened up another butcher's shop in Ardoyne. It was called, ' C & M Meats', for Clarke and Martin Meats. When Patsy wasn't working he loved golf and the Crumlin Star club.

Our house was broken into weeks before Patsy was killed. Patsy heard the glass smashing. He woke me and went downstairs with a golf club. He saw a hand coming in to open the door and he whacked it with the golf club. He ran after them over the back gardens and hedges. I always wondered why someone had tried to break into our house. I thought that maybe they were just hoods.

Bobby Sands was buried the week before Patsy was killed and Francis Hughes had died four days before his death. They were dangerous times. Patsy used to worry about coming home across the Shankill when he had been working at the shop on the Falls. There was an awful lot of hi-jacking and burning and the stress seemed to be getting to him. At that particular time there were businessmen being attacked. Everything went through my head after he was killed. Did they watch the van? Did they take the registration number of the van? Did they look for the van in our street?

The thing about Patsy's murder was that it was carried out so professionally. All of the telegraph wires were cut from the turn of Ligoniel Road, the whole way down the Crumlin Road. This was done in a nationalist area where the RUC and British army were patrolling 24 hours a day. At that time the Crumlin Road was probably the most patrolled road in the whole of Belfast. How could someone cut all of the wires on the telegraph poles along the whole stretch of the road in the early hours of the morning and not be spotted? At that time hardly anyone walked that road at night; someone going up and down telephone poles was sure to be seen by the soldiers. The killers were said to have cut the telephone wires in a way that only an expert could do it; you would have needed to know what you were doing and have special tools.

It was our daughter Elaine who found Patsy's body. I worked all week in an insurance office and I usually slept in on a Saturday morning. Elaine and Patsy would normally have gone out to work early every Saturday morning and I used to sleep in the spare room so I could lie on. Elaine came in and said, 'Mummy, Daddy won't waken'; this was about 7 am or 7.30 am and the alarm clock had already gone off. She kept saying, 'Mummy, Daddy isn't up yet and the door is opened and I can see blood on his nose'. I went into the bedroom thinking that he had decided to lie in. When I walked in, all I could see were the bullets lying all over the bed; I didn't even try to wake him. I just ran. The two of us just ran for the front door, which was already lying open. We started running; we didn't even know where we were going. All that we wanted to do was run. When we got half way up the street we stopped and went back to a neighbour's house. He got the RUC.

Even now none of us know why Patsy was killed. At the time people were talking about collusion and to tell you the truth in those days you thought that people were making it up, but now it isn't so bizarre. A year later there was an inquest and the coroner just said it was a sectarian murder. No one ever claimed responsibility; nobody was arrested for it and the RUC never came back to us to explain what was going on. As I said Patsy was murdered around the time Bobby Sands died. The newspapers tried to say he was murdered because he did not close the shop for Bobby Sands' funeral. But that was rubbish, all of the shops on the road were closed that day; there wasn't one shop opened. I knew my husband's death was a sectarian murder because there wasn't any other reason for it. We had been living with sectarian murders for years; he was just another Catholic.

The newspapers even claimed that I was arrested for my husband's murder because I sued the Northern Ireland Office and they tried to tarnish me by arresting me. But I sued the NIO for compensation on the advice of my solicitor. The RUC arrested me and put me into Castlereagh and they questioned me for a week. When the week was up they just threw me out in the middle of the city centre, with no coat, no money or anything. It was five years after my husband's murder and they were actually saying that it was me who murdered him. They said that I may not have pulled the trigger but I paid for it. One of the detectives eventually admitted to me that it was an old ploy of detectives when you can't find anything to go on; you blame the wife. About ten years later guns were found in Silverstream; one of them was the gun that killed Patsy.

I was always afraid to ask the RUC anything. I was always afraid to ring Tennent Street to ask if there was any news on Patsy's murder. To tell you the truth, I tried to bury it, I was so afraid. All of these years later all I can think of is, 'How dare they!' I am so angry with that. We both suffered after Patsy's death, both Elaine and myself. Before Patsy was killed we had our ups and downs and you thought it was a big deal, but then when you lose someone your life just falls apart. I believe my husband was murdered simply because he was a Catholic.

Micky O 'Neill (friend)

I first met Patsy through playing football at Flax Street. Patsy was a member of the Crumlin Star; they had a golf society and Patsy, myself and Frankie Hamill all joined it together. I remember Patsy and Roisin moving into their house in Abbeydale. Frankie and myself did some work to the new house. Patsy was never one of those people to talk about his own safety; he just laughed things off. He was everybody's friend, he couldn't do enough for you; nothing was a problem.

The night Patsy was murdered we were together in the club. It was a Friday night and I left him at the corner of Mountainview, just beside the garage. I told him I'd see him the next morning. On the Saturday morning Charlie Toner came to my house and told me Patsy had been killed. I ran up to his house and I remember looking at the wooden telegraph pole on the opposite side of the street and the heavy telephone wires had been cut. It looked as if they were hit with a hatchet. Patsy was shot three to four times in the head. No one heard anything because they used silencers. Where Patsy lived was a mixed area; it used to be mostly Protestant but eventually Catholics were moving in. I don't think the attack on Patsy was a random attack. If it had been a random attack they would have booted the door in just like they did with Harry Muldoon [killed by loyalists, Mountainview Drive, 31 October 1984]. But someone went to great lengths to kill poor Patsy. Why did someone want to kill Patsy? He was a great friend not only to me but a good number of people. Patsy was one good friend.

> *I just wanted somebody to come out and say,*
> *'This was a young lad who was sitting at his own door and*
> *he was killed by a British soldier' – the truth.*

Danny Barrett
Killed by the British army,
Havana Court,
9 July 1981

Danny Barrett was born 10 September 1965. His father Jimmy Barrett was born and reared in Hooker Street and his mother Molly (née Hale) was originally from Carrick Hill. The couple were childhood sweethearts and married in June 1963 in St Patrick's chapel. They had four children: Susan, Danny, Conn and Tina. Danny was the second child. For most of their married life they lived in Hooker Street. In May 1980, as a result of redevelopment, they moved to a newly-built house in Havana Court. After rearing their family in a tiny kitchen house, Molly, Jimmy and the kids were looking forward to the new house.

Like most of the young lads in the district Danny went to Holy Cross Boys and St Gabriel's school. While growing up he was a typical young boy; he enjoyed playing pool, going to discos and listening to records. As a teenager, Danny and his friends adopted the skinhead style. They loved the music and wore the obligatory DM boots and cromby coat. The 'gang' of friends were regulars at the disco in the John Paul youth club, parochial hall and Sweat Box club in the Bone. They were popular with their peers and renowned for the youthful pranks and mischievous antics. It was all harmless, good, clean fun. Danny Barrett was just a normal lad who had plenty of friends and everything to look forward to in life.

On 8 July 1981 Joe McDonnell died on hunger strike in the H-Blocks of Long Kesh. As with the deaths of all the hunger strikers tensions were heightened and violence spilled onto the streets. The next day, 9 July, Danny Barrett was shot and killed by the British army as he sat on the wall in the front garden of his own house in Havana Court. At the inquest the British army insisted that Danny had a rifle. A member of the RUC disputed these accusations and said no firearm traces were found on Danny and no spent cartridges were found in Havana Court. To this day no charges have been brought against the British soldier responsible for Danny Barrett's killing. He was 15 years old at the time of his death.

Molly Barrett (mother)

Danny was just a typical young boy while growing up. He was always getting into mischief. He loved playing out in the street and enjoyed playing pool, going to discos and listening to records. He was a skinhead and loved that trend in music. He was just a normal boisterous lad, liked the girls and had plenty of friends. We lived most of our married life in Hooker Street. But in May 1980 we moved into a new house in Havana Court. All of the old houses in Hooker Street and Old Ardoyne were demolished. The new house made a huge difference; it had plenty of space compared to the small house in Hooker Street. Everyone was looking forward to living in the new house, especially Danny; he was really excited and thought it was great. In particular he was looking forward to the big new bathroom.

Danny was only 15 years old when he was shot dead by the British army. He was sitting on the wall at his own front door. It was during the hunger strike in the H-Blocks. That evening Danny had been with his friends to a disco in the Ardoyne youth club but because of the tension in the area, very few children turned up. So Danny and his friends came back to our house in Havana Court.

I was not in the house when Danny was killed. At the time I was visiting a friend, Lily Canavan, four streets away. It was about 9.20 pm. I was sitting with my back to the window. Lily said, 'Here's your Jimmy coming; there must be something wrong'. I said, 'Jimmy what's wrong? Is it our Danny?' He shook his head and I ran out and down the entry. He followed me and said that Danny had been shot. Everybody in Ardoyne was out of their houses. I wanted to go to the hospital. I didn't know he was dead. The soldiers and peelers came and searched my house. They also searched Mickey Holland's home; he was Danny's chum. When I got to the hospital and saw the priest, I just ran away. I knew he was dead. The priest told me Danny was dead and I came back home. While Danny was being driven to the hospital the ambulance was stopped three times, twice by the British army and once by the RUC; each time this took a number of minutes.

Danny was shot from a British army observation post in Flax Street. The British army said he had a gun. At the inquest it took the jury about five minutes to rule out that accusation. No one was ever charged with Danny's murder. He was an innocent child, brutally murdered at his own front door. We have never gotten over his death. The family was never the same. We were robbed of his beautiful life. Danny was very special and he was loved by all of us.

Jimmy Barrett (father)

The evening Danny was killed he and his friends had been to the disco but came back home early. There was some rioting around the corner at the bottom of Brompton Park. A number of plastic bullets were fired at the rioters who were mainly children. I was standing at the front door. It was around 9.30 pm; it was a very clear, warm evening. We were simply standing at the door. The wall around my house is about two feet high. Danny was sitting on it with his hands tucked underneath him. There were a number of shots fired though we didn't see from where or at whom. The shooting seemed to come from the direction of Brompton Park. When Danny heard the first lot of shots he rushed into the house along with my other children. There was a lull of around five minutes or longer and Danny walked back out to the front and I went behind him.

He then sat on the wall again and I stood at the door. We heard another number of shots being fired. Kevin Mullan was standing further down the path. Gerry Ferguson was standing between Danny on the wall and me at the door. I saw Danny fall back over the wall and my first thought was Danny had thrown himself back to get down for cover. Gerry got up and I looked over the wall and saw Danny lying there. He seemed to be bleeding but I thought he had hit his head when he fell over. I jumped over the wall and saw he was losing a lot of blood. I knew then he had been shot. He was unconscious and appeared to me to be dead. I said an act of contrition in his ear and held him in my arms. I took off my shirt and tried to stop the flow of blood. An ambulance was called and Danny was taken to the Mater Hospital; a neighbour went with him and I tried to comfort my family. On arrival at the hospital, Danny was pronounced dead and taken to the morgue. My wife was in a neighbour's house in Strathroy Park and I went to break the news to her.

Immediately after the shooting the police and army came to the scene and searched my home. They looked through my daughter's schoolbooks and the officer in charge told the soldiers they were looking for arms and not to be going through trivial things. Both the police and British army then searched through the yard, bin, coal bunker, and back garden. They also searched all the bedrooms and cupboards, both upstairs and down. They were raiding Danny's friends home in Jamaica Street at the same time. There was no one in their house at the time and they broke the back lock and window. The following morning around 6 am the police and British army and forensic experts came to the outside of the house to examine a bullet hole in my next-door neighbour's wall at number 12. I came out and spoke to them and they were pointing in the direction of a high-rise building in Flax Street that was an army base. There was an observation post on the top of the building and the forensic men told me that was the direction the shot came from. Danny was buried after 10 o'clock mass on 14 July from Holy Cross chapel. The following day the police came and asked me to go to the station and make a statement, which I did.

Danny was still at school at the time of the incident. He and his sister were due to go on a week's holiday to Bray the following week. I had got their money changed to punts for them. Danny was a member of the Ardoyne Youth Club and around 30 of them were going on the trip.

Thomas 'Spider' Stewart (friend)

I was a year older than Danny but we all ran about together in primary school. We started off playing football and then we started to go to discos together. We never really went to them; we just stood outside. Then we went to secondary school. We all got skinheads, me and Danny, Mickey Holland, Jokey Brown, Moe, Ta, Paddy Brown, Butch, Frankie George, Joe, Tony Lynch and Tricky Mc Dade – there was a big squad of us. We went to the disco in Ardoyne youth club and we got barred from the John Paul youth club a few times for being too rowdy; we just didn't look the part and we wouldn't do what we were told. It was all harmless fun. Danny was always out for a laugh and a slag. There was never really any badness in any of us. Before we went out to the disco we used to go over to the Egg factory and mess about in the tunnels telling ghost stories. Most of my memories about Danny would be associated with the parochial hall and the Sweat Box club in the Bone. The two clubs were beside each other; one was a hut and one was a hall. One had a disco on Friday night and the other Saturday night. More times than enough we were barred. Once we pinched all the records out of the youth club but we brought them back again. To us it was all just a good laugh and a bit of fun. I was only going with Sally at the time; I am with her 20 years now.

The day Danny was shot dead, we knew there was going to be trouble. There was rioting everywhere. Our parents wouldn't let us out. We used to stand at either my door or Danny's door and we watched the rioting with Jimmy and Molly. That evening I remember leaving him. I was going down to see my girlfriend Sally. I got down the New Lodge and I wasn't in the house very long when somebody came and said,' Spider, Danny Barrett was shot dead'. I thought it was some kind of joke and they had mixed it up. The next thing we got a phone call that confirmed it was Danny. I ran the whole way up the road. I was praying it wasn't Danny that had been shot. When I got to the house and saw the chaos outside his door, I knew it was true. There was a terrible atmosphere in the area. I was in total shock. Outside the house it was terrible; everybody was crying and screaming.

Danny was just a person sitting on a wall minding his own business. He was a young person who loved life, loved going out and messing about, slagging and having a bit of craic; that was just Danny. After the funeral we all ended up in Jokey Brown's house. We were all sitting talking but none of us could look each other in the face and talk about it. I think we all thought it was a dream – a young lad of 15 years sitting at his own door and suddenly he is shot dead. It's hard to take in. You could really see it taking its toll on Molly and Jimmy. Molly can't hide it and she talks about it right up to this day. They have carried the burden of their young son being shot dead at the front door of their own home; they will carry it to the grave. When you go round to the house Molly loves to hear you talk about Danny still to this day. They still miss him and still hurt over his death to this day.

George McErlean (friend)

Danny and I went to primary school together. I lived in Holmdene Gardens and Danny was from Old Ardoyne. People like to think of Old Ardoyne as the real Ardoyne. I remember Danny in primary school playing in a football match; we played in the class team and we weren't that good. We went to St Gabriel's and knocked about together after school. A crowd of us got skinheads. The music we were into at that time was Ska, Madness, Buster Blood Vessel and all the skinhead stuff. We wore the skinhead type clothes. We wore our jeans turned right up over the DM boots and we wore the big cromby coat. We thought we were great; you thought you were jack the lad. The film, 'The Warriors', was out at the time and we all thought, oh we are the skinheads and we ran about in a big crowd, copying the film. The thing that stood out about Danny for me was he was great craic. When you look back you realise everything that Danny lost out on in life and you realise that you lost a good friend. At the time of his death he was going out with Jokey Brown's sister, Angela; he went with her for a few months. She took his death real bad.

Danny was killed in July 1981. It was a serious political period; it was during the hunger strike. But when you are 15 and you hear there is going to be trouble, it's all excitement to you. You never realised the consequences of what was going on around you. Danny was shot about 9.30 pm. It was a summer's evening. One of the hunger strikers, Joe Mc Donnell, had died the day before and people were telling you to be careful because as darkness fell, the rioting usually became heavier.

There was to be a disco in the youth club that night. When we went round to the club it was empty. We wandered back to Danny's house. We stood at the door talking. Danny sat on the wall. Suddenly there was shooting so we all ran into his house. After a while we went back out. Danny sat on the wall. There was one shot and the next thing, all I saw was Danny's feet going up in the air; it was a gradual thing, it was like slow motion. What I always remember was his feet kicking up into the air and his daddy running over. Tina was in hysterics and the whole place was in turmoil. I couldn't look over the wall; I just couldn't do it. If anybody asked me, 'What is your last memory?', it was probably Danny's feet going into the air.

I went into Danny's house and Tina, who was very young at the time, was in total hysterics. I couldn't bring myself to go out the front door. I went out the back and climbed over his gate and walked to the top of Jamaica Street and I met a few people. I just broke down. It was the worst time of my whole life. I didn't want to hear that Danny had died. I just wanted to keep walking away from it until I got home. I wanted to hide away from it all for a while. I knew the inevitable was going to happen but I just wanted to get away from it rather than face up to it because we were so close. You look back on those years and you didn't realise the full impact it had on his whole family. We lost a good friend but they lost their son who will never be replaced. That family really suffered. Danny was a 15-year-old boy; he was our mate but he was their child and brother who was taken away from them.

The funeral was very hard. There was anger there too. It was a Brit who shot him and it's an anger that you never lose. You look back and you can't believe they killed him. At that time politics wasn't even on our minds; you didn't really understand it. But after his death you just had a different outlook on life. I just wanted somebody to come out and say, 'This was a young lad who was sitting at his own door and he was killed by a British soldier', the truth. There was anger and you wanted somebody to say something that you could have related to. We were all so young and at 15, losing a close friend, you were really screwed up. That person was with you one minute and the next minute he was taken away. We were all in a confused state. You were so cut up inside it took months before you were really able to sit down and talk about Danny as a person and the things he'd done. Those first few weeks I totally avoided the subject because I didn't know how to deal with it. You are a 15-year-old young man, you are hurting but you try not to show too much emotion being at that particular age. You couldn't cry and say, ' I really, really loved him as a friend'. But the reality is we were totally changed because of his death; we were absolutely shattered for months and years.

At 15 we were still very young and there was so much going on around us. There was the hunger strike and there was so much heightened emotion at that time. But that day it really brought reality to our doorsteps; it was happening everywhere else and it was happening to somebody else but it didn't happen to us until we lost Danny. The family hurts every day. You just stand and watch somebody's life being torn apart in front of you, from being a normal happy family getting on with life to being completely broken.

Anthony Braniff
Killed by the IRA,
Odessa Street,
27 September 1981

The family is just looking for the truth. We are willing to take bad news as well as good news.
But if it is possible, we are looking for the republican movement to totally exonerate Anthony because we know that there is a totally innocent man lying in the grave.

Anthony ('Mitch') Braniff's parents were Mary McDonnell from the Falls Road and David 'Curley' Braniff, originally from the Shankill Road [killed by loyalists, Alliance Avenue, 19 March 1989]. The couple married in London where they had gone to find work. They returned to Ardoyne and eventually had thirteen of a family. Anthony was the ninth child. He was quiet by nature, well known for his excellent football skills and great singing voice. He attended Holy Cross Boys and later St Gabriel's school. He had a wide circle of friends that included Joey Quigley, Alex Reid [killed by loyalists, Shankill Road, 3 January 1980] Jap McWilams, Francis Bradley [killed by loyalists, Corporation Street, 19 June 1975], Billy Cairns and a number of others. Anthony married Mary on 3 February 1979; they had three children: Jolene, Anthony and Mary-Lou. At the time of his death Anthony was an IRA volunteer. On 27 September 1981 the IRA killed Anthony Braniff, claiming he was an informer.

Mary Braniff (widow)

Anthony was very quiet and reserved, loveable, and a very good husband. We were only married three years when he was killed. It was early September when he was arrested by the RUC, because the kids had started back to school. About a week later he went and got debriefed by the IRA. My birthday is 21 September; Anthony died on 27 September. We had no money to go out for my birthday so we went out a week later to the Highfield Club with his sisters Cathy and Sheila. We all came back to our house. Anthony fell asleep. But earlier that night he told me that he had to get debriefed for a second time. That's all he said. He didn't seem bothered about it. It was a normal thing to happen. But funny enough I was a wee bit dubious over him being called back the second time. But he wasn't. It was just one of those things.

The next morning as he was going out the door, he said, 'I shouldn't be long, love' and he went where he had to go. When he didn't come back that night, I waited and waited. I ended up falling asleep on the chair. The next morning I went over to Liz Donnelly and I said, 'Liz, I have a terrible feeling about Anthony; maybe he has walked across the Shankill or something like that'. Liz sent her daughter over to look after my kids and I went up to granny B's, Anthony's mummy's house. She was a bit worried too and she got a taxi up to Brian's house. We thought the loyalists had got him. Brian went somewhere; we don't know where but he came back and said that everything was OK. When Brian said that, I knew Anthony was with the republican movement. That night I still waited. My mummy called in from bingo and Geraldine and Gerry came and sat for a while with me. There was still no sign of Anthony. My sister Rita rapped my door and I actually thought it was Anthony. Then she said, 'Sit down; a body has been found in an entry'. I ran out the door and in the distance was Anthony's brother Butch. I thought it was Anthony. I thought, 'Thank God, it's Anthony'. When I got up to Butch he put his arms round me and I knew Anthony was dead. Neither the IRA nor the British security forces came near my house to tell me about Anthony's death.

There was no one charged with the killing. Anthony's clothes and a lot of his personal stuff was never returned by the authorities. He had a lot of wee prayers and a ring on him; they were all missing. His clothes were never returned; the RUC said they had to keep them for forensics. I applied to the authorities to get them back and they said no. That was it; they just went amiss. That is a question that I would like answered: where did his personal belongings go?

There are other questions for me. I remember at Anthony's wake Paddy read a statement out from the republican movement. Skipper Street was mentioned in the statement. Anthony was supposed to have met somebody in the British forces in Skipper Street. But at the time he was supposed to have met these people, he was working with Gerry Tolan. So he couldn't have met anybody at that particular time on that particular date. The statement from the republican movement, I don't know whether Anthony was supposed to have made the statement or they said it. I don't know. I had never heard of Skipper Street. I made it my business to go and find it. Gerry Tolan is a living witness that Anthony was working with him at the particular time and never left him. I don't know if the republican movement ever approached Gerry for evidence. If Gerry can state that as fact, then why was Mitch shot dead?

I think I just lived in a world of my own after Anthony's death. My sister was very good to me and my kids; she took us in because I couldn't go back to the house. The only reason Anthony told me he was involved in the movement was because I accused him of going with somebody because he was coming in late. That is the only reason he told me he was involved and that is the gospel truth. He sat me down during the hunger strike, and he said, 'There are men dying. I have to get out there'. That's why every time I look at Bobby Sands, it brings it all back to me. He thought that because men were dying he had to do something.

Thomas 'Butch' Braniff (brother)

Anthony was the brother next to me; I'm the youngest in the family. He was my big brother and he kept me in check. I used to follow Anthony everywhere he went. Anthony worked all his days; he was labouring to plasterers in the new houses being built in Jamaica Street. He worked with Gerry Tolan and Martin Jones. He was a very fit fella. He was into all those Bruce Lee and kung fu films. I think he was the only person that I ever saw with a six-pack; he was as fit as a fiddle. He was just a natural; he didn't train, he was lean but he was broad and strong. Anthony had a very close relationship with both my parents, especially my mother. If she needed any jobs done, he would do it for her. It was the 1981 hunger strike that brought Anthony into politics. At that time other members of our family were involved in the republican movement. It was a shock to find out Anthony was a member because he hadn't said to many people that he was involved.

Anthony was arrested some time between the 15 and the 19 of September 1981 and held for two days in Castlereagh. When he got out, he went and got debriefed by the IRA. Then seven days later he was dead. It has come to light now that the circumstances have changed a bit regarding Anthony's killing. When he got out of Castlereagh, and the leadership knows, Anthony came forward and said that he had spoken in Castlereagh. The person that debriefed him said he was going to have to go and get this cleared up. So Anthony waited four or five days and he got word on the Friday night that the debriefing was arranged for Saturday at twelve o clock noon. Anthony made his way over and met the people that he had to meet. Thirty- two hours later he was dead.

Every single one of us in the family was totally devastated. I was seventeen at the time. I remember we were living in Cranbrook Gardens and I saw my big brother Paddy banging on the back door; he just fell in through the door and said, 'Anthony's dead! Anthony's dead!' He was shattered. I automatically thought it must have been the Brits or loyalists. To hear a couple of hours later that the IRA had killed him I just couldn't believe it; I was totally devastated. The death had a huge effect on my father. My daddy had to identify Anthony and it took its toll on his health. My mother was absolutely shattered.

It was one of the biggest funerals that I had ever seen; I am not being biased, but he got a huge turn-out. There were plenty of republicans at it and I don't think they would go to an informer's funeral. We are still trying to establish to this day the truth. We hope that the truth will come out about Anthony and that people will do the honourable thing and clear his name.

It is very difficult at the moment for the family as they are at loggerheads with the republican movement. It is hard because the family are still republicans and we don't want to be seen as being in conflict with the movement. We are now in a situation where the family is nearly split over it. The family is just looking for the truth. We are willing to take bad news as well as good news. But if it is possible, we are looking for the republican movement to totally exonerate Anthony because we know that there is a totally innocent man lying in the grave.

In discussions my family have had with the leadership of the republican movement they have stated that the statement made by the IRA in 1981, in regards to my brother's death, was a fabrication of the truth. They claim Anthony pleaded guilty at his court marshal but we are not satisfied with this explanation and would like to know who brought the charges against Anthony and what exactly the charges were. And so to this day that is the way the family is left.

In 1999 Hugh Jordan from the *Sunday World* wrote an article on informers and he had mentioned my brother's name and said he had given information that led to a rifle being caught in Janice and Ronnie Quinn's house. But that is not true. We know it's not true, the IRA knows it is not true. Janice Quinn and Ronnie, God rest him, knew it was not true and it's devastating to read things like that because every day you are living with it and there are people out there thinking that our Anthony was an informer. But I could honestly sit here and have an argument with anybody, or a debate about anything about it, and that's including the leadership of the IRA, that they killed an innocent man – a wee lad of twenty-two who was married with three kids who got involved with the movement and I am sorry to say it cost him his life.

It is very awkward for us as a family to lift papers and read about people saying that he met his handlers here and there. It is not true because he never got the chance, even if he had wanted to. Does an informer get a message at 9.30 on Friday and still goes freely to get debriefed on the Saturday? Does an informer do that? Does an informer go of his own accord? He doesn't do it. It is unheard of and that's a fact. The movement didn't arrest him, they didn't catch him.He went willingly and he never came back; they killed him. This has all been put before the republican movement. But no matter what's done, Anthony is never coming back. But for his kids, and his grand kids, and the history of Ireland … it's one of the most hated things in the world that your father was an informer or your grandfather was an informer; it is really devastating.

As time goes on it doesn't get easy but time heals. Then my father was shot dead by loyalists in 1989. The family still haven't come to terms with my father's death. You just have to carry on but it is very hard. I have fond memories of my father and I wish he were here today. He was a powerful man and a real devastating loss to the family. Anthony to me was someone that I looked up to because he was the brother next to me. He was a very quiet person. The tragedy is we only had him here for twenty-two years.

Paddy Quigley (cousin)

Anthony Braniff was my cousin we were always very close. His mother and my mother are sisters. There was a squad of us that ran about together. Anthony was a cracker footballer. He could mix with anybody; he was a sociable guy. Anthony was a beautiful singer. He had that type of voice that you could have listened to all night. His nickname was Mitch and I really don't know how he got it. It was the same with the scar on his cheek; we never really knew what happened. With the arrival of the troubles it more or less drew people into it. Anthony never really talked much about politics. His family were political and he got his politics from his older brothers. His brothers Paddy and Brian both did time for political offences. Anthony never said he was involved in the republican movement. I sort of guessed he was because he drifted away from all of us.

When Anthony was killed we found out at my mother's house; we received a phone call from the family. Anthony had gone missing for a couple of days and the family were worried about him. He was taken away and murdered. It took a lot out of the family emotionally, because he was a lovely guy; he was a really nice guy. I don't know the politics of it all but I could never see Anthony being an informer. No one has ever been shown any proof that he gave information.

Anthony had a very big funeral and it was very sad. I still think about him and our childhood memories. They were great days. Everybody was poor in those days but the time we spent with each other was brilliant. I would just love to be able to go back to those days. Anthony had no enemies when we were kids. He was just a nice all-round type of guy. Time for us just stopped when Anthony died; he was a very good cousin and his whole family were good; we always stood shoulder to shoulder with each other.

Larry Kennedy
Killed by the UDA/UFF,
Shamrock Club,
Flax Street,
8 October 1981

When he came into the area everybody fell in love with him, all around Ardoyne, from children to the old, because he was a great person. 'Look after the needy not the greedy', that was Larry's philosophy on life.

Larry Kennedy was born in County Tyrone in 1945 where he was brought up by his mother. In the early 1960s he moved to Belfast by himself when still in his teens. In 1962 he met Anthony Keenan from Jamaica Street in Ardoyne. The two became friends. They fell out of contact with one another but two years later Larry turned up on the doorstep of the Keenan's home. He was soon invited into the household where, to all intents and purposes, he was adopted as a brother by the whole family. He took to Ardoyne straightaway. By all accounts, Ardoyne very much took to him too. As a young man Larry was a keen sportsman. He played Gaelic football and represented Tyrone as a junior hurler, winning a championship medal. He later played for Ardoyne GAA and ran a team for the Shamrock Social Club. It was the Shamrock that was probably Larry's most tangible legacy to his adopted district. He was the prime mover in its foundation. Following the burnings of 1969, Larry found the hut in which the Shamrock was first located. He was pivotal in organising the club's growth thereafter. In 1971 Larry was interned in Long Kesh. He put his year of imprisonment to good use by studying for entry onto a sociology degree course at Queen's University. On his release he enrolled and subsequently graduated. This helped Larry earn him his nickname, 'The Brain'. Larry was also a very active worker on behalf of numerous charities. Then (in the midst of the republican hunger strike of 1981) Larry stood for the Belfast city council. He campaigned both as a community worker and as a leading anti-H-Block activist. He won the seat and worked tirelessly for the community in the little time that was left to him. On the night of 8 October 1981 Larry Kennedy was leaving the Shamrock club when a gang of UDA gunmen opened fire on him in the doorway. They then shot indiscriminately into the bar inside. Larry was killed and another man (Michael Lagan) was critically injured. It was less than a week after the last of the hunger strikers had called off their protest. Three days later Larry Kennedy was laid in state in the Shamrock as thousands of people filed past to pay their last respects. He was buried after a massive funeral attended by many of his colleagues from the city council. He was 36 years old.

Sean Murphy (friend)

Larry was a founder member of the Shamrock club. If it was not for Larry there would be no Shamrock. At the start of the troubles, like everybody else, we were building barricades and burning buses. When the [British] soldiers came in we had all the bus seats. We had also saved the off-licence at the bottom of Brompton Park from being looted and burnt down. When the owner came back on the Sunday he gave us a load of drink for saving his bar. Tommy Maguire suggested that we go up to his attic and drink it in the shop. That's where the Shamrock club started from. We cleaned Tommy's attic out and put the bus seats round about it. Larry was the main man organising things. After that he got the big wooden hut we used. He also instigated it when we built more bits on. The happiest day we had was the time the Shamrock won the Lifford Cup. Larry was one of the main men who organised and ran the team. It was the first team from the North ever to win it. No other team in Belfast even came close to winning it. There were some celebrations that night! Larry was a character. They called him 'the Brain' because he knew everything about everything. He went through a sociology course in university and passed with flying colours. He graduated with his scarf and all! He was a great man for charity work as well. When him and me were involved with the Shamrock, we were involved with a lot of stuff for charities, like Cancer Research, Nazareth Lodge. So what happened to him was even more tragic. Larry was a great guy, one of the best friends I ever had. He was a great fella and he is sadly missed, especially from the Shamrock club's point of view. When Larry was shot we were actually in the process of renovating the back room. So when he was killed we named it the Kennedy room after him. We had a big photo of him in the bar, but that is all brushed under the carpet now.

I remember the night Larry was killed; it was a Thursday night, 8 October 1981. I will never forget it. There was a 'do' on for the Knights of Malta run by Mickey Lagan. I was in the club from about 6.30 pm. I used to have a fish shop at Springfield Road and I brought Larry a barbecued chicken up. I used to do that a couple of times a week. I left him at about 7 pm. I think he was still carrying the chicken in a bag he had with him when he was shot later at about 10.30 pm. The wee 'do' was on in the hall and Larry was in the bar. It was just unfortunate that Larry decided to go home about that time. He was just walking out the door when these boys [loyalists] were coming in with guns. They shot Larry first, hit him above the eye and about four times in the chest. Then they stepped over him, came into the bar and shot all round them. It was just luck that no-one else was killed. They riddled the whole bar and shot Mickey Lagan who was on the door of the cabaret in the hall. As far as I can remember the only people injured were Mickey Lagan and Larry.

The guy who did it later turned tout for the RUC. He was going to be a supergrass, then he went back on it. After immunity was withdrawn, the RUC were supposed to charge him with killing Larry. They [RUC] came and asked me to go to court but in the end it never materialised. They wanted me to go to give evidence because I had gone straight down to the club after the shooting. Larry's bag with his washing in was still in the hall and I lifted it. There were two or three bullets that had gone right through him and into the bag. So I brought it down to the barracks for forensics. I thought it might have helped to get the guys that did it. In the end no one was convicted. We were not really kept informed by the authorities about the investigation. I was never asked to go to an inquest or anything. Justice was definitely not achieved for Larry's killing.

Michael Lagan (neighbour and eyewitness)

I worked for the St Lazareth's ambulance corps. The Brits had wrecked the inside of the ambulance one night. They threw everything out into the street and I asked Larry to come round to see it and put a letter into the *Irish News* about it. He said he would but he never got round to do it. Larry was a city councillor and every time you saw him he was very busy. The next time I spoke to him was the night he was shot dead. I was running a 'do' in the Shamrock club to raise money to buy a new ambulance. There was no rioting or anything that night. There was only one peculiar thing which I have never been able to get out of my mind. That was the only night, before or since, when you were not allowed to park just outside the club. Anyway, Larry happened to come in and asked how the night was going. The two of us started talking. He said he was sorry he had not been able to get round to see the ambulance. Then he said, 'I'm away round to get this washing in'. I said, 'Dead on' and he walked out through the door. Then I heard 'bang', 'bang' and a thump. I looked round and Larry was lying back in the hall again. I went over to see what I could do for Larry. Then they [loyalists] opened up again and I jumped back into the corner. As I was lying in the corner they opened up again. I could see blood shooting out of Larry's neck and I thought they were still shooting and hitting him while he was lying there. But I heard later that the vein in his neck was just pumping blood and they were just shooting the wall.

Then a fella wearing a mask came in and stepped over Larry. I thought it was someone from the IRA. I said, 'Oh youse are the brave fellas. Why don't you put your gun down and let us see how brave you are'. He said, 'Shut up, you fenian bastard'. Then I knew it wasn't the IRA. This guy started to shoot at me. The fellas in the bar threw bottles and glasses at him. He hit me seven times and fired 12 other shots. He injured a couple of other people too. My own son got a graze that night. After that I don't know what happened because I was taken away. But, the incident was well thought out; they [loyalists] had tried to get into the club by another door. A lot of children were sitting on rails facing the Shamrock and told them they would have to use the main doors. That was when they came round.

Anthony Keenan (friend and 'brother')

Larry was more than a close friend of mine. He was more like a brother. He was basically adopted into our family and was a much-loved brother to all of us. In fact, when he came into the area everybody fell in love with him, all around Ardoyne, from children to the old. That was because he was a great person. 'Look after the needy not the greedy', that was Larry's philosophy on life. I met Larry in 1962. We were hanging about in the city together; we used to have a few bets and a couple of games of snooker. You could tell by his accent he came from Tyrone. He didn't really know anyone in the city so I said if he ever got stuck to call up to our house in Ardoyne. I didn't see him for a couple of years, then one day I was lying in bed when my father said there was a fella at the door wearing a 'paddy' hat and glasses looking for me. It was Larry Kennedy. So that was the start of Larry staying in our home. He fell in love with the people of Ardoyne. He loved them all, he really did. He thought they were the greatest people he had ever met in his life. He stayed in our house from then until he was murdered by the loyalists.

Larry was a very, very intelligent person. In fact the nickname he got living in Ardoyne was 'the Brain' because he was very, very clever. He was just a great character, great craic. He was a very funny fella, full of life. He was a very sporty person as well, loved racing, hurling, football. He was actually the man behind the Shamrock club. Larry was 'Mr Shamrock'. We all wanted to have this big club so that we could socialise and drink together because, as you know, the people of Ardoyne are a very, very tight-knit family. The Shamrock went from a wee wooden hut at the Jamaica Street end of Brompton Park into one of the biggest and best social clubs in the whole of Belfast. He did a lot of stuff for charity as well. He was the Secretary of the Cancer Research in Ardoyne and ran loads of functions for it. He was a great organiser. He started that off because there was so many young people in the district dying from cancer. I honestly believe that is from the CS gas the Brits fired in the early 1970s. Larry was also an ex-internee; he had been interned in 1971 and was in Cage 7 with all the other lads from Ardoyne for about a year. It was the normal routine. The British army just picked up anybody they thought had a love of Ireland. Larry got picked up like many others; there was no justice. Larry was a great Irishman. I don't think anyone could have beaten Larry in his knowledge of Irish history. It was always his dream to one day see a tricolour flying over the city hall.

In 1981 Larry became a Belfast city councillor. He loved politics and he got me interested in politics. If he had lived, I think he would have made a brilliant politician. Becoming a councillor started off as a sort of joke. I said, 'Larry, you've got the intelligence and the charisma; why don't you run for councillor?' Well, Larry was the sort of person to have a go at things and get them done. He took the bull by the horns and got the Shamrock committee behind him; they helped out tremendously. At the start everybody thought it was a joke because nobody ever dreamed of running for the council. A councillor was supposed to be a big, important person, so nobody gave him a chance of winning. But we turned it into an 'American-style' campaign. Larry loved that. We had a sort of carnival atmosphere. We had flags and bunting out and bands playing on the back of a lorry. We got the people out. We got the message across and through to the people of Ardoyne. Then we were canvassing throughout North Belfast; Ardoyne, Ligoniel, the Bone. 'Vote Kennedy No. 1', we said, 'What the Kennedys did for America we could do for Ardoyne'. Everybody lapped it up. It was something unusual. It was happening in Ardoyne and everybody thought it was great. I remember the day of the count. We were in the city hall and Larry was a bit nervous. We waited for hours and hours and then at the end of it Larry was elected. It was a tremendous result because it was difficult to get people to come out and vote then. After Larry was elected councillor there was no one who put in the effort that he did; I think the people of Ardoyne would agree with that. He was the man that cleaned up Ardoyne. He checked all the entries, filled in people's forms, helped out the old people, organised buses for them and ran outings for the children of Ardoyne.

I spoke to Larry the day that he was murdered. I remember it very, very well. I was in the club the night Larry was murdered. Once again he was being the 'good samaritan' that night. He was organising an outing for the children of Ardoyne. Larry ran two buses every Tuesday and every Friday for the young ones of Ardoyne to go to the swimming pool up in Andersonstown. Larry came over to tell me he was organising the bus for the day after to take the kids up to Andytown. He had just left me, then the next minute the loyalists were shooting all around them. Larry actually gave his life for an awful lot of people because I think Larry made an effort to stop the gunmen. If they had got in they would have murdered a lot more. I don't like to put it this way but Larry sort of sacrificed himself; Michael Lagan did too. If they hadn't been there that night I think there would have been an awful lot more deaths. Along with the rest of the people in the Shamrock I was very lucky myself not to be killed. I was only three or four feet away from the gunman when he pointed the sub-machine gun at me. I just dived on the ground, thinking that was the end for me and a whole lot more. To me, Larry died a hero.

Afterward I just sat there. To be quite honest it was a shock. It knocked me off balance because it happened so quickly. Then I heard somebody shouting, 'I think Larry is dead'. They said to me, 'Your Larry is dead, Anthony'. I flew out to the hall and there was Larry lying there. I remember grabbing Larry, shaking him and shouting, 'Larry, Larry, what's wrong?' I just couldn't believe it. I could see that Michael Lagan had been shot too; Michael was seriously ill but thankfully he lived. I was in deep shock. I just left and went straight round to my house in Holmdene Gardens. Later the police asked me would I go down to the Mater Hospital to identify Larry. When I saw him lying there on the slab I just couldn't believe it. It was just so sad to take away someone that I and everyone loved. I knew everyone would miss him badly. It was so very, very sad.

Larry was taken to my brother Christopher's house for two days. Then he was laid out in the middle of the Shamrock in the big room. It was like a state funeral. It was what he deserved and there were just so many people who wanted to come and see him. There were thousands of people lined outside to come in and see him. It was unbelievable. His mother came too. That was the first time I saw her. She was a lovely wee woman and I could tell by looking at her that she was very, very proud of Larry. I could see that deep down she really loved him and was proud of what he stood for, a man of principle. There was a massive funeral, one of the biggest ever to come out of Ardoyne. Larry was buried in the city and there were a lot of councillors and important people there. Afterward myself, Mary Cameron, Marie McWilliams and a couple other people ran a big function in the Shamrock for Larry. It was a big success and we collected over a thousand pounds. We gave it to the committee and a big Celtic cross was put up on his grave in memory of him from the people of Ardoyne. Larry was just something very special.

> *You imagine when something like that happens that you*
> *would do this or that, that you would fight them.*
> *But fear is the worst thing that you can experience in your*
> *life and it changed my whole life completely.*

Bobby Ewing's mother was called Nora, a Stewart from Butler Street. His father, Brian, originally from Ligoniel and brought up a Protestant, became a Catholic when the two married in 1929. The couple met whilst working in Ewart's Mill where Bobby's father would continue to be employed after his birth. Brian and Nora eventually had seven children, four girls and three boys. Bobby was the second youngest, born on 17 December 1945. At first the family lived with relatives in Herbert Street but eventually they moved into their own home in Butler Street. It was here that Bobby was brought up, attending first the Holy Cross Boys school and then St

Bobby Ewing
Killed by the UFF,
Deerpark Road,
12 October 1981

Gabriel's. As a young man Bobby followed football and developed an early abiding interest in dogs that would later see him keep and train greyhounds. He had also already become a lover of Irish music, another lifelong passion. When he finished school, Bobby went straight into work in the construction industry and soon became a steel erector, a keen supporter of the trade union movement and a declared socialist. By then Bobby's father had moved to England for work. In 1971 he had a heart attack and died. Bobby brought his body home. At virtually the same time his youngest brother was interned. On the brighter side Bobby had started dating Winifred Gillespie and the two were soon married and began a family of their own. They had three boys (David, Brian and Bobby). The family moved from Chatham Street to a new, larger house on the Deerpark Road in 1978. The Deerpark was on the edge of Ardoyne, and that in itself could be a cause of some concern with the threat of attack from nearby loyalist areas. However it offered a chance for Bobby to make a better home and life for himself and his young family. It also gave him the space to build backyard kennels for his much cared-for greyhounds, a hobby that took up most of his spare time and brought him friends from various places and backgrounds. The conflict was not, however, far away. Bobby knew the family of 15-year-old Danny Barrett well [killed by the British army in Havana Court, 9 July 1981]. He was also a friend of Larry Kennedy [killed by the UFF in the Shamrock social club, 8 October 1981]. By then Bobby had become wary for his own safety. He had been receiving threatening phone calls at his home for several weeks. Just a week before his death Bobby was arrested and briefly held by the RUC. However Bobby had never been involved with any political group. Taken alongside other events, this arrest would always lead Bobby's family to have strong suspicions that collusion between the RUC and his loyalist killers lay behind his death. It would certainly have increased his profile as a potential target. At 6.15 pm on 12 October 1981 Bobby Ewing was at home preparing to take his young sons to the scouts when a report on the funeral of Larry Kennedy came on TV. He sat down to watch. With a third waiting in a car outside, two UFF gunmen came into the house, passing two of Bobby's sons on the way. They shot Bobby dead where he sat in front of his wife. No one was ever caught for his killing. He left behind his wife and three young boys, aged twelve, nine and six.

Veronica Clarke (sister)

As a child, Bobby loved football. He was also interested in dogs and animals. He was always a good kid. Bobby was an altar boy and even later in life he was a good Catholic and never missed mass or confession. My mother was a good Catholic and she used to say that she was proud of Bobby because he never missed his duties. Growing up, he hung around with a lot of fellas from the district: Seamie Carland, Con McDowell, Cleaky Clarke, Jim and Pat McAllister. When we were kids I used to take him and Fidelis up to the Forum cinema, to the matinee, every Saturday. We were close because we were the three youngest and Bobby and Fidelis were really close. Bobby was just a good fella, good-looking too. He was my 'ma's heart'; her eyes always lit up when he came into the house. He had big, brown eyes and black, black hair. Having said that, my mother and father loved all of their children with all their hearts. Bobby was a good son, a good brother, a good lad growing up and a good man when he was older. I'm not exaggerating to say that he had no enemies in Ardoyne. He got on with everyone. He loved traditional Irish music from when he was young too and always had records of Irish music, long before the troubles.

The last time I saw Bobby was the Sunday before he died. I had run out of bottled gas and he came over to help me sort it out. We just sat and talked and I always remember him talking about how terrible it was that young Danny Barrett had been shot and that it was frightening to think how anyone could be next. Bobby sat in Molly's house for two nights at young Danny's wake. He would come over and sit up all night, then leave for work in the morning. He was distracted, as if Danny had been one of his own family. Three months later it was him. First it was Danny, then Larry Kennedy was killed and then Bobby was killed himself. Bobby was arrested by the RUC on the Monday after I saw him last. It was just a week before he died. Bobby was getting ready for work at about 5 am or 6 am when they came for him. But he was never in any trouble. They kept him until about 11 am, then they just let him go. The next Monday he was dead and that is why my mother always said that he was set up. She was someone who wouldn't hurt a fly but after that she always blamed the RUC for setting Bobby up. Bobby was killed in 1981 and my mother died in 1991. But until her dying day, even when she was in the hospital and couldn't recognise any of us, at the last she was saying, 'Murder, murder, my son, my son'. Bobby had also been getting threatening phone calls at home for a couple of weeks before he was murdered. There was even a call to the house the night after he was killed. Someone phoned up and asked to talk to him then started laughing. They were sick.

The day Bobby died was the day of Larry Kennedy's funeral, 12 October 1981. It happened about 6.15 pm. He was at home and just about to take his kids to the scouts when he heard the Ulster news coming on and went to watch it. They [loyalists] came in, right past the kids and shot him. They walked right past these two wee children and even that didn't soften their hearts. It was terrible. They went straight to the right room, like they knew exactly where to go. The only consolation for me is that Bobby had his back to the gunmen when they came in and he died instantly so he didn't know anything about it. My brother Billy lived in Jamaica Street and ran up to the house when he found out that Bobby had been shot. At first he was just told that he had been shot in the leg by someone firing from a car speeding past. When Billy got to the house the peelers tried to stop him getting in, but he just pushed past. This was only a few minutes after the shooting but the RUC already had the car the gunmen had used to get away in. It had been found in Ballysillan about five minutes after Bobby was killed, while he was still in the chair where he had been shot.

I was sitting in Molly Barrett's house in Havana Court when I was told that our Bobby had been shot. I had gone down there to see Molly because she had not been well since Danny had been killed. We were just sitting talking when her Susan came running in, squealing, and saying that Bobby had been shot. I went round to my house and a few people came in and said that they thought he had only been shot in the leg. But as it turned out that wasn't what had happened. Bobby had been shot a number of times in the head; he didn't have a chance. It was so sad. The UFF claimed responsibility for murdering Bobby. No one was ever even questioned about it, let alone caught. There was a report in the *Daily Mirror* where the UFF said that they had killed him because of his republican connections. But they have never needed an excuse. He was murdered because he was a Catholic, that's all. He was an easy target, particularly because of where he was living. Bobby used to live in Chatham Street but he wanted to try and bring his kids up as normally as possible and he was worried that they had already seen too many terrible things living there. So the family moved over to the Deerpark Road, though we were all concerned about it.

That was just the way things were. It was terrible; you just didn't know who was going to be next. I remember Mary Stewart saying that very thing to me the day Bobby was killed when I was up at Larry Kennedy's funeral, earlier in the afternoon. It was so hard for people to come through all that. I used to be afraid just sitting in the house afterwards. I had to have the door shut and the lights out and I used to imagine the door being broken in. We had some good laughs in those days but I was always like that, afraid in the troubles. I had been very close to young Danny Barrett too. I had known Molly for 20 years and Danny was in our house all the time. It all just leaves you so angry. I never thought that I would feel hatred but I do, I can't help it. I don't trust the RUC and I don't care what anyone says. I would never let my kids join them. I wouldn't care if Gerry Adams himself said it was ok. Three weeks after our Bobby had been killed some peelers came in two jeeps and picked up my eight year old, Eamonn. They said he stoned their jeep. They brought him into the house and then they started laughing at me about Bobby, tittering and laughing and then waving at me from the back of their jeeps. You don't forget things like that. Bobby was a gentleman. That is the only way I could describe him. He was just good, a good child, a good teenager, a good fella. Anybody would tell you that.

No one ever had anything but good to say about him. He was my brother and I still miss him; it's hard. I'm not saying that I sit around dwelling on it, moping about it, but it never leaves you. First Danny Barrett then Bobby; it was just terrible.

Paddy (brother-in-law)

You would never have heard anybody say a word about Bobby, from when he was young. He grew up at a time when blokes were good blokes, smashing mates. We had a wee football team that started off as 'Kil's Cubs' and then became Ardoyne United. All the guys from around here were members: Paddy McAdorey [killed on active service by the British army, Jamaica Street, 9 August 1971], Seamie McAuley, Cleaky Clarke, Seamy Donnelly, Jimmy Barrett, he was the manager of the team, and I was the treasurer. Bobby was a member of the club too; he didn't play (though his brother Fidelis did) but he would have been one of our best supporters – never missed a match. After the game we would all meet up and go out together. They were good days. Bobby was always good company too. He was a member of the Star and he was sometimes in the League, the Shamrock, the GAA, but he was always a hard-working man. He was good company but his family always came first. He was very independent but a man that never fell out of his religion either. Even when he had moved out of home he always still went to mass. I always remember Bobby as a good-looking man as well, and someone who always kept himself well dressed, even when he was a child. I have always believed that the peelers set Bobby up to be killed. Partly that's because of what happened to me on the night of his funeral. I was over with Winnie [Bobby's wife] in the house on the Deerpark Road and left at about 1 am. I just came out of the gate saying goodnight to Winnie when a car drove past us heading up towards the Oldpark Road. It was going past very slowly and there were three blokes in the car. It looked very suspicious. I started to walk up toward the Oldpark and as I was walking the car went past, swung round down and back up again. Then it was just pacing me. I got to the top of the road and the car just swung in front of me. Someone jumped out yelling, 'Get the bastard'. I saw guns being cocked and I just turned and ran. These fellas were wearing bomber jackets and one of them started shouting 'police' but I kept running, hit Winnie's door and jammed it shut. They were banging on the door but I just shouted for Winnie to call the cops. Two minutes later a landrover pulled up and then these cops started apologising for the other guys, saying that they were just supposed to keep an eye on the house. But I was going to get done that night, the night Bobby was buried.

Joe Stewart (friend)

I knew Bobby from the early 1970s onward, basically through our interest in greyhounds. A friendship just built up through going coursing and the interest in dogs. When he moved into the Deerpark Road Bobby built wooden kennels in the backyard and kept the dogs in there. The first dogs he ever had he reared from pups, which is a great ambition for anyone who keeps dogs. I remember two he had, one was called 'Sarah's Way' and the other was 'Divis View', because from the back of his house Bobby had a great view of Divis. We had some great times, some good laughs, particularly when I used to go over and give a hand with the dogs in the mornings. There was always great humour with the dogs and never any animosity where religion was concerned. Bobby would have had as many Protestant friends as Catholic and that was through the dogs. Keeping greyhounds was always as much a social thing as anything else, a way of relieving tension in yourself and getting away from all the trials of the world. He loved horse racing as well, particularly the classic races like Cheltenham. He read about certain horses, really followed them, watched them. Bobby had a great way with him, a great man for telling a yarn. He was a great family man too, always taking them on holidays at a time when that was not something a lot of people did.

The night before he died Bobby and me were up in the Shamrock along with Con McDowell, another dog man. We had just sold a couple of dogs and were making plans on going to the sales. But it was a plan that never came to fruition because Bobby was killed. I found out that he had been shot when someone phoned me in the house, I didn't realise he was dead. I went over to Bobby's to see what was wrong but the peelers had the street cordoned off. Fidelis his brother was there and they wouldn't let him up to the house. He was going bananas and I couldn't blame him. Bobby and Fidelis were very, very close. It still didn't dawn on me that Bobby was dead. Even after I knew, it didn't really sink in, not even during the wake. It wasn't until after the funeral that I realised he wasn't coming back. There were a lot of his Protestant friends at the funeral too, from Larne, from Kilroot – good friends that we knew through the dogs. They all came to the Star and there was no animosity there, which was a great thing. I was devastated when I heard about Bobby's death. To me Bobby was the last person in the world that should have been shot dead because he didn't do any wrong. I never heard him saying a bad word about Protestants, Catholics, anyone. He wasn't politically minded. He was a nationalist but he wasn't political.

Winnie took Bobby's death very badly. I don't think people realised how much it affected her but I used to call up once a week or so and it took her a very long time to get over it. She ended up having to go to a clinic. Whatever compensation she may have got couldn't do much for her because it was going to somebody that wasn't well. How can she forgive the people who shot her husband in front of her and her children? She can't and I can understand why. I will always remember Bobby as someone who enjoyed life, a man who put his family first and apart from that loved the dogs as his hobby. I always think of him as one of the best-looking fellas in the district, someone who was a great personality, who always took great care over anything he did as well as taking great care over himself. He was a man who thought that you had to have dreams because without them you didn't have life; that's what he always said. I still miss him. He is dead nearly twenty years and I can still see him sitting there in front of me.

Winifred Ewing (wife)

Bobby grew up in Butler Street and I lived in Elmfield Street. I didn't really go around with him when we were young because he was four years older than me. I didn't go out much in the district anyway. He was a wee bit wild when he was young but once he settled down he became a very sensible person and that was the Bobby Ewing I knew. He wasn't a bible thumper or anything like that but he would never miss mass on a Sunday or Holy Day. He just settled down a lot. He liked a gamble when he was single, but nothing serious, and he always liked horse racing. He had a great interest in dog racing as well and after we were married and had moved up to the Deerpark Road we used to keep greyhounds. I started seeing more of Bobby from around 1969, when he used to come around to see my brother Peter. This was at the start of the troubles and everyone used to just go around with people from the district because you couldn't actually go anywhere else. As well as my brother, Bobby used to go around with Neil Somers. The two of them used to come and take me out together and walk me home. We used to go to the Saunders club and we went away for a couple of weekends to Dublin. But at that time there was hardly anywhere you could go. So, even though I knew him from when he was a wee boy, I only really knew Bobby for a couple of years before we were married on 12 May 1972. We went to Dublin for the weekend for our honeymoon. We fitted it in with a big horse race that was on at the same time! I was happy enough with that though; I wasn't much of a one for frilly dresses or anything. At first we got a house in Chatham Street and were there for seven or eight years. Bobby was earning good money and he wanted to move out of the district. He was a steel erector, which paid a good wage. Bobby was a socialist; he was next door to a communist, and a very, very strong union man. He was in the Transport and General Workers' Union and he always held that it was difficult for Catholics to get into good trades, like that of steel erector. Anyway, that was when we moved up to the Deerpark Road, around May 1978. We were only in it about two and a half years before Bobby was killed.

By that time we had three boys, David, Brian and Bobby. We used to take them down South for our holidays with a trailer tent Bobby had bought. He always liked going down around Clare, the Burren and we went down to the cliffs of Moher, Killarney. We went to a fleadh while we were down there too. Bobby always liked traditional music. He used to go to the All-Ireland Fleadh Cheoil with Neil Somers and Eddie Donnelly sometimes, and went up to Buncrana and Bundoran for the music. The conflict had an impact on us but just like it did on anyone else in the district. Bobby had been arrested a couple of times. He had been lifted in 1970 but that was just harassment really. He wasn't interned or anything, though he was arrested when we were over in the Deerpark Road. We hadn't been bothered for a long time then a couple of weeks before he was murdered the Brits came and took him in. They didn't even ask him anything, just kept him for a few hours. We did get some strange phone calls as well, people just calling asking where 'Dallas' was, leaving threats.

The night before he was killed Bobby had been down in the Shamrock. He didn't go out much but that night he had been out with Joe Stewart. He came in, went to his bed and wasn't in work the next day. The next day was a Monday, 12 October. He and our eldest boy, David, were out in the backyard most of the day seeing to the greyhounds, his two favourites, 'Sarah's Way' and 'Divis View'. He was working on a big shed for them. I had to go out for a while, went over to my mammy's house, then picked up the kids from school. Then I came back over to make the dinner. Around 6 pm Bobby said he had to go over to Joe Stewart's house and was going to drop off our Brian at the cubs on his way. He was just on his way out and I remember looking at the clock and saying that it was 6.15 pm so he had better get a move on if Brian wasn't going to be late. He was just going out when Larry Kennedy's funeral came on the TV. Larry had been shot the Thursday before and Bobby turned around to watch it. I was just sitting with a cup of tea and a piece of toast in my hand. Bobby sat down with his back to the door when it was flung open by this fella. Bobby took a bullet in his neck and one went through his head, shooting out his eye. He took three bullets in all and another one missed him and lodged in the wall by the television. Everything was as you see it on TV, in slow motion. I could see every bullet as it went into him and I could smell the gunpowder. I can remember jumping up and saying, 'You've got the wrong man'. I don't know why. There was blood splattered everywhere and then it was as if the world had just stopped. Everything just went into slow motion.

Then I just looked at them [loyalists]. There were two of them. I remember one guy was just standing leaning against the door. They had actually passed two of my kids coming up the path. One of them had a towel wrapped around his hand but because our Brian had seen his daddy cleaning the dogs with towels, he thought they were just doggy men. There was a third guy sat in a car outside. I can't really remember what they looked like even though they weren't disguised or anything. I remember one had on a green jacket. Another had his hair cut very, very short. They were young, 18, 19 or 20. When they bounced in I thought it was a joke. Then in a split second everything just happened, and the realisation hit me. It was all in a split second. The guy leaning against the door was just smiling and I actually thought that they were going to shoot me because there had been women shot around that time. All I could think about was my kids. Then the two of them just turned and ran. I ran after them and there was a fella in the street walking his dogs and he ran after the car as well. I went back into the house and dialled 999. I kept two of the kids out but the oldest fella came running in from the back and saw Bobby lying there. Mr McKenna who lived across from us came running and thought that Bobby was still alive. But my David was just standing saying, 'No, it's just his nerves'. David was just 12 at the time. Then he and I went out to stop the younger two boys coming in. I should have said an Act of Contrition into Bobby's ear but I was just totally scared and terrified. You imagine when something like that happens that you would do this or that, that you would fight them or whatever. But fear is the worst thing that you can experience in your life and it changed my whole life completely. I know it wasn't long but it seemed like an age before the ambulance came. They had Bobby bandaged up but his hands were pure white. They put me in the front of the ambulance and when we got to the hospital I had to give his name and address and then wait in a wee room. Then a nurse came and told me that Bobby was dead. I just started to shake. My sister arrived with a girl from across the street from her. A good friend of Bobby's, Paddy Clarke, arrived down too and Fidel, who went in to formally identify the body for me. The UFF claimed responsibility for killing Bobby. They said it was because of his republican connections. The police came and asked me what happened. I told them and that was that. Nobody was ever charged, never.

There is not a day goes past that I don't think about it but you can't keep dwelling on it because it just drives you mental. But, because I was in the room when it happened, it leaves you with an awful fear. When my kids were younger I was so afraid of the same thing happening again – afraid of this, of that and the other. I went back and lived in the house for six years. It was probably the worst thing I could do but it was partly because Bobby had put so much effort into the house and I dug my heels in, although the Housing Executive also said that they could not give us an emergency transfer because they said we were not under threat. Then Sammy Morrison got shot in the house next door, six years later. It was loyalists again. They had actually parked between our two doors and my middle fella, Brian, was out in the street when Sammy drove up in a taxi and went into the house. The loyalists got out of their car and went down the passageway to try and murder Sammy just as our Brian was coming to the door. It was the second shooting that Brian had been through and a few days later we just moved out to go and live with my sister.

For two years after Bobby died I really struggled. I was forgetting things as I was doing them and had no energy or interest in anything. I was always really, really tired. Then I got up one morning and was looking at myself in the mirror and didn't recognise the face looking back at me. I thought I was going mad. I went into work, in Marks and Spencer's, and was sitting on the till. I just wanted to cry. Then I had what I can only describe as an out-of-body experience. It was as if I was standing beside myself asking myself why it was that I wanted to cry. I didn't know what was real and what wasn't real at that stage. My supervisor took me into a wee room and she just put her arms around me, but I still didn't feel as if I was even here. They sent me home and then the doctor recommended that I should start getting therapy from Alexander Gardens, which I did. They had to teach me how to grieve. They said that the shock was so great that my mind had split into two parts. One part just blocked everything out, the other just wanted to cry. It was really rough going; Then I was alright. But once Sammy got shot it knocked me straight back again. They call it post-traumatic stress syndrome. It just knocks your mind. It's unbelievable. There was no real support for me whatsoever, not from the social services, the chapel, nobody except my own family. I did attend a couple of meetings of a group called Life Line, and there was another similar group I went to for a while, but I didn't find it helped. Everyone was just so involved in his or her own worlds. I just tried to get on with my life.

Bobby was a good-natured big man, a good hard worker who just loved his kids. Being with Bobby was the first time I felt secure in my life and they just took all my security away. They left me so that I missed out on being a mother because I've had to be a mother and a father, and you can't do both. I know my boys would contradict me but I feel that I didn't give them the love that they should have got from a mammy because I had to be strict with them. They did turn out to be three good lads. But it is now that I have grandchildren that I realise that I lost so much of my motherhood. Sometimes when I just wanted to be weak and loving I couldn't; I had to keep being strict and strong. Bobby being killed just robbed us all of so many things. My grandson and granddaughter will just miss out on Bobby completely because nobody can ever take his place, nobody. I don't even feel like I had the time and the chance to truly get to know him.

> *The loyalist gunmen just walked into the shop, singled out Dandy and shot him 17 times. The RUC jeep was parked up at Cliftonville Circus.*
> *I'm sure they heard the shooting. They came down after the gunmen left. The first RUC man that walked into the shop said, 'It's all right, its only Trevor Close'...*
> *I believe the RUC gave his details to the loyalist killers.*

Trevor Close
Killed by loyalists,
Cliftonville Road,
26 May 1983

Trevor 'Dandy' Close was the youngest of four children born to Gretta (née Curry) and Harry Close. Gretta was born and reared in Crumlin Street and Harry was a Falls Road man. The couple settled in Ardoyne, 9 Crumlin Street, and did their best in difficult times to bring up their children; Patsy, Mary, Kathleen and Dandy. Gretta suffered very poor health and as a result Kathleen took on the 'mother role'. Kathleen doted on Dandy and although just a few years older, she more or less reared him. Like most lads in the district he attended Holy Cross Boys and St Gabriel's school. His childhood sweetheart was Marie Maguire from the Bone. Dandy and Marie got married in Dublin on 3 March 1971 and they had four children: Saoirse, Niamh, Fergal and Breda.

Dandy was very sociable. He had a great sense of humour and saw the funny side to everything. He was a terrible 'slagger', had 'the gift of the gab' and could spin a great yarn. He was a popular person with a wide circle of friends, including Harry Mulholland, Paul McAllister, Jamesy Farrelly, Brendan Bradley, Paddy Murphy and Joe Matthews. He enjoyed a pint in Kelly's Cellars where many of his friends drank. But Dandy had a serious side to his character. He was a politically active person.

At the time of his death Dandy was a milkman, which made him a well-known figure throughout north Belfast. Dandy was a decent person who would have gone out of his way to do anyone a good turn. He was a good husband to Marie and a great father to his four children whom he adored. He was well liked by his wider family circle and was particularly close to his mother-in-law.

On 26 May 1983 while Dandy was delivering milk to Hunter's shop on the Cliftonville Road, loyalist gunmen entered, singled him out and shot and killed him in a sectarian attack. Two UVF men were later convicted in connection with his killing. Members of his family believe there was collusion between the RUC and his loyalist killers. Dandy was 33 years of age at the time of his death.

Marie Close (widow)

I always knew Trevor as Dandy. We met when I was about thirteen or fourteen over at the Beltex. The Beltex used to be where the Flax Centre is now. Everybody played there. That's how we met. We were going with each other from we were fifteen years of age. That was about 1962. I was from Ardilea Street in the Bone and he was from Crumlin Street. That's where he was born and reared. His friends at that stage were Frankie Kane, Dutch Doherty and Seanie Meehan. We used to go to the pictures or up to St Gabriel's dance, the Hop. That's all there was to do. The rest of the time we hung about Fusco's chippy on the Crumlin Road.

Dandy went to Dublin in 1971. That's where we got married. Harry Mulholland was our best man. I suppose Harry was always his mate. We stayed in Dublin for about two weeks and then moved into a house in Ardoyne, 39 Chatham Street. I wanted to move back to the Bone and we moved to a house in Oldpark Avenue; it became the family home. We had four children Saoirse, Niamh, Fergal and Breda. When Breda was three months old we moved to 32 Linden Gardens and that is where Dandy lived when he was killed.

I suppose like everybody we didn't really have that much when we were first married. The troubles were on and that's all that seemed important. Your family sort of took second place. Then somewhere along the line something happened. You realise that you have a family and you have kids and that your responsibility is to them. I don't know whether Dandy just grew up or became disillusioned. I don't know what happened but he changed. It was around the time that Fergal was born. He wanted to be with the kids more and to be a daddy and have a normal life, to be able to stay in his own house and just be there. He was arrested dozens of times. Everywhere he went he was stopped and he got a real hard time from the RUC. Dandy was never in jail and never did time. He was constantly harassed, even when he was working on the milk run. I suppose by that time many of his friends had died. His friends changed.

Dandy was the sort of person that you either really, really liked or just couldn't stand. He was a terrible slagger, he was a terrible liar, he was a terrible mixer. Dandy started working with Paul McAllister who had a completely different background, different thinking altogether and the two of them ended up the best of friends. Up until his death Dandy's closest friends were Paul McAllister, Jamesy Farrelly and Brendan Bradley. He was always friendly with Brad. But it was probably Paul and Jamesy that he was friendliest with. They worked together and all they did was rake about. He became a different person. I don't know whether you know that you haven't that much time. Maybe you want to be different and do different things or live a life. He always used to say that his time was short. For about three years before he died that was all I got, 'My time is short. I'll not get old ...'

He loved going to Kelly's Cellars for a drink but he couldn't drink to save his life. But that's where he loved to go. Dandy was a real funny sort of person; nothing was serious and everything was a joke. He wasn't meant to get old and he just enjoyed his life. He always said, 'Smile, sure what difference will it make. If something happens, get on with it and enjoy it and it will be all right tomorrow'. Dandy was a great son-in-law. My mummy had seven sons and I suppose she was closer to Dandy in many ways. He was a good brother-in-law too. He was a really good father, a really good husband and a really good friend.

The last time Dandy got arrested was when Harry Kirkpatrick touted in 1981 or '82. He got arrested and held for seven days. The RUC weren't too happy they couldn't pin anything on Dandy. Dandy said to me, 'They'll stiff me for this', meaning the RUC. At the end of the day that is probably the case and I know that. Before Dandy died he worked for Smith's Dairy on the Oldpark Road.

The morning of Dandy's death I was doing a childcare course in Rupert Stanley College. For some reason I got up earlier than usual. I usually waited for Dandy to come back and waken me up. He left for work around half four in the morning. I was washing my hair and I heard an ambulance. I just knew right away it was Dandy. About ten minutes later the door rapped and it was my brother Eamon who lived two doors below me. It was seven o' clock in the morning. Eamon said, 'Marie' and I said, 'Dandy has been shot' and he said 'Yes'. We went down to the hospital. I think Eamon, Paddy, Paul, Jamesy, Kate, Mary and his father Harry went down to the hospital. At 3.30 pm they told us that he had died. He had been shot seventeen times and there was nothing more they could do.

What had happened that morning was Dandy and the young lad who was working with him went into Hunter's shop at the corner of Elmgrove Street on the Cliftonville Road. The RUC had been in the shop five minutes earlier getting their football pools. They had just left the shop and two loyalist gunmen got out of a car. They walked into the shop, singled out Dandy and shot him 17 times. There was no one else hit in the attack. The young lad, who was only fourteen years old, and the owner of the shop were there at the time. The RUC jeep was parked up at Cliftonville Circus. I'm sure they heard the shooting. They came down after the gunmen had left. The first RUC man that walked into the shop said, 'It's all right; it's only Trevor Close.' I believe the RUC were involved in Dandy's killing. They are never going to admit it and there is never going to be anything done about it. I don't need to prove it. I don't need them to ever say because I know and that is it. I believe the RUC gave Dandy's details to the loyalist killers. The RUC stopped Dandy regularly and told him, 'You're next and you'll be going in a brown box'. At one stage I even phoned Father Faul because I was so fed up with it. I don't think the RUC is ever going to admit to anything or say anything and I don't have the energy to spend on them. I have kids and grandchildren and that is where my life is. It doesn't make any difference as long as I know the truth.

Loyalists later claimed responsibility. A couple of weeks later the RUC said they had arrested loyalists for Dandy's killing. They got the young lad to identify them. They brought him into a room with the loyalists and asked him if they were the ones that did it. When the young lad came to see me I told him not to do that again because it was too dangerous for him. Nine months later they arrested and charged two guys with the murders of Dandy, Stephen Murphy and Joe Donegan. I think it was just a case of 'we've got these two and we'll charge them with Dandy's murder'. One of them got done with setting Dandy up. They said they had been in a pub on the Shankill Road and were given a piece of paper with Dandy's name on it. They were convicted but I don't know how long they got.

Dandy had a big funeral. Everybody from Ardoyne came over. I don't think it made any difference what his beliefs may or may not have been, everybody came to the funeral. In a way it was what Dandy would have loved. He would have seen the funny side of this. At the time I remember thinking he would have hated to live until he was 70 and just died.

You sort of accepted death because that is what happened if you lived in our areas and you were that age. It was 99% certain that was going to happen. You just had to get on with it. That is what I had to do. It was difficult for the kids. The youngest was three and the eldest was ten. You never took time to really see what effect it had on them; you just thought as long as they were getting up and going to school and eating their dinner that everything was all right. It nearly killed my ma. Before Dandy's death she had been living with us and she had just moved back to her own wee bungalow in the Bone two weeks before it. After it she was never the same; it really nearly killed her.

Even though Dandy was my husband, he was also my friend. Dandy was a real good father and a real good brother and son-in-law. He was just Dandy. He was a happy person. There are still people who say to me to this day about him coming to collect the milk money and they hadn't got it and he would give them money. Doing his milk rounds, everybody loved him. All of the kids loved him. I am just happy I married him and had the short time I had with him.

Kathleen O'Kane (sister)

My mother was born and reared in Crumlin Street. My father was from Durham Street in the Falls Road. When they got married, they automatically set up home in Ardoyne. The family house was 9 Crumlin Street; that is were Dandy was born. It was a wee kitchen house; it had three bedrooms and an outside toilet. They called Crumlin Street the 'floating Docks' because the dams used to burst and flood the street and homes. You had an awful time. People talk about the film 'Angela's Ashes'; in those days it was much the same in Crumlin Street and Brookfield Street. There were a lot of those houses with two or three families to one house, particularly in Brookfield Street. In our family there were two boys and two girls. I would say my mummy had about four stillbirths and maybe four or five miscarriages. Four children survived, Mary, Patsy, myself and then Dandy. My mother was always very ill. I took over the mother role even though I was very young. My father worked all his life. He was a bus conductor. Dandy was the baby of the family. He was born on 29 August 1950. He went to Holy Cross Boys school and St Gabriel's. He was terrible for carrying on in school. One day Fr. Myles said, 'See that dandy at the back of the class'. That is how he got his nickname. It stuck with him throughout his life. I even called him Dandy. He was the most loveable creature you could ever have met. He was just the type of person everybody loved. When I got married and got a house in Chatham Street, Dandy more or less lived with me because my mummy was always ill. When I had my son Brian, my husband was away working. Dandy came and stayed with me. Dandy was going with Marie then and both of them were never out of my house.

Then the troubles started. I remember the night the Paisleyites came into Ardoyne and smashed all of my windows and threw petrol bombs. I was stuck in the house with my two kids. I was sitting behind the door trying to keep them out. That was August 1969. I will never forget it until the day I die. It was the night Sammy McLarnon was shot dead. My son Owen was just born. He was born on 7 June '69. I was literally petrified. I remember that night running out of the house because the men had to fight the loyalists down the street. I had two kids in my arms screaming. It was terrible what kids and everybody went through. They just came in smashing windows; they would have burned us totally out. I couldn't believe it. I was so angry. All the Paisleyites and B Specials were in the entry. I ended up getting stuck in Jean Cooney's house that night with my two kids. I always remember I literally couldn't speak with the fright. Jean had two children herself and she brought mattresses from upstairs down into the living room for us. I had no bottle for the child. I had nothing. The next thing we heard Sammy McLarnon had been shot dead and my biggest worry was where Dandy was.

I called the Paisleyites everything for coming in and burning us out. Dandy said to me, 'They are only Protestant people and they are frightened and they are scared'. I couldn't understand this. I had never heard this in my whole lifetime. That was Dandy's views. My father was very pro-British. He never brought us up to be bigots. There were a lot of Protestant people that came in and out of our house. My daddy would have been very much against Dandy being involved with rioting or anything like that. He wouldn't have got into the house if he were involved in anything. So he came to me and I had the whole worry and responsibility of him. It was during that period when everybody would have been involved. I would have literally been involved. The whole street was out helping one another because you were not going to let somebody come in to burn you out. If you call that being involved, everybody was involved. I wouldn't have really understood the politics of the troubles then. All I knew was that they were coming in to burn us out and everybody was trying to help one another.

I remember the day Dandy died like it was yesterday. I had just moved into my new home and Dandy called to see me. He was sitting joking away as usual. I remember he said he was tortured with the police. When I look back on it now maybe he was trying to warn me. He said the police had stopped him and they had taken his photographs out. He always carried photos of his kids and Padre Pio. They stopped him outside Crumlin Road goal and they made him take his shoes off, really, really demoralising him. He was stopped everywhere he went and tortured. Four weeks later, 26 May, I was getting ready for work. The door rapped and it was two of my neighbours from Velsheda Park, Kathleen Campbell and Tilly Toner. When I saw the two of them I said, 'God, what is wrong? Is it a bomb scare? Come on in'. I was going to make them a cup of tea and Kathleen Campbell said to me, 'Have you heard the news?' That was about 8.45 am. Kathleen Campbell looked at me and said, 'Kathleen, sit down'. She knew how close he was to me. She said, 'Dandy has been shot'. Well I just can't explain the shock. I ran out of the house and rang Marie's from a friend's house. Marie's mother answered the phone and she told me Dandy was in the Mater Hospital. All I remember is running down Chatham Street to my daddy. Two men were already in the house putting my daddy's shoes on and tying his laces.

I went down to the Mater Hospital. Dandy was in the casualty department. I remember Marie pacing up and down. I think everybody was just in total shock. He was lying there and he didn't look like he was dying. They then moved him to the operating theatre. All my friends and Marie's friends came down. My daddy just came in and looked and ran out. The nurse came and handed me Dandy's clothes and out fell the photo of the four kids and Padre Pio from his pocket. I should never have been handed those clothes. I remember going into the wee chapel and I couldn't move or speak or do anything. I couldn't pray, I couldn't do anything. I remember just sitting and waiting. I really thought he was going to come out of the theatre and that he was going to be all right. I never once thought he was going to die. It must have been about 3.30 pm when he died. One of the nursing sisters came over and put her arms round me. She said to me, 'You will have to be very, very strong because your sister-in-law is going to need you'. I was probably the weakest of the whole lot of them.

The doctor then brought us all into a wee room; my sister who is deaf was with me. We were all round the doctor in a crowd. I remember him saying, 'We have removed the liver, the spleen, the intestines and the kidneys.' I looked at him and said, 'So is he going into intensive care?' It just shows how much shock I was in at the time. I think he said Dandy died at 3.30 pm or around that time. My sister jumped up and said she wanted to see him. I don't know where I got the strength but I remember getting my sister and literally shaking her. She wanted to go into the theatre and she wanted to see him. I thought to myself that I couldn't let her go in. I don't think I was ready to face it and I didn't want her to face it. I just started haemorrhaging with the shock of it. I don't really remember things clearly after that. I don't know who took us but we went straight over to Marie's house. Marie was standing telling the four children that their father was shot and had died; the squeals of those children I will never forget to the day I die.

There were thousands at his funeral. I remember going up to Milltown cemetery and my daddy was literally shattered. The next day my daddy took pains in his chest and was rushed to the hospital. At that stage you weren't even focusing; I wasn't even focusing on my father. I think I was in shock for months. I was in total shock. There were times I couldn't even dress or wash the children I was so sick. I couldn't go to work. I wasn't able to work. Then I was rushed into hospital and had a major operation. It was just one thing after another. It was total devastation. I'd say it took me ten years to come to terms with his death. I went to Medugorje and that is really where I got healed of the death. I just couldn't accept it. I could accept my mummy dying and my uncle but not Dandy. My father died about three and a half years ago. I nursed him with cancer. It was horrific because it was just my sister and me and the both of us have it. It was really tough to be able to let go and still be at peace with my father's death. But even to this day I find it very difficult to deal with Dandy's death and that was eighteen years ago.

Dandy was the best brother in the world. To me he was the most precious person in the world. He was a very special person. He just wasn't meant to be for this world; he was too good. That is what makes it so painful; he was the loveliest person. I just feel privileged to have been his sister. Dandy would have done anything for anybody. I was just so privileged to have had that time with him and the lovely memories that I have of him. I don't think I ever had an argument with him in all of the time that we were brother and sister. He was just smashing. I'm sure he had his faults; I am not saying he was a perfect person but that is my memory of him. He was a very special person that I couldn't fault in any way whatsoever. I loved him with all of my heart.

I lost my faith for about three years after it. I hated God and I took it out on him. I never thought of the people that killed him once and I still don't to this day. I was so angry. I had prayed so much for protection for him. I felt God took the most precious thing from me, I just found it hard to forgive him. I would be very close to God in my life now; that is the most precious thing in my life and I know he is safe with him. That is what keeps me going. My biggest joy will be going there to meet him. I was anointed three weeks ago and I would have been happy to go because that is my one thing ... to see Dandy again and be with him.

5

1984-1994
Counter-insurgency, Collusion and the Search for Peace – From the Anglo-Irish Agreement to the Ceasefires

The Anglo-Irish Agreement was signed by the London and Dublin governments on 15 November 1985. For both it represented a new and significant diplomatic initiative driven by their (increasingly mutual) political and security interests. Undoubtedly a key determining factor was the rise of support for Sinn Féin within a radicalised northern nationalist population in the wake of the 1981 Hunger Strikes. This was illustrated by the election of Gerry Adams as an MP in 1983 and the party's growing success in local elections. Ardoyne reflected this changing political map. In 1985 Gerard McGuigan was the first Sinn Féin councillor elected for the district. The post-hunger strike atmosphere also ensured that the Northern Ireland Assembly established in 1982 was doomed to failure from the start. The Thatcher government was having to re-consider its approach. The fear that Sinn Féin might become the voice of northern nationalist opinion was also greatly exercising the minds of the government in the South. As a result they set up the New Ireland Forum. The Forum Report (delivered in May 1984) was designed to prop up the position of the SDLP. The British Prime Minister rejected it out of hand. Then on 12 October of the same year the IRA bombed the Grand Hotel in Brighton. Margaret Thatcher narrowly escaped with her life. This may have concentrated British government minds on the need to break the political stagnation that their policies had produced.

The Brighton bomb had also evidenced the continuing capabilities of the IRA in spite of the campaign against it. The supergrass system, after making initial inroads, had soon faltered. The devastating impact in Ardoyne of the Christopher Black trial was not replicated everywhere and even in the district the effect only lasted for a brief period. Allied to the use of supergrasses had been the emergence of a concerted 'shoot-to-kill' policy as the key means of prosecuting a counter-insurgency campaign. The SAS had been at the forefront of such a strategy since the mid-1970s. The killing of Jim Mulvenna, Dinny Brown and Jackie Mailey in a planned SAS ambush in 1978 had already borne witness to that. However, 'police primacy' (introduced in the late 1970s) also led to the greater role of newly-created elements within the RUC in covert activity. In 1980 militarised Divisional Mobile Support Units (DMSUs), Headquarters Mobile Support Units (HMSUs) and Special Support Units (SSUs) were introduced. DMSUs would soon become a common feature of life on the streets of Ardoyne and were involved in most of the controversial incidents in the decade to come. But wider public attention fell upon the SSUs, and one in particular, E4A. This developed after these groups were involved in a series of incidents that resulted in the deaths of (usually unarmed) civilians. Many had been specifically targeted as republicans.

The RUC's contribution to this 'shoot-to-kill' campaign had been both inept and obvious. Widespread international condemnation quickly followed. In turn this led to the instigation of an inquiry into the RUC's use of lethal force. The inquiry was set up in late 1984 and was headed by John Stalker, Deputy Chief Constable of Manchester. In 1986 Stalker was falsely discredited and removed from the inquiry because he was on the verge of unearthing vital evidence to establish that a 'shoot-to-kill' policy did, indeed, exist. The 'shoot-to-kill' controversy had been a particular problem for the Dublin government. Both they and Britain were looking for ways to co-operate on 'cross-border security'. That was difficult for the southern regime when British covert operations were causing such public disquiet. Combined with the desire to win the 'battle for hearts and minds' against Sinn Féin, this provided the impetus for both states to instigate a new political strategy. The Anglo-Irish Agreement was the result.

There was wholesale and angry unionist opposition to the Anglo-Irish Agreement. This resulted in a massive campaign of street protests. It also led to the creation of a common front between unionist politicians and loyalists through the 'Ulster Clubs'. In the wake of the Agreement two important factors therefore merged and produced a deadly outcome. The first was the British government's desire to limit the political fallout of state injustices and infringements of the rule of law. The second was an influx of new, young members into the ranks of loyalist groups. A massive rise of loyalist killings followed. Between January 1977 and December 1987 loyalists killed 72 people. From then until September 1994 they killed 229. The first factor created the need, and the second the means, for a state 'shoot-to-kill' policy by proxy to be put into place. This was the context in which collusion took place in the late 1980s and early 1990s.

Collusion appears to have been an endemic characteristic of British state policy. Evidence of it can be found in all phases of the conflict. Similarly various elements of the massive counter-insurgency apparatus have been key players in this 'dirty war'. For example, there is a great deal of evidence to show that both MI5 and MI6 were always deeply engaged in covert operations involving collusion. They acted as handlers for a network of informers and double agents in both republican and loyalist groups. Ex-British soldiers were often used to infiltrate various organisations (and loyalist groups in particular). They would then operate at the behest of British intelligence. Attempts to recruit ex-soldiers to act as agents was evidenced in Ardoyne by the case of Paul Marlow. Paul was an ex-member of the SAS who bought himself out of the army and returned home to Ardoyne in 1969. He joined the IRA in 1970 and died on active service in 1976 alongside Joey Surgenor and Frank Fitzsimmons from the Short Strand [Paul Marlow, killed on active service in the Ormeau Road, 16 October 1976]. Before his death Paul told others of numerous attempts made by British soldiers and agents to recruit ex-British army personnel to their ranks. Within the British army a number of units have also been the subject of allegations of collusion. For example, in the early 1970s Frank Kitson set up a group called the Military Reconnaissance Force (MRF). MRF has been identified as one of the groups that carried out and co-ordinated extra-legal attacks in co-operation with loyalists. There have also been grave suspicions about the relationship of the SAS with loyalists from the mid-1970s onward. This has been highlighted by the case of the Dublin/Monaghan bombings. In other words, throughout the conflict, collusion was an integral element of British counter-insurgency strategy. It allowed the British state to conduct an aggressive dirty war whilst maintaining the fiction that the 'rule of law' and the norms of liberal democracy were still being upheld. The organised collusion of the late 1980s and 1990s was therefore not entirely new. It was, however, perhaps more important than ever before.

Collusion is a blanket term for many different kinds of activity. It can also take a variety of forms. What might be termed 'unorganised' collusion undoubtedly occurred extensively between individual members of the state forces and loyalists. This usually involved the passing on of information or giving access to weapons. It took place because members of locally recruited security forces and loyalists came from the same communities (and families), shared a similar outlook and empathised with each other's position and politics. However, this 'unorganised' collusion is only part of the story. What has often been more difficult to prove is the level and nature of 'organised collusion'. This is where agencies of the British state (for example MI5 and RUC Special Branch) have given direct and indirect support to loyalists as a matter of policy. Organised collusion meant that the state consciously sanctioned the use of loyalist death squads as (what Frank Kitson once called) 'counter-gangs'. It was probably the most important feature of the conflict in this period.

Organised collusion has also occurred in a range of different ways. In some places (and notably in the border areas of Armagh and Down) there is growing evidence to suggest that collusion was immediate and direct. British security force personnel themselves conspired and participated in a 'loyalist' campaign of assassinations. But organised collusion could take other forms. One was the dissemination of information. This might include details about the appearance, habits, homes and social networks of people from nationalist communities. Such information was garnered from the photographs, maps, log records and interrogation notes held in the thousands of intelligence files the state had complied. Another was in providing loyalists with the means (and specifically the weapons) to carry out attacks. A third concerned the co-ordination and deployment of British state security force personnel. A pattern began to emerge of helicopters, DMSUs, blockades and foot patrols being suddenly withdrawn in the hours and minutes prior to loyalist attacks. It could also involve inexplicably prolonged response times in the immediate wake of such attacks. Similarly, there was often a less than rigorous approach to securing and examining the crime scene by the RUC and British army. Subsequent investigations were often cursory and the authorities proved to be obstructive and uncommunicative to the families of victims. This was all shaped by a 'culture of collusion'. Members of the RUC and British army made threats on a day-to-day basis to people identified as republicans. At the same time information about risks to their lives was often withheld or only partially given for 'security reasons'.

These various forms of collusion had a direct impact on Ardoyne. Joe Austin was a councillor for North Belfast from the early 1990s onward. He describes the impact of British intelligence, RUC and loyalist collusion in the area at that time.

Nationalist North Belfast was always geographically besieged and psychologically isolated. It has also suffered a relentless and continuous record of attacks. These were not, as the media often suggested, 'random' and 'mindless'. Loyalist violence in North Belfast was organised, planned and systematic. The Brian Nelson affair has shown that British intelligence orchestrated attacks. It also shows that they armed loyalist gangs and provided them with information and cover so that they could attack republicans and Catholics in general. Collusion became a securocrat programme designed to break the spirit of nationalists in North Belfast. What is bewildering and almost unbelievable is that it failed to do so. I am sure that British intelligence officers figured that unleashing loyalist violence in the way they did would create such fear, people would be so petrified, that they would keep their heads down and be cowed into submission. But although North Belfast nationalists became very cautious and very angry, they were never cowed. That is quite remarkable and is a tribute to the doggedness of communities like Ardoyne. Resistance took shape through the community caring for itself as a living entity that harnessed repression and exclusion and turned it into something positive. People stepped forward within the community and fought back in spite of the violence and social and economic deprivation inflicted upon it. It happened at every level, even though people lived under the constant threat of attack for doing so. For example, everybody who stood for election in North Belfast was attacked. Bobby Lavery lost a brother and a son. Larry Kennedy was shot dead and Gerard McGuigan's house was attacked on three separate occasions. It is a strange thing, though, that when people are under siege it often brings out the best in them. (Joe Austin, former Sinn Féin city councillor for North Belfast)

In Ardoyne there had always been a well-founded belief that collusion had taken place for many years. The evidence was often not difficult to find. When Ardoyne was invaded on 14/15 August 1969 the RUC had been accompanied by loyalist mobs. From then on they rarely showed themselves to be adverse to siding with (and providing practical support for) 'Ulster's defenders' on a day-to-day basis. As has already been noted, many people were also convinced that British soldiers co-ordinated their actions with loyalists during gunbattles during the 1970s. Indeed, such was the level of identification evident between British forces and loyalist paramilitaries that they often made little or no pretence that they were working in tandem. At times it was far less a case of collusion than a clear and open alliance with the people of Ardoyne cast in the role of their mutual enemy. However, from the early 1980s attacks on leading republican and H-Block political activists by loyalists began to occur with greater regularity throughout the North. A pattern of more coherent and organised collusion was gradually discerned. Gerard McGuigan takes up the story.

It was a couple of years before the pattern became clear. But from the early 1980s onward it was becoming apparent that operations to target republicans were being sanctioned at the highest levels of government. Whether it was the SAS, the UVF or the UFF who actually carried out attacks is immaterial. It was the hand controlling things that matters and that was the hand of government. The RUC were passing on information and that became even more systematic by the late 1980s. They were holding the personal details of literally thousands of people on file and it was deliberately fed to agents like Brian Nelson. I'm not trying to say that a whole unit of the UFF or UVF were taken into Tennent Street barracks for a briefing by MI5, 14th Intelligence, Special Branch or whoever. They didn't need to have control of every loyalist, just certain key figures. Nelson would receive files from his handlers, make copies and return the originals. He and his handlers would then get together to select targets and set people up for assassination. The reality is that the information we have from the Nelson case is only the tip of a very large iceberg because things were never fully investigated.

State intelligence agencies were virtually a law unto themselves. Special Branch could literally do anything they wanted. They were accountable to no one. You knew that if the RUC had your details then so did the loyalists. If you lived in this area that was just a matter of fact. It is like saying that it's light outside so it must be daytime. There were times when this area was like a military camp, then suddenly the RUC and Brits would all be pulled out and then someone was dead. That was the pattern. It was the enemy you couldn't see that you had to worry about. Though for some strange reason people did not let it dictate their lives. Looking back, that's the most remarkable thing of all. But you just knew that, given the opportunity, the RUC would have no problem setting you up for an attack. You knew from the way they would treat you and talk to you at roadblocks. I couldn't count the number of times I was told that I was going to be 'stiffed' – coldly, blankly and boldly told that. I never treated such threats idly. You only have to look at cases like that of Alan Lundy [Alan Lundy, killed by the UFF in Andersonstown, 1 May 1993] or Paddy McKenna [Paddy McKenna, killed by the UVF in the Crumlin Road, 2 September 1989] to see how obvious it is that collusion occurred. The prior knowledge the loyalists had, the way troops were deployed and the way the investigations were conducted makes it as plain as day. The media has to take a lot of responsibility too for the way that they simply accepted the spin put out by the NIO and the RUC press office. The journalists who earned any credit in dealing with this issue are few and far between. This was the most important story you could imagine, state sponsored killings, assassinations sanctioned at the highest possible level, and the media never looked beyond their noses to see the reality that was staring them in the face. (Gerard McGuigan, Ardoyne resident and former Sinn Féin city councillor)

As both Joe Austin and Gerard McGuigan have suggested, the case of Brian Nelson has cast a great deal of light on the nature of collusion in the period from the mid 1980s to the early 1990s. Nelson was a soldier in the British army until 1974 who had joined the UDA in 1972. He served a prison sentence in the late 1970s but by 1983 he had become the intelligence officer for the UDA in West Belfast. He was therefore a leading figure of the UDA's notorious 'C' company based in the Shankill Road. Paramilitaries from this area were responsible for virtually all of the Ardoyne victims of loyalist violence. When he became a UDA intelligence officer Nelson simultaneously started working for the Force Research Unit (FRU). The FRU was a British military counter-insurgency group that had been set up in 1980. Under the guidance of his handlers (including Col. Gordon Kerr, the commanding officer of the FRU from 1987 to 1991) Nelson was given regular access to

British army files on nationalists and republicans. This information was then used to target many for assassination. Loyalist groups carried out virtualy all the attacks on people in Ardoyne in this period.

Evidence of just how freely files were made available to loyalists had already been made apparent in late 1989. An inquiry was set up to look at allegations of collusion in August that year under the direction of Deputy Chief Constable John Stevens. This led to the arrest of a number of leading loyalists. In protest, loyalists pasted up thousands of montages on walls up and down the Shankill Road. These contained the details of people from various nationalist communities leaked to them from British intelligence files. Many were of people from Ardoyne. For people within the district this merely confirmed what they had known for a long time. Indeed, loyalists had often made no secret that they knew intimate details of people's lives. Martin 'Óg' Meehan was on remand in Crumlin Road gaol in 1989. Alongside were many of the loyalist prisoners arrested after the Stevens Inquiry. As he recounts, these prisoners relished the opportunity to evidence the extent of access they had to information.

> They [loyalists] seemed to have every detail imaginable about you. They used to enjoy shouting information about you from the windows of their cells when you were out in the exercise yard. They knew absolutely everything there was to know. They knew where you went, what you did. They knew what social clubs you belonged to. They could tell you what taxi places you used. You name it, they knew it. That was not just me, it was everybody. People from Ardoyne, from the Falls, wherever. The ones who were in because of the Stevens Inquiry had the personal details on over 500 people. The frightening thing was that they knew the details of your home and so they might have targetted your family. (Martin Óg Meehan, Ardoyne resident and ex-political prisoner)

In addition both the UDA and the UVF obtained a large shipment of arms from South Africa in January 1988. It was estimated to have doubled their respective arsenals. British Intelligence had full knowledge of this massive arms consignment (probably through Nelson himself) and yet allowed the importation to take place. This not only protected Nelson's position, it also 'professionalised' this killing machine. It certainly helped to facilitate the stepping up of the loyalist assassination campaign. Again, this impacted directly on the people of Ardoyne. In all ten cases of people from the district who were shot dead by loyalists between January 1988 and the declaration of the ceasefires in 1994 there is evidence to suggest that South African weapons were used. Guns that MI5 allowed to come into Ireland were involved in the murders of Paul McBride, Seamus Morris, Davey Braniff, Paddy McKenna, Hugh Magee, Liam McCartan, Martin Lavery, Alan Lundy, Sean Hughes and Martin Bradley.

The extent of collusion in the cases of all Ardoyne's victims of loyalist violence can still only be guessed at. However, the evidence that has come to light thus far (and not least from the oral testimony of family, friends and eyewitnesses) suggests a pattern of collusion that was endemic, systematic and premeditated. The memories of those who lost loved ones show that all the indicators of collusion are there. In their words can be found a pattern of threats from members of the RUC and army. They show that loyalists appear to have had prior knowledge taken from British state intelligence files. Apparent 'discrepancies' in the way that British army and RUC personnel were deployed are noted. So too are investigations that were conducted in a lacklustre and pointedly slipshod fashion. The following quotes (from the relatives and friends of Trevor 'Dandy' Close, Larry Marley, Paddy McKenna, Martin Lavery, Alan Lundy and Martin Bradley) bear eloquent testimony to the campaign of state-sponsored killing that resulted in the deaths of those close to them.

I believe that the RUC gave Dandy's details to the loyalist killers. They stopped him regularly and would tell him that he was going to be killed, that he would end up in a box. The morning Dandy was murdered he went into Hunters shop at the corner of Elmgrove Street on the Cliftonville Road. The RUC had been in there just five minutes before, getting their football pools. They had just left the shop when two loyalist gunmen got out of a car and walked into the shop. They singled Dandy out and shot him 17 times. The RUC jeep was parked up at Cliftonville Circus so they must have been able to hear the shooting. They came in just after the gunmen left. The first RUC man who walked into the shop said, 'It's alright, it's only Trevor Close'. (Marie Close, widow of Ardoyne victim, Trevor 'Dandy' Close, killed by the UVF in the Cliftonville Road by the UVF, 26 May 1983)

The day Larry was killed he went out to get some motor parts and was gone a good couple of hours. When he came back I remember him saying that he thought it was odd that the RUC or the British army didn't stop him. He was always being stopped. As soon as he walked outside the door he would be stopped. But not that day. I remember him saying that he found it strange. That the RUC and the British army had passed him a number of times but nobody stopped him – that was very, very unusual. (Kate Marley, Ardoyne resident and widow of Ardoyne victim Larry Marley, killed by the UVF in his home in Havana Gardens, 2 April 1987)

Paddy was just going up to the shops on the Crumlin Road when a motorbike pulled up and Brian Robinson [UVF gunman] jumped off and shot him 11 times. There were two undercover Brits sitting just over the road. They could have prevented it. They knew someone was going to get shot and they were just sitting waiting for it to happen. The British army tried to say afterward that they were just a passing patrol that happened on the scene but an eyewitness saw that they were sitting in the car waiting before Paddy was killed. The British army had information that a UVF squad was going to kill someone at that spot on the Crumlin Road. But instead of preventing it happening they decided to let the UVF kill Paddy and then shoot Robinson dead afterward. That was to make it look as if they were even-handed and taking action against the loyalists. So they waited until Paddy was murdered. I have tried to have it looked into properly but the British put a gagging order on the case and you can't get round that; it's impossible. (Joe McKenna, Ardoyne resident and brother of Ardoyne victim Paddy McKenna, killed by the UVF in the Crumlin Road, 2 September 1989)

The week before the UVF shot my father dead the RUC came in to where I worked. When they heard I was one of the Laverys they asked me where I lived and that was all they wanted to know. When I told my da he said that he thought the RUC were up to something. Three days before he was murdered the RUC set up a checkpoint outside the front door of our house. That was strange and had never happened before. Again, I remember that my da was very suspicious about that. Three days later my da was shot dead. After the gunmen had shot my father they took off in a car down to the Woodvale. Someone overheard the RUC radio contacts taking place and listened as an RUC patrol called in to say they were giving chase. They apparently followed them to a loyalist drinking club. They radioed in to say they had found a surgical glove and a balaclava and wanted back up. They never got a reply and ended up waiting outside the bar for a couple of hours. The day after my father was killed I went back into our house to start cleaning it because there was blood everywhere. There was also a big steel hammer that the loyalists had brought with them intending to use to smash in the door. The RUC had not even taken it with them; they just left it there in a bag. The UVF claimed responsibility but there was never anyone arrested. A few years ago the Orangemen were marching past our door on the Twelfth of July. One of them made a gun sign into the house and said, 'I shot your da'. I went for him but the marchers bombarded me with bottles. The whole time the RUC just stood by and let it happen. (Patrick Lavery, Ardoyne resident and son of Martin Lavery, killed by the UVF in his home on the Crumlin Road, 20 December 1992)

The RUC explanation for how the loyalists knew where to find my house was that Alan and I had been down to the funeral of a 'well-known republican' that day and had been followed afterward. That is just farcical and shows that they would try to use anything to explain away what happened. It wasn't a republican funeral and it would not have been hard for them to know where my house was. The whole day that Alan was killed two British army vehicles were parked in my street in full view of my house. They didn't leave until 5.30 pm. The loyalists who shot Alan came in to the road at 6 pm. So the British army was there all day then 'mysteriously' disappeared half an hour before the shooting happened. Nobody was ever arrested for Alan's murder. In fact when I went to meet the RUC in the solicitor's office I saw the file they had on their investigation. There was one page in it. That fitted in with what happened just after Alan was shot. I had a huge row with the RUC at the time because they were taking forever just to secure the scene of the incident. There was absolutely no urgency. They were not even taking any notice of the spent cartridges that had been left on the ground. In the end we had to force them to take the shells as evidence because they were obviously not going to do it themselves. (Alex Maskey, eyewitness and friend of Alan Lundy, killed by the UFF in Andersonstown, 1 May 1993)

Two weeks before Martin was murdered my son Fra ['Sparky' Shannon, killed by the INLA in Turf Lodge, 9 June 1996] was arrested and taken to Castlereagh Interrogation Centre. When the RUC raided the house they made a map of where we had put bulletproof glass, a security gate and drop bars. They had a map of where everything in the house was. I remember the cops saying, 'Murderers on the outside and definitely murderers on the inside'. When Fra was in Castlereagh the RUC told him that in exactly two weeks a top loyalist would kill him. Two weeks and one day later Martin was in my house when the loyalists came in and shot him dead. The UFF first put out a statement saying that they had killed Fra. When I went up to see my other son Paddy in the Crumlin Road gaol he said that loyalist prisoners had been shouting that 'they got Sparky Shannon'. So they obviously had a good idea that there was going to be an attempt to kill him. Martin just happened to be in my house at the wrong time. After they had shot Martin the gunmen escaped on foot. A split second after the gunmen walked out of the house my neighbours came out and saw two RUC jeeps on the Crumlin Road, but it was not until ten minutes later that they came up to the house. (Patricia and Jolene McAllister, Ardoyne residents and aunt and niece of Martin Bradley, killed by the UFF in the Crumlin Road by the UFF, 12 May 1994)

The late 1980s evidenced an upsurge in loyalist killings. However, even in the early 1980s, when loyalists were less active, they continued to present a threat in Ardoyne. Random and nakedly sectarian assassination was an ever-present possibility. On 31 October 1984 Harry Muldoon was at his home in Moutainview Drive. Harry was a taxi driver, a widower and father of two young girls. UVF gunmen broke down the front door. They then beat Harry and shot him dead in front of his daughter Angela. Harry was the first Ardoyne victim since the killing of Trevor 'Dandy' Close the previous year. Dandy had been shot dead on 26 May 1983 by members of the UVF as he stood in a shop on the Cliftonville Road. The manner of Harry's death signalled a pattern of loyalist sectarian murders that would mark the next decade. That of 'Dandy' was a good illustration of how collusion worked.

The aftermath of the Anglo-Irish Agreement also brought with it an attempt to present the RUC as 'professional' in dealing with Orange marches. Loyalist reaction to early efforts at re-routing certain contentious parades was a harbinger of things to come in the 1990s. Using the issue to coalesce opposition to the Agreement, loyalists raised communal tensions considerably in the summer of 1986. This formed the backdrop to the killing of Colm McCallan. Colm was born in Ardoyne but in 1986 he was living in Ligoniel (a small and vulnerable nationalist enclave area close to Ardoyne) and studying at the University of Ulster. Intense rioting had been taking place in many parts of Portadown and Belfast for six nights prior to that of the 13/14 July. That night Colm was standing outside his front door, taking a break from his studies. He was then lured or taken by loyalist gunmen. Colm was found dead several hours later, having been shot three times in the head. It was widely believed that John Bingham (a UVF commander from Ballysillan) was involved in killing Colm. Almost exactly two months later Bingham himself was killed by the IRA. Ian Paisley and the current DUP MP for North Belfast, Nigel Dodds, visited the Bingham home to offer their condolences. Former UUP MP for the area, Cecil Walker, also attended Bingham's funeral on 16 September 1986. Present too was George Seawright, a local loyalist councillor who had previously represented the DUP and had once publicly stated that 'Catholics and their priests' should be burnt in ovens. Seawright was also very active in organising opposition to the Anglo-Irish Agreement. Bingham had recently acted as his election agent. At Bingham's funeral Seawright called on loyalists to avenge his death. Later that day Raymond Mooney (a 33-year-old sales manager and father of four from

Ladbrook Drive) was closing the church hall of the Holy Cross chapel after a religious meeting. Three UVF gunmen grabbed him and a woman he was with. The woman was bound and gagged. Raymond was dragged into some bushes and killed by being shot nine times. This was clearly supposed to be a 'revenge' attack.

The twisted logic that led to the deaths of both Colm McCallan and Raymond Mooney was rooted in the nature of loyalist politics and sectarian ideology. Collusion may not have been immediate and direct in either case. More concrete evidence of collusion is, however, apparent in the death of Larry Marley. Larry Marley was one of the most prominent republicans from Ardoyne. He had been active as an IRA volunteer since the outbreak of the conflict. He had particularly risen to prominence because of his near-legendary involvement in organising and taking part in prison escapes. Most spectacularly of all he had been a key planner of the mass breakout from the H-blocks in 1983. This was when 38 Republican prisoners were involved in the largest ever escape from a British prison. Larry Marley had not taken part in this escape himself because he was due for release in 1985. It was then that he returned to Ardoyne. On 2 April 1987 Larry Marley was at home with his wife and youngest child. He was shot dead by UVF gunmen as he answered a knock at a door. It was the only door in the house that did not have reinforced security. Taken alongside other evidence this raised suspicions that Larry's killers had been primed with prior knowledge of the layout of Larry's home, his circle of friends and his daily routine. There have also been concerns regarding the pattern of surveillance of Larry and the district in general in the days and hours leading up to his death. Certainly Larry's own suspicions had been aroused on the day of his death, as the evidence of his widow Kate shows. Significantly, at the critical moment when his attackers entered Ardoyne the almost blanket presence of troops and RUC, that the area so often endured, evaporated. The loyalist gunmen were also then able to make good their escape. Since then there have been calls for an investigation into these allegations of collusion between the British security forces and Larry Marley's killers.

However, the events surrounding Larry Marley's funeral were as significant, if not more so, than those of his death. During the three days of the wake an ever-growing and increasingly aggressive RUC presence was evident. Then on the morning of Monday 6 April family and friends attempted to leave the Marley house with Larry's remains. They were met with repeated baton charges by members of the RUC. For the next two days DMSUs laid siege to the house and swamped the district. This was an attempt to prevent the funeral going ahead in accordance with the family's wishes. Such was the level of fear and distrust of the RUC that mourners believed they might even attempt to steal the body. There was widespread rioting throughout Belfast and the North in protest at the British state's treatment of the Marley family. In addition, the crowds that gathered in sympathy outside the Marley home grew each day. So great were their numbers that by the Wednesday morning the RUC riot squads could not get near the coffin when it came out of the house. This was in spite of the fact that they mounted repeated charges. In the face of constant attacks the thousands of mourners made their way first through the district to the Holy Cross chapel and then across to Milltown cemetery in the west of the city. This show of solidarity and the strength of purpose of his family eventually allowed Larry Marley to be buried, if not in peace, then with dignity.

The events surrounding Larry Marley's funeral need to be seen in the context of the concerted drive made by the Thatcher government to further 'contain' and 'criminalise' republicans. This campaign had a number of elements. A more censorial approach to the media was clearly evident. Formal and informal pressures were increasingly brought to bear, infringing upon journalistic freedom under the guise of denying the 'oxygen of publicity' to the IRA. This was exemplified by the introduction of the Broadcasting Ban in 1988. But mechanisms of media manipulation were often far less obvious (and consequently all the more potent) than legislative measures. Taken as a whole, the Thatcherite approach to the media represented an onslaught on the very idea that impartial reporting was a desirable goal. It was to be replaced by the sinister euphemism 'responsible journalism' instead. Most journalists, in any case, were either unwilling or unable to adopt a critical attitude toward British state policy. As a result, allegations of 'shoot-to-kill' strategies, collusion or even alternative views on the deaths of people from 'criminalised' communities fell on deaf ears. This contributed to the perpetuation of those policies.

There had also already been systematic harassment of republican funerals. For at least four years prior to the death of Larry Marley a clear policy of funeral disruption could be seen. Nor was Larry Marley's funeral the first in Ardoyne that had been subjected to intimidation and worse. As early as 1971 a tricolour draped on the coffin of Barney Watt was torn off when loyalists attacked the funeral cortege [Barney Watt, killed by the British army in Butler Street, 6 February 1971]. In 1972 paras charged into mourners at the funeral of Davey McAuley [Davey McAuley, killed accidentally in Fairfield Street, 19 February 1972]. As was described earlier, the family of Jamesy McDade found it almost impossible to bury him with dignity after his death in November 1974 [Jamesy McDade, killed on active service in Coventry, 14 November 1974]. Three years later the UVF detonated the car bomb that killed Sean Campbell and Sean McBride at the funeral of Trevor McKibbin [Trevor McKibbin, killed by the British army in Brompton Park, 17 April 1977; Sean Campbell, killed by the UVF in Etna Drive, 20 April 1977; Sean McBride, killed by the UVF in Etna Drive, 21 April 1977]. It is worth repeating that this was the only time that such a bombing took place anywhere in the North in the three decades of conflict. However, there were differences in the case of Larry Marley. The treatment his grieving family, friends and neighbours received was part of a far more deliberate, pre-determined and well-orchestrated state strategy toward republican funerals than had been seen before. It was a British state tactic that continued in the wake of Larry's burial, but only briefly. The stand taken by his family did much to bring this policy to an end.

The campaign of loyalist violence against people from the area did, however, continue. On 3 July 1987, Eddie Campbell, a taxi driver from Etna Drive, was found shot dead near a disused quarry. This was shortly after Nelson's handler Col. Kerr had taken command of the FRU. The gunmen who killed Eddie were from 'C' company of the UFF and the UDA later claimed that Eddie Campbell was involved in gathering intelligence for the IRA. Although he had been interned in the early 1970s this was strongly denied by the family. Sinn Féin also issued a statement saying that Eddie was not a member of the republican movement. The family believes that old British intelligence files had been passed on to the loyalists and that this led to Eddie's death. Just over four months later, on 16 November,

Tommy McAuley from Wheatfield Crescent was shot dead at his place of work on the Crumlin Road. Tommy's death came amidst a spate of loyalist attacks that followed in the wake of the Enniskillen bomb. Six months after that, on 15 May 1988, Paul McBride from Havana Court was enjoying a Sunday afternoon drink in the Avenue Bar in Union Street. UVF gunmen entered the bar and indiscriminately fired at all those inside. Six people were seriously injured and three were killed, including Paul. His brother Sean was one of those killed 11 years previously when the same organisation exploded a bomb at Trevor McKibbin's funeral. The style of attack witnessed at the Avenue Bar was a frequent feature of loyalist violence during the next few years. For example, on 30 October 1993 seven people were killed in the Rising Sun Lounge in the village of Greysteel. Six more died in the Heights bar in Loughlinisland on 18 June 1994. Paul McBride was also the first of the nine people from Ardoyne killed by loyalists over the next 6 years using weapons from the South African arms shipment.

Less than three months after the death of Paul McBride, on the morning of the 8 August 1988, 18-year-old Seamus Morris was standing with his brother on the corner of Brompton Park. It was where he and his friends regularly met. UVF gunmen drove into the district and shot Seamus dead in an indiscriminate and nakedly sectarian attack. As the loyalists tried to escape, the driver of a delivery truck attempted to stop them by blocking their route. The gunmen then opened fire on the lorry and shot dead the driver's mate, Peter Dolan from Andersonstown. The weapon used in this attack was also one suspected of being part of the South African arms haul. On 19 March 1989 Davey Braniff was at his home in Alliance Avenue. Davey was originally a Protestant who had converted to Catholicism when he had married. He was saying the rosary with his wife in the kitchen of their home when loyalist gunmen broke into the house. They came past one of Davey's daughters and a grandaughter who were in the living room. One of the gunmen then shot Davey dead. Eight years earlier Davey Braniff's son had been killed as an alleged informer by the IRA [Anthony Braniff, killed in West Belfast by the IRA, 27 September 1981].

On 2 September 1989 Paddy McKenna from Farringdon Court was walking down the Crumlin Road. A motorcycle pulled up beside him. A gunman sitting on the pillion seat then shot Paddy eleven times, killing him instantly. A few minutes later an undercover British soldier opened fire on the motorcycle and killed the gunman, UVF member Brian Robinson. Initially the RUC suggested that the presence of the British undercover unit had been coincidental. There was a great deal of evidence to the contrary. The UVF later claimed they had evidence that Paddy was a member of the IRA. Certainly both loyalists and the RUC had harassed and threatened Paddy in the past. This claim that he was a member of the IRA was strenuously denied by the family. Paddy's family did, however, suggest that the undercover British presence was proof of premeditated collusion in his death. It is worth noting too that Paddy's death came only a week after that of Loughlin Maginn. In the aftermath of Loughlin's killing the UDA had released RUC files in their possession to support their contention that he had been in the IRA. It was only at this point that the Stevens Inquiry into allegations of collusion was set up. It is within this context that the British army may have seen a number of advantages in what happened to Paddy McKenna and Brian Robinson. They first allowed a supposed 'IRA man' to be killed. They then shot dead a UVF gunman. British Intelligence was therefore able to prosecute its 'dirty war' against republicans while appearing to counter allegations of collusion. Through the pages of their magazine *Combat* the UVF would themselves suggest that such collusion had in fact taken place in the death of Paddy McKenna. The same weapon used in the shooting of Seamus Morris was also used to kill Paddy McKenna.

Another pattern of loyalist violence that had become well established by the late 1980s and early 1990s was to attack Catholic taxi drivers. They were seen as relatively easy, accessible and identifiable sectarian targets. On 10 October 1991 Hugh Magee from Kerrera Street was driving his cab out of Rosapenna Street in the Bone. A UFF gunman shot Hugh dead in a random sectarian attack. This followed the killing of a UDA man on the Shankill Road earlier in the day. Loyalist sectarian killings continued. On 12 March 1992 Liam McCartan was at home with his mother. As he went out his front door to go to the local shops he was shot dead by loyalist gunmen. The UFF later claimed responsibility and suggested that Liam was a member of the IPLO. This was denied vigorously both by that organisation and by Liam's family. Toward the end of the same year, on 20 December, Martin Lavery was at home with his family on the Crumlin Road. He was lying on a sofa in his living room with his four-year-old youngest child sitting on his chest. Two UVF gunmen came in and shot Martin four times, killing him where he lay. The UVF claimed he was in the IRA. Although Martin's brother Bobby was a Sinn Féin councillor, Martin had never himself been a member of any organisation. The UVF's intent was in fact to carry out a sectarian attack as part of an ongoing campaign against elected Sinn Féin representatives. This was another distinctive feature of loyalist activity throughout the 1980s and early 1990s. Less than nine months after Martin was killed, on August 8 1993, Sean Lavery (Bobby's son and Martin's nephew) was shot dead by the UFF. Again there are circumstances surrounding Martin's death that raise grave suspicions of British state collusion in his murder.

By the time Sean Lavery had been killed loyalists had claimed another Ardoyne victim. On 1 May 1993 Alan Lundy was helping the Sinn Féin councillor Alex Maskey to build a porch on his Andersonstown home. The porch was designed to increase the security of the councillor's home. Alan, from Strathroy Park, was a lifelong republican. Alex Maskey had been the intended target of a number of loyalist attacks already. He was particularly hated by them as the first Sinn Féin representative to have taken a seat on Belfast City Council. In one such attack he had already been seriously wounded. In another, Brian Nelson had a direct hand. Nelson had checked the registration number of Alex's car against British Intelligence records when it was parked on the Antrim Road. As Alan and Alex worked on the porch, the British army and RUC presence which had Maskey under almost constant surveillance suddenly disappeared. Within a matter of minutes a car drove up and a number of gunmen got out. They shot Alan in the back several times and then made good their escape. In many ways Alan Lundy's death exemplified the nature of loyalist attacks in this period. A South African weapon was used. The gunmen had enough prior knowledge of their intended victim (a prominent republican figure) and a sense of confidence that they would have a clear route in and out of the area to strike deep into the heart of a republican district. Deep suspicion also surrounded the deployment of British state forces leading up to the attack and in their commitment to the investigation that was subsequently instigated. The last Ardoyne victim of loyalist violence in this period was also shot dead in West Belfast. Sean Hughes had moved to the west of the city when he was still a boy. By 1993 he was a father of three and had his own hairdressing business just off the Falls Road. On 7 September Sean was at work when UFF gunmen came in and asked for the owner. They then shot him dead.

There had, though, been three other Ardoyne victims during this period who had not been killed by loyalists. Each of these deaths, in its own way, indicates the toll that the war had taken by the early 1990s on Ardoyne. They also therefore help to explain why a way out of armed conflict was by that time increasingly being sought. On the morning of 26 June 1991 Gerard Burns left the home he shared with his partner Mary to go to his job in a local chip shop. Mary was never to see him again. Gerard had grown up with the start of the conflict and had been a long time member of first the 'Official' IRA and then the INLA. He had spent several years in prison and had given much of his adult life to the movement. That morning he was abducted by members of the INLA. His body was found in a garden in West Belfast in the early hours of the next morning. Gerard had been shot four times in the head. It was alleged that he had become an informer during interrogation by the RUC in Castlereagh two years before. It is an allegation his family deny.

On 22 August 1992 Isabel Leyland was preparing to return to England. Isabel had come home to Ardoyne several days before in order to visit her sick mother. Isabel was walking down Flax Street when she was killed by the IRA after they opened fire on a British army patrol. Isabel's family name was Bradley. Several of her relatives had spent many years interned and imprisoned. Her brother Francis had been killed in a UVF bomb attack on a petrol station in 1975 when he was just 16 years old [Francis Bradley, killed by the UVF in Corporation Street, 19 June 1975]. A year and nine months after Isabel was killed, and seven months after the loyalist ceasefire was declared, her nephew Martin was shot dead in his aunt's home on the Crumlin Road by the UFF [Martin Bradley, killed by the UFF in the Crumlin Road, 12 May 1994]. Another nephew, Fra Shannon, was also shot dead during a feud within the INLA in 1996 [Fra 'Sparky' Shannon, killed by the INLA in Turf Lodge, 9 June 1996]. The Bradley family represents in microcosm the Ardoyne experience of over 30 years of war.

Then, on 23 October 1993 the IRA in Ardoyne received intelligence that the leadership of 'C' company of the UDA/UFF was meeting in a room above Frizzel's fish shop on the Shankill Road. This was the group that had been instrumental in inflicting years of pain and death on the district. Their meeting place had been a regular spot for the UDA/UFF to hold gatherings for many years. They did have a meeting there that morning. Acting on the information, an active service unit was despatched from the district. One of its members, 23-year-old Thomas 'Bootsy' Begley, carried a bomb into the shop. His intention was to attach it by a chain to an overhanging rack. The plan had been that he would then tell people to evacuate the shop in order to target his intended victims in the room above. However, the bomb exploded prematurely. Thomas Begley, along with nine other people, was killed.

Condemnation for this attack was widespread and wholesale. For a time at least it appeared that it could derail the slowly emerging 'peace process'. When Gerry Adams helped carry the coffin of Thomas Begley to his grave he was denounced throughout the British press. *The Sun* newspaper declared Adams' name to be 'the two most hated words in the British language'. This stood in sharp contrast to the press silence that accompanied unionist politicians when they had 'paid their respects' at the graves of loyalist killers, from members of the Shankill Butchers to John Bingham and beyond. But it was precisely the circumstances that Thomas Begley (like others) had watched shape the lives and deaths of people around him that had led to his actions that day. It was also such circumstances that the peace process was aiming to bring to an end. Working class communities like Ardoyne suffered most from the conflict. It was precisely because people from such areas knew better than any the devastating human costs of the war that they had a greater vested interest in the search for a just peace.

The sources of the peace process were many and had emerged from the mid-1980s onward. In the wake of Sinn Féin's entry into electoral politics and the signing of the Anglo-Irish Agreement, dialogue between Sinn Féin and the SDLP had begun as early as 1988. At first progress was slow. However, secret contacts between the IRA and the British government from 1991 onward helped move things forward. Similarly the formation of an anti-partitionist consensus among a broad base of nationalist opinion in the North, the Dublin government and interested international parties (most notably in the US) began to bear fruit by 1993. Less than two months after the death of Thomas Begley and his nine fellow victims the British and Southern Irish governments issued the Downing Street Declaration. It suggested that Britain would move towards all-party talks if there was an IRA ceasefire.

Given past experience, there was a great deal of scepticism about British intentions within northern nationalist communities. Such distrust was felt nowhere more deeply than in Ardoyne. People in the district had seen British state security policies at their most cynical and destructive over a long period of time. They would take some convincing that the British political establishment had truly changed its spots. At the same time, as elsewhere, the prospect of an end to conflict also created a very real sense of relief. For generations of ordinary people who had grown up amid the most abnormal of circumstances the possibility of 'normality' was something quite extraordinary. These conflicting emotions set a tone of muted optimism when the IRA declared their ceasefire at the end of August 1994. However, fear of future attacks from loyalists did not easily disappear. After all, they had claimed a victim from the area only a couple of months before. On 12 May Martin Bradley was playing with his one-year old nephew in his aunt's home on the Crumlin Road. UFF gunmen came into the house and shot Martin dead as he held the child. Shortly afterward a crowd gathered when it became known that Martin had been threatened only a short time before by members of the British state security forces. However, there is evidence to suggest that the intended victim was Martin's cousin, Fra Shannon. Once more there were also clear indications that the RUC and British Intelligence colluded in the preparation and execution of this attack. That there was a longing in the area for a future without the war is beyond doubt. But people also knew that the path toward that end was likely to prove long, arduous and fraught with continuing danger.

Harry Muldoon
Killed by the UVF,
Mountainview Drive,
31 October 1984

The morning that it happened to my daddy was my mummy's birthday. We'd made arrangements. He was going to pick me up from work after Tracy got out of school and we were going up to the graveyard. We had our flowers to put on my mummy's grave for my mummy's birthday. Then they came in and did that to us.

Harry Muldoon's family were from Brookfield Street in old Ardoyne. His father Patrick (who was originally from the Bone) and mother Mary–Ellen (née O'Connor) had moved there from Crumlin Street not long after they were married. It was in Brookfield Street that Harry was born, the third of seven children. Because he was often unwell as a child Harry left the Holy Cross Boys school with no qualifications. He got a job delivering for Brown's shoe shop at the age of 14. But Harry had always wanted to go to sea. One day he was delivering a pair of shoes to someone on board a ship and he decided that this was his opportunity. There and then he went to work on the boats. He was away for nine months! When he was 20 Harry met his wife-to-be Mary-Ann Flynn from Whiterock at the Plaza. They were married just a year later in October 1961. They first lived in Ardilea Street, before buying their own house in Duneden Park. They lived there until 1972. After that they moved over to Mountainview Drive. By then they had two daughters, Angela and Tracey Ann, to whom they devoted almost all of their time. As someone from old Ardoyne Harry had seen at first hand the outbreak and development of the conflict from the late 1960s onward. Indeed his parents had been burnt out of their home in '69. However, Harry never had any political (never mind 'paramilitary') links. He worked to provide for his family. In early 1978 Harry's wife died of cancer. Harry faced up to the difficult task of bringing up his two young daughters alone. He quit his job working on the boats and started work as a black taxi driver. This was becoming an increasingly dangerous occupation for Catholics by then. Taxi drivers were more and more being seen by loyalists as an easy and convenient sectarian target. On 31 October 1984 three UVF gunmen broke into Harry's home in Mountainview Drive. In front of his daughter Angela they beat Harry and repeatedly shot him until he was dead. His 'crime' was to be a Catholic.

Jimmy McGurk (friend)

Me and Harry came from Brookfield Street in old Ardoyne. I remember him from when I was a kid. When he was young he was a great handball player. He used to play against Brookfield Mill. They used to have different challenge matches on a Sunday. You weren't allowed to play handball then because of the way the RUC treated the nationalist people. Harry was always a great card player too. We would be playing handball or cards in the streets and the cops used to come down on their bikes and chase everybody off the streets. Harry was one of the cuter ones. When everybody ran they left their money lying about and the cops used to come and steal their money. But Harry was that cute he also waited until everybody ran off. Then he scalped the money before the cops got it. He got most of the money. For a time Harry used to run the 'toss' up in Toby's Hall every Sunday. He was a great man for the 'toss', a good footballer and a champion handball player. I remember him in '69 too. Harry was on the barricades, the same as everybody else. Everybody had to defend the whole road from Flax Street right through to Brompton Park – not in a paramilitary sense, but just out defending the area from the opposing factions on the other side of the road and the 'B' Specials.

Harry was always working; he was always a provider. He was a good character. Harry came from a good family, a working family. He worked on the black taxis on the Falls Road for years. He went out early every day and provided for the two kids. He would get home at 3 pm knowing that the kids were getting out of school. He was home to do the mother's role too. To me he was a working class man who had no grievance against anybody because he classed his own fellow worker the same as himself, as working class people. I never heard him talking about anything political and I definitely know that there were never any paramilitary connections. A working class person was equal to Harry whether he was Protestant or Catholic. He didn't see himself as any better than anyone else. He had Protestant friends and he worked with Protestant people over the years through his various jobs. Like myself, Harry was a member of the Crumlin Star [social club]. I can remember having many, many good times with Harry in the Star. We used to go on different away trips, to Dublin and the like. His name would still come up in conversations in the Star because he was well-liked. They even named a snooker cup after him. Harry was a very honest and open fella. He never hid anything from anybody because he had nothing to hide. He always made you feel welcome when you went into his company. On trips away when we were younger he was a famous man for tying people's shoelaces or shaving off their eyebrows or moustache if they fell asleep. He was a character that way. Harry was always thinking and laughing, always being funny. He never spoke about the downs in his life after he lost his wife. He knew he had to keep going for the sake of his two daughters.

I remember Harry coming into the Star once on a Saturday afternoon after he had finished his day's work on the black taxi. This is well before he was shot. We had a few drinks as usual. He said to me that a few times when he was going over the Crumlin Road towards Mountainview a car had slowed down. He had a funny feeling that they were watching him. He was watching them while they were watching him. This happened quite a few times, but he tried to put it behind him. He would tell himself that it might just have been people slowing up or people coming to the side of the road. I was working on the Friday night that Harry was shot dead. I think it was 7 am or 8 am when the word came over from Mountainview. They [loyalists] had broken into Harry's home, went straight up the stairs and murdered him. We met up with Charlie McClean, who was a committee man in the Crumlin Star, at about 11 am and he told us what happened. Charlie lived facing Harry's house. He had gone over to Harry's house with Harry's sister Mary. She lived up there too. Charlie had jumped out of his bed when he heard the door crashing. He saw the gunmen coming down Harry's path. There is a wee lip that you clip your gates into and as Charlie was running over, one of the gunmen was running out and he tripped over the wee lip. He fell on his lip and nose. Charlie tried to grab him but obviously your man jumped in the car and got away. Charlie and Harry's sister went into the house at the same time. There was hysteria in it. Angela and Tracey were there and Harry was shot dead. I think they shot him with a pistol and a shotgun. It was a very, very unfortunate thing.

Mary McCallum (sister)

When he was young Harry always brought money into my mummy when she hadn't got it. He was always a provider. He used to cut sticks up, parcelled them into bundles and put them and my sister in a handcart. Then he would go round doors and sell the sticks to bring the money into my mummy. He did a whole lot of funny things. Harry was the breadwinner. He was great, just full of fun. There was many a laugh in the house. Whenever he came back from the boats he used to bring all of us wee presents. He was good like that. He loved motorbikes and he got himself one when he was coming home from the boats. I remember he put the older brother on the motorbike when he couldn't even ride it. We were running up and down the street after him trying to tell him how to stop. Harry was mischievous like that. Later the only thing that Harry lived for was his children. He just worked. After Mary's death Harry got a permanent job on the black taxis and he stayed there. He kept his black taxi outside the door in the drive. He just provided for the kids and was there to look after them.

I spoke to Harry the night before he died because he was over in the house. He always came in and sat down on the floor with Tracey-Ann on his knee beside the fire. We just talked about casual things, family things. It was Halloween when he was murdered. I heard the bang as the glass of the door went in because he lived just across the street. They used sledgehammers to get in the door because he had bolts on his door. I think there was four of them [loyalists]. I woke up and I said to my husband Paddy, 'There is something wrong over in our Harry's'. We put our shoes on and away we went. It was my husband that went up and found Harry dead. He wouldn't let me into the house. Harry had been shot in the neck first. He tried to fight them off with a stick as he crawled up the stairs. They [loyalists] made the two girls go into the box room and then they shot him. We had to wait for what seemed like hours for the police to come out. There was one strange thing. Every morning there was a police patrol that came around. But that particular morning there was no police around. We asked the police about that but nobody ever made any inquiries about it. Harry was murdered at 5.30 am.

We were never given any support after whatsoever. There was nothing from the Catholic church. I always found that strange, though at the time we never thought about it because our minds were just blank when it happened. Those kids were left without a mother and they were then left without a father. There should have been somebody there to help them along, but there wasn't. I remember I had to fight to get dinner tickets so that Tracey could get free dinners at school. She was turned down for it. But nobody from the clergy ever came; nobody bothered. That made me very angry, very angry. I don't believe justice was done with the ones who were convicted for Harry's murder. I just think that they should never have been let out. Whatever force it was that killed him, they [loyalists] still left those two children fatherless. They had put them into a room to listen to their father being murdered. That's a thing that is never going to go away for them. The only question I would like to be answered is why they murdered him? Why did they leave two children without a father and without a mother? What had they against him when he was only a family man? They [loyalists] never came out and said why they did it. I think he was murdered because he was Catholic. They classed anybody that was on the black taxis as being in the IRA. That is why he was murdered. But Harry wasn't in any organisation at all. He was just a dedicated family man.

Angela Muldoon (daughter)

I remember my daddy used to take me into town every other Saturday. We would go in and get something to eat. He would always have bought me a wee present, like a spirograph or something. It was a delight which I always looked forward to because I knew I was being treated. The four of us would have gone away on holiday every year. There was always just me, my mummy, daddy and my sister. My mummy and daddy only lived for their family. Then in 1977 my mummy took sick. My daddy had gone back working on the boats because he couldn't get work here. Then he was sent for. On 17 January 1978 my mummy died of cancer at the age of 38. That left us with just my daddy. Tracey and my daddy were really, really close. She was just going on five at the time and I was only 14. There was just the three of us and there was an extra bond because we only had him. We didn't have our mummy so we needed him. He was broken-hearted when my mummy died. My mummy and daddy were very close. My daddy ended up working on the black taxis. His heart wasn't in it though. There was many a time he wanted it all to end. He had just had enough; he didn't want to go on without my mummy.

Tracey was 11 at the time my daddy died. She had only started at St Louise's school that September. My daddy use to take her over in the taxi. He was so proud of her. I had a 21st birthday party on 8 October 1984. He had a surprise for me because my aunt Lena came over from England. Then we had a big, big party in the Star. He carried the cake onto the dance floor to me. There is a photo of me and my daddy standing together holding the 21st birthday cake, so I have got those memories that I will cherish forever. The night before my 21st birthday I remember I was standing making chips and I started crying. I went up to his bedroom and I said to him, 'You know, I love you'. He said, 'I know, I know you do'. He said, 'What's brought all this on?' I said, 'I don't know; I just love you'. I don't even know why I said it. I was supposed to be getting engaged and I just said to him, 'I love you and I'll never leave you'. He said, 'You can't think like that if your getting engaged. Go and get married. You have to make your own life'. I said, 'I'll always love you and I'll always make sure you are alright'.

The night before my daddy died he was in the Star. He came home at about 9 pm and I got him his dinner. I went over to my friends but before I left he put on 'The Fields of Athenry'. He was sitting singing it and eating his dinner. Tracey was out playing in the street. I said that I was away and he said, 'Watch yourself'. I went over to my friend Rosemary's, then I came back at about 12 pm. I went in to check on Tracey; she was sleeping. Then I checked my daddy, who was half-asleep. That was it. The next thing I knew, well, I thought it was a nightmare or else that the wind had blown the front door open. There was this loud bang. When I jumped up my daddy was on the stairs and two men were beating him with the end of the gun. My daddy shouted to me, 'Get the police, get the police'. He was looking at me but his back was on the stairs. I was looking over the stairs at him and they were hitting him. I just went into real slow motion. I went in and checked on Tracey. She was just sitting in a wee ball on her own in the bed, squealing. I closed her room door and then I thought, 'I'll go and check on my daddy'. As I opened the room door this big, tall figure was standing there. He pointed the gun at my head. I followed him into my bedroom. That is where my daddy was lying after he had run in. Apparently he had already been shot. He was lying face down on top of my bed and there were these two over him at the side of the bed. There was a big fella and a small one. I remember the tall one; I looked at him and he had fear in his eyes. I thought to myself, 'Is this the first time he was ever on a job like this?' I could feel his eyes looking at me and I always thought, 'I'll know his eyes again'.

The next thing it was just 'bang', 'bang', 'bang'. There were just loud bangs going off. I just covered my ears and closed my eyes and said to myself in slow motion, 'God, my ears are so sore'. When I opened my eyes I ran down the stairs and tried to phone the police. But whenever I phoned it was engaged. I looked at all the glass and said to myself, 'I'm going to cut my feet'. I was standing screaming and shouting, 'They got my daddy, they got my daddy'. Then people grabbed me and I said to them, 'Come on with me. I know which way they went'. I thought they had gone up the Crumlin Road and that's where I was going. But these people pulled me back and wouldn't let me go. To me it seemed to take forever before the police came, but I don't know how long it was. When they did arrive I remember hitting one of them in the stomach saying, 'Why did you take so long, why did you take so long'? Then I was brought over to my daddy's sister Mary across the road from us. Doctors were sent for and I put Tracey to bed. God help her, I told her to go back to bed again, after all that. That was it. The morning that it happened to my daddy was 31 October; it was my mummy's birthday. We'd made arrangements. My daddy was going to pick me up from work after Tracey got out of school and we were going up to the graveyard. We had our flowers to put on my mummy's grave for my mummy's birthday. Then they came in and did that to us. Why?

The day after they killed my daddy I thought to myself, 'Did they just go and get their breakfast like a normal person after that? Did they just go back to their homes and think nothing of it?' Apparently the night before they had been drinking and watching videos. Whenever I eventually went back to work I thought that they would come in and laugh about it. Sometimes I think that even now. I'm still waiting on a phone call saying, 'We killed Harry Muldoon'. Or I find myself looking at people and wondering if that is them. Eventually the UVF claimed responsibility for my father's murder. I only read about the name of the person who killed my father in the paper. Dennis McClean he was called. He admitted another two murders along with my daddy's murder. There was never any explanation for my father's murder. The police never ever said why. I just took it that it was because he was a black taxi driver and he was a Catholic. He [McClean] served time but the other two that were in the house were never caught; they never got them. They were masked. All I can do is hope and pray that God will punish them.

At the hearing the fella who had his car taken by them over in the Shankill wanted to come and talk to me because he felt so sorry. He felt so guilty, but it wasn't his fault at all. Me and my aunt drove down once to where that man lived. I don't know why I did. I actually tried to find out where Dennis McClean lived whenever I read his name in the paper. But what was the point? At the time no one ever came and offered us support, only my daddy's and my mummy's family and friends. No legal groups or anything like that came near us. Eventually a girl from Cruise came out every so often to see how me and Tracey were. The Catholic church only visited us at the time it happened. In the few days after it happened, when my daddy was being waked, people were coming in, but not after. At the time I had many friends but the one who I will always remember for her kindness and friendship is Margaret. She was always there for me and Tracey. I will never forget her for that. She is a very special person to me. I could never thank her enough. She was and still is always there for me. People say time is a healer. For some that may be true, but for us it just means another way of trying to accept life without him and it is very hard.

In the hours after my father was murdered the police were 99.9 per cent sure of getting the ones who did it; that is what they said at the time. I thought that the RUC would have known that night who had done it and that they could have got them right away. I was hoping that there would have been somebody got for it there and then. There was a milkman who used to go round our way and he said that the police were there every day. But the morning my daddy was killed, when he was delivering the milk, there was no police in the area of Mountainview at all. In the end no-one was convicted until about 1987. At that time I got a phone call to tell me to come down to the police station. When I got down there a policeman said to me, 'You'll be happy to know there has been somebody charged with your daddy's murder'. I started crying because I was on my own. Nobody rang to tell me to take somebody with me. Obviously I knew it was about my daddy's case, but I didn't expect to hear that somebody was charged with his murder. But that was the end of it. I never heard another thing from the police about it. The papers actually sent me stuff; that is when I knew that somebody had been convicted.

I just think that it is very unfair that my daddy isn't here today. There have been times when it has been very, very hard. Like when I got married and he wasn't there to walk me up the aisle. Then in 1989 his first grandson, Ryan, was born. My daddy had had no sons. In 1991 we had Nicole and he never got seeing her either. They are missing out because they are saying, 'Why did the bad man have to take our granda away?'

Colm McCallan
Killed by loyalists,
Millview Court,
14 July 1986

At the end of the day, what did the people who killed Colm achieve? Nothing. It was just a complete waste of human life. Colm was from a deprived working class background and so were the people who killed him. They were not privileged; they were fighting for something because they had nothing themselves, and all it resulted in was Colm's death.

Colm McCallan was born on 25 March 1961. His father, Frankie, was from Kingston Street on the border between Ardoyne and the Bone. His mother, Kathleen O'Kane, had been brought up by the McKenna family in Chatham Street, where, after marrying in 1952, Colm's parents started to raise their family. Colm was one of seven children, four boys and three girls. In the early 1960s the family moved to Farringdon Gardens, then to a house in Bray Hill. However, they were soon intimidated out of there. Then they lived opposite the Ballysillan playing fields in Wheatfield Gardens. Once again they were forced to move by the threat of possible violence in 1969 and made their home in Alliance Avenue. By then Colm had already been sent to the Holy Cross Boys school and the Christian Brothers school on the Antrim Road. Colm's whole family was involved in the GAA, as they had been for generations. Colm himself played both Gaelic football and hurling for the Ardoyne Kickhams in his teens. He was also active in the trade union movement and in the socialist group, Militant, following his brother Frankie into both. But Colm was as much interested in the craic as he was in any great political cause. He had a number of different jobs. He worked in the Michelin factory in County Antrim and set up a small building business with a couple of friends. But shortly before his death he began life as a student at the University of Ulster, Jordanstown. By then Colm had married Bernie Winters from the New Lodge. The two had moved into a house together in Ligoniel where they also started to bring up their two young sons. Ligoniel is a North Belfast Catholic enclave area that had seen more than its fair share of attacks. In the summer of 1986, the marching season brought added tension with ongoing loyalist protests over the Anglo-Irish Agreement signed less than a year before. Areas like Ligoniel were under a state of virtual siege. On the night of 12 July a number of loyalist gunmen walked into the area seeking out a Catholic target. Colm had gone to his front door for a smoke after finishing some work for his course. It is unclear exactly what then happened but he was found a short distance away, about an hour later, with three bullet wounds to the head. After fighting for his life for two days in intensive care, Colm McCallan died. He was 25 years old when he was shot dead by loyalists in a purely sectarian attack.

Mickey McCallan (brother)

We were a big GAA family; my grandfather and my great grandfather were all tied up with it. The whole family were. The GAA was one of the few social outlets in this parish so, alongside the sport, it always had a big social impact. When he was growing up,

Colm played football and hurling for the GAA club and he used to go around with our brother Rory a lot; they were close. We were a big, extended, close family but Rory and Colm were particularly close. Like all big families, there were arguments, sometimes serious ones, but there was also always a tremendous sense of unity, a real strength there too. Colm was friends with a lot of different fellas in and around the area, like Gerard McFarlane. He was reasonably quiet but he also had his wilder moments, particularly in his teens. By the time he was 18 or 19 he had also developed an interest in girls, like all fellas growing up. In late 1984 he married a girl from the New Lodge, Bernie Winters, and they got a house and moved up to Ligoniel around that time. My parents had always pushed us all educationally. We all got the 11-plus but Colm didn't. I think Colm carried that around with him like a wound for years. So it was all the more important to him when he got into university. When he got into Jordanstown it was a very big deal to him. He had just finished his first year at Jordanstown when he was killed.

Our eldest brother Frankie was very involved with the trade union and Colm ended up following him in that direction, though I'm not sure how seriously he took it all. I don't think the conflict impacted upon Colm when he was growing up anymore than any other kid in the area at the time. He wasn't arrested outside the normal thing when they [RUC and British army] would scoop people up from the street, take them down to Flax Street barracks and process them. It just affected him like everyone else. You were restricted where you could go, particularly through the '70s with the murders and assassinations all around Ardoyne and on the Cliftonville Road. It meant that your social life was fairly much restricted to the clubs in the district. Maybe that was one of the attractions of socialist politics in Belfast at that time; it got you into parties on the Lisburn Road! When we moved out of Wheatfield Gardens, at the start of the conflict, we weren't exactly put out but there had been a number of incidents. At one point a bomb was left outside and there were a couple of petrol bombings. Something similar happened when we were in Alliance Avenue. A couple of shots were fired at Frankie and me coming home one night. But that was no different than for anyone else, particularly as we lived in the middle rather than the on the fringes of Ardoyne.

I've never been entirely sure about what happened when Colm was killed. There were a lot of different stories that went around about the exact circumstances; some of them may have been just rumours. I know that the night he was killed Colm had been working on a drawing he had to do for his final year university exams. He had finished it and gone outside for a bit of a walk and a smoke. It seems that some fella who was out walking his greyhound came over and him and Colm were just talking to one another. The next thing was these guys were on to them. The fella with the greyhound ran and so did Colm. But it would seem he was hit once as he ran and then he was shot another couple of times after that. The doctors said that Colm must have crawled some distance after that but the damage had been done. Even if someone had come along then I don't think he would have made it. The Protestant Action Force claimed responsibility for his killing. They had attacked a number of people around Ligoniel since the start of that year. Colm's was about the fourth or fifth such shooting. At that time John Bingham [UVF leader shot by the IRA in September 1986] held the reins of power in loyalist circles around Ballysillan and he was probably involved. But I imagine that history will probably prove that he had strings on his back.

At the time of Colm's death I was living where I am now in Glengoland. I got a phone call around quarter to four in the morning from my sister's husband at the hospital to say that Colm had been shot. I went down to see him in intensive care at about 10 am the next morning. He looked like he wasn't going to make it. He had head injuries and his head was all bandaged up. I drove up to Ligoniel, to where he had been shot and spoke to a couple of people to try to find out what had happened. There was one wee woman I talked to who was in a bad state; it had a hard effect on her. She had heard the shots and could hear Colm moaning but had been afraid to go out. It was tormenting her; she was wracked with guilt. But as I said to her, anybody would have done the same; she couldn't blame herself. Different people told me that there were two or three guys in a car who had been driving around the estate for quite some time, half an hour to an hour, depending on who you talked to. It wasn't a case of a car just driving in and somebody being shot. I thought that was strange and there were a lot of strange things happening around that time. When Frankie and me were at the hospital two well-dressed men came up to us, produced a card and wanted us to go down to Tennent Street barracks, they said to pick up our Colm's clothes because they had finished with them. It got a bit heated with them because they were a bit pushy and I was in no form for any of that. But there was something about it that I found strange. There was a well-known branch man from Tennent Street who was also hanging around the hospital that morning. It was just very peculiar. They were bad times, with the like of John Bingham going around, and there always appeared to be a more sinister hand behind things.

That morning my grandfather was also awoken by a reporter for the *Irish News* at 8.30 am telling him that Colm had been shot. The journalist then drove my grandfather down to the hospital and tried to convince him that he should be allowed to take a picture of all of the family around Colm in his bed. It was ghoulish. Then some kids were paid a few bob to break into Colm's house and take a photo of him that was on the mantelpiece and that photograph appeared in the paper. We were tormented by the press. We made up our minds that we were not going to talk to them because it just felt that no one really cared; it was just today's story and tomorrow it would be some other poor fella. My father died three years before Colm was killed and the only thing that is good about that is that Colm's death would have killed him. My mother was a very strong woman; her life revolved around the home and my father's death hit her hard. But Colm's death took a big, big part of her. It had a huge impact on everyone in the family; it affected all of us. I suppose it was the first time the troubles had hit us directly. We had been very fortunate as such a large family to be living in this area and to have escaped anything like that happening up to that point. My brother Rory ended up inside [for INLA involvement] and I have always believed that it was because of that. He listened to people after that who got him involved in things. I don't think that would have happened if it hadn't been for Colm being killed. I was just supposed to be starting a two-year law degree at Queen's that October. But after Colm's death I just couldn't concentrate on anything, so I ended up not doing it. Colm's death had a big effect on me, even more than when my father had died. Out of all of us he would have been the least likely to ever have been involved in anything, even rioting. I always think of Colm as just a fella who enjoyed life; he was good company, good craic. It's funny, this is probably the first time I have sat and spoken about Colm at any length for years; it's just a bit strange to me.

Gerard McFarlane (friend)

I knew Colm's family for years through the GAA. It was through the club that I got to know Colm well. His father had been the chairperson and his family were all playing members. They were steeped in GAA tradition. Colm came up through the ranks; he played football and hurling for the Kickhams until he was about 18 or so. He was just a typical young lad who knocked about the GAA, a loveable rogue. After he got married, Colm and his wife came and lived up near me in Ligoniel. I don't think he knew a lot of people up around that way. I would bump into him the odd time and we would stand and have a bit of a yarn. He would always ask about the club, the family, how things were going. He was a very nice young lad. That made the circumstances of his death all the more tragic.

There was a lot of tension around the period Colm was killed. It was just after the 12th of July and not a year on since the signing of the Anglo-Irish Agreement. Ligoniel is a very isolated nationalist area and there had previously been a few sporadic attacks by loyalists into the area. Another young lad had been shot two or three times just about a week before. They [loyalists] had come up from the Ballysillan area through the kids' football pitch and fired about 10 or 20 shots at a guy walking down the steps towards Ligoniel Road. Fortunately he lived. The tension had been growing for weeks and weeks. I don't think people really grasp what it was like to live in Ligoniel; it was like a siege. There was one way in and one way out. One night they even cut all the telephone wires which meant that we were totally isolated. There was general panic among the ordinary people that night wondering why they had cut all our phone lines. Everybody thought that the loyalists were going to do something big and attack the whole area. After that vigilantes began appearing on the streets, blocking and checking for any strange cars coming in. On the night Colm was shot I had actually been in Ardoyne. There were vigilantes up on the Ligoniel Road who stopped the car just to check and see who was in it. I was only in the house 15 minutes after that when I heard four or five shots. I looked out the front window because it sounded to me as if the shots came from the street. It transpired later that the sounds had come from out the back of the house. Colm was still alive at that stage. It wasn't until later that I realised that he had been lying there, only 20 or 30 yards away, for about an hour until a couple of young fellas found him. People had heard the shots but where his body lay was behind a big set of railings at the end of the estate. There was talk that some young lad had seen two or three hooded men coming through the bus terminus about 15 or 20 minutes before Colm was shot. He didn't know who they were so he ran off. I think someone saw Colm standing at his door, that he had just come out for a bit of a smoke and had said goodnight to someone when they passed up the street. Some people have said that the ones that killed Colm may have spoken to him because there was no sign of a struggle by his door. It may be that they [loyalists] said they were there defending Ligoniel from loyalist attack and that is why he walked away with them. I'm fairly sure that they then gave him a severe beating before they shot him.

It wasn't until the next day that I found out that Colm had been attacked. There was obviously a lot of police activity and someone came to the door and said that it was Colm who had been shot. He was still alive at that stage and died later in the hospital. I felt terrible about it when I heard; I think I just switched off. I kept thinking about the fact that I had heard the shooting. It was in the back of my mind all the time that he had been lying 20 yards from my house for an hour and a half. Maybe if he had been found five or ten minutes after he was shot, he might have survived. A lot of people were hurt by the fact that he lay there in agony, in such an isolated spot, and nobody knew.

Manus Maguire (friend)

I got to know Colm through his brother Frank. Frank was a union man, involved in the socialist movement and so was I. We hooked up together through the GAA and we used to go out a lot together socially. I got a job up in Derry after that and Colm used to come up. We would get a car and tour around Donegal of a night looking for a session or a bit of craic. Colm was a real live wire. He loved going out and he really liked Irish music. When we were sat in a pub during a session Colm would sing a few songs; he knew all the songs. He was a real character and when I knew him he just knew no fear. Colm mixed in a lot of different circles, the sort of fella who didn't like to let the grass grow beneath his feet. You could be just sitting in a pub in Letterkenny or wherever and the next thing, Colm would just come walking through the door. He was someone with a real sense of adventure and loved a bit of excitement. Colm got involved in socialist activities through his brother, Frank, who was a fairly senior figure in the civil service union. Frank was also a member of Militant and Colm followed him into it. He wasn't really into politics that much, but he did understand the nature of injustice and that was what bothered him. I remember one time we went up to Coleraine for a big demonstration against the National Front. They were trying to get organised in the north and the socialist movement was setting up counter-demonstrations to oppose them. Colm organised a group of fellas to go down from Ardoyne and sometimes he would act as a steward on such marches.

Colm moved up to Ligoniel when he got married to Bernie. I remember going up there one night with him after we had been out and it was a little scary. This was in the early 1980s when a lot of people were being attacked and shot and Ligoniel was very vulnerable. It was pitch black at night up around there and there was just one road in and out. People were very nervous about living up there because there was a real sense of threat. I remember when Colm was killed hearing the news on the radio that someone in Ligoniel had been shot. Like everyone else the first thing I thought about was who I knew that lived up there. I was living just off the Antrim Road at that time, a spot that was a bit vulnerable itself. About an hour later there was a rap on my door. Apparently it was a fellow union member who had come to tell me the news. But it was about 1.30 am and at that time you just didn't answer the door at that time of night. The next morning I read in the *Irish News* that the person who had been shot was 25 and a student. That's when I really started thinking that it might have been Colm. A bit later that day at work Frank phoned me to say that Colm was in intensive care.

Colm had been shot three times in the head but even then he had tried to get up. For me that said everything about Colm. He would take nothing lying down. There were a lot of different stories about what happened to Colm but I know that he was physically fit and fairly athletic. So if there had been any chance of him getting away he would have been able to take it. I presume that he was shot in the back of the head and that he didn't know anything was wrong until it was too late. Colm's murder happened against the background of loyalist opposition to the Anglo-Irish Agreement. There were also ructions going on at that time down in Portadown over Orange parades. But Colm was shot for no other reason than that he was a Catholic. People in Ligoniel were just innocent civilians; there was no escape for them. They were very, very easy targets.

His funeral was a very big affair. I brought a van load of people up from Dublin. There were a lot of union people there and I always remember that there was a wreath from the Dee Street Community Centre. Frank worked for the community service, so it was partly to do with that. But it was also very much about showing opposition to sectarianism and paying respects to the family. I think it had been organised by a woman who worked at the centre, Maggie Barr, who was from a Protestant background. There were a lot of senior union people there as well. I remember Colm's mother being so proud that there was such a huge turnout from Ardoyne. There was also a big public meeting in Ligoniel after the funeral to discuss how the community could defend itself against such attacks. In the mid-1980s there was such a threat that a large proportion of the community were at the meeting, probably about 300. People were so frustrated with the murders that were happening all around them that they were just desperate for something to be done.

Colm was the first close friend of mine who was killed during the conflict. I was from Strabane and had lived in Derry for years and there was not the same sectarian division there. What you worried about in those areas was getting shot by the British army and the RUC. When I came to live in Belfast the real difference was the sense that you could be just going out for a newspaper or a pint of milk and you might get attacked. There were enough examples of things like that happening; It just made you realise how vulnerable you were. It also brought home to me who was being killed in the conflict. It was ordinary working class people from deprived areas. Then their families were left with virtually nothing to support them if it were not for the community that rallied around. Colm was a real live wire, totally indestructible, full of youth. Like everyone else there was good and bad in him. He was someone who knew how to take care of himself, someone who stuck up for himself, his mates, his family and the community, someone who cared for those around him too. At the end of the day, what did the people who killed him achieve? Nothing. It was just a complete waste of human life. I remember his brother Frank making that very point, that Colm was from a deprived working class background and so were the people who killed him. They were not privileged; they were fighting for something because they had nothing themselves, and all it resulted in was Colm's death.

Raymond Mooney
Killed by loyalists,
Holy Cross chapel,
16 September 1986

I was told by the gunmen that I was to be clear why this was happening. It was in retaliation for a friend of theirs who had been shot and buried that day and they were members of the Protestant Action Force. They then sat me on the ground and tied my feet. As they did this shots rang out and they ran, leaving me tied up on the ground and Raymond dead.

Raymond Mooney was born in Ardoyne and raised in Highbury Gardens. His parents, Thomas and Catherine Mooney, had four sons: Patrick, Gabriel, Raymond and Martin. Raymond went to Holy Cross Boys and St Gabriel's school before attending St Mary's Training College. He left St Mary's before finishing the course and took up employment with the Northern Ireland Electricity Service. He lived in Ladbrook Drive with his wife Briege and their four children: Michael, Lisa, Christopher and Fiona. Raymond was a keen GAA supporter and did voluntary work for Holy Cross chapel.

On 16 September 1986 Raymond Mooney was killed in the grounds of Holy Cross chapel, after chairing a meeting of 'The Living Church' group. As Raymond and a female friend locked the doors of the Family Centre, gunmen attacked them. They tied the woman up and shot Raymond dead. The Protestant Action Force (cover name for the UVF) told their victims during the attack that Raymond was shot in retaliation for the death of leading UVF man John Bingham, killed by the IRA a few days earlier.

Briege Mooney (widow)

We met, believe it or not, in Benidorm, Spain. I had never set eyes on Raymond before. Then we started going out together. At that stage Raymond was working in NIE. He was a member of the GAA and played for Ardoyne Kickhams. He worked behind the bar as well. His nickname was 'Stitchy' because every weekend he ended up with some injury. He helped out in the monastery as well. He had been an altar boy and never sort of cut his ties. I remember the year that we got engaged he still served midnight mass on Christmas Eve. He was a devout Catholic and his family were the most important thing to him. No matter how many kids we had, he always provided well for them. He was very old-fashioned regarding things like that. He thought his place was out working and my place was in the house. Michael was five, Lisa was four, Christopher was two and Fiona was three months old when Raymond died, so it was a pretty big handful. Nobody expects to be left to rear a young family alone.

He was very active in the community. He was in the People's Defence and helped out when people were burned out. That was before I met him. But I know people spoke very highly of him because of the work he did during that time. At one stage he had actually talked about joining the priesthood but then decided that it wasn't for him. Everything in his life always seemed to revolve around the church. He was chairing a meeting of 'The Living Church' the night he was killed. The meeting was actually supposed to be held on the Monday night but that was our wedding anniversary. He said to Sister Helen, 'It's more than my life is worth to go to that meeting on Monday night; it will have to wait until Tuesday'. For a long time that made me feel that it was my fault. I know now that it was stupid to even feel like that. It was a revenge shooting by loyalists in reaction to John Bingham's killing.

That Tuesday, 16 September, was an awful day. It was the day that John Bingham was buried. We collected our Lisa from Mercy Primary school and both sides of the Crumlin Road were lined with loyalists waiting for the funeral. The tension on the Crumlin Road was really high. When the funeral was over everybody gave a big sigh of relief; people were thinking, 'Thank God, it's over'. Raymond went on up to the Family Centre that night for a meeting of 'The Living Church'. The meeting was well attended. Aileen Toal had the keys and her and Raymond had to wait until everybody cleared the hall. Normally he would have come out the front door. But because Aileen had her car parked in the grounds of the monastery, and she was giving Raymond a lift home, they went out the back door. As they came out the back door of the Family Centre, three fellas from the Protestant Action Force jumped on them. The strange thing was that the last two people to leave the meeting before Raymond and Aileen were Fr. Victor and Fr. Michael, two new priests who were coming to Ardoyne. The gunmen could obviously identify them because of their collars, and didn't touch them. They took Aileen to the side of the chapel doors where the St Paul of the Cross altar is and they took Raymond into the grove. They tied Aileen up but made Raymond kneel down and shot him. After they had gone, Aileen got herself loose and went round to the monastery where they phoned for an ambulance and the police.

It was so strange. I didn't hear the shooting that night because I was out the back making the baby's bottle. I was actually thinking that it was Raymond's turn to make the bottles. The phone rang and it was Bridie McKillen, a friend of mine. She told me there had been shooting on the road and asked if Raymond was home yet. I phoned Aileen's house and as I was speaking to Aileen's husband, Jim. There was a knock at my door. It was Fr. Pat and Fr. Michael. I knew as soon as I saw them that Raymond was dead. My automatic reaction was to ring my mummy and I screamed, 'You better come round because Raymond Mooney has been shot dead'. Then neighbours in the street came over; Our house was absolutely packed. I must admit that the people in Ladbrook Drive were very, very good, Maureen Crossan particularly. I had brilliant support from my family and the welfare officer from the NIE, Dermot Davie, was an absolute gem.

The strange thing was that they took Raymond's body away on Wednesday to Forster Green to do x-ray's, apparently for evidence. I was told that he was now the property of the coroner. It was hard to believe he was dead because there was no body; it was ridiculous. People came on the Wednesday night thinking the body was home and to pay their respects but there was no body there. He had died on Tuesday night at half ten but we didn't get his body home until Thursday at twelve. He was buried on Friday at twelve. So that literally left us with one night for people to come and pay their respects. He was buried from Holy Cross church.

The police never came to my door throughout the whole time. They have never come to my door to tell me what has been found out about the case. To the best of my knowledge nobody has ever been charged with the killing; if they have the police have never come to tell me.

Aileen Toal (friend)

I knew Raymond when we were growing up in Ardoyne because we both went to Irish dancing classes. I didn't see Raymond for many years until I became very friendly with his wife Briege through the Ardoyne Family Centre where we both attended classes. I went on to become supervisor of the centre. Through my work in the centre I got involved in a project called 'The Living Church'. Raymond was very involved and became a leader in the project. On the night of Raymond's murder, September 16 1986, there was a meeting of 'The Living Church' project in the Ardoyne Family Centre. Raymond was chairing the meeting. As there had been trouble on the Crumlin Road earlier that day I offered Raymond a lift home at the end of the meeting. My car was parked in the monastery grounds, so we left by the back door of the Family Centre. We locked all doors and then noticed we had left a light on, so we went back inside, turned the light off and locked the doors once again. As we went down the pathway three men jumped from the hedges, pushing us against the wall. They pointed a gun and said they were members of the Protestant Action Force, and told us to be quiet and do as they said. The men took us across the church grounds, and the front of the church, keeping us close to the walls to avoid outside lights.

We were brought down the disused steps at the front of the church and into the green where we were both told to kneel down. Raymond was then asked for identification, which he produced. I was also asked for ID. They stayed behind us a lot of the time and were talking amongst themselves, but I couldn't make out what they were saying. They then removed Raymond's tie and tied it round my mouth, and tied my hands behind my back. One man in particular was constantly shouting at me to stop looking at him, pushing my head to the ground. I wasn't aware that I was looking at him. Suddenly from behind I was brought to my feet. Two of the gunmen walked me to the side of the church. The third stayed with Raymond. They stood me against the wall and spoke very sharply to me. The gunmen said that I was to be clear why this was happening. It was in retaliation for a friend of theirs who had been shot and buried that day and they were members of the Protestant Action Force. They then sat me on the ground and tied my feet. As they did this, shots rang out and they ran, leaving me tied up on the ground and Raymond dead.

I sat for a few minutes not knowing what to do. I was unsure if they had completely gone and did not know if I was going to be shot as well. I eventually struggled, freed my feet, and ran to the monastery. With my hands still tied, and my mouth gagged, I pressed the monastery bell with my head. It was opened by one of the priests to find me hysterical.

Gabriel Mooney (brother)

Raymond and I went to Holy Cross and St Gabriel's together. We were both in the GAA and played hurley and gaelic for the Kickhams. Raymond worked in the head office of the Electricity Board up until he died; he would have been very influential in the

Electricity Board. I remember the guy he worked for telling me after his death that it took three guys to do the job that Raymond had done. This guy cried at Raymond's funeral; That was the effect Raymond had on people. Raymond's life was basically the chapel because when Raymond wasn't at home or at work he was at the chapel. From day one he was an altar boy and he was very religious. He was always running functions for the chapel and ran a lot of schemes, functions and dinners for old-age pensioners. Raymond presented me with the Margaret McCorry Memorial Cup at one of the pensioners' functions [Margaret McCorry, killed accidentally by the IRA in Crumlin Road, 20 December 1971]. The cup was in appreciation of the work that my Irish dancers had done for the old-age pensioners. Raymond and Margaret Mc Corry had been very close friends. Her death had a terrible impact on Raymond; it really hurt him. It was actually Raymond's idea to come up with the Margaret McCorry Cup in her memory. I still have it. I won't part with it simply because Raymond presented it to me himself.

The night Raymond was killed, Aileen Toal was with him at a meeting and her car was parked out the back of the chapel. I found out later that the gunmen had marched him across from the back of the chapel right round to the front where they shot him. Apparently the gunmen jumped on them when they came out the back door and they asked if there was anybody else in the hall. Raymond and Aileen just clicked and said it was empty. Aileen said Raymond was very calm, but that was just Raymond. He was talking away to the gunmen saying different things and trying to calm them down. But they weren't having any of it. Aileen said to me that they tied her up and they didn't even have anything with them to tie her up. So they asked her for her tights and they tied her up. They took Raymond's ID so they knew who Raymond was before they shot him. Up to the time that they actually shot Raymond he was talking and trying to calm them down. The temperament of the guy who did the shooting was completely different than the other two guys. When he shot Raymond he executed him; he fired the four rounds into Raymond. To this day I believe that Raymond's death wasn't a one-off and he wasn't in the wrong place at the wrong time. To me Raymond was shot and picked out because of the type of guy he was. He was good, he was involved in everything; everybody knew him and knew how good he was. They wanted to shoot someone like Raymond, to keep things going. If they'd shot an IRA man, that's it, he deserved it. If you want to keep things going then kill somebody like Raymond.

The next day Martin and I went to Tennent Street police station and they took us over to Forster Green to identify Raymond. It is a devastating thing identifying your brother like that. I remember going home in the police car and looking out the window and finding it unbelievably hard to take in. They sent his body for special x-rays to find out exactly how many times he had been shot. The coroner's report said he had been shot nine times with a 9mm and once with a sawn-off shotgun.

The impact on the family you can imagine; we had gone through a lot when my Patrick disappeared. When Patrick disappeared we couldn't really get together without talking about it and then there were stages that we didn't want to get together because of it. So when Raymond was killed, it was the whole thing over again. It was me who had to go and tell my mum and dad. I called my daddy and Martin out into the hallway and mummy was at the bottom of the stairs. I told them and mum just totally lost it, totally and utterly lost it. The effect on our family was just total devastation. I couldn't talk to anybody; I couldn't go out or go into crowds. It nearly destroyed our family. Since Raymond died I have had 50 or 60 jobs. A few months in a job was long enough; once I got to know the people and they got to know me that was that, I was gone. It got to the stage were I had to go for help. I would love to go on as if this had never happened… I would love to go up and put my arms round Martin and have a good hug and talk about our family.

Raymond was my brother and as a person he was very special. Raymond would have done anything for anyone and he loved God. Raymond is always with me; he will always be with me. He was special to everyone. I just wish to God my brother Raymond was here today; I wish to God they were all here.

Larry Marley
Killed by UVF,
Havana Gardens,
2 April 1987

I just sensed that no matter what it took to get Larry a burial with dignity in a peaceful way Kate was prepared to do it. Her love for him was so strong; she had such respect for what he stood for in his life, as a republican…
I felt that no matter what was going to happen from that point onward Larry Marley was going to be buried with dignity and in a way that any family deserves.

Laurence 'Larry' Marley was born on 24 July 1945. He was one of the three sons and daughter of John Marley from Jamaica Street and his wife Kathleen (née Molloy, originally from the Lower Falls). Larry went to the Holy Cross Boys school and (despite passing his 11-plus) went to St Gabriel's. After leaving school Larry became a self-taught motor mechanic. In 1966 he married Kate and the two would go on to have a family of six boys. Larry was known as a good father; however for much of their childhood it was Kate who brought their sons up by herself. Like so many of his peers, Larry became an IRA volunteer in the wake of the outbreak of the conflict. He was arrested numerous times and would eventually spend 13 years of his life as a political prisoner in the cages of Long Kesh and the H-Blocks. It was in prison though that Larry became widely known for his capacity to escape. Larry launched many escape attempts and a number were successful. He was a key organiser of the breakout from the H-Blocks in 1983 when 38 republican prisoners took part in the largest single prison escape in the history of the British penal system. Larry did not take part in the breakout himself because his release date was coming up soon after. He was released in November 1985 and was therefore able to spend a few months with his family. On 2 April 1987 Larry was at home with his wife and youngest son Sétanta (who was only two weeks old) when there was a knock at the door. When he answered the door, UVF gunmen shot Larry several times as his wife Kate protected the body of their baby with her own a few feet away. Larry died in hospital shortly after. Larry Marley was an IRA volunteer at the time of his death. The story did not, however, end there. The Thatcher government and the RUC had been targeting and attacking republican funerals since 1983. It was a campaign that culminated in an attempt to prevent a dignified burial for Larry Marley. There was a tense three-day standoff between massed RUC men and mourners outside the Marley family home. It only ended when public opinion and the sheer weight of numbers of the mourners forced the funeral through. The determination of his wife Kate and family ensured that Larry Marley was buried with dignity.

Kathleen Marley (wife)

I knew Larry all my life. We grew up in the same street and we were always chums. From when I was about 11 or 12 we used to socialise together down at the bottom of the street. Larry was friends with Jim and Bobby Reid and we all used to hang about at Granny Reid's wall, or down the side at Lizzie Whelan's. I started going with Larry when I was about 19. In 1966 we got married, then we stayed with his family in Estoril Park. After that we got a flat on the Antrim Road and then moved from there up to Jamaica Street. We had a family of six children together: Laurence, Manuel, Joseph, Seamus, Sean and Sétana, six boys. Laurence was just starting school, Manuel was two, Joseph was just over a year and I was three months pregnant with twins when Larry was lifted in 1973. That was a hard time for me because they were only babies. In 1975 Larry escaped from Newry Court House with 11 others and was on the run in the South for about a year. Then he was caught on the M1 motorway on a motorbike. The RUC stopped to help them; they recognised Larry's face and he was recaptured. He didn't get out until November 1985. That was his first Christmas home in years. Laurence was 18 that February; we had the following Christmas together and then Larry was killed in April 1987.

The morning of Larry's death the kids went out to school as usual. Larry was running in and out the back door fixing the car because it wasn't working right. Then the two of us went out in it to get some shopping and afterwards came back home. He was away a couple of hours, looking for parts for the motor and he got back about a half an hour or so late for his supper. When he came back he said that it was strange because he hadn't been stopped. I remember him saying that he had been passed by the British army and the RUC loads of times but he hadn't been stopped. That was very unusual. He was always stopped as soon as he walked out the door. I remember him saying how strange that was. Anyway, he got his supper and then he was just holding the child and playing with the kids, trying to coax them all to go out to the disco down at the Ardoyne Community Centre. One of the kids, Seamus, never went out much. Even when he said he was going to the disco he used to just go down to his granny's and sit with her. We said to him to just go down with the others. Seamus was just gone about 10 minutes when the shooting started. I was sitting on the settee with the baby. Larry was kneeling down beside me and we were looking at all the clothes people had brought for the child. We were laughing because people had brought so many. The two of us hadn't a penny and we were just laughing because people had brought two or three suits for the baby where they would usually have just brought one. Larry was sitting with the child on his knee, still playing with him and he just said, 'I told them we were having a christening party' and he was laughing.

The next thing was there was a rap at the door. Larry got up, went over and stood at the side of the wall. Then he opened the living room door and asked who it was. Someone shouted 'Sean'. We thought it might have been someone we knew, though he looked over at me and I looked at him because it didn't sound quite like the person we knew. It was a very loud, deep voice. Then Larry went out into the hall and I just put my head down to feed the child. The next thing there was just this sound like an explosion. I thought that it was a bomb. It turned out it was a shotgun, but it was just this big bang. I looked up at Larry; he was hunched over in the hall. I remember him sitting at one point, sort of staring at the floor. Then he just looked over at me. After that he stood up and waved for me to get down. He never spoke. The whole time there were bullets whizzing past; there seemed to be hundreds and hundreds of bullets. It went on and on. I just sat and squealed, covered in bits of glass and splinters of wood. I didn't know what to do. I lifted my knees up to cover the child and just sat there squealing. Then Larry took one or two steps and his eyes went back in his head. His two legs went like jelly and he fell back into the hall again. I put the child down on the settee, ran out into the hall and just kept shouting into Larry's ear. I opened the door and a young lad I knew was there. I yelled to him to get an ambulance. It took a while for the ambulance to come; then they took Larry to the Mater Hospital. He died about 90 minutes later. We thought he might make it because he had been through so much down the years. When the doctor told me he was dead I just squealed and collapsed; I could not believe that he had died. I was completely numb. Then someone drove me home. When we got back to the house the RUC were not allowing anyone in. They threw Manuel out of the hall; they were really aggressive. So we went up to my mummy's. We just sat there until we were allowed to go back into the house. I don't think I slept that night; I just sat on the settee. The next afternoon they brought Larry home. After that people just kept bringing me cups of tea. Then I remember Pat McGeown sitting on the end of the settee. I said to him that I couldn't even talk or keep my eyes open any longer. This was Saturday. Larry had been shot on the Thursday and that was the first sleep that I got.

I try not to think about Larry's funeral; it really upsets me to think about it. Because of the actions of the RUC we were unable to bury Larry for a number of days. I remember we were going down the steps to take the coffin up to the chapel and the RUC were trying to provoke a confrontation by pushing and harassing everyone. I thought that we needed to wait until it had quietened down a wee bit, But it just kept getting worse. The priest came down and Laurence was interviewed for the TV. We made it clear we were postponing the funeral till the next day. Larry was actually waked for five days in the house. He had been brought home on the Friday evening and was supposed to be buried on the Monday, but he didn't get buried for two days after that. Even then the RUC were still there in their hundreds. We got to the chapel but the priest said very little about what type of person Larry was. I don't think there was even a candle lit on the altar; it was all dark. That really upset me. Afterwards I was told that the priests were reluctant to conduct the service at the graveside. I felt angry and bitter about that because I used to attend mass regularly and I have brought the kids up to believe in God. I hold that very strongly. But the way they treated Larry really, really annoyed me. It still annoys me now; I hate to think about it. I think it was a disgrace the way we were treated by the Catholic church. The boys all went to chapel and holy communion; some of them were altar boys, I still have all their bibles. If someone dies now I go up to the chapel, but I only do it for the sake of the person that has died. I don't go to mass apart from that now. Even when Sean went back to school, just a couple of weeks after Larry's funeral, we had a wee bit of bother. He was told to write an essay saying what a great man Bishop Daly was. Sean came back to the house nearly crying, saying that he wouldn't do it because of the stance Bishop Daly adopted during Larry's funeral. It was just a total disgrace.

After Larry died the house was packed for about three months. There was no drink or anything like that; it was all just talking. It was all men, friends of Larry's, who would just come in to talk about him. When they came in and told stories about him it was like he hadn't gone away, as if he was still alive. It kept the kids going too. They were told tales of the things that Larry had done and what he got up to in the Kesh. He was always full of devilment. Larry was full of humour; he would have kept you going. Fellas would come in and tell the kids all about him and I was all right as long as they were all right. But I remember one night plainly. It was only a few days after the funeral; everyone had gone. I think they thought it was best to leave us on our own for a while to start to get used to it. Manuel came in and sat down on the kitchen unit next to me as I was cooking. Then I just burst out crying. I think that was the first time I had cried since I had been told he was dead. Manuel just sat staring at the floor and the rest of them were just sitting in the other room staring. The house was so quiet you could have heard a pin drop. That was a bad night. I never had a woman to sit and talk to. There was a nun who came just after Larry's death and just sat with me. My mummy would come over and talked but all I could do was cry. A lot of people were around but then it just stops and there is just the odd person; it gets worse then. We all just hit rock bottom. I remember telling the children to pretend Larry was still in gaol but that we couldn't visit him. Maybe that was wrong but that's how we coped with the loss. But nobody came to offer us counselling; there was nothing like that.

Seán Mag Uidhír (friend)

I first met Larry Marley in prison in 1976 when I was on remand and he was already a sentenced prisoner. He had already done a few years and had escaped a couple of times. Even then he was a bit of a legendary figure in the camp. He was in Cage 12 at that stage, for about a year or 18 months. Everybody knew that Larry's whole thing was to escape. People used to name their pet birds Larry Marley if they liked to get out of their cage. His name was just associated with escape. Larry was one of the main movers behind digging an escape tunnel out of Cage 12. Then he was moved out of the cages. After him, Pat McGeown and Bik McFarlane were caught trying to escape. They dressed up as screws and made it to the front gate before they were recognised. So Larry was moved down to the H-Blocks around March 1978; then he went on the blanket. I didn't see him again until after his release in November 1985. But from then until his death I got to know him really well because we spent a lot of time together.

Larry had a great sense of humour, great craic. When he went into one of his happy half hours he could have you lying on the floor. In some of the darker moments we had to go through he had a way of lifting your morale and raising your spirits. In a very humble way he would remind you that the whole conflict was just about ordinary Joe Soaps like us and what we were doing was a response to the state presence, to oppression. I came to love Larry as the person he was. He was a good father, a good husband and he loved his kids intensely. He was a person with a lot of commitment and love for the people in his community. Larry was very, very down to earth; there were no frills to him. He was also an intelligent man who could have had a conversation about anything under the sun. He was very interested in religions and very curious about other people's beliefs. A genuinely broad-minded character who was also very interested in socialist politics. But my biggest memory of him was as a really nice human being, someone who was good company to be around and who genuinely cared both for his family and for the broader community.

The last time I spoke to Larry was two days before he was killed. He was in and out of the house a lot at that time. In the short time that he had been out of prison he had been arrested three times and he was constantly being harassed. So he would stay home a lot at night. His house had been very heavily raided just a couple of weeks before. But on that Tuesday I called into the house to see him. Sétanta had only been born a couple of weeks before and he was playing with the child. What I remember of that last visit was his concern for me. His last words were for me to take care and watch out for myself. On the Thursday he was killed I was actually in the Shamrock for a do for the local nursery school. Someone came in and said that a man had been shot in Ardoyne Avenue. I thought it was a random attack from a passing car so I never thought about Larry. About 20 seconds later someone else came in and said that Larry Marley had been shot. The Shamrock was about 50 yards from his door so I just ran out. The RUC were already there. I met Pat McGeown, who was a very close friend of Larry's, at the gate. At that stage Larry was lying slumped on his side in the hallway at the door with his eyes closed. My immediate feeling was, 'Comrade, you're not going to make it'. The RUC wouldn't let either me or Pat any closer. The patrol was led by a sergeant who for years had tortured me, stopping me anytime he saw me. So Pat and me just headed down to the hospital and we met up with Kate, Manuel, Laurence and some of the kids. Bobby Lavery came down as well and eventually there were about 15 or so of us in casualty. The medical team were working on him from about 9 pm to 10.30 pm. Larry was a strong guy, fairly fit, and you just hoped against hope that he would pull through. The RUC who had been at the house were there too. They could see into the room, could see he was dying, and I suppose a sense of humanity came through because they talked to Bobby Lavery as he came in and said that things were looking bad. At about 11 pm they called Kate and a couple of us in because he was dead. I remember he still looked alive. I touched him, trying to take it all in, and to say goodbye. I came out of the room and I really wanted to cry. But there were members of the RUC all around the room and I couldn't cry in front of them. A young lad started crying but I thought that I had to hold it together until I got back to their house so I could help clean it up before

Kate went home. We went back to the house and some of the neighbours had already started to clean it up. When Kate came home we tried to make her take a cup of tea and get a lie-down, but she couldn't. She started to tell me what had happened and how the UVF squad had come to the front door. Larry had put bullet-proof glass in the back door because it backed onto the road; he thought that was the most likely point of attack. I think the killers had been briefed so they came to the front instead. When they [loyalists] called out they said that it was me so I think these people were even told what to say. I just felt terrible with the loss.

I went down with young Laurence the next morning to formally identify the body. I felt terrible for the young lad; he was only 18. As we went through the town in the car we were spotted by the RUC in an armoured car and pulled over. To be honest I was really angry for the wee fella; he didn't need that harassment at a time like that. It got quite heated and then they let us go on. Laurence did the formal identification and we headed back to Ardoyne. Laurence wanted to make the funeral arrangements. He was an intelligent young man and very interested in religion; he used to go up to talk to the priests. He may have been thinking about the priesthood at that time. So he knew the priests well but they were a bit difficult with him. It was then we began to realise what the political implications were and that this was not going to be a normal funeral. For four years IRA volunteers' funerals had been the scene of confrontations and baton charges. I think, even sub-consciously, the priests realised what might be at stake. I felt badly for Laurence because he was really let down by the church. As a body the Catholic church really let down the Marley family and Kate and Laurence in particular. But none of us expected what was going to happen.

Larry's body was brought back at about 4 pm that day. Almost as soon as the body was brought home, the RUC and British army appeared on the scene. For most of the next four or five days there were jeeps parked all around the house and there was constant heavy patrolling of the area. Inside the house there was a wake going on and the IRA mounted a guard of honour. Myself and Rab McCallum acted as a bridge between the family and the movement to make sure that whatever Kate's wishes for the funeral were would be done. Kate was adamant from the word go that if the RUC didn't allow the funeral to be carried out in a dignified and peaceful way then she was prepared to stop it and if necessary bring Larry's body back. The RUC were just there to keep the pressure on. There was a particular cop and his crew that stopped me on the Saturday, asking me what my name was and whatever. It just brought it home that it was back to 'business as usual'. It didn't matter that my friend had been killed, it didn't matter how anybody in Ardoyne felt, they were just there to keep the boot at the throat. The humanity was out the window. One of the DMSUs brought in to cover the wake eventually assaulted me at the bottom of Havana Gardens. It was only due to the intervention of Gerard McGuigan (who was a councillor at the time) that it didn't get a lot worse. By the Saturday night the wake went quiet and I got half an hour on my own with Larry. The emotion just got too much for me. I went up the stairs into a room, locked the door and just cried my eyes out. There were hundreds of people coming from everywhere into the house. Larry had been 13 years in prison and republicans from all over the country knew him. The IRA carried out a volley of shots at the Ardoyne Centre for Larry. That gave you a bit of a lift with the area crawling with peelers and Brits. It was a fitting tribute. I remember his son Manuel had been walking down the road near there at the time and he felt proud that his father's comrades had done that. Then the IRA said that there would be no open military funeral so that there would be no excuse for the RUC to attack it or prevent a peaceful, dignified burial.

On the Monday morning there was a build-up of riot squad peelers from about 8.30 am. They were right outside in the gardens virtually opposite the house. We moved out of the house with Larry's body. His sons were carrying the coffin and a few of the younger lads were looking very frightened by the whole thing. As we came out, the RUC surged to push through the crowd, trying to get right to the coffin. You have to understand that at that time you wouldn't have put it past the RUC to take the body. Eventually we got back into the house but the commotion kept on outside. I remember Martin McGuinness and others outside calling for calm. I asked Kate how she was and she was a bit shaken up, like all of us, but she said to me, very clearly, 'If it takes a week, I'm keeping him until they pull back. I don't care what they do; he's not going out there until they pull back'. I have to admit, inside myself, I knew the RUC were beaten there and then. The minute that woman said that to me, so determined, I knew that the RUC had never met anything like that. I just sensed that no matter what it took to get Larry a burial with dignity in a peaceful way Kate was prepared to do it. Her love for him was so strong; she had such respect for what he stood for in his life, as a republican, and because of his experiences. It was quite obvious to me that Kate Marley was not for bending; she was not for turning on this. I felt that no matter what was going to happen from that point onward Larry Marley was going to be buried with dignity and in a way that any family deserves.

Laurence appealed to the Catholic bishops to ask the church to intervene and help ensure a peaceful funeral. There were negotiations going on between Martin McGuinness and the RUC commanders but after an hour or two we realised the funeral was not going to happen that day. As soon as it was called off there was a flurry of activity. There were a series of hi-jackings and IRA operations around Belfast. There were 30-40 bomb scares and one or two bombs so that the RUC couldn't concentrate their numbers to deal with the funeral. For us the family remained the main concern and we kept a good presence in the house because there was a real fear that the RUC might come in to take the body. There was a black flag march held up the Falls that night as well with several thousand people. I was still in the house when the SDLP councillor Pascal O'Hare came in. At first I thought he might be just looking to make political capital out of the situation because it was highly unusual for an SDLP figure to show his face at a republican funeral. But it showed the anger that was in the community. Pascal said a prayer at the coffin and told us he would do whatever he could to help because what was happening to Kate was wrong; he was very genuine. It made me feel that opinion had completely turned against the British and the RUC on this issue.

We stayed in the house through that night. Next morning the peelers started gathering in numbers again. If anything, there were even more of them and they looked like they couldn't wait to get stuck into the crowd. But people were just fed up, disgusted and angry with what was happening. Even more turned up for the funeral to show their response to what had happened the day before. It was a tense and nervous situation because we were just trying to bury a friend and you were worried about what was going to happen when the body was brought out. So we braced ourselves for another confrontation. We didn't even get as far as we had done the day before. In no time at all the batons were out, the RUC were beating people and they were fighting back. So we brought the body back inside and Kate and Laurence announced that the funeral was off again that day. A funeral arranged for Monday morning was now delayed until at least Wednesday. We had a terrible dilemma; we were told that under public health regulations if the body was not buried within 48 hours of the funeral being announced that the RUC might legally be able to take the body. We had to tell Kate and she had to give her permission for the body to be embalmed, which is not a particularly nice procedure. We cleared the house that afternoon to allow some privacy and the undertakers opened up the coffin and embalmed Larry's body.

By that stage everyone was exhausted. I hadn't really slept for four and a half days, since the night of the shooting. I felt at times like I was going to collapse, but we all just had to keep going and catch a few minutes rest whenever we could. Then on that Tuesday night there was by far the biggest demonstration in Ardoyne since the hunger strikes. I could see that there were a lot of people there who weren't republican, some you wouldn't even have thought of as nationalist. There were people who would never have gone to a political demonstration in their lives. It was a clear signal that people believed that there was a fundamental human right at stake, that everyone has a right to bury their dead and that the RUC and the Brits had gone too far in their attempt to prevent this burial. I remember Fr. Des Wilson addressing the crowd that night and I just felt that we were going to come through this. Kate was still very determined and there was such a huge turnout that you just knew the Brits were going to be beaten on this.

Wakes are sad occasions but they are a time too for telling stories, having a bit of craic to keep spirits up and to remember the person who is gone, particularly when it is somebody who had such a great sense of humour like Larry. There was great morale there and it somehow felt like you were identifying with Larry's spirit. On the third morning there was a large number of RUC again, but the crowd had grown hugely and it was far harder for the RUC to get close to the coffin. They kept trying to push through but by that stage the sheer numbers of people locking arms that they were facing stopped them. You just felt that the funeral was going to go ahead because they would not physically be able to stop us. We got out, even though the peelers were everywhere and you could tell they were struggling to try to keep control. With the road so narrow and so many people, confrontations were inevitable and rows broke out again half way up Brompton Park. There was some close quarters fighting. You could see fear in the eyes of some of those RUC who had spent the last number of days harassing and growling at you. There was another set-to at the Crumlin Road, but again there were just too many bodies for the RUC to get through. We got to the chapel and after the funeral mass we went back down through the district. We had to stop some of the young ones throwing things at one point. We wanted to keep things dignified for the sake of Kate and the family. As we moved down the New Lodge Road there were thousands of people joining us. Despite a couple more scuffles, by the time we got to the bottom of the Falls we knew that it was all over because there were thousands more waiting to join the cortege at Divis Flats. People lined the street all the way up the Falls; it was incredible. The road looked like a battlefield after nights of rioting. But amidst all that I remember seeing all these old women in dressing gowns and slippers outside the Royal Victoria Hospital who had gotten off their sick beds to show their respects. At Milltown cemetery Martin McGuinness gave the oration. At one point he asked everyone to turn round and look at the RUC riot squad. 'You are staring into the face of defeat', he said. It sort of summed it all up. They had set Larry up to be killed, they had all the guns, they had everything, but we had beaten them. We had buried our friend and comrade.

About three months after Larry was killed I was being interrogated in Castlereagh by the Special Branch and getting the usual treatment: 'You're getting killed next'; 'We're getting the UVF for you'. Then they sang a popular Belfast song called 'Mickey Marley's Roundabout', only they sang, 'Larry Marley's Roundabout' with a load of different words. I totally despised them for that. This is the so-called guardians of British law and order. Someone losing their life is no topic for a song or trying to wind somebody up. I felt such a mixture of emotion afterwards. I was very proud of our community for showing how they thought what was happening was just wrong and for doing what they did when the chips were down. But the politicians and the church leaders really let the Marley family down. Fr. Des Wilson was an honourable exception; there was also a presbyterian minister and Fr. Gerry Reynolds from Clonard who came up and offered to act as mediators. At a personal level I felt that I couldn't show my emotion for a long time. The abnormality of the situation we were put in robbed me of the chance to grieve properly. Like a lot of other people I don't think I had the chance to grieve until after the ceasefires. But Larry's funeral, and how the community reacted to the situation, that is something that you just never forget. It is burnt into my consciousness. I remember thinking how much Larry would have loved all this. He had a tough, tough life but he always came through things because of his sense of humour and his spirit. There he was still having such an effect even in death. Kate was the one I felt sorry for. She had had such a hard life bringing the wee lads up on her own for years. Then having to handle such a difficult situation as the funeral, which she did so well. Knowing too that she was going to be doing things on her own again, except this time knowing too that Larry wasn't going to be coming back. There were a few more serious attacks on republican funerals, at Finbar McKenna's and at the funerals in Derry of Paddy Deery and Eddie McSheffrey. But outside of those, and the attack by Michael Stone, most were peaceful for years after. The reason for that was the stand taken by Kate Marley, the courage and determination she showed, and the dignity of her 18-year-old son in dealing with the media while coping with the loss of his father. The damage it all heaped on the Marley family was great. Kate had such a hard time having to bring up six boys on her own. It has always been difficult to talk about all this. What is needed is for the friends of Larry to really talk about what happened with the family and with Kate.

Joe Marley (son)

I was 15-years-old when my father was murdered. For 13 of those years myself and my four brothers were only able to see my father on visits in Long Kesh. My memories of the visits in Long Kesh are good. Some people may find that strange, but we only had one half hour visit a week so we would try and cram an entire week's happenings into that time. My father never felt inadequate or embarrassed about expressing his feelings for us; it was one of the qualities I admired most in him. He was released in November 1985 and we spent our first Christmas together as a family that year. There was a real feeling of contentment and that no matter what happened we could cope because he was there. When I was around him I always felt safe and that nothing could harm me; that is the sort of person he was. I have some very special memories of my father which I will cherish forever, too many to squeeze into a few paragraphs in a book. I prefer to share them with my own sons when they get older.

From November 1985 when he was released until his death in April 1987 my father was constantly harassed by the British army and the RUC. He was held at Castlereagh several times. On one occasion there he was told by a senior RUC detective that they would feed his name and the names of two other local republicans to a loyalist death squad in the Ballysillan area. Only two weeks before his murder he was told by a British army major that he wouldn't live much longer. He said that if they [British army] couldn't do it they could get ones to do it for them. They were true to their word. On 2 April 1987 my father was shot at our home in front of my mother and my youngest brother, Sétanta, who was just two weeks old. I was at the local disco when I was told. I remember Rab McCallum bringing myself and my younger brother to the hospital. I saw my mother sitting on a chair as I entered the casualty; her blouse was soaked in blood. We all waited, hoping to hear that he was going to pull through but they came out and told us that he had died. They let us go in and see him; he was lying on a table. He looked like he was asleep and we all just stood around him. My 16-year-old brother Manuel was always very deep and kept his emotions to himself. But he began to really cry. I had never seen him pour his emotions out like that. I wanted to hug him and tell him that it was all right but I couldn't; a horrible feeling of despair saturated me. It is a feeling I will never forget. The next day we began the wake and as soon as my father's body came back, the RUC had taken up positions around the house. They harassed mourners who had come to pay their respects. At night they would shine the light from the land rover up at the front door and at the living room window where his body lay.

My father was a volunteer in Oglaigh na hÉireann. His comrades had made it clear that they had already paid their tribute to him and that there would be no formal presence at the funeral. This did not stop the RUC from attacking the funeral and we had to postpone the funeral twice. My father lay in our house almost a week before we were able to bury him. The actions of the RUC and British government were despicable at the funeral. But we expected nothing more and their actions came as no surprise. It is not my intention to offend anyone but the silence of the Catholic church inflicted more hurt and pain on my family than the British ever could. The day before my father was buried a member of the British army who was killed in Divis Flats was buried in England. He was a Catholic. His union jack-draped coffin was carried out of the Catholic church by six uniformed members of the British army, taken to an adjoining graveyard and a volley of shots were fired. During my family's ordeal, my oldest brother, Laurence, appealed to the Catholic church hierarchy to intervene. Their silence was deafening. My youngest brother, Sétanta, was robbed of ever getting to know our father. My mother had to raise myself, Laurence, Manuel, and Sean while my father was in the Kesh. History was repeated on 2 April 1987 when my mother was left again with a two-week-old son to raise on her own. My father never got to meet his five grandsons and granddaughter. Most people who knew my father will have their own memories of him: comrades, ex-POW's and friends. But for myself and my family we will remember him as a loving husband and father.

Eddie Campbell
Killed by loyalists,
Horseshoe Bend,
3 July 1987

> *It's in my memory and it will always be in my memory until I die. I am saying again, I forgive them. I do really. I pray for them. I do really,*

You couldn't but like Fast Eddie Campbell, a jolly fella who adored his wife, doted on his mother and kept pet birds. He was born in 1947, the second son of Alice (née Totten) and Thomas Campbell, a joiner. Alice was from Ardoyne, where her father kept a sweet shop; Thomas's people had moved to the area from Lincoln Avenue. They would work all their adult lives and rear five of a family in Brookfield Street – Thomas, Eddie, Rosaleen, Marie and Wilfie. He attended Holy Cross Boys and then St Gabriel's school and played football and hurling. In later years, he enjoyed watching boxing and snooker. As he grew older, Eddie became known as Fast Eddie, an ironic reference to his deliberate manner.

He met Betty (née Weir) when they were still at school. It was love at first sight. They were married by Fr. Sylvester in Holy Cross on 15 April 1964 and moved into the front room of Betty's parents' house. Eddie and Betty moved to Canada but homesickness brought them back to Belfast in June 1969. In the same year Eddie became an IRA volunteer. Comrades remember him as deeply committed. Above all, he was reliable. In 1972 Eddie was interned and served over two years in Cage 3. After his release he opened a pet shop but eventually gave it up and started working as a taxi-driver with Rambo Fusco, a close friend. His health, however, was beginning to cause concern and he was diagnosed with sclerosis of the liver. After several years confined to the house and hospital, he pulled through and by the mid-1980s, he was out working nights for D-Cabs on King Street.

On the night of 3 July 1987, a loyalist death squad hired Eddie's taxi, shot and killed him, and dumped his body in Ligoniel. It is unclear if Eddie was simply unlucky, the loyalists not caring which Catholic they murdered, or if he had been specifically targeted using old intelligence files supplied by the RUC or British army. Either way, he was an ordinary man doing an ordinary job killed in a purely sectarian attack. Eddie Campbell was forty years of age when he was murdered. He and Betty would have been twenty-five years married the following April.

Alice Campbell (mother)

In '69 I was very house-proud. I looked after my house and I loved my children. I didn't do anybody any harm. But in '69 they came up to the top of the street with motors, lorries and their petrol bombs. I say 'they'; a prominent unionist politician was there and a couple of other men that I have seen on the television were there. When they came down the street they had guns and they burned from the top of the street right down and my house went with all the rest. I didn't get one thing out of my home that I worked for and my husband worked for. My mother left me stuff that she had had for years. Money wouldn't buy what she left me because it was all sentimental stuff.

After we were burnt out, my children were very young and we stayed in Holy Cross school for a while. Then we moved into my mother-in-law's house. We stayed there until we bought a house in Farringdon Gardens. We brought my son Eddie and his wife Alice with us. Eddie worked in Michelin and when he was on night shift they used to come down and write UVF slogans on my windows. And I knew that some day the same thing would happen again and in '71 the same crowd, same men — I'll never get them out of my sight — burned my house again and all in it. That was twice that happened…

That was nothing losing two homes. You can build them up again. You can work and build them up which I did and I'm still doing. But they took my son. He was a taxi driver and he was only 40 and he worked for D Cabs. That morning he got a call to the house. I was making his breakfast and he got a call saying he was needed down in D Cabs to take three men to Ligoniel and up he got. If I only had kept him five or ten minutes later he wouldn't have been there. But he went and the three boys got into his car and they asked him to go up the Hightown Road. So he took them up the Hightown Road and he stopped the car and they pulled a gun and they shot him. He got hit in the shoulder and the arm. They threw him into the back and they took him away up over the Horseshoe Bend. They took him out and put him in the boot of the motor and shot him through the head. It's all down in the paper. I could show you the paper today because I read it manys a time and I think about what they did to my son that never did harm to anybody. That's hard.

I heard it on the news first of all that a body had been found in Ligoniel. Eddie hadn't come home that night and Betty came up and she said to me, 'Mum, Eddie didn't come in last night and there was a body found in Ligoniel' and I said 'Surely to God, Betty it isn't?' and she said, 'Well, he didn't come home' and I said 'I'll ring different places. Maybe he is playing a hand of cards. He stays out like that, Betty. You know that'. He would stay out and go to his mate's and play a hand of cards and come home the next day. But she said, 'It's on the news'. So Rosaleen said to her husband, 'Take the car and away up the Ligoniel Road and see whose body it is; see who it is and see is it our Eddie'. He did that and he came back and he said 'Rosaleen, it's Eddie. He is lying on the Ligoniel Road bend in a plastic bag'. Then Betty rang me and said, 'Don't you be looking at the television. They will be showing you this'. But I watched the television and I saw what they did and that's in my mind until the day I die. I saw him on the television getting put in a black sack that you put in the bin and six RUC men carrying him out. And what was that for? I don't know; it's hard to know. It's in my memory and it will always be in my memory until I die. I am saying again I forgive them. I do really. I pray for them. I do really.

I remember wee simple things. He was a boy that played football, hurling, you name it he was in it. Because he was very fat and stout and they use to call him 'Barrel.' He would come home when he had been fighting and I would say to him, 'What did you do now?' and he said, 'They are calling me "Barrel"' and I'd say, 'Did you tell them that it cost money to put that there?' But he lost all his weight he grew up. Like any other wee fella he loved fun and he loved life. He had plenty of friends but a good lot of his mates have died.

There were three boys charged with the murder of my son. I didn't go to the court that day with Betty. Whenever they were passing Betty, she said 'God will never forgive you' and they said, 'We would do the same thing again if we got the chance'. They are the words they said. No remorse. No nothing. They got out a few months ago; I was watching the television. I got a phone call from Betty saying that they were getting out and she said, 'When you see it don't let it upset you.' I said 'Oh, it will never bring him back.' I don't care whether they get out or not. My Eddie was a good boy and I lost him. They say forgive and I forgive them boys for what they did but I can't forget it. I always pray for them but those sort of people that do those things, they don't believe in God.

Betty Campbell (widow)

Eddie was murdered on the 3 July. He was a night driver for D Cabs. He left at about twenty past twelve. I went out and sat in the car with him for a couple of minutes and he said to me 'I better go on here because I'll be late for going into work' and he said, 'By the way I have something to tell you, something good to tell you in the morning'. I never found out what it was. He had sclerosis of the liver and we were saving up to go to Lourdes. We were 24 years married when he was murdered so we were intending to go on our 25th wedding anniversary which would have been in April 1988.

When he got down to the depot there was a cab in front of him and the taxi man was about to put these three fellas into it. But the night driver always gets the job. So the three of them were put into Eddie's car. They said they wanted to go to Ligoniel. I know this through the court; whenever the case came up I was at the court. When they got up to the turn of the road they told him to stop. When he stopped two men came out of an entry and they got Eddie out of the taxi and they knocked him out and put him in the boot of the car. They were going up to the Horseshoe Bend to shoot somebody up there. But they couldn't get in through the gates and they appear to have forgotten that they had put Eddie in the boot. Whenever he started to move they realised and they turned round and said, 'What are we going to do with this bastard in the back because he has heard everything?' They took him up a lane at the Horseshoe Bend. Eddie said to them, 'You're not going to shoot me are you?' Your man pulled the gun and the gun jammed. 'If I get this fucking thing to work I am,' he said and he shot him. The three of them took turns. They shot him in the head, one bullet in the back of the head which the judge said killed him right away. They shot him in the back; they shot him in both arms and they shot him in the head. Then they took the car away and it was found up in Ballysillan burnt out.

The taxi drivers hadn't got any radios in their cars at that time and I didn't have a telephone then so the men in the depot thought that maybe Eddie had gone on home. It was 7 am the next morning and the door rapped and it was the boss of D Cabs. He was wondering did Eddie take bad with his illness. I was thinking that maybe he was in one of the hospitals. I went round to a niece's house and I telephoned all the hospitals to see what was happening. Then a nephew said, 'I'll ring the RUC and see if there is anything happened to him. Maybe he has been in a car accident or something.' As soon as he rang there they said, 'Give us your number and we'll ring you back again.' They rang back and he came in and his face was white and he said to me, 'Betty, we have to go round with the log book of the car; we have to go down to Tennent Street.' So me, Michael and my brother Joe went down to Tennent Street and I kept saying to Michael in the car, 'What's wrong? Has he been in an accident?' It never crossed my mind that he was shot dead... never crossed my mind...

When we got to Tennent Street, an RUC woman took me up the stairs into a room and said to me, 'We've got bad news for you' and I said, 'What's wrong?' and she said, 'Your husband was shot dead last night'. I said, 'No it couldn't be.' She said, 'Yes, they found his coat and we found his ID in his pocket'. I just lifted the table and flung it up and I shouted 'I want my brother. I want my brother'. When I was coming out with my brother and nephew, Eddie's car was sitting there and it was burnt. I knew it was his car. I thought that instead of them bringing me down there they should have come to the house and told me in the house. I used to have an altar sitting there; I have it in my bedroom now. I used to have it sitting there because we always said our wee prayers at night-time before he went out. Him and me always said our wee prayers together and I just came in and my brother Joe knew what I was going to do. I just smacked the whole thing right down; the statues were in wee bits. My brother, he sat months later and he put every piece of the statues together.

About two weeks after Eddie was buried they asked me to go down to the RUC station down in Tennent Street. So I took my two nephews down with me and there was three big detectives sitting and they wanted me to go into the room with them. I said I wasn't going in unless the two nephews came in. One was asking me one question, one was asking me another question as if I was under interrogation. One was saying to me, 'What time did he leave the house at?' Before I could answer him the other one was saying, 'When was the last time you saw him? What was the last thing you said to him?' I broke down and one of my nephews said, 'I think she has had enough. With the murder of her husband and the funeral, she has had enough'.

The RUC came and told me they had got two fellas. They couldn't tell me their names until they were being charged. Then they came the following week after that and told me they had got another one. The court case came up then and I got a summons to go to the court. Why they asked me to go to the court I don't know but I had to go. The three fellas that murdered Eddie were just sitting looking up and grinning at me. There were actually four of them up; they were up in court for three murders. They got life and they got out last year; they did seven years, something like that.

I don't feel that justice was achieved. I'm not up on politics; I don't know anything about it. But the only reason I went round and voted 'Yes' for the Agreement was because of the young children coming up. I don't want the rest of the families to suffer what a lot of other people have gone through. All them guys got out of that Maze Prison. I had the news on and the three of them came walking out of the gaol and I wasn't even told that they were getting out. I wasn't made aware of them getting out. It was very hard for me… very, very hard for me.

Eddie was a very jolly fella. I remember one 12th of July Eddie came down Estoril Park and he had the big orange sash on him, a hat and a black umbrella. The whole of Estoril Park was out laughing at it. I was out and I was shouting, 'Will you get that off you? Get that off you!' I don't know where he got it from. For two years before he died he had sclerosis of the liver and he went off the drink; he just stayed in the house in Estoril Park. We were 24 years married. I was going into 16, he was going into 17 when we married. And we had a good marriage and we did love each other.

Thomas McAuley
Killed by loyalists,
Crumlin Road,
died 16 November 1987

My brother Tommy was just a very happy and cheerful person. He was a character. He made people laugh and that was his aim, just to make people happy. Tommy was one of life's true gentlemen.
He is very sorely missed every day by each and every one of us.

Tommy McAuley was one of seven children (Alice, James, Thomas, Rosemary, Paul, Patrick and Marian) born to Thomas and Mary (née Mathews). Tommy attended Sacred Heart Boys school and finished his education at St Gabriel's. He was a keen weight lifter and won the All Ireland Champion title three times. He was full of life, always pulling pranks and out to make people laugh. On leaving school, he worked delivering bread and then as a dispatch rider for the *Belfast Telegraph*. For a number of years he worked on the buses before opening up a restaurant, Bon Appetit, on the Crumlin Road. He married Patricia Gourley from Farringdon Gardens in Holy Cross chapel in 1976; they had two children, Clare and Stephen. Tommy was involved in various charity works and was regularly organising fund-raising events. By all accounts he was extremely likeable and a well-respected person.

On 11 November 1987 a loyalist gunman entered the restaurant and fired several shots at Tommy, seriously wounding him. Five days later he died in hospital from his injuries. The killing of Tommy McAuley was purely sectarian. He was killed simply because he was a Catholic.

Mr and Mrs McAuley (parents)

Most people called Thomas, Tommy. He was born on 20 September 1955. He lived in Jamaica Street most of his life, until he got married. Tommy was named after his father Thomas. His father was originally from Ardilea Street, in the Oldpark area and there were sixteen children in his family. I am Mary Mathews, his mother, and I married Thomas in St Patrick's chapel on 14 October 1947. I am originally from Upton Street, off the New Lodge Road. I am one of eight children. Thomas senior was a chief stewart in the Merchant Navy and I worked as a tailoress for C&A.

Tommy married Patricia Gourley. Fr. Ailbe did the wedding ceremony in Holy Cross chapel. Fr. Ailbe married the entire McAuley family. Patricia was originally from Farringdon Gardens, Ardoyne. They had two children, Clare and Stephen. Tommy owned his own restaurant and catering business on the Crumlin Road. Before that he worked on the buses based at the bus depot in Ardoyne. The management of the bus depot asked Tommy if he would consider carrying out the Ulsterbus tours as he had such a good way with people; he had a great personality. He was very well-known and liked by all. The restaurant was called Bon Appetit, where you could sit in or have a take-away service. Bon Appetit was situated close to Flax Street on neutral ground as Tommy was trying to cater for both sides of the divide. Thomas was a very friendly, kind-hearted man who would have done anything for anybody.

About ten days prior to Tommy's death he was approached in his restaurant by persons whom he believed to be members of the UDA. They demanded that he pay them protection money. Tommy informed them that he didn't think it was necessary for him to pay the protection money as his business was small and that he wasn't going to pay protection money to any organisation. Shortly after this confrontation on 11 November a lone gunman walked into his restaurant and shot him at point blank range. He never stood a chance; he was shot eight or nine times. Miraculously he didn't die immediately but died five days later in the Mater Hospital on 16 November. A group claimed responsibility for his murder and made a statement that it was revenge for the Enniskillen bomb.

On the day of Thomas's funeral Holy Cross chapel was packed to capacity and crowds of people had to stand in the chapel grounds because there was no room inside. People from all areas of Belfast and further afield, Protestant and Catholic alike, came to mourn the death of Thomas. We were heartened by the amount of letters and support we received from everyone, including members of the Protestant community.

Paul McAuley (brother)

Tommy was known as a character. He was always up to something and always laughing. He made you laugh, no matter what. When he left school he was a dispatch rider for the *Telegraph* for two or three years. They supplied him with a motorbike. I used to follow him about and do things that he was doing. We were a very, very close family. There were seven of us living in a small house in Jamaica Street. Tommy used to go out with a girl in Farringdon and at night you could hear his motorbike echoing through all the streets on his way home. I used to jump into his bed, keep it warm for him and listen with the window open until I heard him coming into the house. We were close that way. I would have done anything for him and he would have done anything for me.

Tommy liked cooking and he liked the catering end of things. He didn't want to spend the rest of his life as a bus driver. Three of us [brothers] worked on the buses at the same time. He wanted to open his own restaurant, which he eventually did. He put everything he had into the restaurant on the Crumlin Road. It was tough going and he started to do outside catering as well. He did every kind of function, weddings, christenings and parties. The catering business was going well but the shop itself was very, very, slow probably because of where it was. He was thinking about giving the shop up and concentrating instead on the outside catering; that's what he told me. The family worried about his safety because of where the shop was situated on the Crumlin Road. There was a lot of tension around the shop.

Before Tommy was shot, his wife told me that he was becoming moody and that he was changing. She said she found him sitting on the step outside the house, just sitting thinking. She found it very strange because he wasn't his normal cheerful self. As far as I know, and I'm going by what his wife said, there was something bothering him. Whether or not he was threatened, or he sensed he was in danger, it was starting to get to him. I would definitely say he had worries about working in the shop because it was very, very tense. It used to drive me crazy just thinking about him every day over there; it was a dangerous spot. I was worried sick about him. The first chance I got off the bus I would ring to make sure he was home safely.

It just so happened that I was on the Shankill run the night he was shot. I got to the top of Twaddell Avenue and the Ardoyne junction and it was sealed off by the police. I thought there was a bomb scare. I drove the bus on up the road. I was worried about Tommy and I tried to get to a phone to ring him, but it was dangerous to leave the bus. I eventually had to take the bus back down the road again. I was trying to get as close to the town as possible so I could get to a phone to see if he got home all right. It was then my brother Jim met me with another bus driver and took me off the bus. The other driver took over my bus. Jim told me that Tommy had been shot by loyalists. We went straight to the Mater Hospital.

When we got to the hospital Tommy was in the intensive care unit. I saw them rushing him to the theatre and I could see his wounds. At that stage we didn't know how bad he actually was. We just stayed there morning, noon and night and never went home. Tommy was there for five days before he actually died and we just never left him, it was as simple as that. And we weren't going to leave him just in case somebody tried to come back and finish the job that they had done.

I went in and spoke to him in the intensive care unit. He put his hand up to me and held my hand. He told me he loved me, even though he was really ill. It was pretty hard for the whole family; it was chaos. My mummy and daddy were going out of their minds. It was very, very hard to watch. It was unbelievable; it will be with us for years. The entire time he was in hospital the bus drivers constantly called and asked about him. It came to the point that the whole Citybus, no matter who was on that road, sounded their horns going past the hospital. They hit the horn for him to let him hear it, to help him fight the thing. The whole time the nurses played his Queen tapes; he had his own wee hi-fi there. You were just going in and looking at him and talking to him but whether he heard you or not I don't know because he was eventually put on a ventilator. They decided to take him off the machine to make him try and fight it more. Once they turned the machine off that was it; he just didn't pull through.

It was a total nightmare. It was really very hard and traumatic for the whole family. My mother died suddenly a year after it; she never came to terms with it. I was on nine anti-depressant tablets a day for eight years after it. I am still on them to this day and that is twelve years later. Tommy was buried on the Thursday and I stayed with my mother and father to try and help them cope. I couldn't cope myself but I was trying to help them. My father collapsed in the living room with a burst ulcer. We were back down in the Mater Hospital and back down in the same intensive care for five days watching my daddy. I came home to my own house for the first time after two or three weeks of being in hospitals. My wee girl was only a baby and she started to go into convulsions in my arms. She had blocked tubes in her wee body and the next thing I was in the hospital again for another five days. It really was so unreal at the time. How could it happen?

At the funeral the house was full – all of his friends, the insurance people he worked with, the people from the bakery where he had worked, the weight lifting club, bus drivers, you name it. There were hundreds there, Protestants and Catholics. It was a big funeral in Ardoyne chapel. I didn't know but apparently he had wanted to be cremated. We didn't know this until the actual day. We didn't know what to expect because we were never at a cremation. The hearse wasn't stopped the whole way from Ardoyne. The police made sure it was okay going the whole way up the Castlereagh Road and there was no bother at it. Fr. Fernando did the requiem mass. He was a very good friend of Tommy's for years.

My brother Tommy was just a very happy and cheerful person. He made people laugh and that was his aim, just to make people happy. Tommy liked to do things for people; if they needed him he was there. Tommy did bed pushes for charity; anything for charity he did it. The family actually did a bed push and raised a couple of thousand pounds to buy a dialysis machine for the Mater Hospital. There's a plaque with his name dedicated to his memory. He advised me in everything throughout my life. So when he died that was a big thing for me; I was on my own, sort of thing. All our family are very, very close but he was the one who was leading me throughout my life and he is sadly missed. He was a gentleman who loved his family; he really loved his daughter and son.

My brother was killed for no reason other than his religion. Tommy never had any enemies and never did anything to harm anybody. It was purely sectarian. There was nobody ever charged with my brother's murder. After all of these years it bothers me that nobody has ever been brought to justice for it; they are still out there walking about. At the time it didn't bother me who did it or who didn't do it because I was so messed up with losing my brother.

Paul McBride
Killed by the UVF,
Avenue Bar,
Union Street,
15 May 1988

Ever since our Sean had been killed, whenever any of us were not in the house overnight, we always phoned my ma ... Paul had been out and remembered he had not phoned. So he went into the Avenue bar to phone my ma.

Paul McBride was born on 31 January 1961 in Hooker Street, Old Ardoyne. He was the fifth born child of 11. Paul was the son of Jimmy and Mary McBride (née Gillen) He went to the Holy Cross Boys school and St Gabriels and was particularly close to the three brothers nearest in age to him; Sean, Joseph and Henry. Because of the conflict his family moved to Herbert Street in 1970. Times remained difficult. Whilst saying the rosary one evening a bullet was fired in through the window of the family home, bursting a water pipe. The final straw came when a British army landrover knocked down a gable wall, collapsing on the family's outside toilet. They decided to move to England. However, after spending just three months in Stoke-on-Trent homesickness brought a return to the district. At first they went to Herbert Street but the McBrides were soon on the move again when they were burnt out in 1971. Briefly they went back to Hooker Street before finally settling in Flax Street. Paul grew up a quiet, gentle man. He was an avid reader and very interested in cookery. He could find only casual work though. For a time he was a volunteer worker for the Northern Ireland hospice. As a gay man in the Belfast of the 1970s and 1980s life was not always easy. He socialised mostly in town, though even here acceptance was often hard to find. He always remained, however, very close to his family. The death of his brother Sean in a loyalist car bomb explosion in 1977 hit Paul particularly hard [Sean McBride, killed by the UVF in Etna Drive, 21 April 1977]. He would always say that he felt he too would die young. On the afternoon of Sunday 15 May 1988 Paul was socialising in the Avenue Bar in Union Street. In an indiscriminate sectarian attack two UVF gunmen came in and fired repeatedly with automatic weapons at the crowd of customers. Many were injured and Paul was killed along with two other victims, Stephen McGahan from the New Lodge and Damien Devlin from Andersonstown. Paul was 27-years-old.

Henry and Seamus McBride (brothers)

Henry: There was only 11 months between Paul and me. I was born on 15 February 1962 and Paul was born on 31 January 1961. We were very close and grew up and went to school together. I remember that my da used to get up at the crack of dawn, because he worked laying asphalt, so Paul and I were always first at the school in the morning. We were always playing chasies in the mornings, even when it was freezing cold, to keep warm. When we were young we all used to say the rosary in the house during Lent. Our Paul was always tittering and laughing through it. Once he started laughing, that was it. We would all laugh and our da would crack up.

Seamus: I was 10 years older than Paul, so when we were growing up, he was just a younger brother to me. He was a really good-looking kid. Just like any other younger brother he would tap you for money if you were working. He knew when to be about when you got paid! When he was younger he used to get up to a bit of mischief. I remember catching him stealing the chocolate buttons from inside the Easter eggs and putting the eggs back together so as no one would notice. Another time my ma sent him to the shop to buy her a crème egg. She used to like to sit and read in bed eating a crème egg. He came back from the shop and gave her the egg in a bag. The next thing my ma was biting into the paper to take it off and it turned out to be a fresh egg. It went all over the bed. My ma was calling him a stupid 'so and so' and my da nearly fell out of the bed laughing. Paul thought my ma had sent him for a real egg! When he was older he moved out of the house and had his own flat. He used to like to dabble in a bit of cooking. I will never forget the day he phoned my wife up and asked her how to cook a duck. The next time I saw him we had a good laugh about that. He said he had put it in as a duck and when it came out it had shrunk so much it was a pigeon! To me, our Paul was an 'ace' because he was never any trouble. There was never any hassle with Paul. He never gave my mother or father any bother. I don't think he had ever been in a row.

Henry: Paul's death was a total shock to all of our family. The day Paul got shot I was with Tommy 'Butch' Braniff. It was a lovely summer's day and we had gone for a walk. We had been told that there had been a shooting in the Avenue Bar and that about five people from Ardoyne had been shot dead. There was a rumour that a relative of mine, Arter Corbett, was dead. That turned out to be untrue. Then we heard that my brother Gabriel's brother-in-law (Stephen McGahan) had been there and had been shot. He was a regular in the Avenue Bar so they knew that he would have been there. My father was running around try to find Gabriel to let his wife know that her brother was in the bar. The whole time my da didn't know that his own son was lying on that same floor. He was still looking for Gabriel when the cops came to the house.

Our Paul never went into that bar. He was never in it in his life. The reason he was there was because he had been at an all-night party. Ever since our Sean had been killed, whenever any of us were not in the house overnight, we always phoned my ma. At that time they [loyalists] were coming into Ardoyne, kicking people's doors down and shooting people dead. They were taking people away and assassinating them. So if you were not at home you had to phone to let my ma know you were all right. Paul had been out and remembered he had not phoned. So he went into the Avenue Bar to phone my ma. There was someone on the phone when he went in and Stephen McGahan called him over to have a pint with him. From what I know, he never even got to taste it. Two gunmen entered, one with a handgun and one with an AK 47. They emptied both of them, reloaded and emptied them again. Paul was one of the first hit because the phone in the Avenue Bar is right beside the front entrance. Apparently there was a UDR patrol stopping cars by the Avenue Bar just before our Paul was killed. Two witnesses testified to that but nothing was ever taken on. They never investigated things when they were fresh. It was always a couple of years later when everything was gone and forgotten about. It was the same carry-on with Paul's death as it was with Sean's. Everyone knew who had done it but nobody got charged with it. There was a guy who got six years for handling weapons and one who got three years for hijacking the car.

I found out Paul was dead that evening. Butch and I had gone over to the Bone to baby-sit because my wife was going out that night. We were just sitting down to watch a couple of movies. It was a lovely evening. At about 8.30 pm I was upstairs getting changed. I looked out of the window and could see my wife coming toward the house. She was distressed, crying, and my sister was holding her arm and she was crying too. At first I thought it must have been true about Arter, or that they had just found Gabriel's wife. Then my wife told me that our Paul was the other one lying on the floor of the Avenue Bar. I still thought that they must have gotten it wrong. My next door neighbour drove me and Butch up to my ma's house. My father was just leaving to go and see if it was Paul who had been killed. My da's stepbrother, Tommy Clarke, ran us up to Forster Green because that is where my da had gone to identify the body. We missed him there again. I was there with my brother Anthony and my uncle Tommy. The doctor who did the autopsies came out and asked us if we were family and if we loved our brother. He said that he had been doing the job for 20 years and had seen some terrible sights but that our Paul was in a very bad way. He said that if I loved my brother I was better remembering him the way he was and that I should not go in to see him. I became very distressed. It is hard to explain the way I felt. My stomach was turning. I felt like it wasn't really happening. I was waiting for someone to wake me up and tell me it was all a dream. I was insisting on going in. My brother Anthony was very distressed and in a bad state too. So the doctor said again that we were better remembering him as he was and that he was very sorry for our troubles. Then we went home. In hindsight I am glad that I didn't go in. I had found it very, very hard to get over Sean; the whole family did, but it was even harder with Paul.

Seamus: I found out Paul had died when I got a phone call. My wife Theresa was at bingo and I went up there with Eugene Farley in his car. I did not want anyone stopping her and telling her before I could see her. This was about 9.30 pm. I saw her coming down the road with Mrs Farley, got out of the car and she ran over to me. I told her Paul was dead. She started crying and asking me what had happened. I said that all I knew was that he was dead. Eugene took us over to Ardoyne. We had to go through Tennent Street, the police were standing at the turning for the Crumlin Road and stopped the car. Eugene told them that he was taking me to Ardoyne because my brother had just been shot dead. They made us get out of the car. I had to grab hold of Eugene to calm him down; I think that if I hadn't grabbed Eugene he would have ended up in Tennent Street police station. Eugene thought that by telling them the situation they would have directed us through. Then they searched the car. They took out the back seats and everything. They asked me and my wife for ID and to look at Eugene's licence. They checked the tax disc and everything. It showed how much remorse they had; they held us back for about 20 minutes. Within that 20 minutes the anger was building up inside me and Eugene but I just wanted to get over to the house, to my parents. That policeman's face will never leave me; he was a young lad, about 25 or 26. He just didn't want to know. His attitude was, 'I am here to inconvenience you'. If you weren't bitter, the like of that would make you bitter. When I got over to Ardoyne my daddy was just numb; he wasn't saying anything. I went in and threw my arms around him. My mummy had been sedated by the doctor; she was in bed. When the coffin went up to the chapel I was standing with my daddy. Everybody was moving out and me and my daddy were walking up the middle aisle. We got to the door and he said to me, 'Well, thank God there is enough of you left to look after your mummy'. I told him not to talk like that. He said, 'Son, I have lost all taste for life.' I asked him what he meant and he said, 'I'll tell you some day.' My Daddy only lived for nine months after that.

Paul's funeral was like Sean's; it was massive. He always said he would die young so he had songs picked out for the funeral. He said that he didn't want any hymns because he wanted to go out with a bang. I remember they played 'Hey Big Spender!' There were three people buried and our Paul was the first one buried that day. There was a fella called Dee Devlin, from Andersonstown who was killed in the bar with Paul. The other fella killed was Stephen McGahan, who was our brother-in-law. Our Gabriel had married Stephen McGahan's sister, Ann. They were actually three brother-in-laws indirectly, all related by marriage. There was one other coincidence. When the bomb went off in Etna Drive that killed our Sean, Patsy 'Coco' McAuley was sitting in a car beside the bomb. He was badly blown up that day. Then he was in the Avenue Bar when Paul was killed and he got pellets in his back. I think he was actually shot five times. It is ironic; 10 years apart and he was involved in both incidents. At that time tensions were very high in all nationalist areas. The loyalists were just going into nationalist areas and wiping people out; people were living in fear. When the doorbell rang in a club everybody's head would turn to see who was coming in. That was the kind of conditions we were living under. So when something happened it was like a kind of release of tension. It was as if people were saddened or shattered but at least perhaps we could get a bit of peace for three days until the burial – although the place would be swamped with Brits and cops after the event. They were always around the houses of those who had been killed and in mourning. They never went to those of the perpetrators and closed their homes off. Paul was cremated and his ashes were buried with Sean's body.

Henry: The chapel was packed for the requiem mass; it was a powerful turnout. Most people went onto the other funerals afterward. Our Paul's was first, then Stephen McGahan's in New Lodge and Dee Devlin's in Andersonstown. It was to show solidarity. After burying our Paul, my brother Gabriel had to go with his wife and bury her brother who was killed alongside Paul in the Avenue Bar. The grief was doubled for him. His wife's family were grieving and then when he came over to us he was getting no relief. My mother was never really a healthy woman after our Sean's death. My mother is the type of woman who does not need a lot in life. She was happy with a cupboard full of messages and a big lit fire; she was never a hard woman to please. But I remember there would be nights when my father would deliberately pick a row with her just to get my mother's mind away from going down the road of thinking about our Sean and our Paul. There were nights when she just couldn't stop crying. My da would tie a hanky around her head as tight as he could because she was suffering with migraine headaches. My mother is still living; she is a strong-willed woman, though she is not well at the moment. Our brother Hockey [Patrick] was never the same after what happened to Sean and Paul. He grew up with hatred in his heart and his bitterness was understandable. He was older and knew what the crack was. He knew that Catholics were getting treated unfairly, getting killed for nothing and that more and more of us were being killed. He dealt with it as best as he could until he couldn't take anymore. Now he is dead too and a lot of that stems from the troubles.

It hit my father very badly and he died shortly after. My da and I were like mates and my ma got me to talk to him about how Paul's death affected him because he wasn't going to his bed or getting any sleep. I came home from the Star (social club) one night to find him crying and talking to himself. It was a lovely evening and he had the front door open and I could hear him crying. I went in and said to him, 'Da, what are you doing talking to yourself?' He just burst out crying. I asked him why he was not going to his bed. He said that since he had gone to identify Paul, every night, when he closed his eyes, he could see what he had identified on the table. My da found it very hard to close his eyes. In the nine months he lived after our Paul died I don't think he went to bed at the proper time with my mother for more than a week. When he closed his eyes he saw the image of our Paul lying on that table with no face. Paul had been shot nine times; he was riddled. It destroyed my father. But even though my brothers had been killed, my father never wanted any of us to go out and kill anyone else. He didn't believe in violence. He worked hard all his life; he had to because there were 13 of us. He brought us up with the same morals and those morals still live on in our family.

Seamus: My father always said that he couldn't kill anyone and that we should never think about taking another person's life. If he saw some one bigger being violent toward a younger one, he would always take the smaller one's part. That was his way. My daddy told me that he identified our Paul by the tattoo, his forehead and a ring. My father knew the ring because it had been his and he had given it to Paul only the week before. Paul had been hit with a dum dum bullet in the back of the head and it had taken the best part of his face away.

Henry: My father died of a broken heart. The night he died the nurse in the hospital said that there was nothing really wrong with him; he just didn't want to live. It was very peaceful that night. Just before my father died, I remember the sky was the nicest colour of blue that I have ever seen in my life; it was like the painted ceiling in Ardoyne chapel. He pulled himself up, turned to the window and let out a big sigh. I knew he was dead. My brother Joseph and I both wanted to be there when his eyes were closed. His eyes were a gorgeous colour, just like the sky; then our Joseph closed his eyes. I think he was relieved to die. Is it any bit of wonder that my father died of a broken heart? He knew he couldn't get justice and he knew there was no way that he could win. My father was someone I could always have turned to if things weren't going well but after Paul died that went away too. You could turn to nobody because everybody was just in their own grief. No one ever called to offer us counselling after Paul died. At the end of the day, when your brother, sister or cousin has been killed, people tend to forget about it. It maybe takes six weeks or six months, but they do forget. They don't know the burden that relatives have to carry afterward. After my da died, my ma kept getting letters from the city hall addressed to my da to come and collect Paul's death certificate. He was Paul's next of kin, so they were addressed to him. It was really distressing for my ma. The letters kept coming so I went down to collect the death certificate. This was about a year and a half after he was killed. I couldn't believe what I read. Everything my da had said came back to me. It told you all the places where Paul had been shot. He got two or three in the back of the head, through to the face. He was also shot two or three times in his back and in his arms, torso, legs. I don't know how my father survived for nine months. When Paul was killed it also brought back to him what had happened to Sean.

Paul had his own philosophy on life. His attitude was, 'Live and let live'. He used to be tortured because he was gay. That was why he drank in the town, because he used to get such a hard time. He was quite withdrawn and quiet. He was a guy who his family understood but not a lot of other people because he only let himself be really known by those closest to him. He did things in a quiet way – like when his sister-in-law Elizabeth [Patrick's wife] died. He used to walk up to their house without calling in just to check on the family. If you bumped into him he would just say that he was watching over his wee nieces. The only time he let himself go was when he had a few drinks on him. Then he used to throw his arms around you and tell you how much he loved you. It was Paul who gave my wife the money to buy the headstone for Sean's grave; he worked hard and saved up for it.

Henry: He got the sack from that job not long after that. He was packing shelves, took one Mars bar and lost his job. But they sacked him because he was gay and a Catholic. It went on his record and he couldn't get work after that. Paul was only 27 at the time he was killed. He had a tattoo on his hand that said, 'Sean, Skin'. Our Paul took it really bad over our Sean too. Paul was a lonely type; he was very quiet and shy. He didn't express himself in front of everybody, only with certain people that he felt free to be himself with. Paul was a very caring and very loving person. He always cared and worried about others. He was very thoughtful. He used to come up and clean my ma's house from top to bottom. It wasn't the kind of thing blokes would have done then but our Paul didn't give a fuck. He just did it and that was it. Paul was just a 'nice gentleman', a kind, discrete person. Paul had a premonition that he was going to die young; he always thought that he would die young.

Jim McWilliams (friend)

Paul was a character. I first met him at school; we both went to St Gabriel's and were always getting into trouble together. We were a bad influence on one another. They used to try and keep us apart but we were like two cheeks; if Paul was there, I was there with him. We once let down the tyres and put sugar in the tank of the car of the woman from the school board. We were always getting letters sent home for getting up to mischief. Paul was just good craic. The teachers loved him, even though he had them all tortured. When we were older we used to go to discos together and to the John Paul youth club. We used to help out in Bridie Maguire's youth club in Herbert Street. Even there they used to try and split us up because we were always messing. Paul loved gardening too, and music. He loved clothes and was always combing his hair; he would take 20 minutes to comb his hair. Paul was always a practical joker. He once handcuffed me to a fire escape and left me sitting there with everybody looking at me for half an hour. After he had a few drinks, though, he always used to say that he would never see 30 and that he just wanted to see his brother again. It had really broken his heart when his brother Sean had been killed. They were a very close family and he really missed Sean. It dampened Paul's spirit when Sean was killed.

Paul was gay. This was in the 1970s and 1980s and people were very narrow-minded about gays. We used to go to the Carpenters club in Lower North Street. That was one of the first gay clubs opened in Belfast. Paul and I used to get a lot of stick. There were a lot of gay bashers around who used to jump you in gangs of three or four. Some of them used to come out of a club around the corner and stone us. At first Paul was very worried about how people would perceive him; he didn't know how his family would react to his being gay and he was afraid that his brothers would turn against him. But he had a talk with his brother Henry one night and his family did accept it. That made Paul feel a lot better. Paul never really worked. He may have worked part-time sometimes in the Europa; he worked in the function room preparing tables and things like that. At the time of his death Paul had a partner with whom he was living in a flat in Kinnard Terrace.

We had been out drinking the night before Paul was killed and he had cried about his brother that night. The next day he came up to my house. I was getting ready to go out and Paul said that he wouldn't wait even though I was insisting that he did; he went on out. This was just an hour before he was killed. If he had waited for me he would still be alive today. He went down to the Avenue Bar, which is not a place he usually went to. In fact, I don't think he had ever been in it before. I was supposed to meet him later at his flat, at 6 pm. I got there but there was no sign of him. He was usually punctual so I knew that there was something wrong. I heard that he was dead later that night when our John came over and told me. I was totally devastated. He was a friend and I had known him a long time. It was like having a part of me just ripped away. I couldn't face going to Paul's funeral; I was just frozen and my mind was not functioning. I went to the graveyard but I didn't go to the requiem mass. I couldn't bear to hear them playing his favourite music. His family had asked me what his favourite song was and they played, 'I will always love you' by Dolly Parton. Paul loved that. He had wanted his ashes scattered over the Cavehill but I know that the family wanted to bury some of his ashes with the body of his brother Sean. Paul was a very kind-hearted person. If someone had been lying out in the street he would have brought them in and fed them. I still miss Paul very much. It was like losing a part of me; we were like two pages of the one book. Anything I couldn't remember he would have remembered and vice versa. We were very close. That is why when Paul was killed everybody thought that I was killed too because I was always with him.

After Paul's death I went to see a psychic because we always said to one another that if anything ever happened we would find a way of letting each other know if there is life after death. I went to see this psychic, a blind girl, who immediately asked me if I knew someone called Paul. It was like having a phone call waiting for me. She said that Paul had walked into the room with me. That was Paul's way of letting me know there was a life after death. I felt as if I was having a conversation with Paul being relayed through her. I had a terrible headache before I went in; it was gone when I left. That was exactly one year after Paul died.

That was it, birth, death and marriage in the same family on the same date. What used to be one of the happiest days in our family turned out to be one of the most heart-breaking. There was no more celebrating Roisin's birthday or our parents' anniversary. It was just too hard.

Seamus Morris
Killed by loyalists,
Etna Drive,
8 August 1988

Seamus Morris was born on 14 January 1970. He was the oldest son of five children born to his parents Seamus and Madeline who had been married on 8 August the previous year. He had two brothers (Conor and Kieran) and two sisters (Lisa and Roisin). Seamus went to Holy Cross Boys school and then after passing his 11-plus, went to St Malachy's grammar school. He grew up in Brompton Park, where most of his closest friends were to be found, although his family moved to Highbury Gardens shortly before his death. Throughout his youth he was a keen Gaelic football player. Seamus played for St Malachy's with whom he won an Ulster medal. In his early teens Seamus benefited from a project that took children from school to stay for a time with a family in the US away from the conflict. After he left school Seamus worked for a time for the civil service and then started a government work training scheme with his brother Conor. By this time Seamus had been seeing a girl, Elaine Shevlin and the two had begun to make plans for the future. On the morning of his death Seamus and Conor were standing outside Whelan's shop in Etna Drive on their way to enjoy a game of snooker. A car containing three loyalist gunmen pulled up alongside them and opened fire. Seamus was killed instantly. As they drove away the loyalists also shot and killed another man, Peter Dolan from Andersontown. Peter was travelling in a lorry that tried to prevent Seamus' killers from making good their escape. Seamus Morris was only 18-years-old when he was shot dead. He was the random victim of a purely sectarian attack. Being a Catholic from Ardoyne made him a legitimate target in the eyes of loyalists.

Conor, Kieran, Lisa and Roisin Morris (brothers and sisters)

Seamus was our big brother and we loved him to bits. He was a quiet lad, everybody will tell you. Even when he was young he helped raise the youngest ones in the family. Seamus was the eldest and looked after us; he never let us down. There was no hassle with him and he always did what we wanted. Our ma worked night shift for years, first in Mossley Mill, then for a long time in Edenderry and finally in Mallusk. Seamus was the one who watched us and got us up in the morning. Him and Conor were working in Boucher Road together and Conor would lie on to the last minute. But Seamus was up from the crack of dawn, getting ready and fixing his hair. He was always in front of the mirror as he liked to look his best. When he was at school he went over to America, as part of a project that took children away from the troubles. The family that took him asked our ma if they could take Seamus back over to America and put him through college. But our mummy didn't want him to go because he was still so young. He was only 14. It is actually documented though that Seamus was the only 'project child' who was killed in the troubles. Seamus also played Gaelic football with Conor for years. It was great, two brothers playing for St Malachy's together. We used to trail our wee brother Kieran with us to watch the games in Casement Park trying to get him interested but he wasn't keen at all. Seamus was into music as well, Pink Floyd, things like that. The first concert he ever went to was the Jesus and Mary Chain along with his mate Paddy. The two of them were all dressed in a check suit and straw hat. Everyone around them was all in black from head to toe. What fools they felt; we had such a laugh about that. He was just an 18-year-old who went along with the in-thing at the time; that was him. He didn't go out to clubs and wasn't a big drinker. He loved his snooker though, and that is where he was heading, for a game in Ta Lockey's, when he was killed.

Conor: Seamus was killed on Monday, 8 August 1988, at about 11.15 am. Seamus and I should have been in the Tech that day but the instructor didn't show; we came home. Seamus phoned and arranged to meet his girl later that morning, but first we were going to play a game of snooker. I remember a knock came to the door. Seamus called me and told me my mates were at the door.; it was the Jehovah's Witnesses. They had me for about half an hour. I could hear Seamus and my ma laughing the whole time upstairs in the bedroom; mum had worked the night-shift the night before so she was still in bed. The two of them thought this was hilarious. Seamus went on out and I met him halfway down the street and he was still laughing. So I said, 'Come on, let's go for a game of snooker'. We went down to Whelan's shop where we stopped to talk to big Martin McClafferty. That was when it happened. I was standing right beside Seamus when a car pulled up alongside us. I heard the bang, put my head down and saw the gun. I got a few yards down the road before I realised what was happening. I turned round to see that Seamus was dead, and that was the hardest moment of my life. There were three loyalist gunmen, two in the front and one with an AK rifle in the back. The one in the back had fired from the car; they didn't get out. Seamus was hit five times, four in the body and one in the head. He was killed instantly. They fired at the three of us, Seamus, me and Big Martin, but only Seamus got hit. I think they concentrated on making sure that they got one. The car sped off towards Flax Street. There was a beer lorry there and the guy driving it tried to ram the car to prevent the killers from making good their escape, but the loyalists fired at the lorry and shot the passenger, Peter Dolan, dead. He was from Andytown, he was shot in the groin. The driver of the beer lorry tried to take him straight to the hospital but he was stopped by the cops in Flax Street. They [RUC] took Peter Dolan from the beer lorry and into the jeep. He died just after getting to the hospital.

It wasn't even his [Peter Dolan's] job, working on the lorry that day. He was just filling in for someone who was off sick. Apparently they drew straws and Peter drew the shortest one. The fella who was supposed to be working that day was Fr. Kenneth's brother. Fr. Kenneth had come down to comfort us straight after Seamus' death while he still thought that the passenger in the lorry was his own brother. There he was consoling us and not once did he say that he thought that his brother had been shot too. About a year after, we got a phone call from the CID informing us that they were 99%

sure that they knew who had been the trigger man. It was a UVF man apparently called Brian Robinson who had just been shot dead by the British army, although not until after Robinson had killed Paddy McKenna as well [from Farringdon Court, killed by the UVF on 2 August 1989 amid allegations of possible collusion]. When Seamus was shot, the driver of the car had a pistol, the gun that Peter Dolan was shot with, and apparently it was the same pistol that Paddy McKenna was killed with too. Seamus had been going with a girl before he was killed, Elaine, a lovely wee girl. They had a good time together and they were going places. Elaine ended up as a schoolteacher. A month after Seamus was killed we got a letter offering him an accountant's job back with the civil service. Elaine took Seamus' death really badly; it just wrecked her. She came and visited my mum every Sunday for years after. My mum looked forward to seeing her as did the rest of us; she was like part of the family. She even asked for mum's approval to go with someone else years later. My mother died of cancer about four years after Seamus' death and we definitely believe there was a connection. Seamus getting killed destroyed her and she got the cancer less than a year later. For us, not just one person was killed; it totally destroyed the whole family. My father took it really bad and to this day he still cannot bring himself to talk about it; it just hurts too much. The loyalists took Seamus from everybody. He was a loving son, a great big brother and most of all a best friend; we loved him. It is something that you never get over. I know that our Lisa feels that it ruined her life and that she has never felt the same afterwards. She should have been finishing school when it happened. She just couldn't go back because she couldn't bring herself to go near where Seamus was shot. Lisa moved out of Ardoyne not long after and finds it difficult to come back to the district because of that.

The day Seamus was killed was my sister Roisin's birthday; she was 13. The same day was my mum and dad's wedding anniversary too. That was it, there was birth, death and marriage in the same family on the same day. My father and mother were married on 8 August, Roisin was born on 8 August and Seamus was killed on 8 August. The 8th of the 8th '88 was the day Seamus was killed, such an unlucky number. We just stopped celebrating Roisin's birthday and my parents' wedding anniversary after his death. And there was no Christmas in our house; it was never Christmas for us after that day. Seamus was just the nicest guy you could have met. He had such a lot to live for, a smart guy with a lot going for him. He wasn't just a brother to me; there was only a year between us, he was a great friend to me as well. We were the best of mates and went everywhere together. No one could replace him. We all really miss him; we miss him all the time.

Elaine Shevlin (girlfriend)

I met Seamus in March 1988 when he was sitting with his best friend, Patrick Connolly, on the wall at the bottom of Brompton Park. He used to sit with his friends at that corner. On bright evenings, when it was lovely, everybody used to sit out. It was so tragic that he was eventually killed there. At first we were just friends but a great spark developed between us, even at such a young age. I was just 14 at the time. His friend Paddy started going out with my cousin Tracey. Seamus and I were like chaperones for them at first; that was how we got to know one another. He often appeared shy to people at first because he used to just take in what was going on around him. He had a lovely smile, a sparkle in his eyes and a great sense of humour. Seamus was always impeccably dressed and he was very, very attractive. He was just a gorgeous and a beautiful person. He had a lively personality, a great wit and there was a very sensitive side to him as well. Seamus was very family-orientated; he adored his family and he was the big brother and protector of them all. He was very close to his younger brother Conor in particular. It was a young, innocent relationship. Seamus was my first love. In some ways that can never be beaten or broken. Everything about it was perfect and beautiful and that hasn't been changed with time. His death was so tragic and hard to get through. I found it difficult to cope for a long time, although I was helped through it by my best friend and future husband, the Morris family and my parents. Seamus and I used to just do teenage things together. We would go for walks around the Waterworks, sometimes went to Ta Lockey's to play snooker or pool and went into town a few times. After a while Seamus became a regular visitor to my house and we used to sit listening to records and talking for hours. The last record he ever bought was a Tracey Chapman tape, 'Talkin' about a Revolution', the Thursday night before he was killed. There is one of the songs in particular, 'Baby can I hold you?', that is still so poignant and disturbing when I listen to it today. It helped me to get through everything and at the same time tortured me to listen to it. The day before Seamus was killed was a Sunday. I remember he told me that he couldn't sleep and had got up early and gone to mass. He wasn't really that religious and that is something that has always just stuck in my mind. The next day was the Monday and I received a phone call from Seamus at around 10.50 am. That surprised me because he would usually have been at the Tech at that time. He asked me to go for a walk and I said that I would get ready and meet up with him at about midday. We were going to go up to the Waterworks so I said I would meet him at the corner on Brompton Park, where we always met. I was getting ready when I heard the shots. I remember that very clearly. I knew the shooting was close so I just had a sense of uneasiness. I was coming down the stairs when the phone rang. It was my cousin Tracey phoning from my granny's house, just around the corner in Jamaica Street. She told me that Seamus had been shot. Tracey had gone around and witnessed the aftermath. At first I thought she was joking. Then my granny came on the phone and I passed it over to my mother. I remember her trying to put her arm around me and saying, 'Elaine, Seamus has been shot and they think he is dead'. I just felt the same sense of disbelief as I feel today. I think I tried to run out of the house at that stage, fighting everybody off. I did manage to get up the street and some of the neighbours came out. News spreads so quickly and the neighbours in Moutainview were very good. Some of them brought me back down to the house. I think I was given some tablets and by that stage things were just unreal and very difficult to comprehend. My parents were very supportive under such difficult circumstances; my dad took me down to Seamus' house. I remember still thinking that I had to go down to meet Seamus. I was saying to people that I had to go, that he was waiting for me. Then I remember thinking that I shouldn't have arranged to meet him on the corner, that I should have told him to come up to my house. That was the whole thing with the words of the Tracey Chapman song, 'Baby, if I told you the right words, at the right time'. I thought that if I hadn't said I would meet him at the corner then he wouldn't have been there then. I know everybody says the same sort of thing; we all blame ourselves. Seamus was supposed to have been at the Tech but the instructor was sick so he had come home. I know the instructor was from Ardoyne and I am sure he had to cope with a sense of guilt as well. But there was just such a set of circumstances that meant that he was there at that moment. At the end of the day, I suppose he was meant to be there, but it is very hard to understand why.

When I got to Seamus' house his whole family were there and his mother, Madeleine, was in an awful state. That was the first time I had really met Seamus' mother and father and they were so good to me, they really were. I don't know how I could have got through those years without their help. I was such a very small part of Seamus' life and his mother, who had lost her first-born child and saw her poor son lying dead at the corner, she was just so good to me. I could not praise Seamus' family enough; they were so supportive, so giving and caring to me. I was a young teenage girl going through horrendous emotions and Madeleine brought me in as if I were her own daughter. It had such a profound effect on me because Seamus had been such a special, caring, considerate person. He had a great love of his family and was loyal to his friends. I can't find the words to say what a lovely person he was with his great sparkling eyes and his sense of humour. I feel honoured to have known Seamus, to have shared his life and grown close to him that fateful summer. I known we were meant to be together. It was so tragic that his life was cut so short when things were just beginning to look up for him. It had such a devastating effect on his family. They all went through such terrible suffering and immeasurable loss. It was all so unfair. Why?

Brendan Whiteway (friend)

Seamus grew up in the same street and he lived about six or seven doors above me. There was a whole crowd of us who hung about together growing up. There was myself, Seamus and Conor, Thomas and Martin Begley [Thomas Begley, killed on active service, Shankill Road, 23 October 1993], Tommy and Mark Mervyn. Most of us went to school together, the Holy Cross, and then on to St Gabriel's, though Seamus and Conor passed the 11-plus so they went on to St Malachy's. But after school, we were all back together in the same street, just kids, running about in wee gangs, like most kids. Old Ardoyne was getting knocked down about then so we used to go into the houses for the scrap, lead and copper mainly, and get a bit of money together, particularly during the summer. Every summer, when we were about nine or ten we all used to go to Bray, County Wicklow as part of a summer trip scheme. It was with the Ardoyne Youth Club. That was how we spent our summers, running about, trying to stay out of mischief, playing best man's fall in people's gardens, rapping doors in the dark when no-one could see us and playing football. Seamie played as a winger or a striker, though he played more GAA. He ended up playing for the Kickhams. I think he was still with them when he was killed. That's what we grew up with. When we were in our late teens we'd play a bit of snooker, have a little bet on the football or the odd horse, play a bit of darts.

Seamus didn't have any political views; none of us did really. We were just growing up, having fun and trying to keep ourselves out of trouble. He was down-to-earth and easy-going, that's the way I would describe Seamie. He would have gone places in life because he was very smart. Conor and him both made a real effort with school. He was just beginning to learn about computers, which at that time would have been a real asset. I'm sure he would have ended up with a really well-paid job. He always kept himself straight, fit, well-dressed and well-groomed. When we got a bit older, me and Seamie sort of broke away a bit and used to hang about together at the bottom corner of the street, at Lizzie Whelan's garden. We just played cards at night-time and sat with a few drinks, chit chatting. As the years went on, me and Seamie used to dander across the Antrim Road, round the Waterworks and across the Bone, just going for walks looking for girls, as boys do. He met Elaine Shevlin, who was from Mountainview, through me. I had a bit of a thing for her cousin at the time. They were going together at the time Seamie was killed. It always looked like something that was going to carry on for a long time.

Right up until the day Seamie died we would all spend a lot of our time up in Ta Lockey's playing a bit of snooker. Lizzie Whelan's corner was our corner. There were a lot of us who always hung about there playing cards and talking till the early hours. Whoever pulled the gun on Seamie may have known that we were always there. The loyalist killers probably did a couple of pre-runs and they couldn't have missed the fact that as soon as the summer came there was always life about that corner. It was our corner, until that fateful morning that Seamus was killed. I was in the house that morning. He had called up for me earlier. Then I saw him standing down at Lizzie Whelan's wall. I went back up to the house to get myself ready and meet up with him. I was standing in the bathroom when I heard the gunfire. I ran down the path and saw the crowd gathering at the corner of the street. I pushed my way through the crowd, looked at the ground and saw Seamus lying there dead. I knew he was dead as soon as I looked at him. It is something that has always lived with me that when I saw him lying there dead I just walked back up the street to the house and told my mummy that Seamie had been shot dead. Then I went out into the yard, lifted a mop bucket, filled it with soapy water and started washing my da's car. Fr. Kenneth, who was the rector at the time, went flying past running down the street to give Seamie the last rites. People were going past me as I washed the car saying, 'Seamie's dead. Does Brendy know?' I just carried on washing the car. I knew he was dead but it was just an instinct to do something normal. I was just in shock; basically I just couldn't understand it. I thought I would wake up and it was all like a dream. It is a sad world that we live in that somebody as innocent as Seamie could be taken away just because he was a Catholic. I still go up to the graveyard five or six times a year to tend to his grave and sit and talk to him. I have never forgotten about him and I keep my own memories of him – not so much about the way he met his demise but about all of us growing up and the laughs we had. I go up and talk to him out loud, tell him how I am getting on and how everyone else is doing, just to keep in contact with him. I see Conor up there sometimes. He was devastated by what happened. Seamie's whole family was devastated really because they were all very, very close. His mummy got cancer after Seamie was murdered and she just went downhill, just gave up the fight. Seamie's gone but in a sense he is not gone because his family and friends always keep him in their minds.

> *Then they started shooting my husband. We fell beside each other like spoons in a drawer. They kept shooting him and I thought it would never stop. I screamed out, 'Please, please don't shoot him; he is an old man.'*

Davy Braniff
Killed by loyalists,
Alliance Avenue,
19 March 1989

Davy Braniff was born a Protestant and came originally from Snugville Street, just off the Shankill Road. He later moved to Alliance Parade near Ardoyne. He attended Everton School. Davy's father and brothers worked in the shipyards, as did Davy for a time. That is where he trained as a plumber but went on to work as a steel erector. Davy also liked to go dancing. It was in the Avoca Street dance hall that he met a young Mary McDonnell. Mary was a Catholic, originally from Nazarene Street off the Falls Road, who had recently moved up to Ardoyne. In 1945 the pair married in London where they had gone to find work. Davy had also converted to Catholicism. Davy and Mary soon had a family of their own. They set up home in a two-bedroom house in Jamaica Street. They eventually added a third bedroom to house their 13 children (Mary, David, Patrick, Anne, Billy, Brian, Joseph, Geraldine, Anthony, Catherine, Sheila, Theresa and Thomas). Davy was a hard-working man and turned his hand to whatever he needed to do to provide for his family. In his time off, Davy (or Curly as he was known by friends because of his dark curly hair) liked to play darts and cards. He also supported Manchester United and Celtic football clubs. Even before Davy's death the family was far from untouched by grief. His daughter Mary died in childbirth on 12 August 1975. Later, and maybe worst of all, Davy's son Anthony (a volunteer in the IRA) was shot dead by the same organisation as an alleged informer in 1981. The family has always denied the claim. Anthony's death had a terrible effect on Davy to whom he was particularly close. On 19 March 1989 Davy was in the kitchen of his home saying the rosary with his wife. UFF gunmen burst into the house and made their way to the kitchen and living room. Two of them shot Davy Braniff dead while the other gunman held his daughter Sheila and granddaughter Jane at gunpoint. Davy was 63 years old and left behind not only a wife but by now 11 children and 60 grandchildren. The killing of Davy Braniff was a blatant sectarian attack.

Mary Braniff (wife)

All of my family were raised in Jamaica Street. We had seven boys and six girls. Davy was a very good person. He was very good-hearted. When I met Davy, I was only 16. I remember when he brought me to meet his mother she asked me to go upstairs to one of the bedrooms to get a parcel. I did this; so she opened it and said, 'This is the sash that David's father wore.' I didn't realise what she was talking about but I later discovered that they never wanted me to marry Davy. But our love for each other was very strong and we got married in 1945 and of course Davy converted to Catholicism. In doing this he had to go for catechism every week; he stuck to this with great conviction and as our marriage progressed Davy became in my eyes a devout Catholic. The night he was killed was Palm Sunday and we had been to mass earlier that morning. Davy was upset to find there was no palm left in the church to bring home. Little did we know that Davy would be dead that same evening. We were saying the rosary at home and were on the second decade of the glorious mysteries when the gunmen kicked the door off its hinges. I remember there were three of them. One went to the sitting room and the other two stood there for what seemed forever (though I now know was only moments). Then they started shooting my husband. We fell beside each other like spoons in a drawer. They kept shooting him and I thought it would never stop. I screamed out, ' Please, please don't shoot him; he is an old man.' My whole family took what had happened to their father very hard. My youngest son Thomas took it particularly hard. All of my children would visit on a Sunday. That Sunday they didn't come round, so thank God they weren't there because they too may have been killed. I'll end by telling you about Davy's funeral. It was huge and I never saw a funeral like it in my life. It seemed as if the whole of Ardoyne was there. Some of my 60 grandchildren were singing and Bishop Daly presided over the mass. I also remember one of my children telling me that when they looked around the cortege looked like a river of people flowing slowly behind them. I will always love him and my faith will keep me strong in my defence.

Sheila (daughter)

On the night my father was killed three gunmen burst into our home. One of them held my niece Jane at gunpoint. I tried to get up from my chair but the gunman just signalled to get down. I was on my knees on the floor squealing, 'Please don't shoot my daddy, please don't shoot him'. The gunmen never spoke a word; it all seemed so very professional. They were dressed in black from head to toe. After the shooting stopped the gunmen backed out still pointing their guns. I ran after them but one of the other men who was in the car started banging the window and pointing towards me. At that one of them turned back, pointed the gun at me and backed off into the waiting car. I ran back into the kitchen, but when I got there I could see two bodies lying on the floor. My mummy was wrapped around my daddy and there was blood everywhere. I thought that they were both dead. Then my mummy sat up and I just thought, 'She's alive, she is alive'. The first thing she said was, 'Quick, get the holy water,' which I did. Then I ran out squealing for help and the neighbours started running in. It was horrific, really terrible. What was terrible too is that none of the family visited that day as most of them normally did. I can remember what I was thinking once the shooting stopped. I know it might seem strange but I was saying to myself, 'What will happen when they find out daddy is dead?' Then I ran up the street to my sister Cathy's house. I was screaming, 'Daddy's dead' and we both ran back to the family home. My brothers Joe and Paddy were running down also. When we got to the house the police had arrived. We were treated with hatred and bitterness by the RUC. I know they had to get into the house to do whatever they had to do but my brother's wouldn't let them touch daddy. Then they lifted him into the mortuary van. My father will never be forgotten and he will be loved and remembered by his family and friends. My daddy was a very loving father and he was always there for us; he worked hard all of his life.

Billy Braniff (son)

My father and mother got married in 1945. My dad's family didn't get on too well with him after that because he gave up his Protestant tradition as he loved my mum so much. As their family growing up, we could see how much they loved each other. My dad was shot dead in 1989. My mum and dad were in the kitchen of their home in Alliance Avenue when three gunmen burst in. One of them went to the living room and held my sister Sheila and my daughter Jane at gunpoint. The other two went to the kitchen and between them shot my father nine times in the head and torso. My mother lay at his side the whole time pleading, 'Don't kill him; he is an old man; please don't kill my husband.' Her cries fell on deaf ears and they just kept on shooting. The gunmen couldn't have known my mother and father were saying the rosary as they both said it every night. I can remember my daughter Jane running into our home screaming, 'Granda Braniff has been shot.' I ran to my parents' house in what seemed like moments. In the kitchen my dad lay bleeding. I still remember clearly that he was lying on his right side and I could see his rosary beads still in his hands. There was nothing I could do but pray. The rest of my family started arriving and then it was total pandemonium. I remember my dad still feeling warm to the touch. We all said our goodbyes to him as he lay on the floor. The heartache my family went through was horrific and the pain still goes on. No one ever claimed responsibility for the murder of my father, but we, the family, know who did it. To this day, through all her pain and loss, my mum still prays for the people who murdered him.

> *I have no doubt that the British army and RUC could have prevented Paddy being killed … The Angel of Death was sitting at the top of Brompton Park and the other undercover agent was at the roundabout. The British army had information that a UVF squad was going to hit somebody at the front of the road that morning, but instead of preventing it, they decided to let them kill someone.*

Paddy McKenna
Killed by loyalists,
Crumlin Road,
2 September 1989

Paddy McKenna was 43 years of age when he was shot dead by loyalists in front of undercover British army soldiers on the Crumlin Road in 1989. Paddy was the son of Catherine and Joseph McKenna. He had five sisters and one brother. The family had originally lived in Carolina Street in Sailortown before moving to Cranbrook Gardens in the 1950s. An exceptional goalkeeper, Paddy played for a host of local teams in the area, as well as winning trophies with other Belfast clubs. In the years before he died, Paddy was living in the family home with his mother Catherine and cousin Stephen Murphy. He had been working for the Corporation but had been forced to give up the job due to loyalist intimidation. Paddy had been seriously injured in the 1970s when loyalists posted him a booby-trapped Valentine's Day card, which blew up in his face.

Paddy was shot dead as he walked along the Crumlin Road on the morning of Saturday 2 September 1989. He was shot 11 times by UVF gunman Brian Robinson, who was a pillion passenger on a motorbike. An undercover British army unit was in the immediate vicinity of the shooting and witnessed Paddy's killing. Minutes later Brian Robinson was shot dead by a female undercover soldier, dubbed the Angel of Death, who was herself later questioned during investigations into a number of killings involving collusion between loyalists and the British army.

Joe McKenna (brother)

Paddy was the youngest of the family; there was Peggy, Sally, Tina, Bridget, Alice, myself and then Paddy. We were burnt out of our house in Cranbrook Gardens during internment in 1971. Everyone that was burnt out stayed in the school until they found somewhere to live. Paddy and my mother eventually moved to Farringdon Court. As a teenager Paddy spent a long time in hospital; he had a hair lip and no palate but they couldn't do much for him in those days. Paddy had a lot of friends. He was a great goalkeeper. A lot of the teams he played for were mixed religion. Paddy was football crazy; he would have played football 24 hours a day. He played for Crumlin Star, John Paul and Ardoyne Youth Club. When he was with Dunmurry Rec, they won the league. He had loads of medals and trophies for football, but they were all lost when my mother's house was burnt in Cranbrook.

Ewarts Mill was Paddy's first job. When we were burnt out in 1971, Ewarts sent him his cards saying that they had to get somebody in to take his place. They were looking rid of him because he was a Catholic; it's as simple as that. Then he got a job in the Corporation as a bin man. He swept the streets around Smithfield. Paddy never married, although I think he always had an eye for one girl in particular. After we all grew up and my mother and father died, it was only Paddy in the house. Around this time the loyalists were giving Paddy a terrible time. A lot of them knew him from when we were living in Cranbrook and they were always hassling him. He eventually had to give up his job street cleaning because they were always deliberately sending him to loyalist areas. In 1974/75 the loyalists sent Paddy a bomb in a Valentine's Day card. It exploded and he was badly scarred around the face.

Paddy was shot at 10 o'clock, Saturday morning. My son-in-law phoned to tell me and I ran round to the shops. I lifted Paddy up, but as soon as I lifted him I knew he was dead. Paddy had been helping Tina Gallagher in her fruit shop. He had just left the shop when he was shot. He gave her a hand every Saturday morning to put out her stall. The two loyalists were on a motorbike. A loyalist called Robinson jumped off the motorbike and shot Paddy dead. Two undercover British soldiers sat and watched the whole thing. The woman soldier, who was dubbed the Angel of Death, was sitting at Brompton Park in an Astra, the other undercover soldier was sitting at the roundabout, covering the Shankill. The two of them watched the whole thing happening. When Robinson and the other guy sped off on the motorbike, the Angel of Death went after them. There were roadworks at Flax Street and the motorbike slowed down to go into Cambria Street. Her car hit the bike and they came off and she shot Robinson as he lay on the ground at the bus stop. Days after, they had a shrine set up at the spot where Robinson was shot. On the Monday the cops closed the road off; when they were asked why, they said that a VIP clergyman was coming to pray at the spot where Robinson was shot; you can guess who the clergyman was.

I have no doubt that the British army and RUC could have prevented Paddy being killed. I think anybody on the front of the road that morning was getting it. Later they said it was just a passing patrol that came on the scene, but it wasn't. The Angel of Death was sitting at the top of Brompton Park and the other undercover agent was at the roundabout. The British army had information that a UVF squad was going to hit somebody at the front of the road that morning, but instead of preventing it, they decided to let them kill someone.

Tina Gallagher (friend)

I knew Paddy from we were kids. Paddy just lived across the street. He always helped me out in the fruit shop, weighing out potatoes, lifting veg in and out. He was a good friend. On the Saturday morning he was killed I asked Paddy to help me out. At the time he was shot Paddy, myself and my daughter Carly were just coming out of our shop. Paddy and Carly had walked out of the shop and I was talking to someone on my way out the door. The next minute I heard noises; then the gunman just seemed to be there. He had a helmet on… and the next minute bang, bang. But it was like everything had slowed down and I saw Paddy falling. Paddy wasn't even moving and the gunman came right over and shot him another ten times. Then he just jumped on the motorbike and sped off and a car followed them. We had noticed a particular car moving around all morning. We didn't think; we just noticed the car; you were always aware of unusual things because you were on the front of the road. I think that the Brits and RUC knew what was going to happen, maybe not to Paddy, but to someone. I don't think they meant to kill Brian Robinson but I think they did it to say, 'Look, we're here, we're on the ball; we are looking out for the Catholics'. But they allowed the loyalists to shoot Paddy and did nothing.

Patricia McClaferty and Una Smith (friends)

I first met Paddy when he was helping rebuild the houses in Farringdon that were burnt out by the loyalists. Paddy was a kind person; if he won in the bookies he would always share his winnings. I remember when the loyalists sent him a Valentine's Day bomb. His mother kept the card in the house all day until he came home. He opened it at the door and it blew up in his face. After that he was living on his nerves. He seemed to think that they were coming back to get him. Paddy loved music; he loved Linda Rondstat and country music. He had thousands of LPs. He was very self-conscious because of his speech impediment but he was relaxed with us. About nine months before Paddy was killed, we were in the youth club and we had a stupid argument. He asked me, 'Will you come to my funeral?' Then he just said, 'I'm going to be killed soon'.

Paddy was a good friend, he really was; you didn't realise it until he was gone; you didn't realise how good he was. The night after Paddy was killed, we were driving out on the Crumlin Road for petrol and the loyalists were making a shrine where Brian Robinson was shot, but there wasn't a thing about Paddy being killed, just Robinson.

Gerard Burns
Killed by the INLA,
New Barnsley Park,
West Belfast,
29 June 1991

I would just like to know the truth and I would like someone to come and tell me why my brother was shot three times. Why would he become an informer for them? Can somebody come and tell me what was really behind all this? After all these years, I want to know.

Gerard 'Skin' Burns was born on 21 November 1953, the son of John and Jane (née Brown) of 125 Jamaica Street. John Burns was known to most people as 'Rocky'. He was a clothes dealer and originally came from the Falls Road area. His mother Jane was from Carrick Hill. They were married in 1938. Gerard was the second youngest boy of six children, one of whom had died at birth. The five surviving children were all brought up in the family home in Jamaica Street. Gerard attended the Holy Cross Boys school and St Gabriel's along with his brother John. When he left school, he worked in the cutting room of what was then known as the Beltex factory. Like most young boys, Gerard was full of mischief. He and John were always at loggerheads with each other. However, when the conflict began, Gerard grew up before his time as he became one of those who defended his district. Gerard was shot on three occasions during the early 1970s. The first time was on the morning of internment; he was shot four times and seriously wounded by the British army on the Crumlin Road. Then he was shot by loyalists at the top of Ardoyne Avenue. Finally he was shot in the leg by a member of the paras following rioting in the Bone. In 1972 Gerard was arrested and convicted for throwing nail bombs. He served his time in the 'Officials' Cage, Cage 21. Gerard was someone who always took his political commitments seriously. In 1975 Gerard was released and was a member of the INLA. By then he had married his wife Olive Johnstone who was originally from Divis Flats in West Belfast. They set up home in Oldpark Avenue and had three children, two boys and a girl (Gerard, Karan and Darran). However, the marriage did not last. Later, Gerard moved in with his new partner, Mary and her two children in Kingston Court, Ardoyne. By then he was working in the Jamaica Inn and spent much of his spare time either participating in various club teams or organising events for charities.

He was, however, still also a member of the INLA. Feuds within the ranks of the movement led Gerard, along with many others, to seek refuge in the South on a number of occasions. He spent six months in Dundalk in the year prior to his death. Gerard was interrogated by other members of the INLA on 29 June 1991. The next morning his body was found at the bottom of a back garden in New Barnsley Park in West Belfast. His arms and feet were tied; he was gagged and blindfolded and had been shot three times in the head. During Gerard's wake a member of the INLA read out a prepared statement to the family alleging that Gerard had been killed as a paid RUC informer. It was a claim denied by members of his family.

Mary Burns (sister)

Gerard was always known as 'Skin' because of his light build. My other brother was known as 'Fat' because he was well-built. Gerard was always quiet and just mingled with other boys his own age. After the troubles started Gerard was injured and later imprisoned. He was shot in the back in 1971 by the British army and the Knights of Malta tended to him in the school in Butler Street. Afterward the Brits would re-open his wound by unpicking the stitches with a pencil. My mother and sister would have to take him back down to the Knights of Malta to get them re-done. Shortly after, he ended up in gaol for the attempted murder of seven soldiers in Jamaica Street. He was in Crumlin Road gaol first and then he was in Long Kesh for quite a number of years. I remember when he got out of gaol, I just came walking into the house, after all those years, and there he was just standing in the kitchen shaving. I couldn't believe it. I hadn't known he was due for release.

Gerard knew a lot of people in Ardoyne. Among his old friends were John Fennell, Joe Matthews, Victor Cummings, Brendan Bradley and Seamus Clarke. He socialised in the Highfield Club that used to be in Etna Drive and he used to play a bit of football on Oldpark playing fields. Not long after he got out of prison he married a girl called Olive, from Divis Flats. They set up home on Oldpark Avenue and had two boys and a girl. Olive and Gerard split up later, although Gerard always tried to look out for the children. He would go and visit them as often as he could when Olive moved with them to England soon after. Gerard then lived with a girl called Mary from Ardoyne in Kingston Court. He was living there and working in the Jamaica Inn when he was killed. Gerard had also been in our house when it went on fire. He and my daddy escaped with burns but my mother was killed trying to save my first-born. That incident had a terrible effect on all the family, especially Gerard.

Gerard died on 29 June 1991. He was 37 years old. Gerard was found with his arms and legs tied. He was barefoot and blindfolded. His mouth was taped and he was dressed in a boiler suit. Apparently he had been questioned by the INLA all night. At one point it would appear he tried to get away by jumping through a window but it didn't work. His body was found near Ballymurphy, in the back of garden in New Barnsley Park. He had been shot three times in the head and his body was thrown over the wall of the garden. A fourth bullet hit the garden wall. He was shot as an alleged informer by the INLA. I was at home when I heard that my brother had been killed. This was on the Sunday, at about 4 pm or 5 pm. A priest from the Sacred Heart chapel on the Oldpark Road came to tell me. I was just sitting having a cup of tea and I hadn't heard the news so the priest told me our Gerard was dead. I just broke down and started crying; I couldn't take it in. The priest took me to Tennent Street police station but first I went up to try and tell my brother Davy. But he wasn't in. I also went over to tell Gerard's girlfriend, Mary, in Kingston Court. She screamed and broke down when I told her. My sister Bell was also there with her daughter Sharon and I had to break the news to her too. Bell took it very, very badly and the priest had to try and console her and calm her down. It was Bell and I that had to go down to the morgue and identify the body. During Gerard's wake a member of the INLA read out a statement to the family from that organisation stating why they said they killed him –

although personally I wasn't listening. Some people went up the stairs to talk to a priest while the statement was being read. I didn't, but I didn't want to listen to it either. We buried Gerard from Kingston Court.

The RUC never came near us and never came to tell me that my brother was dead or anything else. What I would really like to know is where the INLA got their information from that Gerard was a police informer. I would like to know why he was shot because, within my own heart, I don't believe the accusations that were made against him. He did not do what he was accused of. Gerard was not a police informer. I don't believe he was getting paid as an informer because he never had any money. Gerard's girlfriend and my eldest brother were taken upstairs on the day of the funeral to be told by a member of the INLA as to what had happened but my sister and I wouldn't go. I didn't want to listen to that on the day of his funeral.

Gerard was a down-to-earth person who wouldn't let anybody harass or hassle him. I would just like to know the truth and I would like someone to come and tell me why my brother was shot three times. His face and head were shot, his jaw was broken and I had to go and identify that body, my brother's body. I want to know why they brought his body up an alleyway and shot him while he was lying on his back. I want the RUC to come and tell me if he was a police informer. He was always being lifted by the RUC from the Oldpark police station. The army had my mother tortured with coming in and out when we all lived in Jamaica Street. So why would he become an informer for them? Can somebody come and tell me what was really behind all this? After all these years, I want to know.

Joe Matthews (friend)

Skin's father and uncle were both local clothes dealers. When he was growing up, Skin used to get a bit of slagging from other kids about that. But Skin's father, Rocky Burns, was a real character. I came from Stratford Gardens and Gerard came from nearby Jamaica Street. There was a group of eight or nine of us who grew up together. There was Skin [Gerard], Seamus Clarke, Paddy Teer and others. We were all really close. We used to get up to all the deeds of the day but there was no bad harm in it. Nobody had any money in those days. This was back before 1969. Skin never had much of an interest in school, like the rest of us. Growing up at the start of the troubles your main problem in school was getting to and fro without getting into any trouble with the RUC or the ones from Somerdale. Skin would always have been in the front line if anything did happen. He was as game as a badger. If there was rioting going on we always hung around at Alliance Avenue because there were always problems with Alliance Road and Glenbryn. At the start of the conflict Skin would have been involved in rioting and I remember he joined the Fianna of the 'Sticks' ['Official' IRA] in 1970. He was shot in Ardoyne Avenue in the early troubles by a member of the UVF. There was rioting going on and the next thing this fella came out with a .22 rifle and shot Skin in the neck. After that Skin always had that bullet lodged in his neck. They were afraid to operate on it because it was too close to a nerve and he might have ended up paralysed. He was shot on two other occasions. In 1971 he was shot over by St Gemma's school. He was hit four times in the back from a sterling sub-machine gun during another riot by the Brits. He was in a bad way that time. I think he went down South to recover but it wasn't long before he was back again. Anywhere he went that summer Skin would take his shirt off and show off his war wounds. Then he was shot again, in the leg this time, when he was up at the front of the [Crumlin] road. That was during another riot. A passing car opened up. I'm not sure if that was the police or loyalists. That all happened within about a year or 18 months. Skin had bullet holes all over him and nobody could ever understand how he was still alive.

He did a couple of years inside in the early 1970s when he got caught with a nail bomb. He was in at the time of the Long Kesh burning. People have told me that Skin was the same inside as out. If there was anything to be done people would give Skin a call and he would do it. When he came out of jail Skin stayed with me for a while and he was different to before. He was always well-groomed and spotless and when he was talking about politics, he would use words that I could only understand half the time. He had definitely had a political education while he was in jail. This was about 1974 or 1975 when the INLA was formed. Skin went into jail as a volunteer of the 'Official' IRA and came out a volunteer of the INLA. They were strong at that time and had broken from the 'Official' IRA because they wanted to be more militarily active. That would have been a major motivation for Skin joining them. The fact that most of the people he was active with in Ardoyne before he went inside had also gone over to the INLA was also important. As far as I know he was a member of the INLA until the day he died.

Skin was staying with me at the time that there was a fire in his mother's house. We were just going down Etna Drive when we saw that the house was burning. We rushed round and as we got there, Skin's brother Fat came rushing out the door. I remember Joe McAlea was in a terrible state because he had seen one of Skin's sister's children stuck upstairs through the window. There was no hope for the wee one and the child died in the fire. Skin's mother had also been caught in the fire and died of her burns two weeks later. It was really terrible. After the fire Skin was devastated. Around that time, after his marriage had ended, Skin fell for a girl called Patricia Varndell. She later committed suicide and that really wrecked Skin too. Skin and I were also in the Shamrock the night that Larry Kennedy was killed [Larry Kennedy, killed by the UFF in the Shamrock social club, 8 October 1981]. We heard the rattle of gunfire from the doorway and everyone ducked to get out of the way. But Skin was one of the first ones out of the door. He was throwing stones at the car as the gunmen were making their getaway. One of them was hanging out of the door firing shots behind him. There was no doubt about it, Skin had nerves of steel.

Skin always maintained his links with the INLA. People who were involved together always kept close and sort of looked out for each other. That was important in the days when the feuds were going on. When the connection with Harry Kirkpatrick developed things began to get out of hand. There was too much power being concentrated in certain hands and there were a lot of touts running around. This was in the early 1980s when the Christopher Black trial was going on. There were too many wee gangs with people who were becoming power crazy. I know that Skin broke away from the INLA at that time but he rejoined again in the mid to late 1980s. On the night that Skin was killed I was in Australia and I got a phone call to say that he was dead. His body was found up in New Barnsley and the INLA said he was an informer. I was surprised to hear it. Skin was a decent soul; it's a real pity the way things turned out for him and his family.

Mary (partner)

I was born on the Falls Road but my daddy was from Ardoyne. When my granny died we moved into her house in Duneden Park so I knew Gerard when we were young. But I wasn't going with him then. He used to help run discos in Toby's Hall in the early 1970s. That was where we met. I didn't see him again until 1987. I had left my husband after marital problems and had come back to Ardoyne. I met Gerard in the GAA. He walked me home and we just started seeing each other after that. Gerard had been married to his wife Olive and had three kids from the marriage. They were all young when he died. I had two kids of my own. Olive went to England with the kids after they broke up and he really missed them. He was close to his kids. He loved them and they loved him. I was living in my mother's house in Duneden, then I got a house down in Kingston Court and Gerard and I started living there together. We did so up until the time of his death.

Gerard was a jolly person, very witty, and he loved chatting up women even when he was with me! He loved doing things for charity and was always planning and running events in the Jamaica Inn. If he came up with an idea to do something he would put his whole heart and soul into it, especially if it was for a children's charity or for someone who had died. He was also into different sports. He was in the darts, pool and snooker teams for the Jamaica Inn and used to organise matches with other bars and clubs. He also liked to follow local football and particularly all the boys' teams in the district. He loved anything to do with the district.

I never knew the exact circumstances about how he had been shot earlier in his life but I know that a couple of them were serious. He had bullet holes over his body. He still had a bullet fragment inside him, up around by his shoulder blade. Now and again that would cause him pain and he was told that he had to be careful because if it shifted it could kill him. Gerard had been in a house fire when he was younger too. He and his daddy escaped with bad burns but his mother was badly burnt and died in hospital after a couple of weeks. His nephew was burnt to death as well. I remember him telling me about how he tried to get his nephew out of the house. The child had been in the back bedroom and his mother was upstairs too. Gerard had tried to get to them out; he got into the bedroom where the child was but because the wee boy was so afraid, he had hidden behind the wardrobe and then the smoke drove Gerard back. When Gerard and I were living in Kingston Court there was a house fire beside the Jamaica Inn. It brought it all back to him and really knocked him for six. There was a girl who lived there with two children. When they started screaming Gerard went into the house. But he could not get them out either. It really played on his mind. Everything came flooding back. He just kept saying that he couldn't save the child, that there was nothing he could do. He was very kind-hearted and would have done anything for anyone.

During my time with Gerard the British army and the RUC raided the house a couple of times and every time he went out they stopped him. They used to strip search him. He was tortured by them. He told me that he had been taken into Castlereagh and beaten before. This was when his bullet wounds would still have been tender. They used to poke them to try to get him to squeal. But he was very staunch. He used to run around with

John Fennell and a number of other known INLA members. Almost all the people Gerard hung around with then were shot and killed. Most of them were INLA men. He knew a lot of other people, just about everyone in Ardoyne really, but they were the people he ran around with. He was sometimes worried about being shot. I was aware that Gerard was a member of the INLA. He made that clear to me. He never stayed with me when there was any trouble, with disputes going on, for the safety of my children and me. During the time of the feud he had to go down to the Free State, like a lot of others. He was in Dundalk for six months about a year before he was killed. I used to go down with my kids and see him until things calmed down and he was able to come back. It wasn't long after he returned that he was murdered. Gerard was a political person. He was very politically minded and very staunch in his beliefs. I remember one night we were having a bit of an argument and I said to him that I thought that he would put the cause before me. He said that he was sorry to say it but that was true, that his political views had to come before me and the children. So I just learned to live with that. I remember when he died I got a letter from a prisoner and a good friend of Gerard's. He said that he could not believe that they had killed Gerard as an informer because he just wasn't like that.

Gerard was living with me at the time of his death. The last time I saw him was that Saturday morning, 29 June. I got him his breakfast and he went to work. He was working in a chip shop on the Oldpark Road at the time. About an hour after he left the house (about 11.55 am) I sent my eldest over to see if Gerard had any money. But he came back and said that Gerard wasn't there. He said that some other person had answered the door and said that he was not there. This person had come to my house just after Gerard had left looking for him. He had appeared a bit out of breath. I went out over to my aunt's at about 12.15 pm but my aunt and cousin were actually coming down to my house for me and got there at around 12.30 pm. While they were waiting there for me to come back the person who had been at my door earlier came up and asked them if they had seen either Gerard or me. They thought that he looked in a bit of a state. I didn't get home until about 4 pm. This person called back again later but I just told him that I did not know where Gerard was and left it at that.

At about 8 pm I went over to the Jamaica Inn to see if Gerard had been in, but he hadn't been. I was a bit concerned by this time and I wondered if Gerard had been lifted. I went back and forth between the house and the Jamaica Inn a few times. I was just asking to see if he had turned up. But there was no sign of him. At about 11.50 pm I went up to his sister Bell's house but they hadn't seen him either. I was just asking anybody I knew that knew him but the answer was always 'no'. About 11.55 pm I was in the club asking again. Some of those he would have hung around with said they had not seen him. But I also thought that they were looking at me in a rather strange way. In the meantime there had apparently been a news flash but I had nor heard it. I rang around a couple more people but there was no sign of him. Because I couldn't do anything else I just went to bed.

The next morning my sister and her husband came into the house to see if Gerard was back yet. A few minutes later Mary, Gerard's sister came in and a priest was with her. I was in the kitchen and as they came in, I asked Mary what was wrong. She burst into tears and told me that he had been shot. I started squealing and asking where he was. The priest started to say that he was sorry and then I just collapsed on the floor. For ages after that I couldn't take in what was being said to me. So the priest explained what had happened to Gerard. It was only about a day later that I think that I began to understand what was going on. It only really hit me when his body came home and it was explained to me how he had been found, what had happened to him. It was so callous; it was terrible. At the wake people from the INLA came to talk to me, and they said that the INLA had shot Gerard as an informer. They said they had a tape. But I said that it was a lie, that Gerard could never have been an informer. I asked one of the INLA men who I knew very well what he thought. He said that he had heard the tapes and he thought it was true. I couldn't believe he said that, and I told him so. Gerard had always treated him so well. I told them to get out of the house so they left. They claimed that they did not beat Gerard but they did beat him; I saw the bruising on his body.

I was told what happened later. Apparently there were two men waiting for him when he went to his work and they went off in a taxi with him. They took Gerard to New Barnsley, saying that they just wanted to talk to him, to ask him questions. They said that he broke down and that they never laid a hand on him. But I saw the bruises on his body. He actually died between 11.20 pm and 11.25 pm, roughly 12 hours after he had been taken. They shot him and dumped him over into a back garden. The man of the house heard the shots and he ran out to where Gerard was lying in the garden. The man didn't touch him but just rang for the police. They would not go near the body at first in case it was booby-trapped. By the time the coroner came it was after 12 pm so they put the date down as 30 June. But he was actually killed on 29 June. The RUC took a statement from me and said they would get back to me after they investigated the matter. But they never did. I asked them to tell me whether or not Gerard was an informer but they would neither confirm nor deny it.

The only problem at the funeral was the press. They just would not go away. There was a lot of people that Gerard had known for years who stayed away from the funeral. I felt let down by that. There was talk about having some sort of a do for Gerard at the Jamaica Inn. But in the end nothing came of it because of the circumstances in which he died. I have my own opinions on why I think Gerard was killed. He held a high rank in the INLA and I think someone wanted his position. The only way they could do it was to claim that he was a tout. I think it was part of the internal feuding. In my heart, from that day to this, I have never accepted the reason they gave for killing him. I would love it to come out publicly that it was untrue. Because he was so well-known, and his family were as well, it was really hard for them. There was such hurt and shame for them to deal with given the terrible circumstances of his death. It wouldn't have been as bad if he had been shot by the cops or the army. But to die like that, tortured, trussed up, shot in the head and thrown over a garden wall. It was just terrible. At that time Gerard was everything to me; he was a good friend and he loved my kids. They took it all very, very hard. Gerard was just such a loveable person; everybody liked him. It was all such a terrible shame.

> *They waved Hugh's taxi down and he thought he was getting a fare. There were a few people in the taxi with Hugh, but the gunman just walked over from the wee bakery and put the gun through the window and shot Hugh.*

Hugh Magee
Killed by loyalists,
Rosapenna Street,
10 October 1991

Margaret Ann and Hugh Magee (senior) were born and reared in Ardoyne. They had eleven of a family, five boys – Owen, Hugh, Jim, Tommy and Martin – and six girls – Alice, Kathleen, Mary, Maureen, Patricia and Theresa. The family were reared in a small terrace house in Chatham Street. Hugh was the eldest son. He went to Holy Cross Boys school and like most of his peers left with no qualifications. He boxed with Down and Connor Boxing Club in his youth, won quite a few trophies and reached the Ulster finals. His first job was in Brookfield Mill; he then joined the Merchant Navy for a short spell and at the time of his death worked as a taxi driver in Ardoyne. Hugh Magee was a quiet person and very much a family man. His brothers and sisters looked up to him and if ever in trouble, it was Hugh that they turned to. On 10 October 1991 loyalists killed Hugh Magee as he drove his black taxi in Rosapenna Street.

Josie (widow)

My maiden name is Josie Travers. I came from Crumlin Street. I met Hughie in Brookfield Mill where I worked. Hughie started to get very great with me and he gave me an apple every day. He asked me out. I was going with him for about two years and then he went away to join the Merchant Navy. He was writing to me for a least a year and a half and you could say the heart grew fonder. He wanted me to get married in England but my father wouldn't hear of it, so Hugh came home. We got married on 15 July 1961 in Holy Cross chapel. Fr. Denis married us. Hugh's brother Tommy and my sister Maureen stood for us; we had our reception in the Crumlin Star, Butler Street. I had two miscarriages before I had a son in 1977. We called him Paul. We were both over the moon when he was born. Paul was only 14 years old when Hugh was murdered. We had two good friends, Alice and Paddy Wade. Paddy ran about with Hugh from school days right up until Hugh was murdered.

The day Hugh died he came in as usual for his dinner at 4.20 pm and he told me that a man had been shot dead in the Shankill. He said as far as he heard they got the wrong man. I started putting out his dinner and Hughie said that he was going out at about 6 pm again. I said, 'Hughie, there's the helicopter out. If I were you, I wouldn't go out again'. He said, 'Sure I've only started back again, Josie, this two days'. You see, he was off for a fortnight with the flu and he'd just started back again on Tuesday. Hughie said, 'They are hardly going to shoot me'. I said, 'Hughie, they'd shoot anybody', and he just said to me, 'Don't be worrying'.

I went on to bingo and the next thing I saw my brother John coming through the door. He was waving at me to come out. I went towards him and I said, 'What's wrong? Is there something wrong with Paul?' He said, 'Josie, you'll have to come. Hugh has been shot', and that was all I can remember as I collapsed. When I came round, the fella that drove the Star mini-bus at the time drove us down to the Mater Hospital. As I was walking through the doors the priest met me and I knew then Hughie was dead. He told me that he had been with Hughie in his last few minutes.

Our Paul had been waiting at the gap in Brompton Park for his dad to come as he did every Thursday night for his pay. But two lads who knew him told him that his daddy had been shot dead. Paul just ran amok.

Declan Liggett (eyewitness)

Myself and Roisin and my eldest child got into Hughie's taxi the night he was murdered. When the taxi was full, Hugh began to drive up the usual route. As we went along Rosapenna Street two peeler jeeps were coming in the opposite direction, so Hughie stopped to let them pass. Just as we were coming up to the corner of Rosapenna Street I saw a man standing at O'Hara's bakery. As we pulled up at the junction I could see the man pulling out a gun. Hughie looked down the road at this point. Then Hugh seemed to notice what was happening and his whole expression just changed. I saw everything happen in slow motion. I couldn't even shout for Hughie to watch out; it must have been shock. I saw a puff of smoke and then the next thing he shot Hughie; he fell down beside the hand brake.

We were all in a bad way by this time. Roisin and the child were trying to lie on the floor and the gunman was running down the Oldpark Road. I think four bullets hit Hughie. The taxi was still in first gear and it crashed into the railings across the road. When we looked around, we could see people coming running toward us. At that point I pushed the glass across to try and get at Hughie and lifted him up a bit. He was still alive at that stage but I really mean barely as you could hear him gasp for breath. We couldn't get the taxi doors open as Hughie had child locks on. We were locked in the back of the taxi. One of the other black taxi men came and was able to open the doors. Hughie started to fall out of the taxi and the fella was trying to hold him. Then a fella called Jimmy Crawford stopped a taxi going by and put Hughie into the back of the car and took him to the Mater Hospital.

There was one thing that was very strange to me when we had to go to Tennent Street police station to make statements. They brought us into a room and I started to tell them what happened. I got to the bit were I started to tell them about the one who did the shooting and that he had ran down the Oldpark Road towards the bungalows. One of the CID men kept trying to change my mind as to where the gunman had run. He said, 'You mean he ran toward Tennent Street'. It wasn't until later that I remembered about the two peeler jeeps passing Hughie seconds before he was murdered. So by right the peelers must have seen the gunman.

Paddy and Alice Wade (friends)

I knew Hugh throughout my adult life. Houses were difficult to get in those days in Ardoyne and my mother and I were living in Beechmount. A room became vacant at number eight Chatham Street and Hugh Magee and John Brown from Herbert Street walked all the way over to Beechmount to tell me. From that day Hugh and I became very, very good friends; that lasted about fifty years.

When Hugh was younger he was a very good boxer. He boxed for St Gabriel's. Charlie McAuley, the man with the one hand, was his trainer. Hugh was a lovely singer, he loved country and western music; him and Alice used to harmonise together. If you asked him to sing a song he would have sung the Ardoyne song, 'In the middle of August in the year '69'. Hugh was a great guy, all for his home, a real one hundred percent family man. Let's put it like this, if he had a shilling, he would have given his wife eleven pence out of it. He was dedicated to his wife.

I was sitting in the Crumlin Star the day it happened. A bloke had been shot dead in the Diamond Bar on the Shankill Road. I said, 'Somebody will go tonight for that'. Later I was in my house and my mate Paddy from across the street opened the door and said, 'Your mate has been shot'. My wife and I went straight to the hospital. The UFF claimed responsibility, although no one was ever arrested or changed with the murder. The police told Josie they had an idea who they were looking for but they hadn't enough evidence to arrest them.

Hugh's death had a terrible impact on me psychologically, for months in fact maybe even going into a couple of years, every time I thought of the violent way he died. Hugh always feared that corner where he was shot; you have to stop there. Everybody knew Hugh, he had the best of Protestant friends. There were Protestants at his funeral; they came to me and said, 'We are sorry about your mate; he was one good guy'.

I have fond memories of Hugh. Chatham Street holds a bag of memories and a bag of tricks. Hugh was a real hard-working guy throughout his life. Hugh and I made a pact with each other. Whoever died first, the other would lower his friend into the grave, which I did. Hugh was quiet and reserved. He was a very good son who was dedicated to his mother and father and also his sisters and brothers. He loved his whole family and they always looked up to Hugh.

> *We were all in shock afterwards and it was only later that you started to ask questions about why the RUC had done what they had done. Why did the RUC checkpoint disappear just before the shooting? Why did the patrol move away from the house and not towards it? I believe what a lot of Catholics believe, that there has definitely been collusion between the RUC and loyalists.*

Liam McCartan,
Killed by the UFF,
Alliance Avenue,
12 March 1992

Liam McCartan's mother Rose came from South Derry. Her family was from Toomebridge and Bellaghy. The family of his father James was from the Ormeau Road and the Falls Road in Belfast. That is where James had been born but he moved to Desertmartin after his mother died when he was still a boy. The two met at a dance in Desertmartin, married, and moved to Belfast in 1965. By then Liam had already been born. He was the third of eight children (five boys and three girls). For a few years the family lived in the Ballybone then moved to Rathcoole to be close to James' job helping to build the ICI plant in Carrickfergus. In 1974, during the Ulster Workers' Council Strike, the family was forced out of Rathcoole by loyalists. They moved to Ardoyne and set up home in Alliance Avenue, close to the 'peace line' with nearby loyalist areas. When in Rathcoole Liam had attended Stella Maris school and when he arrived in Ardoyne he went to St Gabriel's. He left school with few qualifications and worked intermittently. He did work for a while in a community house on Alliance Avenue, helping with elderly neighbours and delivering meals on wheels. Liam was known as a quiet but sociable fella. He liked to read a lot and followed the local football team Cliftonville. At weekends he would meet up with family and friends in the local clubs (particularly the Highfield) for a night out. However, like many other families living in the 'hotspots' close to loyalist areas, there was also an ever-present threat of attack. Liam himself had been targeted on a number of occasions in the past. On 12 March 1992 Liam was setting out from his home to meet up with his brothers for the regular Thursday might get-together in the Highfield. He was the last of the family still living with his mother in Alliance Avenue. His father had died of cancer in 1989. As he walked down the path UFF gunmen came towards him. Liam tried to get back inside the house and close the door but it was too late. He was shot five times and died from his wounds shortly after. For his family the disappearance of an RUC checkpoint and the movement of a foot patrol around the time of the shooting raised suspicions of collusion between the RUC and his loyalist killers. The UFF subsequently claimed Liam was a member of the IPLO but this has been strenuously denied by both his family and that organisation. Liam's mother, who had witnessed the attack on her son, had to move house after his death. She was subsequently raided a number of times by the RUC. She was also later held at gunpoint by loyalist gunmen who came looking to kill one of her other sons. Liam McCartan was 32 years old when he was shot dead in an overtly sectarian attack.

Brian McCartan (brother)

We moved to Ardoyne after we were put out of Rathcoole. It was during Paisley's strike [UWC strike] in 1974. They put a lot of Catholic families out then. They [loyalists] put a large white X on your door. That meant you were supposed to get out otherwise they would be round to petrol bomb, burn and wreck your house. The next morning a coal lorry and people from Ardoyne came out to us. I remember Coco McAuley was one of them. I was about nine or ten at the time and I remember getting lifted up onto the lorry. We just took whatever stuff we could. We got the house in Alliance Avenue from the Housing Executive and that became our home for the next 20 years, until the shooting of Liam. We had really gone from bad to worse. The house was on the 'peace line' and there was a murder match every week. There were petrol bombs thrown at the house and every 11 July night my daddy would sit with soaked towels ready in case petrol bombs were thrown through the windows. We never got any protection from the RUC or the British army. The only protection you had was yourself and people coming up from Ardoyne. Sometimes loyalists would come down in their droves and you had to have people coming from Ardoyne to come up and stand their ground. There were three or four years between Liam and myself. He used to run about with Paul Grieve and a group of other fellas. Liam was just a quiet fella; he just kept himself to himself. He loved reading and read anything and everything. He was a real bookworm. That's all he really did, read books and listen to the radio. He wasn't a loner or anything; he just liked sitting reading and listening to the radio. He used to go out drinking with Paul Grieve in the old Hole in the Wall in the Bone and in the Highfield.

On a Thursday all us brothers used to meet up for a drink in the Highfield. But the week Liam was killed our older brother Frankie was away in Wales and the youngest Jim was in England. We weren't going to bother but I phoned Liam and he said we should still meet up. So I arranged to go up to the house. I first had to go over and visit my wife and kids. Then as I was making my way up to the house I was told in the street that there had been a shooting and Liam had been hit. By the time I got to the house the cops were all over the place and they wouldn't let me inside. I thought Liam was still there and wanted to get in. They dived on me in the garden and there was a bit of a scuffle. Liam had actually been taken to the hospital. He had been shot at 7.40 pm and he died at 9 pm that night.

I found out later what had happened to Liam from people in the street and my mummy, who was in the house at the time. Apparently there were two carloads of them [loyalists]. One of them went up the path of a house up the street first and then they realised it was the wrong house. They got back in the car and came down the road. About that time Liam had just asked my mummy for the loan of a couple of pound to go down to the Highfield. The loyalists didn't rap on the door because Liam was on his way down the path when they came up to him. He must have seen them and ran back into the house because his footprints were on the door where he tried to kick it closed. It was then that my mummy just heard banging. She went out into the hall and saw a figure standing there. She couldn't see Liam and didn't think he was there at first. They actually went up the hall and fired three rounds at my mother. The shots missed her and went into the walls and the wooden frame of the door. Then the gunmen went running down the path and into the car. My mummy ran down the path after them. Then she came back into the house and that was when she saw Liam lying there.

At the time of the shooting there was an RUC foot patrol at the top of Alliance Avenue. When we asked the RUC about this they said there was but they did not stop because they were not sure where the shooting was coming from and whether or not it was directed at them. They ended up going in completely the opposite direction to the one the shooting was coming from. They were safeguarding their own lives; that was the explanation they gave. There had also been a permanent RUC roadblock outside my mother's door stopping cars going in and out of Ardoyne for the week before Liam was shot. It had been almost constant and had only rarely been broken off. Ten minutes before Liam was shot it disappeared. I and other people felt that was very, very strange. The RUC never gave an explanation for that. When Liam was in the hospital my mother, myself and my brother Michael had to go there to identify him. There was a lot of hassle there with the cops too. They were looking over toward me and laughing, like it was all a big joke. We were all in shock afterwards and it was only later that you started to ask questions about why the RUC had done what they had done. Why did the RUC checkpoint disappear just before the shooting? Why did the patrol move away from the house and not towards it? I believe what a lot of Catholics believe, that there has definitely been collusion between the RUC and loyalists. There was a person charged with the shooting but then the charges were dropped. The RUC came round to tell us that this guy was being released. That was the only time they were round at the house apart from coming and raiding it. After the murder, my mother moved from the family home she had lived in for 20 years into a house in the Oldpark Road. It was that house the RUC raided several times. It was as if the RUC were rubbing salt into the wounds. That house was also hit three times by loyalists. On two occasions no one was home but the third time my mother was there on her own. This was around 1993 or 1994. The loyalists held a gun to her head while they searched the house to see if there were any fellas at home. The RUC just laughed in her face when they were called out and said that they had no information of anything having happened. My mother eventually had to leave the Oldpark and moved into Ardoyne because of everything that happened.

As far as support for the family went she was never offered anything by the RUC. The priest from the Sacred Heart parish who performed mass at Liam's funeral could not have done more for my mother and the family. The Survivors of Trauma Group has written letters to us and Brendan Bradley has offered help, but I would rather deal with things myself. My mother will never be the same. She doesn't say a lot and tries to keep a strong face for the rest of us but you can see the way it affected her inside. I think we need to come out and tell the truth about the way that things are set up here in the north. Bodies dealing with victim's families are set up for the like of RUC families. Even the compensation is a joke. Not that you want any money but the amount of money my mother got was like spitting in her face. I don't think Liam was specifically targeted. I think that our house was targeted because we were a Catholic family and that they [loyalists] would have shot anybody who was in the house. That is why they fired at my mother. It was just a sectarian attack on a Catholic family. The UFF claimed my brother's death and said that he was a member of the IPLO but that was just a load of rubbish. The IPLO actually made a statement to the *Irish News* to deny that Liam had ever been a member of their organisation. Liam was just an ordinary young Catholic man growing up. He was just like the rest of us. He liked a joke and messing about. He believed, like the rest of our family, that Catholics have been trampled on here for years. But he wouldn't have talked about things much. He was just a fella who kept himself to himself.

Paul Grieve (friend)

I first met Liam at school in St Gabriel's when he was about 13 or 14. His family had to move from Rathcoole and they came to live in Alliance Avenue. Everything was new to him and his family at first so they were sort of outsiders. Liam was a quiet fella but within a couple of weeks we just sort of clicked and became friends. No matter how smart you were you were never going to get far if you went to St Gabriel's but Liam and me both tried. Up until fifth year we were both in the 'A' classes and we were annoyed when we were dropped down at that time. Liam was always good at English, maths and technical drawing. He wasn't bad at anything, a good all-rounder. There were about seven or eight of us who knocked about together and everyone liked Liam because he was an easy fella to like. He was quiet and never a fighter, though you knew not to mess with him. We all used to go away on holiday together. In 1976 or 1977, when we were about 16 or 17, a whole squad of us hired a caravan down south. We always used to go away in the summer to Bundoran, Salthill, places like that. Liam always liked travelling and he would get away at any chance he got. We used to go to the fleadhs and although he couldn't play any instrument, Liam really liked traditional music. He was a big follower of Planxty and Christy Moore. His nickname was 'the Blade'. When he was about 17 he got caught with this wee penknife. The Brits were always searching us and Liam had this idea that he could hide this wee knife behind his wristwatch. But he got searched and caught with it one night over in the Bone. So he got the nickname 'the Blade' after that!

Liam was very close to his family. His father had died when Liam was young and he was very close to his mother. Liam was always the sensible one in the house and his mother could always count on him. The two of them were very close. Liam was just an honest, sound type of guy. As far as work went Liam did whatever jobs he could get. He worked in the building trade with me and did some voluntary work. Because I am originally from the Sacred Heart when Liam and me started to go out drinking we used to go to the old Hole in the Wall. Then we used to socialise in the Highfield at the back of Etna Drive. Liam used to just go out at weekends, a social drinker. He liked playing pool and was happy playing all day on a Saturday. We were also both Cliftonville supporters and we used to go to all the matches, home and away, together. There was a girl Liam went with when he was about 17 or 18 called Jennifer, the daughter of the woman who owned the chippy at the bottom of Butler Street. She was the most serious he was about a woman. There were a couple of other girls on the scene after that but Jennifer was the most serious. Liam was just a quiet sort of man. I got married at the time of the hunger strikes in 1981. Liam never forgave me for that! We were all republican minded before the hunger strike but I think that reinforced Liam's views more than anything else. When you really got to know Liam you could have a good conversation with him because he knew what he was talking about. Liam was interested in news and current affairs and he would have known a lot about the politics of the situation here. He did a lot of reading on the politics of the country. He was like that right up until the last time I saw him alive.

A couple of days before he was shot, Liam handed me an old book in the Highfield. It belonged to my da and Liam was just returning it after having read it. The book was about sectarian murders in Belfast [Andrew Boyd's Holy War in Belfast]. What a coincidence, two days later Liam was shot dead. Liam always had a premonition of dying at the spot he was killed. He said that to me a few times. It is a bad spot because a lot of people have been shot there. For years Liam thought they [loyalists] had been watching him and that they nearly got him a few times before. They had tried to get him one time but he saw them coming. They tried to pull him into a car but he managed to get away. He was threatened quite a few times. I remember one in particular in about 1978. We were drinking just across the road from Liam's house on Alliance, just by the Deerpark. It was after a Cliftonville match. This UVF man actually pulled a gun out standing next to the RUC and one of the peelers just told him to put it away again. The UVF guy knew the names of all the fellas there who lived in dodgy areas. He said to Liam, 'See you McCartan, you are getting blown up'. We were all arrested after that. There were times when we had run-ins with the cops. Once, in about 1979, Liam and me came out of a party on the Cliftonville. We were walking home in the early hours when this car pulled up. There were no markings and no uniforms but when these guys got out with guns they told us to get up against the wall. If it had been the other lot [loyalists] they would have just shot us. They didn't search or ask us our names. In fact they didn't say anything. They knew who we were. They just pistol whipped us then got back in the car and drove off. Liam had his tooth chipped that night.

On the night Liam was shot I was in my own house. My wife's aunt phoned at about 10 pm and told my wife that Liam had been shot dead; then she told me. I went round to the house the next morning at about 7 am. I found out later that he had been going round to the Highfield but when he opened his front door they [loyalists] were just standing in the garden waiting for him. Liam tried to close the door but they kicked it in. They started shooting at Liam and his mother Rose. They put a couple of bullets right into Liam's head. He didn't die instantly but a couple of hours later. Liam had a big funeral because he had a lot of friends. He was a person who didn't have an enemy. Liam's death had a terrible impact on me because he was a very close friend. We had fallen out for a while but had made up a couple of months before. Then all of a sudden he was killed. Liam was always a very good friend of mine and he never deserved what he got. He was just a good, solid Irishman, an intelligent man, and he did not deserve to die in that way. His house had been targeted before. A house beside them had been blown up a few years before and I always felt that the intended target had been the McCartan's because there were six male adults in the house. Liam's death was purely sectarian.

Rose McCartan (mother)

The night my son Liam was murdered, Maureen Magee and my grandson, Thomas, were also in the house. Liam had just gone out for a few drinks. Maureen and I were having a cup of tea. Things were quiet. Then the door was kicked in and all these dark figures were moving about. Then I heard gun shots. When I ran out into the hall my son, Liam was lying on the floor. He was breathing very low. I tried to speak to him and said, 'Please son, don't die'. I said a prayer in his ear. His breathing was getting worse so I ran and phoned an ambulance. It arrived very quickly. I got into the ambulance along with Maureen. I was in a daze. Maureen stayed very close to me. When we eventually arrived at the Mater Hospital Liam was rushed into a small ward. We were put into a room to wait. When the doctor arrived in to see us he said Liam was holding his own. Then not long after that he came back and said, 'I'm sorry, Liam has gone'. I felt as if Liam had just walked through me. Things were never the same after that terrible night. I miss him so much.

> *I heard a bang and Isabel pushed me to the ground. Then there were another two bangs. I had never heard shooting before so I didn't know what it was. Then I heard, 'I'm hit, I'm hit'. I turned round and there was blood all over Jim Clarke's hand and then I heard this wee voice saying, 'I'm hit too' and I looked and there was blood coming out of Isabel's mouth.*

Isabel Leyland
Killed by the IRA,
Flax Street,
21 August 1992

Isabel Leyland's mother Bessie (née Boyd) was originally from the Newtownards Road; her father Johnny Bradley was from Ludlow Street, New Lodge Road. Isabel was the ninth of fourteen children born to Bessie and Johnny. She attended Chief Street school, left at the age of 15 and started work in Rosebank Mill. She had a wide circle of friends that included Lizzie Fennell, Phyllis Doherty and Joanne and Maura Clarke. In 1969 Isabel moved to Rochdale, England, where she eventually settled with her husband Brian Leyland. During those years she worked as a care assistant in an old people's home. Isabel was a regular visitor home and made the trip two to three times a year.

On 21 August 1992 while home on a visit, and just hours before leaving, Isabel was accidentally killed by the IRA in an attack on a British army patrol in Flax Street. Three other members of the Bradley family have been killed as a result of the conflict [Francie Bradley, killed by loyalists, Corporation Street, 19 June 1975; Martin Bradley, killed by loyalists, Crumllin Road, 20 December 1994; and Fra Shannon, killed by INLA, Turf Lodge, 9 June 1996].

Mary Bradford (sister)

Isabel went to England around 1969. Three of our brothers, John, Davey and Bernard, were already over in Rochdale along with myself. Isabel was 41 when she was killed. She lived in Rochdale at the time of her death and had come over to Belfast to see my mother who was ill. She was staying in our house in Northwick Drive. Isabel visited Ardoyne as often as she could. Her family nickname was 'Ruby'. She was going to collect photographs from a friend the day she was killed.

The day she died Isabel had been in Ardoyne ten days. She was supposed to leave later that day on the 4 pm flight. That morning we went up the road and she bought soda bread, soup vegetables and stuff you can't get in England to take back with her. About 12.30 pm we came down from the Crumlin Road and made lunch because she was going back in a few hours. Then my sister Patricia's daughter, Jolene, came in. She told us it was her birthday and showed us a bracelet her mummy had bought her. She was 11 that day. Isabel asked Jolene to go with her to Phyllis Doherty's shop. This was about 1.30 pm. Isabel was looking to get photos from Phyllis. The photos had been taken years ago when they were all in Waterfoot. Isabel left the house around 1.50 pm with Jolene. At about 2.30 pm I saw Maggie Scullion coming up our path. I went out to the door to meet her because I thought she was looking for someone. Maggie told me that Isabel had been shot. She was shaking. I ran over to Tony Wilkinson's house and asked Tony's daughter Linda to come over and look after my mummy. When I got to Flax Street Isabel wasn't there. There were just crowds of people. She was with Jolene when she was shot. They were coming from the Shamrock Club direction up towards Phyllis Doherty's house. The main reason she wanted the photographs was because her daughter, who is 16 years old, always wanted to know what her mammy looked like when she was that age. Isabel had intended to get the photos and take them back to England to show the kids.

My brother Brendan and myself went down to the Mater Hospital. When I got down there I immediately phoned Isabel's family. I didn't know she was dead at this stage. Someone had told me that she was all right, that she was talking. I just took it for granted she had been grazed. I was saying to myself, 'Jesus, I hope she's alright and can make the 4 pm flight because her family are waiting on her'.

Jolene McAllister (niece)

21 August 1992 was my 11th birthday. Me and my mummy had gone into town that morning. When we came back I said I wanted to see Isabel before she went back to England. That was round about 12.30 - 1 pm. I went round to 52 Northwick Drive and Isabel was there with Mary and my granny eating lunch. Isabel asked me to go with her to see Phyllis Doherty and I said yes. We went to Phyllis's shop and Isabel was told that she should call to Phyllis's house to collect photographs she had been looking for. After we left the shop we were walking down towards Flax Street and we met my uncle Tommy at the Shamrock Club. Tommy was behind the wire gate at the Shamrock door and he said to me, 'Give Isabel a hug'. He said he would see her the next time she was over and Isabel said, 'You'll never see me again'. When Isabel was talking to Tommy they were touching each other's fingers through the wire mesh of the front door. We walked on and just as we turned the corner into Flax Street we saw Jim Clarke and Isabel said, 'hello'. Then I heard a bang and Isabel pushed me to the ground. Then there were another two bangs. I had never heard shooting before so I didn't know what it was. The peelers were there and there was a lot of running about. Then I heard, 'I'm hit, I'm hit', and I turned round and blood was all over Jim Clarke's hand. Then I heard this wee voice saying, 'I'm hit too' and I looked and there was blood coming out of Isabel's mouth. I got up to run and a peeler got out of a jeep, pointed a gun at me and said, 'Get down on the ground'. I told him my aunt was shot and I just ran. I went up past the community centre and a girl asked me what had happened. I told her and she offered to walk me home. As we were walking up the street I met my brother's mate and he brought me home. When we got to the house I told my mummy Isabel had been shot and she went down to the hospital. The shooting happened around 3 pm. I didn't know she was dead until later when my cousin told me.

Phyllis Doherty (friend)

I knocked about with Patricia and Isabel Bradley at school. We were all mates – Patricia, Isabel, Lizzie Fennell, Joanne Clarke and Maura Clarke. We used to go to the 'Hop' and we knocked about Freddie Fusco's chippie. Years ago Nailer Clarke brought us to Waterfoot in his van. The whole crowd of us stayed in one tent. We were going camping and Isabel brought a wee bag of coal with her! That's when all the photos were taken. It was around 1967. Isabel moved to England but whenever she came back we always contacted each other.

During her last stay in Ardoyne Isabel had been in my shop a few times looking me. But we kept missing each other. The Thursday night before she was due to go home Isabel spent a few hours in the shop and we talked about everything. We talked about the old times and what we did before 1969. She said to me, 'Phyllis, I'm going back tomorrow. Remember those photos of us in Waterfoot? Could I have them?' I told her I'd hunt them out for her and Isabel said she would call the next day to collect them. I looked for the photos and I could only find one wee small one. Isabel called to the shop the next day and I had left word that she was to call to my house. So Isabel left the shop and she rang me; this was before 1 pm. I told her to come up to my house and she said she would dander up with Jolene. I said I would leave the key in the door. I waited for a while and then went upstairs and fell into a sleep. I never even heard the shooting. The last words I heard from Isabel was she was on her way up to my house. A couple of people told me later that they had phoned me so I must have gone into a really deep sleep.

I remember wakening up and getting washed. I left the house and walked through the gap in Brompton Park. I'm nearly sure it was Geraldine Conrad told me Isabel had been shot. I think it was about 4 pm. I was numb. I didn't know what to do so I made my way round to the Bradley's house. Mary Bradley arrived from the hospital with Janis. I didn't know what to say, I was just in shock. The only photo I found wasn't even taken in Waterfoot; it was taken down in Woolworth's, and it was of me and Isabel and another girl. I gave the photo to her husband because he wanted to show it to his kids.

The gunmen walked into our house through the back where they found my wee brother. They were wearing masks and boiler suits. One of them put a gun to his head while the other one went into the front room. My da thought it was someone messing about. They then shot my da and took off out the back again where my wee brother chased them, throwing scissors at them. My ma ran to the front of the house where she threw a flowerpot at them. One of the gunmen turned and fired a shot at my ma. It missed her and hit the wall behind.

Martin Lavery
Killed by loyalists,
Crumlin Road,
20 December 1992

Martin Lavery's parents were Jane McClean from the Bone and Patrick Lavery, originally from Leeson Street, Falls Road. The couple had sixteen children, eleven sons and five daughters. Martin was the youngest son, born 18 July 1952 in Carrick Hill, Unity Flats. He attended St Patrick's primary school in North Queen Street and St Patrick's Secondary school on the Antrim Road. He left school in 1967 and had a couple of different jobs before working for the Housing Executive in 1977. Theresa McShane from Ardoyne was Martin's childhood sweetheart. Both played in St Patrick's accordion band. That's how they met and started dating. In 1973 they married in Holy Cross chapel and eventually had four children: Patrick, Therese, Danielle and Martin.

Two years before Martin's death the couple bought a house on the Crumlin Road. Martin spent all his spare time carrying out the renovations. That was typical of Martin. He was the 'handy man' of the Lavery clan, able to turn his hands to anything. Martin was an ordinary, decent family man devoted to his wife and children and wider family circle. A few days before Christmas, 20 December 1992, loyalist gunmen entered the Lavery family home and killed Martin while he relaxed with his four-year-old daughter Danielle. It was a blatant sectarian attack. His wife and three of his children witnessed the killing. Less than a year later, Martin's nephew, Sean Lavery, was killed in a similar loyalist attack.

Danny Lavery (brother)

Martin was shot dead on 20 December 1992. His closest friends were his brothers, Martin, Kevin, Bobby and myself. We hung about together when we were growing up and into adulthood. We went to the Plaza until it closed down and we went to Romano's. Martin frequented the Highfield Club and the Star. He played the drums in the Sacred Heart accordion band. That's where he met his wife Theresa. Martin was known as a constant worker. At his funeral Fr. Kenneth said what he remembered most about Martin was that every time he saw him he had the shirt off, working out in the garden or in the house. He could put his hands to anything. If you gave him a book to read it would have taken him three or four months to read it. But if you gave him work to do, he had it done in three or four days. He was the 'handy man' of the family.

Martin was arrested when he was 17 years old for riotous behaviour in the Unity Walk area. He got nine months. He appealed and got a further nine months. This was in 1969/70. He served his time in Crumlin Road gaol. He did his full sentence as a non-political prisoner; that was before the days of political status. I remember going up to see him and he was wearing a prison uniform.

I was in the house the day Martin died. I got a phone call from Bobby saying that there had been a shooting at Martin's house. I said I would go straight to the hospital. In the hospital the Special Branch came up to us and said, 'We are sorry about your brother'. Bobby said, 'I'm sure you are'. Then their attitude changed. They said, 'One of you bastards has to go in and identify him because he's dead'. That's how we were told.

The day he was killed, two gunmen entered the back door of Martin's house. He was repairing the house. He was building an extension. It was about 7 o'clock at night. It was dark. Martin had a sore back and he was in the living room lying on the chair with his child Danielle; she was four at the time. The gunmen came in and fired four bullets into him. When his wife realised what happened she ran after the gunmen and threw a flower plant at them. His eldest daughter, his youngest daughter and his youngest son were in the house at the time. The UVF claimed responsibility for the murder, saying he was an intelligence officer for the IRA and was the brother of former Sinn Féin councillor Bobby Lavery. Nobody was ever arrested for his killing.

Patrick Lavery (son)

My mother was married when she was 18 and I think my daddy was 21. They went out with each other for years, so they must have met when they were about 13 or 14. My mother was originally from Andersonstown. Her granny took very ill and the family moved over to Ardoyne to look after her. They moved to a house in Eskdale Gardens. My mother's maiden is McShane and her granny was called Prenter, the Prenters from Hooker Street.

My daddy taught me how to play the drums; he taught me how to draw. He was just the best daddy in the world to me. When I was a child I collected toy soldiers and every week on his way home from work, he bought me a box of toys. I remember as I was growing up if anybody gave me a hard time he was out in the street sticking up for me. My da could put his hands to anything; he could have built you a wall, a fireplace, hang a door, knock walls down. He had a wee bar built in the house so that he could bring all of his brothers up for a drink. He had the kegs of beer connected and everything. The house was a wreck when it was bought. But my da always said it had potential. He said when he finished the renovations he would sit down, have a drink and say, 'I did that'. He hadn't got a chance to get it finished because they came and shot him before he had it finished.

I remember the day my daddy was murdered. I was working in McLaughlins Bar, down the New Lodge. I was a barman there. In those days you worked from 12.30 pm to about 2.30-3 pm; you then went home and started back about 7 pm. My ma drove me to work at about 7 pm. At roughly quarter past seven a phone call came to the bar for me. It was my uncle; he just said to me, 'Get home, get home now'. I knew that something was seriously wrong and deep down in my heart I knew that my da had been shot. I thought back to the very first day that we all went to see the house before we moved in. My first words were, 'Don't buy this house, cause my da is going to be shot here'. Anyway on the way home I met a black taxi man, Mickey Reid. I asked him would he please drive me up to the house. I then told him that I thought my da had been shot. As we proceeded up the Crumlin Road we saw an ambulance flying down with all the lights flashing, I said to the taxi man, 'I told you; that's my da in that ambulance'. The taxi man put the boot down and as we arrived at the house the whole place was cordoned off. The RUC were everywhere and there were people outside. I jumped out of the taxi and ran into the house and my ma was standing crying. I started shouting and screaming, 'What's happened? What's happened?' She said, 'They just came in and shot him'. I started punching walls and asking for a gun. I went outside and the RUC told me not to worry, that my da had only been shot in the side.

When we arrived at the hospital a lady doctor came over to us. My mother just looked at her and said, 'He's dead, isn't he?' She said, 'Yes'. My ma wailed and wailed and wailed. I went over and hugged her and told her to be strong. We were walking out when we saw Bobby and Danny (Martin's brothers). I had a few words with them. I was extremely angry. They told me to calm down. I was then asked to go in and identify my daddy and I said 'No'. So my mother went in with my kid brother and I went outside.

The next day I went to our house to get it cleared for the wake. There was blood everywhere, up and down the radiators where he had been shot. There was also a big steel hammer left behind by the gunmen. They were obviously intending to use it to smash their way into the house. The RUC hadn't even taken it with them. They just left the hammer in our house in a big clear plastic bag.

The night before my da was to be buried there were cars and buses flying up and down past our house from Hesketh to Woodvale. They were loyalists guys in the cars and they were taunting and laughing and giving my family the fingers. I just went mad. I hit the drink. I just couldn't take any more.

I asked my ma to go over what happened when my da was killed. My da was lying down with my wee sister on the sofa. They were in the front parlour; my thirteen-year old brother was sitting in the back parlour at the time and my other sister was using the phone. The gunmen must have thought the front door had security so they went to the back of the house to use a hammer to smash their way in. But the back of the house was not locked as my da had been out earlier feeding the dog. The gunmen then walked into our house through the back where they found my wee brother. They were wearing masks and boiler suits. One of them put a gun to his head while the other one went into the front room. My da thought it was someone messing about. They then shot my da and took off out the back. My wee brother chased them and threw scissors at them. My ma ran to the front of the house and threw a flowerpot at them. One of them turned and fired a shot at my ma. It missed and hit the wall behind her. The bullet hole can still be seen. The gunmen then took off down towards the Woodvale. According to news reports, the RUC gave chase after them. The gunmen went into a pub, but the RUC wouldn't go into it. After a couple of hours they entered the pub where they found a surgical glove and balaclava.

The week before my da was killed I was working in McLaughlins Bar. We were constantly tortured by the RUC in those days. They were constantly raiding the bar. One day they came in and I went up the stairs with them. One of the RUC asked me my name. When he heard I was one of the Laverys, he asked me where I lived. When I told him, he said that was all he wanted to know. I told my da when I got home; he said, 'You watch, I think those cops are up to something'. Three days prior to my da being murdered there was an RUC checkpoint set up outside the door of our house, which was very strange as it had never happened before. I said to my da, 'You watch; I think they're up to something'. Three days later my da was shot dead. The UVF claimed responsibility. There was never anyone arrested.

> *It just didn't seem right that it would be in somebody else's house and in the middle of doing work. It was difficult to accept; he was in the wrong place at the wrong time. For me that's the whole tragedy of it.*

Alan Lundy
Killed by loyalists,
Andersonstown,
1 May 1993

Alan Lundy's parents were Jeannie and Danny Lundy. They had four children: Alan, Elizabeth, Patricia and Danny. After leaving St Gabriel's school Alan worked for a short time in a local factory and later became a plasterer by trade. He was a popular, very likeable fella. He had plenty of good friends including Rab McCallum, Gerard McGuigan, Charlie McAuley and Seamus Stewart. After his release from Long Kesh in 1978 where he served time as a political prisoner, he met Margaret McArdle, his future wife. They soon got married and eventually had five children: Alan, Daniel, Clare, Ciaran and Elizabeth.

Alan was a hardworking family man and is remembered for his willingness to help others. 'A nicer guy you couldn't have met'. Alan was a life-long republican and an active member of Sean McCaughey/James Saunders Sinn Féin cumann. On 1 May 1993, while working in the home of his close friend, Alex Maskey, loyalists attacked the house and Alan was killed.

Margaret (widow)

Alan was one of those people that everybody liked. He was a brilliant worker; he did jobs for people and wouldn't take any money. That's the kind of person he was. I met Alan in the Shamrock. He had just been released from gaol after doing five years for a political offence. We started going out with each other on a regular basis and got married on 9 December 1978. I knew Alan before he was released from gaol because he went about with my brother Frankie, who is also dead now. They were good buddies and Alan sometimes stayed in my mummy's house. Seamus Stewart was the best man at our wedding and Teresa Mullan was the bridesmaid. We had five children. Alan was brilliant with the kids.

The night before he was killed we were at the pictures. I always remember that when it comes to his anniversary. I can't remember what we went to see but we went back to the Shamrock for a couple of drinks. I remember we were talking about the kids growing up. His friend Charlie McAuley had moved to Dundalk and Alan was thinking about selling the house and moving there too. That was his plan, to take the children away out of this place, out of this environment. The kids were getting older and he was worried about their safety. That's what we were talking about that night. The next morning he had to go and do a plastering job in Alex Maskey's house.

I remember it was a lovely sunny day. I never thought in a million years that he wasn't coming back. At about 5 pm my son Daniel was sitting on the wall outside and he said, 'Mummy, the priest wants you'. Fr. Ralph came in and asked me if I was Margaret

Lundy and did I have a husband called Alan Lundy. Then he asked me if Alan was working with a man called Alex Maskey. I just stood there and I knew something was wrong right away. He asked if Alan had left the house in a car. He said, 'Well, he has been hurt'. My first reaction was he had been in a car crash. I never thought in a million years that Alan had been shot; it never entered my head. The priest didn't really seem to know the details. I said to him, 'If anything had happened I would have got a phone call from Alex Maskey'. Then I started to panic. I remember squealing and getting my Daniel to get Rosaleen Mailey, a neighbour across the street, and she came over. The next thing was a car pulled up and Gerard McGuigan and Phyllis Doherty, and I think Janis Quinn, came in. That's when I knew, when they came up to the door. Gerard McGuigan came in and he said, 'Margaret, he is dead', and I kicked Gerard McGuigan. I hit out at everybody; I just collapsed and I squealed. Two of my children were away at the time on a wee break with the community centre. The next minute the house was just packed.

It wasn't really explained to me what happened, just that he had been shot. I suppose I put a barrier up there and then. I didn't know what was happening. I wanted to go up and be with Alan. I regret that very much that I didn't get up to Alex Maskey's house. I wanted to go up but I was told it would be better if I didn't. I really regret that, because Alan lay up in that house for hours and hours before the RUC would even release his body. I am still so angry about that.

It was explained to me later what happened. Alan was clearing up the job they'd been doing. Brits were sitting outside. Alex went into the house and the next minute the Brits disappeared. This is what Alex or Liz Maskey told me, I can't remember which one. Alan saw his killers coming. He saw the car and the gunman getting out. He ran. He ran into the house and slammed the door and threw a hammer at them. He said to Liz, 'Get out the back'. Liz and her two sons got out the back. As Alan was running through the house they opened up and he was killed outright.

The UFF claimed responsibility but nobody was ever charged. I think they found the car and the gun in it. The inquest was, I think, two years or more after his death. I can't remember the verdict; they just closed it unsolved. They still haven't found anybody for it. At Alan's funeral the cops were everywhere. Gerard McGuigan said the cops wanted to come and give their condolences. I was angry because the British army knew what was happening the day Alan was killed.

Alan was a good man, an honest man going out to do a day's work. I remember watching the TV and it showed you Alan getting carried out in a body bag and it showed the gun that was used. But yet they never got anybody for his murder. They didn't arrest anybody. I think there was something more sinister that went on. The RUC and Brits were in on it. The Brits were outside Alex's house all day and then disappeared to let the loyalists get in. There was no explanation; it was just thrown to the side and it has never been brought up again. But I do think the cops knew who they were, I really do. There was a programme on about Johnny Adair and about the shooting of Alan up at Alex Maskey's house. It was about a year after his death. I didn't know that the programme was coming on TV. I saw it unawares and I was shocked. I got no prior warning that this programme was coming on. But apparently they are allowed to do that. They just apologised for upsetting me.

I was left with five children. I went through a terrible time. My kids and me ended up going to counselling. My wee girl had nightmares. Everybody just fell apart. I fell apart. I couldn't handle it. Things still come up; things would bring back memories. My eldest son still hasn't talked about his daddy; he's really deep. He has an awful lot of hatred in him and I don't blame him. He has never spoken about it; he keeps it all in and you can see the anger in him. I got no compensation. They said that because Alan had been charged, and did time for a political offence, I wouldn't get any compensation. And they said that my kids weren't entitled to anything either. It's not about the money...

I have to say that Sinn Féin really were there for my children and me. They organised the funeral because I couldn't, and they erected Alan's head stone. They supported my family and me. They still do to this day and I am really grateful to them. It helps an awful lot knowing that they still remember Alan and they remember us. His funeral was massive, a big, big turn out; everybody came and the chapel was packed. I remember they gave me a tri-colour off Alan's coffin. They had a do for him and they presented me and his mother with a lovely medal with his photo on it, which I thought, was lovely, very touching. It's good that I know somebody cares and they haven't forgotten.

Alex and Liz were devastated. Liz was there with him, holding him and comforting him and I wished that I had been there, that is my regret. It must have been a terrible trauma for Alex and Liz and their kids to see Alan being killed. I'm sure it will always be there with them that hurt. He was a good friend of Alex. I'm sure they are suffering too and my heart goes out to them. It was just that Alan was at the wrong place at the wrong time. They witnessed it and I'm sure it was a terrible thing to see. I know they will never forget Alan.

Rab McCallum (friend)

I ran about with Alan from I was a kid of about 12 or 13 years of age. We all knocked about together, joined the Fianna together, joined the IRA together, went to gaol together and spent time in the same cages together. Alan got out of gaol and I went back inside again. He always came up to visit me and we kept in contact with one another. When I got back out again Alan, myself, Gerard McGuigan and Charlie McAuley would have regularly gone out and had a drink together. We were very close.

What I remember most about Alan was just how continuously helpful he was, no matter what you were doing. If I had been working on the house, regardless of what it was, he would have offered to give me a hand. But it was always the same way with him; no matter what you wanted he would help. One of the last things he did was plaster my hall. When he got killed he was doing Alex a favour. It is something that just stuck with me that he was always there for me. Sometimes when I walk out and see the hall that he plastered and coming through on the old brickwork you can see were he actually stood and worked beside you. If anyone ever asked me to take it down, it just wouldn't happen because it is one of the things I remember; we had a bit of craic doing the work together. He was a really good person. I never heard anybody say a bad word about him. I can't ever remember having a cross word with him. Alan was the one who made the peace and smoothed things over. He was just a great fella.

I think it was Gerard McGuigan phoned me and said 'Alan is dead'. It just didn't sink in. It was a Saturday and I think we were actually due to go out for a drink. That's what always happened; we use to end up in the League on a Saturday afternoon and then we went on out that night. I was shocked by the phone call and couldn't comprehend it. I just couldn't comprehend how it actually happened. I didn't envisage an attack on Alex's house and Alan being in the middle of it and him being dead. A lot of different things went through my head. It just didn't seem right that it would be somebody else's house and in the middle of doing work. Because of his involvement in the republican movement if anybody had come to his door and shot him dead you would have accepted it as part of life of being a republican. But that's the tragedy of it, that it wasn't intended for him probably and that he ended up getting it. For me that is the whole tragedy of it. That's the thing that sort of sticks with me; it was difficult to accept that he was in the wrong place.

Thoughts of him always creep into my mind; I think about him now and again and I know that I miss him at times. I remember the day the ceasefire was called. I heard the horns beeping and I went round to the Gap to see what was happening. All the cars were flying by with the flags out the windows. Alan was the first thing I thought about. It was very emotional. That was a big one for me to deal with.

Alex Maskey (friend)

I first met Alan in 1973 when I was on remand in Crumlin Road gaol. Alan had been interned but he was taken out of internment and charged with a political offence. He went on remand in Crumlin Road gaol and ended up coming into a cell with myself. We shared a cell for several months and we got to know each other very well. That was a particularly difficult period in Crumlin Road gaol. The governor was trying to establish a very strict brutal regime. Brits were brought in every other weekend, wrecked the place and beat a lot of us up. So I suppose there were a lot of strong friendships forged around that particular period.

I always found Alan a sort of happy-go-lucky person. One thing that really struck me during that period was that the republican movement changed its policies regarding recognising the court. Up until that point Alan had refused to recognise the court. With the new policy he was given the option to recognise the court. It was quite clear that on the evidence presented by the RUC regarding his case he would have walked out of the court. Despite the fact that people said to him, 'You should recognise the court because you'll get out and you won't face a long prison sentence', he refused to do so. He said that some people he had been with in Ardoyne, before he had gone into gaol, had not recognised the court and were serving prison sentences. He didn't think in all conscience that he could recognise the court and get out earlier. I thought that was a very courageous decision he took. I thought that was a very important indicator of his strength of character and the type of person that he was; he decided to take the harder route.

Certainly in the earlier days, like most other republicans, if not all of us, things had to be done and you had to get on with it. He wouldn't have had any doubts about what he was doing. He wouldn't have had any doubts about the direction the republican movement was going in and what had to be done. He was absolutely committed to his objectives and what he had to do to achieve them. I know that in later years of course he embraced the electoral strategy. He worked very hard at elections and he worked at building Sinn Féin in his own area. In my estimation he would have been one of those very credible people in his community. He was well into fund-raising for most of that time for the party. Although he was a very personable person I don't think he was too keen on the public side of a lot of the work. But he was always very much into building the infrastructure. He was an organiser. He made a very huge contribution to the party. He brought his own credibility to the whole electoral strategy within his own community.

Over the years any work I would have got done in the house, any plastering work, Alan would have done it. He converted my loft and did all of the plastering work. He was very reliable, one of those people you could always call on to do a bit of work at home for you. Around 1993 period I was told that I had to ensure that my house had extra security because of the ongoing loyalist threat. I decided I would get a small porch built on the front and back of the house, just basically an extra door either side of the house. Obviously that required plastering as well and Alan was one of the people I asked to do that bit of work for me. That day Alan and I went over to my house and worked basically throughout the day. We took time out to go to Angelo Fusco's father's funeral. After Alan was killed, I had to give a statement to the RUC. Two RUC officers were being queried by my solicitor Peter Madden about the circumstances of the shooting and the allegations about collusion. The RUC explanation was that Alan and I had been at Angelo Fusco's father's funeral, which they said was a well-known republican funeral, and in all likelihood loyalists had followed us from the funeral. I thought that was an interesting position being put to us by the RUC. It was obviously farcical. But it just shows you they would use anything. Angelo Fusco's father's funeral was not a republican funeral. The RUC had the nerve to use that as a possible reason as to how the loyalists were able to follow us to my house. They didn't need to follow anybody; they knew where my house was.

That day there were a few other lads working at the house because there was a lot of building material, rubble and stuff to be moved. Everybody else more or less packed up; the job was finished. Alan had to do a bit more work. Alan and myself went in and had our dinner with my family. When we finished our meal and as we were leaving our kitchen to finish off the work, both of us were saying we had to go to the toilet and we actually pushed each other to one side, a bit of a joke: 'I'm going first; no I'm going first'. We both sort of jostled in our living room and basically I won the jostle and went upstairs to the bathroom. Alan went on into the porch. I was in the bathroom and I heard the shooting. At that stage my kids actually didn't know what had happened. We had all just been sitting together a few minutes earlier eating our dinner. When I came down the stairs Alan had actually made an attempt to run through the living room and into the back of the house. He got shot and just fell dead in the living room, just across the threshold of the doorway into the dinning room.

The loyalists pulled up and got out of the car. There was a skip at the front path and they leaned over the skip and just raked the front of the house with gunfire. Alan got shot just once in the head. He died almost instantly. Myself, Alan, my wife Liz and our two boys were in the house at the time. They were sitting in the dining room just behind the living room. When Alan came running in he actually fell on the threshold of the living room and the dining room. They were sitting at the table finishing off their dinner and Alan just fell in front of them. Liz grabbed the children and pushed them into the back of the kitchen. They didn't know what had happened. Liz then tried to put them out the back of the house. But they wouldn't go because obviously they just took it for granted I was out the front. They didn't know I had been upstairs when the shooting occurred. Obviously there was pandemonium. The kids were very fond of Alan because he talked to them a lot, especially about football. They just couldn't take it in.

After the shooting, all the neighbours in the street were out very quickly. It was a bright, good, clear evening. The whole street were remarking immediately about the fact that the British army had been parked down the street the entire day and yet they had just mysteriously disappeared about half an hour before the incident happened. Of course as the day went on everyone, including the local clergy and even Joe Hendron, who was the MP at the time, knew that from early morning there had been two British army vehicles parked in my street. They were parked in full view of my house and they didn't leave the street until 5 pm or 5.30 pm in the afternoon. The loyalists came at 6 pm and did the shooting.

Nobody claimed responsibility and there was nobody arrested. In fact when I went to meet the RUC in the solicitor's office they opened the file and they had one page in it. It was just so obvious that there was nothing being done about it. As far as I'm concerned the powers-that-be within the RUC were well aware; there was certainly no investigation, not even an attempt to have an investigation. Everybody knew the UDA was involved in it. There was a car found but there was never anything said by the RUC to indicate that it was the car involved in the killing or anything else of that nature.

We phoned the local priest and he went down and actually spoke to Margaret. I know the priest told Margaret that he wasn't sure what had happened; obviously they were trying to break it to her gently. I didn't want to leave our house until Alan was taken from it. I just didn't want to leave Alan really and I sat with him, as did Liz also. I was sort of torn. I kept in touch with Gerard McGuigan who was talking to Margaret and talking to the priest. I knew Margaret was obviously very distressed. But probably even at that point she didn't actually really know he was dead; she wasn't sure. So for me I was caught because I didn't want to leave until Alan's remains were removed. In fact I had a huge row with the RUC over all that because it seemed to us that it was taking forever. Certainly there was no urgency on their behalf to do the scene of the crime or anything else. There were spent cartridges left round the place; in fact we actually picked them up and forced the RUC to take them because they certainly weren't doing it themselves. Then I went over and just tried to explain to Margaret myself the whole terrible details of it. What sticks in my mind is the way in which Margaret greeted me when I arrived at her house. Obviously she was stunned and heartbroken but she just wanted to know every detail, and needed to hear Alan was not left alone. She kept insisting that I was not to blame. She was so hurt but thinking of my family also.

For me I just felt very dirty; that's the only way I can really describe it, because here is a situation where there is a person dead because of me. He left his house with five kids and a wife and didn't come back. In one sense you couldn't take it on board. But as I've said, the only way I could describe how I felt was dirty. Here was somebody doing me a favour and lost his life and his family have lost him.

I know his family are left to carry his death over a long number of years. It's coming up to eight years now. For me he'll always stand out, not because it happened in my family home, but because I came to know him in the prison setting and got very friendly with him over the years, got to know him and his family very well. He was just a very personable, likeable fella but deeply committed to what he knew had to be done here. I think it's just really, really sad that he had to lose his life the way he did.

It was just an indiscriminate attack. They never even asked for Sean by name. We believe as a family that our son was killed solely because he was a Catholic.

Sean Hughes
Killed by the UFF,
Falls Road,
7 September 1993

Sean Hughes' mother was born Marie Monaghan. She was originally from Concorde Street but the family had been bombed out of their home by the Luftwaffe in 1940. Two years later they got a house in Highbury Gardens in Ardoyne. It was there that Marie met Sean's father Seamus, from Butler Street. The two married in August 1952. At first they raised their family in Marie's family home. The first-born was Sean, on 14 March 1953. He was the eldest of what was eventually a family of three boys and three girls. Sean went to the Holy Cross Boys school but by then the Highbury Gardens house had become too small for the growing family and they moved to Knockdhu Park. Sean finished his education at the Christian Brothers secondary school on the Glen Road. When he finished school Sean worked as a waiter before getting a job in a hairdresser's. At around the some time he started to go out with Marie McCarney. Marie lived in Riverdale too, although her mother was from Jamaica Street. They eventually married when they were both just 20 on 11 August 1973. They soon started their own family and lived in Trench Park for a while before setting up home in the Four Winds area. Sean and Marie had three children, David, Lisa and John. After he got married, Sean set up his own hairdresser shop called 'John David'. It was located at the top of Donegall Road, just off the Falls. Sean did well. He had another shop for a time and became secretary of the hairdressers' association. Sean lived for his family and his work. However, in the context of the loyalist sectarian assassination campaign of the early 1990s, owning a business on the Falls was not without its dangers. On 7 September 1993 UFF gunmen first tried to attack people in a butcher's shop next door to Sean's salon. Then they ran up the stairs into his shop and asked for the owner. The gunmen shot Sean dead. Afterwards there were accusations that an RUC roadblock near the scene of Sean's death had disappeared half an hour before his killing. The gun he was shot with was also one of the UFF's South African weapons. Sean Hughes was a member of no political or military organisation. He was shot dead in a sectarian attack because he was a Catholic.

Marie and Seamus Hughes (mother and father)

Marie: We moved over to West Belfast in 1964 when Sean was 11. We had been living in my mother and father's house and there were five of us sleeping in the one room. There wasn't enough room so we moved across to Knockdhu Park. Sean never wanted to leave Ardoyne. As a child Sean never gave us any trouble. He was a good lad; all my children were lively, happy youngsters. Even when he grew up, Sean was a quiet lad. He had a sense of humour and would have joked with his family. But if he was out, he was always quite quiet and reserved. He lived for his work, home and family. He loved all kinds of music, traditional, opera, everything. When he was young he tried to pick up music himself but didn't have the ear for it. His father bought him a guitar. Him and his mates were going to start a band but it never materialised. Sean's brother Thomas was always his closest friend and he got very close to his youngest brother Seamus before he died. Seamus always went to Sean for advice. He missed Sean terribly after he was killed. When he left school, Sean at first wanted to be a chef. Then I saw an ad looking for someone for a unisex hair salon, Sonya's in Chapel Lane. He decided to give it a try and got a start. He never looked back after that. He was very good at hairdressing and after that place closed down he worked in Ann Street. He was 16 when he started hairdressing and that was also when he met his wife Marie. She came to his birthday party. They went with each other for four years and married when they were both 20. It was at that point that Sean decided to start his own hairdressers. After Sean and Marie married they lived with us for a while, then they got a wee bungalow in Twinbrook. They lived for a while in Trench Park, then got the house up by Carryduff, in the Four Winds area. That is where they lived and brought up their three children until Sean was killed. At one time Sean had two hairdressers' shops but the main one was 'John David'. That is where Sean was murdered. I was always worried about Sean. I used to say to him that someone could come right up the stairs and shoot him. I don't think he was ever threatened, but there was always a worry.

I will never forget the day Sean was murdered. Sean's father and I were both sitting in our home when we found out. I had a terrible feeling all day that something was wrong. I am not normally superstitious but I had cracked a mirror earlier on. I always go down to the chapel to say the stations of the cross and even as I was praying, I had this horrible feeling. Then, as I came in the back door of the house, the phone rang. My husband took the phone. It was my brother and he told us there had been a shooting in Sean's shop. All I could say was, 'Sean, Sean'. Then we got a call from our niece confirming that it was Sean who had been shot. My daughters Ann and Paula were in a shop on the Stewartstown Road when they heard it on the radio. They were totally stunned and went straight down to Sean's shop. My brother then came to the house and went down to the hairdressers with Sean's father. I just sat praying and asking God to give me the strength not to feel hatred and anger.

Seamus: I went down to the shop. The cops were there. People were shouting at them saying that they had been sitting in their jeeps for an hour and 15 minutes without doing anything. Apparently the RUC had a roadblock in place for about an hour or so before Sean's death. Then they disappeared and the UFF came in and killed him. Afterwards they got away down the Donegall Road without being touched. I didn't have any hassle from the RUC when I got there myself; that was because Gerry Adams was there. They just said I wasn't allowed up and then they brought Sean down in a plastic bag. It is then that I found out what had happened. The gunmen [loyalists] had gone to the butcher's shop around the corner. The guy in there had seen them and pulled the shutter down. They may have tried another shop, then they ran up Sean's stairs and asked for the proprietor. Sean answered and then they riddled him. There were a few other people there. There was one wee man who had been a commando in World War II and he was annoyed that he could not do anything. Another fella was behind the counter answering phones and they shot at him too. There was a young girl called Clare who worked with Sean and he died in her arms. She said the act of contrition in his ear. It was just an indiscriminate attack. They never even asked for Sean by name.

Just after, the *Irish News* put out a statement saying that Sean was an OC in the IRA. I think it was because Gerry Adams had been there. I saw red about what the *Irish News* did. I phoned the editor and told him that Sean was just a lad who lived for his family and his home. They had put him down as a 'terrorist'. I said that it was bad enough that Sean's life had been taken without doing that to his good name. They apologised and put a retraction in but they never explained to me why they had said that in the first place. The UFF released a statement claiming responsibility for killing my son. We believe as a family that our son was killed solely because he was a Catholic. He was murdered for his faith. They probably didn't like the fact that he was a Catholic and a businessman. But Sean had a lot of Protestant friends. There was one wee woman from the Shankill Road he used to talk about who had a hairdressing business there. She had her place burnt down because she wouldn't pay protection money to the loyalists. I met her a couple of years ago through the hairdressing association. They have a John David trophy that they have asked various members of our family to give. She said that Sean was like a son to her. The UDA burnt that wee woman out. We didn't go to the court case. We couldn't face it. The men who killed Sean had not worn masks so there were descriptions of them. There were two of them brought up on charges but they both got off. One of them is dead himself now. I think it was something to do with drugs. Another one was later shot during elections.

Marie and Seamus: Sean was not a political person. He just lived for his family and did his best to provide for them. To us, we couldn't have had a better son. He was loving, kind and there for you if you needed him. All our kids are good but he was the oldest and he took responsibility for the younger ones. Sean's murder had a devastating impact on the whole family. They were all close. They always stuck up for one another and when they went out together they always had great fun. His sisters were crushed by what happened. Thomas was closest to Sean and he took it very badly.

Mary Glennon (aunt)

The day Sean was murdered my niece Elizabeth phoned me to tell me what happened. He was just dusting a man down after cutting his hair when the loyalists came in and shot him. His younger brother Seamus has since been putting together a family tree and he has been over to the Falls to piece together what happened. Next to Sean's shop was Aldo's café and next to it was a space where cars could be parked. Apparently the police had been moving cars from around there as if setting it up for a getaway. The butcher who worked next door to Sean was also shot and injured a couple of months after Sean was killed. He had been going to give evidence in relation to Sean's case. The butcher left that shop after that. The UFF claimed Sean's death though they never gave any reason for it. It was because he was a Catholic. They were just trying to prove that they could go into the Falls and kill people. They had killed the fella who owned the 'seven eleven' across the road from the shop a couple of weeks before. There were a couple of people charged for Sean's death. I went to the court just one day. The person I saw giving evidence was brilliant. He identified one of the killers. But they still got off. At the end of the day it was a case of pure, blatant sectarianism. All those lads killed round there were killed solely because they were Catholics. To me Sean was a good, very kindly fella. He used to come up to Ardoyne all the time and I would drop into the shop for a chat every week. He was just a good, kind man who lived for his work and his family.

Thomas Hughes (brother)

When Sean and me grew up in Ardoyne we would have knocked about with a load of fellas. There was Frankie and Jackie Donnelly, Martin Bean, Paul McKibbin, Davy and Terry Agnew and our cousins, Coco and Gerard McAuley. We used to play a lot of football together, although Sean wasn't much of a player. He was a good runner though. Sean was into Irish and he was great at it. He was into music too. He was a great disco dancer and if he had a couple of drinks he loved to sing Frank Sinatra songs. But he never did drink much. Sean was religious but not overtly so, only in the sense that he insisted that his own family went to mass on a Sunday. But Sean was never into politics at all. He was definitely 'anti-terrorism'. He never liked any aspect of the conflict. He wouldn't have put anyone else down for their views but he definitely would not have supported Sinn Féin or the IRA. I actually introduced Sean to his wife-to-be Marie. He was about 14 then. Marie was his first serious girlfriend. They married in August 1973 and I was Sean's best man. After school he worked as a waiter for a while, then he took up the hairdressing. When he started that people used to say that he was going into it because he was gay. But I knew exactly why. It was because there were women involved in it! Sean was the only bloke in the shop with all these girls standing in miniskirts around him. Whenever we all went in he would just turn and laugh as if to say, 'I know why you are here'! Sean was a very quiet bloke until you got him started and he got on with everybody.

The last time I saw Sean was the Saturday before he was killed. He was shot the following Tuesday. I called into the shop to have a bit of a laugh with him. Sean was brilliant and loved talking when he was working in the shop. He just loved his job and when you were in that chair you got a great conversation out of him. The day Sean was killed I was actually working on a heating job in Lisburn. I had a bad feeling all day. I always carried a saw with me for protection, especially when I was in a loyalist area. I remember that day a mate came through the door and I swung at him with the saw. I just missed him by inches. I packed the job in for the day at that stage. This was only about 1 pm. I was just mentally and physically shattered. So I was lying in the bed when my uncle Tommy phoned. He was just shouting, 'Sean has been shot'. He said it had been on the radio. I ordered a taxi and when I got in the driver said that there had been a fella shot dead in a hairdressers on the Falls Road. I went straight to the hairdressers. I tried to go up the stairs but the police stopped me. I was told then that there had been a big roadblock on the Falls Road up until about 3 pm that afternoon. Sean was killed at 3.30 pm. It had been choc-a-block with police and army, then 30 minutes later my brother was dead. The loyalists ran to the butchers first, then into Sean's place. Then they shot him. After we got there my father and I went into Aldo's café and Gerry Adams came in and told us about what had happened with the roadblock. There was a load of newsmen in there and one took a photo of my father. The look of grief on his face I have never seen on anyone before or since.

A couple of people were later lifted for Sean's death but they were not convicted. They were UFF men. I never paid much attention to whoever killed my brother because I knew nothing would happen to them anyway. I actually felt sorry for the people who did that to my brother. Sean was completely innocent, so what satisfaction they got out of killing him I don't know. I don't know how they had the nerve to do it. They just shot him because he was a Catholic man. The family was really devastated by Sean's death. Sean's wife and kids were shattered. Everybody took it bad. I never thought anything would happen to Sean with him working on the Falls Road. If anyone was going to be shot I thought it would be me because I worked in risky areas. So afterwards, wherever I was working after that I was far more careful. Sean was just a great older brother. He was easy to talk to and would give you advice. He could be sarcastic and you had to know him well to get on with him but he was funny and a smashing bloke. If you were in need he was there for you.

> *The IRA did not go out to kill innocent people. I myself deeply regret innocent people dying that day. The intended target was the UDA leadership who were responsible for numerous murders in our areas throughout the years.*

Thomas Begley
Killed on active service,
Shankill Road,
23 October 1993

Thomas Begley's father Billy was originally from Carrick Hill and his mother Sadie (née Pentagast) was from Brompton Park, Ardoyne. Billy and Sadie met in the Plaza in 1959 and two years later were married in Holy Cross chapel. They lived for a while in Carlisle Circus but eventually moved back to Ardoyne, to Sadie's family home. The couple had five children: Billy, John, Ann-Marie, Martin and Thomas.

Thomas (Bootsy) Begley attended Holy Cross Boys and St Gabriel's school. He had a number of casual jobs and worked with his father in the building trade. He was close to his brothers and particularly fond of his sister Ann-Marie. His lifelong friend was Sean Kelly. Although he was a shy, quiet fella, Thomas enjoyed socialising and 'the craic' with his mates. He loved fishing, fixing old cars and was a member of Carrick Hill Martyrs flute band.

Thomas Begley was an IRA volunteer. On 23 October 1993 he was killed while on active service with his friend and comrade Sean Kelly. Thomas was killed and Sean Kelly was seriously injured when the bomb they were planting exploded prematurely in Frizzell's fish shop on the Shankill Road. The intended target was the UDA leadership whom they believed were meeting upstairs in the premises. Since the 1970s the offices above Frizzell's fish shop had been the UDA West Belfast brigade headquarters. The IRA intended to plant the bomb, timed to allow the evacuation of the shop, but not enough time for those upstairs to escape. Nine Protestant civilians were also killed in the explosion. This was a devastating human tragedy for the Shankill Road community and the family and friends of the innocent Protestant civilians killed who understandably viewed the incident as an indiscriminate attack.

Sean Kelly later wrote to the *Irish News* expressing deep regret at the loss of innocent life. He also repeated the IRA statement that the target had been UDA/UFF members meeting upstairs in the building.

Mr and Mrs Begley (mother and father)

We knew that Thomas was sympathetic to the republican movement but at no time did we know that he was involved in the IRA. At the time of his death Thomas wasn't going out with any girl in particular. Thomas was a very polite, quiet, and shy young lad. His friends were Sean Kelly, Brian and Raymond Wootton and the Reids.

Thomas died instantly along with nine other people when the bomb he was carrying exploded prematurely while he was inside Frizzell's fish shop on the Shankill Road. The Ulster Defence Association (UDA) had used the offices upstairs above the fish shop as their headquarters. We understand that the IRA's intention was to plant the bomb, and to give time to allow people in the fish shop to get out. But there wouldn't have been enough time for the UDA/UFF, who had been holding a meeting upstairs, to escape. Sean Kelly, Thomas's close friend, was with him. He was severely injured in the explosion and pulled from the rubble. Later Sean wrote to the *Irish News* expressing deep regret at the lost of innocent life in the bombing; he also said that their target had been UDA/UFF members whom they believed were meeting upstairs in the building. Sean regularly calls to visit us and keeps in touch with the family.

We were totally devastated at Thomas's death, as we were with everyone who died during this tragic incident. The family found it difficult to come to terms with. The first year was probably the worst. He is very sadly missed by all of us.

Ann-Marie Thomson (sister)

Thomas was quiet when he was younger. But he was very outgoing at the same time. He was next to me in age and we were close. Thomas was into cars and motorbikes and loved mechanics. If my kids needed their bikes fixed it was Thomas who did it. Thomas would have done you a good turn; he was my baby sitter. He had loads of friends and he was very popular in the street. All of the ones he grew up remained close friends right up to his death. His best friend was Sean Kelly; they would have fought with one another and were the best of friends the next day. Thomas never held a grudge.

Thomas was a member of the Carrick Hill Martyrs Flute Band; he carried the flag. He was the first one to carry the tricolour to the city hall; he was as proud as punch. He wasn't a big drinker. Me and my husband used to laugh because if Thomas had more than two pints he was giddy. He was the quiet man, he didn't tell you an awful lot; his business was his own. I was aware of his involvement in the republican movement; I was quite proud of him to be honest.

I will never forget the day Thomas was killed. It was a nice day and my mummy and I walked into town. The tension in North Belfast was really high because there had been so many loyalist sectarian shootings. When we reached the New Lodge Road we saw a crowd standing round a car listening to the radio. I heard somebody saying, 'Jesus there has been a bomb on the Shankill'. We were shocked. First reports were that it was at the UDA headquarters and six UDA men had been killed. We walked on into town. As we were crossing the Crumlin Road my mummy blessed and said, 'Thomas is going to be brought home to me in a box'. My mummy went on and met up with my daddy in town. I went over to my husband's mother's house in the Short Strand.

The word was filtering through that the bomb had been in a fish and chip shop and it was all civilians that had been killed. Everybody's nerves were on a knife-edge. I phoned home to Ardoyne a couple of times but the phone was engaged. I thought to myself that that was strange. Several hours later I eventually got through to my mummy's house and my aunt Ann answered the phone. She told me to come home straight away. I asked what was wrong; I thought there had been trouble. She eventually told me Thomas had been killed. I still didn't think about the bomb; I thought loyalists had come in to the district and shot him. That was about 12.15 am.

Going from the Short Strand to Ardoyne seemed like miles and I thought I was never going to get there. The first person I met at the door was Eddie Copeland. The peeler jeeps were everywhere. I went into the house and it was packed. Everything was going through my head, but no one knew exactly what had happened. The atmosphere was unbelievable. They didn't know who was alive and who was dead. At this stage there was still that wee bit of hope that Thomas wasn't dead. My mummy's friend Helen and my aunt Ann went to the Royal Hospital but couldn't find anything out. They then went to Grovesnor Road RUC station. Apparently the words the RUC used were, 'These are the bomber's relatives; escort them off the premises'.

The bombing happened at 2 pm on Saturday and it was about 7.45 am next morning before we found out who was dead and who was still alive. I can't remember talking to Sean's mummy before we found out it was Thomas that had been killed. Sean's sister Philomena just threw her arms round me and said how terrible the whole thing was. From that day to the funeral everything was a blur to me; it was as if one day it happened and the next thing he was getting buried. The body came home and we weren't allowed to open the coffin; we had his photograph on top of the coffin. Throughout the wake there was harassment from the RUC and British army. Eddie Copeland ended up getting shot in our garden by a British soldier.

The harassment continued well after the funeral. During the first Easter commemoration we were going up the Falls Road to lay a wreath and on the way back an RUC man was eating an apple and he shouted, 'Here Begley' and threw the apple and said, 'There is the other half of your brother'. The family got hate mail, it was terrible. But you rise above that and don't let it drag you down. My whole family lived in fear; my father had to leave his job. I think the first year was definitely the worst year of it all.

The people of the district gathered round and gave us their support; they couldn't do enough. When the funeral cortege was going to Milltown cemetery there were protests by loyalists. Everybody was in a panic because the loyalists had taken over the bridge at the flyover from the Shankill and were waiting on the funeral with bricks, bottles and eggs, everything to attack the funeral. My mummy was squealing; the expression on her face was that of severe shock. A lasting memory of the funeral is the people running from Unity Flats towards the Shankill to save the cortege.

My mummy and daddy put a statement out about the deaths on the Shankill Road saying that they regretted what had happened, that they had grandchildren too and they thought of the wee ones that were killed. There was a wee 7 and 13 year old killed. My parents said that they were living with feelings of guilt too as regards to the civilian deaths. It was 11 months after Thomas's death that the cease-fire was called; I started to feel everything then. I had very mixed feelings at that time. I grieve every day for Thomas but the first year was like a total nightmare. We were grieving that much for Thomas we didn't know what day of the week it was. It took a while to be able to think straight.

Thomas was a happy-go-lucky kid and he was always there for me when I needed him. I think about him a lot. He was 22 when he was killed; it was two weeks before his 23rd birthday. So that was another blow; you had just buried him and then it was his birthday and the pain was unbearable. I have learnt to live with it now but the first couple of years were a mixture of emotions. I had a lot of anger inside me but thank God, now I accept it. I will always remember him with great pride and am so proud to say he was my brother.

Billy Begley (brother)

Bootsy and I were very close. He was more than just a brother to me; he was also one of my best friends. From he was about 13 years old he visited my family in Unity Flats and him and Kells his best friend would regularly baby-sit for us. My wife Isobel was very fond of them both. They were a joy to have around. The kids loved them both and the craic was great when they were in our company. As a young man I carried the tricolour for the Carrick Hill Martyrs flute band. But as time went on I passed the honour down to Bootsy. He loved it, especially when accompanied by Kells on the drum.

I can remember visiting my mum's house and going to Bootsy's room and sitting for hours just talking to him. I think my mum had an idea that he was involved. She knew he was sympathetic to the republican struggle. She would often ask me to talk to Thomas and try to convince him otherwise. I told her there was no use because that's what he believed in from an early age and he had already made his mind up regarding the issue. My mum's biggest fear was that one day Thomas was going to be brought home to her in a coffin. I use to tell her to stop thinking like that and not to worry about him.

I'll never forget the day Bootsy was killed. I called to my mum's house that morning. I remember laughing and saying to Bootsy, 'I can't believe my eyes. What are you doing up this early on a Saturday?' But he never replied. My mum was at the shops. It was about 8.45 am and Thomas was kneeling on the living room floor raking the fire. Just then my mum came in, I said hello to her and then Thomas and myself went outside to talk. Next thing I realised it was 10.45 am; we had been talking for about two hours. I then decided that I was going to make my way home. Thomas said he would walk me to the corner of the street. On the way down he asked if he could stay for a few nights in my house. I said, 'no problem' and thought nothing of this. Thomas often stayed the night with us. I even told him that he could come hunting with me the next morning. We got to the corner and said our good-byes. I made my way home not knowing that they were the last few moments I was ever going to spend with my younger brother.

Since 23 October 1993 there hasn't been a day that goes by that I have not thought of Bootsy. He was my brother and my best friend and he will always be loved and missed dearly.

Sean Kelly (friend and comrade)

I grew up with Thomas Begley; I have known him all my life. We did all the basic things you do when you are young and growing up. Our base was the bottom of Brompton Park where we played cards with a group of other lads. We never really ventured too far when we were younger but as the years went on, we started going out to the clubs. We went to the GAA on a Sunday night and the Jamaica Inn on a Thursday night. When Bootsy was young he was like the rest of us, but quiet and shy in his own way. He never held a grudge and he wasn't a fighter. His main interest was work and he liked working with his daddy, Billy. Bootsy loved cars; I think he would like to have been a mechanic. He was always buying scrap cars. He spent more money doing the car up than he did buying it; it was a hobby. He was always content when he was round cars or when he was working. His favourite music was country music: Patsy Cline, Dolly Parton and Kenny Rodgers. But he also liked Rave and Dance music. His favourite poem was by Seamus Heaney. It's a poem about taking the hard road to freedom; he had that poem on his bedroom wall.

I was already in the republican movement and we were having a discussion about the situation in the district and the heavy-handedness of the RUC and the DMSUs. We were talking about the conflict in general and Bootsy said to me, 'I would like to join the movement. I would like to do something about this'. Bootsy would have been a bit like myself at that particular time; he wasn't fully politically aware. There is no use pretending we were fully tuned in to everything politically at that time. But we knew that we didn't like what was happening to our community and we wanted the Brits out of Ireland. We were young, we were eager; we knew what we were about. We knew what was going on around us wasn't right and wasn't proper and we wanted to do something about it. Later, I would say, we became more fully politically aware. Bootsy took the step and joined the republican movement. When he was involved there was no job too big or too small for him; he was always at hand. Bootsy never had a complaint and he was always coming forward with ideas. He just did what he had to do and that was it.

The night before the operation on the Shankill, Bootsy was like myself; we knew what was ahead of us the next day and what we had to do. That night I think he just wanted a bit of time on his own and to go and see his brother. The next morning he was up from the crack of dawn. He knew it was a big task ahead. That morning I met him. I remember us walking up the entry, the last moments that we spent together. We were saying how important it was to get our intended target, the UDA leadership and the Inner Council of the UDA. From 1990 Ardoyne had suffered an awful lot; the UFF / UDA were slaughtering Catholics and it was time for us to take the people responsible out of circulation. We were not gloating about killing anybody but we knew it had to be done.

I am not afraid to admit, I was nervous; I knew I was on a difficult operation. I knew I had to be careful because of the risk of civilian lives being lost. Bootsy was also aware of this. Everybody knew what the target was, the UDA/UFF meeting. There was absolutely no intention whatsoever of killing innocent people that day. We were talking about that even when we got out of the car on the Shankill Road; we were saying, 'Hope to God that we get the right people here; hope to God there are no innocent lives lost'. Our intention was to go in, give the warning, plant the bomb and get out. But obviously it didn't happen like that. All I can remember is me and Bootsy walking and exchanging a couple of brief words to each other. We were concentrating on what we had to do, that is all I remember. I can't remember another thing after the bomb went off.

It was devastating that so many people lost their lives that day. The media has portrayed us as deliberately wanting to slaughter innocent people. Even when I was up in court the judge said, 'This is for the wanton slaughter of innocent people', but it wasn't. It was an operation that went terribly wrong; the bomb went off prematurely and there was nothing we could have done about it. There was nothing I could have done about it, not a thing. I am not saying that it was right; obviously it was not. It had a huge impact on us; it had a big impact on the nationalist communities with the revenge attacks, the Greysteel massacre and the other sectarian killing of Catholics that followed. At the end of the day you could go into any Protestant area, you could go down the Shankill, up the Sandy Row or anywhere and plant a bomb if innocent people were your target. You would not go out on a military operation taking the risks that we took and the consequences that were suffered in order to target or kill innocent people. That definitely wasn't our intention. Bootsy was not sectarian. I have nothing whatsoever against the Protestant community. To me the conflict is not based on Protestant against Catholics or Catholics against Protestants; this conflict is based on the British presence in our country.

I was in intensive care for two weeks and I remember my mummy coming in. My first words when I started to come round a bit were, 'Where is Bootsy?' and she said to me, 'Bootsy is lying in the next bed'. I can remember she just burst into tears and I grabbed her hand. I'm not sure how many days passed and I said to my mummy again, 'Where is Bootsy?' and she said, 'He is dead and buried a week ago'. I just broke down. I still didn't fully know the extent of what had happened and then my mummy told me there were nine civilians killed including women and children and then I broke down again. I took it really bad. It really wrecked me. It was also hard on both sets of parents.

When the Good Friday Agreement was signed and they started the prisoner releases and paroles, I sat in my cell one night and I had Bootsy's photograph up on the wall. I looked up and said, 'I wish to God you were here. I wish you were here getting out with me today'. I thought how Sadie, Bootsy's mother, would feel about me getting out. I thought she would be thinking, 'My Thomas is dead'. I know now that the family wouldn't think like that but those thoughts were going through my head. I was conscious of calling to her door and being happy, saying that I was in a relationship and saying that I had a girlfriend. Then when my child was born it was hard for me to tell them and their son was lying dead.

I know what it is like to lose someone now; I lost a close friend that day and a comrade and it is very hard. I think about it every day of my life without fail. I try not to let it mess my head up but I think about it and try to keep it under control. I have a very close bond with the Begley family; I would say that that relationship if anything has grown stronger. I go to his grave regularly on anniversaries and at Christmas. That is just a promise that I made to him, that I wouldn't let him down and that I would always keep in contact with his family.

The IRA did not go out that day to kill innocent people. I myself deeply regret innocent people dying that day; the intended target was the UDA leadership. Our war was with the British establishment and the UDA/UFF, the forces who were slaughtering our people. On that specific day that's who our intended target was, not innocent people, not children, not women out doing their shopping and that is fact. It just happened that me and Thomas got the task of going on the operation and it went terribly wrong.

I have no doubt in my mind that had Bootsy survived that operation he would, like myself, have remained a dedicated republican and would have been fully supportive of the peace process. He was an IRA volunteer and I am certain he would have shown the same discipline and commitment as all other volunteers to achieving the objectives of republicanism, despite the provocations and difficulties we have experienced, particularly in this area over recent years. Bootsy is sadly missed and republicans should re-double their efforts to bring about the re-unification of our country so that deaths like Bootsy's were not in vain.

Eddie Copeland (friend)

I knew the Begley family all my life. I went through both primary and secondary school with Bootsy. We started to run about together in the early 1990s and he became a very close friend. He was a real character, the heart and soul of the company he was in.

The day he was involved in the bombing was a very sad day for the people of Ardoyne, especially for us his friends, and obviously for the Shankill Road community who had lost nine innocent civilians. I heard about Bootsy's death later that evening when it was confirmed that he had been killed. Bootsy was an IRA volunteer and as a republican I offered my help to his family. I helped out and did whatever I could at the wake. From the time Bootsy was killed until he came home we barely left his house. We wanted to be there to support the family.

When Bootsy's body came home there was a huge military presence. Ardoyne was swamped with RUC and British army. There were, for example, British army jeeps constantly sitting outside the Begley home. There was a lot of aggravation; the RUC and British army were hurling abuse and shouting sick remarks and comments about Bootsy. Tension was really high in the area. People were fearful that there was going to be a sectarian attack on the actual Begley house.

The British army shot me at Bootsy's wake. He was killed on Saturday 23 October and the Brits opened up and shot at us outside his home on 26 October. There was myself and other local republicans, and republicans from outside the area, who were there in support of the family. I was standing talking to a friend; it was after lunch, roughly about 1.30 pm. There was an RUC jeep sitting outside the Begley house. There were two British army landrovers constantly circling the area and they were doing a lot of finger pointing, shouting and all the rest of it. I was standing looking down towards Etna Drive as the jeeps drove up Brompton Park. Then that was it, I got shot.

I think I was shot from the second jeep. The Brit was standing up looking out of the hatch. I didn't know it was the British army shooting at the time. I thought it was a sectarian attack. I was just lying in the garden wondering what was going to happen next. I was shot twice, once in the back and badly grazed on the shoulder. I was in total agony. The force of the bullet spun me around. I may have travelled as much as ten feet. It was a frightening experience. Then my mother and brother came on the scene. My mother was constantly slapping my face trying to keep me awake and alert. She kept saying, 'This is history repeating itself'. In 1971 my father was shot dead by the British army, he was only 23 years old. He was shot on 28 October and died on the 30 October [Johnny Copeland, killed by the British army, Strathroy Park, 30 October 1971]. I was 23 years old when the British army shot me and it was October 26th. My father was shot in the back and I was shot in the back; the similarities were scary. It was only when I started to feel better and got back on my feet again that I fully realised the dates and the ages and the circumstances. That is what my mother meant when she said history is repeating itself. I was only one year old when my father was killed.

Bootsy was a real character. I was gutted at his death. He was probably the closest person to me, as a friend, to be killed. It was heart breaking to see the family; it was hard to try and speak to them, and I just didn't know what to say.

> *I turned round and I saw a gunman; he was wearing a black monkey hat, a scarf and black sunglasses, black bomber jacket and black running shoes. As Martin turned round I just saw a flash, then I looked and Martin was on the floor and my wee brother Jamesy was lying beside him screaming.*

Martin Bradley
Killed by loyalists,
Crumlin Road,
12 May 1994

Martin Bradley was born on 12 July 1970. His father was Hugh Bradley from 52 Northwick Drive, Ardoyne and his mother, Mary Ward, was from Carrick Hill. The couple married and eventually had five children: Colette, Anthony, Angela, Martin and Thomas. In 1978 the family moved to Cranbrook Court. Martin attended Holy Cross Boys and St Gabriel's school and like most lads in the area left with no qualifications. His nickname was 'Marty Dander' because of his distinctive walk, 'the Bradley dander'. Martin was just an ordinary decent young lad who was keen on the odd bet and loved a game of snooker. He was very close to his wider family circle, in particular his younger cousins and aunts who loved his humour.

On 12 May 1994 while visiting his aunt Patricia, a loyalist gunman burst into her house and killed Martin, narrowly missing her one-year-old son. The UFF later claimed responsibility for the killing. Martin was 23 at the time of his death. Three other members of the Bradley family have been killed as a result of the conflict [Francie Bradley, killed by loyalists, Corporation Street, 19 June 1975; Martin Bradley, killed by loyalists, Crumllin Road, 20 December 1994; and Fra Shannon, killed by INLA, Turf Lodge, 9 June 1996].

Patricia McAllister (aunt)

Martin used to come to my house and tap me for either 50p or £1. He would give me a whole big story about what he needed it for. He got this old black car, 'Night Rider', that's what we called it. He used to go over to the Jamaica Inn and give people lifts home. He never got paid for it. Whenever he called to the house none of the kids would go out because you always got a good laugh. He always exaggerated his stories. If he won anything in the bookies he would have given you a few pounds. No matter who asked him to do a favour he would have done it for them. That was the type of him.

Two weeks before Martin was murdered, my son Fra (Sparky) was arrested for the shooting of a loyalist. That was two weeks and one day before Martin was killed in my house. When Fra was in Castlereagh interrogation centre the RUC told him they would give him two weeks and a top loyalist would be out to kill him. Fra told his solicitor about the threat and who made it. Local people told us that a well-known loyalist had been spotted driving up and down the road around our house. This was after Fra had been arrested. I went to see our Paddy in the Crumlin Road gaol the Saturday after Martin had been killed and he said the night that it happened he heard loyalist prisoners shouting, 'They got Sparky Shannon (my son Fra), they got Sparky Shannon'. Poor Martin just happened to be in the house at the wrong time. When Fra was arrested, the

RUC raided the house. They saw the bullet-proof glass and the security gate and drop bars. One of the cops said, 'Look at this: murderers on the outside, definitely murderers in the inside'. They drew a map of the house and where everything was in it. They didn't tell me Fra had been arrested.

Martin came in the back way to my house; nobody would ever have known Martin was in my house. He came down Kerrera Street and in the back. Martin, myself, Joe and a couple of the kids were in the kitchen. This was about 5.05 pm. Joe brought Thomas out to show him the doghouse. The child, Jamesy, started squealing after his daddy and Martin lifted him up on his shoulders. So we were standing there talking and I had the dinner on. Then Jolene and her friend Ann-Marie came in. I asked Jolene to shut the front door and she said no. Jolene actually blamed herself as a matter of fact and was attending the hospital. She said that if she had done what I had asked her and shut the door the gunman wouldn't have got in.

When Martin was shot I thought it was my gas bottle exploding and I sort of went down along with him. It was just a handgun the gunman had. Martin was only in the house about twenty minutes when he was killed. They must have been coming for my son Fra. That particular day Fra was on his way here but ran out of petrol at the top of Alliance Avenue. He went to Gerry 'Wiffle-Waffle' and got a container to get petrol. If Fra's car hadn't ran out of petrol he would have been in the house. Martin was shot around 5.30 pm and wasn't taken out of my house until around 9 pm. I thought that was very long. They made us stay in the living room and took everybody's fingerprints.

There were two statements released by loyalists. The first stated the UFF had killed Sparky. But the second statement mentioned Martin's name. Funny enough the first peeler that got out of the jeep outside my house said, 'Did they get Sparky?'

Martin was a big gentle giant. He would never have hurt anybody. He was very fond of his aunt Angela and she was very fond of him.

Jolene (niece and eyewitness)

When I came into the house my mummy asked me did I close the front door and I said no. She said to me, 'Go and shut the front door'. And I said, 'No'. But as I got up to shut the door I heard, 'Yo'. I thought it was my daddy's friend shouting Joe. I turned round and I saw a gunman; he was wearing a black monkey hat, a scarf and black sunglasses, black bomber jacket and black running shoes. As Martin turned round I just saw a flash then I looked and Martin was on the floor and my wee brother Jamesy was lying beside him screaming. Martin had my wee brother on his shoulders at the time and the bullet that hit Martin just missed my wee brother's leg. Martin tried to run at the gunman but he slipped in his own blood. The gunman pointed the gun at Martin's head and shouted, 'Die, you fenian bastard' and shot him twice. Then he walked out. My friend Ann-Marie was sitting in our living room and the gunman told her to 'fuck off' and booted her in the legs.

I actually blamed myself and was attending the hospital. I thought if I'd done what my mummy had asked and shut the door, the gunman wouldn't have got in. Then I had to come to an understanding that the gunman would have got in some way. But I always thought it funny, and always said to myself, if the gunman had come in and I had been standing on my own in the kitchen what would he have done? Would he have shot me? Or what if my mummy had thrown the chip pan at the gunman? There must have been somebody waiting outside to help the gunman get away. There was no car. One of our neighbours saw him. They were wondering why he was putting a scarf on coming up our path. So the gunman must have got 'ready' in our hall. I didn't hear anything. The gunman pushed past me and nearly knocked me under the stairs. Then I went into convulsions. Immediately after the shooting, when everybody ran out to the Crumlin Road, there were two RUC jeeps parked down the Crumlin Road. That was only a split second after the gunman walked out of our house. But it took the RUC about ten minutes to come up the road to our house.

Colette Bradley (sister)

Martin was born on 12 July 1970 and he died on 12 May 1994. He was 23 when he was murdered. My mother told him that the bands came out for his birthday on the 12th of July and he believed that when he was younger. Martin loved playing snooker. He frequented the Jamaica Inn and Ta Lockey's but he wasn't really a drinker. Martin drank with our neighbour Martin McErlean. Martin brought him out for a drink one night and our Martin ordered a pint of beer and a bottle of coke. Martin McErlean said he couldn't figure out why. Our Martin was only 17 or 18 years old at the time. Apparently he took a swig of the beer and went 'Ooh' and then took a swig of the coke to wash it down.

Martin loved the bookies. He loved gambling on the horses and the dogs. I would describe Martin as a very happy- go-lucky person; he didn't take things too seriously and he didn't really plan ahead. He just got up in the mornings and whatever came, came. He was friendly with Christy Davidson who now lives in Estoril Park and Angelo Falloni who came from Alliance Avenue. As far as I'm aware they were his friends at the time of his death.

I was living up in Ligoniel when Martin was shot dead. The last time I saw him was four or five days before his death. He had just got a new car; it wasn't new but it was new to him. He came up to see me and he took me out for a spin in the car. That was the last time I saw him. The day that Martin was killed I had been at Queen's University all day. It was a lovely day and it was coming up to exam time. I went to Botanic Gardens and it was bustling with people; it was such a beautiful day. I went into town that afternoon. I got a number 57 bus up the Crumlin Road. Martin was killed on the Crumlin Road just facing the chapel. It was probably around 5.00 pm and that was close to the time Martin was killed. When I got home I remember I turned on the TV to hear the news. UTV came on and Mike Nesbitt the presenter said, 'News has just come in of a shooting in north Belfast, the Crumlin Road'. Automatically I thought, 'Thank God it's not a street that anyone belonging to me lives in'. I wasn't thinking of Patricia's house on the Crumlin Road at the time.

Then at 6.45 pm I saw my brother Anthony coming up the path. I opened the door and he said, 'Did you hear about Martin?' and I said, 'No'. I just started crying and the next thing my mother came up the path and said, 'Come on and get your coat; the priest is out in the car'. I didn't know it then but Martin's body was still lying round in the house in 393 Crumlin Road. My father had gone round there and neighbours were in the house. There was nothing you could do because we didn't know anything. Then Patricia came round and she said that Martin and Thomas had called to her house and they were standing in the kitchen talking. Patricia said the next thing she turned round and there was a masked man standing with a gun. The gunman shot Martin. I think he was shot four or five times, once in the head. Patricia said she just didn't realise what was happening and looking back, she should have lifted the chip pan and thrown it round him. But she said it was all over so quickly and Martin died on the spot. That night there was different reports given out and the first was that loyalists (I can't remember which group) had shot 'Sparky' (Fra Shannon) dead. They went in to shoot Francis but shot Martin by mistake. Nobody was ever arrested for Martin's killing. That was a time when there was really heightened tension and there had been a few people arrested but not necessarily in relation to Martin's killing. No one was ever charged with Martin's killing.

British army observation post (now demolished) at the junction of Crumlin and Woodvale Road. The post occupied the site of an old house from which British soldiers ambushed Bernard Fox, 4 December 1972.

6

1994-2002

Peace, What Peace? To the Good Friday Agreement and Beyond

The IRA called a ceasefire on 31 August 1994. As has already been noted, it came after years of formal and informal negotiations and seemed to open the door to full and inclusive all-party talks within a matter of months. The initial reaction within Ardoyne was mixed, although generally charged with a real sense of hope and euphoria. People were unsure of exactly what the future might hold in store. Many (on the basis of past experience) were deeply suspicious. There were undoubtedly some who were downright hostile and wondered what the sacrifices of the previous three decades had been for. Distrust of both the British state and the intentions of unionists and loyalists was widespread. Some feared too that any sign of 'weakness' could leave Ardoyne vulnerable to attack again. However, this was a community that had for too long been on the frontline of conflict. In the main people were therefore relieved that it might finally be coming to an end. If the ceasefire was 'unknown territory' there was a general feeling that the worst of times might be about to be consigned to the past, a sense that real political progress could be made. As in many other nationalist areas, news of the ceasefire was greeted by a cavalcade of tricolour-flying cars making its way through the district. Virtually every corner it passed was a marker in someone's mind of a violent incident of the past, where a friend was hurt or a loved one lost. Conor Stiobhard is a teenager from Ardoyne. He describes something of what it was like to grow up in the district in the 1980s and early 1990s and what significance the 1994 ceasefire held for him.

I was born in 1981, just after the hunger strike. As a youth growing up in Ardoyne in the 1980s and 1990s you were obviously conscious of Brits in the streets and that people were stopped and harassed by the RUC. Because I was so young I just remember that there were times when I was not allowed out to play in the street. The next day you would find out that there had been house raids or the like going on at the bottom of the road. If that sort of thing is going on around you then you soon start to ask questions. I remember the day of the Shankill bomb very well. I was not allowed out in the evenings for quite a while afterward. My parents explained to me that they were afraid of a backlash against Ardoyne. That was the first time I remember my parents talking openly about the rights and wrongs of such things, though they always left it up to me to make my own mind up as to what I thought.

The day the first IRA ceasefire was called was a very important one to me. I was about 13 at the time. I remember watching the cavalcade of cars with tricolours driving through the district. It really felt as if something had been achieved. It came as a bit of a shock to some people and there were those who felt that it was a backward step. For young people it meant that you might not have to go through what others had in the past. On the other hand you might not get the chance to 'play your part'. But there have been a lot of good things that have come about because of the ceasefire. There is now real progress in terms of 'bread and butter issues' like housing, employment and education. There is a sense of a future. (Conor Stiobhard, a youth from Ardoyne)

Republicans believed that within three months of the ceasefire being called 'inclusive dialogue' would take place. This belief was based upon the many years of protracted (and mostly secret) negotiations that had previously taken place. Gerry Kelly (today an elected representative in the Assembly for North Belfast) was one of those deeply involved in negotiations both before and after the ceasefire was declared. He gives a personal recollection of what that period was like and the tenor of the debate amongst nationalists in North Belfast at the time.

Calling a ceasefire in 1994 was not an easy decision for republicans to take. There are good, empirical, logical reasons for republicans to be suspicious of ceasefires. History has taught us to be wary. The debate as to whether it was a wise move was something going on within all of us. If you had gone into any household or pub in a nationalist working class area at that time you would probably have heard the self-same arguments that were taking place at all levels of the republican movement. It was an emotional time, a period of great personal and collective turmoil about what was the best thing to do. If people had asked me if I trusted the Brits then I would have said 'No, of course not, but this is what they are saying to us'. Ultimately we believed we had got to the point where it was necessary to create the conditions to sit down and talk. That is what the ceasefire was designed to do. It also gave people a real sense of empowerment, that it was republicans who were taking the leading role and providing the engine to drive the peace process forward. When the ceasefire was first called I think there was a real wave of hope and people really want to give it a chance to work. (Gerry Kelly, MLA for North Belfast)

In the immediate wake of the ceasefire real progress seemed to be a distinct possibility. This was despite the initial response from loyalists which did not bode well for the future. On the first day of the IRA cessation the UFF killed a Catholic, John O'Hanlon, in Skegoniel Avenue in North Belfast. However, on 31 October the 'Combined Loyalist Military Command' (representing the UVF, the UFF and the Red Hand Commandos) declared a joint ceasefire on the grounds that the 'union was safe'. In February 1995 the British and Irish governments published their 'Joint Framework Document'. It was presented as a blueprint for a future constitutional settlement. Unionists were, however, opposed to it. In addition the Conservative administration (dependent on unionist support in parliament shortly) introduced the issue of decommissioning weapons into the equation shortly after. The peace process began to stall. The political vacuum thus created was soon filled by more direct loyalist actions.

In July 1995 the first 'stand-off' at Drumcree took place. 500 Orangemen were briefly halted and then allowed to march down the Garvaghy Road, the Catholic quarter of the overwhelmingly loyalist town of Portadown. A few days later the RUC and British army forced an Orange parade down the Ormeau Road despite protests from the residents. By 12 August there were further clashes as an Apprentice Boys parade was once again permitted to march down the Ormeau Road. Protestors were beaten from the street. In Derry the Apprentice Boys marched around the city walls for the first time in 25 years. It appeared that unionism and loyalism was 'drawing a line in the sand' over the issue of disputed parades as a last rallying cry against political change. The next few years would be marked by successive upheavals on the 'parades issue'.

Still full all-party talks did not get underway. Frustration with this situation was clearly expressed at a special Sinn Féin conference held to discuss the ceasefire in September. Bobby Lavery was a city councillor for the Oldpark ward from the mid-1980s and 1990s and represented Ardoyne at that conference. He also lost a brother and son in loyalist gun attacks in 1992 and 1994 and remembers how people viewed developments at the time.

There is rarely a bad situation, no tragedy, out of which no good can come. My brother Martin and my son Sean were both shot dead by loyalists. The impact of their deaths on my family and myself was terrible, absolutely terrible. But, because of what had happened I think people were willing to listen to me when I said that the peace process had to be given a chance. If I was not bitter and seeking revenge then people could not dismiss what I was saying. They had to listen to why I was determined that this was the right way forward. But I remember there was a Sinn Féin conference called in September 1996. I was in the Ardoyne Cumann at the time. There was a motion put forward opposing the continuation of the ceasefire. I was the only one who voted against it. People were arguing that we had moved a long way to try and get the peace process going but the Brits had given nothing. A lot of that was right. The Brits were prevaricating over everything. The language they were using was an insult to everyone. They were talking about the 'decontamination' of Sinn Féin, things like that. At the same time there had been a lot of suffering in this area. So many of the deaths had been concentrated in North Belfast. People here want to see the war finished once and for all. Because of what they have gone through, because they know there has been collusion and all that, they don't trust the Brits. So understandably people were very, very wary of the Brits. But I believed we had the ability to make them move. That was why I still argued then that the ceasefire should continue to be supported. Nevertheless the vote went the other way but I was still elected as one of two delegates to the conference. So even though I was for the ceasefire I had to give a speech against it. I said as much at the start of the speech but afterward half the hall ended up cheering a speech that I wrote and gave but totally disagreed with! (Bobby Lavery, former Sinn Féin city councillor and brother of Ardoyne victim Martin Lavery)

In late November responsibility for resolving the decommissioning issue was given over to a special commission set up under the chairmanship of former US Senator George Mitchell. This paved the way for the visit of President Bill Clinton two days later. Mitchell issued his report on 24 January 1996. He argued that getting rid of weapons should not be a prerequisite for talks to begin. It seemed that the breakthrough had finally arrived. However, on the very same day John Major announced that elections for a 'Northern Ireland Forum' would have to take place prior to negotiations. Apart from anything else, setting up an elected assembly before talks had even begun looked like a return to Stormont by the backdoor. In addition loyalist attacks had not ended. Indeed at certain times they were stepped up. Demilitarisation had only occurred slowly and, despite an IRA ceasefire that was now in its 17th month, 'inclusive dialogue' seemed as distant a prospect as ever. Gerry Kelly describes how this period was experienced in North Belfast.

> After the ceasefire was called I think the community was watching to see what would come out of it and how things would change on the ground. That is obviously very pertinent to North Belfast which has often been seen as the cockpit of the conflict. Nationalist North Belfast is a series of small enclaves surrounded by loyalists and the area witnessed one-fifth of all casualties. The communities live cheek by jowl so the bitterness is door to door. People know those on the other side who have been involved. Nationalists in North Belfast, from the youngest to the oldest, knew that the RUC and the British army were behind the loyalist murder gangs. They didn't need a welter of documents to prove it. But they wanted to give the peace process a chance; they wanted to believe in it. However, that belief and commitment was put to the test on virtually a daily basis through from 1994 to 1996. The British government were just stalling and they brought up the issue of decommissioning to delay matters. Giving up weapons had not even been mentioned before. Every time there was a vacuum the loyalists reacted by carrying out attacks and North Belfast saw wave after wave of them. That was basically why the ceasefire eventually broke down, because on the ground Catholics were being attacked and the British government showed by their actions that they lacked the will to move things forward. (Gerry Kelly, MLA for North Belfast)

On 9 February 1996 the IRA called off their ceasefire and exploded a large bomb in Canary Wharf, London. In the following weeks and months people in Ardoyne wondered what direction the future would take. In the summer they were to find out. Before that, however, feuding within one of the smaller republican organisations (the INLA) had led to the deaths of two more people from the area. On 4 March John Fennell from Eskdale Gardens was found dead near his caravan in Bundoran, Co. Donegal. John had been a long-time and prominent member of the INLA. He had been beaten to death with a breeze block by members of the same group. Just over three months later Fra Shannon from Velsheda Court was leaving a house in Turf Lodge when he was shot dead. He was the fifth person to die as a result of the INLA feud. Just over two years before, Fra's cousin Martin Bradley had died in a loyalist gun attack of which Fra was probably the intended target [Martin Bradley, killed by the UFF in the Crumlin Road, 12 May 1994].

On the political stage things also looked bleak. Despite making significant gains in elections for the Forum, Sinn Féin were excluded from 'all-party' talks when they began in June. Then in July the second 'Drumcree stand-off' was accompanied by widespread loyalist rioting. It seemed to bring the North to the brink of civil war and created fear and tension in enclave nationalist communities. The RUC showed itself to be extremely reluctant to use force to prevent loyalist demonstrations and riots. However, after the British government reversed its initial decision and forced both the Drumcree and Ormeau marches through the RUC were far less reticent in using all means at their disposal to quell the nationalist rioting that was the inevitable consequence. In a three-day period they used over 5,000 rounds of plastic bullets, something not seen since the days of the 1981 hunger strike.

Throughout the late 1990s Orange marches were the occasion of a build-up of sectarian tension. This often resulted in (almost always Catholic) families being forced or burnt out of their homes. Such was the case for a number of families who lived in Torrens (a small mixed area on the fringes of Ardoyne) in 1996. One of those was a young single mother of two, Christine Corbett. Christine's testimony bears witness to the terrible cost that such events could bring in their wake.

It all happened during the Orange marching season and the Drumcree stand-off in 1996. I had been living in Torrens for just over a year. There was just myself and my three young children. The street I lived in was mixed and if anything it probably had more Catholics than Protestants in it. There had not been any trouble on the previous 12 July but in 1996, unlike the year before, loyalists put flags up and painted the whole street. There was also a build up of threats. Someone scrawled, 'Fenian cunt, you are the next out' on my backdoor. Remarks were being made to my kid when they were playing in the street. On another occasion there was a man standing at my gate at about 11 pm at night. He was calling me a 'Fenian bastard' and telling me to get out. The police came but they just let him walk away. I knew that there was no point phoning the police again after that.

On the eighth of July two minibuses arrived up in the street. They contained a crowd of loyalists who knocked on all the doors of the Protestant houses. This was to organise a protest over Drumcree outside the RUC barracks at the top of the road. After about an hour they all came down the street. There was about 30-50 of them. I was out closing the front gate and when I turned round I could see the whole crowd jumping over gardens and running toward my house. I rushed inside, closed the front door and pushed some furniture up against the living room door. The loyalists bust down the front door and I could hear them running through the house. They were pushing at the living room door and it was banging in and out as I tried to keep it closed. Then some of them lifted one of my kids' bikes that was in the garden and threw it through the front window. They threw a big plank of wood in as well and the glass went all over a young girl who was sitting in the room with me. We were just in total shock by this time because we knew that they were going to come in through the window.

About five minutes later three RUC men appeared at the window and said that they were going to escort us out. The crowd was still at the bottom of the street shouting that they were going to petrol bomb our house and kill us. There were some known loyalists there too who were taking photos of us. Two of the policemen were actually laughing as they took us out, saying that the Protestants only wanted their houses back. One of them was ok but the police basically just stood back and let everything happen. As we were leaving, this Protestant woman who lived next door to me and who I used to say 'hello' to was squealing at me. 'Get out you Fenian bastard, these are our houses', she was shouting. I was just standing there, alone with my three kids. The people round there just turned and we knew we couldn't stay. It made me realise I could never trust the police again. When word got round to Ardoyne anyone with a van came down to help my brother take out all our furniture. Then all the other Catholics in the street started to move out too. There were about 10 or 12 families in total. Some of them had lived there for years and there were some elderly people amongst them. Billy Hutchinson went on TV claiming that we had not been put out but that was simply not true. We were put out. It was made clear to us that it was dangerous to stay. That is what we were told and loyalist gunmen were seen with masks on at the back of the street.

Afterwards the various families were put into a hotel for a couple of weeks. The social services and the dole treated us very badly. There was no counselling offered to us and we were hardly given any financial help at all. Then we were all split up and moved into different hostels. My children and I were put into a hostel which was actually an assessment centre. There were wee girls with problems in there as well as child molesters and drug dealers. The whole place was like an open prison. They monitored anyone coming to see you. If you were out of the hostel more than two nights in a row you lost your place. The kids had to be in bed by 9 pm. We basically never went down the stairs and just lived in one bedroom because I wanted to keep the kids away from the hostel environment. We were there for two years. That whole time was awful, an absolute nightmare.

The whole thing had a terrible impact on my family. My son began to have panic attacks. My daughter was about ten then and she started to suffer from migraines. They also became very, very aware of the division of Protestants and Catholics. They would get very frightened and upset when they saw loyalist flags being put out or if there was any trouble. I became very depressed and agitated and ended up on medication. I never went out. I thought it would be alright when we eventually got a home of our own again but I have never felt the same since. It has also been really difficult to build up the confidence of my children again. They still get very nervous and panicky about things. We had a home and lost everything. The security of a normal family life was taken away from my children – all because we were Catholics who were living in Torrens. Now we just take it all day by day. (Christine Corbett, victim of intimidation, Torrens 1996)

Throughout the coming months and years loyalists were to threaten, harass and attack many people from Ardoyne. On countless occasions people and their homes have been shot at and firebombed. Many attacks were directed at high-profile republicans. For example, on 22 December 1996, a loyalist bomb placed under his car injured the well-known Ardoyne republican Eddie Copeland. Eddie's father Johnny had been shot dead by the British army in 1971 (Johnny Copeland, killed by the British army in Strathroy Park, 30 October 1971). Eddie himself had been shot three times by a British soldier in 1993 while he was attending the funeral of his friend Thomas Begley, who died in the Shankill Road bombing [Thomas Begley, killed on active service in the Shankill Road, 23 October 1993].

Ex-prisoners were often specifically targeted and living with the possibility of attack and regular death threats has become a way of life. This is particularly so at times of heightened tension. The killing of Billy Wright by the INLA in the H-blocks in December 1997 was one such occasion. Eight Catholics were killed in the wake of Wright's death. None of these were from Ardoyne but there were numerous attacks. Martin 'Óg' Meehan describes the pattern of loyalist attacks directed at him and his family in recent times.

> Since 1997, when Billy Wright was shot dead, I have received word via the RUC of death threats by loyalists against me every month or so. They only ever give a minimal amount of information, just 'your life's in danger', that sort of thing. You end up just taking it in your stride. But on 22 January 2001 the RUC got in touch with my girlfriend and said that they had to speak to me urgently. That was a bit different. I was told that wherever I had been planning to spend the night I should not go there. It was the night that the South Antrim and North Belfast branches of the UDP said they would no longer support the peace process. The threat to me was coming from the Red Hand Defenders, which is a cover name for the UDA. So I took my girlfriend and our child over to my house because I had been intending to stay at hers. At about 5.30 am shots were fired in through the living room window. Then they shot into the hall at the stairway. They obviously knew what they were doing. My brother lived in the same street. About five or six days later his house was attacked. Five shots were fired into the back window. We had been told that one of the sons of Martin Meehan was going to be assassinated. My brother has never had any political connections at all. It just goes to show that the RUC seem to know exactly what is going to happen but they don't disclose details. There needs to be fuller disclosure than they give at present. Attacks like that are inevitable when things like the loyalist feud happen. You just have to take all the precautions you can: change your car, watch where you go and have as much security fitted as possible. It's the fact that they might attack your family that is frightening. They could throw a pipe bomb through the window of the house and wipe your whole family out. That fear and the threats have a terrible effect. It is particularly stressful for your family. It is always in the back of your mind. If an electrician or a postman that you don't recognise comes to your door you are immediately suspicious. But there are about 15 Republican ex-prisoners living in my street so we all look out for one another. (Martin 'Óg' Meehan, Ardoyne resident and republican ex-prisoner)

Significantly, most of the attacks launched by loyalists are not, however, necessarily directed against 'known' republicans. Throughout the years of the peace process countless Ardoyne families with no republican connections have been subject to loyalist violence and intimidation. A favoured method of attack in recent years has been the pipebomb. There have been scores of occasions when such devices have been thrown at the homes of people on the fringes of the area. Verbal threats, daubed slogans, attacks with bricks, acid or petrol have also been the reality with which many have lived. As a result numerous families have been intimidated out of their homes.

In June 1997 a Labour government came to power at Westminster. Only then was the logjam of a Tory administration dependent upon a recalcitrant Unionist Party for its slender majority removed. The 'peace process' now seemed capable of moving forward again. The IRA renewed their cessation in July and this provided the space for all-party negotiations to take place. Unlike the first ceasefire of 1994, on this occasion the response in Ardoyne was extremely muted. There was no cavalcade of cars. The experience of the last few years had taught people to lower their expectations. Yet, although the party negotiations that followed were often difficult, protracted and acrimonious they finally resulted in the signing of the Good Friday Agreement on 10 April 1998. The Agreement was a truly historic document. It contained measures to deal with a wide range of matters from new and novel constitutional arrangements to human rights and equality legislation. It also held out the possibility of reform of the RUC, the release of political prisoners, decommissioning and demilitarisation. The Agreement was also historic because, for the first time in modern Irish history, a majority of the populations of Ireland as a whole, within the Six Counties and of both the nationalist and unionist communities in the North all gave their consent to the same constitutional settlement.

There were still, though, great problems to be overcome and difficult days ahead. That summer saw the by now almost annual organised mayhem ignited by the Orange marching season. It followed another seemingly perpetual 'stand-off' over the Drumcree parade in Portadown. In addition, the 'Real IRA', a breakaway republican group, exploded a car bomb in Omagh that August. The Omagh bombing resulted in the deaths of 29 people. It was the greatest loss of life from a single incident in the whole 30 years of conflict. In many ways Omagh caused everyone to stand back and reflect. Within the nationalist community, and from the republican movement itself, criticism of the Omagh bombing was significantly pointed, terse and forthright. This was a mark of changing times.

Deep divisions were certainly not swept away by the Agreement, and many outstanding issues remained. But there were now grounds for optimism, particularly after the vote in favour of the Agreement in June 1998 was so decisive. Over 70 per cent of the total population (and an estimated 96 per cent of northern Catholics) supported it. The events in the Garvaghy Road, Omagh and elsewhere that summer had shown that such hopes might still prove to be forlorn. Yet there were grounds to believe that the war was slowly being left behind. Certainly the reinstated IRA ceasefire had remained remarkably solid despite often severe provocation and the worrying machinations taking place within loyalism. This was quite as much the case in Ardoyne (an area often looked to as a barometer of grass-roots republican opinion) as elsewhere. In addition, there was an evident lessening in the state security force presence on the streets. Troop numbers were being reduced. Demilitarisation (through the removal of watchtowers and checkpoints) was not progressing swiftly but it was beginning to happen. For the first time in a generation the appearance of the British army and the RUC was becoming an exception rather than the rule. Political and communal tensions remained but Belfast, in general, was starting to relax. So too, tentatively, was Ardoyne.

Given what had happened to their community, people in Ardoyne had always been more conscious than most of the need to take all due precautions for their personal safety. But even they too had begun to ease their vigil a little. Houses that would have been seen as too close to 'frontline' areas abutting Protestant estates were being bought by an Ardoyne population bursting at its artificially restricted sectarianised seams. Young people (or at least those who could afford to) went into the bars, clubs and pubs in the city centre in a way unimaginable just a few years before. And at night, as they made their way home, many now began to walk when and where they would not have done previously. If 'peace' and normality were by no means assured, Belfast was beginning to feel that the war might really be coming to an end.

It was in this seemingly changing environment that (like many others) Brian Service was making his way home at around midnight on 30/31 October 1998. He was heading along Alliance Avenue back to his home in Duneden Park after a usual Friday night out at his brother's house. Brian had grown up and spent almost all his life in Ardoyne. He was only six years old when the conflict began in 1969. Like all those of his generation he had known little besides the realities of the war around him and the violence it had bred. Indeed, a few years before he had been attacked and severely beaten by a gang of loyalists. Brian knew he had to be vigilant. However, random sectarian attack is ultimately difficult to completely guard against. whatever vigilance is maintained and precautions are taken. Brian Service was just a Catholic from Ardoyne going home when two loyalist gunmen ran up to him and shot him dead. Minutes before they had chased and tried to kill another Catholic man. Brian's death was the result of a random, unprovoked sectarian killing. The war for Ardoyne was evidently not yet over. The men who murdered Brian Service claimed to be members of an organisation called the Red Hand Defenders (RHD). This loyalist 'splinter' group had first appeared in the same month that Brian was killed. It is one of a number of such groups that have emerged in recent years. Many were merely 'front' names for the UFF and UDA. Along with the Loyalist Volunteer Force (LVF), founded by Billy Wright in early 1997, such groups were to keep up a sectarian war of attrition.

As part of the Good Friday Agreement a power-sharing executive for the government of the North including (for the first time) members of Sinn Féin, was due to be set up on the day that Brian Service was killed. The executive was not, in fact, established that day, due to an issue that has dogged the process throughout; decommissioning. In similar vein the problem of disputed Orange parades has continued to raise tensions in recent years. In and around Ardoyne the annual Orange 'Walk of the North' and July Twelfth parades have almost invariably led to heightened sectarian tensions and clashes. Since 1996 Ardoyne has found itself vulnerable to being closed off and hemmed in during such periods. Clashes between groups of youths, gun and firebomb attacks by loyalists and a general atmosphere of threat has marked the weeks of the 'marching season'.

However, there have been real attempts by community activists to establish ways and means to diminish these street clashes. Much of this work has been aimed at the young. One such initiative was the setting up of the Ardoyne Fleádh. The first such event dated back to the early years of the conflict. In the late 1980s and early 1990s there was a concerted effort to make these community festivals bigger, better organised and more spectacular. In part this was seen as offering an alternative avenue for young people to channel their energies from the rioting. That had often led them to be badly beaten by the RUC. Through the Fleádh the people of Ardoyne could find a better way to express themselves and their identity. It offered them a way to show pride in their district and to demonstrate a sense of community. Similarly initiatives have been undertaken to establish community-based interface mechanisms to reduce tensions, allay fears and pre-empt an escalation of confrontations. Rab McCallum is a community worker who has been involved in many of these initiatives.

In the early 1990s some community activists started to develop the Fleádh. This was in order to provide the kids in the district with an alternative to the violence that often occurred at that time of year. Then people started to think that something had to be provided all year round. The Ardoyne/Oldpark playground committee grew from that and got the first playground built for this area. Then the ceasefire began to focus minds on what was missing in the district and how to overcome certain social issues it was facing. At first we were just reacting to particular problems. But gradually we have become more strategic and are looking for structured, sustained and well-funded programmes to develop the area over several years. One of the main problems we have to deal with is how to diminish conflict at the interfaces with Protestant areas. In the immediate wake of the ceasefire people thought the 'peace walls' would come down in a year or two. It soon became clear that was not going to happen. The reality is that people do not really think about the other community unless there is a problem. There is a certain naïvety in what peace and reconciliation initiatives can actually achieve. There is still too much hurt, fear, anger and suspicion on both sides. All we can try to do is create some sort of a buffer where 'normality' can flourish. Reconciliation is going to come when ordinary people use ordinary services across the interface.

We have also developed a mobile phone network as a way to try and nip impending trouble in the bud. That came after the trouble that occurred because of the Drumcree stand-off in 1996. It was clear that there were times when things blew out of proportion because of lack of communication. If Protestants see a van coming from Ardoyne to move out someone who felt threatened or intimidated, then they might think that they were going to be attacked. Things could escalate from there. The mobile phones open up a channel to avoid such misunderstandings. Community workers, most untrained in conflict resolution, volunteer their time and energy all summer to try to limit trouble. Sometimes they can stop a car being burnt or a riot starting. But in the end, if things develop a momentum, there is very little they can do. What we have also found is that trouble at the interfaces is often less to do with sanctioned attacks than with kids who create just as much of a problem for their own communities. Alongside all that there is also the issue of policing. Most people in this community do not trust the RUC and until they are changed sufficiently, the community will not have confidence in them. The people who can most effectively police a community are those from the community. (Rab McCallum, Ardoyne resident and community worker)

Such efforts are not, however, always successful. In June 2001 rioting was sparked off by clashes that occurred during the Orange 'Walk of the North'. Tensions in North Belfast had been raised by loyalist reaction to Sinn Féin gains in Westminster and local elections. At the end of June a threatening loyalist crowd began gathering every day to block the Ardoyne Road as the RUC looked on. The loyalists did so to prevent primary school children from Ardoyne attending the local Holy Cross primary school. The RUC then moved en masse into the district. Rioting was inevitable and clashes with the RUC lasted for several nights. An uneasy calm returned thereafter but the potential of future trouble was signalled by a number of failed loyalist attacks in the following weeks. On 12 July a peaceful protest by people from Ardoyne against Orangemen returning from their annual march up the Crumlin Road was met with arrests, baton charges and plastic bullets by the RUC. Severe rioting was again the predictable result. Isobel McGrann and Philomena Flood were two of the parents whose children had been blocked from going to the Holy Cross school by the loyalist crowds. Their story is worth telling at length for the insight it gives into what happens in such situations.

Isobel: It all started on the 19 June. Apparently a taxi driver was taking a 14-year-old in a Celtic shirt up to the [Holy Cross Girls] school to collect his sister. Loyalists began stoning the car, the taxi driver swerved out of instinct and nearly hit some fella on a ladder. The loyalists thought this was done deliberately and within the space of a few moments the street was full of them. There were masked men amongst them. I was going up to collect my seven-year-old child from her school as usual. As I got to the top of Alliance Avenue I could hear people screaming. I looked up the road and saw a crowd of men and women standing with sticks. Then a car came at me on the footpath and I had to run back down the road. My first thought was that loyalists might have gone up to the school and shot some of our children dead. Then the RUC arrived and blocked the whole road. They stopped us from getting up to the school and even though we were begging them to help us to get up to our children they wouldn't. Instead of coming down and protecting us and our children they stopped us seeing them. They stopped cars getting through by putting a line of landrovers across the road. They wouldn't let any parents get in contact with their children.

Philomena: We could see men and women in the loyalist crowd. Some of them were masked and many of them were holding sticks, hammers, knives, everything. In the middle of all that were some of our children who had already come out of the school and who were trying to make their way down the road. They were caught up as these men with hammers and things were running past them. That is what we had to stand and witness.

Isobel: Cars and taxis were sent up from Ardoyne to try and get our children down from the school via the Crumlin Road. We had to run through the Everton School Complex to get there because some of the loyalists were making their way round there too. That was terrible because there are handicapped children in that school and they were very frightened by what was going on. At that point I saw my young daughter. She was incredibly upset and I just grabbed hold of her. Children were standing all around the place, crying, hysterical and wetting themselves. It was terrible. The children should have been home by 2.15 pm and by this time it was nearly 4 pm. All that time we did not know if our children were hurt, where they were, nothing.

Philomena: I went up the road and watched as children were coming down screaming. I remember seeing Isobel holding onto her daughter as she was wetting herself. It was very, very distressing and I still could not find my little girl. Nobody knew where she was. I went back to my house in case she had been able to make her own way home and found her in the house. She was very badly shaken up. Just as I got in the door I heard squealing coming from up the road. I ran out and there was a group of kids crying. They were really badly shaken up and clinging to a woman for their dear lives. I brought them all into my home. There was actually a health visitor in my house trying to treat my daughter at the time and she tried to help with these other children as well. The whole atmosphere was terrible. Kids and parents were all anxious. There was a complete state of distress. My wee girl is seven, a timid, fragile child. Since all this happened she has reverted to acting like a baby again. Her whole character has changed and her behaviour has become very difficult to cope with. She says she never wants to put a Holy Cross uniform on her back again because she feels like she is a target when she wears it.

Isobel: The next morning at about 7.30 am I came into the living room to find my seven year old watching the news. I asked her what she was doing and she said that she was looking to see if her school had been burnt down because she never wanted to go back to it or walk up that road again. I had to try to explain to her, a seven year old who did not even know what a Catholic or Protestant was, why we had to try and go back up that road. Just after that we called a meeting in the Ardoyne Community Centre to discuss what had happened and what to do next. We eventually set up a committee with representatives from the various schools in the area. That was because by that stage the attacks had widened to include St Gabriel's, the Convent and Our Lady of Mercy [schools] as well. Most of our schools are actually in Protestant areas and are attacked regularly. The committee is called RTE, the Right to Education Committee. We started to organise a peaceful protest. Every day the road was blocked off and we would walk up to the RUC line with our children as a way of protesting against what was happening and demanding that our children be protected on their way to school.

Philomena: We had loyalists driving by in cars shouting things at our kids. One of them was a member of the Glenbryn Residents' Committee that we are supposed to negotiate with. I was coming down the Crumlin Road one day when a car pulled up and this person started shouting sectarian abuse, mostly directed at my daughter. The RUC were stood a few feet away and just let this man do it. After all this my child is just not the same wee girl she was three months ago.

Isobel: The contrast with all of that is what happened on 12 July [2001]. That morning there was a peaceful, silent protest as usual when the Orange marchers with two bands went past. The RUC were there but they did not have on riot gear or anything like that. The Orangemen were returning at about 7.30–8.30 pm and another silent protest was planned to take place at the shops on the Crumlin Road. When I got up there the RUC were going crazy. They were just beating everyone around them. They fired water cannons right into people's houses. People who were just walking up the road were being shot with rubber bullets. One wee 16-year-old girl was at her friend's house and was hit in the face with one. Another child of 14 was going up to his aunt's and was hit on the leg. Then Philly and I witnessed one man in particular getting very badly beaten.

Philomena: Everything had happened in the space of five minutes. Everything had been relaxed and peaceful and suddenly these RUC men came in and wreaked havoc. We were stuck in a garden with a 70-year-old man. A couple of doors away from us about 8 RUC officers were beating this fella. I just remember watching this man's eyes just opening and closing. I thought I was witnessing a man being beaten to death. It was just like that Rodney King case in America. I was panicking and crying. Isobel and I got down on our knees and pleaded with them to stop hitting him. But the RUC just swore at us and called us 'Fenian bastards'. Then they started beating up this 70-year-old-man. They were beating the hell out of him. That was all for a loyalist band. On the one hand there are innocent schoolchildren aged between three and eleven who have never done anything to anybody. On the other you have a group of people, the Orangemen, and everyone that isn't blind or a bigot knows what they stand for. But the RUC can act like that to protect one and not the other. The way that I see it, what the RUC did on 12 July was just a continuation of what the loyalists did to our children on 19 June. The RUC are loyalists in uniform.

Isobel: We have tried to do things to get our kids settled again but it is not easy. We held a fun day because they missed their sports day at the school. The RTE has also tried to organise counselling. I just want to see things getting back to normal so that we can take our kids back up to their school up the Ardoyne Road. If it doesn't happen we will have to start protesting again. I tried to get my child a new uniform the other day but when I picked it up in the shop she just went into hysterics. That's where we are at the moment. (Isobel McGrann and Philomena Flood, Ardoyne residents, mothers of a Holy Cross primary school pupils and members of the Right to Education Committee)

The loyalist protest against the Holy Cross Girls has now been 'suspended' but the situation has continued to be a difficult one. The effects of the trauma visited on parents and children alike is also likely to be long-lasting. Coping with the legacy of lost loved ones has also been a marked feature of recent years. The peace process has given many people in the area the space, often for the first time, to think about what has been endured in their past. Until then coping with the ongoing reality of the state's military presence and the threat from armed loyalists precluded time for reflection. With 'peace' came the possibility of contemplation. For many this has been a difficult, painful process. Sean Mag Uidhír provides an insight into what many people were going through by talking about his own feelings on this emotional subject:

The ceasefires gave us all the time and space to look back and start really dealing with things that we had not been able to deal with before. For so long, because the struggle was still going on and there was always something else that they had to cope with, people had to suppress their emotions and put them on the backburner. Not long after the second ceasefire was called I remember watching the episode of Peter Taylor's programme, 'Provos' that looked at the period from 1983-1992. I was almost traumatised for a couple of weeks afterward because it brought back so much pain. It all began to hit me at once and I was very low for a time. So I began to wonder why it was that such feelings were only coming out now. What I came to realise is that I had known so many people who had died but I had never been given the opportunity to grieve. At the time all those people had died I had to bury the pain I felt even as I buried them. My family and close friends got me through that period. But I think this is a major problem for this society right now because a lot of people have no one to whom they can turn, no one to listen to them when they feel low. We need to have the support provided for the families of victims to deal with their loss.

I think it is particularly difficult at times for people in a place like Ardoyne. For the last five years we have had to listen to large sections of the media speaking about victims but only in terms of those from one side of the community. When the media talk about victims they mean the relatives of the members of the military and RUC who were killed. I think the important thing is that this community, the people of Ardoyne, respects everyone's grief. I don't think there is anyone here who would deny that a mother in Birmingham, or the Shankill, or in Bangor, or anywhere feels any less about the loss of a loved one than a mother or a family in Ardoyne. However, I feel very strongly that that has not been reciprocated. I do not feel as if the grief of Ardoyne has been given equal recognition. They do not feel as if their pain is seen as on a par with those of the relatives of British military or even Protestant civilian victims whose grief, quite rightly, is given recognition. More than anything people here would simply like to see and hear the truth about what happened to their loved ones. The state has been involved in cover-ups and lies throughout the last 30 years, from the deaths of Sam McLarnon and Michael Lynch onward. People feel genuinely aggrieved that their suffering has not been recognised, particularly in cases of state killings. People have a burning need for the truth and that we must have. Whatever form it takes, whether it is a 'truth commission' or not, we need some mechanism for obtaining the truth that really opens up the state's files and opens the books on state killings. We need this not for the sake of revenge but as a means of coming to terms with what we have all been through. Without that, how can there be real reconciliation? Without that, how can people have real closure in their lives? I still meet people today who cannot find that closure because they know that there has been an active effort made to deny them the truth. More than anything I would like to see us all do more for the relatives of all the victims, no matter what their politics or their religion. If there is anything we can do to help we simply must do it. That includes requiring the state to admit that they were party to the conflict too. The state has to concede that they bear their share of responsibility for the war just as I believe that this community and republicans have been prepared to acknowledge the part they too have played. (Sean Mag Uidhír, journalist and local resident)

In the midst of the peace process many people have argued that the past must be put to one side and that it is time to 'move on'. No one wants to 'move on' more than those who have lost someone dear, as too many people have in Ardoyne. In addition this is a community defined by a tight network of interlocking kin and friendship ties. As a result, loss has been a truly collective experience, although suffering has always been felt most deeply by the immediate family of those killed. Yet people in Ardoyne are also keenly aware that 'moving on' should not preclude the importance of memory. Dealing with the past is also a way of mapping out the future. These are lessons being learnt in areas like Ardoyne amongst people who have been too used to not having their voices heard. Gerry Kelly, who has lost many friends in the conflict himself, gives his perspective.

> To me a victim is a victim is a victim. We have to get away from what might be called the 'hierarchy of grief'. It is the people who survived that are the issue. The focus must be on the loved ones, no matter who the victim was or what they did. If an RUC man or woman was killed then they left behind relatives who loved them and who face hurt and trauma. If it was someone who was totally uninvolved then their family suffered equally. In just the same way, if it was an IRA person that was killed, then they also had a husband, wife, father, mother, son or daughter who has had to deal with the same pain. We all have to deal with ghosts. All the relatives of victims are entitled to the same treatment and access to help and support. Everyone deserves to be treated equally. Unfortunately the Bloomfield Report didn't do that and appointing the security minister to have responsibility for victims was a very negative step. It all indicated that the relatives of some victims are still not accepted as such. We have to fight to change that. I suppose, to show leadership we also have to be the first to change. It is hard for the IRA (and all the other combatants) to come to terms with the extent to which people have suffered at their hands and that mistakes have been made. But if we are in a conflict resolution process then there is a need to move things in that direction. Those who have been oppressed do not want to oppress others and we have to develop that to build the necessary bridges. I think that the way you do so is by involving the community. People need to take things into their own hands. They may need the state for funding and facilities but in the end it is people themselves who know what they need and the best way to achieve it. I don't know if a South African style truth commission is the answer, the circumstances here are very different. I think things will develop by local groups doing the work on the ground. That will be the other side of the fact that north Belfast has been the cockpit of the conflict. Because people have faced the worst of things then it is also the place where the greatest steps toward truth, justice and reconciliation are also going to take place. (Gerry Kelly, Sinn Féin MLA for North Belfast)

Ardoyne is in many ways a far more confident, buoyant community than in the past. Some might feel that the district has lost some of the characteristcs that sustained it in years gone by. It is a community that faces different kinds of problems than was once the case. Yet those problems are still less than half the story. Ardoyne is an area that (perhaps in no small part because of the conflict) still has a sense of community and purpose. Initiatives to deal with the social and economic problems to be found in the district have, as often as not, emerged from within. A network of groups and bodies, workers in the voluntary sector, public representatives and ordinary members of the community has taken shape, evidencing that sense and purpose. Years of struggle called upon the deepest wells of resourcefulness and self-reliance. At least this is a positive legacy in their wake. The young Conor Stiobhard again:

My ma and da tell me stories of what has happened to the community over the last thirty years. Sometimes they joke about things. They like to tell me that us young ones would not have the education we get today If they had not gone out and thrown stones in 1969! Or that in the early '70s you couldn't go out for a carton of milk because there were shots ringing all around you. They talk about internment too, and what a huge effect it had on everybody. They talk about what impact the hunger strike had. I have read a lot about the hunger strike and talked to people who lived through it. It just comes up in conversation and people pass on their stories. I suppose it is through that you become conscious of what the community has suffered. But you also learn how it has grown together and developed its own spirit.

If people had been told in 1969 that Sinn Féin would be in control of Belfast City Hall they would have laughed at you. The community is more relaxed too. But there are also still a lot of problems. There are still sectarian attacks and harassment from the RUC. There is still surveillance from the British secret services. There has also been a huge rise in anti-social behaviour amongst young people. Drug-related crime, joy-riding and under-age drinking have really increased because of the lack of presence of the IRA in the area. But there is still a real sense of community here too. There are loads of different community groups in the district. There are cultural activities like the Irish-language schools. There is a real sense of a future. There was a chain of solidarity that bound the community together in 1969 and I think those bonds of community are still there today. (Conor Stiobhard, Ardoyne youth)

Those experiences have equally left many deep and painful memories. However, they are memories that might prove to be a positive resource for the future. There are many young people in Ardoyne today who were not born when the hunger strikers died in 1981 let alone when the conflict began in 1969. The stories of the lost loved ones of Ardoyne are a legacy that may help them make sense of, and change, the world around them.

To my knowledge nobody has ever claimed responsibility. I think they were too ashamed to claim it, to be honest with you, and that is the truth of the matter.
But it is widely known that it was the opposing faction of the INLA; they did it but they wouldn't claim it.

John Fennell
Killed by the INLA,
Bundoran,
6 March 1996

John Fennell was born on 6 December 1955 to Alice (née Deeds) and James Fennell. Alice was born and reared in Brookfield Street and James originally came from Leeson Street in the Lower Falls. The couple were married on Christmas Day 1941 in Holy Cross chapel. They eventually had thirteen children, seven girls (Mary, Bridget, Alice, Elizabeth, Eileen, Lena and Ann) and six boys (Pat, Frankie, Jimmy, John, Paul and Joe). John attended Holy Cross Boys school and after passing his 11+, went to St Mary's grammar school but finished the final months of his education in St Gabriel's. John was a very likeable, sociable, popular fella who had a wide circle of friends. He was an avid reader and loved travelling abroad. Just eleven months before his death, John's partner Deirdre gave birth to twin boys, Fionntan and Ruaidri. John Fennell was a lifelong republican and founding member of the INLA. On 6 March 1996 he was beaten to death in Bundoran. Since its inception the INLA was plagued by a series of feuds. It split into two rival factions in 1995. John belonged to the GHQ staff faction. It is widely believed that the rival Army Council faction killed him. To date no one has claimed responsibility for his death.

Deirdre Owens (widow)

I met John in May 1988 and we got engaged. John was a really smart person but he left school without many qualifications. It was the height of the troubles and he just got caught up in things. I think he would have gone far if the troubles hadn't happened. His daddy was a foreman in the building trade, all his of brothers went into the trade and it was just protocol for John to go into it too. But he just didn't like it. He wasn't a bricklayer; it was too rough for him. He then got into catering. He actually helped to get a lot of businesses off the ground. He helped get the Shaftesbury restaurant off the ground whenever it started up. He wanted something where you didn't have to clock in and clock out; he didn't like the shifts. He had a chip van in Etna Drive. After that he worked in different chippies. John really enjoyed books. He was a great reader. It was because he could switch off when he read. He enjoyed travelling. The two of us tried to make sure we went away every year. Then the twins were born on the 21 March 1995. They were 11 months when John was murdered. He was murdered three weeks before their first birthday.

John left the house on the Monday morning and said he was going away. It was quite strange. That was Monday 4 March. I didn't find out until the next night that he had died. I hadn't been well and I had taken time off work. We were putting the house up for sale that week. We had found a house out in the country and we had been bidding for it. We were thinking of moving out of Ardoyne because of the kids being born and we wanted to get married.

That night John's brother Joe and his wife were over visiting. They left about 9 o'clock and everything was fine; the kids were in bed. I got a phone call and somebody said to me, 'I have seen something on the RTE text about a body being found'. But there was no name given. The person said, 'Maybe you should phone up'. I got nervous then. I phoned the Bundoran Garda station and the Guards just said, 'Can you give me a description of your friend and what he was wearing?' and I did. He said, 'Would it be possible for you to come down here with somebody to identify the body? I am not saying it is who you say it is but just to eliminate him'. I went into complete and utter shock. I ran up and got changed. I was saying to myself, 'Please, please don't be dead'. The minute I had put the phone down I heard a jeep outside the house. I opened the blinds a wee bit and they shone a spotlight into the house, so they had been listening to the phone calls. I phoned John's brother and I said, 'I think John's dead; you better get over here'. Joseph came over within five minutes and the next thing there were people pouring into the house. I phoned my mummy and daddy and asked if they could come and take the kids.

I never got to go down to Bundoran. John's brothers went on ahead. They must have thought it would be better if I stayed here. Paul, Joe and Jimmy went down and by then I still had no confirmation he was dead. By that stage the house was just crammed with people; people were outside and they were coming from all over the place. I was thinking, 'It can't be true'. It must have been about 2 o'clock in the morning and somebody said I should phone John's solicitor and get him to phone the gardaí. So we did that and the solicitor phoned back and he said, 'Deirdre, I am sorry'. Somebody took the phone off me, and the next thing everybody was in tears. So it was actually the solicitor who confirmed John was dead. His brothers weren't even allowed near him for two days before they identified John.

There were millions of special times John and I had together before he died. But there is one I suppose I remember most. It was one of those special memories. It was after the kids were born. The two of us were sitting here and John said, 'You know, I'm just so lucky, I have never been happier in my life and I am so lucky to have you and I am so lucky to have these two baby boys. I'm just so happy'. Some people never hear that in their lives from somebody. I feel that if I made John's last lot of years on this earth like that, then it was something; at least he was happy.

I am disgusted with the way I was treated by the state authorities and the gardaí. I have been down to Bundoran a few times to collect John's personal things. They were always pressurising me as if I had done something wrong. I wasn't happy with the way

I was treated. You can tell that they are just turning a blind eye to it. I had no bother at all from the police or British soldiers up here.

John's inquest was an open verdict. I felt that the media and press coverage was pretty disgusting. I have actually challenged reporters for things they have written because it was lies, complete and utter lies. They didn't do any investigating; they just ran with what they first heard. It is really a slur on my family because John, me and the kids are a family. John's death just completely wrecked his family. John's mummy just went down hill. And the way we were treated by the people who killed him as well was disgusting. They never let it drop; they just kept it up, malicious phone calls from them. The family doesn't feel that justice was achieved. I have spoken to the gardaí about how unhappy I was about things, I have been in touch with the Minister for Foreign Affairs and I am going to contact the Minister for Justice. I was offered support after John's death. The whole family and friends rallied together from the start. There is the Survivors of Trauma; without it I would have felt that there was absolutely nothing, nowhere to go to. It really has been a lifeline, because you know you are sitting with people who know what you are going through.

Paul and Joe Fennell (John's brothers)

The conflict had a big impact on him. When he was younger he was in the 'Official' Republican Movement. John was one of the founder members of the INLA; all the founder squad left the 'Officials' in late 1974. It had been brewing for maybe a year before that but the actual spilt came in late '74, early '75. During the feud with the 'Officials' his life was threatened; they were all on the death list at the end of it. The road he took was with the INLA and eventually that's how he came to his end. The organisation was plagued with feuds over the years. The first INLA feud came around 1987, late '86 when they all got out after the Harry Kirkpatrick supergrass case. It was inevitable what was going to happen. I remember saying to him, 'You better get out of the road'. He just sort of dismissed it. John was a senior member of the movement. He held the position of Adj. General, up until the day he died. There were always disgruntled people in the movement. I think it had just lost its way; there was no backbone there, no real base from what I could see. John just stayed on. I don't know why he did that. But he just stayed on, there was no talking to him that way, once he had made his mind up that was it.

I had a drink with John on Boxing Night in the Clifton Tavern and the problems within the INLA must have been brewing maybe even then but nobody knew. It all came to a head when Cue Ball and a few others were arrested in Balbriggan with weapons. When they went to court, they declared that the INLA had been observing the cease-fire although it wasn't public. Then Gino Gallagher got shot. He had made his move for the leadership when the others were arrested. He became the Chief of Staff. Cue Ball and the rest weren't having any of it and he was killed. That was when it actually all came out in the open. As far as I know what happened was John went to Bundoran to meet them. Cue Ball and all were hiding out there because they had already jumped bail in the Free State. So they were more or less on the run both sides of the border. It seemed to be, it was last man standing or whatever way they were going to operate.

We went to Bundoran to try and establish if it had been John that was killed. It was the early hours of the morning when we arrived. Eventually the guard came out and described more or less what seemed to be John. But it took two days before they would let us see him. He had been lying outside all night where he had been killed and the next day for the forensics. They had the place sealed off and they wouldn't let us up to see. From what I heard we wouldn't have recognised him because he had been hit on the head with a concrete block. He wasn't shot; he was beaten to death. When we eventually did get to view the body we had to go to Sligo morgue. We asked to take the sheet off him to see the extent of the injuries. They objected and I said, 'We are the family and we want to see the extent of his injuries'. It was horrific. They eventually took the sheet down; you could see he had been badly beaten.

To my knowledge nobody has ever claimed responsibility. I think they were too ashamed to claim it, to be honest with you, and that is the truth of the matter. But it is widely known that it was the opposing faction of the INLA; they did it but they wouldn't claim it. During a TV programme on the two factions, they asked the opposing faction if they had killed John. They refused to comment on it. Nobody has ever come near the family. There were a lot of allegations in the papers. The truth be told, if he had been shot in a shoot out it mightn't have been just as bad. I'll be honest with you, we were expecting that sort of thing but none of us were prepared for what we actually saw.

Everybody was just totally devastated. My mother just recently died. She was never the same after John's death. My father has never really said anything either. It was the way they killed him and the whole thing over the funeral. The body was in that bad a condition we couldn't leave the coffin open. That caused grief because people thought they could never really say goodbye. That caused stress. The funeral was big. A lot of people turned up. I just wanted to get him buried with a bit of dignity. He was given a military funeral.

John was very, very intelligent. He was fearless, I don't think there was anything John truly feared; he would have faced anything. He always had a place in his heart for the underdog. All kinds of people came to his funeral and cried over him. A very charismatic person, any company he went into he just stole the company; he was just one of those guys. All in all, John was a good guy. He would have helped you out when you needed it. I'm just sorry to see the way he went. It's hard to swallow really. I think it's just a waste.

I don't care what anyone says about Fra, to me he was one of the best kids I ever had.

Fra Shannon's mother Patricia was living at his grandmother's home in Northwick Drive when Fra was born on 30 August 1974. He was the third oldest in the family, with five brothers and two sisters. Fra went to the Holy Cross Boys school and St Gabriel's (which he left when he was 15). He did, though, also have some behavioural problems as a child. After leaving school Fra never found work. He was an avid football fan and loved playing and following his club, Liverpool. Amongst his friends were Tambo Bradley, 'Danso' Murphy and Tambo Cairns. As Fra grew up his behavioural problems did not go away. By the time he was 16 he had been arrested for joyriding. It was to be a regular feature of what was

Fra Shannon
Killed by the INLA,
Turf Lodge,
9 June 1996

left of his young life. It also resulted in Fra being seen as 'anti-social' within the area, though his family saw him quite differently. Whilst his family were never specifically told as much, it has been suggested that Fra was involved with the INLA. A feud within that organisation had erupted in 1996 following the death of the INLA chief of Staff, Gino Gallagher [killed by the INLA in Falls Road, 31 January 1996]. In late May 1996 Fra Shannon had completed another gaol sentence and returned to live at his family home in Velsheda Court. On 9 June Fra was leaving a house in Turf Lodge when a gunman shot him three times in the head. His death was said to be part of the feud. Fra Shannon had one child, Leah, with his then girlfriend, Teresa Slane from the Falls Road. However, Fra never got to see his daughter. Leah was born on 1 July, just over three weeks after Fra was killed. Fra Shannon was 21 years old at the time of his death.

Patricia Shannon (mother)

I was in my home when I found out Fra had been killed. This was the day he was shot, 9 June 1996. My sister Mary, brother Hughie and his wife Mary came to tell me that Fra had been shot in Turf Lodge. At first I thought he had just been hurt and was still living. I thought that he had been kneecapped or something. Then I went to the Royal Victoria Hospital but they told me I had to go over to Forster Green. I thought that was another hospital. When we got there the RUC were standing at the door and they started to ask me questions. They asked me if Fra had any distinguishing marks, things like that. They still had not given me any indication that Fra was dead. It was only after all the questions were over that an RUC man said, 'Who is going to identify him?' It was only then that it struck me that Fra was dead. He had been shot in the head three times. His brother Paddy identified him.

Afterward I could not understand the reports that said that Fra had been killed as part of the INLA feud. Fra had been in gaol whilst the feud was going on. He had been inside for seven months and had only been out for two weeks and two days when he was shot. Fra had been in gaol a few times. As everybody in Ardoyne knows, he was a local joyrider and that is what he was mostly lifted for. His first term of imprisonment had been served in Lisnevin when he was 16. After that he had been in Hyde Bank, Crumlin Road gaol and then Magilligan. In fact, he never spent much time out. I think he only had one Christmas at home after he was 16. He got a beating once as well and was put out of the country. He went to England to see Paddy's father. But with the beating, his legs were full of poison and he ended up in hospital in England for the three weeks. Whenever he was going through security at the airport after that the metal detector went off because of the metal pieces in his body. They stripped him because they thought he was carrying something. Anyway, the thing is that he was inside when the feud had been going on. No one ever came to tell me that he was in any organisation. I also spoke to people who would know about such things after and all they told me is that Fra had 'been warned'. But I was never told what he had 'been warned' about. Nobody has ever told me what exactly it is that Fra was supposed to have done that got him killed and the people who I went to see did not have much time for him in the first place. What I was told later is that Fra had been driving his mate's car at the time he was killed in Turf Lodge. I do not know whose house he was going into when he was shot. The RUC said that he was also wearing a wig and glasses and had a bulletproof jacket on at the time of his death. I never saw these things when I went to identify the body. They were not produced at the coroner's court either, though they were mentioned at that point.

I don't care what anyone says about Fra, to me he was one of the best kids I ever had. Fra always helped me and did anything I asked him to do. I used to preach at him about his joyriding but I suppose that was just his life. I always thought that if Fra was killed that is how it would happen, in a car crash whilst he was joyriding. But he was an awful good kid in the house and he always helped me look after the younger ones. He had no sense of money and would have given you whatever you needed. He used to help me with phone bills, clothes for the kids, anything. Fra would have given you his last penny. That was the type of him. He had bad ways. But I have never really told people about the fact that from when Fra was around five he had a child psychiatrist coming to see him in the house. Doctors had been looking to assess Fra from when he was about three years old. So he had these problems from when he was very young. Fra just lived in a wee world of his own. In my eyes Fra was very quiet. He loved kids and would do anything for the three younger ones. He never really asked for anything. The last time I saw Fra was the day before he was killed. He was staying at his girlfriend's most of the time but he came over and had just got a wash and a bit of breakfast. He just said to me, 'I'll see you later ma' and then he went out. I never saw him alive again.

> *The people that killed Brian never give a reason why.*
> *It was probably because he was a Catholic going into a*
> *Catholic area. I have no bitterness towards them.*
> *I just hope that no other family has to suffer and that*
> *Brian is the last victim.*

B rian Service was born April 15, 1963. He was the second eldest of three sons born to Ann and David Service. At that time the family lived in Joanmount but shortly after Brian's birth they moved to Mountainview Park, which became the family home. Brian attended Holy Cross Boys and then St Gabriel's secondary school, which he left at 16 years old. As a teenager he was well liked by his peers and socialised with a group of friends including Alex Thompson, Eddie Boulter, Mickey McKee and Paul Fleming. During those early years Brian had a couple of relationships but none of them led to marriage. He was a social drinker, a big U2

Brian Service
Killed by loyalists,
Alliance Avenue,
31 October 1998

fan and basically kept himself to himself. Brian was close to his brothers David and Martin; in later years he developed a particularly strong bond with his eldest brother David.

Brian was a painter and decorator by trade. After a spell of unemployment he went to England to find work. He settled in London and made many friends. By all accounts he thoroughly enjoyed his five years there and felt that it had widened his horizons and changed his perspective on life. When the recession hit London in the late 1980s, and work became scarce, he decided to return home.

Brian was the 'quiet man'. He was, as everyone said, a really nice fella. On 30 October 1998 Brian spent the evening in his brother David's home. It was a nice evening, the 'cease-fires' were on and Brian decided to walk home; it was after midnight. He said his goodbyes to his brother. As Brian walked along Alliance Avenue he was shot and killed in a blatant sectarian attack. A loyalist group called the Red Hand Defenders claimed responsibility for the killing. Brian was 35 years old at the time of his death.

Stephen Arthurs (witness)

I work in a theatre as a light and sound engineer. On the night of 30 October 1998 I got a call at about 11.30 pm to strip the equipment out of the theatre after a performance. The guy who phoned told me he would pick me up in Alliance Avenue in about 10-15 minutes. I started walking towards the Oldpark Road. It was the night before Halloween. It was cold, pitch black and there were fireworks going off. I crossed over to the left-hand side when I approached the corner of the Deerpark Road. Two fellas were walking toward me as if they were drunk, one on either side of the road. I saw my friend's car on the corner of the Deerpark and walked toward it. All of a sudden I heard someone coming running behind me. I turned and saw a fella with a hood and scarf covering his face. I could see the other guy coming up from behind on the other side of the road as well. I was caught in the middle. My mate in the car flicked on the car headlights to try and stop them and I jumped in the car and we drove off. The fella ran up the Deerpark Road. I didn't see a gun. I just thought I was going to be mugged. It was exactly midnight because the news was on the radio as I got into the car.

I came home from work at about 5 am. I couldn't get into Alliance Avenue because the cops had it sealed off. I was told that there had been a sectarian shooting and a Catholic had been killed. The shooting had taken place at around five past twelve on the corner of Deerpark Road. I told the cops what had happened to me and gave them a description of the two masked killers. The next morning, the CID took me to the barracks to make a statement. They said I was lucky to be alive, though they later denied saying that.

I felt so guilty the day after. I felt that I should have told the cops. But I thought they were just trying to rob me. It sunk in afterwards and I felt a sense of guilt. I feel for Brian's mother and I feel guilty because I didn't do anything. I was afraid to go to his funeral in case his family were annoyed. Sometimes I still think about it, when I'm just listening to a bit of music; I still feel guilt. I was too relaxed and had dropped my guard; I hadn't thought it could happen because the ceasefire was on.

David Service (brother)

There were three boys in our family, Brian, Martin and me. I am the eldest, Brian was next and Martin is the youngest. There was a three-year gap between Brian and me. In our younger days the age gap meant that we weren't as close. Brian and Martin would have been closer then. It was when I got married that our relationship gradually got stronger.

Brian was never really into any sports. He was just a typical young fella growing up. In his teenage years he was into music. One of the first albums he ever bought was 'Parallel Lines' by Blondie. When he heard U2 for the first time that was it for him; he thought they were the best band he had ever heard. Bono actually heard about Brian's death and that he was a great fan. He sent us a letter saying how sorry he was to hear about his death. Brian had a great knowledge of music; you could say that music was one of his hobbies. He was a social drinker and he frequented the clubs in Ardoyne.

Brian went to England because of the lack of work here. He said going to England was the best five years of his life. His first job was a kitchen porter. Then he got a job as night porter in the Ritz Hotel. He said it was a marvellous experience because he met all sorts of famous people and the tips were great. He worked there for about a year and a half. In London he shared a flat with a number of guys from Australia and New Zealand. I went over to London for a while myself and shared the same flat. Brian said that those first two to three years his mind opened up to the world – meaning in comparison to the wee back streets of Ardoyne and Mountainview.

When Brian returned from England he went back to the family home. My mum always had his room for him. He wasn't long back and one night coming out of the Chinese take-away on the front of the Ardoyne Road he was attacked by a gang of loyalists. Brian made a run for it but they caught him at the top of Brompton Park. Three of them pinned him to the ground. One of the guys got his head and smashed it off the wall, while the other two guys pinned his arms to the wall and tried to scratch UVF slogans on the back of his hands with a knife. Brian called down to my house later that night in a state and I took him to the hospital. That incident brought Brian back to reality, because when you have been away for a long period of time your whole person changes; you relax and don't constantly look over your shoulder every five seconds.

The night Brian was shot dead he had been up in my house. It was a Friday night. Brian would have regularly visited us. Brian bought a few cans of beer and called to the house. We sat and watched TV. Brian left our house about midnight. I left him to the door and we had a few words together. He wasn't fearful leaving the house. Because of the so-called ceasefire at the time everybody was in a more relaxed way of thinking and he just decided to walk home that night. It took me a while to come to terms with that; I felt a certain amount of blame. But Brian had made his decision and that is what he wanted to do. I couldn't have forced him to take a taxi if he didn't want to. They were all on ceasefire and he thought there was no problem walking home, just like most people walking down Alliance Avenue that night.

Brian was dead within twenty minutes of leaving the house. The thing I'll always have to live with is he was dead and I didn't know. That was a massive shock to me and my whole family. My mother phoned me about 7.45 am and you don't expect to hear bad news. It was one almighty scream down the phone, 'Your brother is dead; he was shot last night'. Ann my wife was out at work. I basically went into automatic mode. I was the oldest brother and I just felt that I had to be strong for my mother and father, no matter how I felt. I think your body goes into shock but you are allowed to function to a certain degree. I felt I had to function, to hold everything together.

That morning I walked into the room and my mother and father went to pieces. I tried to hold it all together, for Ann, for the kids and for our Martin. When I saw Martin he just went to pieces in front of me. There was a policewoman there and she was crying. I had to identify Brian at the coroner's and I didn't want to do that. I told my father that I didn't want him to go. I thought it was too much for him, so Martin and I went. I spent the rest of that day with my mother and father. My mother's world just fell apart that day and she didn't know how she was going to cope. People came to help. I always said if the Lord is anywhere at all, he shows it in those moments. We didn't have to lift a finger; family and friends did everything for us.

It didn't really hit until I got home that night. I was sitting on the bed and I took my shoes off and it just all went then. It was as if I was allowed to release all the emotions. I just cried sore. I thought when I woke up the next morning I would feel a bit better but my whole system just went again. I knew it was part of my grieving process. You don't realise how close you are to your brother until a personal thing of that immensity happens to you; that is when you really feel it. My wife Ann says that her love for Brian will always be with her to the day she dies. My love goes back to the wee boy, the sibling, when I was growing up. I have all of that to remember. I have come to accept it but there is still an emptiness that you cannot fill. It was like a part of me had died with Brian and it can never be replaced. Part of my life was very much focused around doing things with him. We would drink together; he went on holidays with me Ann and the kids. It has been difficult for me but it has been far more difficult for my mother and father. When I lost my brother Brian, I lost my best friend.

Ann Service (mother)

I brought my boys up to be moderate and not to hurt anyone and that no one had the right to take a life, even though they lived in a violent world. But I never really thought that anyone would take one of my son's lives. Their father Davey was always really worried but I never thought too much about it. Brian lived in England for a few years and when he came home eventually got a house in Duneden Park. But he came here every day for his dinner. He used to say to us in the summertime, 'You two have it made' and I used to say 'Do you think so at our age?'

When Brian died the police came to the door. Davey was in bed and I was awake. When I saw the police I thought 'trouble... my son'. That is what came into my head. We just couldn't understand who could do such a thing, why anybody would take a gun and kill Brian. It is difficult for me to talk about Brian. There is deadness in me now and I can't easily tell his story the same as I once did. I was going over bits of paper with things I had written about him. This is one of them:

> *It was early on Saturday morning*
> *I was awake as if waiting.*
> *Why the knock upon the door?*
> *Who'd be calling so early?*
> *Maybe Brian was seeking warmth away from his cold place.*
> *It's my son,*
> *Has something happened to my son?*
> *As I looked into their faces I hoped, please smile; let this be all right.*
> *So formal, so efficient, so legal.*
> *I became as a child humbled by their presence,*
> *Paralysed by my fear.*
> *It's my son,*
> *Has something happened to one of my sons?*
> *I looked into their faces, shaking like a child.*
> *Wounded. Afraid.*
> *Trouble, my mind was screaming,*
> *Police, breaking the law, trouble.*
> *Please smile, make it all right.*
> *It wasn't.*
> *It wasn't really.*
> *Saturday morning,*
> *Nothing happened on a Saturday morning.*

Because it's your child, I was hoping a miracle would happen. I wanted things to be all right. The police came to my door about a quarter past seven and they didn't tell me right away what actually happened. I was trying to guess and everything entered my head. They had a set of keys in their hands and they were Brian's. He had no identification on him. We never got the full details. That is one of the hardest things to bear. As I said to someone recently, 'We'll never forget because of the way that he died'.

As you know Brian's death occurred on 31 October, Halloween. The whole of the city was blazing with fire works the night Brian's body was brought home. But I was bringing home a coffin that had lay all night in a morgue. I didn't know what had happened to Brian and I couldn't be with him. Part of me was degraded and mocked for the loss of his dignity. When his body was being brought in things didn't stop; the world still went on.

That evening he had dinner with us. He left our house with love that night. He went up to his brother David's' house. That was all I knew until the next day. He had only left David's house about ten minutes when it happened. Brian would usually have taken a taxi. But it was a nice night, it was early and so he decided to walk. My added distraction was that Brian had died alone and I was not with him. I'm still distracted to this day. It hurts. Two of the young lads that were with him after he had been shot came and told me that they had held Brian while one of them ran to get an ambulance. They were having a party in their house and heard the shooting; they thought it was fireworks. I am hurting myself by telling you this but I wanted to be with Brian and hold him. Somebody said to me, 'You can go back and hold him in your mind'. Many people have died like Brian, worse than Brian died. But death is a very lonely thing.

I cried a lot. I was so sorry. People kept asking me, 'Why are you saying you're sorry?' It was because I couldn't save him from life and I couldn't save him from death. Why couldn't I? I said, 'Every child in this community deserves to live. They deserve to live, to experience life, to go skiing, to go canoeing, to do everything that people take for granted. They think anything is good enough for the working class, the working class kids. Well, no it's not'.

When Brian died I thought he is going to be waked in this house. How am I going to cope? What am I going to do? People came and helped out I was so grateful for that. That will never leave me. People let me mourn in the way I needed to mourn. I was so surprised that everybody came, supported and got us through. That was lovely. All his friends and all his old mates lifted his coffin. That was beautiful.

I still write about my son. Here is one of the poems.

> *Waiting for a future without a life*
> *Waiting for the seasons to change*
> *Waiting to light candles (which we do every night)*
> *Closing the curtains*
> *Wearing the night as a shawl*
> *My comfort, my shroud*
> *Waiting for someone to listen*
> *To bring about a sense of justice*
> *To comfort the living and the dead*
> *You tell me, his mother, his life was worth nothing*
> *That his existence was worthless to be stamped out like an ant on the ground*
> *The law of the land insults our intelligence*
> *It twists the knife, it degrades his memory and our self-respect*
> *Brian was born into the troubles and he died in them*
> *We paid the price of peace so no word of...*
> *Injustice lies cold and silent in the grave*
> *The dead can make no demands*
> *Have you lost a son?*

Ardoyne early 1990s. Above, mural urging the withdrawal of British troops from Ireland and below, women commemorating the 1980/81 hunger strikes outside Shamrock Social Club. Among those present are: Bernie Brown, Mary Clarke, Jeannie Hamill, Kate Lagan, and Maria Williams

Above, children in fancy dress on a float at the Ardoyne Fleádh Cheoil opening parade, corner of Berwick Road and Brompton Park. Below, children's talent competition on the stage at Holy Cross Boys pitch.

RUC in riot gear (top) prepare to escort parents and their young children from Holy Cross School through the Glenbryn residents' protest. Above, terrified children walking to and from Holy Cross School as loyalist protestors hurl abuse, missiles and, on one occasion, a bomb, autumn 2001.

Conclusion

'Whoever defines the past may also control the future'

It is extremely difficult to accurately convey the enormity of the devastation and pain disclosed in the testimonies of this book. Perhaps the words do not exist to describe such loss. Those directly involved in the project, most of us born and reared in Ardoyne, were at times overwhelmed with what we heard. In many ways the book tells a 'hidden' history, a literally 'unspoken' story that might even shock members of our own community. The personal testimonies, the most important part of the book, are often very moving and painful to read. It is the first time that many individuals have spoken of these experiences. Clearly they are very personal and private memories. Yet, equally distressing is the similarity of experience recounted by different people spanning three decades of conflict. These testimonies are accounts of ordinary people who are not normally part of public discourse. It is usually the powerful and privileged who write history. If this book has value it is in providing an opportunity to understand, through the voices of ordinary people themselves, the reality of recent history and the ways in which people responded. What emerges clearly is the indomitable spirit of the Ardoyne community. The personal testimonies speak of individual and collective courage, survival, struggle and active resistance. This is not a story of passive victimhood, but of people living their lives in the most difficult circumstances.

The 99 deaths of people from Ardoyne between 1969 and 1998 did not take place in a vacuum. However, in the trauma and confusion of the time people often did not have the space to reflect upon and fully analyse the context of the killings. The conflict was ongoing and the deaths continued, sometimes on a daily basis. In such circumstances the community had no other option but to 'get on with things'. It was a way of coping with the brutality and loss endured. One of the things this book hoped to do is to provide just such a space for reflection. The book has also therefore set out to put those deaths into political and historical perspective. It describes how the killings occurred in the context of deliberate counter-insurgency strategies employed by the British state to 'manage' the conflict. It demonstrates how an entire community was targeted by counter-insurgency violence and how the legal system became little more than an arm of such an approach. Central to this analysis is an insight into the terrible consequences of such strategies for the ordinary people of Ardoyne. The testimonies should not, however, be seen in isolation. They are part of a bigger picture and a wider history of the conflict in the north of Ireland.

To document such experiences prevents them from being misrepresented or written out of history. In this context, the manner in which the conflict is 'remembered and forgotten' is a key arena for struggle. Even though the British security forces were directly responsible for a number of deaths (and there is evidence of collusion with loyalist paramilitary groups in numerous other cases) their role and culpability in the conflict is frequently omitted from public discussion on the past. The 'two traditions' model of conflict management has obscured the role of the British state as an active and violent agent in the conflict. This book represents an effort by ordinary people to redefine who gets heard and what is remembered. It represents a counter-discourse to the 'organised forgetting' and culture of denial propagated by the British state.

The most important issues raised by the book are the enormity of the suffering and the prevailing sense of injustice. It should be stressed that the ACP did not set out to research and analyse the impact of the conflict on individuals in the Ardoyne community. But as more and more testimonies were taken we were shocked by the extent and gravity of what people had experienced and what they were continuing to go through. In a sense this book became as much concerned with the lives of those who grieved as it was about those who died. As a result, and although the testimonies are more than able to speak for themselves, the ACP felt that it was important to try and piece together more comprehensively some of the consequences and effects on relatives, friends and neighbours. The 'whole picture' had to be told as fully and effectively as possible, highlighting the scale and nature of the private suffering. While this research and analysis is far from exhaustive, it is representative of ordinary peoples' experiences. It also, significantly, strikes many chords with other recent research findings in this area.

A State of Closure: The Family Experience of the Project

The ACP has placed a great emphasis upon the issues of accountability, equality and transparency in the various processes involved in producing the book. There was always a great concern that 'stirring up' memories and strong emotions could have a negative and traumatic effect on those giving their intimate testimonies. As a consequence, we have attempted to find out what value this work has had for those who have shown great courage and compassion in taking part. The feedback received from those individuals interviewed has been overwhelmingly positive. The edited interviews were returned to participants for comment and approval before publication. Several individuals included additional details or made minor adjustments. There is no doubt that recalling the traumatic events frequently aroused emotions and many tears were shed in the giving and receiving of testimonies. However, most people found the experience to be positive and beneficial. That people were so willing to speak also ensured that a truer picture of the devastating consequences of the conflict on Ardoyne could be drawn.

A State of Distress: The Personal Cost of Loss

To begin with, we found that in the vast majority of cases the immediate impact of death caused immeasurable grief. That grief was deepened still further by enduring feelings of injustice. People frequently described the terrible emotional cost that the death of their loved one had on all family members. It is noticeable, for example, how many times the early deaths of parents or partners were ascribed to the impact of their loss. Such people are the hidden victims of political violence. Many interviewees also spoke of how the emotional toll was exacerbated by a sense of powerlessness engendered by the way in which they were treated by official agencies and institutions. Undoubtedly this has had long-term physiological and psychological consequences. Many of the individuals interviewed talked of experiencing ill health, both mental and physical. In a significant number of instances it is clear that there has been long-term distress and profound emotional disturbance.

There were very real and direct social and economic consequences too. The vast majority of those killed as a result of political violence in Ardoyne were men. This meant that many women were left with the responsibility of bringing up their (often young) family. A high percentage of women spoke about the great difficulties they faced coping with the stresses of bereavement alongside their new role and responsibilities as sole providers and carers. Many also noted the extent to which they were left to fend for themselves, with only their wider family network to provide them with support. This situation often created tremendous financial problems. That was in addition to terrible emotional strain made all the worse by intense feelings of loneliness. This often led to a sense of being overwhelmed. Several women also spoke of how their experiences had a profound impact on their characters. A significant number also talked of developing a dependency on sedatives, drugs and alcohol as they tried to cope with their circumstances. The words of one woman could find echoes in the stories of many others: 'Afterward I became addicted to prescription drugs; I couldn't go through life without them. I didn't want to live; I just wanted to do myself in … I was on maybe 50 to 60 valium a day … I ended up having two nervous breakdowns'. Such are the hidden costs of losing a loved one in violent circumstances.

Many interviewees also had feelings of misplaced guilt. Even though they often knew it was illogical, many believed they had somehow contributed to the victim's death. This both evidenced and deepened their psychological pain. One young woman describes her feelings after witnessing the killing of her cousin: 'I actually blamed myself and was attending the hospital. I thought if I'd done what my ma had asked and shut the door, the gunman wouldn't have got in. Then I had to come to an understanding that the gunman would have got in some way'. This was a very common reaction. In addition many testimonies evidenced the extent to which people could not grieve properly whilst the conflict was ongoing. This was particularly apparent in the interviews carried out with those who had been directly involved in the armed struggle. The words of one republican activist (discussing the death of a close comrade and friend) illustrate the point: 'At a personal level I felt that I couldn't show my emotion for a long time, that the abnormality of the situation we were put in robbed me of the chance to grieve properly. Like a lot of other people I don't think I had the chance to grieve until after the cease-fires. But … it's something that you just never forget; it's burnt into my consciousness'. In such circumstances individuals found their own way of coping. That almost invariably involved not talking about what happened, particularly at a personal level. Such silences leave a lasting psychological legacy too.

The situation for many bereaved families was often compounded by economic hardship. In many instances the main breadwinner of the family had been lost. If public mechanisms of emotional and psychological support were often absent, financial help was also found to be in short supply. A further knock-on economic effect for relatives was their loss of employment. This was often due either to related ill health or because the individuals could not return to work for security reasons. Whether or not victims had been involved in any political or military activity their death often left their family at additional risk from future attack. 'Guilt by association' has hardly been an unfamiliar experience for many relatives.

A large number of both men and women also spoke of how difficult it was to rebuild their lives and of how things were changed forever. For many the death put severe stress on family relationships. The effects on children are probably incalculable. It is again notable how many victims (themselves often still young) left children who were in their early years. The testimonies of these sons and daughters, now grown, illustrate the deep distress that the death of their parent created for them. Every aspect of their young lives was disrupted and redefined thereafter. The sense of loss was amplified for some because they never had an opportunity to really know their mother or father at all. The pain of bereavement for the living parent was undoubtedly often intensified by watching the effect that events had upon their children, as the words of this young mother show: 'I was left with five children. I went through a terrible time. My kids and me ended up going to counselling. My wee girl had nightmares. Everybody just fell apart. I fell apart. I couldn't handle it'. The effects on friends, eyewitnesses and the wider community who have suffered distress as a result of the deaths are, similarly, probably immeasurable.

There is no doubt that the conflict had a huge and terrible impact on the lives of the men, women and children left to grieve. Indeed, for almost all, the lack of the space to grieve (at either an individual or collective level) was one of the most difficult issues of all. The bereaved also had to rely on their immediate circle of family and neighbours where no official support, counselling or advice was available. On the other hand, there was one positive consequence to such adversity. Ardoyne women were not only the backbone of the district's family and social structures. Circumstances forced many to assume higher profile public roles within the community. Struggle and loss ensured that women became key actors working for social change. Again, the testimonies help illustrate a process whereby the community itself became the source and site of solidarity and support. As one interviewee explained: 'Resistance took shape through the community caring for itself as a living entity. It harnessed repression and exclusion and turned it into something positive. People stepped forward within the community, in spite of the violence and social and economic deprivation inflicted upon it, and fought back'.

A State Apart: Harassment and Alienation in the Wake of the Death

A clear theme to emerge from the testimonies is the overwhelming sense of alienation that ordinary people have felt from the state and its institutions. Many testimonies speak of the brutality of a system that treated ordinary people with utter contempt and colluded to ensure lack of disclosure, accountability and justice. Relatives themselves were often viewed as subversives, and dehumanised as a result. Many were not accorded the common civility those who find themselves in such traumatic circumstances should expect. Such treatment provoked a growing sense of mistrust of state authorities, even for the most moderate and unpoliticised citizen. This was a marked tendency from the earliest days of the conflict. For example, a number of people noted that they expected the Scarman Tribunal to address the views and concerns of the community at the outbreak of the conflict. It soon became apparent that this was not to be the case. People realised that the shooting dead of two unarmed young men from the district by the RUC was to be left uninvestigated. A disbelief in the legal system was the inevitable and widely shared result. This sense of astonishment and growing cynicism was mirrored in countless other instances. People were confronted by state structures that violated their own laws and ignored or misrepresented 'inconvenient' truths. They were also seen to act in a manner that flew in the face of natural justice. It would be surprising if alienation from the state was not the consequence of such a situation.

Although not in all cases, a substantial number of testimonies provide evidence of systematic abuse and discrimination by official agencies and institutions in their treatment of the relatives of the dead. Verbal and physical abuse, intimidation, taunts, threats and obstructive and inhuman treatment have been the order of the day in far too many instances. This process often began with the way in which families were informed of their loss. Indeed, some people have never been officially informed that their loved one was killed. A common practice (particularly in the early days of the conflict) was for the victim's home to be raided by the RUC or British army. News of the death filtered to the family only afterward via friends of neighbours. One woman recalls the way in which her family learnt of the death of her brother: 'My mother and father found out about Jackie's death when a young lad came up to our house and he said, "Sadie, your Jackie was killed last night; your Jackie was shot dead last night". Numerous testimonies tell similar stories. Several individuals describe how they learnt about the death of a family member in the most callous of ways whilst in prison. One individual found out his son had been killed through a news flash on television.

In other cases house raids took place shortly after news of the fatal incident reached the family. Such actions were particularly evident when the state forces were responsible for killings in disputed circumstances. They often seem to have been used as a pretext for gathering information that might later be used in a damage limitation exercise. This would occur even in instances where the victim quite evidently had no political or military involvement. During such raids relatives could be subject to the most appalling harassment, as the experiences of one interviewee shows. 'The house was raided before his remains came home; they said they were looking for evidence, weapons. I went mad, berserk, saying they had done enough harm; my mother and my brother-in-law had to restrain me. They [British soldiers] literally wrecked the house. They pulled electric fires out of the walls in the bedrooms, they tore off the built-in wardrobe doors, they lifted nearly every floorboard in the house. My children weren't used to that and it was so frightening for them. They were so young; the baby was only seven and a half weeks. I was feeling bad; my husband had been shot dead and then them bastards came round and raided me'.

For some individuals harassment began immediately after the incident occurred. At the scene of a number of killings, relatives, eyewitnesses and friends were subjected to taunts, aggressive behaviour and verbal and physical abuse from the British security forces. Several eyewitness testimonies describe how they were subjected to harassment and even arrested at the scene of the crime. Francis Bradley's death is a case in point. After friends had witnessed Francis' fatal wounding in a booby-trap bomb, they were arrested and held in custody for several hours. During that time plastic bags were put over their hands, they were aggressively interrogated by the RUC and subjected to taunts and abuse. They learnt that Francis had died when an RUC man came into the interrogation room and said, 'Your friend Francie the bomber has just died in hospital'. It was only when the Protestant Action Force claimed the killing later that evening that they were released from custody. The anguish of relatives, friends and neighbours was often compounded when they arrived on the scene of the killing to be (often violently) prevented from attending to the dying. In the case of Brian Smith, for instance, British soldiers viciously attacked local women as they attempted to offer consolation to Brian as he lay dying and the other wounded individuals.

Several testimonies describe how friends and relatives were deliberately obstructed from reaching hospital, either by arrest or prolonged questioning and detention on the street. In several cases the wounded travelling either in ambulances or private vehicles were deliberately delayed from reaching hospital, sometimes for up to several hours. This is what the family of Anthony McDowell experienced after the shooting of their twelve-year son and brother by British soldiers. 'We only got as far as Flax Street coming down the Crumlin Road and we were stopped by the paras. They took us out, put us against the wall and then took us to Tennent Street for questioning. One of the things I always remember in Tennent Street was they said they shot the wee bastard who was shooting out of the car and that now they have got the other fucker, meaning me … Hours later the three of us were taken in a car and thrown back into Ardoyne. Then we walked down to the house and that's when we found out Tony was dead and he was in the morgue'. One can only imagine the distress caused to relatives and friends when they are denied the right to spend last precious moments with a loved one. The pain of loss for relatives was, at times, intensified when they reached hospital due to inappropriate and aggressive questioning by the RUC and British army. Several relatives described how they were taunted and verbally abused by the British security forces. When Pat Mailey was taken to the morgue to identify the body of his brother Jackie (killed alongside Jim Mulvenna and Dinny Brown) he was deliberately first shown the bodies of Jim and Dinny. Such premeditated acts of emotional cruelty would leave a bitter legacy. In addition, eyewitnesses and neighbours who brought the victims to hospital found themselves under suspicion and arrest. The neighbours who brought Pat McCabe's fatally wounded body to hospital were themselves arrested and questioned for several hours.

A State of Unrest: The Mistreatment of Funerals

For some relatives and friends the harassment did not stop there. A number of testimonies describe how they were unable to grieve in peace and bury their loved one with dignity. Numerous testimonies describe how homes came under heavy surveillance or siege by the

British security forces. Everyone entering or leaving a wake was stopped, searched and p-checked. As one relative recalled, 'Nobody got peace to come and pay their respects to Gerard. The soldiers crucified them; they were everywhere'. At the wake of 12-year old Anthony McDowell (shot by British soldiers while sitting entirely innocently in a passing car) paratroopers attempted to enter the family home, claiming they had seen IRA personnel entering the house. The family tried to prevent the paras from entering their home. Scuffles broke out and one relative was shot with a rubber bullet.

Several testimonies describe how funerals were subjected to attacks, harassment and attempts by the British security forces to dictate arrangements. British paratroopers rushed young David McAuley's funeral cortege. Mourners were thrown into pandemonium when the coffin was nearly knocked off the pedestals on which it stood. In the case of James McDade the Catholic church prohibited his corpse from entering the chapel, British Airways staff refused to transport the body back home from England and the National Front in Coventry and loyalists in Belfast attacked the funeral cortege. The targeting and attack of republican funerals became more systematic during the 1980s. It was a campaign that culminated in an attempt to prevent any dignified burial for Larry Marley in 1987. A three-day stand-off including massed RUC men and local residents outside the Marley family home only ended when the sheer weight of numbers of the mourners forced the funeral through. In 1993 mourners at the funeral of Thomas Begley were fired on by the British army. One prominent republican was shot and seriously wounded in the incident.

Throughout the conflict surveillance of funerals by the British security forces was a common occurrence. Mourners were photographed, stopped, detained at roadblocks and frequently arrested going to and returning from the graveside. This type of harassment was not confined to republican funerals. It was very much part of the surveillance of daily life in the community. Yet despite such heavy surveillance, funerals leaving Ardoyne were frequently attacked or subjected to taunts and abuse by loyalist mobs. These attacks were not confined to republican funerals but included civilians killed by loyalists. In the worst such example, Trevor McKibbin's funeral in 1977 was the target of a loyalist car bomb. Two of the mourners (Sean McBride and Sean Campbell) were killed. The carnage that this attack caused could very easily have led to the deaths of many more.

Even after the funeral relatives were subjected to relentless taunts and abuse from the British security forces. There are dozens of accounts that illustrate this point. One example is the death of Eddie Sharpe. Eddie was an unarmed civilian killed by paratroopers. Afterwards his widow Alice and their children were routinely subjected to a campaign of harassment. As she recalls in her testimony, 'My house had never been raided before this incident. But the Brits tortured me for a whole year afterward. They raided the house and every time they passed me in the street they were stopping me and searching me. If I didn't let them search me they would send saracens to come and take me. They were singing, 'Where's your daddy gone?' and things like that to the kids'. What such an account illustrates is that the relatives of victims themselves often became victimised and were treated as if they had done something wrong. Again, this practice was not reserved solely for the families of republican activists. However, when the British security forces were responsible for the killing (whether of a civilian or activist) it was particularly prevalent and vicious.

A State of Illusion: The Nature and Impact of Media Misrepresentation

There are many reading the accounts held within this book who may ask themselves how such things could have happened without there being a huge public outcry. That assumes, of course, that people were either aware, or cared, about what happened to these families. Very often this was not the case. One of the main reasons for this was the way in which the conflict and these deaths were reported. The role of the press, and the control of information, had a devastating effect on the lives of the ordinary people of Ardoyne. At the heart of the conflict in the north of Ireland was a struggle over the legitimacy of the state and its institutions. The battle for legitimacy was fought out as much in the media as elsewhere. A fundamental duty of the state is to protect the right to life of all its citizens. Given its counter-insurgency policies, the British state could not therefore admit that its agents had been involved in unlawful killings. To do so would have shown to the wider world that it failed to treat all its citizens equally. At the same time people in areas like Ardoyne could quite plainly see that what official bodies were saying was not true. Widespread disbelief in the state was the inevitable consequence. This was a propaganda war in which the families of the dead of Ardoyne were often little more than pawns.

For example, in the immediate aftermath of killings (and again particularly when they involved disputed circumstances) the British state would disseminate misinformation, misrepresent victims and constructed a version of events that was at odds with local peoples' accounts. A whole structure of disinformation was instituted in order that the British security forces' description of events was the first, most widely (and sometimes sole) version heard and read. If competing accounts followed they were invariably overshadowed and seen as lacking credibility. Given the location of many incidents, people from Ardoyne were often the only eyewitnesses. However, Ardoyne was demonised as being socially and politically 'deviant'. As a result it was all but impossible for their evidence to be given equal weight. In such circumstances the truth can become buried all too easily. Relatives faced an uphill struggle getting the media to listen to their side of the story. In the case of Eddie Sharpe, for example, at least two different versions of events were released by the NIO in quick succession. As his widow Alice explains, 'The first statement the Brits put out was that Eddie was shot dead climbing over a yard wall. They must have realised that they'd got their stories mixed up. The next statement said that he was a gunman standing pointing a rifle at them from his garden. At the inquest they admitted that he wasn't a gunman and he should never have been killed'. Misinformation was not restricted to state killings. In the case of Bernard Rice the media quoted RUC sources alleging that the IRA had killed the victim for being a supporter of Rangers football team. Bernard Rice was actually the victim of a 'random' loyalist sectarian attack.

Such media manipulation was part of a much wider pattern. Channelling the nature, content and flow of information (particularly with regards to the use of lethal force by agents of the state) was a central component of counter-insurgency strategies from the early 1970s onward. Journalists were highly (often exclusively) dependent upon official bodies for the detail of events. At the start of the conflict the British army press office had primary responsibility for dealing with this area. In late 1971 it was supplemented by the setting up of the Army Information Policy Unit. Based at the British army's HQ this structure was recently described by the journalist David McKittrick as the 'Lisburn lie machine'. Information Policy was run by British intelligence and was designed to engage in 'psychological operations' through the dissemination of 'black propaganda', as its one-time key member Colin Wallace would later reveal. This British military structure was specifically established to manipulate the media. 'Misrepresentation' was therefore not so much due to 'oversights' or an absence of information as to a deliberate policy carried out by agencies that were set up with this express purpose in mind. Within minutes of a fatal incident taking place this machine would go into full swing. A story would swiftly appear that supposedly 'explained' and condoned the actions taken by the British army. Whatever the circumstances of the death, victims would be vilified, usually through (entirely unsubstantiated) accusations of armed aggression. Having ensured that this 'primary definition' of events was put into the public realm, other eyewitness accounts were disparaged and discredited. Even after Information Policy ceased to operate after the mid-1970s this approach still dominated official responses to such incidents. The move toward 'police primacy' would mean that the RUC Public Relations Department and the Northern Ireland Information Service would later become more important conduits for such state control of information. If they were less crude in their methods, they were no less effective in conditioning how disputed events were understood. Again, their representation of reality has been most questionable when state security forces have been directly involved in a killing, or where there have been allegations of collusion.

Yet this process could not have worked if there had not been a willingness within the media to go along with these official readings of events. Direct and indirect censorship combined with self-censorship in keeping these stories from the public's attention. Nor would it have been possible to discredit the accounts of families and eyewitnesses from Ardoyne given at the time the killings occurred unless they were themselves seen, and reported, in a particular way. Over the years the media has demonised and labelled Ardoyne a 'terrorist community', implying that both victims and relatives alike were less than innocent. What is apparent from testimonies is that many relatives have suffered great distress as a result of sections of the media intruding on their grief, misrepresenting events and giving less than equal recognition to all victims. One woman's words speak for many: 'I felt that the media and press coverage was pretty disgusting. I have actually challenged reporters for things they have written because it was lies, complete and utter lies. They didn't do any investigating; they just ran with what they first heard and it is really a slur on my family because John, me and the kids are a family. How dare they slur us like that.'

Relatives have further complained that they have had no control over what was written or published. Indeed, many expressed this as one of the most important reasons why they wanted to be involved in this book. This lack of control could take a variety of forms. In one particular case the Northern Ireland Office used a black and white image of a victim at the scene of his death for the confidential telephone advertisement. The publication took place without the family's consent and caused great hurt. In several other testimonies relatives describe the long-term distress caused by the media's use of very explicit photographs of their loved one immediately after they had been killed. As Davy Glennon remarked: 'Not only did my father's death affect everybody in the family but the photographs of his death still haunted the family for years after it and still haunt my mother'. Some families have also felt let down by books, based primarily on newspaper records, which purport to tell the stories of those who have been killed. Longstanding pain caused by the original 'errors' in reporting have been rekindled and compounded as they continue to falsify the past. Preventing media misrepresentations becoming 'history' has spurred on many to become involved with the ACP.

A State of Denial: State Killings and Collusion

Of the 99 people killed in Ardoyne between 1969 and 1998, two were killed by the RUC and 24 by the British Army. This represents 28% of the total. In all 26 cases no charges were ever brought, no court proceedings instigated, no prosecutions made, no sentences served. None. This is despite the fact that in very many cases it is quite clear that the victim was unarmed, had committed no crime and posed no threat. In other instances evidence suggests that the British army and RUC acted in direct contravention of the rules and guidelines laid down to govern their use of lethal force. In other words, they broke the law and got away with it. A culture of unaccountability was the result. The treatment families subsequently received from the security forces should be seen in this light. This was not a case of a 'few bad apples'. It was a consequence of the culture the state helped foster. For many victims of state violence their relative's sense of loss was greatly increased by the denial of the status of 'victim' to their loved one. There are silences that still shroud these deaths. Time and time again the testimonies show this to have had a deeply traumatic effect on grieving families. Every death in Ardoyne matters equally. However, there are a great many questions that remained unanswered with regards to state killings. For the relatives of these dead, state denial of wrongdoing is not merely a thing of the past; it is an active process in the present. As a result, many of these families continue to call for the state to publicly acknowledge its culpability for acts of violence through some form of truth-telling process.

Fifty (or just over 50% of the Ardoyne dead) died at the hands of loyalist paramilitaries. As was discussed in chapter 5, the extent and nature of collusion is far less easy to determine. Undoubtedly not every one of the 50 Ardoyne deaths caused by loyalist groups involved collusion. However, it is equally beyond doubt that the evidence which has so far come to light shows collusion to have been central to the nature of the conflict as a whole. The testimonies of relatives and eyewitnesses is critical in helping to piece this bigger picture together. Their words illustrate the various ways that collusion took place. It may be worth summarising some of these forms. First, there was both direct and indirect involvement of state security forces in killings carried out by loyalist paramilitaries. Second, collusion was a long-term element of British counter-insurgency strategy. However, it came to the fore in the late 1980s. Such collusion happened in a number of ways. Information was passed on from intelligence files concerning what people looked like, where they worked and lived, where and with whom they socialised. Loyalist 'information officers' doubled as British agents and acted as the main channel for this data. Weapons were either provided or permitted to enter the country that were then used in loyalist attacks. State forces were deployed in ways that allowed loyalists to enter and exit areas in order to carry out shootings. In the aftermath of a killing the RUC were often slow to respond or failed to conduct a thorough search of the crime scene. Investigations were often perfunctory and carried out with little or no contact with the victim's family. A culture of collusion compounded a culture of unaccountability that extended into a legal system shaped to service the counter-insurgency strategy of the state.

An Unaccountable State: Inquests, the Legal System and Lethal Force

As has already been noted, there were 26 state killings in Ardoyne but no member of the British security forces ever faced criminal prosecution for any of these deaths. It would appear that blanket immunity applied in such cases. In the absence of prosecutions the only opportunity relatives had of finding out facts about the killing was the coroner's inquest. However, it is clear that the inquest system was used as a mechanism to protect members of the security forces involved in disputed killings. In 1981 changes were introduced to the rules governing inquests in the north of Ireland. As a result, inquests were unable to bring in verdicts as they could in Britain. They could only produce findings. The inquest therefore became a purely inquisitorial process restricted to establishing the immediate causes and circumstances of the death. This limited the power of the inquest to act as a check against the discretion of the police to not fully investigate and of the prosecutor to not criminally prosecute fatal incidents.

Even before the 1981 changes there were problems with the nature of 'verdicts'. A disturbingly large number of 'open verdicts' were recorded at inquests when deaths had been caused by the British state. An open verdict was returned despite evidence that 'lethal force' was used in many cases of the Ardoyne dead. For instance, the British army admitted that the killing of 50-year-old Sarah Worthington had been a mistake [Sarah Worthington, killed by the British army in Velsheda Park, 9 August 1971]. However, no criminal sanction was sought against the soldier responsible for her death. An open verdict was also returned in the case of 76-year-old Elizabeth McGregor [Elizabeth McGregor, killed by the British army in Highbury Gardens, 12 January 1973]. This was in spite of the fact that it was admitted that there had been an 'error' resulting in the 'fatal discharge of the weapon'. In the case of Eddie Sharpe the British army admitted that he was not a gunman, as was earlier claimed, and that he should never have been killed [Eddie Sharpe, killed by the British army in Cranbrook Gardens, 12 March 1973]. Yet an open verdict was returned. The list could go on, but these examples point toward a wider pattern. Prior to 1981 open verdicts in inquests were used as a way to suppress the truth and protect members of the British security forces involved in disputed killings from prosecution.

The constraints imposed on the inquest system did not end with the problems of verdicts. They have been further hampered by the imposition of Public Interest Immunity Certificates. These have prevented relevant and material information being made available to the court. In addition, inquests could not compel those suspected of carrying out killings to attend the court. The non-compellability of witnesses meant members of the security forces responsible for causing a death could submit unsworn statements to be read out in court. Their non-attendance also removed the possibility of cross-examination. In short, those responsible for the killing were not required to give account of their actions. Inquests have not therefore had the effective powers to uncover all the facts related to any death. Nor could they truly protect the legitimate interests of the relatives of the victim. This has obviously been most problematic in killings where the circumstances are hotly disputed. In effect the process has 'hidden the truth' from relatives and has shackled any semblance of accountability. This raises very grave doubts as to whether the legal system sufficiently protected the rights of victims and their relatives.

The established rules governing the way that inquests were to proceed have therefore proved deeply problematic. This was compounded further by the way they were actually conducted. The whole inquest procedure was not only traumatic but (as relatives explain) it was also an often-demeaning experience. The attitude of the judiciary and their treatment of relatives have left a lot to be desired. This is painfully recalled in a significant number of testimonies, as the following example illustrates: 'I just couldn't believe what happened that day in the court and I couldn't wait to get out of it. I felt like I was the one to blame for my husband's death, like it was me on trial instead of being the victim... I always remember what he [the judge] said, that I was better off financially with my husband dead. That is what the judge said. That always stuck in my mind'. In a number of cases key civilian witnesses were not called to give evidence. Those civilian eyewitnesses who did give evidence were often treated with suspicion. Their accounts were frequently written-off, challenged or simply not treated with the same validity as security force sources.

Blame was also frequently attributed to the victim: 'They just said he was running and that they shot him and that he was a wanted man ... it's not a capital offence to run' [Gerard McDade, killed by the British army in Brompton Park entry, 21 December 1971]. Similarly, in the case of the killing of 12-year-old Anthony McDowell, it was implied that his uncle had endangered Anthony's life by driving through a checkpoint [Anthony McDowell, killed by the British army in Etna Drive, 19 April 1973]. This claim is and was strongly denied. However, this is what happened at the inquest. 'They [the paras] said they stopped us and it was death by misadventure because I [the uncle] drove on. Who drives on past the paras? If they had stopped us I would have stopped... They kept on saying that there was gunfire coming from the car we were in, which is a load of rubbish. Whenever they did the forensics, there was nothing ever found in the car; there was never nothing on Tony; there was never anything on me, nothing. But at the end it was still death by misadventure... That was their explanation and the way they washed their hands of it... I categorically stated that I was never stopped, never, ever stopped'.

Few relatives had any experience of inquest proceedings. Nor did they receive any advice and assistance from state authorities. In some cases there is evidence of obstruction. Relatives were not kept informed by the RUC about the ongoing investigation. Important information may therefore have been denied to them. Several relatives were not even informed that the inquest was taking place. Many others were officially told just 24 hours beforehand. As a result families were not fully aware of their rights. This produced a tremendous sense of alienation and powerlessness. It could also exacerbate undeserved feelings of guilt as relatives later felt that they should have done more to bring out the truth. What is even more important is that the lack of information undermined the ability of families and their legal representatives to protect their interests within the legal process.

The testimonies reveal that the inquest process has been wholly unsatisfactory. Serious concerns about its functions and practices have been raised. For many relatives the inquest process was little more than a farce. Furthermore, it is illustrative of the way in which the legal system was used by the British state in conflict management despite a political rhetoric of normality. Since the inquest is the first mechanism of accountability within the legal process it is vital that it has the authority, determination and integrity to pursue the truth. This is particularly so in the case of state killings. Not surprisingly, campaign groups have called for a critical review of the present inquest process and the establishment of a new system. Such demands are emanating from no one more vocally than the families of those killed by state forces.

A State of Change? The Search for Truth and Justice

Despite the odds stacked against them many families attempted to achieve justice for their loved ones at the time of their deaths. They continue to do so. More recently a number of families have issued a call for cases of deaths in disputed circumstances to be re-opened. Nor are they passively waiting for the state to act. These families have begun the job themselves. They have accessed inquest papers and are finding out details about the circumstances of the death, in a number of cases some twenty or thirty years after the event. In itself this is an important step on the road to discovering the truth and finding justice, as one relative describes: 'I have only found out recently, when I read the inquest papers, the extent of injuries and what happened to my brother (Jackie Mailey) ... I just really couldn't believe what I was reading. I really honestly couldn't. I can't emphasise that enough'.

This is indicative of a wider reality. Many relatives have a deep and fundamental need to know 'the truth' whether the death of their loved one was a result of state, loyalist or republican actions. Public acknowledgement of 'the truth' is seen as an essential part of the healing process for many families. The fact that relatives have never been told 'the truth' about the circumstances of the death of their loved one has greatly compounded their grief. For them there is no closure. It is not always clear how such closure can be achieved. There may not be a single road to that goal. In fact it is up to each individual and family how they approach the issue of seeking truth and justice. Some may prefer to let 'sleeping dogs lie'. Others may choose to take legal action, campaign for a public inquiry or push for a mechanism (such as a truth commission) to reveal the truth about the past. There may be a need for a range of mechanisms to be available. Different approaches are not necessarily mutually exclusive.

What the Ardoyne testimonies show is that victims of state violence (and their relatives) must receive the same recognition as other victims of the conflict. A simple maxim has to be central: 'a victim, is a victim, is a victim'. Given this perspective there are two main reasons why the issues of direct state killings and allegations of collusion matter so much. The first is that these cases have been treated differently in the past. The state has prosecuted and imprisoned thousands of republicans accused of being involved in killing members of the security forces, loyalists and civilians. It has been estimated that a total of 100,000 years have been served by republican prisoners during the last three decades. On the other hand, on-duty members of the RUC and British army have killed 360 people. Yet, only 22 individuals have been prosecuted as a result. Only four of those were convicted. None served more that three years in prison. All members of the British army found guilty of murder returned to their regiment after their release. No RUC officer has been successfully prosecuted for a killing committed while on duty. This suggests a pattern of impunity in cases where the state has been (or is suspected of having been) involved in the killing. State agents involved in the use of lethal force have not therefore been treated the same as others. As a result, the rights of their victims have not been protected equally within the legal system.

The second reason concerns the burden of responsibility of the state itself. The state claims to protect all citizens and is entrusted with upholding law and order. As such there is an even greater requirement for accountability and transparency to be applied in cases where agents of the state have been involved in the use of lethal force. Indeed, this is a principle recently re-iterated by the British prime minister. In 1998 Tony Blair laid out the reasons why the events of Bloody Sunday needed to be the subject of a new judicial inquiry. This was due to the fact, he claimed, that 'Bloody Sunday was different because, where the state's own authorities are concerned, we must be as sure as we can of the truth, precisely because we pride ourselves on our democracy and respect for the law'. In other words a basic, fundamental duty of the state is to protect the right to life of its citizens. It is on its record in fulfilling that duty that any state must be judged.

It is for this reason that a European Court of Human Rights decision delivered on 4 May 2001 was so significant. Unable to gain satisfaction from domestic courts, a number of families of victims of state violence and collusion took their cases to the European Court. They did so on the basis of Article 2 of the European Convention on Human Rights. Article 2 establishes the right to life as a human right. It also therefore calls upon the states that are signatories to the Convention to uphold that right. In the cases of Kelly, Jordan, McKerr and Shanaghan grounds were found that called into question the British state's record to do so. The court severely criticised the British government's failure to carry out effective and thorough investigations into state killings and allegations of collusion. The inquest system came in for particularly sharp rebuke. The inability to compel witnesses to attend inquests was denounced. In fact, the coroner's rules in this regard have only recently been changed. However, that does not take away from the fact that those inquests conducted under the old system did not therefore conform to Article 2. In addition the lack of disclosure of information to the next-of-kin of the victim was seen to have prevented families from protecting their interests. In other words, they were not treated fairly and equally. Again, this contravened Article 2 by not allowing for an effective investigation.

The emphasis on the rights of families was critical. As the evidence of the testimonies in this book have shown, the four cases involved in the 'Article 2' decision were not unique. The interests of Ardoyne families were rarely protected equally. What was also extremely important was the European court's finding (in the case of Patrick Shanaghan) that allegations of collusion should have been treated as legitimate and worthy of investigation. Evidence that had been dismissed as inadmissible should have been looked at by the court. The implications of this for the families of many of the Ardoyne dead are also massive. The 'Article 2' ruling has effectively opened up a can of worms for the British government. Families now have the potential to reopen similar cases, even if the incident took place 20 or 30 years ago. The testimonies in this book indicate that the state failed to fully investigate circumstances surrounding state and loyalist killings. These cases were subjected to the same mechanisms that were severely criticised by the European Court. The possibility of pursuing cases through the courts on the basis of the Article 2 ruling is very real.

The British government's response to the ruling has been to try and minimise the impact. Attempts are currently being made by the state to apply the ruling to future cases only and not in retrospect. Relatives will undoubtedly challenge this interpretation in the courts in the coming months. At the same time it is highly probable that the government may attempt to introduce ways to subvert this ruling, possibly by initiating a truth commission-style process. Truth commissions have been employed in a number of countries going through the transition from conflict to peace. They have a mixed record of success and there are arguments both for and against them. They can undoubtedly provide a series of important functions. For example, truth commissions can be important in establishing a mechanism for victims to air their pain. They can also provide official acknowledgement of a long-silenced past, outline needed reforms and reduce the likelihood of such atrocities being repeated in the future. However, there are concerns that such a broad-based truth process may become a mechanism to reduce the truth-telling process in relation to state and collusion case killings. It can become a means of the state continuing to escape its responsibilities. The lesson from elsewhere is that truth commissions are rarely effective if there has not been a real and fundamental political change. Where the state has retained its power, it can continue to manage the truth. A truth commission can become the means of doing so. The recent antics of the British state with regards to the Bloody Sunday inquiry (weapons being destroyed, state witnesses obtaining anonymity) do not bode well for the potential of any state-sponsored truth commission. Quite simply, if a truth commission were to be driven by the British state it has the power to control the process and protect its interests. Worse, it could then claim the moral high ground for initiating such a process and apparently addressing such thorny issues.

Another mechanism open to families would be to campaign for full, public and independent inquiries. This may be particularly pertinent over the issue of collusion. There have been very few prosecutions in cases where collusion is alleged or suspected. The legal process has clearly failed in this regard. Some victims' families (for example, those of Pat Finucane, Rosemary Nelson and the victims of the Dublin and Monaghan bombs) have already demanded independent public inquires. It may be that a wider focus is needed that allows for the full pattern of collusion to be examined. The implication of the Article 2 ruling is that collusion can no longer be ignored in the legal arena that investigates deaths. Given that the ruling has retrospective meaning, it can again mean that relatives may seek to reopen such cases through the courts. Evidence of collusion that had previously been excluded could now form the basis of 'serious and legitimate' concerns. This could prove critical in the future.

The search for truth and justice does not only involve the families of victims of state violence and collusion. Republicans were also responsible for killing people in Ardoyne over the past thirty years. In most cases the IRA claimed responsibility, made contact with the family and attempted to explain their actions. In many instances this process was seen by the family as sufficient. However, this was not always the case. In some cases relatives were either not informed of what had happened or continue to dispute the circumstances of their loved ones' death. Non-state groups such as the IRA do not have the same resources and power at their disposal as the state. The British state also employed its resources to investigate, prosecute and imprison those to which it was opposed. In other words, accountability for killings has not been equal. However, there remains a moral obligation for the republican movement to address any unresolved issues.

There may, again, be lessons to be learnt from elsewhere. In South Africa the ANC held two internal commissions of inquiry into abuses committed in ANC refugee and detention camps. Senior members of the ANC acknowledged that an organisation which is 'built upon respect for human rights has an obligation to acknowledge and redress the wrongs of the past and to prevent them from happening in the future'. The circumstances in South Africa are not the same as those in the north of Ireland. As a result, the specific form a republican mechanism of truth-telling may differ from that adopted in the ANC. Yet the precedent is important. There is an onus on the leadership of the republican movement to seriously consider its own structure for investigating cases where families believe they have not been treated fairly. It needs also to consider the form and forum through which it communicates those findings. It is incumbent for those who have been the subject of a 'hierarchy of victimhood' to ensure that equality is their guiding principle.

This book was itself an attempt to engage in the process of truth-telling. Whatever the potential of legal routes to pursuing the truth, recording, archiving and publishing people's stories is a path open to any family or community. Projects like the Ardoyne Commemoration Project are important because they create the space for victims and survivors to tell their story. Oral history has often been used as a tool in liberation and resistance struggles throughout the world. It has been used as a tool to challenge official accounts of history in countries such as Cuba, South Africa, Chile, Argentina and Guatemala. It is important that ordinary people get the opportunity to tell their story from their perspective. The ACP would encourage other communities to initiate similar projects in order to challenge official versions of history currently prevalent in public discourse.

Select Bibliography

Amnesty International. Political Killings in Northern Ireland, London, Amnesty International, 1994

Bew, Paul. Northern Ireland: A Chronology of the Troubles, 1968-96, Dublin, Gill & Macmillan, 1999

Boraine, Alex. A Country Unmasked: Inside South Africa's Truth and Reconciliation Commission, South Africa, Oxford University Press, 2002

Burton, Frank. The Politics of Legitimacy: Struggles in a Belfast Community, London, Routledge, 1978

Cohen, Stanley. States of Denial: Knowing about Atrocities and Suffering, London, Polity Press, 2000

Coogan, Tim Pat. The Troubles: Ireland's Ordeal 1966-1995 and the Search for Peace, London, Hutchinson, 1995

Dillon, Martin. The Shankill Butchers: a Case Study in Mass Murder, London, Arrow Books, 1990

Dillon, Martin. The Dirty War, London, Arrow Books, 1990

Ellison, Graham & Smyth, Jim. The Crowned Harp: Policing Northern Ireland, London, Pluto Press, 2000

Faligot, Roger. Britain's Military Strategy in Ireland: the Kitson Experiment, Dingle, Brandon Books, 1983

Faul, Denis & Murray, Raymond. The Hooded Men, Belfast, 1974

Farrell, Michael. Northern Ireland: the Orange State, London, Pluto Press, 1990

Fay, Marie-Therese et al. Northern Ireland's Troubles: the Human Costs, London, Pluto Press, 1999

Gifford, Tony. Supergrasses: the use of Accomplice Evidence in Northern Ireland, London, Cobden Trust, 1984

Hamber, Brandon. Past Imperfect: Dealing with the Past in Northern Ireland and Societies in Transition, Derry, INCORE, 2000

Hamber, Brandon. How Should We Remember? Issues to Consider when Establishing Commissions and Structures for Dealing with the Past, Derry, INCORE, 1998

Hayner, Priscilla. Unspeakable Truths: Confronting State Terror and Atrocity, London, Routledge, 2001

Kelly, Kevin. The Longest War: Northern Ireland and the IRA, Dingle, Brandon Books, 1982

Kitson, Frank. Low Intensity Operations, London, Faber and Faber, 1971

Krog, Antjie. Country of My Skull, London, Vintage, 1999

Lundy, Patricia & McGovern, Mark. 'The Politics of Memory in Post-Conflict Northern Ireland', Peace Review, Vol. 13, No. 1, March 2001, pp. 27-34

McKitterick, David et al. Lost Lives: the stories of the men, women and children who died as a result of the Northern Ireland troubles, Edinburgh, Mainstream Publishing, 1999

Miller, David. Don't Mention the War: Northern Ireland, Propaganda and the Media, London, Pluto Press, 1994

Mullan, Don. The Dublin and Monaghan Bombings, Dublin, Wolfhound Press, 2000

Mullan, Don. Eyewitness Bloody Sunday, Dublin, Wolfhound Press, 1997

Murray, Raymond. State Violence: Northern Ireland 1969-1997, Cork, Mercier Press, 1998

Murray, Raymond. The SAS in Ireland, Cork, Mercier Press, 1990

Ní Aoláin, Fionnuala. The Politics of Force: Conflict Management and State Violence in Northern Ireland, Belfast, Blackstaff, Press, 2000

Perk, Robert & Thomson, Alistair. The Oral History Reader, London, Routledge, 1998

Relatives for Justice. Collusion 1990-1994: Loyalist Paramilitary Murders in the North of Ireland, Derry, Relatives for Justice, 1995

Rolston, Bill. Unfinished Business: State Killings and the Quest for Truth, Belfast, Beyond the Pale Publications, 2000

Rolston, Bill. War and the Words: Northern Ireland Media Reader, Belfast, Beyond the Pale Publications, 1996

Sieder, Rachel. 'The Politics of Remembering and Forgetting in Central America', in Alexandra Barahona de Brito & Paloma Aguilar (eds.), The Politics of Memory, Oxford, Oxford University Press, 2000

Sutton, Malcolm. Bear in Mind These Dead: An Index of Deaths from the Conflict in Ireland, 1969-1993, Belfast, Beyond the Pale Publications, 1994

Unknown. British Intelligence, Brian Nelson and the Rearming of the Loyalist Death Squads, 1994

Walsh, Dermot. Bloody Sunday and the Rule of Law in Northern Ireland, Dublin, Gill & Macmillan, 2000

Walsh, Dermot. The use and abuse of Emergency Legislation in Northern Ireland, London, 1983